COOK'S
ILLUSTRATED
Texas-Style Barbecue
Best Grilled Chicken
Rating Garlic Presses
Perfecting Pasta Caprese
Best Blueberry Scones
Grilled Garlic Potatoes
Tasting Teas

COOK'S
ILLUSTRATED
French-Style Mashed Potatoes
Fuss-Free Turkey
Best Stovetop Steak
All About Chocolate
Dinner Frittatas
Apple Strudel
Rating Cinnamons

COOK'S
ILLUSTRATED
Rich Chocolate Tart
Julia Child's Turkey
Hearty Chicken Stew
Testing Stand Mixers
Holiday Pork Roast
Twice-Baked Sweet Potatoes
How to Make Pizza

COOK'S
ILLUSTRATED
Grilled Glazed Chicken Breasts
Grown-Up Grilled Cheese Sandwiches
Rating Bacons
Fresh Peach Pie
Testing Inexpensive Chef's Knives
French Pork Stew
Kitchen Myths

COOK'S
ILLUSTRATED
Best Chicken Breasts
Easy Cheese Soufflé
Pressure-Cooker Pot Roast
Cooking Oil Guide
Quick Yeast Bread
Shrimp Fra Diavolo
Testing Baking Pans
Almond Cake

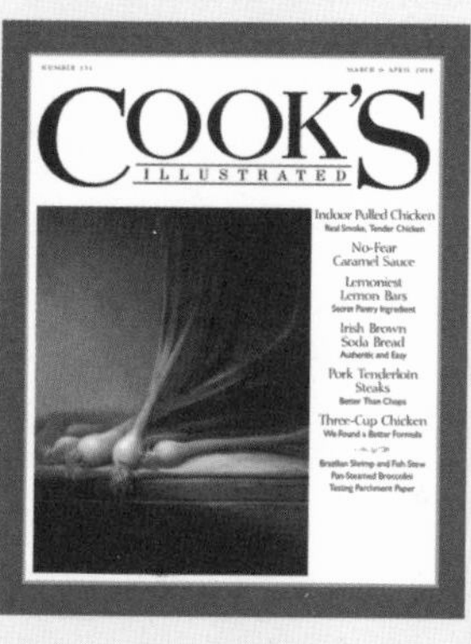
COOK'S
ILLUSTRATED
Indoor Pulled Chicken
No-Fear Caramel Sauce
Lemoniest Lemon Bars
Irish Brown Soda Bread
Pork Tenderloin Steaks
Three-Cup Chicken

COOK'S
ILLUSTRATED
Rating All-Purpose Flours
Pasta Primavera Simplified
How to Buy a Gas Grill
Oven-Fried Chicken
Discovering Great Gumbo
Improving Custard Pie

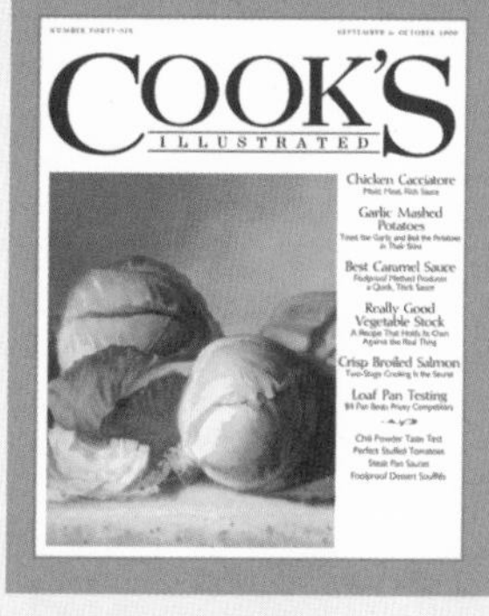
COOK'S
ILLUSTRATED
Chicken Cacciatore
Garlic Mashed Potatoes
Best Caramel Sauce
Really Good Vegetable Stock
Crisp Broiled Salmon
Loaf Pan Testing

COOK'S
ILLUSTRATED
Double Chocolate Sheet Cake
Beef Burgundy
Crisp and Tender Thin-Crust Pizza
Is a $200 Saute Pan Worth the Money?
Chicken Piccata
The Truth about Yeast

COOK'S
ILLUSTRATED
Best Blueberry Cobbler
BBQ Ribs
Kachos Done Right
Tuscan Grilled Steak
Buttermilk Coleslaw
Rating Tortilla Chips
Ice Cream Sandwiches

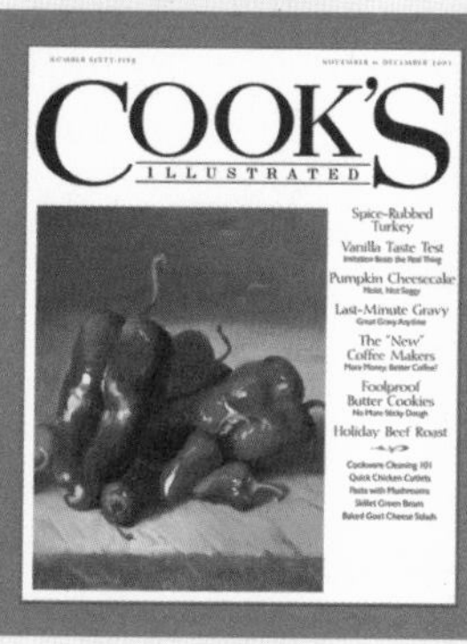
COOK'S
ILLUSTRATED
Spice-Rubbed Turkey
Vanilla Taste Test
Pumpkin Cheesecake
Last-Minute Gravy
The "New" Coffee Makers
Foolproof Butter Cookies
Holiday Beef Roast

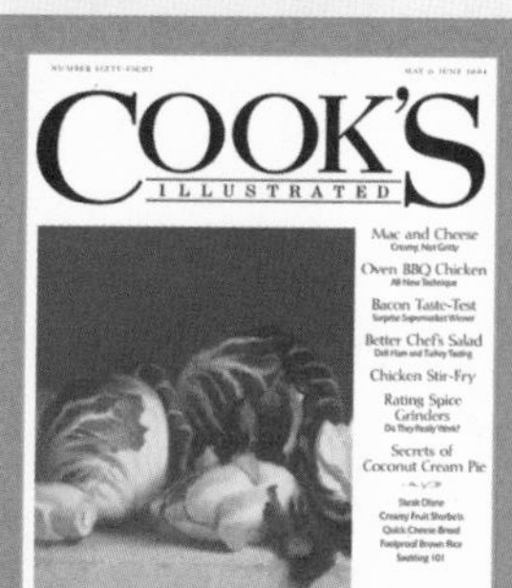
COOK'S
ILLUSTRATED
Mac and Cheese
Oven BBQ Chicken
Bacon Taste-Test
Better Chef's Salad
Chicken Stir-Fry
Rating Spice Grinders
Secrets of Coconut Cream Pie

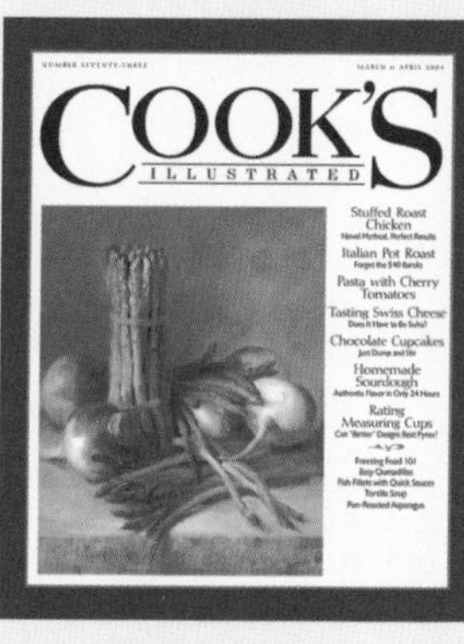
COOK'S
ILLUSTRATED
Stuffed Roast Chicken
Italian Pot Roast
Pasta with Cherry Tomatoes
Tasting Swiss Cheese
Chocolate Cupcakes
Homemade Sourdough
Rating Measuring Cups

COOK'S
ILLUSTRATED
Ultimate Chicken Pot Pie
Flaky Biscuits 101
Perfecting All-Beef Meat Loaf
Oven-Smoked Ribs
Best Chocolate Mousse
Rating Grill Pans
Bistro-Style Potatoes

COOK'S
ILLUSTRATED
Real Jerk Chicken
Grilled Beef Short Ribs
Best Raspberry Sorbet
Grill-Smoked Salmon
Juicy Turkey Burgers
Tasting American Cheddars
Quick Corn Salsas

COOK'S
ILLUSTRATED
Grilled Chicken Secrets
Summer Vegetable Gratin
Authentic Drive-In Burgers
Supermarket Olive Oil Tasting
Best Blueberry Pie
Keeping Produce Fresher Longer

COOK'S
ILLUSTRATED
Best Beef Tenderloin
Glazed Roast Chicken
Reviving Baked Ziti
Rating Blenders
Keeping Pantry Staples Fresh
French Mashed Potatoes
Real vs. Fake Vanilla

COOK'S
ILLUSTRATED
Memphis-Style Barbecued Ribs
The Perfect Spatula?
Argentine Grilled Steak
Extreme Banana Bread
Grilled Stuffed Chicken Breasts
Diced Tomato Tasting
Creamy Gazpacho

COOK'S
ILLUSTRATED
Easy Grilled Pork Roast
Real Pub-Style Burgers
Barbecued Chicken Kebabs
Fresh Strawberry Pie
Real Pasta Primavera
Rating Greek Yogurts
Liquid Measuring Cups

COOK'S
ILLUSTRATED
Chicken Adobo
Hearty French Potato Casserole
Cinnamon Swirl Bread
Italian Meatball Soup
Shrimp 101
Tasting Canned Whole Tomatoes
Testing Saute Pans

COOK'S
ILLUSTRATED
Naked Grilled Chicken
Herb-Crusted Salmon
Blueberry Bundt Cake
Best Charcoal Grill
Stir-Fried Asparagus
Quick Grilled Ribs
The Frugal Kitchen

COOK'S
ILLUSTRATED
Shredded Beef Tacos
A Whole New Way to Poach Chicken
Higher, Lighter Scones
Complete Guide to Classic Sauces
Best Orange Juice
Thai Chicken Curry
Lemon Pudding Cake

COOK'S
ILLUSTRATED
15-Minute Grilled Country Ribs
Superflaky Biscuits
Spanish Chicken
Carbon-Steel Skillets
Chocolate-Caramel Layer Cake
Indoor Flank Steak
Freezer Tips and Tricks

D1089054

AMERICA'S
TEST KITCHEN

ALSO BY AMERICA'S TEST KITCHEN

Tasting Italy: A Culinary Journey
The New Essentials Cookbook
Dinner Illustrated
The Complete Diabetes Cookbook
The Complete Slow Cooker
The Complete Make-Ahead Cookbook
The Complete Mediterranean Cookbook
The Complete Vegetarian Cookbook
The Complete Cooking for Two Cookbook
Cooking at Home with Bridget and Julia
Just Add Sauce
How to Roast Everything
Nutritious Delicious
What Good Cooks Know
Cook's Science
The Science of Good Cooking
The Perfect Cake
The Perfect Cookie
Bread Illustrated
Master of the Grill
Kitchen Smarts
Kitchen Hacks
100 Recipes: The Absolute Best Ways to Make the True Essentials
The New Family Cookbook
The America's Test Kitchen Cooking School Cookbook
The Cook's Illustrated Meat Book
The Cook's Illustrated Baking Book
The Cook's Illustrated Cookbook
The America's Test Kitchen Family Baking Book
The Best of America's Test Kitchen (2007–2019 Editions)
The Complete America's Test Kitchen TV Show Cookbook 2001–2019
Sous Vide for Everybody
Multicooker Perfection
Food Processor Perfection
Pressure Cooker Perfection
Vegan for Everybody
Naturally Sweet
Foolproof Preserving
Paleo Perfected
The How Can It Be Gluten-Free Cookbook: Volume 2
The How Can It Be Gluten-Free Cookbook
The Best Mexican Recipes
Slow Cooker Revolution Volume 2: The Easy-Prep Edition
Slow Cooker Revolution
The Six-Ingredient Solution
The America's Test Kitchen D.I.Y. Cookbook

THE COOK'S ILLUSTRATED ALL-TIME BEST SERIES

All-Time Best Brunch
All-Time Best Dinners for Two
All-Time Best Sunday Suppers
All-Time Best Holiday Entertaining
All-Time Best Appetizers
All-Time Best Soups

COOK'S COUNTRY TITLES

One-Pan Wonders
Cook It in Cast Iron
Cook's Country Eats Local
The Complete Cook's Country TV Show Cookbook

FOR A FULL LISTING OF ALL OUR BOOKS

CooksIllustrated.com
AmericasTestKitchen.com

PRAISE FOR AMERICA'S TEST KITCHEN TITLES

"*The Perfect Cookie*. . . is, in a word, perfect. This is an important and substantial cookbook. . . . If you love cookies, but have been a tad shy to bake on your own, all your fears will be dissipated. This is one book you can use for years with magnificently happy results."
THE HUFFINGTON POST ON *THE PERFECT COOKIE*

Selected as one of the 10 Best New Cookbooks of 2017
THE LA TIMES ON *THE PERFECT COOKIE*

"This cookbook from the staff at America's Test Kitchen deserves a place on the bookshelf of every cake baker. More than 200 recipes, all written in the confident voice of the Test Kitchen, will inspire home cooks and offer a master class in baking and decorating."
PUBLISHERS WEEKLY (STARRED REVIEW) ON *THE PERFECT CAKE*

Selected as the Cookbook Award Winner of 2017 in the Baking category
INTERNATIONAL ASSOCIATION OF CULINARY PROFESSIONALS (IACP) ON *BREAD ILLUSTRATED*

Selected as one of Amazon's Best Books of 2015 in the Cookbooks and Food Writing category
AMAZON ON *THE COMPLETE VEGETARIAN COOKBOOK*

"Cooks with a powerful sweet tooth should scoop up this well-researched recipe book for healthier takes on classic sweet treats."
BOOKLIST ON *NATURALLY SWEET*

"This book upgrades slow cooking for discriminating, 21st-century palates—that is indeed revolutionary."
THE DALLAS MORNING NEWS ON *SLOW COOKER REVOLUTION*

"A beautifully illustrated, 318-page culinary compendium showcasing an impressive variety and diversity of authentic Mexican cuisine."
MIDWEST BOOK REVIEW ON *THE BEST MEXICAN RECIPES*

"Some 2,500 photos walk readers through 600 painstakingly tested recipes, leaving little room for error."
ASSOCIATED PRESS ON *THE AMERICA'S TEST KITCHEN COOKING SCHOOL COOKBOOK*

"This book is a comprehensive, no-nonsense guide . . . a well-thought-out, clearly explained primer for every aspect of home baking."
THE WALL STREET JOURNAL ON *THE COOK'S ILLUSTRATED BAKING BOOK*

"This encyclopedia of meat cookery would feel completely overwhelming if it weren't so meticulously organized and artfully designed. This is Cook's Illustrated at its finest."
THE KITCHN ON *THE COOK'S ILLUSTRATED MEAT BOOK*

"Some books impress by the sheer audacity of their ambition. Backed up by the magazine's famed mission to test every recipe relentlessly until it is the best it can be, this nearly 900-page volume lands with an authoritative wallop."
CHICAGO TRIBUNE ON *THE COOK'S ILLUSTRATED COOKBOOK*

"The 21st-century *Fannie Farmer Cookbook* or *The Joy of Cooking*. If you had to have one cookbook and that's all you could have, this one would do it."
CBS SAN FRANCISCO ON *THE NEW FAMILY COOKBOOK*

"The go-to gift book for newlyweds, small families, or empty nesters."
ORLANDO SENTINEL ON *THE COMPLETE COOKING FOR TWO COOKBOOK*

"The sum total of exhaustive experimentation . . . anyone interested in gluten-free cookery simply shouldn't be without it."
NIGELLA LAWSON ON *THE HOW CAN IT BE GLUTEN-FREE COOKBOOK*

"A one-volume kitchen seminar, addressing in one smart chapter after another the sometimes surprising whys behind a cook's best practices. . . . You get the myth, the theory, the science, and the proof, all rigorously interrogated as only America's Test Kitchen can do."
NPR ON *THE SCIENCE OF GOOD COOKING*

"It's all about technique and timing, and the ATK crew delivers their usual clear instructions to ensure success. . . . The thoughtful balance of practicality and imagination will inspire readers of all tastes and skill levels."
PUBLISHERS WEEKLY (STARRED REVIEW) ON *HOW TO ROAST EVERYTHING*

COOK'S ILLUSTRATED

REVOLUTIONARY RECIPES

GROUNDBREAKING TECHNIQUES.
COMPELLING VOICES. ONE-OF-A-KIND RECIPES.

AMERICA'S TEST KITCHEN

Library of Congress Cataloging-in-Publication Data
Names: America's Test Kitchen (Firm), publisher.
Title: Cook's illustrated revolutionary recipes : groundbreaking techniques, compelling voices, one-of-a-kind recipes. / America's Test Kitchen.
Description: Boston, MA : America's Test Kitchen, [2018] | Includes index.
Identifiers: LCCN 2018017995 | ISBN 9781945256479 (hardcover)
Subjects: LCSH: Cooking, American. | LCGFT: Cookbooks.
Classification: LCC TX715 .C78548 2018 | DDC 641.5973--dc23
LC record available at https://lccn.loc.gov/2018017995

America's Test Kitchen
21 Drydock Avenue, Boston, MA 02210

Manufactured in the United States of America
10 9 8 7 6 5 4 3 2 1

Distributed by Penguin Random House Publisher Services
Tel: 800.733.3000

Editorial Director, Books **Elizabeth Carduff**

Associate Editors **Melissa Drumm and Rachel Greenhaus**

Editorial Assistants **Kelly Gauthier and Alyssa Langer**

Design Director, Books **Carole Goodman**

Deputy Art Director **Allison Boales**

Associate Art Director **Katie Barranger**

Production Designer **Reinaldo Cruz**

Photography Director **Julie Bozzo Cote**

Photography Producer **Meredith Mulcahy**

Contributing Photography Direction **Mary Ball**

Senior Staff Photographer **Daniel J. van Ackere**

Staff Photographers **Steve Klise and Kevin White**

Additional Photography **Keller + Keller and Carl Tremblay**

Food Styling **Catrine Kelty, Chantal Lambeth, Kendra McKnight, Marie Piraino, Elle Simone Scott, and Sally Staub**

Photoshoot Kitchen Team

Manager **Timothy McQuinn**

Lead Test Cook **Daniel Cellucci**

Test Cook **Jessica Rudolph**

Assistant Test Cooks **Sarah Ewald, Eric Haessler, and Mady Nichas**

Cover Art **Robert Papp**

Line Illustrations and Section Openers **John Burgoyne**

Graphic Illustrations **Jay Layman**

Production Manager **Christine Spanger**

Imaging Manager **Lauren Robbins**

Production and Imaging Specialists **Heather Dube, Dennis Noble, and Jessica Voas**

Copy Editor **Cheryl Redmond**

Proofreader **Elizabeth Wray Emery**

Indexer **Elizabeth Parson**

Chief Creative Officer **Jack Bishop**

Executive Editorial Directors **Julia Collin Davison and Bridget Lancaster**

Editor in Chief, *Cook's Illustrated* Magazine **Dan Souza**

CONTENTS

WELCOME TO AMERICA'S TEST KITCHEN

This book has been tested, written, and edited by the folks at America's Test Kitchen. Located in Boston's Seaport District in the historic Innovation and Design Building, it features 15,000 square feet of kitchen space, including multiple photography and video studios. It is the home of *Cook's Illustrated* magazine and *Cook's Country* magazine and is the workday destination for more than 60 test cooks, editors, and cookware specialists. Our mission is to test recipes over and over again until we understand how and why they work and until we arrive at the best version.

We start the process of testing a recipe with a complete lack of preconceptions, which means that we accept no claim, no technique, and no recipe at face value. We simply assemble as many variations as possible, test a half-dozen of the most promising, and taste the results blind. We then construct our own recipe and continue to test it, varying ingredients, techniques, and cooking times until we reach a consensus. As we like to say in the test kitchen, "We make the mistakes so you don't have to." The result, we hope, is the best version of a particular recipe, but we realize that only you can be the final judge of our success (or failure). We use the same rigorous approach when we test equipment and taste ingredients.

All of this would not be possible without a belief that good cooking, much like good music, is based on a foundation of objective technique. Some people like spicy foods and others don't, but there is a right way to sauté, there is a best way to cook a pot roast, and there are measurable scientific principles involved in producing perfectly beaten, stable egg whites. Our ultimate goal is to investigate the fundamental principles of cooking to give you the techniques, tools, and ingredients you need to become a better cook. It is as simple as that.

To see what goes on behind the scenes at America's Test Kitchen, check out our social media channels for kitchen snapshots, exclusive content, video tips, and much more. You can watch us work (in our actual test kitchen) by tuning in to *America's Test Kitchen* or *Cook's Country* on public television or on our websites. Listen in to test kitchen experts on public radio (SplendidTable.org) to hear insights that illuminate the truth about real home cooking. Want to hone your cooking skills or finally learn how to bake—with an America's Test Kitchen test cook? Enroll in one of our online cooking classes. However you choose to visit us, we welcome you into our kitchen, where you can stand by our side as we test our way to the best recipes in America.

facebook.com/AmericasTestKitchen
twitter.com/TestKitchen
youtube.com/AmericasTestKitchen
instagram.com/TestKitchen
pinterest.com/TestKitchen
google.com/+AmericasTestKitchen

AmericasTestKitchen.com
CooksIllustrated.com
CooksCountry.com
OnlineCookingSchool.com

Cardamom
Nutmeg
Star Anise
Fenugreek
Turmeric
Mint
Saffron
Curry Leaves
Cassia Bark
Indian Bay Leaves

INTRODUCTION

Twenty-five years ago the premier issue of *Cook's Illustrated* hit newsstands and mailboxes. It featured an oil painting of spring produce on its cover; tips on how to zest citrus, shop for the best eggplant, and string rhubarb on pages 4 and 5; a guide to breaking down poultry on pages 16 and 17; and recipes for, among other things, flaky biscuits, roast chicken, and grilled pizza peppered throughout its 32 pages. It cost 4 dollars and contained no advertising. The year was 1993.

I have a copy of the issue at my desk and I love to flip through it. It's dense with the kind of information I've always craved as a cook—clear illustrations of core techniques, no-nonsense approaches to dishes I love, and science-backed answers to common cooking questions. The magazine even feels good in my hands, with its heavy, smooth, still-white pages. *Cook's Illustrated* has always stood out to me as a singular, unique publication that, quite frankly, shouldn't have worked. At a time when food magazines were glossy, colorful, and laser-focused on the food of chefs and restaurants, *Cook's Illustrated* proclaimed—through hand-drawn illustrations and black-and-white photography—that the home cook was king. The magazine's success and growth over these 25 years is, to me, proof positive that Americans, now more than ever, care deeply about cooking, spending time in the kitchen, and feeding family and friends.

Our mission at *Cook's Illustrated* is actually quite simple: Methodically break apart a dish, figure out how and why it works, and test every variable in pursuit of a foolproof recipe. (We approach equipment testing and product taste tests with the same scientific rigor.) That process lasts at least six weeks for every recipe we publish. And it works. Our recipes are trusted by millions of home cooks to work the very first time. But another really special thing happens when you give talented cooks time, resources, and a goal. They make some pretty incredible discoveries. The book you are holding contains 25 years' worth of such discoveries, tucked into 180 recipes for everything from scrambled eggs and weeknight chicken to pan-seared scallops and no-knead brioche.

What kind of discoveries? You'll find perfect corn on the cob that never gets boiled. An ultracreamy tomato soup that's completely dairy-free. A perfectly grilled steak that begins its journey in a very low oven. And ingenious low-key approaches to traditionally high-fuss recipes like risotto, ratatouille, and sandwich bread. These recipes tell the story of how *Cook's Illustrated* has changed American home cooking over the past 25 years.

It also tells the story of American food writing. *Cook's Illustrated* was the first publication to pull back the curtain and take readers deep into the process of recipe development. Rarely published since they originally appeared in the magazine, each feature-length story celebrates the art of food writing and the extensive work that goes into every recipe. By recounting our failures, successes, and discoveries we teach you how and why the recipe works.

A decade ago I left the restaurant world and landed the job of test cook for *Cook's Illustrated*. Coming from the lightning-fast world of a production kitchen I was awestruck by the resources, effort, and time dedicated to recipe development. To see from the inside that *Cook's Illustrated* was as authentic, focused, and dedicated as it had always appeared to me as a reader was inspiring. Ten years on I'm proud to say that we are as committed as ever to our singular purpose: helping home cooks make amazing food. This book is both a gorgeous celebration of what we've accomplished over a quarter of a century and a promise of what's to come.

Sincerely,

Dan Souza

EDITOR IN CHIEF, *COOK'S ILLUSTRATED*

Jelly
Doughnut Holes
Cinnamon-Sugar Cake
French Cruller
Coffee Roll
Beignet
Cruller
Boston Cream
Chocolate Glazed
Honey Glazed

EGGS AND BREAKFAST

FOOLPROOF SOFT-COOKED EGGS

ANDREA GEARY, *January/February 2013*

In retrospect, I can see why some stages of my quest for the perfect soft-cooked egg caused my coworkers to think I had gone off the deep end. I can understand why they were surprised and even alarmed to see me furtively slipping into a darkened restroom armed with a high-powered flashlight, an empty toilet paper roll, a permanent marker, and two cartons of U.S. grade A eggs, size large. (For the record, I was trying to determine the precise location of the yolk within each egg, because I was convinced that it influenced the way the egg cooked.) And I concede that it was a mistake to spend five weeks vigorously shaking raw eggs in their shells in an effort to encourage even cooking; the fact that 25 percent of the shaken eggs exploded in the saucepan probably should have tipped me off.

But I figured that achieving my goal would be worth a little embarrassment along the way. A soft-cooked egg—its smoothly gelled white encasing a sphere of warm liquid yolk—is every bit as satisfying to eat as a poached egg, but it looks tidier, and preparing it requires less equipment. It's a one-ingredient recipe; how hard could it be to get it right?

Turns out that soft-cooked eggs are a bit of a crapshoot because you can't rely on any visual cues to monitor the eggs' progress. You don't know if you've succeeded or failed until you're already seated at the breakfast table.

Granted, many people successfully make soft-cooked eggs every day, but here's the thing: Those folks have precisely tailored their individual methods to suit their kitchens. They use the same saucepan, the same amount of water, the same burner, and the same number of eggs every time. If any one of these variables changes, all bets are off.

That wasn't good enough for me. I wanted a method that would produce consistent results for any cook, in any kitchen, using any equipment, whether he or she was cooking one egg, four eggs, or even a half-dozen.

TAKING THEIR TEMP

The problem with eggs is that they aren't just one ingredient. Tucked within that porous shell are really two very distinct ingredients: the white and the yolk. Each is composed of different types and ratios of proteins, fats, and water, which means that they react differently to heat. Most important: The white and the yolk begin to coagulate, or solidify, at very different temperatures. The egg white begins to coagulate at 142 degrees and is fully solid at around 180 degrees, while the yolk solidifies at about 158 degrees.

Combining fridge-cold eggs and ½ inch of boiling water delivers set whites and fluid yolks every time.

What does this mean? When cooking an egg that we want to be ultimately both solid (the white) and liquid (the yolk) at once, we have to bring the whites up to a much higher temperature—and do so carefully.

To begin, I figured that I had two choices for cooking: aggressively high heat or low-and-slow heat. In the past, the test kitchen has made hard-cooked eggs with a low-heat cooking method: Place the cold eggs in a saucepan, cover them with cold water, bring them to a boil, and then turn off the heat. Cover the saucepan and let the eggs finish cooking in the cooling water for 10 minutes. A quick chill in ice water, and voilà! Eggs with fully set whites and firm yolks. Could the key to soft-cooked eggs be as simple as halting the process a little earlier, before the heat penetrates to the center and sets the yolk?

No such luck. I followed our hard-cooked egg method, but to monitor the progress of the eggs, I cracked one open as soon as the water came to a boil and then another at each 1-minute interval after that. Sure, that first egg had a beautifully fluid yolk, but it also had a lot of slippery, transparent white. After 1 minute, part of the yolk of the next egg had started to solidify, but there was still a lot of undercooked white. By the time the white was fully set at the 3-minute mark, about half of the yolk had already coagulated and was beginning to turn chalky.

High heat it was. So I would simply take cold eggs from the fridge, drop them into boiling water, and then remove them as soon as the whites were cooked but before the heat penetrated all the way to the yolks.

Admittedly, this is your basic soft-cooked egg recipe, and folks have been doing it this way for millennia. It took a bit of testing to find the timings and quantities that worked for me in the test kitchen, but after some trial and error, I landed on the following method: I placed two large, cold eggs in 4 cups of boiling water in a small, heavy saucepan and fished them out after 6½ minutes. After running cold water over them for 30 seconds, I peeled them and sliced them open to reveal set whites and warm, liquid yolks.

However, this was not a flexible method. When I added extra eggs, some watery whites were in evidence after 6½ minutes. That's because adding the cold eggs to the saucepan temporarily lowers the temperature of the water. With more eggs, the water's temperature dipped lower and took longer to return to 212 degrees; with fewer eggs, the water recovered more quickly. So changing the number of eggs changed the amount of time that it took for the eggs to cook perfectly.

FULL STEAM AHEAD

If only I could somehow use boiling water to cook the eggs without actually submerging them in it, I thought. That seemed like an absurd idea—until it occurred to me to try a steamer basket. I brought 1 inch of water to a boil in a large saucepan while I loaded the steamer basket with two large, fridge-cold eggs. I lowered the steamer into the saucepan, covered it, and let the eggs steam for

6½ minutes, after which I transferred the steamer to the sink and ran cold water over the eggs before breaking them open. They were perfect. Eggs cooked in steam took exactly the same amount of time as eggs that were submerged in an ample amount of boiling water.

When I tested batches of one to six eggs with exactly the same cook time and got exactly the same results, I was sure I had cracked the case: The key to a perfect yet still flexible recipe for soft-cooked eggs was not to boil them but to steam them. But could I simplify it even more? I wondered about steamerless steaming. If an egg cooked in steam takes the same amount of time to cook as an egg that is submerged in boiling water, doesn't it follow that if you cook the same egg partially in water and partially in steam, it will still cook evenly?

This time I brought a mere ½ inch of water to a boil in my saucepan, and then I placed two cold eggs directly on the bottom of the pot, covered it, and steamed/boiled them. Because of the curved exterior of the eggs, I reasoned, they wouldn't make enough contact with the water to lower the temperature significantly, so the cook time would remain the same as it did with the steamer. At the end of 6½ minutes, I cooled the eggs by transferring the whole pot to the sink and running cold water into it for 30 seconds. I peeled the eggs and cut each one in half, revealing two beautifully tender yet fully set whites cradling warm, fluid yolks.

Subsequent tests with different-size batches (from one to six eggs) worked equally well using exactly the same timing. And with only ½ inch of water to heat, this recipe was not only the surest and most flexible but also the quickest. Just in time, my reputation as a serious and sane test cook was restored. Never again would I stress about producing perfect soft-cooked eggs for breakfast anytime, anywhere, under any conditions.

Soft-Cooked Eggs

MAKES 4 EGGS

Be sure to use large eggs that have no cracks and are cold from the refrigerator. Because precise timing is vital to the success of this recipe, we strongly recommend using a digital timer. You can use this method for one to six large, extra-large, or jumbo eggs without altering the timing. If you have one, a steamer basket makes lowering the eggs into the boiling water easier. We recommend serving these eggs in eggcups and with buttered toast for dipping, or you may simply use the dull side of a butter knife to crack each egg along the equator, break the egg in half, and scoop out the insides with a teaspoon.

4 large eggs
Salt and pepper

1. Bring ½ inch water to boil in medium saucepan over medium-high heat. Using tongs, gently place eggs in boiling water (eggs will not be submerged). Cover saucepan and cook eggs for 6½ minutes.
2. Uncover saucepan, transfer to sink, and place under cold running water for 30 seconds. Remove eggs from saucepan and serve, seasoning with salt and pepper to taste.

WHAT DOES PERFECTLY COOKED MEAN?

The proteins in egg whites and egg yolks solidify at different temperatures, making the perfect soft-cooked egg an exercise in precision. Firm yet tender whites must reach 180 degrees, while the yolk must stay below 158 degrees to remain runny. To achieve this temperature differential, it's essential to start cooking the eggs in hot water (versus the cold-water start that we've proven works best for hard-cooked eggs) so that the whites will be blasted with enough heat to solidify before the heat has time to penetrate to the yolks.

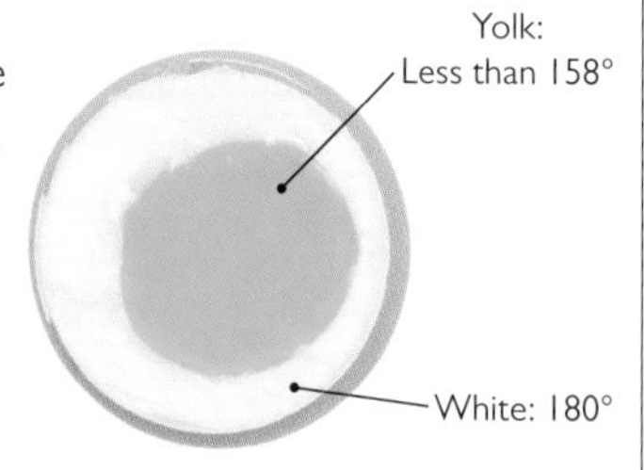

variations

Soft-Cooked Eggs with Salad

SERVES 2

Combine 3 tablespoons olive oil, 1 tablespoon balsamic vinegar, 1 teaspoon Dijon mustard, and 1 teaspoon minced shallot in jar, seal jar, and shake vigorously until emulsified, 20 to 30 seconds. Toss with 5 cups assertively flavored salad greens (arugula, radicchio, watercress, or frisée). Season with salt and pepper to taste, and divide between 2 plates. Top each serving with 2 peeled soft-cooked eggs, split crosswise to release yolks, and season with salt and pepper to taste. Serve.

Soft-Cooked Eggs with Sautéed Mushrooms

SERVES 2

Heat 2 tablespoons olive oil in large skillet over medium-high heat until shimmering. Add 12 ounces sliced white or cremini mushrooms and pinch salt. Cook, stirring occasionally, until liquid has evaporated and mushrooms are lightly browned, 5 to 6 minutes. Stir in 2 teaspoons chopped fresh herbs (chives, tarragon, parsley, or combination). Season with salt and pepper to taste, and divide between 2 plates. Top each serving with 2 peeled soft-cooked eggs, split crosswise to release yolks, and season with salt and pepper to taste. Serve.

Soft-Cooked Eggs with Steamed Asparagus

SERVES 2

Steam 12 ounces trimmed asparagus (spears about ½ inch in diameter) over medium heat until crisp-tender, 4 to 5 minutes. Divide between 2 plates. Drizzle each serving with 1 tablespoon extra-virgin olive oil and sprinkle each serving with 1 tablespoon grated Parmesan cheese. Season with salt and pepper to taste. Top each serving with 2 peeled soft-cooked eggs, split crosswise to release yolks, and season with salt and pepper to taste. Serve.

TRIAL AND ERROR: SHAKIN' EGGS

I did a lot of crazy things in the name of perfect soft-cooked eggs, but it was my weeks-long obsession with the position of the yolk within the raw egg that really caused my colleagues to worry about my mental health. I'd discovered that with a bright light, or candler, focused on the shell of a raw egg, it's possible to see the placement of the yolk inside. So I fashioned my own candler from a flashlight, a toilet paper roll, and tape and holed up in a dark room, where I marked the position of the yolk on dozens of eggs before cooking them. Sure enough, I found that when the yolk was positioned closer to one end or the other, it overcooked, while the white remained too wet. But I also found a way to coax an off-center yolk back to the middle of the egg: by vigorously shaking the raw egg for 15 seconds. This did indeed produce soft-cooked eggs with the right consistency, but it also led to a new problem: It moved the air sac from the broad end of the egg to the side, giving the egg a 25 percent greater chance of exploding during cooking. What to do? Well, I prefer the occasional imperfectly cooked egg to one that actually erupts in the pot. But if you really want your friends and family to think you're nuts, fashion a candler, find a dark room, and when you spot an egg with an extremely off-center yolk, stick it back in the carton for a different use.

YES, YOU CAN PEEL A SOFT-COOKED EGG

Though it seemed unlikely to us, soft-cooked eggs are actually easier to peel than are hard-cooked eggs. This is because the soft-cooked white is more yielding. Start by cracking the broad end of the egg against a hard surface and then peel away both the shell and the inner membrane. A quick rinse in warm water removes any remaining wisps of membrane and shards of eggshell. Split the egg in half and serve it over toast, or have it your usual way.

TROUBLESHOOTING SOFT-COOKED EGGS

THE PROBLEM A POT OF BOILING WATER

The biggest problem with the most widely used soft-cooked egg technique—dropping cold eggs into boiling water—is that you can perfect the cook time for a set number of eggs, but every time you add or subtract an egg (or even use a different pan), that timing is thrown off. That's because the number of eggs added to the pot (and how well that pot can hold heat) affects how little—or how much—the water temperature drops from the boiling point of 212 degrees. Even a 1- or 2-degree drop significantly influences the cook time. Here's how much the temperature changed immediately after we added one egg, four eggs, and six eggs to a quart of boiling water.

STEADY BOILING
The water temperature was unchanged by one egg.

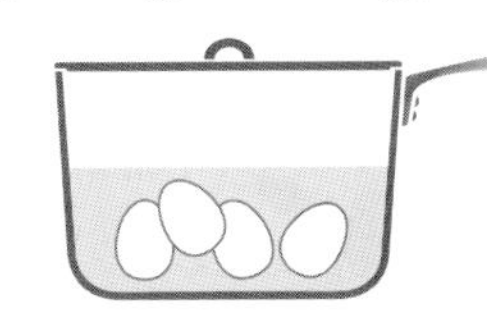

NOT BOILING
With four eggs, the water took a full minute to return to a boil.

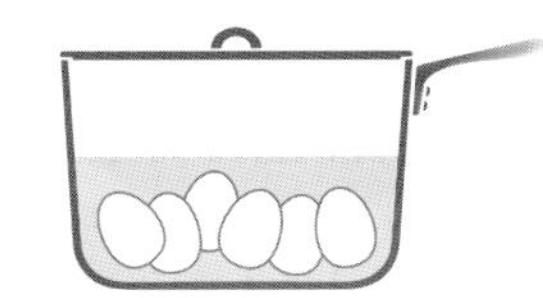

NOT BOILING
With six eggs, the water took 2 minutes to get back to 212 degrees.

THE SOLUTION A POT OF STEAM

Steaming eggs over ½ inch of boiling water cooks them in exactly the same way as a pot of boiling water, allowing us to create tender yet firm whites with luscious runny yolks. It also removes the big problem with the boiling technique: Because steaming involves so little liquid, the water returns to a boil within seconds, no matter how many eggs you add to the pot. By steaming your eggs, you can cook up one, two—even six—perfect soft-cooked eggs every time.

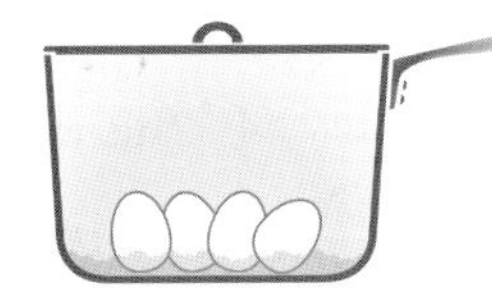

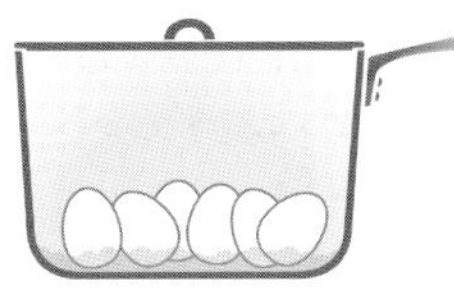

DETERMINING THE AGE OF EGGS

The age of eggs doesn't really matter when you're frying or scrambling, but we prefer the freshest specimens possible for our Soft-Cooked Eggs. To determine the pack date (which is typically the same day that the eggs were laid), check the end of the carton for a three-digit code known as the Julian date; this is often beneath or above the sell-by date when one is provided. The numbers run consecutively, starting with 001 for January 1, so 078 would indicate that the eggs were packed on March 19. (The Julian date may follow a set of numbers beginning with a "P"; this is a code indicating the packing plant.)

While some sources suggest that you can check freshness by putting eggs in a bowl of water—fresher eggs are more likely to sink, while older ones are more likely to float because the air sack expands over time—we found that wasn't a reliable test since eggs didn't float until they were four to six months old. It's a safer bet to just check the Julian date; try to find eggs that are less than three weeks old.

DATE CHECK
The three numbers on the second line indicate when the eggs were packed.

EASY-PEEL HARD-COOKED EGGS

ANDREA GEARY, *March/April 2016*

The test kitchen has a surefire method for producing perfect hard-cooked eggs: Put the eggs in a saucepan, cover them with an inch of cold water, bring the water to a boil, cover the pot, let the eggs sit off the heat in the cooling water for 10 minutes, and then transfer them to an ice bath for 5 minutes before peeling. You'll get tender whites and uniformly opaque (but not chalky) yolks every time.

But eggs cooked this way can be difficult to peel—a problem that has more to do with the membrane that lines the shell than with the shell itself. When that membrane cements itself to the egg, it must be painstakingly peeled away and often takes pieces of the white with it, leaving an unappealingly pitted exterior—an unacceptable result when you need flawless eggs for deviled eggs or garnishing a salad.

THE IMPACT OF AGE

"Fresh eggs are harder to peel than older eggs." This piece of conventional wisdom seemed like the natural place to start my testing. Could the key to success really be as simple as choosing the proper eggs to cook?

Here's the science behind the claim: The white in a fresh egg is slightly alkaline. As the egg ages, the white becomes more alkaline as the dissolved carbon dioxide (a weak acid) it contains dissipates—and the more alkaline the white, the easier it is to peel when cooked. Why? Because the higher alkalinity causes the egg white proteins to bond to each other, not to the membrane directly under the shell. That's the theory, anyway.

To test it, I used our foolproof method to cook 18 fresh and 18 month-old eggs, peeling them all right after they'd cooled. As expected, many of the fresh eggs were difficult to peel, and a few were downright impossible. But the older eggs weren't a guarantee for easy peeling either—some were actually quite difficult—so I moved on.

ENVIRONMENTAL INFLUENCES

Having exhausted my options in terms of ingredients (there was only one), I examined the cooking method. Our foolproof approach makes it impossible to overcook the eggs, but if another method would make peeling easier, I was willing to branch out.

I compared five methods—our foolproof method, boiling in already-boiling water, steaming in a pressure cooker, steaming over boiling water, and baking—cooking 10 eggs each way and peeling them all right after cooling them in a 5-minute ice bath.

I graded each method from A to F: If most of the eggs cooked a certain way peeled easily, the method got an A. If the shell clung stubbornly to most of the eggs, forcing me to tear the whites, it received a lesser grade.

The foolproof and baking methods produced eggs that were challenging to peel; they each scored a C (but unlike the nicely cooked foolproof eggs, the baked ones sported green rings around their yolks). The pressure-cooked eggs were nicely cooked, and the method earned a B. But the steaming and boiling methods each earned an A. Their shells slipped off to reveal perfectly smooth whites. What made them (and the pressure-cooked eggs) succeed?

PEELING AWAY THE ANSWER

The only real common denominator of the boiled and steamed eggs was that both went directly into a hot environment, whereas eggs cooked by our foolproof method started out cold and warmed up slowly as the water came up to a boil. The baked eggs also qualified as using a cold start because the oven's air is a slow and inefficient conductor of energy.

Our science editor explained what was happening: Plunging raw eggs into boiling water (or hot steam) rapidly denatures the outermost proteins of the white, which reduces their ability to bond with the membrane. Plus, those rapidly denaturing proteins shrink as they start to bond together, and that causes the white to pull away from the membrane. Thus, these eggs are easy to peel. (The pressure-cooked eggs are a unique case: Though they start out in cold water, the water gets hot very rapidly and can reach as high as 250 degrees, which likely causes additional shrinkage of the proteins, making the eggs easy to peel.) Conversely, proteins that rise in temperature slowly, as in the eggs started in cold water or baked in the oven, have more time to bond to the membrane before they bond with each other, so the membrane is difficult to remove.

The key to easy peeling is starting the eggs directly in hot steam, not in cold water.

STEAMING AHEAD

As for which hot-start method it would be—steaming or boiling—I had an idea. When I developed a recipe for Soft-Cooked Eggs (page 4), I determined that steaming was a superior method to boiling because adding eggs to a pot of boiling water lowers the temperature of the water, making it hard to nail down a precise cooking time that will give you dependable results every time. Eggs that steam in a steamer basket, on the other hand, don't touch the water, which means they don't lower the water temperature, so the same cooking time produces consistently perfect results. Plus, steaming is faster because there's less water to bring to a boil.

To prove the point, I compared the two methods: I filled one saucepan with water, brought the water to a boil, carefully lowered six eggs into the water, covered the pot, and then turned down the heat slightly so the eggs wouldn't jostle and break. In another saucepan, I brought 1 inch of water to a boil and then placed a steamer basket loaded with six eggs into it before covering the pot. After 13 minutes (which a few tests showed was ideal), I transferred all the eggs to an ice bath and chilled them for 15 minutes.

Sure enough, I preferred the texture of the steamed eggs. Their yolks were uniformly cooked but not chalky, while the yolks of the boiled eggs were just a tiny bit translucent at the center, just a bit undercooked—likely due to a temporary dip in temperature when the cold eggs went in.

I had one last challenge: Would my steaming method make even notoriously difficult fresh eggs easy to peel? Indeed it did. With my new cooking technique, it couldn't have been easier; I was able to peel six eggs in just over 2 minutes. (When I used a novel method of enclosing eggs in a plastic container with water and shaking them vigorously, I cut that time to mere seconds.)

A REPORT CARD ON PEELABILITY

We compared five methods, cooking 10 eggs per method and peeling them all after letting them cool for 5 minutes in an ice bath. We then assigned a grade to each method based on the condition of the peeled eggs. Our takeaway: The steaming and boiling methods each earned an A, as nine of the 10 peeled eggs cooked each way were flawlessly smooth.

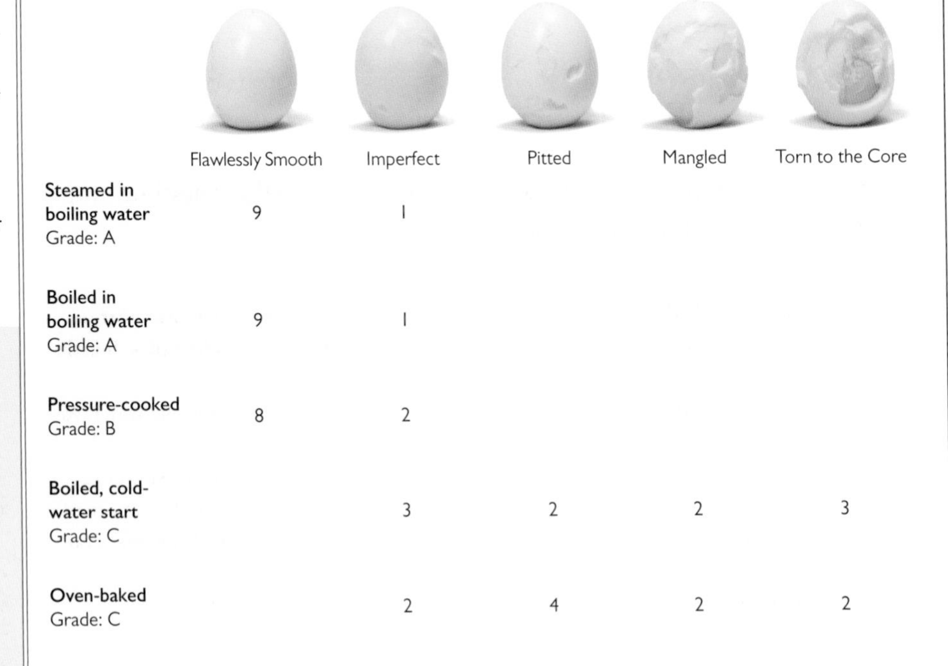

	Flawlessly Smooth	Imperfect	Pitted	Mangled	Torn to the Core
Steamed in boiling water Grade: A	9	1			
Boiled in boiling water Grade: A	9	1			
Pressure-cooked Grade: B	8	2			
Boiled, cold-water start Grade: C		3	2	2	3
Oven-baked Grade: C		2	4	2	2

Easy-Peel Hard-Cooked Eggs

MAKES 6 EGGS

Be sure to use large eggs that have no cracks and are cold from the refrigerator. If you don't have a steamer basket, use a spoon or tongs to gently place the eggs in the water. It does not matter if the eggs are above the water or partially submerged. You can use this method for fewer than six eggs without altering the timing. You can also double this recipe as long as you use a pot and steamer basket large enough to hold the eggs in a single layer. There's no need to peel the eggs right away. They can be stored in their shells and peeled when needed.

6 large eggs

1. Bring 1 inch water to rolling boil in medium saucepan over high heat. Place eggs in steamer basket. Transfer basket to saucepan. Cover, reduce heat to medium-low, and cook eggs for 13 minutes.
2. When eggs are almost finished cooking, combine 2 cups ice cubes and 2 cups cold water in medium bowl. Using tongs or spoon, transfer eggs to ice bath; let sit for 15 minutes. Peel before using.

PEEL SIX EGGS IN 41 SECONDS!

Combined with our hot-start cooking method, this novel approach to peeling is so efficient that the shells slip right off. Instead of preparing the ice bath in a bowl, use a plastic container with a tight-fitting lid. Once the eggs are chilled, pour off half the water and, holding the lid in place, shake the container vigorously using a vertical motion (the eggs will hit the top of the container) until the shells are cracked all over, about 40 shakes. Peel, rinse, and use as desired.

BLAME THE MEMBRANE

Most cooks assume that when an egg is difficult to peel, it's because the shell is sticking to the egg white. But it's the membrane between the shell and the white that's really the problem. When an egg is very fresh or when it's cooked slowly, the proteins in the white bond to the membrane instead of to one another, and the membrane becomes cemented to the white and impossible to peel away.

Our solution to this issue was to plunge the eggs directly into hot steam, which causes the egg white proteins to denature and shrink, reducing their ability to bond with the membrane and thus making hard-cooked eggs that are much easier to peel.

PERFECT POACHED EGGS

ANDREW JANJIGIAN, *March/April 2017*

You could argue that poaching eggs is an ambitious goal from the start. Drop a delicate raw egg, without its protective shell, into a pot of simmering water in the hope that it will emerge perfectly cooked. That means a tender, fully set white—no ring of gelatinous, translucent goo surrounding the yolk—and a yolk that's fluid but thickened, almost saucy. Equally important: The white must not be raggedy or wispy at the edges and must boast a plump, ovoid flying-saucer shape that's ideal for nestling atop an English muffin or a bed of salad greens.

Since a raw egg cooked in simmering water wants to spread out in all directions, it's this latter issue that's the trickiest to overcome. I was determined to figure out a solution, and I would have plenty of help: There are dozens of recipes, essays, and videos claiming to produce perfect results. I would try them all and see where I landed.

DOWN THE DRAIN

First I experimented with the more novel suggestions I found. These ranged from poaching eggs in a muffin tin in the oven to microwaving each egg individually in a small bowl of shallow water to parcooking them in the shell. I wasn't too surprised when most of these ideas proved to be dead ends. Conventional methods worked better, but they also had limitations. The most common trick was to swirl the water around the eggs to create a vortex that kept the white from spreading while folding any loose stragglers back on the yolk. This worked, but I could only poach one or two eggs at a time. Another approach involved lowering an egg into the water in a large metal spoon and using a second spoon to block the loose white from straying too far. The results were perfect—but who wants to juggle spoons like that to cook a single egg?

The most useful trick I found didn't try to corral the white during cooking but instead started by draining the raw eggs in a colander. At first I found this step counterintuitive—wouldn't all the white just drain off through the holes? It turns out that every egg contains two kinds of white, thick and thin. The thicker portion clings more tightly to the yolk, while the thinner, looser portion can slip through the colander holes. It is this thinner white that is most prone to spreading out into wispy tendrils in the water, so eliminating it went a long way toward fixing this issue. Starting with the freshest eggs possible increased the chance that more of the white was thick, so less of it would drain away, leaving a plumper poached egg.

ACID TEST

I next tried a common method targeted at a different issue: ensuring that the yolks stay runny while the whites, which solidify at a much higher temperature, reach the right degree of tender firmness. This approach calls for adding a few splashes of vinegar to the simmering water. Acid lowers the water's pH, which makes the proteins in the white set faster. The only issue? For the vinegar to be effective, you have to add so much that it gives the eggs a sour taste. I found the upper limit was ½ teaspoon per cup of water, which wasn't enough to be much help. But there was something else I could add that also makes egg proteins bond faster: salt. Using vinegar and salt together meant I didn't need much of either one. After a few tests, I worked out my formula: 1 tablespoon vinegar and 1 teaspoon salt to 6 cups water.

TESTING THE WATERS

But there was still more I could do to keep the whites tidy—I could get the eggs into the water as gently as possible. Gingerly sliding them into the water from bowls held close to the water's surface, as many recipes suggest, kept the white contained, but pouring multiple bowls at once was awkward. Cracking all the eggs into a 2-cup liquid measuring cup and pouring them in one by one at different spots in the water was easier. Plus, I could retrieve them in the order they were added, so they cooked to the same degree. It made sense at this point to switch from a large saucepan to a broader Dutch oven, which made it easier to bring the measuring cup close to the water.

Picture-perfect poached eggs need an assist from a few simple tools: a colander, a liquid measuring cup, and a lidded Dutch oven.

After bringing the water to a boil, I added the vinegar and salt, deposited the drained eggs around the water's surface, and then considered whether to lower the heat to a bare simmer or shut it off completely and cover the pot, allowing residual heat to do the cooking. I'd seen recipes calling for both methods, and after a quick test, I settled on the latter for two reasons: First, even though it was very gentle, the residual heat was still enough to allow the egg whites to set, and it was extra insurance that the yolk would stay beautifully runny. Second, in the covered environment, steam could cook the white at the very top of the eggs, which can be the most stubborn to set. Though timing varied slightly depending on the size of the eggs, I found that it took about 3 minutes for the white, including the top, to become nicely opaque. Plus, one advantage of poaching eggs as opposed to cooking them in their shells is that you can actually see the results and return the eggs to the pot if necessary.

And with that, I really had it: a foolproof recipe for perfect poached eggs. As ambitious as it had seemed at first, poaching eggs now felt like a quick, simple way to add protein to any meal, from eggs Benedict and corned beef hash to a salad or pasta to fried rice to polenta.

Perfect Poached Eggs

SERVES 2

For the best results, be sure to use the freshest eggs possible. Cracking the eggs into a colander will rid them of any watery, loose whites and result in perfectly shaped poached eggs. This recipe can be used to cook from one to four eggs. To make two batches of eggs to serve all at once, transfer four cooked eggs directly to a large pot of 150-degree water and cover them. This will keep them warm for 15 minutes or so while you return the poaching water to a boil and cook the next batch. We like to serve these eggs on buttered toast, on toasted and buttered English muffins, or on salads made with assertively flavored greens.

4 large eggs
1 tablespoon distilled white vinegar
Salt and pepper

1. Bring 6 cups water to boil in Dutch oven over high heat. Meanwhile, crack eggs into colander. Let stand until loose, watery whites drain away from eggs, 20 to 30 seconds. Gently transfer eggs to 2-cup liquid measuring cup.
2. Add vinegar and 1 teaspoon salt to boiling water. With lip of measuring cup just above surface of water, gently tip eggs into water, one at a time, leaving space between them. Cover pot, remove from heat, and let stand until whites closest to yolks are just set and opaque, about 3 minutes. If after 3 minutes whites are not set, let stand, checking every 30 seconds, until eggs reach desired doneness. (For medium-cooked yolks, let eggs stand in pot, covered, for 4 minutes, then begin checking for doneness.)
3. Using slotted spoon, carefully lift and drain each egg over Dutch oven. Season with salt and pepper to taste, and serve.

POACHING APPROACHES THAT DIDN'T PAN OUT

TEST 1 POACH IN MUFFIN TIN
Poach eggs in 350-degree oven in muffin tin with 1 tablespoon water added to each muffin cup. Results: Whites stayed neat, but eggs cooked unevenly, setting faster in outside cups.

TEST 2 POACH IN MICROWAVE
Place each egg in small glass bowl with ¼ cup water. Microwave for 1 to 2 minutes. Results: Whites stayed contained, but cooking time and heat level varied for different microwaves.

TEST 3 PARCOOK IN SHELLS
Briefly boil eggs in shells, then scoop each parcooked egg out of shell into water. Results: Too involved; eggs had to be cool before removing from shells, which was messy and tended to break up white.

TEST 4 CREATE VORTEX
Swirl water vigorously around eggs to create whirlpool. Results: Effective at keeping whites neat but too fussy and only worked for one or two eggs at a time.

TEST 5 ENCLOSE IN SPOONS
Lower 1 egg at a time into boiling water in large metal spoon, using smaller second spoon to keep loose white from straying too far. Results: Effective but fussy and only worked for one egg at a time.

TOOLS FOR SUCCESS

One key step to our perfect poached eggs is adding salt and vinegar to the poaching water, which helps the whites set at a lower temperature off the heat before the faster-cooking yolks get too thick. Beyond that, we also use a few special tools in order to achieve the perfect results.

COLANDER Draining the eggs before cooking removes the loose whites, preventing messy, wispy tendrils.

LIQUID MEASURING CUP Pouring the eggs from a measuring cup allows us to add them to the water gently, minimizing jostling.

DUTCH OVEN WITH LID Covering the pot allows residual heat to finish cooking the eggs, even the gooey white at the top.

MAKE-AHEAD POACHED EGGS

Here's a neat trick: Poach eggs ahead of time and serve them later (a common practice in restaurants). Start by transferring up to four cooked eggs to a bowl of cold water (for more than four eggs, use ice water). Refrigerate the eggs in the water for up to three days. To reheat, transfer the eggs to a pot of water heated to 150 degrees on the stove (use 6 cups of water for two to four eggs or 10 cups for six to eight eggs) and cover them for 3 minutes, by which time they should be at serving temperature.

PERFECT FRIED EGGS

ANDREW JANJIGIAN, *July/August 2013*

To me, a fried egg should be fried. I'm talking about the sort you find at the best diners: sunny-side up and crisp on its underside and edges, with a tender and opaque white and a perfectly runny yolk.

Ideally, I'd whip up this diner-style breakfast in my own kitchen, but the fried egg recipes I'd tried (and I'd run through my fair share) had failed to produce the results I wanted. Perhaps seasoned short-order cooks can consistently turn out great fried eggs because of their years of sheer practice. Or maybe a hot, slick commercial griddle is the key. All I knew for sure was that my home-cooked sunny-side up eggs always had one of two possible defects. The first was undercooked whites—specifically, a slippery, transparent ring of white surrounding the yolk. The second was an overcooked yolk—often it was fluid on top but cooked solid on the underside.

We cracked the code to perfectly fried eggs: It involves knowing when to walk away from the heat—and taking the eggs with you.

These faults are due to a predicament that plagues most types of egg cookery: Yolks and whites set at different temperatures. This means that yolks, which start to solidify at around 158 degrees, are inevitably overcooked by the time the whites, which set up at 180 degrees, are opaque. My objective, then, was to get the whites to cook through before the yolks did. I also wanted whites with beautifully bronzed, crispy edges. I had my work cut out for me.

GETTING FRIED

There are two basic approaches for tackling an egg's disparate doneness temperatures: Cook low and slow or hot and fast. The former calls for breaking the egg into a warm, greased nonstick skillet and letting it gradually come to temperature over low heat, which can take 5 or more minutes. If the flame is low enough, the heat will firm up the white before the yolk sets. The downside: This technique doesn't add browning or crispiness. Raising the heat toward the end of cooking only overcooks the entire egg.

The opposite method blasts the egg with fierce heat from the start in an attempt to cook the white so quickly that it is out of the pan before the yolk even considers setting up. The best example that I've tried comes from Spanish chef José Andrés, who calls for shallow-frying an egg in a tilted skillet containing an inch or so of very hot olive oil. Within seconds, the bottom of the white bubbles and browns, and as you continuously baste the egg with hot oil, the top of the white cooks through as well. The whole process happens so quickly (just 30 seconds or so) that the yolk can't possibly overcook, and the result—a filigree of browned, crispy egg surrounding a tender white and a runny yolk—is just what I wanted.

And yet, there were drawbacks. The flavor of the egg wasn't quite what I had in mind. Olive oil gave it a great savory taste, but it lacked the buttery richness of a diner-style egg. What's more, the sputtering oil made a mess of my stovetop and threatened to burn my forearms. The method also required cooking only one egg at a time. Sure, they cooked quickly, but I wanted to produce two or four eggs at one time. Could I use high heat and far less oil and be able to feed two people breakfast in one go?

HATCHING A PLAN

I reviewed what I had learned: First, it was difficult to get the eggs to cook evenly when I broke them one by one into the pan. Breaking the eggs into small bowls ahead of time so that all I had to do was slide them into the pan saved time—and went a long way in a recipe in which mere seconds make a difference. Plus, it worked equally well with two or four eggs. Second, it was important to let the pan fully preheat low and slow. A quick blast of high heat can cause hot spots to form and, thus, the eggs to cook at different rates. I got the best results by adding a teaspoon of vegetable oil to the skillet and setting it over low heat for a full 5 minutes. You also need a pan roomy enough for the eggs to spread out but not so roomy that large areas of the pan remain empty, which could cause the fat to burn. A 12- or 14-inch pan works best for four eggs, an 8- or 9-inch pan for two. Finally, adding a couple of pats of butter to the pan right before slipping in the eggs resulted in great flavor and browning due to the butter's milk proteins.

Going forward, I fried a few rounds of eggs on medium-high heat after preheating the skillet on low. The butter and oil sizzled nicely and the eggs started to brown almost immediately. But (perhaps predictably) things deteriorated from there, with the whites undercooking or the yolks overcooking, depending on when I reached for my spatula. Lowering the heat once the whites were browned at the edges did let them solidify before the yolks set up, but that process took so long that the whites, in effect, oversolidified, turning tough and rubbery.

For a moment I was stumped—until I thought back to the key to Andrés's shallow-fried eggs: basting. Basting the eggs with hot fat helped quickly cook the top and bottom of the white before the yolk could set up. I wasn't up for basting due to its accompanying splatter, but how else could I rapidly generate heat from above? I pictured myself in a diner, watching a line cook perch an overturned aluminum bowl on top of griddle-fried eggs to speed cooking. How about a lid? The reflected heat and steam trapped by a lid might just work.

For my next test, I covered the pan as soon as the eggs were in place. Ninety seconds later, I lifted the lid for a peek, fingers crossed, before using a spatula to quickly remove my specimens. The good news was that the vexing ring of jiggly, uncooked white around the

yolk was gone, and the white was perfectly tender, with a nicely browned underside and edges. The bad news was that the lid had trapped too much heat: The yolk was now a bit overcooked.

Instead, I slid the covered skillet off the burner entirely, hoping the gentle residual heat of the pan would firm up the white but not the yolk. It took a few dozen more eggs to get the timing just right but—stopwatch in hand—I finally nailed down the proper intervals: One minute over medium-high heat followed by an additional 15 to 45 seconds off the heat produced beautifully bronzed edges; just-set, opaque whites; and fluid yolks every time.

Mission accomplished: perfect diner-style fried eggs—no diner necessary.

Perfect Fried Eggs

SERVES 2

When checking the eggs for doneness, lift the lid just a crack to prevent loss of steam should they need further cooking. To cook two eggs, use an 8- or 9-inch nonstick skillet and halve the amounts of oil and butter.

2 teaspoons vegetable oil
4 large eggs
Salt and pepper
2 teaspoons unsalted butter, cut into 4 pieces and chilled

1. Heat oil in 12- or 14-inch nonstick skillet over low heat for 5 minutes. Meanwhile, crack 2 eggs into small bowl and season with salt and pepper. Repeat with remaining 2 eggs and second small bowl.
2. Increase heat to medium-high and heat until oil is shimmering. Add butter to skillet and quickly swirl to coat pan. Working quickly, pour 1 bowl of eggs into 1 side of pan and second bowl of eggs into other side. Cover and cook for 1 minute. Remove skillet from heat and let stand, covered, 15 to 45 seconds for runny yolks (white around edge of yolk will be barely opaque), 45 to 60 seconds for soft but set yolks, or about 2 minutes for medium-set yolks. Slide eggs onto plates and serve.

variation

Spaghetti with Fried Eggs and Bread Crumbs

SERVES 4

Be sure to cook the eggs just before serving, so that the yolks will still be runny and help create the sauce. Rather than using vegetable oil and butter, fry the eggs in 4 teaspoons olive oil.

2 slices hearty white sandwich bread, torn into quarters
½ cup extra-virgin olive oil
Salt and pepper
4 garlic cloves, minced
1 pound spaghetti
1 ounce Parmesan cheese, grated (½ cup), plus extra for serving
1 recipe Perfect Fried Eggs

1. Adjust oven rack to middle position and heat oven to 375 degrees. Pulse bread in food processor to coarse crumbs, about 10 pulses. Toss crumbs with 2 tablespoons oil, season with salt and pepper, and spread over rimmed baking sheet. Bake, stirring often, until golden, 8 to 10 minutes.
2. Cook 3 tablespoons oil, garlic, and ¼ teaspoon salt in 12– or 14-inch nonstick skillet over low heat, stirring constantly, until garlic foams and is sticky and straw-colored, 8 to 10 minutes; transfer to bowl.
3. Meanwhile, bring 4 quarts water to boil in large pot. Add pasta and 1 tablespoon salt and cook, stirring often, until al dente. Reserve 1 cup cooking water, then drain pasta and return it to pot. Add Parmesan, remaining 3 tablespoons oil, garlic mixture, and ½ cup reserved cooking water and toss to combine.
4. During final 5 minutes of pasta cooking time, wipe now-empty skillet clean with paper towels and place over low heat for 5 minutes. Fry eggs as directed, making sure yolks are still runny.
5. Season pasta with salt and pepper to taste, and add more reserved cooking water as needed to adjust consistency. Top individual portions with bread crumbs and fried egg and serve, passing extra Parmesan separately.

FLAWLESS FRIED EGGS: IT'S ALL IN THE DETAILS

Our method for foolproof fried eggs uses a few key tricks to ensure that both the yolk and the white come out perfectly done.

PREHEAT PAN Preheating your pan on low heat for 5 full minutes guarantees that there will be no hot spots in the skillet that could lead to unevenly cooked eggs.

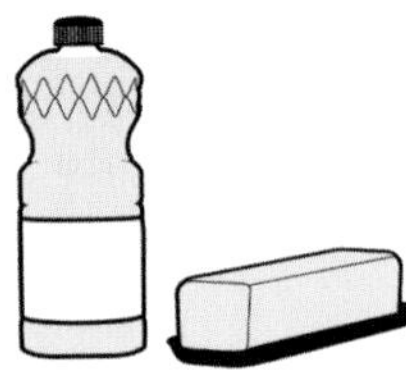

USE TWO FATS We use vegetable oil, which has a high smoke point, while preheating the pan. Butter, added just before the eggs, imparts a diner-style richness.

ADD EGGS ALL AT ONCE Cracking the eggs into small bowls makes it possible to add them to the skillet simultaneously so they cook at the same rate.

COVER IT UP Covering the skillet traps heat and steam, so the eggs cook from above as well as below, firming up the whites before the yolks overcook.

FINISH OFF HEAT Moving the pan off the heat after 1 minute of cooking allows the whites to finish cooking—gently—while keeping the yolks liquid.

PERFECT SCRAMBLED EGGS

DAN SOUZA, *July/August 2011*

I take pains with just about everything I cook, but not scrambled eggs. Usually my goal is just to get them on the table, fast. My method, such as it is, goes something like this: Whisk eggs, add a splash of milk, pour the mixture into a hot skillet, and stir over medium-high heat until the eggs puff up into large, moist curds. Trouble is, that's not what usually happens. All it takes is the merest distraction for my eggs to go from glossy, fluffy, and wobbly to tough, dry slabs. But even when I take my time and gently stir the eggs over lower heat, I still don't get the results I want. Instead, I end up with spoon food: curds so pebbly and fine that the mixture looks like oatmeal.

It was time to get serious, to stop leaving everything to chance and nail down an approach to foolproof, fluffy, tender scrambled eggs.

OF EGGS AND BONDAGE

I did a little investigation into the science of cooking eggs, and the first thing I discovered was that to produce the ideal voluptuous curds, my slapdash approach over higher heat wasn't far off. Only relatively high heat will produce enough steam (from the dairy and the water in eggs) to puff up the scramble. As the proteins in the eggs continue to heat, they unfold and then bond together to form a latticed gel in a process known as coagulation. The texture of the eggs depends on exactly how much unfolding and bonding occurs. To create moist curds, I needed the egg proteins to bond enough to transform from a liquid into a semisolid, but not so much that they seized up into a tough mass. Fortunately, I could fall back on some lessons learned in the test kitchen over the years to address this problem.

Lesson one: Adding salt to the raw eggs makes for more-tender curds. In the same way that soaking a piece of pork in a brine solution tenderizes its protein network, salt dissolves egg proteins so that they are unable to bond as tightly when cooked.

Lesson two: Don't overbeat the eggs or you'll have a tough scramble. This may seem counterintuitive (since physical agitation usually destroys structure), but the principle is easily illustrated by what happens when you whip egg whites into peaks. Vigorous whisking unfolds proteins in much the same way that heat does; once unfolded, the protein strands readily bond together to form a tighter structure. Since the last thing you want to do is accelerate the unfolding process before the eggs hit the heat, beat them until just combined with the gentler action of a fork rather than a whisk.

THE DAIRY GODMOTHER

I kept those points in mind as I assumed the role of short-order cook, whipping up batch after batch of scrambled eggs to see how the other major component in the mix—dairy—affected the texture. Some of the recipes I consulted called for milk, others for half-and-half or heavy cream, but all three options contain two important tenderizers: water and fat. What I needed to know was how the water-to-fat ratio in each would affect coagulation; I also needed to know exactly how dairy-rich my tasters liked their eggs.

To feed four people, I beat eight eggs with both salt and pepper and varying proportions of all three dairy options; poured the eggs into a medium-hot, butter-slicked 12-inch skillet; and dragged a heatproof rubber spatula around the pan for about 2 minutes, until the eggs appeared clumpy but still shiny and wet. My tasters and I mulled over the pros and cons of each dairy ingredient. Milk produced slightly fluffier, cleaner-tasting curds, but they were particularly prone to weeping. Heavy cream, on the other hand, rendered the eggs very stable but dense, and some tasters found their flavor just too rich. One-quarter cup of half-and-half fared best: Though everyone agreed that these curds could stand to be fluffier, they were decently puffed and stable thanks to the tandem effects of the liquid's water and fat.

The benefit of adding dairy is threefold: First, the water it contains (80 percent in half-and-half) interrupts the protein network and dilutes the molecules, thereby raising the temperature at which eggs coagulate and providing a greater safety net against overcooking (and disproving the classic French theory that adding the dairy at the end of cooking is best). Second, as the water in the dairy vaporizes, it provides lift (just as in a loaf of baking bread), which causes the eggs to puff up. And third, the fat in the dairy also raises the coagulation temperature by coating and insulating part of each protein molecule so that they cannot stick together as tightly.

A combination of high and low heat, plus a fat boost from dairy and extra yolks, produce the pillowy scrambled eggs of our dreams.

Half-and-half wasn't a perfect solution, however: Some tasters still found the dairy flavor too prominent. Less dairy would only make the recipe less foolproof, so I researched ways to boost egg flavor. The best suggestion came from a colleague. She mentioned that when her grandmother makes fresh pasta, she adds an extra yolk or two to the dough to approximate the richer flavor of farm-fresh eggs. I followed suit, and sure enough, the more yolks I added to the mix, the richer the results. There was no need to overdo it, though: Two yolks per eight eggs balanced the flavor nicely. Even better, the high proportion of fat and emulsifiers in the yolks further raised the coagulation temperature, helping to stave off overcooking.

Before I moved on to fine-tune the cooking method, I tried a couple of unconventional stir-ins that promised either fluffier or more

tender eggs: vinegar and baking powder. The acidity in the former tenderized the eggs in much the same way that salt did but far more drastically: Just a drop rendered the curds mushy. A dash of baking powder was also too much of a good thing, puffing the eggs like a diner-style omelet as well as imparting a chemical aftertaste.

I also experimented with the advice of old-school French cookbooks to start with room-temperature eggs. While we've proved that egg temperature can influence the structure of some delicate cakes, I found that cold eggs and room-temperature eggs produced virtually identical scrambles.

So much for "secret weapons." It was time to face the fire.

BEATING THE HEAT

The bottom line was that no matter how perfectly I balanced the amounts of protein, fat, and water, the scrambled eggs would still fail if they overcooked. Low heat would curb overcooking, but I needed higher heat to produce nicely puffed curds. Suddenly it hit me like a whack with a cast-iron skillet: What if I used both high and low heat?

I mixed up another batch of eggs, tossed a piece of cold butter into the pan, and turned the heat to medium-high. Once the butter was melted but not brown (a cue that a pan is too hot), I added the eggs, constantly scraping the bottom and sides of the skillet to form large curds and prevent any spots from overcooking. As soon as my spatula could just leave a trail in the pan with minimal raw egg filling in the gap (about 2 minutes in), I dropped the heat to low and switched to a gentle folding motion to keep from breaking up the large curds. When the eggs looked cooked through but still glossy (about 45 seconds later), I slid them onto a plate to stop the cooking process. To my delight, the results were almost perfect—fluffy and tender, for sure—and the method was far more fail-safe than my high-heat-only attempts.

My tasters' only holdover request? Larger curds, please. I tried scraping a bit less frequently, but while the curds were certainly bigger, they were also overcooked in spots. Stymied, I looked over all the elements in my recipe and realized that there was one component I hadn't addressed: the size of the pan. In theory, my vessel choice mattered more here than in any other recipe, since a smaller skillet would keep the eggs in a thicker layer, thereby trapping more steam and producing heartier curds. Whisking together one more batch of eggs, I put aside my 12-inch skillet and grabbed a 10-inch pan instead, and then proceeded with my recipe. About 3 minutes later, I had the best batch of scrambled eggs yet: big billowy curds that were perfect with or without a last-minute sprinkle of fresh herbs.

I was finished with slapdash. A simple, foolproof version of my favorite breakfast was finally served.

Perfect Scrambled Eggs

SERVES 4

Follow visual cues when cooking the eggs; your pan's thickness will affect the cooking times. To dress up the eggs, add 2 tablespoons of minced fresh parsley, chives, basil, or cilantro or 1 tablespoon of minced fresh dill or tarragon after reducing the heat.

8 large eggs plus 2 large yolks
¼ cup half-and-half
Salt and pepper
1 tablespoon unsalted butter, chilled

1. Adjust oven rack to middle position and heat oven to 200 degrees. Place 4 heatproof plates on rack.
2. Using fork, beat eggs and yolks, half-and-half, ¼ teaspoon salt, and ¼ teaspoon pepper in bowl until thoroughly combined and mixture is pure yellow; do not overbeat.
3. Melt butter in 10-inch nonstick skillet over medium-high heat (butter should not brown), swirling to coat pan. Add egg mixture and, using heat-resistant rubber spatula, constantly and firmly scrape along bottom and sides of skillet until eggs begin to clump and spatula leaves trail on bottom of pan, 1½ to 2½ minutes. Reduce heat to low and gently but constantly fold eggs until clumped and just slightly wet, 30 to 60 seconds. Immediately transfer eggs to warmed plates and season with salt to taste. Serve immediately.

variations

Perfect Scrambled Eggs for Two

Use 4 large eggs plus 1 large yolk, 2 tablespoons half-and-half, ⅛ teaspoon salt, ⅛ teaspoon pepper, and ½ tablespoon butter. Cook eggs in 8-inch nonstick skillet for 45 to 75 seconds over medium-high heat and then 30 to 60 seconds over low heat.

Perfect Scrambled Eggs for One

Use 2 large eggs plus 1 large yolk, 1 tablespoon half-and-half, pinch salt, pinch pepper, and ¼ tablespoon butter. Cook eggs in 8-inch nonstick skillet for 30 to 60 seconds over medium-high heat and then 30 to 60 seconds over low heat.

Smoked Salmon Scrambled Eggs with Chive Butter

Mash 3 tablespoons softened unsalted butter with 3 tablespoons minced fresh chives. Toast 4 (1-inch-thick) slices rustic white bread, then spread with 2 tablespoons chive butter. Cook eggs as directed, first melting remaining chive butter in pan. Immediately spoon eggs on top of buttered toasts, top with 3 ounces smoked salmon, and serve. Garnish with extra chives if desired.

SCRAMBLED EGG EXTREMES

The best puffy scrambled eggs aren't hastily cooked over high heat. Nor are they gently cooked over low heat.

RUBBERY
Blasting the eggs over higher heat gets breakfast on the table in a hurry—but produces dried-out, rubbery curds.

WET
Keeping the heat low might prevent the eggs from overcooking, but the result will be loose, tiny curds that look like lumpy custard.

TRANSLATING HUEVOS RANCHEROS

ERIKA BRUCE, *January/February 2006*

Huevos rancheros, or "rancher-style eggs," is a dish born of ease and convenience: a quick, satisfying meal that makes use of leftover salsa and corn tortillas to serve as a simple Mexican breakfast alongside hearty refried beans. While there are many variations on this theme, most often the eggs are quickly fried, slipped onto a corn tortilla base, and then napped with a fiery roasted tomato-chile salsa.

North of the border, it's a different story: The huevos rancheros found on American brunch menus more closely resemble heaping plates of nachos. The eggs are lost under any number of untraditional ingredients—meat, gobs of melted cheese, shredded lettuce, and slices of avocado—the tortillas become soggy, and the flavors are muddied.

But even with an authentic recipe, making this dish at home is no less problematic when the cook is faced with mediocre supermarket ingredients such as pale, mealy tomatoes and rubbery packaged tortillas. I wanted to do right by this dish and produce a version as close to authentic as I could with the materials at hand.

THE SALSA DANCE

Salsa is the star in most authentic versions, so improving it was my first move. Traditionally, a cooked salsa is used (often fried in a little hot oil), and I thought canned tomatoes might give me better flavor than fresh. Armed only with the basics—tomatoes, jalapeños, and onions—I sautéed my way through a few simple salsas, substituting pureed, diced, and whole canned tomatoes for fresh. Pureed tomatoes were too thin and smooth, diced tomatoes were on the overly firm and chunky side, and whole tomatoes tasted too cooked. Tasters were looking for the bright, tart flavor that only fresh tomatoes can offer.

Back in the produce aisle, I reexamined my options. I tried diminutive cherry and oblong plum tomatoes as well as the usual round orbs. The cherry tomatoes held the most promise with their puckeringly tart flavor, but tasters couldn't get past the amount of skin and seeds in the salsa. The plum tomatoes had slightly more complexity than the round tomatoes and a more compact, less watery texture. In an effort to increase their flavor, I turned to the broiler but despite blackening and blistering their skins, the high heat did little to improve the flavor on the inside of the tomatoes. I decided to reduce the oven temperature and give the tomatoes more oven time. At 375 degrees, the tomatoes stayed intact, their flesh smooth and velvety.

With a little attention, even mediocre supermarket ingredients can be made to shine in this homemade version of a Mexican classic.

Because I was now roasting the tomatoes and thus effectively enhancing their flavor (and then pulsing them in the food processor), I wondered if the chiles and onions would also benefit from roasting. I halved the jalapeños and cut the onions into thick wedges and tossed them with a little vegetable oil along with the tomatoes. Indeed, roasting improved their flavor, adding a deeper, sweeter intensity. Heady garlic was a welcome addition to this mix, as were cumin for its nutty flavor and cayenne pepper for extra zing. For more color and depth of flavor, I coated all the ingredients with a tablespoon of tomato paste before putting them in the oven. All I needed now was some brightness to round out the salsa. Once I had given the roasted vegetables a quick turn in the food processor, I added lime juice and fresh cilantro. As a final touch, I reserved one jalapeño and added it, finely chopped, at the end for a zesty, clean chile flavor.

NOT SO OVER-EASY

After the rigmarole of roasting the salsa ingredients (though it was certainly worth the effort), I was chagrined to find that the simple fried-egg preparation I was expecting turned out to be a sloppy mess on the plate. Four gently fried eggs looked beautiful in the skillet but, once separated, appeared haphazard and irregular on top of a round tortilla—if I didn't break the yolks getting them there. While poaching the eggs is not traditional, I had seen this technique in a few recipes; indeed, these eggs were easily (and neatly) scooped out of their poaching liquid.

As I monitored my two adjacent cooking vessels full of bubbling liquid—poaching eggs and simmering salsa—I realized I might be able to make things even easier. Adding all the hot salsa to a skillet, I scooped out four small wells and cracked an egg into each, then fit a lid over the top for even cooking. Although the edges of the whites were disrupted from the bubbling salsa, the eggs were just as easily transferred to the plate as before. Lowering the heat while the eggs were poaching solved the frayed-edge matter, and I finally achieved the look I was after. Even better, the eggs benefited from the flavor boost, and I had only one pot to watch (and one less to wash).

TORTILLA REFORM

Most authentic recipes call for fresh, handmade corn tortillas. I was stuck with all-but-stale supermarket versions. Some recipes attempt to "soften" the tortillas with a 5-second shallow-fry, but this produced sodden, greasy results. Longer frying eliminated the sogginess but not the greasiness. Toasting the tortillas in a thin coating of oil in a skillet made them tough. Finally, I returned to the oven. Brushed lightly with oil, sprinkled with a little salt, and toasted until golden brown at 450 degrees, these tortillas were crisp and dry—a perfect foil for the soft, creamy poached eggs and the deep, roasted flavors of the fiery salsa. My translation was complete.

Huevos Rancheros

SERVES 2 TO 4

To save time in the morning, make the salsa the day before and store it overnight in the refrigerator. For extra-spicy salsa, add some of the reserved jalapeño ribs and seeds to taste. If you like, serve with refried beans.

Salsa

3 jalapeño chiles, stemmed, halved, and seeded
1½ pounds plum tomatoes, cored and halved
½ onion, cut into ½-inch wedges
2 garlic cloves, peeled
2 tablespoons vegetable oil
1 tablespoon tomato paste
Salt and pepper
½ teaspoon ground cumin
⅛ teaspoon cayenne pepper
3 tablespoons minced fresh cilantro
1–2 tablespoons lime juice plus lime wedges

Tortillas and Eggs

4 (6-inch) corn tortillas
1 tablespoon vegetable oil
Salt and pepper
4 large eggs

1. *For the salsa:* Adjust oven rack to middle position and heat oven to 375 degrees. Mince 1 jalapeño; set aside. Toss remaining 2 jalapeños, tomatoes, onion, garlic, oil, tomato paste, 1 teaspoon salt, cumin, and cayenne together in bowl. Arrange vegetables cut side down on aluminum foil–lined rimmed baking sheet. Roast until tomatoes are tender and skins begin to shrivel and brown, 35 to 45 minutes.

2. Let roasted vegetables cool on baking sheet for 10 minutes. Process onion, garlic, and jalapeños in food processor until almost completely broken down, about 10 seconds. Add tomatoes and process until salsa is slightly chunky, about 10 seconds. Stir in minced jalapeño and 2 tablespoons cilantro. Season with salt, pepper, and lime juice to taste. (Salsa can be refrigerated for up to 24 hours.)

3. *For the tortillas and eggs:* Increase oven temperature to 450 degrees. Brush both sides of each tortilla lightly with oil, sprinkle with salt, and place on clean baking sheet. Bake until tops just begin to color, 5 to 7 minutes. Flip tortillas and continue to bake until golden, 2 to 3 minutes. Remove tortillas from oven and cover baking sheet with aluminum foil to keep tortillas warm.

4. Meanwhile, bring salsa to gentle simmer in 12-inch nonstick skillet over medium heat. Off heat, make 4 wells (about 2 inches wide) in salsa using back of spoon. Crack 1 egg into each indentation and season eggs with salt and pepper. Cover and cook over medium-low heat until eggs are cooked through, 4 to 5 minutes for runny yolks or 6 to 7 minutes for set yolks.

5. Place tortillas on individual serving plates and gently top with cooked eggs. Spoon salsa around eggs to cover tortillas. Sprinkle with remaining 1 tablespoon cilantro. Serve with lime wedges.

BUYING EGGS

There are numerous–and often confusing–options when buying eggs at the supermarket. Here are a few things we've learned in the test kitchen about buying eggs.

COLOR The shell's hue depends on the breed of the chicken. The white-feathered leghorn chicken produces the typical white egg. Brown-feathered birds, such as Rhode Island Reds, produce ecru- to coffee-colored eggs. Our tests proved that shell color has no effect on flavor.

FARM-FRESH AND ORGANIC In our taste tests, farm-fresh eggs were standouts. The large yolks were bright orange and sat very high above the comparatively small whites, and the flavor of these eggs was exceptionally rich and complex. Save these for use in egg-centric dishes where they can really shine. Organic eggs took second place, with eggs from hens raised on a vegetarian diet in third place and standard supermarket eggs last.

THREE STEPS TO BETTER *HUEVOS RANCHEROS*

Enhancing simple store-bought ingredients with a few easy tricks and rethinking how the elements of this rich and spicy breakfast dish came together helped us create a more flavorful, streamlined version of huevos rancheros.

ROAST Slow roasting improved the flavor of supermarket tomatoes while intensifying the other salsa ingredients.

TOAST Crisping store-bought tortillas in the oven yielded the best texture—light and crispy, not tough or greasy.

POACH Poaching the eggs in small wells made in the salsa improved their flavor and left us with just one pan to watch.

DEFINING HASH BROWN POTATOES

SUSAN LOGOZZO, *September/October 1998*

The recollection of fragrant, crisply fried potato cakes being served in a diner by a short order cook provided the inspiration for me to perfect my own hash brown recipe.

After researching potato recipes, I decided I had to make a distinction between hash browns and their close relatives—home fries, potato pancakes, and roesti. To my mind, home fries, a close relative of hash browns, are made from potatoes that are always cooked first, then chopped or sliced, sautéed, tossed with onions in oil or bacon fat, and served in a mound. Potato pancakes are a more distant ethnic cousin, always made with egg and a starch binder, which give them a different appearance and a softer texture. Roesti, raw grated potatoes cooked in a large skillet, are the most similar to hash browns. However, they are much thicker and are usually cut into wedges and served as a potato accompaniment at dinner. I concluded that hash browns are best defined as thin, crisply sautéed potato cakes made with grated or chopped potatoes, raw or precooked.

No need to precook the potatoes for perfectly crispy, rich hash browns; just don't forget the butter.

THE POTATO

Even though I assumed a starchier potato would be best suited for this assignment, I began by testing every variety of potato in my local market. After thorough testing, the only type I completely eliminated were the waxy or low-starch varieties, such as Red Bliss, which did not stay together or brown well and were also lacking in flavor. The all-purpose potatoes sold in plastic bags in the supermarket, which have a medium starch content, worked well enough to be considered an adequate choice. I also liked the buttery color, as well as the taste, of Yukon Golds, another medium-starch potato. But the russet or Idaho, a high-starch potato, yielded the best results overall. It adhered well, browned beautifully, and had the most pronounced potato flavor.

My next challenge was to decide between raw and precooked potatoes. My guess was that precooked potatoes would be my choice, but side-by-side taste tests convinced me I was wrong. Precooked potatoes tasted good, but when cut into chunks they did not stay together in a cohesive cake, and when grated they needed to be pressed very hard to form a cake. Unfortunately, this meant they ended up having the mouthfeel of fried mashed potato. Although this is an acceptable alternative if you have leftover cooked potatoes, I found that I preferred using raw, grated potatoes. Because they stayed together well while cooking, they could be made into individual rounds or formed into a single large round that could be cut into wedges or folded over, omelet-style. I also liked the more textured interior, the pronounced potato taste, and the way the raw shreds of potatoes formed an attractive, deeply browned crust.

Choosing the best method for cutting the potatoes was easy. For the initial tests, I used raw potatoes and tried them coarsely chopped and diced as well as grated, since these three methods were mentioned in several recipes. The chopped potatoes never stayed together in the pan, nor did the diced version. They browned up nicely, but in my opinion, they were simply chopped, sautéed potatoes, not hash browns. I did the remainder of my testing with potatoes grated on the large-hole side of a box grater, which gave the hash browns the texture I was looking for. This could also be done with the shredding attachment of a food processor.

To peel or not to peel the potato is a matter of personal preference, based on nutritional and aesthetic factors. The presence of the grated peel altered the taste a bit, but it did not negatively affect the overall cooking method and desired outcome.

COOKING THE HASH BROWNS

After cooking countless batches of hash browns, I found that the pan itself was an important factor. A skillet with sloping sides made it considerably easier to press the potatoes into a flattened shape, invert them, and slide them from the pan. All these tasks were more difficult with a conventional straight-sided frying pan. As for browning, properly seasoned cast-iron pans and uncoated stainless steel pans produced the best exterior, with potatoes that were evenly colored and crusty; however, nonstick pans browned adequately and, obviously, were easy to use and clean.

I also found that butter, brought just to the browning point over medium-high heat before adding the potatoes, provided good color and a very rich, satisfying taste. Since I find the aroma and taste of fried bacon irresistible, though, I was still anxious to cook my hash browns in bacon fat. But while the rendered fat did add a bacon taste, the potatoes did not achieve the same golden brown color they did with just plain butter. I also found the overall flavor of the potatoes diminished by the lack of butter. Of course, if you're frying bacon for breakfast and have the fat sitting in your pan, add a little butter and use it to cook your hash browns. At this point in my testing, I could predict the outcome of using vegetable oil (canola or corn). The resulting crust was not as golden brown and the taste not as interesting.

My last cooking-method test was to cover the potatoes during cooking. What I found was that the cover trapped steam in the pan, which reduced the crispness of the crust. This was usually not necessary anyway, because I began with a thin layer of potatoes in the pan, which cooked through adequately without covering.

While testing, I used only salt and freshly ground pepper for seasoning, planning to experiment with other ingredients at a later time, but I became so fond of the buttery salt and pepper taste that I decided to use only these seasonings for the master recipe. Of course, adding grated onion or chopped

scallions and parsley (or other fresh herbs to suit your taste) is certainly an option. The onion or herbs can either be tossed with the grated potatoes before cooking or sprinkled over the potatoes in the pan before pressing them with the spatula.

I found that my hash browns could be made into one or more individual servings or one large portion (folded or not) that could be cut into wedges. I also liked using hash browns as the base for toppings or folding them over fillings like omelets. Regardless of how you choose to present the hash browns, however, serve them steaming hot.

FLIPPING HASH BROWNS

1. After browning first side, slide hash browns onto large plate.

2. Invert hash browns onto second large plate.

3. Slide, browned side up, back into skillet to brown second side.

Classic Hash Browns

SERVES 4

Shred the potatoes on the large holes of a box grater or with the large shredding disk of a food processor. To prevent the potatoes from turning brown, grate them just before cooking. You can leave the potatoes unpeeled, if desired. Garnish the hash browns with chopped scallions or chives before serving, if desired.

1 pound russet potatoes, peeled and shredded
Salt and pepper
2 tablespoons unsalted butter

1. Wrap shredded potatoes in clean dish towel and squeeze thoroughly to remove excess moisture. Toss potatoes with ¼ teaspoon salt and season with pepper.
2. Meanwhile, melt 1 tablespoon butter in 10-inch skillet over medium-high heat until it begins to brown, swirling to coat skillet. Scatter potatoes evenly over entire skillet and press to flatten. Reduce heat to medium and cook until dark golden brown and crisp, 7 to 8 minutes.
3. Slide hash browns onto large plate. Melt remaining 1 tablespoon butter in now-empty skillet, swirling to coat pan. Invert hash browns onto second plate and slide, browned side up, back into skillet. Continue to cook over medium heat until bottom is dark golden brown and crisp, 5 to 6 minutes longer.
4. Fold hash brown cake in half; cook for 1 minute. Slide onto plate or cutting board, cut into wedges, and serve immediately.

variations

Hash Brown "Omelet" with Cheddar, Tomato, and Basil

The crisp potatoes offer a nice contrast to many filling ingredients. Try filling with ¼ cup chopped ham, bacon, or sausage and/or ¼ cup cooked vegetables, such as mushrooms, peppers, or onions.

After melting butter in step 3 and sliding potatoes back into skillet, top hash browns with 1 seeded and finely chopped tomato, ¼ cup shredded cheddar cheese, and 1 tablespoon chopped fresh basil. Proceed with recipe, folding potato cake in half and cooking until cheese melts.

Open-Faced Hash Browns with Ham, Tomato, and Swiss Cheese

As with the Hash Brown "Omelet," these individual potato cakes can be topped with a host of ingredients. For an interesting variation, you can top the fully cooked hash browns with smoked salmon and sour cream after you remove them from the skillet.

After melting butter in step 2, divide potatoes into 4 equal portions and reduce cooking time to 5 minutes per side, turning them with spatula rather than inverting them using plate. Once potatoes are fully browned, top each portion with 1 thin slice deli ham, quartered, 1 thinly sliced small tomato, and 1 ounce shredded Swiss cheese. Cover and continue to cook over medium heat until cheese melts, 1 to 2 minutes. Serve immediately.

STRESS-FREE SPUD STORAGE

When buying potatoes, look for firm specimens that are free of green spots, sprouts, cracks, and other blemishes. We generally prefer to buy loose potatoes, so that we can see what we are getting. Stay away from potatoes in plastic bags, which can cause potatoes to sprout and rot. If stored under unsuitable heat and light circumstances, potatoes will germinate and grow. In addition, when potatoes are stored improperly, the level of naturally occurring toxins increases, causing a greenish tinge known as solanine. If your potatoes have solanine spots, those portions of the potato should be totally cut away, since solanine is not destroyed by cooking. To avoid these issues, keep potatoes in a cool, dark, dry place and away from onions, which give off gases that will hasten sprouting. Most varieties should keep for several months. The exception is new potatoes—because of their thinner skins, they will keep no more than one month.

BEST BUTTERMILK PANCAKES

MARCUS WALSER, *July/August 2009*

When our forebears set out to make pancakes enriched with the sweet tang of buttermilk, they had a built-in advantage: real buttermilk. Instead of the thinly flavored liquid processed from skim milk and cultured bacteria that passes for buttermilk today, these earlier Americans turned to the fat-flecked byproduct of churning cream into butter. This rich, flavorful buttermilk thickened and increased in tanginess the longer it was stored.

The switch from churned buttermilk to cultured buttermilk would account for the lack of true tang in most modern-day buttermilk pancakes—but not for flaws in texture. The ideal flapjack boasts a slightly crisp, golden crust surrounding a fluffy, tender center that has just enough structure to withstand a good dousing of maple syrup. Unfortunately, my attempts to create such perfection gave me a tall stack of pancake pitfalls. Some were thick and cottony; others were dense and gummy or oddly crêpe-like. This short-order cook had a long way to go.

The secret to full-flavored, fluffy pancakes in every batch is in the chemistry of the acids and leaveners in the batter.

NO (PAN)CAKE WALK

Straightforward as it may seem, pancake-making is fickle work, more akin to unleashing a series of volatile chemical reactions in a pan than mixing up a quick batter of flour, sugar, salt, milk, buttermilk, leavening agents, eggs, and melted butter. Here are just some of the dynamics at work: The proteins in flour combine with the water in the milk and buttermilk to form gluten, the network of proteins that gives pancakes their basic structure. Eggs add more structure-reinforcing protein, plus moisture that evaporates as the pancake cooks, creating bubbles that help it rise. Baking soda responds to the acid in the buttermilk, producing carbon dioxide gas that further aerates the pancake; baking powder reacts to the heat of the pan to release more carbon dioxide.

The problem is that changing any one of these ingredients sets off a chain reaction that affects the others, with dramatic consequences for the final flapjack. And buttermilk, it turns out, is one of the most potent triggers for such a domino effect.

Case in point: A recipe I tried early on called for 2 cups of flour, 2 tablespoons of sugar, 1½ teaspoons of baking powder, 1 teaspoon of baking soda, ½ teaspoon of salt, 1 cup of milk, 1 cup of buttermilk, 4 tablespoons of melted butter, and two eggs. I mixed the wet and dry ingredients in separate bowls and then gently combined them with a few quick whisks to form a batter (with pancake recipes, less is more when it comes to whisking), which I cooked on a hot, oiled griddle, flipping once during the process. Though the pancakes weren't terrible, they needed to be lighter and, as I'd come to expect, they had only weak buttermilk flavor.

Swapping out regular milk for just the tangy stuff seemed like an obvious solution—until that plan deflated. Literally. More buttermilk means a greater concentration of acid in the mix, which in turn causes the baking soda to bubble too rapidly. The result: pancakes that overinflate when they first cook and then collapse like popped balloons, becoming dense and wet by the time they hit the plate. OK, simple enough—just cut back on the baking soda, right? Wrong. Baking soda promotes browning. Reducing it leads to pale pancakes completely missing their flavorful, golden brown crust.

MORE TANG FOR THE BUCK

Just a few tests in, and I was already in a jam. The batter needed more acid for flavor, but upping the acid content meant overinflated, dense pancakes. My only hope was to concentrate on getting the buttermilk flavor just right and keep my fingers crossed that I could backtrack and fix what would almost certainly be a ruined texture.

Next I tried increasing the amount of buttermilk from 2 to 2½ cups. Not surprisingly, more made the pancakes spread out too thin. They had no real interior—just two crusts smashed together. What about dehydrated buttermilk powder? Technically, it should consist of pure buttermilk with just the liquid component removed. But tasters complained that these pancakes tasted soapy. Maybe a more concentrated acid would help boost flavor. I tried adding a few teaspoons of lemon juice to the batter, but tasters objected to its distinct citrus flavor and aroma. Similarly, vinegar added a sour odor that tasters detected immediately. What about other dairy ingredients? Yogurt has an acidity comparable to that of buttermilk, but is thicker. I figured I could add at least ¼ cup of it without throwing off the consistency of the batter too much. No such luck. Once whisked into the batter, yogurt turned as loose as buttermilk.

Sour cream was my last hope. Since it's cultured with the same bacteria as buttermilk, it has many of the same flavor compounds, but in much higher concentration, yielding more acid per cup. It also boasts far less moisture. Just ¼ cup gave my pancakes the rich tang I was after, without diluting the batter. Tasters didn't even know there was a buttermilk impostor in the mix.

INFLATION NEGATION

I still had some work to do on texture. As expected, the added acid from the sour cream exacerbated the leavening problem; plus, the pancakes had an extremely wet, gummy crumb. As I thought about it, I realized why: A quarter-cup of sour cream has the same amount of fat as a tablespoon of butter. Too much fat can stunt gluten formation by coating the flour proteins so they don't bond with water. Backing off to 3 tablespoons of butter reduced gumminess significantly. Once I fixed the problem of overinflation, it should rid the cakes of gumminess entirely.

I knew that my hyperactive leaveners had to be cut down. Due to its critical role in flavorful browning, removing baking soda was out of the question. What if I removed the baking powder instead? "Double-acting" baking powder is called so for a reason. It has a dual impact, reacting with its own built-in acid (usually cream of tartar) to create carbon dioxide as soon as it encounters moisture; it then reacts again to a second built-in acid (sodium aluminum sulfate) to create more gas when exposed to heat above 120 degrees. Eliminating baking powder would cut out both these reactions.

As I pulled my first batch of tender, fluffy, perfectly risen pancakes off the griddle, I thought I had solved my problem. But over the course of a few batches from this batter, the quality of my pancakes slowly declined. By the time I got to my fourth batch, the cakes were so dense and underrisen as to be nearly inedible. The problem is that baking soda reacts as soon as it gets wet, instantly enlarging the tiny bubbles of gas created by whisking. The first batch gets the full benefit of these bubbles, but subsequent batches are shortchanged as the bubbles dissipate. Without the compensating effect of baking powder creating more gas when the cakes hit the pan, a dense texture is the inevitable result.

Eliminating either of these leaveners wasn't an option, but what about cutting back on each of them? I reduced both by ½ teaspoon and instantly proved my earlier assertion that with pancakes, even the smallest change can make the biggest difference. Thankfully, this time the change was for the better. My pancakes had gone from collapsed, flat, and unpalatably dense to light, fluffy, and full of their trademark tang. Finally, I had buttermilk pancakes that lived up to their name. Pass the syrup, please.

Best Buttermilk Pancakes

SERVES 4 TO 6

The pancakes can be cooked on an electric griddle. Set the griddle temperature to 350 degrees and cook as directed. This recipe works best with a lower-protein all-purpose flour such as Gold Medal or Pillsbury. If you use an all-purpose flour with a higher protein content, such as King Arthur, you will need to add an extra tablespoon or two of buttermilk.

2 cups (10 ounces) all-purpose flour
2 tablespoons sugar
1 teaspoon baking powder
½ teaspoon baking soda
½ teaspoon salt
2 cups buttermilk
¼ cup sour cream
2 large eggs
3 tablespoons unsalted butter, melted and cooled
1–2 teaspoons vegetable oil

1. Adjust oven rack to middle position and heat oven to 200 degrees. Spray wire rack set in rimmed baking sheet with vegetable oil spray; place in oven. Whisk flour, sugar, baking powder, baking soda, and salt together in medium bowl. In second medium bowl, whisk together buttermilk, sour cream, eggs, and melted butter. Make well in center of dry ingredients and pour in wet ingredients; stir until just combined. Do not overmix. Let batter sit for 10 minutes.
2. Heat 1 teaspoon oil in 12-inch nonstick skillet over medium heat until shimmering. Using paper towels, carefully wipe out oil, leaving thin film of oil on bottom and sides of pan. Using ¼-cup dry measuring cup, portion batter into pan in 4 places. Cook until edges are set, first side is golden brown, and bubbles on surface are just beginning to break, 2 to 3 minutes. Using thin, wide spatula, flip pancakes and continue to cook until second side is golden brown, 1 to 2 minutes longer. Serve pancakes immediately or transfer to wire rack in preheated oven. Repeat with remaining batter, using remaining oil as necessary.

BAKING SODA'S BROWNING BOOST

We've always heard that baking soda boosts browning, so even when we found that the high concentration of acid in our pancake batter was overreacting with the baking soda, causing our pancakes to rise too high and then deflate, we still left this leavener in. But would taking baking soda out really be so bad if it led to fluffier pancakes?

EXPERIMENT We mixed two batches of pancake batter—one leavened with baking powder and baking soda; the second leavened with baking powder alone—and cooked pancakes from each batter side by side.

RESULTS Pancakes made without baking soda not only lacked color, they lacked flavor, tasting unacceptably bland. The pancakes leavened with both baking powder and baking soda cooked up deeply golden with rich, nutty flavor.

EXPLANATION When baking soda (an alkali) meets up with buttermilk and sour cream (acids), the baking soda reacts immediately to produce tiny carbon dioxide bubbles that leaven the batter. At the same time, it neutralizes the batter's acidity to create a more alkaline environment that promotes browning and the creation of hundreds of new flavor compounds. These are what make pancakes taste far more complex and interesting.

THE BOTTOM LINE For better flavor, the baking soda had to stay in. To ensure fluffy pancakes from batch to batch, we'd have to adjust both its amount and the amount of baking powder.

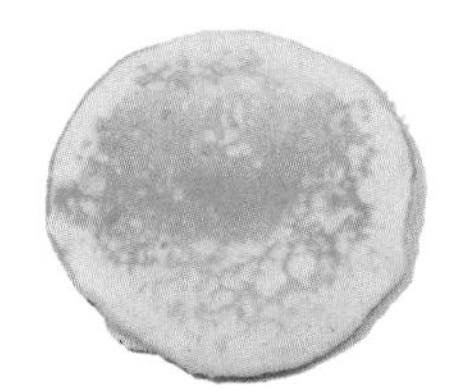

PALE AND BLAND

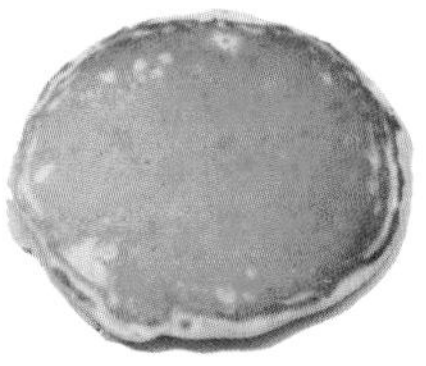

BROWN AND FLAVORFUL

RESURRECTING RAISED WAFFLES

KERI FISHER WITH GARTH CLINGINGSMITH, *March/April 2004*

Raised waffles are barely on the current culinary radar, and that's a shame. Instead of being leavened with baking powder or baking soda, raised waffles rely primarily on yeast, which yields breakfast fare with a unique texture and flavor. Raised waffles are much more interesting than basic waffles; they are at once creamy and airy, tangy and salty, refined and complex.

The concept is simple enough. Most of the ingredients (flour, salt, sugar, yeast, milk, melted butter, and vanilla) are combined the night before and left to rise on the counter. The next day, eggs and baking soda are added and the batter is baked off. In fact, yeasted waffles involve less work than traditional waffles when it comes time to make them in the morning. But as I soon found out, many of the old recipes still in circulation are not reliable.

THE BASICS

Most raised waffle recipes call for the batter to be left out at room temperature overnight to rise. A warm kitchen provides a fertile field in which the yeast can feed. During my initial tests, however, I discovered that these recipes had too small a window of time before tangy turned downright sour. Batter left to rise unrefrigerated overnight (for me, from 5 o'clock in the afternoon—the end of the work day—until 9 o'clock the next morning) rose and fell, leaving behind a thin, watery batter that yielded an unpleasantly sharp-tasting waffle. A more flexible option, I discovered, was to leave the batter to rise—more slowly—in the refrigerator. Now I could prepare the batter before dinner and let it sit safely overnight. This simple change made the rest of my testing go much more smoothly.

Because most home cooks now use instant (rapid-rise) yeast, which does not require proofing, this was my leavener of choice. The question was, how much? A full packet of yeast (2¼ teaspoons) yielded an overly fluffy, insubstantial waffle; the large amount of yeast was producing a glut of gas. Waffles made with a scant 1 teaspoon of yeast were too bland, so I settled on 1½ teaspoons, which imparted a pleasant tangy flavor and a texture halfway between airy and earthbound.

Choosing the right flour was confusing because raised waffles are part bread (think yeast bread) and part cake (think griddle cakes). Tests quickly determined that waffles made with bread flour were bready, tough, and chewy. Cake flour produced a sour, thin waffle. All-purpose flour lived up to its name and was the flour of choice, providing a solid base for both good flavor and good texture.

Plan ahead for superior waffles: Letting this yeasted batter stand overnight in the fridge helps control fermentation and maximize flavor.

Tasters overwhelmingly preferred waffles made with milk to those made with heavy cream or buttermilk. The batter made with cream was too heavy for the leavening power of the yeast, and the resulting waffles were dense. The waffles made with buttermilk, on the other hand, were thought to taste "like cheese" (the yeast provides more than enough flavor), so I crossed it off my list, along with sour cream and yogurt. Too much milk made the waffles delicate; the right amount was 1¾ cups. Whole, reduced-fat, and skim milk all yielded similar results, a big surprise until I recalled that I had already added a stick of melted butter; the total fat content of the batter wasn't changed much by the type of milk used. (I had tested 2 and 4 tablespoons of butter, but tasters preferred the extra-crisp exterior and rich flavor provided by a full stick.)

Just 1 teaspoon of vanilla added depth of flavor, and a full teaspoon of salt complemented the waffle's tangy flavor. A tablespoon of sugar gave the waffles a sweetness that wasn't cloying.

THINKING AHEAD

At this point, my working recipe called for only two ingredients to be added in the morning: eggs and baking soda. Wondering if the eggs could be mixed in the night before, I prepared a batch and found that these waffles had the same great texture and flavor as a batch made with eggs added at the last minute. Best of all, adding the eggs at the outset made for even less last-minute work than was called for in the old-fashioned recipes. (Recipes that call for leaving the batter on the counter overnight add the eggs in the morning for safety reasons. Because I was letting the batter rise in the refrigerator, I could safely add the eggs at the outset.)

The next question concerned the baking soda called for in some recipes. Did these waffles really need it? Tests proved that waffles made with and without baking soda were virtually indistinguishable. Why, then, do most recipes call for it? Because batters left at warm room temperature for too long are usually batters that contain dead yeast in the morning (as I found out in an early test). The baking soda, then, is a fail-safe ingredient, one that ensures raised waffles. Because my recipe has the batter rise in the controlled environment of the refrigerator, the yeast is not given the chance to die off. In dozens of tests, the yeast still had plenty of leavening power the next morning, making the baking soda redundant.

Now there was nothing to add in the morning except syrup. I had discovered that raised waffles not only taste better than the traditional variety but that a tiny bit of advance planning makes them easier to prepare at breakfast time as well.

Yeasted Waffles

SERVES 4

The batter must be made 12 to 24 hours in advance. We prefer the texture of the waffles made in a classic waffle iron, but a Belgian waffle iron will work, though it will make fewer waffles. While the waffles can be eaten as soon as they are removed from the iron, they will have a crispier exterior if rested in a warm oven for 10 minutes. (This method also makes it possible to serve everyone at the same time.) These waffles are quite rich; buttering them is not compulsory and, to some, may even be superfluous.

1¾ cups milk
8 tablespoons unsalted butter, cut into 8 pieces
2 cups (10 ounces) all-purpose flour
1 tablespoon sugar
1½ teaspoons instant or rapid-rise yeast
1 teaspoon salt
2 large eggs
1 teaspoon vanilla extract

1. Heat milk and butter in small saucepan over medium-low heat until butter is melted, 3 to 5 minutes. Let mixture cool until warm to touch.

2. Whisk flour, sugar, yeast, and salt together in large bowl. In separate bowl, whisk eggs and vanilla together. Gradually whisk warm milk mixture into flour mixture until smooth, then whisk in egg mixture. Scrape down bowl with rubber spatula, cover tightly with plastic wrap, and refrigerate for at least 12 hours or up to 24 hours.

3. Adjust oven rack to middle position and heat oven to 200 degrees. Set wire rack in rimmed baking sheet and place in oven. Heat waffle iron according to manufacturer's instructions. Remove batter from refrigerator when waffle iron is hot (batter will be foamy and doubled in size). Whisk batter to recombine (batter will deflate).

4. Spray preheated waffle iron with vegetable oil spray. Add ⅔ cup batter to waffle iron and cook according to manufacturer's instructions until crisp, firm, and golden, 4 to 6 minutes. Serve immediately or transfer to wire rack in oven. Repeat with remaining batter.

THE EFFECTS OF TEMPERATURE ON YEAST

Fermentation is arguably the oldest of cooking techniques. Even the early hunters and gatherers must have noticed that meat and berries tasted and smelled quite different a few days after collection. Louis Pasteur made the seminal discovery that the changes in food over time often result from the metabolic activity of microbes; Pasteur was observing the action of yeast, which converts sugars to ethyl alcohol and releases carbon dioxide gas as a byproduct.

In our waffle recipe, yeast plays two roles, providing leavening and flavor. Initial tests convinced us that leaving the yeasted batter out all night at room temperature yielded an exhausted, sour-tasting batter. Curious to see how much faster yeast respiration occurred at room temperature than in the 40-degree environment of the refrigerator, we fashioned a simple respirometer using a test tube and a balloon. As the yeast breaks down sugars into carbon dioxide, gas becomes trapped in the balloon, causing it to inflate.

Within a short period of time (3 hours), the room-temperature batter had produced enough carbon dioxide to inflate the balloon, indicating healthy yeast activity. But after 18 hours, the batter was spent and no longer produced carbon dioxide. The refrigerated batter produced carbon dioxide at a very slow but steady rate—which is good news for the cook. Rather than having to closely monitor a waffle batter left at room temperature, we refrigerate ours, thereby affording ourselves one of the greatest luxuries of all: sleeping in.

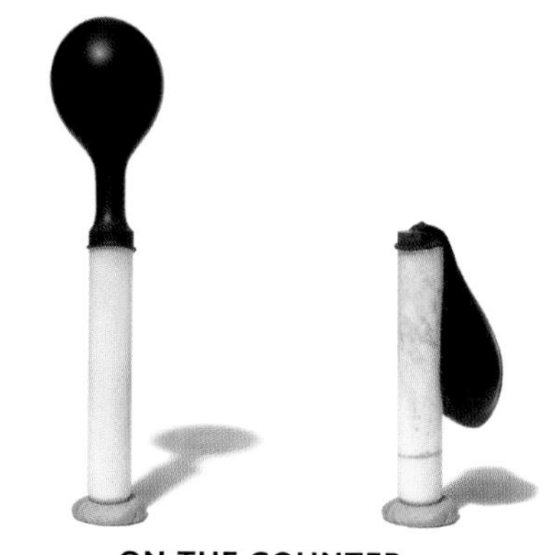

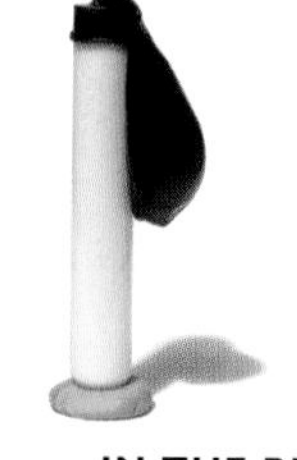

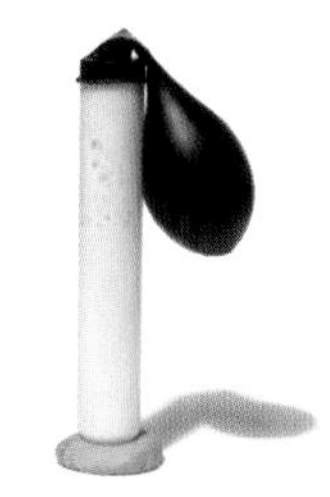

ON THE COUNTER

AFTER 3 HOURS
The batter quickly produces enough carbon dioxide to fill the balloon.

AFTER 18 HOURS
Yeast cells have died and the batter has collapsed and separated.

IN THE REFRIGERATOR

AFTER 3 HOURS
The batter produces a little carbon dioxide to partially fill the balloon.

AFTER 18 HOURS
The batter continues to produce carbon dioxide at a steady rate.

PREPARING YEASTED WAFFLES

1. Spray waffle iron with vegetable oil spray, and add ⅔ cup batter to iron. Cook until waffle is crisp, firm, and golden, then transfer to wire rack in oven to keep warm.

2. To keep waffles warm while preparing remaining waffles, transfer to wire rack set in rimmed baking sheet in 200-degree oven.

TEN-MINUTE STEEL-CUT OATMEAL

ANDREA GEARY, *September/October 2012*

The motto of the kings of ancient Scotland was "Nemo me impune lacessit." It means "No one attacks me with impunity" or, more plainly, "Don't mess with me." I resided in Scotland for several years, and I can confirm that, though the kings are long gone, that fiercely proud and sometimes downright pugnacious spirit lives on. It takes a brave (or perhaps foolish) person to criticize any aspect of Scottish identity, but as it happens I have a serious problem with one of the country's most iconic dishes: oatmeal.

I would eat traditional Scottish oat porridge every day if I could. It's delicious and sustaining, and preparing it couldn't be simpler: Steel-cut oats, which are dried oat kernels cut crosswise into coarse bits, are gently simmered in lightly salted water until the hard oats swell and soften and release some of their starch molecules into the surrounding liquid. Those starches bond with the liquid, thickening it until the oatmeal forms a substantial yet fluid mass of plump, tender grains. So, what's the problem? That transformation from gravelly oats to creamy, thick porridge takes 30 minutes minimum; 40 minutes is preferable. There's just no way I can squeeze that into a busy weekday morning.

To reduce the prebreakfast rush, some cooks allow steel-cut oats to just barely bubble in a slow cooker overnight, but I've never had luck with that approach. After 8 hours the oats are mushy and blown out and lack the subtle chew of traditionally prepared oatmeal. If I was going to work my favorite kind of oatmeal into regular breakfast rotation, I'd have to find a quicker way to cook it. My goal: perfect porridge that required fewer than 10 minutes of active engagement.

DON'T BE GRUEL

Oat cookery has changed very little over the centuries, which explains why I had so few leads on alternative timesaving methods. In fact, the only Scot-sanctioned shortcut I knew was one I'd learned while working as a breakfast cook at a small hotel in Scotland: soaking the steel-cut oats in tap water overnight to initiate the hydration of the grain. Thinking that I'd give this approach some further scrutiny, I prepared two batches of oatmeal using a fairly standard ratio of 1 cup oats to 4 cups water. I soaked one measure of the grains overnight in room-temperature water and cooked the other straight from the package and then compared their respective cook times. As it turned out, presoaking saved some time, but not enough. Almost 25 minutes passed before the soaked oats morphed into the loose yet viscous result I was after—only about 15 minutes faster than the unsoaked batch. I wasn't quite convinced that some sort of presoak treatment wouldn't help, but for now I went back to the drawing board.

As a matter of fact, I had a trick in mind. We'd had the same timesaving goal when developing our Creamy Parmesan Polenta (page 337), and we'd discovered an unlikely addition that sped things up considerably: baking soda. Introducing just a pinch of the alkali to the pot raised the pH of the cooking liquid, causing the corn's cell walls to break down more quickly, thereby allowing water to enter and gelatinize its starch molecules in half the time. I thought that the baking soda might have a similarly expediting effect with my steel-cut oats, so I dropped a pinch into the pot and waited. And waited. Twenty minutes later, I had the creamy porridge I was after, but a mere 5-minute savings wasn't going to do it. I decided to ditch the baking soda idea.

I hadn't abandoned the notion of jump-starting the hydration process with a presoak, but I obviously needed a more aggressive method. That's when my thoughts turned from presoaking to parcooking. Surely boiling water would hasten the softening of the oats faster than room-temperature water, right? To find out, I brought the oats and the water to a boil together, cut the heat, covered the pot, and left it to sit overnight. When I uncovered the pot the next morning, I knew I was getting somewhere. Thanks to this head start, the coarse oats I'd started with had swelled and fully softened. I was encouraged and flipped on the burner to medium to see how long it would take before the cereal turned creamy and thickened. About 10 minutes of simmering later, the porridge was heated through and viscous—but was also mushy and pasty like the slow-cooker oats. Simmering the oats for less time wasn't the answer: It left the liquid in the pot thin and watery. As surprising as it seemed, I could only conclude that parcooking by bringing the oats up to a boil with the water was too aggressive, causing too many starch molecules to burst, which turned the oats to mush and caused the liquid to become pasty.

By adding an overnight sit, you can have perfectly cooked steel-cut oatmeal in no time in the morning.

Still, things were looking up. A 10-minute cook time was a major step in the right direction. In my next test, I decided to split the difference between the Scottish room-temperature soak and the mushy boiled-water method. Instead of bringing the oats to a boil with the water, I boiled the water by itself, poured in the oats, covered the pot, and then left them to hydrate overnight. The next morning I got the pot going again. With this slightly more gentle method, 10 minutes later the oatmeal was perfectly creamy and not at all blown out or sticky.

I had just one other problem to solve—this one a classic oatmeal quandary. Though the finished oatmeal looked appropriately creamy in the pot, the mixture continued to thicken after I poured it into the bowl as the starches continued to absorb the water. By the time I dug in, the result was so thick and pasty that I could stand my spoon in it.

That's when I seized on my last adjustment: I would cut the heat before the oatmeal had achieved its ideal thickness and then let it sit for a few minutes, until it thickened up just enough. I gave it a whirl, simmering the oatmeal for a mere 5 minutes and then moving the pot off the heat to rest. Five minutes later my tasters and I dug into a bowl of perfect porridge: creamy and viscous and not the least bit pasty. Goal achieved.

OAT CUISINE

My tasters' only critical comment: Though a bowl of unadulterated oatmeal might be traditional in Scotland, on this side of the Atlantic we like ours loaded up with toppings. Of course I could easily serve my cereal with the usual fixings (brown sugar, maple syrup, dried fruit, etc.), but I wondered if I could change the flavor of the porridge more fundamentally by swapping out some of the water for more flavorful liquids and by adding some punchier ingredients.

Our science editor and I agreed that letting milk or juice sit out overnight might be pushing food-safety limits (water was fine, he assured me), so I looked over my recipe and came up with an alternative approach that worked brilliantly: rehydrating the oats in just 3 cups of boiling water and withholding the last cup of liquid until the following morning, when it could be replaced with milk, juice, or something else right before simmering. This way, I could adjust the ingredients to make a few varieties of oatmeal to please even the most jaded palate. I came up with apple-cinnamon made with cider, a carrot cake spin made with carrot juice, and a cardamom-scented cranberry-orange variation made with orange juice.

As much as the Scots are known for being proud and stubborn, they are also known for their inventiveness and imagination. It is, after all, Scots whom we have to thank for penicillin, Sherlock Holmes, and television. I'm confident that my 10-minute steel-cut oatmeal will appeal to the innovative side of the national character.

Ten-Minute Steel-Cut Oatmeal

SERVES 4

The oatmeal will continue to thicken as it cools. If you prefer a looser consistency, thin the oatmeal with boiling water. Customize your oatmeal with toppings such as brown sugar, toasted nuts, maple syrup, or dried fruit.

4 cups water
1 cup steel-cut oats
¼ teaspoon salt

1. Bring 3 cups water to boil in large saucepan over high heat. Remove saucepan from heat; stir in oats and salt. Cover saucepan and let stand overnight.
2. Stir remaining 1 cup water into oats and bring to boil over medium-high heat. Reduce heat to medium and cook, stirring occasionally, until oats are softened but still retain some chew and mixture thickens and resembles warm pudding, 4 to 6 minutes. Remove saucepan from heat and let stand for 5 minutes. Stir and serve.

variations

Apple-Cinnamon Steel-Cut Oatmeal

Increase salt to ½ teaspoon. Substitute ½ cup apple cider and ½ cup whole milk for water in step 2. Stir ½ cup peeled, grated sweet apple, 2 tablespoons packed dark brown sugar, and ½ teaspoon ground cinnamon into oatmeal with cider and milk. Sprinkle each serving with 2 tablespoons coarsely chopped toasted walnuts.

Carrot Spice Steel-Cut Oatmeal

Increase salt to ¾ teaspoon. Substitute ½ cup carrot juice and ½ cup whole milk for water in step 2. Stir ½ cup finely grated carrot, ¼ cup packed dark brown sugar, ⅓ cup dried currants, and ½ teaspoon ground cinnamon into oatmeal with carrot juice and milk. Sprinkle each serving with 2 tablespoons coarsely chopped toasted pecans.

Cranberry-Orange Steel-Cut Oatmeal

Increase salt to ½ teaspoon. Substitute ½ cup orange juice and ½ cup whole milk for water in step 2. Stir ½ cup dried cranberries, 3 tablespoons packed dark brown sugar, and ⅛ teaspoon ground cardamom into oatmeal with orange juice and milk. Sprinkle each serving with 2 tablespoons toasted sliced almonds.

KNOW YOUR OATS

The cereal aisle stocks a variety of oat products—but not all of them make for a good bowl of oatmeal. Make sure you know which options are best for which applications.

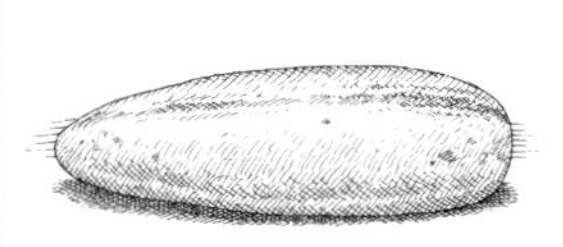

GROATS Whole oats that have been hulled and cleaned (also called oat berries). They are the least processed oat product, but we find them too coarse for oatmeal. Think of them more like a grain. Try them in salads and pilafs.

STEEL-CUT OATS Groats cut crosswise into coarse bits (sometimes called Scottish or Irish oats). We strongly prefer them in oatmeal; they cook up creamy yet chewy with rich, nutty flavor. They're usually not used for baking, though.

ROLLED OATS Groats steamed and pressed into flat flakes (also called old-fashioned oats). They cook faster than steel-cut but make for a gummy, lackluster bowl of oatmeal. They are our favorite for baking.

SUPERCHUNKY GRANOLA

ADAM RIED, *March/April 2012*

Whether paired with milk, fresh fruit, or yogurt—or eaten by the fistful as a snack—granola is a must-have in my kitchen. Too bad the commercially prepared kind is such a letdown. Whether dry and dusty, overly sweet, infuriatingly expensive ($10 for a 12-ounce bag?), or all of the above, it's so universally disappointing that I recently vowed never to purchase another bag.

Of course, that meant that if I wanted to enjoy granola, I had to make my own. I expected a homemade version to dramatically improve matters, but it only partially helped. Sure, do-it-yourself granola afforded me the opportunity to choose exactly which nuts and dried fruit I wanted to include, as well as how much. But there was a downside: The slow baking and frequent stirring that most recipes recommend results in a loose, granular texture. I wanted something altogether different: substantial clumps of toasty oats and nuts. My ideal clusters would be markedly crisp yet tender enough to shatter easily when bitten—I definitely didn't want the density or tooth-chipping crunch of a hard granola bar.

Starting from square one, I laid out my plan of attack: I would nail down particulars about the oats and nuts first and then set my sights on achieving substantial chunks.

STARTING WITH THE BASICS

I got down to business and set up my own little granola factory, baking test batches using instant, quick, steel-cut, and old-fashioned whole rolled oat varieties. It was no surprise that instant and quick oats baked up unsubstantial and powdery. Steel-cut oats suffered the opposite problem: Chewing them was like munching gravel. Whole rolled oats were essential for a hearty, crisp texture.

Nuts, on the other hand, offered much more flexibility. Almost any type—I chose almonds for my working recipe—did just fine, contributing rich, toasty flavor that developed as the cereal roasted in the oven, along with plenty of crunch. While many recipes advocate adding them whole, I preferred chopping them first for more even distribution.

As for other potential dry add-ins, more unusual grains (such as quinoa or amaranth) and seeds (sunflower, flax, pumpkin, and so on) are terrific choices, but since I planned on making granola often, I wanted to keep things simple, with ingredients that I routinely stock in my pantry.

With two of the primary players settled, I mixed up a batch using 5 cups of rolled oats and 2 cups of chopped almonds coated with my placeholder liquids: honey and vegetable oil (plus a touch of salt). I used a rubber spatula to spread the sticky concoction onto a baking sheet that I'd first lined with parchment for easier cleanup. I deliberated over what oven temperature to choose, and I settled on a relatively moderate 375 degrees to ward off scorching and allow the ingredients to brown slowly and evenly. I stirred the mixture every 10 minutes or so until it was evenly golden, which took about 30 minutes. The granola boasted a fantastic toasty scent coming out of the oven, but just as I had feared, there were no hearty chunks.

For big, satisfying clusters, we make a granola "bark" and then break it up into crunchy clumps.

Temporarily setting the textural issue aside, I considered the other ingredients, starting with the sweetener. Honey and maple syrup are the most common choices, but even in small amounts, the honey struck many tasters as too distinct. Maple syrup was preferred for its milder character, especially when I balanced it with the subtle molasses notes offered by light brown sugar. One-third cup of each for 7 cups of nuts and oats gave the granola just the right degree of sweetness.

The other major component in most granola recipes is fat. But because fat-free commercial versions are so popular and I didn't want to leave any stone unturned, I whipped up a batch in which I left the oil out of the recipe completely. No dice: The fat-free cereal was so dry and powdery that no amount of milk or yogurt could rescue it. I eventually determined that ½ cup was the right amount of oil for a super crisp—but not greasy—texture. Our science editor explained that fat is essential for a substantial crisp texture versus a parched, delicate one: Fat and liquid sweeteners form a fluid emulsion that thoroughly coats ingredients, creating crunch as the granola bakes. Without any fat, the texture is bound to be dry and fragile. I did two final fat experiments, swapping butter for the oil in the first, only to find that it was prone to burning. In a subsequent trial, extra-virgin olive oil gave the cereal a savory slant that divided tasters, so I stuck with my original choice: neutral-tasting vegetable oil.

PUTTING THE PRESSURE ON

My granola now possessed well-balanced flavor and perfectly crisp oats and nuts, but I still had to deal with the issue of how to create big clumps. As I paged through cookbooks looking for a magic bullet, I uncovered a lot of interesting suggestions, including adding dry milk powder, egg whites, and sweet, sticky liquids like apple juice or cider to the mix. Sadly, none produced the clusters of my dreams.

If an additional ingredient couldn't help create the substantial chunks I sought, how about adjusting my technique? I'd been reaching into the oven to repeatedly stir the granola as it baked, so I decided to try skipping this step. To make sure that the cereal wouldn't burn in the absence of stirring, I dropped the oven temperature to 325 degrees and extended the cooking time to 45 minutes. Sure enough, some olive-size pieces did form in a no-stir sample—but I wanted more (and larger) chunks. For my next try, I used

a spatula to press the hot granola firmly into the pan as soon as it emerged from the oven so that the cooling syrup would bind the solids together as it hardened. This worked, but only to a point. Could I take this idea to the next level?

Since the raw granola mixture was so sticky with syrup and oil, I wondered if muscling it into a tight, compact layer in the pan before baking would yield larger nuggets. I gave it a try, happily finding that when I pulled the cereal from the oven, it remained in a single sheet as it cooled. Now the end product was more of a granola "bark," which was ideal, since I could break it into clumps of any size. Not only had I finally achieved hefty—yet still readily breakable—chunks, but as an added boon, this granola was now hands-off, aside from my having to rotate the pan halfway through baking.

FINISHING WITH FRUIT

All that my chunky granola needed now was sweet bits of dried fruit. I tested a variety of choices—raisins, apple, mango, pineapple, cranberries, and pear—finding that they all either burned or turned leathery when baked with the other ingredients. To rectify this, I tried plumping the fruit in water or coating it with oil to help prevent moisture loss.

And yet time and time again, it emerged from the oven overcooked. It eventually became clear that the best way to incorporate the fruit was to keep it away from heat altogether, only stirring it in once the granola was cool.

My simple recipe was nearly complete, but I wanted to create a tiny bit more depth. After some tinkering, I found that a healthy dose of vanilla extract (I used a whopping 4 teaspoons) was just the ticket, accenting the maple, nut, and fruit flavors without overwhelming them.

Finally, I developed a few twists on my basic formula by switching up the fruit-and-nut pairings and accenting them with flavor boosters like coconut, citrus zest, and warm spices. Forget the store-bought stuff. Home is where you'll find the holy grail of granola: big, satisfying clusters and moist, chewy fruit.

Almond Granola with Dried Fruit

MAKES ABOUT 9 CUPS

Chopping the almonds by hand is best for superior crunch. If you prefer not to hand chop, substitute an equal quantity of slivered or sliced almonds. Use a single type of your favorite dried fruit or a combination. Do not substitute quick or instant oats.

⅓ cup maple syrup
⅓ cup packed (2⅓ ounces) light brown sugar
4 teaspoons vanilla extract
½ teaspoon salt
½ cup vegetable oil
5 cups (15 ounces) old-fashioned rolled oats
2 cups (10 ounces) whole almonds, chopped coarse
2 cups (10 ounces) raisins or other dried fruit, chopped

1. Adjust oven rack to upper-middle position and heat oven to 325 degrees. Line rimmed baking sheet with parchment paper.
2. Whisk maple syrup, brown sugar, vanilla, and salt in large bowl. Whisk in oil. Fold in oats and almonds until thoroughly coated.
3. Transfer oat mixture to prepared sheet and spread into thin, even layer (about ⅜ inch thick). Using stiff metal spatula, compress oat mixture until very compact. Bake until lightly browned, 40 to 45 minutes, rotating sheet halfway through baking. Transfer sheet to wire rack and let cool completely, about 1 hour. Break granola into pieces of desired size. Stir in raisins. (Granola can be stored at room temperature for up to 2 weeks.)

variations

Pecan-Orange Granola with Dried Cranberries

Add 2 tablespoons finely grated orange zest and 2½ teaspoons ground cinnamon to maple syrup mixture in step 2. Substitute coarsely chopped pecans for almonds. Use 2 cups dried cranberries for dried fruit.

Spiced Walnut Granola with Dried Apple

Add 2 teaspoons ground cinnamon, 1½ teaspoons ground ginger, ¾ teaspoon ground allspice, ½ teaspoon ground nutmeg, and ½ teaspoon pepper to maple syrup mixture in step 2. Substitute coarsely chopped walnuts for almonds. Use 2 cups chopped dried apple for dried fruit.

Tropical Granola with Dried Mango

Decrease vanilla extract to 2 teaspoons and add 1½ teaspoons ground ginger and ¾ teaspoon ground nutmeg to maple syrup mixture in step 2. Substitute coarsely chopped macadamia nuts for almonds and 1½ cups unsweetened shredded coconut for 1 cup oats. Use 2 cups chopped dried mango or pineapple for dried fruit.

Hazelnut Granola with Dried Pear

Substitute skinned and coarsely chopped hazelnuts for almonds. Use 2 cups chopped dried pear for dried fruit.

FOR BETTER GRANOLA, ADD FAT

When we mixed up a batch of granola in which we left out the oil, the resulting cereal was a real flop, the oats having taken on a crisp but overly dry consistency. It turns out that fat is essential for creating a likable crispness.

Here's why: When the water in a viscous liquid sweetener (such as the maple syrup in our recipe) evaporates in the heat of the oven, the sugars left behind develop into a thin coating on the oats and nuts. But without any fat, the sugar coating will become brittle and dry. Only oil can provide a pleasantly crisp coating with a sense of moistness.

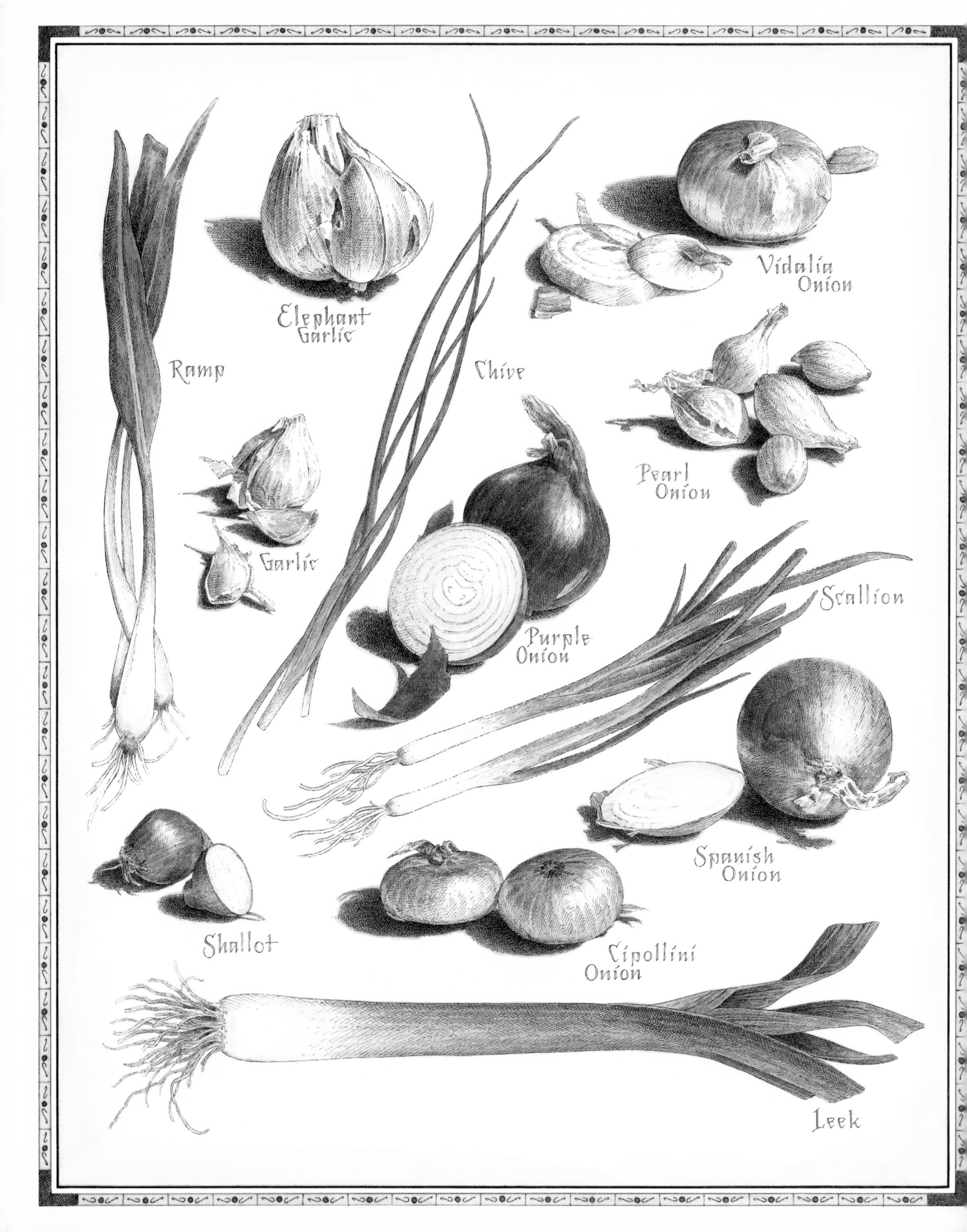

Elephant Garlic
Vidalia Onion
Ramp
Chive
Pearl Onion
Garlic
Purple Onion
Scallion
Spanish Onion
Shallot
Cipollini Onion
Leek

SOUPS, STEWS, AND CHILIS

CREAMLESS CREAMY TOMATO SOUP

J. KENJI LOPEZ-ALT, *September/October 2008*

Tomato soup should have it all: good looks, velvety smoothness, and a bright, tomatoey taste. But poor versions are the norm, either featuring an acidic, watery broth or an overdose of cream. Though it's meant to tame tartness and lend body, I've always found that adding cream goes hand in hand with muting flavor. I wanted soup with rich tomato flavor and a satisfying texture. Could I get there without the cream?

The first step in the process was to pass over fresh tomatoes for canned, which are almost always far better than your average supermarket tomato, with more consistently rich and concentrated flavor. Plus they're already peeled—a big timesaver for soup. I opted for whole tomatoes rather than diced or crushed; the latter two types contain more calcium chloride, an additive that prevents them from breaking down completely, compromising texture. I then developed a simple working recipe, sautéing onions and garlic in butter, stirring in the tomatoes and some chicken broth, and blending the whole thing. The results were decent, but dull.

Sandwich bread creates a luxurious-textured soup without dulling the bright tomato flavor.

If cream subdues tomato flavor, could the milk solids in the butter be tamping it down as well? I substituted extra-virgin olive oil for the butter and found that the soup brightened as a result. To compensate for the flavor the oil lost as it cooked, I drizzled a little more over the soup before it went into the blender. Most tasters also welcomed a couple tablespoons of brandy.

TAMING TARTNESS

Now that I had my flavor profile nailed down, I was on to bigger problems: tartness and thin texture. Sugar is often used as a means to combat tartness. We preferred brown sugar to one-dimensional white sugar and corn syrup, but sugar could only take us so far—when I added enough to tone down tartness the soup became unpalatably sweet. I needed a thickener that would also help temper the acid. Dairy ingredients were definitely out, but what about a starch? Cooking flour along with the onions to form a roux made for a thicker soup, but the texture turned slimy instead of creamy, and it did nothing for flavor. Cornstarch produced similar results. I scoured our cookbook library before I found inspiration in another tomato-based soup: gazpacho. This Spanish classic is made from tomatoes, olive oil, and garlic, along with an unusual element for thickening: bread. But gazpacho is served cold. Would bread work as a thickener for hot soup?

I tore several slices of sandwich bread into pieces and stirred them into the pot as the soup simmered. When I processed the mixture, I ended up with bread chunks that resisted being sucked down into the blender's spinning blades. I decided to try leaving out the broth until the very end. With my next batch of soup, I pureed the tomatoes with the aromatics and bread before returning the mixture to the pan and whisking in the broth. One taste and I knew I'd hit on just the right solution. My tomato soup had the same velvety texture as the creamy kind, but with bright, fresh flavor. None of my tasters even guessed that my soup contained a secret ingredient.

Creamless Creamy Tomato Soup

SERVES 6 TO 8

Make sure to purchase canned whole tomatoes packed in juice, not puree. If half the soup fills your blender by more than two-thirds, process the soup in three batches. You can also use an immersion blender to process the soup directly in the pot. For even smoother soup, pass the pureed mixture through a fine-mesh strainer before adding the chicken broth in step 2.

¼ cup extra-virgin olive oil, plus extra for serving
1 onion, chopped fine
3 garlic cloves, minced
1 bay leaf
Pinch red pepper flakes (optional)
2 (28-ounce) cans whole peeled tomatoes
3 slices hearty white sandwich bread, crusts removed, torn into 1-inch pieces
1 tablespoon packed brown sugar
2 cups chicken or vegetable broth
2 tablespoons brandy (optional)
Salt and pepper
Chopped fresh chives

1. Heat 2 tablespoons oil in Dutch oven over medium-high heat until shimmering. Add onion, garlic, bay leaf, and pepper flakes, if using. Cook, stirring often, until onion is translucent, 3 to 5 minutes. Stir in tomatoes and their juice. Using potato masher, mash until no pieces bigger than 2 inches remain. Stir in bread and sugar and bring soup to boil. Reduce heat to medium and cook, stirring occasionally, until bread is completely saturated and starts to break down, about 5 minutes. Discard bay leaf.
2. Transfer half of soup to blender. Add 1 tablespoon oil and process until soup is smooth and creamy, 2 to 3 minutes. Transfer to large bowl and repeat with remaining soup and remaining 1 tablespoon oil. Return soup to clean, dry pot and stir in broth and brandy, if using.
3. Return soup to brief simmer over medium heat. Season with salt and pepper to taste. Serve, sprinkling individual bowls with chives and drizzling with extra oil.

BUTTERNUT SQUASH SOUP

RAQUEL PELZEL, *November/December 2001*

With its brash orange color, luxurious texture, and unapologetic squash flavor, butternut squash soup should be anything but meek. Unfortunately, many recipes bury the bold flavor of the butternut squash beneath chicken stock, an excess of cream or milk, or an overabundance of spices. The consistency of the soup is another problem, with some being too thin and others too thick, like a porridge. I set out to preserve the natural flavor of the squash while transforming it into a silky smooth soup.

First, I needed to cook the squash. Most recipes simmer, sauté, or roast it. When simmering or sautéing the squash, the first step is to remove its tough outer skin. Then the flesh must be cut into manageable pieces. After pureeing, the sautéed squash tasted gritty, and although the simmered squash had a smooth, satiny mouthfeel, all of the peeling and chopping was too much work.

To highlight the pure butternut squash flavor, this recipe makes use of the whole vegetable—even the fibers and seeds.

Simpler is oven-roasting, for which the skin can be left intact. I rubbed the squash with oil and placed it in a hot oven. The roasting took a while, but it was easy to slip the squash meat away from the shell.

Happy with the simplicity of roasting, I pureed the squash with water. To my surprise, the puree was mealy and caramel-flavored. I gave roasting another chance, this time pureeing the squash with chicken broth in one batch and milk in a second batch. The chicken broth interfered with the flavor of the squash, while the milk made the puree taste like melted squash ice cream.

Clearly simmering the squash did it more justice than sautéing or roasting, but that meant peeling and cutting. Thinking that moist heat might be the key, I decided to try steaming. I placed cut, seeded, unpeeled squash in a steamer basket, lowered the basket into a 6-quart Dutch oven, covered the pot, and let the squash steam until tender. Not only did the squash cook in a half-hour, but the cooking liquid was perfumed with the squash's essence. After pureeing the squash with some of the cooking liquid, I found it neither mealy nor sugary. Plus, I had avoided peeling the squash by steaming the cut pieces and then scooping the softened flesh from the skin with a spoon.

Now I needed to bolster the flavor of the puree, which consisted only of water and steamed squash. I tried three separate tests in which I sautéed garlic, onion, and shallots in butter and then left each in the pot during steaming. Before pureeing, I strained the sautéed bits from the squash-infused broth. The garlic and onion were overpowering, but the shallots complemented the squash nicely. I added salt, and while the soup now tasted good, it still lacked depth of flavor.

As I pored over my notes, it occurred to me that perhaps I was throwing away the answer to more squash flavor—the seeds and fibers. In my next test, instead of ditching the scooped-out remnants, I added them to the sautéing shallots and butter. In a matter of minutes, the room became fragrant with an earthy, sweet squash aroma, and the butter turned a brilliant shade of saffron. I finished the recipe by straining out the shallots, seeds, and pulp. The resulting soup was boldly flavored and intensely orange.

Finishing touches included sugar (brown sugar added sweetness plus nuttiness) and heavy cream (some recipes call for as much as 2 cups, but I found that ½ cup was sufficient). Velvety and permeated with a heady squash flavor, the soup was thick but not custardy, sweet but not pie-like. Finally, a butternut squash soup worthy of its title.

PREPPING SQUASH FOR SOUP

To save on prep time, we simply cut the unpeeled squash into quarters and then steam it.

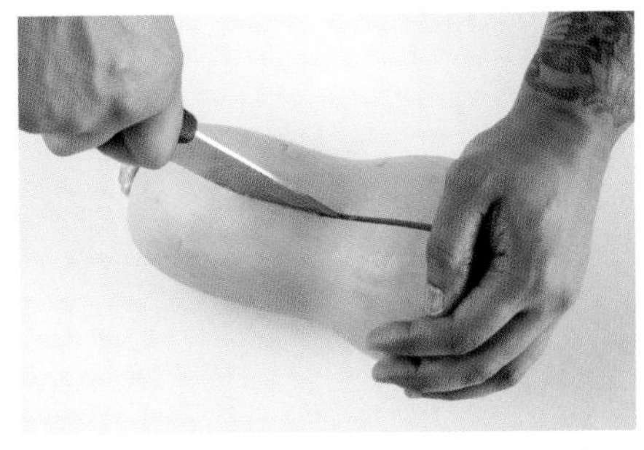

1. Drive chef's knife into center of squash; press down through end of squash. Repeat on opposite side.

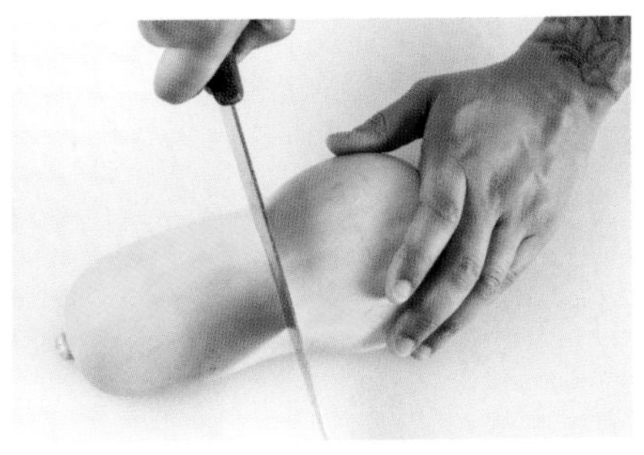

2. Halve each squash piece widthwise, separating narrow top end from wider, seed-filled bottom end.

3. Scrape out seeds and fibers using spoon, and reserve.

Butternut Squash Soup

SERVES 4 TO 6

If you don't own a folding steamer basket, a pasta pot with a removable pasta insert works well. Some nice garnishes for the soup are a drizzle of balsamic vinegar, a sprinkle of paprika, or Buttered Cinnamon-Sugar Croutons (recipe follows).

4 tablespoons unsalted butter
1 large shallot, chopped
3 pounds butternut squash, quartered and seeded, with fibers and seeds reserved
6 cups water
Salt and pepper
½ cup heavy cream
1 teaspoon packed dark brown sugar
Pinch ground nutmeg

1. Melt 2 tablespoons butter in Dutch oven over medium heat. Add shallot and cook until softened, 2 to 3 minutes. Stir in squash seeds and fibers and cook until butter turns orange, about 4 minutes.

2. Stir in water and 1 teaspoon salt; bring to boil. Reduce to simmer, place squash cut side down in steamer basket, and lower basket into pot. Cover and steam squash until completely tender, 30 to 40 minutes.

3. Using tongs, transfer cooked squash to rimmed baking sheet. Let squash cool slightly, then scrape cooked squash from skin using soupspoon; discard skin.

4. Strain cooking liquid through fine-mesh strainer into large liquid measuring cup. Working in batches, puree cooked squash with 3 cups strained cooking liquid in blender until smooth, 1 to 2 minutes. Return pureed soup to clean pot and stir in cream, sugar, nutmeg, and remaining 2 tablespoons butter. Return to brief simmer, adding additional strained cooking liquid as needed to adjust consistency. Season with salt and pepper to taste, and serve.

accompaniment

Buttered Cinnamon-Sugar Croutons

MAKES ABOUT 1 CUP

2 slices hearty white sandwich bread, crusts removed, cut into ½-inch cubes (1 cup)
1 tablespoon unsalted butter, melted
2 teaspoons sugar
½ teaspoon ground cinnamon

1. Adjust oven rack to middle position and heat oven to 350 degrees. Combine bread and melted butter in medium bowl and toss to coat. Combine sugar and cinnamon in small bowl, then add to bowl with bread and toss to coat.

2. Spread bread in single layer on parchment paper–lined rimmed baking sheet and bake, stirring occasionally, until crisp, 8 to 10 minutes. Let cool completely on sheet. (Croutons can be stored for up to 3 days.)

variations

Curried Butternut Squash and Apple Soup

A tart apple, such as a Granny Smith, adds a nice contrast to the sweet squash, but any type of apple may be used.

Reduce amount of squash to 2½ pounds. Add 1 large apple, peeled, cored, and quartered, to steamer basket with squash. Substitute 2 teaspoons curry powder for nutmeg.

Southwestern Butternut Squash Soup

Substitute 1 tablespoon honey for brown sugar and ½ teaspoon ground cumin for nutmeg. Stir 2 tablespoons minced fresh cilantro and 2 teaspoons minced canned chipotle chile in adobo sauce into soup before serving.

Creamy Butternut Squash Soup with Fennel

Reduce amount of squash to 2 pounds and add 1 teaspoon fennel seeds to pot with squash seeds and fibers. Add 1 large fennel bulb, cut into 1-inch-thick strips, to steamer basket with squash.

BUILDING FLAVOR IN BUTTERNUT SQUASH SOUP

1. Sautéing the seeds and fibers from the squash builds a potent, squash-forward flavor base.

2. Steaming the squash gives it a silky texture and clean flavor.

3. Incorporating the flavorful strained steaming liquid into the soup ensures that no squash flavor is wasted.

4. Using a small amount of cream gives the soup richness, while brown sugar gives it nutty depth.

CHICKEN NOODLE SOUP, UPDATED

J. KENJI LOPEZ-ALT, *January/February 2009*

If I wanted to make chicken soup the old-fashioned way, I'd scrupulously freeze the scraps every time I butchered a whole chicken. Once I had saved enough, I would simmer the collected backs, ribs, and wing tips for hours, hovering over the pot with a skimmer in hand, until I had intensely flavored stock, to which I'd add vegetables, shredded chicken, and noodles.

But is this time-honored method really the best way to make stock? Sure, it made sense in the past as an economical way to get a second meal from the carcass of a spent bird. These days, however, spending hours to make a pot of soup from scraps and bones just isn't practical. I wanted deeply flavorful chicken soup, full of vegetables, tender meat, and soft noodles, but I also wanted to find a faster, more convenient way to make it.

SCRAPPING SCRAPS

I figured that making my stock with a mixture of canned chicken broth and water would jump-start its flavor. The trick would be to add enough real chicken flavor to the broth so that tasters wouldn't be able to detect its canned origins. Instead of blindly accepting conventional wisdom about how to do that, I decided to take a scientific approach, isolating the variables and testing each one. Using a ratio of 2 quarts of canned broth to 1 quart of water, I made six different stocks, using 1 pound each of various chicken parts (bone-in breasts, boneless breasts, bone-in dark meat, boneless dark meat, wings, and just bones and scraps) to analyze the flavor that each lent to the finished stock. To my surprise, the stock made from bones and scraps—the traditional choice—was the weakest-tasting of all. Clearly, these parts are traditional on account of frugality, not flavor. Wings produced flavorless, fatty stock, and bone-in dark meat produced dishwater-colored stock with a mineral flavor (caused by the blood around the joints of the thighs and drumsticks). Boneless breasts and dark meat, which had the cleanest chicken flavor, were the best choices.

My stock now had decent flavor, but I wanted it to be much more intense. In restaurants, stocks are cooked at a bare simmer for hours to keep them crystal clear. But I discovered that letting the stock cook at a medium boil emulsified some of the chicken fat, turning the stock slightly cloudy but greatly enhancing its taste. A few more quick tests determined that a bay leaf plus the usual trio of vegetables—onion, carrot, and celery—added desirable complexity. But the flavor still needed greater depth. The easy solution was to add more chicken. A full 3 pounds created a wonderfully rich stock, but spending money on a large quantity of chicken that would eventually be discarded (once simmered in stock, chicken is bland and lifeless) seemed a bit absurd. I was at a dead end. I decided to get out of the kitchen and into the library.

Enhancing store-bought broth with ground chicken and aromatics yields a rich-tasting base for this easy soup.

THE GROUND RULES

Many stock recipes advise starting with raw chicken parts, but I wondered if the chicken would benefit from sautéing before it was simmered in water and broth. I cooked the chicken pieces in a tablespoon of oil along with the aromatics just until the meat lost its pink color. The direct heat encouraged the release of flavorful juices from the chicken and vegetables, contributing additional layers of complexity to the stock. Conclusion: The sautéing step was well worth a few minutes of extra time.

Another fact: Flavor extraction happens quickly on the surface of meat, but the molecules deeper inside (say, at the center of a chicken breast) take more time to travel to the surface. So, in order to increase the rate at which the flavor was extracted, I would need to increase the surface area of the meat. For my next stock, I chopped the meat into 1-inch pieces. Tasters found this stock to be far more flavorful than one made with whole chicken pieces. Cutting the meat into ½-inch pieces was better still. Could I take this notion to the extreme?

I got out a food processor and pulsed the chicken pieces until they were very finely chopped. Tasters claimed that the stock I made from this pulverized meat had the richest flavor of any I'd made yet. To preclude any second-guessing, I sent samples to a lab to determine what quantity of dissolved solids had been extracted from the ground meat versus from the whole chicken pieces. The results confirmed what I already knew: Ground chicken releases a lot more flavor than whole chicken pieces. But why bother with the food processor when ground chicken is available at the supermarket? Good question. A pound of store-bought ground chicken gave up its flavor so readily that in just about an hour, I had an intense, golden, chickeny stock.

SOUP'S ON

Though my stock now had great flavor, it lacked the body of stock made with bones, which contain connective tissue that converts to gelatin when heated, thus thickening the liquid. I tested various thickeners and finally settled on 1 tablespoon of cornstarch per quart of liquid. (Cornstarch is cleaner-tasting and makes a more translucent stock than flour, and it's easier to incorporate into stock than gelatin.)

I also needed to introduce a second form of chicken to the soup—there was no way I was going to serve the spent ground chicken. Tasters preferred white meat to dark meat, and two bone-in breast halves provided just the right amount. Leaving the skin on protected the chicken from drying out, and adding it to the pot when I added the water allowed it to cook gently and evenly, ensuring that the meat remained moist (I removed it during the last 20 minutes to let it cool before shredding).

Finally, the vegetables that I had used to make the stock were now limp and lifeless. After discarding them, I added fresh onion, carrots, and celery to the stock, cooking them until they were just tender. Rich egg noodles were a prerequisite, plus potatoes to make the soup truly hearty. For a final burst of color and flavor, I added a few handfuls of torn Swiss chard leaves right at the end of cooking, along with the shredded chicken and some minced parsley. Though it had taken a month of testing, I had finally ushered chicken noodle soup into the 21st century with a recipe that was not only faster than the traditional method but also yielded a soup that was every bit as satisfying.

Hearty Chicken Noodle Soup

SERVES 4 TO 6

When skimming the fat off the stock, we prefer to leave a little bit on the surface to enhance the soup's flavor. The soup can be prepared through the end of step 2 and refrigerated for up to two days or frozen for up to three months.

Stock

1 tablespoon vegetable oil
1 pound ground chicken
1 small onion, chopped
1 carrot, peeled and chopped
1 celery rib, chopped
8 cups chicken broth
4 cups water
2 (12-ounce) bone-in split chicken breasts, trimmed and halved crosswise
2 bay leaves
2 teaspoons salt

Soup

¼ cup water
3 tablespoons cornstarch
1 small onion, halved and sliced thin
2 carrots, peeled, halved lengthwise, and cut crosswise into ¾-inch pieces
1 celery rib, halved lengthwise and cut crosswise into ½-inch pieces
1 russet potato, peeled and cut into ¾-inch cubes
4 ounces egg noodles
2 ounces Swiss chard, stemmed, leaves torn into 1-inch pieces (optional)
1 tablespoon minced fresh parsley
Salt and pepper

1. *For the stock:* Heat oil in Dutch oven over medium-high heat until shimmering. Add ground chicken, onion, carrot, and celery. Cook, stirring frequently, until chicken is no longer pink, 5 to 10 minutes (do not brown chicken).
2. Reduce heat to medium-low. Add broth, water, chicken breasts, bay leaves, and salt; cover and cook for 30 minutes. Remove lid, increase heat to high, and bring to boil. (If liquid is already boiling when lid is removed, remove chicken breasts immediately.) Transfer chicken breasts to large plate and set aside. Continue to cook stock for 20 minutes, adjusting heat to maintain gentle boil. Strain stock through fine-mesh strainer into large pot or container, pressing on solids to extract as much liquid as possible; discard solids. Let liquid settle, about 5 minutes, then skim off fat.
3. *For the soup:* Return stock to Dutch oven set over medium-high heat. In small bowl, whisk water and cornstarch until smooth slurry forms; stir into stock and bring to gentle boil. Add onion, carrots, celery, and potato and cook until potato pieces are almost tender, 10 to 15 minutes, adjusting heat as needed to maintain gentle boil. Add noodles and continue to cook until all vegetables and noodles are tender, about 5 minutes longer.
4. Meanwhile, remove skin from reserved chicken breasts, then remove meat from bones and, using 2 forks, shred into bite-size pieces; discard skin and bones. Add chicken; Swiss chard, if using; and parsley to soup and cook until heated through, about 2 minutes. Season with salt and pepper to taste, and serve.

FAST TRACK TO FLAVORFUL CHICKEN SOUP

1. **SAUTÉ GROUND CHICKEN** Sauté ground chicken with aromatics to deepen flavor.

2. **POACH CHICKEN BREASTS** Add water, broth, and breasts; poach breasts about 30 minutes and remove.

3. **THICKEN STOCK** Strain stock and thicken with 3 tablespoons of cornstarch.

4. **ADD CHICKEN** Shred breasts and add to pot with vegetables to create fast, hearty soup.

PROVENÇAL VEGETABLE SOUP

KEITH DRESSER, *May/June 2015*

Nearly every Western cuisine lays claim to a vegetable soup, but my favorite is the version native to the south of France called *soupe au pistou*. The French equivalent of minestrone, this broth is chock-full of vegetables, beans, and herbs—a celebration of the fresh produce that returns to the markets in early summer.

Virtually any vegetables can and do go into the pot, but carrots, celery, leeks, zucchini, and the thin French green beans called haricots verts are typical. Pasta is often included, along with a white bean known as *coco de Mollans*. The only component that's an absolute constant is the pesto-like condiment for which the soup is named; stirring a spoonful into each bowl lends the broth a fresh jolt.

But when I've made the soup with supermarket produce, what should be a flavorful, satisfying soup often lacks character and body. I also find that when I don't have time to soak and simmer dried white beans (cannellini or navy are a typical substitute for hard-to-find coco de Mollans) and instead shortcut with canned ones, the soup suffers. What if there was a way to have both—that is, a hearty, full-flavored soupe au pistou that I could throw together anytime?

Including the liquid from canned cannellini beans gives this vegetable soup body and character.

Most classic versions use water for the soup base, but for more flavor I would make a vegetable broth. Ordinarily, that's a labor-intensive process, but our homemade Vegetable Broth Base (page 74) takes only minutes to make. I made 3 cups of broth and added an equal amount of water, to produce a base that was flavorful but delicate enough to let other ingredients come forward.

I wanted the mixture of vegetables to be abundant but not cluttered. I softened a leek with celery and carrot, added minced garlic, poured in the broth and water, and brought it all to a simmer. I added 8 ounces of haricots verts that I had cut into short lengths. When they were bright green but still crisp, I added a can of drained cannellini beans and some chopped zucchini and tomato, which added fresh flavor and brightness.

Within minutes, the soup's flavors seemed balanced and on target and the vegetables were tender. But there was the thin broth to address. Adding pasta to the soup helped: Not only did it make the soup heartier, but the pieces sloughed off starch as they boiled, giving the broth more body—though not enough.

But there was an ingredient already at my disposal that I hadn't yet employed: the starchy liquid from the canned cannellini beans. This viscous, seasoned "broth" produced a soup that was still brothy but also had some body.

As for the namesake pistou, I simply pureed a generous handful of fresh basil with Parmesan, a clove of garlic, and plenty of extra-virgin olive oil to yield a bold, grass-green sauce that was sharp and rich—the perfect accompaniment for the fresh, clean soup.

And with that, I had soupe au pistou that was both fast and flavorful, not to mention satisfying enough to stand on its own.

Provençal Vegetable Soup (Soupe au Pistou)

SERVES 6

We prefer broth prepared from our Vegetable Broth Base (page 74), but store-bought vegetable broth can be used.

Pistou

¾ cup fresh basil leaves
1 ounce Parmesan cheese, grated (½ cup)
⅓ cup extra-virgin olive oil
1 garlic clove, minced

Soup

1 tablespoon extra-virgin olive oil
1 leek, white and light green parts only, halved lengthwise, sliced ½ inch thick, and washed thoroughly
1 celery rib, cut into ½-inch pieces
1 carrot, peeled and sliced ¼ inch thick
Salt and pepper
2 garlic cloves, minced
3 cups vegetable broth
3 cups water
½ cup orecchiette or other short pasta
8 ounces haricots verts or green beans, trimmed and cut into ½-inch lengths
1 (15-ounce) can cannellini or navy beans
1 small zucchini, halved lengthwise, seeded, and cut into ¼-inch pieces
1 large tomato, cored, seeded, and cut into ¼-inch pieces

1. *For the pistou:* Process all ingredients in food processor until smooth, scraping down sides of bowl as needed, about 15 seconds. (Pistou can be refrigerated for up to 4 hours.)
2. *For the soup:* Heat oil in Dutch oven over medium heat until shimmering. Add leek, celery, carrot, and ½ teaspoon salt and cook until vegetables are softened, 8 to 10 minutes. Stir in garlic and cook until fragrant, about 30 seconds. Stir in broth and water and bring to simmer.
3. Stir in pasta and simmer until slightly softened, about 5 minutes. Stir in haricots verts and simmer until bright green but still crunchy, 3 to 5 minutes. Stir in cannellini beans and their liquid, zucchini, and tomato and simmer until pasta and vegetables are tender, about 3 minutes. Season with salt and pepper to taste. Serve, topping individual portions with generous tablespoon pistou.

BEST FRENCH ONION SOUP

REBECCA HAYS, *January/February 2008*

Legend has it that a hungry King Louis XV of France invented onion soup after returning home to an empty larder late one night from a hunting excursion. He took the few ingredients he could find—a sack of onions, leftover beef stock, and a bottle of Champagne—and created the now-famous recipe.

These days, the ideal French onion soup combines a satisfying broth redolent of sweet caramelized onions with a slice of toasted baguette and melted cheese. But the reality is that most of the onion soup you find isn't very good. Once you dig through the congealed cheese to unearth a spoonful of broth, it just doesn't taste like onions. I discovered the source of these watery, weak broths when I looked up some recipes. One was particularly appalling, calling for a mere 7 ounces of onions to make soup for six! Even more disturbing were those that advised sautéing the onions for only 5 or 6 minutes—not nearly enough time for them to caramelize.

THE FRENCH CONNECTION

The good news is that I really didn't need these lackluster recipes. I knew of a terrific one introduced to the test kitchen by a friend visiting from France. Henri Pinon patiently cooked 3 pounds of onions in butter over very low heat until they were golden brown (this took about 90 minutes), then deglazed the pot with water. Nothing unusual there—deglazing is common in onion soup recipes. What followed, however, was something entirely new. Henri allowed the onions to recaramelize, and then he deglazed the pan again. And again. He repeated this process several more times over the course of another hour, finally finishing the soup by simmering the onions with water, white wine, and a sprig of thyme. He garnished the soup in the traditional way, with a slice of crusty toasted baguette and a very modest amount of shredded Gruyère, passing the crocks under the broiler to melt the cheese. How did it taste? Beyond compare—the broth was impossibly rich, with deep onion flavor that burst through the tanginess of the Gruyère and bread.

Having watched Henri make his soup, I couldn't wait to give the recipe a try. But before I started cooking, I pondered his technique. When onions caramelize, a complex series of chemical reactions takes place, producing new colors, flavors, and aromas. Each time Henri deglazed the pan and allowed the onions to recaramelize, he was ratcheting up the flavor of the soup in a big way. Back in the test kitchen with Henri's recipe in hand, I started cooking, and a long while later, the soup was on. It was as delicious as when Henri had made it, yet after standing at the stove for more than 2 hours, I barely had the energy to enjoy it. Was there a way to borrow Henri's technique while cutting down on the active time?

To coax impressive flavor out of humble onions, we start cooking them in a covered pot in the oven.

I cranked the heat from low to high to hurry the onions along, and my risk-taking was rewarded with burnt onions. I needed steady heat that wouldn't cause scorching—the stovetop was concentrating too much heat at the bottom of the pot. Why not use the oven? I spread oiled sliced onions on a baking sheet and roasted them. Instead of caramelizing, however, they simply dried out. Lower temperatures caused the onions to steam. Next, I cooked as many sliced onions as I could squeeze into a Dutch oven (4 pounds), with far more promising results—the onions cooked slowly and evenly, building flavor all the while. After some trial and error, I finally settled on cooking the onions covered in a 400-degree oven for an hour, then continued cooking with the lid ajar for another hour and a half.

With my new hands-off method, the onions emerged from the oven golden, soft, and sweet, and a nice fond had begun to collect on the bottom of the pot. Even better, I'd only had to tend to them twice in 2½ hours. Next, I continued the caramelization process on the stovetop. Because of their head start in the oven, deglazing only three or four times was sufficient (the process still took nearly an hour—but this was far better than the 2-plus hours Henri spent on his dozens of deglazings). Once the onions were as dark as possible, I poured in a few splashes of dry sherry, which tasters preferred to sweet sherry, white wine, Champagne, red wine, and vermouth.

FINISHING TOUCHES

Settling on a type of onion from standard supermarket varieties was a snap. I quickly dismissed red onions—they bled out to produce a dingy-looking soup. White onions were too mild, and Vidalia onions made the broth candy-sweet. Yellow onions, on the other hand, offered just the sweet and savory notes I was after.

Henri had used only water for his soup, but after making batches with water, chicken broth, and beef broth alone and in combination, I decided the soup was best with all three. The broths added complexity, and my goal was to build as many layers of flavor as possible.

At last, I could focus on the soup's crowning glory: bread and cheese. So as to not obscure the lovely broth, I dialed back the hefty amounts that have come to define the topping in this country. Toasting the bread before floating a slice on the soup warded off sogginess. As for the cheese, Emmenthaler and Swiss were fine, but I wanted to stick to tradition. A modest sprinkling of nutty Gruyère was a grand, gooey finish to a great soup.

Best French Onion Soup

SERVES 6

Use a Dutch oven that holds 7 quarts or more for this recipe. Sweet onions, such as Vidalia or Walla Walla, will make this recipe overly sweet. Use broiler-safe crocks and keep the rims of the bowls 4 to 5 inches from the heating element to obtain a proper gratin of melted, bubbly cheese. If using ordinary soup bowls, sprinkle the toasted bread slices with Gruyère, return them to the broiler until the cheese melts, and then float them on top of the soup.

Soup

4 pounds onions, halved and sliced ¼ inch thick
3 tablespoons unsalted butter, cut into 3 pieces
Salt and pepper
2¾–3 cups water
½ cup dry sherry
4 cups chicken broth
2 cups beef broth
6 sprigs fresh thyme, tied with kitchen twine
1 bay leaf

Cheese Croutons

1 (12-inch) baguette, sliced ½ inch thick
8 ounces Gruyère cheese, shredded (2 cups)

1. *For the soup:* Adjust oven rack to lower-middle position and heat oven to 400 degrees. Generously spray inside of large Dutch oven with vegetable oil spray. Add onions, butter, and 1 teaspoon salt. Cook, covered, for 1 hour (onions will be moist and slightly reduced in volume). Remove pot from oven and stir onions, scraping bottom and sides of pot. Return pot to oven with lid slightly ajar and continue to cook until onions are very soft and golden brown, 1½ to 1¾ hours longer, stirring onions and scraping bottom and sides of pot after 1 hour.
2. Carefully remove pot from oven (leave oven on) and place over medium-high heat. Cook onions, stirring frequently and scraping bottom and sides of pot, until liquid evaporates and onions brown, 15 to 20 minutes (reduce heat to medium if onions brown too quickly). Continue to cook, stirring frequently, until bottom of pot is coated with dark crust, 6 to 8 minutes, adjusting heat as necessary. (Scrape any browned bits that collect on spoon back into onions.) Stir in ¼ cup water, scraping pot bottom to loosen crust, and cook until water evaporates and another dark crust has formed on pot bottom, 6 to 8 minutes. Repeat process of deglazing 2 or 3 more times, until onions are very dark brown. Stir in sherry and cook, stirring frequently, until sherry evaporates, about 5 minutes.
3. Stir in chicken broth, beef broth, thyme sprigs, bay leaf, 2 cups water, and ½ teaspoon salt, scraping up any browned bits on bottom and sides of pot. Increase heat to high and bring to simmer. Reduce heat to low, cover, and simmer for 30 minutes. Discard thyme sprigs and bay leaf and season with salt and pepper to taste.
4. *For the cheese croutons:* While soup simmers, arrange baguette slices in single layer on rimmed baking sheet and bake until bread is dry, crisp, and golden at edges, about 10 minutes. Set aside.
5. Adjust oven rack 8 inches from broiler element and heat broiler. Set 6 broiler-safe crocks on rimmed baking sheet and fill each with about 1¾ cups soup. Top each bowl with 1 or 2 baguette slices (do not overlap slices) and sprinkle evenly with Gruyère. Broil until cheese is melted and bubbly around edges, 3 to 5 minutes. Let cool for 5 minutes before serving.

variation

Quicker French Onion Soup

If you don't have a bowl large enough to accommodate all the onions, microwave them in a smaller bowl in two batches.

Combine onions and 1 teaspoon salt in large bowl and cover (cover should completely cover bowl and should not rest on onions). Microwave for 20 to 25 minutes until onions are soft and wilted, stirring halfway through microwaving. (Use oven mitts to remove bowl from microwave and remove cover away from you to avoid steam.) Drain onions (about ½ cup liquid should drain off) and proceed with step 2, melting butter in Dutch oven before adding wilted onions.

GOLDEN ONIONS WITHOUT THE FUSS

Forget constant stirring on the stovetop, which can take hours of active work. Cooking onions in the oven takes time but requires little attention, making our Best French Onion Soup recipe much more hands-off.

1. **RAW** The raw onions nearly fill a large Dutch oven.

2. **AFTER 1 HOUR IN OVEN** The onions are starting to wilt and release moisture.

3. **AFTER 2½ HOURS IN OVEN** The onions are golden, wilted, and significantly reduced in volume.

BETTER BLACK BEAN SOUP

REBECCA HAYS, *January/February 2005*

Black beans (or turtle beans) have always been a staple in Mexican, Cuban, and Caribbean kitchens, but they really came into vogue in the United States with the introduction of black bean soup in the 1960s. The Coach House restaurant in New York City popularized the soup, which was an all-day affair. It started with soaked beans that simmered for hours with, among other ingredients, parsnips, carrots, beef bones, and smoked ham hocks. The pureed soup was finished with a splash of Madeira, chopped hard-cooked eggs, and thinly sliced lemon. Refined? Yes. Realistic for the modern cook? No. The good news is that today's recipes, heavily influenced by Latin American cuisine, are easier to prepare. The bad news is that as restaurant recipes have been simplified, flavor has suffered.

Testing five soups shed light on specific problems. Asked to record their impressions, tasters chose the words "watery" and "thin" to describe the texture of most soups and either "bland" and "musty" or "overspiced" and "bitter" to describe the taste. The soups were given low marks for appearance, too—all had unattractive purple/gray tones; none were truly black.

BEAN TOWN

When beans are the star ingredient, it's preferable to use the dried variety, not canned—the former release valuable flavor into the broth as they cook, while the latter generally make vapid soup. (I simmered five brands of dried beans and there were only minor variations in flavor. In short, brand doesn't seem to matter.) We've also learned that there's no reason to soak dried beans overnight—doing so only marginally reduces the cooking time and requires too much forethought. Similarly, the "quick-soak" method in which the beans are brought to a boil, then soaked off the heat for an hour, is disappointing in that it causes many of the beans to explode during cooking.

As for seasoning, a teaspoon of salt added at the outset of cooking provided tastier beans than salt added at the end of cooking. We've found that salting early does not toughen the skins of beans, as some cooks claim. In addition to salt, I threw a couple of aromatic bay leaves into the pot.

I knew I didn't want to make from-scratch beef stock, so I focused on more time-efficient flavor builders, starting with a smoky ham hock. While tasters liked its meaty flavor, it also made them want more—not just more meat flavor (hocks are mostly bone) but real meat. I turned to untraditional (for black bean soup) cured pork products: salt pork, slab bacon, and ham steak. Ham steak contributed a good amount of smoky pork flavor and decidedly more meat than any of the other options, making it my first choice.

Ham steak adds meaty flavor to a black bean soup flavored with cumin, garlic, and lime juice.

Aside from the ham flavor, the soup tasted rather hollow. I found improvement with a *soffrito*, a Spanish or Italian preparation in which aromatic vegetables and herbs (I used green pepper, onion, garlic, and oregano) are sautéed until softened and lightly browned. But my soffrito needed refinement.

Fragrant oregano was replaced with cumin, which had a warmer, more likable taste. I slowly incorporated the ground spice, working my way up to 1½ tablespoons. Sound like a lot? It is, but I was after big flavor, and when the cumin toasted along with the aromatics, its pungency was tempered. I also replaced the bitter green pepper with minced carrot and celery for a sweeter, fresher flavor.

My colleagues urged me not to be shy with minced garlic and hot red pepper flakes: I added six cloves and ½ teaspoon, respectively. The soup was now a hit, layered with sweet, spicy, smoky, and fresh vegetable flavors. While the Coach House recipe called for homemade beef stock, my aggressive seasonings meant that a mixture of water and canned broth was all that was needed.

THROUGH THICK AND THIN

My colleagues were united in their request for a partially pureed soup, refusing both ultrasmooth mixtures and chunky, brothy ones. Even after pureeing, though, a thickener seemed necessary. Simply using less liquid in the soup and mashing some of the beans ameliorated the texture somewhat, but the soup still lacked body. A potato cooked in the soup pureed into an unpleasant, starchy brew. Flour, cooked with the oil in the soffrito to form a roux, and cornstarch, stirred into the soup at the end of cooking, both worked. I decided to call for cornstarch, which lets the cook control the thickness (or thinness) of the finished soup by adding more or less of the slurry (cornstarch and water paste) to the pot.

I was finally satisfied, save for the soup's unappealing gray color. The solution came to me in a roundabout way. While our food scientist was looking into remedies for the gas-causing effects of beans in digestion, we noticed that a side effect of cooking beans with baking soda is that the beans retain their dark color. The coating of the black beans contains anthocyanins (colored pigments) that change color with changes in pH: A more alkaline broth makes them darker, and a more acidic broth makes them lighter. I experimented by adding various amounts of baking soda to the beans. The winning quantity was a mere ⅛ teaspoon, which produced a great-tasting soup (there was no soapy aftertaste, as was the case with larger quantities) with a darker, more appetizing color than unadulterated beans. Problem solved.

Classic additions to black bean soup include Madeira, rum, sherry, or scotch from the liquor cabinet and lemon, lime, or orange juice from the citrus bin. Given the other flavors in the soup, lime juice seemed the best fit. Because it is acidic, too much lime juice can push the color of the soup toward pink. Two tablespoons added flavor without marring the color.

Without an array of colorful garnishes, even the best black bean soup might be dull. Sour cream and diced avocado offset the soup's heat, while red onion and minced cilantro contribute freshness and color. Finally, wedges of lime accentuate the bright flavor of the juice that's already in the soup.

ALL ABOUT DRIED BEANS

For our black bean soup, dried beans are central to the success of the recipe. Here's what to know about dried beans.

BUYING When shopping for beans, it's essential to select "fresh" dried beans. Buy those that are uniform in size and have a smooth exterior. When dried beans are fully hydrated and cooked, they should be plump, with taut skins, and have creamy insides; spent beans will have wrinkled skin and a dry, almost gritty texture.

STORING Uncooked beans should be stored in a cool, dry place in a sealed plastic or glass container. Beans are less susceptible than rice and grains to pests and spoilage, but it is still best to use them within a month or two.

SORTING AND RINSING Prior to cooking, you should pick over dried beans for any small stones or debris and then rinse the beans to wash away any dust or impurities. The easiest way to check for small stones is to spread the beans on a large plate or rimmed baking sheet.

Black Bean Soup

SERVES 6

Dried beans tend to cook unevenly, so be sure to taste several beans to determine their doneness in step 1. For efficiency, you can prepare the soup ingredients while the beans simmer and the garnishes while the soup simmers. Garnishes are essential for this soup, as they add not only flavor but texture and color as well. Our favorites are lime wedges, minced fresh cilantro, finely diced red onion, diced avocado, and sour cream.

Beans

1 pound (2½ cups) dried black beans, picked over and rinsed
5–6 cups water
4 ounces ham steak, trimmed
2 bay leaves
1 teaspoon salt
⅛ teaspoon baking soda

Soup

3 tablespoons olive oil
2 large onions, chopped fine
3 celery ribs, chopped fine
1 large carrot, peeled and chopped fine
Salt and pepper
5–6 garlic cloves, minced
1½ tablespoons ground cumin
½ teaspoon red pepper flakes
6 cups chicken broth
2 tablespoons cornstarch
2 tablespoons water
2 tablespoons lime juice

1. *For the beans:* Combine beans, 5 cups water, ham, bay leaves, salt, and baking soda in large saucepan. Bring to boil, skimming any impurities that rise to surface. Cover, reduce heat to low, and simmer gently until beans are tender, 1¼ to 1½ hours. (If after 1½ hours beans are not tender, add remaining 1 cup water and continue to simmer until beans are tender.) Discard bay leaves. Transfer ham steak to carving board and cut into ¼-inch pieces; set aside. (Do not drain beans.)
2. *For the soup:* Heat oil in Dutch oven over medium heat until shimmering. Add onions, celery, carrot, and ½ teaspoon salt and cook until vegetables are softened and lightly browned, 12 to 15 minutes.
3. Stir in garlic, cumin, and pepper flakes and cook until fragrant, about 1 minute. Stir in broth and cooked beans with their cooking liquid, and bring to boil. Reduce heat to medium-low and cook, uncovered and stirring occasionally, until flavors have blended, about 30 minutes.
4. Puree 1½ cups of beans and 2 cups of liquid in blender until smooth, then return to pot. Whisk cornstarch and water together in small bowl, then gradually stir half of cornstarch mixture into simmering soup. Continue to simmer soup, stirring occasionally, until slightly thickened, 3 to 5 minutes. (If at this point soup is thinner than desired, repeat with remaining cornstarch mixture.) Off heat, stir in lime juice and reserved ham, season with salt and pepper to taste, and serve. (Soup can be refrigerated for up to 3 days. Add water as needed when reheating to adjust consistency.)

variation

Black Bean Soup with Chipotle Chiles

Chipotle chiles are spicy; for a spicier soup, use the greater amount of chipotles given.

Omit red pepper flakes. Add 1 to 2 tablespoons minced canned chipotle chile in adobo sauce to soup with chicken broth.

THICKENING BLACK BEAN SOUP

Adding only half of the cornstarch slurry at a time allows us to better control the final consistency of the soup.

HEARTY LENTIL SOUP

ELIZABETH GERMAIN, *January/February 2004*

Run-of-the-mill lentil soup always reminds me of the scene from the film *Oliver!* when Oliver Twist begs, "Please, sir, may I have some more?" The problem, of course, is that no one who isn't truly, deeply hungry would ask for a second helping of the thin slop or flavorless mud that often passes for this common soup. Even a picture-perfect bowlful of lentil soup can be an illusion because it still may have no flavor whatsoever. Yet this earthy dish ought to be a winner. It's cheap, it's quick, and it tastes just fine—maybe even better—the next day. I was determined to develop a master recipe for my cold-weather repertoire that would be a keeper. I wanted a hearty lentil soup worthy of a second bowl.

I started by preparing five representative recipes, and two discoveries quickly came to light. First, garlic, herbs, onions, and tomatoes are common denominators. Second, texture is a big issue. None of my tasters liked the soup that was brothy or, at the other extreme, the one that was as thick as porridge. They also gave a big thumbs down to those that looked like brown split pea soup. Consequently, recipes that included carrots, tomatoes, and herbs were rewarded for their brighter colors (and flavors). There was also a clear preference for the subtle, smoky depth meat provides. The next step was to determine which lentils to buy and how to cook them.

LENTIL LESSONS

Brown, green, and red lentils are the most common choices on supermarket shelves. At specialty markets and natural food stores, you can also find black lentils and French green lentils (*lentilles du Puy*), the latter being the darling of chefs everywhere. In addition to color differences, lentils can be divided according to their size—large or small—and to whether they are split, like peas, or not. Ordinary brown and green lentils are large, while red, black, and lentilles du Puy are small. Red lentils are often sold split and are used most frequently in Indian dishes such as dal.

To make some sense of all of this, I made five pots of lentil soup, each one using a different colored lentil. Red lentils were out—they disintegrated when simmered. All four of the remaining choices produced an acceptable texture, but tasters preferred, as expected, the earthy flavor and firm texture of the lentilles du Puy. To our surprise, however, the larger green and brown lentils also fared reasonably well.

Next, I set out to test cooking methods. Some recipes call for soaking the lentils for a few hours before cooking. Not only did I determine that this step was unnecessary—lentils cook up rather quickly—but I also discovered that soaking increases the likelihood of a mushy texture. Even without soaking, some varieties, especially the large brown and green lentils, have a greater tendency to fall apart if overcooked. Searching for a way to avoid this problem, I employed a common Indian culinary trick: sweating the lentils in a covered pan with aromatic vegetables prior to adding the liquid. Using brown lentils, I cooked up two batches and, bingo, I had solved the problem! The sweated lentils remained intact, while the unsweated lentils had broken down.

To better understand this phenomenon, I set up a series of tests with our staff science editor, John Olson. We sweated one batch of lentils with just onions and carrots. In the second batch, we added salt, and in the third batch we added vinegar to test the role of acids. The results were clear. The first batch—without any salt or acid—was the worst, with a very mushy texture. The lentils sweated with salt were the most intact; the vinegar helped keep the lentils firm, but it was not as effective as the salt (at least in amounts that would taste good). Why did we get these results? When legumes are cooked, pectin-like compounds break down into a gelatinous goo similar to jam. Salt and acids (such as those found in vinegar or canned tomatoes) reinforce the original insoluble pectic compounds and retard their conversion to gel. Sweating lentils with bacon, canned tomatoes, and salt (as well as aromatic vegetables and herbs) not only ensured an ideal texture but boosted the flavor of the legumes as well.

One issue concerning texture remained. Tasters wanted a chunkier soup and did not like the brothy base. I tried pureeing a few cups of the soup and then adding it back to the pot. Tasters praised the contrast of the now-creamy base with the whole lentils and found the entire soup more interesting.

Sautéing the lentils before simmering them helps them retain their texture and bite.

FLAVOR DEVELOPMENT

Pork was the meat of choice in all of the recipes I examined. I found that the lentils cooked too quickly to extract the smoky flavor that a ham bone or hock can impart. Prosciutto and pancetta were too mild. Tasters preferred the smoky flavor of bacon and liked the textural addition of the bacon bits. Another advantage bacon offered was rendered fat. I used it to sauté the vegetables and aromatics, which further infused the soup with smoky flavor.

From early testing, I knew that onions, carrots, garlic, and tomatoes were a given for flavor and color. When crushed or pureed tomatoes were added to the pot, the soup took on the dispiriting color of tomato sauce. Tasters preferred drained diced tomatoes, which allowed the lentils to remain center stage. Turnips were out of place, and potatoes were too starchy. Tasters also rejected celery, saying its flavor was too prominent. A bay leaf, thyme, and parsley rounded out the other flavors and added a touch of bright green to the pot.

Last, but not least, was the question of liquids. I prepared two batches, one with water and one with chicken broth. Neither was ideal. Water produced a soup that was not as rich in flavor as desired, while the broth-only version tasted too much like chicken soup. After several more tests, I concluded that a mix of 3 parts broth to 1 part water produced a hearty depth of flavor without being overpowering.

Now I turned to ingredients to brighten the soup and found that dry white wine worked wonders. Because the acidic wine had noticeably improved the soup, I tried one final adjustment. Many recipes call for the addition of vinegar or lemon juice just before the soup is served, so I stirred a touch of balsamic vinegar into the pot at completion. Now my tasters came up and asked, "Please, Elizabeth, may I have some more?"

LENTILS 101

Lentils come in various sizes and colors, and the differences in flavor and texture are surprisingly distinct. For our Hearty Lentil Soup, the best type was clear.

LENTILLES DU PUY These lentils are smaller than the more common brown and green varieties. While they take their name from the city of Puy in central France, they are also grown in North America and Italy. Dark olive green, almost black, in color, with mottling, these lentils were praised for their "rich, earthy, complex flavor" and "firm yet tender texture."

BLACK LENTILS Like lentilles du Puy, black lentils are slightly smaller than the standard brown lentils. They have a deep black hue that tasters likened to the color of caviar. In fact, some markets refer to them as beluga lentils. Tasters liked their "robust, earthy flavor" and "ability to hold their shape while remaining tender." A few tasters found the color of the soup made with them "too dark and muddy."

BROWN LENTILS These larger lentils are the most common choice in the market and are a uniform drab brown. Tasters commented on their "mild yet light and earthy flavor." Some found their texture "creamy," while others complained that they were "chalky." But everyone agreed that they held their shape and were tender inside.

GREEN LENTILS Another larger lentil, this variety is the same size as the brown lentil and is greenish-brown in color. Although tasters accepted the "mild flavor" of these lentils and liked the way they "retain their shape while being tender," most complained that the soup made from them was "a bit anemic-looking."

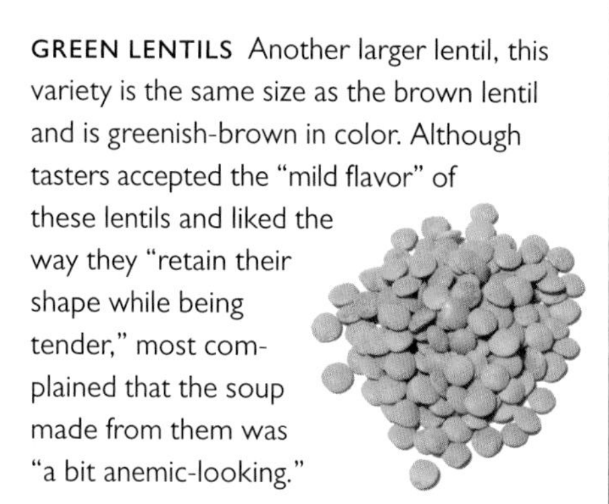

RED LENTILS These small orange-red lentils "completely disintegrate when cooked." They made a soup that looked "anemic."

Hearty Lentil Soup

SERVES 4 TO 6

We prefer lentilles du Puy, sometimes called French green lentils, for this recipe, but brown, black, or regular green lentils are fine, too. Cooking times will vary depending on the type of lentils used. The soup can be made in advance: After blending the soup in step 3, let the soup cool completely and refrigerate it in an airtight container for up to two days. To serve, heat it over medium-low until hot and then stir in the parsley and vinegar.

3 slices bacon, cut into ¼-inch pieces
1 large onion, chopped fine
2 carrots, peeled and chopped
3 garlic cloves, minced
1 teaspoon minced fresh thyme or ¼ teaspoon dried
1 (14.5-ounce) can diced tomatoes, drained
1 bay leaf
1 cup lentilles du Puy, picked over and rinsed
Salt and pepper
½ cup dry white wine
4½ cups chicken broth, plus extra as needed
1½ cups water
3 tablespoons minced fresh parsley
1½ teaspoons balsamic vinegar

1. Cook bacon in Dutch oven over medium-high heat, stirring often, until crisp, about 5 minutes. Stir in onion and carrots and cook until vegetables begin to soften, about 2 minutes. Stir in garlic and thyme and cook until fragrant, about 30 seconds. Stir in tomatoes and bay leaf and cook until fragrant, about 30 seconds. Stir in lentils and ¼ teaspoon salt. Cover, reduce heat to medium-low, and cook until vegetables are softened and lentils have darkened, 8 to 10 minutes.
2. Increase heat to high, stir in wine, and bring to simmer. Add broth and water and bring to boil. Partially cover pot, reduce heat to low, and simmer until lentils are tender but still hold their shape, 30 to 35 minutes.
3. Discard bay leaf. Process 3 cups soup in blender until smooth, about 30 seconds, then return to pot. Heat soup gently over low heat until hot (do not boil) and adjust consistency with extra broth as needed. Stir in parsley and vinegar and season with salt and pepper to taste. Serve.

FRESH CORN CHOWDER

ELIZABETH GERMAIN, *September/October 2000*

While it is most easily appreciated on the cob, fresh corn also lends itself well to another American favorite: corn chowder. The ingredients in most recipes are relatively standard and certainly simple enough. There are the corn and other vegetables, usually potatoes and onions at minimum; there are the liquids, water or corn or chicken stock enriched with some sort of dairy; and there's some sort of fat, be it butter, bacon, or salt pork. Most recipes also have in common a reliance on the time-honored technique of first cooking the onions in fat to develop flavor and then adding the liquids and vegetables. Comfortable with this basic approach, I decided to build my master recipe from the ground up.

FLAVORFUL FAT

I knew from the outset that I wanted my chowder to be loaded with fresh corn flavor. What became apparent after testing a few recipes was that the texture and flavor of the base is also critical to a great chowder. The first contributor to that flavor is fat. Because lots of people haven't cooked with salt pork and some shy away from bacon, I was hoping that butter or oil would prove to be adequate substitutes, but tests proved otherwise. Chowders prepared with corn oil were bland and insipid. Butter was better, but it failed to add complexity of flavor to the chowder. Somewhat surprisingly, rendered bacon fat also failed to add much interesting flavor. Tradition, in the form of salt pork, served the chowder best, giving the base a deep, resonant flavor. (Salt pork comes from the pig's belly and consists mostly of fat, striated with thin layers of meat.)

The best corn chowder is made by grating some of the fresh corn for the soup's base and stirring in whole kernels at the end of cooking.

The next question concerning the fat was how to use it. What was the best way to render the fat? Was it necessary (or desirable) to cut the salt pork up into small pieces? Should the salt pork itself be removed from the pan after rendering, or is there an advantage to leaving it in the pot? The chowder developed a truly delectable flavor when the salt pork stayed in the pot throughout cooking. Cutting it in bits, though, proved to be undesirable; I found those little pieces to be tough and chewy. My solution was to use two big chunks that could easily be removed at the end of cooking. One shortcoming of this technique is that the same amount of salt pork cut into a couple of big pieces produces less fat than all of those small pieces, and it wasn't quite enough to sweat the onions. I compensated by adding a little butter to the pan.

LIQUID GOLD

With this first important building block of flavor in place, I could go on to consider how best to infuse the chowder base with the flavor of corn. Corn stock, corn puree, corn juice, and corn pulp were all possibilities.

I made two quick stocks with corn cobs and husks, using water in one and chicken stock in the other. Although both brews had some corn flavor, their overall effect on the chowder was minimal; making corn stock was clearly not worth the effort. I did learn, though, that water diluted the flavor of the chowder while chicken stock improved it; this would be my liquid of choice for the base.

Looking for a quick and easy solution, I next tried pureeing the corn kernels and dumping them into the chowder. This wasn't going to work: the hulls made for an unpleasantly rough texture.

In an earlier Cook's article, "Corn Off the Cob," Rebecca Wood identified grating and scraping as a good means of extracting flavor from corn to be used for chowder. This approach is time-consuming and messy, but the result convinced me that it is worth the effort. Here was one of the secrets to great corn chowder. The pulp was thick, lush, smooth-textured, and full of corn flavor. When added to the chowder, it improved both flavor and texture dramatically.

HOT CORN ICE CREAM?

My next concern was the dairy, and, as it turned out, the thickener to be used. A problem with the dairy component of chowder is its tendency to curdle when heated, with lower-fat products such as 2 percent milk more likely to curdle than high-fat products such as heavy cream. It's the protein component of dairy that causes curdling, and heavy cream is not susceptible because it has so much (about 40 percent) fat; the protein molecules are thus completely surrounded by fat molecules, which keep the proteins from breaking down. But I would not be able to rely entirely on heavy cream to prevent curdling, as my tasters rejected this version. In their collective opinion, it tasted "like hot corn ice cream."

While some heavy cream was needed to give the base some depth of character, whole milk, which is wonderfully neutral and therefore capable of being infused with corn flavor, would make up the larger part of the dairy. This composition gave me some concern about curdling, which is where the thickening factor came in. I realized that the most practical thickener to use would be flour, which is known to help stabilize dairy proteins and so prevent curdling. Having a dual objective of both thickening the base and stabilizing the dairy made my work easier. To prevent curdling, the flour has to be in the pot before the dairy is added. The logical choice of technique, then, would be to make a roux, stirring the flour into the fat and onions at the beginning of the cooking process.

THE SOLIDS—EASY AS 1, 2, 3

Determining the chowder solids was a relatively simple matter. Onions, potatoes, and corn kernels were a given; the questions were what variety of onion and potato and how much of each? Yellow onions and leeks were serviceable, but Spanish onions proved best, adding flavor without dominating the other ingredients. The favorite potatoes were red potatoes, which remained firm and looked great with their skins left on. I celebrated the symmetry of batch 41 when I realized that 3 cups of kernels, 2 cups of potatoes, and 1 cup of cooked onion (the volume of 2 cups raw) was perfect. Whole corn kernels add authenticity to the chowder, and I learned that adding the kernels after the potatoes have been cooked till tender, then cooking the kernels just briefly, results in a fresh-from-the-cob corn flavor. A bit of garlic added some depth and fullness, while thyme, parsley, and a bay leaf helped to round out the flavors.

MILKING THE CORN

1. Start by grating corn ears on box grater.

2. Finish by scraping any remaining kernels off cob with back of knife.

Fresh Corn Chowder

SERVES 6

Be sure to use salt pork, not fatback, for the chowder. Streaks of lean meat distinguish salt pork from fatback; fatback is pure fat. We prefer Spanish onions for their sweet, mild flavor, but all-purpose yellow onions will work fine, too.

10 ears corn, husks and silk removed
3 ounces salt pork, rind removed, cut into two 1-inch cubes
1 tablespoon unsalted butter
1 large onion, chopped fine
2 garlic cloves, minced
3 tablespoons all-purpose flour
3 cups chicken broth
2 cups whole milk
12 ounces red potatoes, unpeeled, cut into ¼-inch cubes
1 teaspoon minced fresh thyme or ¼ teaspoon dried
1 bay leaf
1 cup heavy cream
2 tablespoons minced fresh parsley
Salt and pepper

1. Using chef's knife, cut kernels from 4 ears corn (you should have about 3 cups). Grate kernels from remaining 6 ears on large holes of box grater into bowl, then firmly scrape any pulp remaining on cobs with back of butter knife or vegetable peeler (you should have 2 generous cups grated kernels and pulp).

2. Cook salt pork in Dutch oven over medium-high heat, turning with tongs and pressing down on pieces to render fat, until cubes are crisp and golden brown, about 10 minutes. Reduce heat to low, stir in butter and onion, cover, and cook until onion is softened, about 12 minutes. Remove salt pork and reserve. Add garlic and cook until fragrant, about 1 minute. Whisk in flour and cook, stirring constantly, about 2 minutes. Whisking constantly, gradually add broth. Add milk, potatoes, thyme, bay leaf, grated corn and pulp, and reserved salt pork and bring to boil. Reduce heat to medium-low and simmer until potatoes are almost tender, 8 to 10 minutes. Add reserved corn kernels and heavy cream and return to simmer. Simmer until corn kernels are tender yet still slightly crunchy, about 5 minutes. Discard bay leaf and salt pork. Stir in parsley, season with salt and pepper to taste, and serve immediately.

EXTENDING THE CORN CHOWDER SEASON

To extend the fresh corn chowder season into the colder months, I tested freezing fresh corn three ways: one batch on the cob frozen raw; another batch of kernels, with the requisite amount of grated and scraped corn frozen separately, also raw; and another batch blanched on the cob before freezing.

Three months later, I made chowder from each of the batches of frozen corn. Chowders made from the corn frozen raw on the cob and the pregrated and scraped corn were stale-tasting and looked curdled. However, the chowder prepared with corn blanched on the cob and then frozen conveyed the fresh flavor of summer corn, and its texture was perfect.

Why? A good part of what gives fresh-picked corn its wonderful juiciness and flavor are its sugars. Once picked, however, these sugars start to break down, turning into starch. Primarily responsible for this unfortunate transformation are two groups of "marker" enzymes, peroxidase and catalase. Cold temperatures slow down the action of these enzymes considerably (which is why fresh-picked corn should go straight to the refrigerator and remain there till cooked), but the right amount of heat can stop them dead in their tracks. Blanching the corn completely disables the enzymes, thereby protecting the corn from decay.

To freeze corn for chowder, husk 10 ears of corn and bring 1 gallon water to boil in large pot. Add half of the corn, return the pot to a boil, and cook for 5 minutes. Remove the cobs and place immediately in a bowl of ice water for 4 minutes to stop the cooking. Spread the cooled ears out on a clean kitchen towel to dry, and repeat the blanching and shocking process with the remaining corn. Freeze the dry corn in zipper-lock freezer bags. When preparing the chowder, cook the whole kernels in step 2 for just 2 to 3 minutes to maintain their crunch.

BEST GROUND BEEF CHILI

ANDREW JANJIGIAN, *November/December 2015*

I'm not from Texas, so I've never had the mindset that chili by definition could only mean a bowl made with hand-cut chunks of beef. If anything, I'm always more drawn to ground beef versions, since they skip the tedious step of breaking down a whole roast. That said, ground beef chili often suffers from dry, grainy, somewhat tough meat. I set myself the challenge of changing that.

I wanted a big batch of thick, spicy, ultrabeefy chili—the kind I'd pile into a bowl with tortilla chips or rice and enjoy with a beer. In order to create that, I would first have to sort out how to give the ground meat the same juicy, tender texture found in chili made with chunks of beef.

GROUND PLAN

As a first step toward improving dry meat, I opted to use 2 pounds of 85 percent lean (15 percent fat) ground beef. The fat in the mix would lubricate the meat fibers, creating a sense of moistness. As for how to cook it, most chili recipes—whether using ground beef or chunks—call for browning the meat in oil to build a flavor base. Since ground beef sheds a fair amount of liquid as it cooks, and liquid precludes browning, I cooked it in three batches so that any moisture could evaporate quickly.

The next big question was how long to simmer the meat for the most tender results. Recipes vary widely: Some suggest an hour, others call for 2 hours, and more than a few say "the longer the better." But would the fact that the meat was ground make its proteins and collagen break down more quickly than stew meat, which requires roughly 2½ hours of simmering? I knew this could be cleared up by one simple test.

But first I needed a basic chili recipe to work from. After setting the browned meat aside, I sautéed a few spoonfuls of store-bought chili powder (a stand-in for the homemade blend I planned to mix up later), diced onions, and minced garlic in the residual fat. Once the aromatics were softened, I returned the beef to the pot along with a can of pinto beans and a small can of whole tomatoes that I pureed in the food processor. Finally, I stirred in 2 cups of water. I brought the mixture to a boil, put the lid on the pot, and transferred it to a 275-degree oven where the ambient heat would cook it gently. After about an hour, the result was only mediocre: The flavors were no longer raw-tasting, but they were somewhat blah. Plus, the beef still had the dry, tough texture I was trying to avoid.

For moist and tender ground beef in chili, baking soda and a long simmer are key.

TRYING FOR TENDERNESS

Sixty minutes of simmering clearly wasn't long enough to tenderize the meat. I put the chili back into the oven, pulling it out and sampling it every 15 minutes or so. The Goldilocks moment, when the meat was fairly tender, came at the 90-minute mark.

This suggested that just because meat is ground doesn't mean it doesn't take time to tenderize: The pieces might be smaller than meat chunks, but the muscle fibers are made of the same proteins and collagen that require similar exposure to heat to break down. Heat penetrates the fibers more quickly when they are in small pieces, which is why chunks of chuck roast might take 2 to 2½ hours to tenderize, while ground beef requires only 90 minutes.

I had made progress, but the ground beef still wasn't living up to its full potential: I wanted it to be even more tender, and it wasn't as moist as chunks of beef would be. That's because fine pieces of ground meat give off far more moisture during the browning step than larger meat chunks do. The muscle fibers tighten up when heated, squeezing out some of the liquid they contain. And the smaller the piece, the more liquid will be lost to the surrounding environment.

There are a few tricks to help keep ground beef tender and juicy. One of them I was already doing: using meat with a relatively high fat content. Another is to add salt and let the meat sit for about 20 minutes. In addition to seasoning the meat, salt alters the structure of the meat proteins to better allow it to retain moisture. Finally, you can raise the pH of the meat with a little baking soda to help the proteins attract more water and hold on to it.

Indeed, incorporating baking soda—¾ teaspoon plus 2 tablespoons of water to help it dissolve—not only kept the meat juicy and made it even more tender, but it also produced an unforeseen benefit: Since the beef now barely shed any moisture during cooking, and a higher pH significantly speeds up the Maillard reaction, the meat browned much more quickly. This meant that I could cook it in a single batch rather than in three—a major timesaver.

FAT AND FLAVOR

With that, I shifted my focus to giving the chili memorably spicy flavor. Store-bought chili powder is convenient, but it's not that much trouble to make a homemade blend that tastes significantly better. I started with six dried whole ancho chiles, toasted to bring out their raisin-like sweetness and fruity heat. But it was hard to grind the small quantity of chiles in a food processor, since the pieces just bounced around the workbowl. One trick we've used in the past is to add cornmeal to the mix to bulk it up. The cornmeal also serves to slightly thicken and add corn flavor to the chili. I used the same approach, but substituted a few tortilla chips for the cornmeal, since I always have them on hand to serve with chili.

For another layer of heat and smokiness, I stirred in minced chipotles in adobo. And to boost the chile notes without adding more heat, I threw in some sweet paprika. Of course, chili powder isn't made from just chiles. I also added a generous amount of ground cumin, plus garlic powder, ground coriander, dried oregano, black pepper, and dried thyme.

Finally, about that fat. After the chili came out of the oven, it was covered in a layer of bright orange grease. When I reflexively skimmed it off, my tasters complained that the chili tasted a little flat and lean. The Day-Glo color should have been a giveaway that the fat was loaded with oil-soluble compounds from my spice blend. Discarding it robbed the chili of flavor. So for my next batch, instead of removing the fat, I just stirred it back in. Now the chili boasted deeply spiced complexity.

To cut some of its richness, I added 2 teaspoons of sugar and a couple of tablespoons of cider vinegar. I served the chili with lime wedges, fresh cilantro, chopped onion, and plenty of tortilla chips and/or steamed white rice. This chili was full-flavored and rich but certainly not so rich that my guests didn't come back for seconds.

WHEN IT COMES TO COOK TIME, CHUCK IS CHUCK

You might think that just because ground beef is made up of tiny pieces of meat, it doesn't need much time to cook. But ground chuck is exactly that—cut-up pieces of chuck roast—and as such contains the same proteins and collagen that require adequate exposure to moist heat to properly break down. Many chili recipes cook the ground meat for 45 minutes or even less. For optimally tender results, we simmer ours for 1½ to 2 hours—almost as long as we do stew meat.

=

CUBED VS. GROUND
Both benefit from longer cooking.

Best Ground Beef Chili

SERVES 8 TO 10

Diced avocado, sour cream, and shredded Monterey Jack or cheddar cheese are also good options for garnishing. This chili is intensely flavored and should be served with tortilla chips and/or plenty of steamed white rice.

2 pounds 85 percent lean ground beef
2 tablespoons plus 2 cups water
Salt and pepper
¾ teaspoon baking soda
6 dried ancho chiles, stemmed, seeded, and torn into 1-inch pieces
1 ounce tortilla chips, crushed (¼ cup)
2 tablespoons ground cumin
1 tablespoon paprika
1 tablespoon garlic powder
1 tablespoon ground coriander
2 teaspoons dried oregano
½ teaspoon dried thyme
1 (14.5-ounce) can whole peeled tomatoes
1 tablespoon vegetable oil
1 onion, chopped fine
3 garlic cloves, minced
1–2 teaspoons minced canned chipotle chile in adobo sauce
1 (15-ounce) can pinto beans
2 teaspoons sugar
2 tablespoons cider vinegar
Lime wedges
Coarsely chopped cilantro
Chopped red onion

1. Adjust oven rack to lower-middle position and heat oven to 275 degrees. Toss beef with 2 tablespoons water, 1½ teaspoons salt, and baking soda in bowl until thoroughly combined. Set aside for 20 minutes.

2. Meanwhile, place anchos in Dutch oven set over medium-high heat; toast, stirring frequently, until fragrant, 4 to 6 minutes, reducing heat if anchos begin to smoke. Transfer to food processor and let cool.

3. Add tortilla chips, cumin, paprika, garlic powder, coriander, oregano, thyme, and 2 teaspoons pepper to food processor with anchos and process until finely ground, about 2 minutes. Transfer mixture to bowl. Process tomatoes and their juice in now-empty workbowl until smooth, about 30 seconds.

4. Heat oil in now-empty pot over medium-high heat until shimmering. Add onion and cook, stirring occasionally, until softened, 4 to 6 minutes. Add garlic and cook until fragrant, about 1 minute. Add beef and cook, stirring with wooden spoon to break meat up into ¼-inch pieces, until beef is browned and fond begins to form on pot bottom, 12 to 14 minutes. Add ancho mixture and chipotle; cook, stirring frequently, until fragrant, 1 to 2 minutes.

5. Add beans and their liquid, sugar, tomato puree, and remaining 2 cups water. Bring to boil, scraping bottom of pot to loosen any browned bits. Cover, transfer to oven, and cook until meat is tender and chili is slightly thickened, 1½ to 2 hours, stirring occasionally to prevent sticking.

6. Remove chili from oven and let stand, uncovered, for 10 minutes. Stir in any fat that has risen to top of chili, then add vinegar and season with salt to taste. Serve, passing lime wedges, cilantro, and chopped onion separately. (Chili can be refrigerated for up to 3 days.)

BETTER BROWNING THROUGH CHEMISTRY

Browning ground beef is a challenge since it expels juices more rapidly than chunks of meat do, and most of that moisture needs to evaporate before browning can occur. To limit the amount of liquid, the usual solution is to brown in batches. We stick with one batch but toss the meat with baking soda before cooking, which helps lock in moisture. How? By raising the meat's pH levels. Raising the pH of meat increases its water-holding capacity, meaning that the proteins attract more water and are better able to hold on to it—not just during browning but throughout cooking. Besides keeping the meat from losing water that would make it steam versus brown, a higher pH also speeds up the Maillard reaction, making the treated meat brown even better and more quickly.

THE ULTIMATE BEEF CHILI

ANDREA GEARY, *January/February 2011*

Chili devotees (or "chiliheads," as they are known) are an opinionated, even cheerily belligerent bunch. Each cook will swear that the only chili worth eating is his or her own: rich with slow-cooked meat and redolent with chile peppers and spices, all bound in an unctuous sauce. But chili is basically just meat cooked with ground chiles; how could one be so much better than another? The key, any chilihead will tell you, lies in the all-powerful "secret ingredients."

I lost count of the references unearthed in my research to the intriguing additions that could magically improve a humble pot of chili, but the specifics were hard to nail down. (Chiliheads are as secretive as they are argumentative.) It took a lot of digging to compile a list. The Internet yielded fascinating new leads, like prunes floated atop the simmering chili (removed before serving), and obscure cookbooks revealed a couple of others (chocolate, beer). Chiliheads were reluctant to reveal the key to their own success; luckily, they could occasionally be coaxed to divulge the details of other cooks' recipes, including one chili that was thickened with "just a touch of peanut butter."

Inspired by these inventive (some might say wacky) cooks, I was determined to make my own ultimate chili. Before I began developing my recipe, I looked one more place for ideas: chili cook-offs. Who, I reasoned, would know more about producing the ultimate chili than these die-hard cooks who labor 40 weekends per year to defend their bragging rights? It turns out that the chili cook-off circuit is a fascinating world unto itself, but my sleuthing yielded little in the way of practical instruction.

WHAT'S YOUR BEEF?

Enticing as my ever-increasing list of secret ingredients was, it was getting me nowhere until I developed a basic recipe that these strange additions could embellish. Adopting the opinionated swagger of a veteran chili cook, I brashly laid down my own ground rules: To live up to my high expectations, my chili would have to be all beef (diced, not ground), and it would have pinto beans, tomatoes, onions, and garlic. These last four ingredients are actually highly controversial in some parts of the United States, but: my recipe, my rules. It's the chilihead way.

I began by testing five different cuts of beef: flap meat, brisket, chuck-eye roast, skirt steak, and short ribs, all in ¾-inch dice, and all browned before going into the pot with sautéed onions, jalapeños, and garlic; diced tomatoes; beef broth; and quick-brined pinto beans. For the sake of simplicity, I seasoned each pot with ⅓ cup of chili powder.

Though the short ribs were extremely tender, some tasters felt that they tasted too much like pot roast. (Not to mention that it took $40 worth of them to make just one pot of chili.) The brisket was wonderfully beefy but lean and a bit tough. The clear winner was chuck-eye roast, favored for its tenderness and rich flavor. The beans were praised for their soft, creamy texture (attributed to the hour-long brine), and tasters embraced the addition of the tomatoes and aromatics. But I was far from home free: My tasters also complained that the chili powder gave the dish a gritty, dusty texture, and the flavor was "less than vibrant."

GETTING DOWN TO THE NITTY-GRITTY

Making my own chili powder seemed the best way to solve both of those problems, so I decided to give it a try. Of all the dried chiles that are available in most supermarkets, I chose anchos for their earthiness and arbols for their smooth heat. I removed the stems and seeds from six dried ancho chiles and four dried arbol chiles, then toasted the anchos in a dry skillet until they were fragrant (the very thin arbols burned when I tried to toast them). After cooling the anchos, I ground them in a spice grinder along with the arbols and 2 teaspoons each of cumin and oregano, both common seasonings in commercial chili powder blends. The sauce in chili made with my own blend was not only much more deeply flavored but also remarkably smooth. Why was the batch made with the supermarket chili powder so gritty in comparison?

Our "secret" chili ingredients are really just pantry staples: lager, molasses, cocoa powder, and cornmeal.

Research revealed that at many processing plants dried chiles are ground whole—stems, seeds, and all. The stems and seeds never break down completely, and that's what gives some commercial powders that sandy texture. Making chili powder is undeniably a time-consuming step, but for my ultimate chili it was worth it.

Nevertheless, before venturing into the world of secret ingredients, I wondered if I could streamline my recipe a bit. Finding I was spending far too much time trimming the chuck-eye roast of fat and sinew, I switched to blade steak, which also comes from the chuck and was simpler to break down into ¾-inch chunks; it took half the time and my tasters were none the wiser. Rather than grind the chiles in successive batches in a tiny spice grinder, I pulverized them all at once in the food processor, adding a bit of stock to encourage the chile pieces to engage with the blade rather than simply fly around the larger bowl. The puree still wasn't quite as fine as I wanted it to be, but I'd address that later. I also used the food processor to chop the onions and jalapeños. Since stovetop cooking required occasional stirring to prevent scorching, I moved the bulk of the cooking to the gentler heat of the oven, where it could simmer unattended for 90 minutes.

SECRET WEAPONS

Happy with my basic recipe, I was ready to spring a series of unlikely ingredients on my colleagues. My research had indicated that chili cooks' secret weapons tended to fall into five categories: cooking liquids, complexity builders, sweeteners, meat enhancers, and thickeners. In a series of blind tastings, I set out to separate the wonderful from the simply weird.

At this point, the only liquid in my recipe was the predictable beef broth. In my next four pots of chili I added Guinness, red wine, coffee, and lager to the mix. The stout gave the chili a bitter edge and flattened out the bright notes of the jalapeños and tomatoes, and the wine was too tangy. Tasted just 30 minutes into the cooking time, the coffee seemed promising, but it did not end well, becoming as bitter and acidic as the dregs in the office urn. The lightly hoppy flavor of the lager, however, complemented the tomatoes, onions, and jalapeños beautifully—not so surprising, perhaps, since chili and beer pair well by tradition. Lager was in.

Next up: the complexity builders, ingredients that add depth without being readily discernible. Cloves and cinnamon were deemed too identifiable and sweet, but members of the chocolate family—unsweetened chocolate, unsweetened cocoa, and bittersweet chocolate—performed well, with tasters appreciating the complexity that each provided. Since I would be sweetening the pot in the next test, I named the unsweetened cocoa the winner in this round and added it to my recipe.

The aim of adding a sweet ingredient to chili is to smooth out any sharp or acidic flavors without making the dish noticeably sweet. I had high hopes for the two prunes left to float on the top of the simmering chili, but that technique was too subtle for my tasters. Four ounces of Coca-Cola added to the pot had the surprising effect of enhancing the tomato flavor too much, and brown sugar was "OK but kind of boring." The winner in this round? Molasses, which lent the chili an "earthy, smoky depth" that tasters loved.

The next category, meat enhancers, yielded the most surprising results. Many cooks swear by the practice of augmenting their chili with "umami bombs" in the form of anchovies, soy sauce, mushrooms, or even Marmite (and competitive cooks tend to go straight for the MSG in the form of stock cubes or Sazón Goya). I found that adding such ingredients dramatically increased the meaty flavor of the chili, but in doing so they threw the balance of chiles, aromatics, and spices out of whack. It was just too meaty, or as one taster observed, "like chewing on a bouillon cube." Tasters even persuaded me to switch from beef broth to chicken broth, citing better balance. Good-quality meat was meaty enough, thanks.

On to the most eagerly anticipated test of them all: peanut butter. Intended to thicken the chili, it's not as bizarre as you might think. Mexican cooks often add ground seeds and nuts to mole to give it richness, texture, and depth, so why not add peanut butter to chili? I tested more prosaic thickeners as well: flour and the traditional masa (dough made with limed corn, then dried and ground).

The flour subtly thickened the chili, but it didn't offer anything in terms of flavor. The peanut butter, on the other hand, lent a "big roasted flavor" to the chili, but it also left a strange aftertaste that had tasters simply saying "yuck." The masa was well received for its thickening properties and the subtle corn flavor it contributed, but even for ultimate chili I balked at buying a 4-pound bag of masa just to use 3 tablespoons. This is where I introduced my own quirky ingredient to the pantheon of secret ingredients. I found that when I added 3 tablespoons of cornmeal to my food processor chili paste, its bulk helped me achieve a finer grind, and it accomplished the thickening goal admirably.

Other cooks might accuse me of being full of beans, but this chili, with its tender beef and complex sauce, plus its own secret ingredients, is one I will defend with the vigor of the most seasoned chilihead.

BUILDING THE ULTIMATE CHILI

1. **MAKE PASTE** by grinding toasted anchos, dried arbols, spices, cornmeal, and broth.

2. **SAUTÉ** onions, jalapeños, and garlic in Dutch oven, then add chili paste, tomatoes, molasses, broth, and beans to Dutch oven. Stir to combine.

3. **SEAR** beef in batches in skillet until well-browned; transfer to Dutch oven. Deglaze skillet with lager between batches and scrape up fond; add to Dutch oven.

4. **TRANSFER** chili to oven and cook until meat and beans are fully tender, 1½ to 2 hours.

Ultimate Beef Chili

SERVES 6 TO 8

A 4-pound chuck-eye roast, well trimmed of fat, can be substituted for the blade steak. Because much of the chili's flavor is held in the fat, refrain from skimming it from the surface. Dried New Mexican or guajillo chiles make a good substitute for the anchos; each dried arbol may be replaced with ⅛ teaspoon cayenne pepper. For a spicier chili, use the larger amount of arbols. If you prefer not to use any whole dried chiles, the anchos and arbols can be replaced with ½ cup of commercial chili powder and ¼ to ½ teaspoon of cayenne pepper, though the texture of the chili will be slightly compromised. Good choices for toppings include diced avocado, finely chopped red onion, chopped cilantro, lime wedges, sour cream, and shredded Monterey Jack or cheddar cheese.

8 ounces (1¼ cups) dried pinto beans, picked over and rinsed
Salt
6 dried ancho chiles, stemmed, seeded, and torn into 1-inch pieces
2–4 dried arbol chiles, stemmed, seeded, and halved
3 tablespoons cornmeal
2 teaspoons dried oregano
2 teaspoons ground cumin
2 teaspoons unsweetened cocoa powder
2½ cups chicken broth
2 onions, cut into ¾-inch pieces
3 small jalapeño chiles, stemmed, seeded, and cut into ½-inch pieces
3 tablespoons vegetable oil
4 garlic cloves, minced
1 (14.5-ounce) can diced tomatoes
2 teaspoons molasses
3½ pounds blade steak, ¾ inch thick, trimmed and cut into ¾-inch pieces
1½ cups mild lager, such as Budweiser

1. Combine 4 quarts water, beans, and 3 tablespoons salt in Dutch oven and bring to boil over high heat. Remove pot from heat, cover, and let stand for 1 hour. Drain and rinse well.

2. Adjust oven rack to lower-middle position and heat oven to 300 degrees. Place anchos in 12-inch skillet set over medium-high heat; toast, stirring frequently, until flesh is fragrant, 4 to 6 minutes, reducing heat if chiles begin to smoke. Transfer to food processor and let cool. Do not clean skillet.

3. Add arbols, cornmeal, oregano, cumin, cocoa, and ½ teaspoon salt to processor with toasted anchos; process until finely ground, about 2 minutes. With processor running, slowly add ½ cup broth until smooth paste forms, about 45 seconds, scraping down sides of bowl as needed. Transfer paste to small bowl. Pulse onions in now-empty processor until coarsely chopped, about 4 pulses. Add jalapeños and pulse until consistency of chunky salsa, about 4 pulses, scraping down sides of bowl as needed.

4. Heat 1 tablespoon oil in Dutch oven over medium-high heat. Add onion mixture and cook, stirring occasionally, until moisture has evaporated and vegetables are softened, 7 to 9 minutes. Add garlic and cook until fragrant, about 1 minute. Add tomatoes and their juice, molasses, and chile paste; stir until thoroughly combined. Add beans and remaining 2 cups broth; bring to boil, then reduce heat to low and simmer.

5. Meanwhile, heat 1 tablespoon oil in now-empty skillet over medium-high heat until shimmering. Pat beef dry with paper towels and sprinkle with 1 teaspoon salt. Brown half of beef on all sides, about 10 minutes; transfer to pot. Add ¾ cup beer to skillet, scraping up any browned bits, and bring to simmer. Transfer beer to pot. Repeat with remaining 1 tablespoon oil, remaining beef, and remaining ¾ cup beer; transfer to pot. Stir to combine and return mixture to simmer.

6. Cover pot, transfer to oven, and cook until meat and beans are fully tender, 1½ to 2 hours. Let chili stand, uncovered, for 10 minutes. Stir well, season with salt to taste, and serve. (Chili can be refrigerated for up to 3 days.)

SECRET WEAPONS ... OR WEIRD EXTRAS?

When chili cook-offs proved a bust, we combed the Internet for claims of "secret" ingredients to see if any would actually improve our recipe. Most were better left on the shelf.

YOU'RE IN!
Cornmeal brought great body to the sauce, while beer, molasses, and unsweetened cocoa added depth and complexity.

DIDN'T CUT IT
We'll pass on ingredients like peanut butter, red wine, cola, prunes, and coffee. "Umami bombs" such as anchovies and shiitake mushrooms are also off our list.

GETTING THE FUNDAMENTALS RIGHT

Many chili recipes rely on commercial chili powders, but these lack depth, and the ground seeds and stems they often contain will turn the stew gritty. We up the ante by using whole chiles. For complex chile flavor, we grind dried ancho and arbol chiles into a paste. Fresh jalapeños bring grassy heat.

BETTER THAN CHILI POWDER

THE BEST BEEF STEW

J. KENJI LOPEZ-ALT, *January/February 2010*

Every winter, I lock myself in the kitchen with a piece of beef chuck, vegetables, and my Dutch oven and set about the alchemic task of turning a tough cut of beef tender. And every winter, I emerge a few hours later, disappointed. It's the smell that keeps me going at it: As the stew simmers, it fills the house with a rich aroma, but the taste is never as complex as the scent would lead you to believe. It's not that my beef stew is bad—the tender meat, flavorful vegetables, and brown gravy are good, but nowhere near good enough to merit the several hours of waiting.

Of all the dozen or so recipes I tried, ranging from quick-and-easy versions with canned beef broth, heavy thickeners, and tiny pieces of beef to better (but still disappointing) 4-hour versions, the only one that delivered truly satisfying flavor came from the famed Michelin-starred chef Thomas Keller. The problem? It took four days, a dozen dirty pots and pans, and nearly 50 ingredients to make. Sure, the results were fit for royalty, but it was hardly the approachable, home-cooked meal I was aiming for. There had to be a reasonable compromise between the dim, underdeveloped flavors in the shortcut recipes and Keller's no-holds-barred version.

MEATY MATTERS

The basic process for beef stew is straightforward: Brown chunks of beef in a Dutch oven, add aromatics and thickener, cover with liquid, and simmer until everything is tender and the flavors have melded. The key to developing complexity is to maximize flavor in every step. American beef stew is first and foremost about the beef—all other ingredients exist merely to support or complement it—so picking the right cut is essential. Using packaged "stew meat" from the supermarket was a nonstarter; the jumble of scraggly bits and large chunks was impossible to cook evenly. Cuts like tenderloin, strip, or rib eye turned mealy with prolonged cooking; they're better for searing or grilling. More esoteric cuts like hanger or skirt steak offered great flavor, but their texture was stringy. While well-marbled blade steaks and short ribs (favored by Keller) worked well, in the end they were no better than chuck-eye roast. It's one of the cheapest, beefiest cuts in the supermarket, and it turns meltingly tender when it's properly cooked.

The first key to rich, meaty flavor is proper browning, which means searing in two separate batches for a big pot of stew. Otherwise, the meat releases too much moisture and ends up steaming in its own juices. After browning the beef, I decided to caramelize the usual choices of onions and carrots (rather than just adding them raw to the broth, as many recipes suggest) to start the stew off with as much flavor as possible. Though at first I planned to remove the meat while sautéing the vegetables, I found that by leaving it in the pot, its residual heat helped the onions and carrots cook faster and more evenly. Crushed garlic, I decided, was essential. I sautéed it with the rest of the ingredients for 30 seconds before adding ¼ cup of flour to lightly thicken the stew. I then deglazed the pan with 2 cups of red wine, scraping the bottom of the pot to release the flavorful browned bits and allowing the liquid to reduce for just a few minutes to give its raw flavor a chance to dissipate. I then added 2 cups of chicken broth (favored over tinny canned beef broth) and let the stew simmer for 2½ hours in the oven (which provides a more even heat than the stovetop).

The stew was bare-bones, but I'd worry about other additions later. For now, I wanted to see how the flavor of the broth was developing. Not very well. Despite the little tweaks in the browning steps, my stew still lacked real meatiness. I decided to attack the problem in a more scientific manner.

SOUPING UP THE BROTH

We've long known that ingredients rich in glutamates—compounds that give meat its savory taste—can enhance the flavor of a dish. Tomatoes are one such ingredient. I experimented with various canned tomato products, finally landing on tomato paste, which lent just the right background note.

Thinking of other glutamate-rich ingredients, I wondered about cured meats, such as bacon, that have a superconcentrated flavor. Bacon was too smoky for the dish, but salt pork worked well. A small piece added a subtle depth to the broth and the beef. Then I remembered another salted product that's packed with glutamates: anchovies. I mashed one up and incorporated it along with the garlic and tomato paste. It was a smashing success, with tasters praising the newfound beefiness. In fact, I found I could add up to four fillets with increasingly better results before the fishiness revealed itself. Finally, my stew was packed with the depth I was looking for. But one problem remained: texture.

A couple of teaspoons of gelatin, stirred into the stew at the end of cooking, offer rich body.

THROUGH THICK AND THIN

Keller's stew starts with homemade veal stock. As it cooks, collagen in the veal bones is transformed into gelatin, which gives the final stew a luxurious, mouth-coating texture—something that my flour-thickened broth lacked. Theoretically, powdered gelatin should work just as well as the real deal. But once I removed the flour, I needed to add nearly ½ cup of gelatin powder to thicken the stew sufficiently. Flour or gelatin alone didn't work, but what about a combination? I made the stew with ¼ cup of flour just as before but added a single packet of bloomed gelatin after removing the stew from the oven. After just 3 minutes of simmering on the stovetop, the liquid developed a rich, glossy sheen that looked (and tasted) every bit as rich as the veal stock–based version.

With my stew perfected, the rest of the recipe was simple: I added a handful of frozen pearl onions toward the end of cooking along with some frozen peas. As for potatoes, starchy russets broke down too easily, turning the stew grainy. Medium-starch Yukon Golds added halfway through cooking were the way to go. As I ladled myself a steaming bowl of the supremely meaty and satisfying stew, I couldn't help but appreciate that, sometimes, the little things really do matter.

TRIMMING A CHUCK ROAST

To ensure consistent texture and flavor, avoid packaged stew meat (which can include odd-sized pieces from all over the cow) and start with a chuck roast.

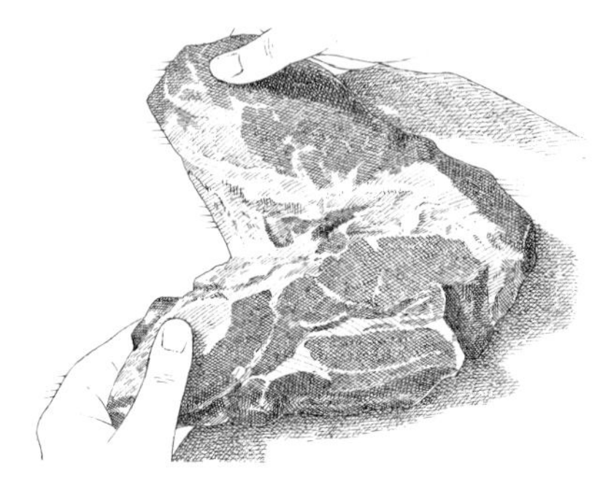

1. Pull apart roast at its major seams (marked by lines of fat and silverskin). Use knife as necessary.

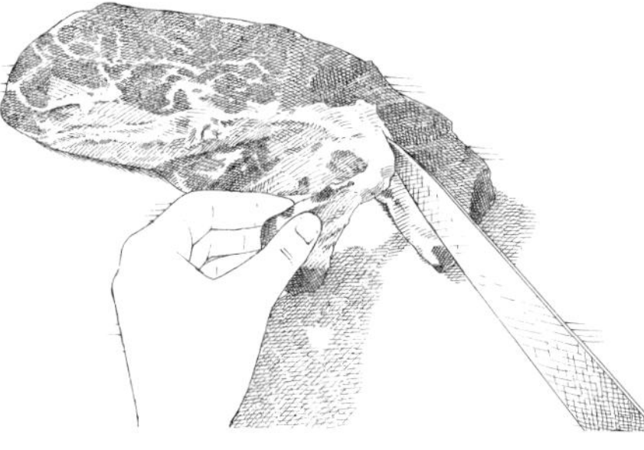

2. With sharp chef's knife or boning knife, trim off thick layers of fat and silverskin.

Best Beef Stew

SERVES 6 TO 8

Use a good-quality medium-bodied wine, such as Côtes du Rhône or Pinot Noir, for this stew. Try to find beef that is well marbled with white veins of fat. Meat that is too lean will come out slightly dry. Four pounds of blade steaks, trimmed of gristle and silverskin, can be substituted for the chuck-eye roast. While the blade steak will yield slightly thinner pieces after trimming, it should still be cut into 1½-inch pieces. Look for salt pork that is roughly 75 percent lean.

2 garlic cloves, minced
4 anchovy fillets, rinsed and minced
1 tablespoon tomato paste
4 pounds boneless beef chuck-eye roast, pulled apart at seams, trimmed, and cut into 1½-inch pieces
2 tablespoons vegetable oil
1 large onion, sliced thin
4 carrots, peeled and cut into 1-inch pieces
¼ cup all-purpose flour
2 cups red wine
2 cups chicken broth
4 ounces salt pork, rinsed
2 bay leaves
4 sprigs fresh thyme
1 pound Yukon Gold potatoes, unpeeled, cut into 1-inch pieces
1½ cups frozen pearl onions, thawed
2 teaspoons unflavored gelatin
½ cup water
1 cup frozen peas, thawed
Salt and pepper

1. Adjust oven rack to lower-middle position and heat oven to 300 degrees. Mash garlic and anchovies in bowl to paste, then stir in tomato paste.

2. Pat beef dry with paper towels. Heat 1 tablespoon oil in Dutch oven over medium-high heat until just smoking. Add half of beef and brown on all sides, 7 to 10 minutes; transfer to bowl. Repeat with remaining 1 tablespoon oil and remaining beef, then return first batch of beef to pot.

3. Reduce heat to medium and stir in onion and carrots. Cook, scraping up any browned bits, until onion is softened, 1 to 2 minutes. Stir in garlic mixture and cook until fragrant, about 30 seconds. Stir in flour and cook for 30 seconds.

4. Slowly stir in wine, scraping up any browned bits and smoothing out any lumps. Increase heat to high and simmer until thickened and slightly reduced, about 2 minutes. Stir in broth, salt pork, bay leaves, and thyme sprigs and bring to simmer. Cover, transfer pot to oven, and cook for 1½ hours.

5. Remove pot from oven. Discard salt pork and bay leaves and stir in potatoes. Cover, return pot to oven, and cook until potatoes are nearly tender, about 45 minutes.

6. Using large spoon, skim any fat from surface of stew and discard thyme sprigs. Stir in pearl onions and cook on stovetop over medium heat until potatoes and onions are tender and meat offers little resistance when poked with fork, about 15 minutes. Meanwhile, sprinkle gelatin over water in bowl and let sit until gelatin softens, about 5 minutes.

7. Increase heat to high, stir in peas and gelatin mixture, and simmer until gelatin is fully dissolved and stew is thickened, about 3 minutes. Season with salt and pepper to taste, and serve. (Stew can be refrigerated for up to 2 days; adjust consistency with extra broth as needed when reheating.)

WHY ADD GELATIN?

Thomas Keller's recipe for beef stew uses homemade veal stock. Veal bones contain collagen, which is converted to gelatin as it cooks, giving the stew a luxurious texture. To re-create this effect without the labor-intensive homemade stock, we add powdered gelatin (bloomed in water) at the end of cooking.

THE BEST CHICKEN STEW

DAN SOUZA, *November/December 2013*

Living in a nation of chicken lovers, I'm always surprised at how rarely I find chicken stew on a menu or in a cookbook. We have great chicken pot pies, plenty of chicken casseroles, and some of the best chicken noodle soups going, but in the stew category we seem almost exclusively drawn to beef. The few chicken stews I have seen are either too fussy or too fancy, derivatives of French fricassee or coq au vin, or seem more soup than stew, with none of the complexity and depth I expect from the latter. It was time to make an adjustment to the American canon. I'd develop a chicken stew recipe that would satisfy like the beef kind—one with succulent bites of chicken, tender vegetables, and a truly robust gravy.

WHERE'S THE BEEF?

Since my clear goal was to develop a beef stew–caliber chicken stew, that's exactly where I started. Beef is practically designed for stew. Chuck roast (cut from the shoulder) can be easily cubed into even pieces, seared hard to develop a rich-tasting crust, and simmered for hours until fall-apart tender, all the while remaining juicy. This treatment is made possible by the meat's tough network of connective tissue, which slowly converts into lubricating gelatin during cooking. This turns the beef tender while the gravy is infused with rich beefiness and body—a culinary win-win.

I couldn't make chicken behave like beef, but obviously fattier, richer-tasting dark meat was my best choice. I could start by subbing boneless, skinless thighs for the meat in a basic beef stew recipe, shortening the cooking time drastically for the quicker-cooking chicken. I didn't expect perfection, but perhaps I'd have a good jumping-off point from which I could tweak and adjust as needed.

I heated a couple of tablespoons of oil in a large Dutch oven and seared 2 pounds of halved thighs. After they browned, I transferred them to a bowl. In the then-empty pot I softened some basic aromatics in butter and then sprinkled in flour to create a roux for thickening. Next I stirred in store-bought chicken broth, the browned chicken, and chunks of red potatoes and carrots. After an hour of gentle simmering, the vegetables were soft and the chicken was tender. The stew looked pretty good. But its appearance was deceiving: One bite revealed a weak-flavored gravy. Not to mention that the chicken, though not desiccated, showed a disappointing lack of juiciness. In fact, the vegetables were just about the only redeeming things in the pot.

To make a supersavory gravy for our chicken stew, we brown and then simmer chicken wings.

I had a radical thought: What if, instead of trying to preserve some of its flavor and juiciness—which didn't work anyway—I cooked the life out of the chicken so that at least it would enrich the gravy? Then, I would discard it and cook more chicken in the stewing liquid just until tender. It didn't make sense to treat thighs or even drumsticks this way. But wings are another story. They actually have a decent amount of collagen, and because they're more about skin and bones than about meat, discarding them after they'd enriched the gravy wouldn't seem wasteful. (Wings are fun to pick at during a football game, but shredding them individually after cooking and stirring the meat into a stew would be a hassle that most cooks would prefer to avoid.)

WINGING IT

I split a pound of wings at their joints to ensure that they'd lie flat and brown evenly, allowing me to maximize the flavorful Maillard reaction. After browning the wings on both sides, I removed them and built a gravy just as I had before. I then added the browned wings back to the pot along with potato and carrot pieces. I covered the pot and let everything simmer in a 325-degree oven for about 30 minutes.

Next I stirred in the halved boneless, skinless chicken thighs (I skipped searing this time to prevent them from drying out) and returned the pot to the oven until they were fork-tender, about 45 minutes longer. When I removed the wings from the pot, they literally fell apart in my tongs, a sure sign that much of their connective tissue had been converted into gelatin. I also tasted the meat to see what flavor it might have left to give. The answer: not very much, meaning that I'd effectively extracted it into the gravy. Indeed, the stew had improved dramatically. The thighs were tender and juicy and the gravy was more chicken-y and velvety. It wasn't beef-stew good, but I was making progress.

FLAVOR SAVIOR

Next I focused on really ramping up flavor. While good chicken soup is all about attaining pure chicken flavor, stew requires more depth and complexity. Browning the wings was a step in the right direction, but I needed a lot more reinforcement. I rounded up some big flavor boosters: bacon, soy sauce, and anchovy paste. A few strips of bacon, crisped in the pot before I browned the wings in the rendered fat, lent porky depth and just a hint of smoke. Soy sauce and anchovy paste may sound like strange additions to an all-American chicken stew, but their inclusion was strategically sound. When ingredients rich in glutamates (such as soy sauce) are combined with those rich in free nucleotides (such as anchovies), flavor-boosting synergy is achieved. The nucleotides affect our tastebuds so that our perception of meaty-tasting glutamates is amplified by up to 30 times.

I added 2 teaspoons of anchovy paste with the aromatics—minced onion, celery, garlic, and thyme—and a couple of tablespoons of soy sauce along with the broth. Just as I'd hoped, things took an immediate turn to the more savory—without tasting salty or fishy. My colleagues were finally going for seconds. I was feeling pretty good, but I knew that I could take things further.

I decided to try cooking my stew uncovered to evaporate water and concentrate flavors. Not only did the stew gain a bit more intensity, it got an extra boost of browning on the surface and around the rim of the pot. Deglazing the sides of the pot by wetting them with a bit of gravy and scraping it into the stew with a spatula produced a considerable flavor boost. Still, I wondered if I could put these powers of reduction to even better use.

I started another batch. This time after the aromatics turned golden brown, I stirred in a cup of the broth along with the soy sauce and a cup of white wine and brought everything to a boil. When the liquid had fully evaporated, the aromatics started to sizzle again and I proceeded to prepare the roux, add the rest of the broth, and continue with the recipe. The reduction had concentrated flavors and also mellowed everything for a rounder-tasting, soul-satisfying stew.

All I had to do to finish the stew was remove the wings, add a splash of fresh white wine for some bright acidity, and sprinkle the pot with some chopped fresh parsley. This was truly a stew worthy of the name; the proof was in the pot, no beef necessary.

Best Chicken Stew

SERVES 6 TO 8

Mashed anchovy fillets (rinsed and dried before mashing) can be used instead of anchovy paste. Use small red potatoes measuring 1½ inches in diameter.

2 pounds boneless, skinless chicken thighs, halved crosswise and trimmed
Kosher salt and pepper
3 slices bacon, chopped
1 pound chicken wings, cut at joints
1 onion, chopped fine
1 celery rib, minced
2 garlic cloves, minced
2 teaspoons anchovy paste
1 teaspoon minced fresh thyme or ¼ teaspoon dried
5 cups chicken broth
1 cup dry white wine, plus extra for seasoning
1 tablespoon soy sauce
3 tablespoons unsalted butter, cut into 3 pieces
⅓ cup all-purpose flour
1 pound small red potatoes, unpeeled, quartered
4 carrots, peeled and cut into 1-inch pieces
2 tablespoons chopped fresh parsley

1. Adjust oven rack to lower-middle position and heat oven to 325 degrees. Arrange chicken thighs on baking sheet and lightly season with salt and pepper; cover with plastic wrap and set aside.

2. Cook bacon in Dutch oven over medium-low heat, stirring occasionally, until fat renders and bacon browns, 6 to 8 minutes. Using slotted spoon, transfer bacon to medium bowl. Add chicken wings to pot, increase heat to medium, and cook until well browned on both sides, 10 to 12 minutes; transfer wings to bowl with bacon.

3. Add onion, celery, garlic, anchovy paste, and thyme to fat in pot; cook, stirring occasionally, until dark fond forms in bottom of pot, 2 to 4 minutes. Increase heat to high; stir in 1 cup broth, wine, and soy sauce, scraping up any browned bits; and bring to boil. Cook, stirring occasionally, until liquid evaporates and vegetables begin to sizzle again, 12 to 15 minutes. Add butter and stir to melt; sprinkle flour over vegetables and stir to combine. Gradually whisk in remaining 4 cups broth until smooth. Stir in wings and bacon, potatoes, and carrots; bring to simmer. Transfer to oven and cook, uncovered, for 30 minutes, stirring once halfway through cooking.

4. Remove pot from oven. Use wooden spoon to draw gravy up sides of pot and scrape browned fond into stew. Place over high heat, add thighs, and bring to simmer. Return pot to oven, uncovered, and continue to cook, stirring occasionally, until thighs offer no resistance when poked with fork and vegetables are tender, about 45 minutes longer. Discard wings.

5. Season stew with up to 2 tablespoons extra wine and salt and pepper to taste. Sprinkle with parsley and serve.

BUILDING A RICH, FLAVORFUL GRAVY

START WITH BACON AND WINGS Brown chopped bacon, then sear halved wings in rendered fat to develop meaty depth. Set bacon and wings aside.

ENHANCE FLAVOR BASE Sauté aromatics, thyme, and anchovy paste in fat to create rich fond. Add chicken broth, wine, and soy sauce, then boil until liquid evaporates.

COOK GRAVY Cook reserved bacon and wings (with potatoes and carrots) in more broth. This extracts flavor from meats and body-enhancing collagen from wings (later discarded).

HOMEMADE VEGETABLE BROTH

ANDREA GEARY, *January/February 2015*

Ask someone to make a list of extravagant foods and they're unlikely to mention vegetable broth. But consider how it's traditionally made: You take a lovely pile of produce, chop it up, and boil it for about an hour. Then you fish out all the food, throw it away, and keep the liquid. And after all that, what you have is not a meal but an ingredient.

It's no surprise that most cooks opt for store-bought vegetable broth (or even water). But even the best of the commercial stuff is not ideal, which is a shame, since a good broth can be the difference between a ho-hum vegetarian dish and a flavorful one that satisfies all diners, vegetarian or otherwise.

I wanted to make a broth that would boost my vegetarian meals the same way that chicken or beef stock boosts my meat-based cooking. But since vegetarian dishes can be more nuanced and subtle in their flavor, I would need a broth that wouldn't overpower the other ingredients or call too much attention to any one vegetable. If possible, I also wanted my recipe to generate minimal waste and be economical and simple to produce, so I could consider it a staple rather than a luxury.

TAKING STOCK

Meat broths are a straightforward concept: Chicken broth tastes like chicken, and beef broth tastes like beef. But extending that logic to vegetable broth doesn't work because all vegetables taste different. To begin, I worked my way through several recipes using various vegetables and methods. I was drawn to one that was made almost entirely from scraps: carrot peels, celery leaves and ends, parsley stems, onion skins, and leek greens. But the earthy flavor of the carrot peels and celery ends dominated. A modern sous-vide broth made with 10 vegetables and herbs and cooked in a 185-degree water bath for 3 hours was flavorful, but the yield was only 1½ cups. I couldn't see myself going to that kind of trouble for such a small amount.

One recipe made with roasted vegetables required both the oven and the stove and took longer than 2 hours to make, and the caramelization of the vegetables made it too sweet. And my wild card, a raw puree whizzed in the blender like a vegetable smoothie and then strained through a fine-mesh sieve, was also a bust: Heavy on celery and watery tomatoes and cucumbers, the strained liquid had a murky orange-brown color and an unsuitably tangy flavor reminiscent of bad gazpacho. I considered changing the vegetables, but doing so would still result in what was basically vegetable juice. I was certainly getting an idea of what I didn't want.

The key to the best vegetable broth? Forget about the liquid and make a flavor-packed puree instead.

I had almost given up when I happened upon a recipe in *The River Cottage Preserves Handbook* by Pam Corbin. For her Souper Mix, vegetables, herbs, and salt are ground in a food processor. Stir a spoonful of this paste into boiling water and there you have it: vegetable broth. These days, commercial options abound for vegetarian bouillon cubes and concentrates, but I had never seen a homemade version.

The potential was clear. Grinding vegetables was quick, with no cooking required. And unlike the failed smoothie concept, this base was undiluted and kept all the flavorful ingredients in the final product—those flavors would be extracted by the hot water to make an infusion. I appreciated that there was little waste, along with an unexpected advantage: more compact storage. Instead of ending up with several quarts of broth, I'd just have one container.

I loaded chopped leeks, fennel, carrots, celery root, sun-dried tomatoes, garlic, parsley, cilantro, and more than ¾ cup of salt into the food processor, as the recipe directed. The reasoning behind all that salt was persuasive: It would discourage spoilage so the base could be stored for weeks in the refrigerator. There was also a benefit Corbin didn't mention: The salt prevents the base from solidifying in the freezer, so it's easy to scoop out only what is required.

Compared to the previous versions, this broth was fresh-tasting. The leeks, carrots, and celery root gave it a balanced flavor, and the sun-dried tomatoes, rich in savory amino acids, contributed depth.

But there were problems. The vegetable flavor was weak, and the 7 ounces of herbs (a huge amount; consider supermarket bags of greens that weigh 6 ounces) dominated the broth and turned swampy during storage. The garlic didn't fare well either. Its flavor continued to develop and became too hot. With their sweet-sour undertone, the sun-dried tomatoes were too identifiable to be an anonymous umami booster. Although fennel added a pleasant licorice-like flavor, it wouldn't be welcome in every application. And, yes, ¾ cup of salt was too much. Still, I was intrigued by the possibilities.

FROM THE GROUND UP

A *mirepoix*, a mixture of two parts chopped onion to one part each of carrots and celery, is the classic base for many broths, so I started there. Corbin's recipe featured celery root and leeks, but I hoped that regular celery and onions would work just as well. I pureed 6 ounces of chopped onion, 3 ounces each of chopped carrots and celery stalks, and 2 ounces of salt, which was less than half the amount in the previous batch. (I measured by weight for consistency since chopped vegetables pack unevenly.) Since cilantro has a more prominent flavor than parsley, I stuck with the latter and added only ½ ounce of it.

Celery root was in the recipe for a reason. The regular celery added bitterness and a slightly sour flavor. It turns out that celery root is not just milder than celery; it also has a more complex, creamy flavor. Both celery root and celery get their characteristic flavor from several phthalide compounds, but celery has more of one called sedanolide, which has a notably bitter flavor. Celery root was back in.

It was a similar story with the leek/onion swap. The higher moisture content of the onions made the base watery, so it solidified in the freezer. Worse, it was simultaneously sweeter and more sulfurous than the base made with leeks, which also possess the least sugar of all the alliums. So leeks went back in as well. My broth was better now, but it still tasted a bit lightweight, so I went in search of an extra boost.

A PUNGENT PUNCH

The onions had been a failure, but their diluting effect did give me an idea. What if I took the opposite tack and concentrated my vegetables' flavor? That way, I could use more of them. I sliced leeks, carrots, and celery root and dried them for hours in a low oven. Then I ground them up in the food processor and added parsley and salt. Despite my starting with twice the amount of vegetables as in my previous batch, the vegetable flavor was weaker.

It turns out that water was not the only thing my vegetables lost in the oven; a lot of their volatile flavor compounds had evaporated, too. But this test was not a waste. It got me thinking about concentrated sources of flavor, which in turn led me to consider an option I've been quite snooty about in the past: those dried minced onions found in bottles in the spice aisle.

Dried minced onions aren't simply dehydrated; they're freeze-dried. Our science editor filled me in on the process: Frozen food is placed in a vacuum-sealed chamber. In this vacuum, the ice transitions into vapor and is pulled out of the food. Whereas the heat of a conventional oven pulls out flavor compounds along with the water, freeze-drying leaves many more of those compounds in place, just waiting to be reactivated by water.

I'll admit that I went overboard at first. When I swapped them for more than half the leeks, the broth tasted like onion soup. But a little experimentation led me to the sweet spot: 5 ounces of leeks augmented with 3 tablespoons of dried minced onions.

SAVORY SALVATION

The distinct flavor of the sun-dried tomatoes in the first batch had been problematic, but I appreciated their umami quality, so I considered other options. Canned and fresh tomatoes took my base back to a slurry, so next I tried tomato paste. Just 1½ tablespoons contributed an appealing savoriness.

That hint of umami left me wanting more. I went to the pantry and pulled out savory non-meat powerhouses. Shiitake mushrooms were too earthy, and miso paste was too subtle in small amounts and too identifiable in larger. Kombu, a dried seaweed, worked well, but I settled on a less exotic option: soy sauce. Three tablespoons gave my broth the muscle it had lacked. To compensate for the added sodium, I cut the salt back to 2 tablespoons, which was still enough to prevent the mixture from freezing solid.

This broth had it all: easy preparation, minimal waste, convenient storage, and, best of all, fresh, balanced vegetable flavor that worked well in everything from soups and sauces to pastas and risotto. If I had to find a fault with this recipe, it would be that because it lasts about six months I don't get to make it very often. But I can live with that.

Vegetable Broth Base

MAKES ABOUT 1¾ CUPS BASE; ENOUGH FOR 7 QUARTS BROTH

For the best balance of flavors, measure the prepped vegetables by weight. Kosher salt aids in grinding the vegetables. The broth base contains enough salt to keep it from freezing solid, making it easy to remove 1 tablespoon at a time. To make 1 cup of broth, stir 1 tablespoon of fresh or frozen broth base into 1 cup of boiling water. If particle-free broth is desired, let the broth steep for 5 minutes and then strain it through a fine-mesh strainer.

2 leeks, white and light green parts only, chopped, and washed thoroughly (2½ cups, 5 ounces)
2 carrots, peeled and cut into ½-inch pieces (⅔ cup, 3 ounces)
½ small celery root, peeled and cut into ½-inch pieces (¾ cup, 3 ounces)
½ cup (½ ounce) fresh parsley leaves and thin stems
3 tablespoons dried minced onion
2 tablespoons kosher salt
1½ tablespoons tomato paste
3 tablespoons soy sauce

Process leeks, carrots, celery root, parsley, dried minced onion, and salt in food processor, pausing to scrape down sides of bowl frequently, until paste is as fine as possible, 3 to 4 minutes. Add tomato paste and process for 1 minute, scraping down sides of bowl every 20 seconds. Add soy sauce and continue to process for 1 minute. Transfer mixture to airtight container and tap firmly on counter to remove air bubbles. Press small piece of parchment paper flush against surface of mixture and cover tightly. Freeze for up to 6 months.

A BROTH BASE YOU CAN FREEZE—AND NEVER THAW

Our recipe calls for 2 tablespoons of kosher salt (we use Diamond Crystal). That might seem like a lot, but once the base is diluted, it contains just 399 milligrams of sodium per 1-cup serving; commercial broth ranges from 240 to 1,050 milligrams per cup.

Furthermore, because salt depresses water's freezing point, the concentrate will never freeze solid. This means that you can keep it in the freezer for months and scoop out exactly the amount you need without ever having to thaw it.

SCOOP AND RECONSTITUTE
Mix 1 tablespoon of base with 1 cup of boiling water.

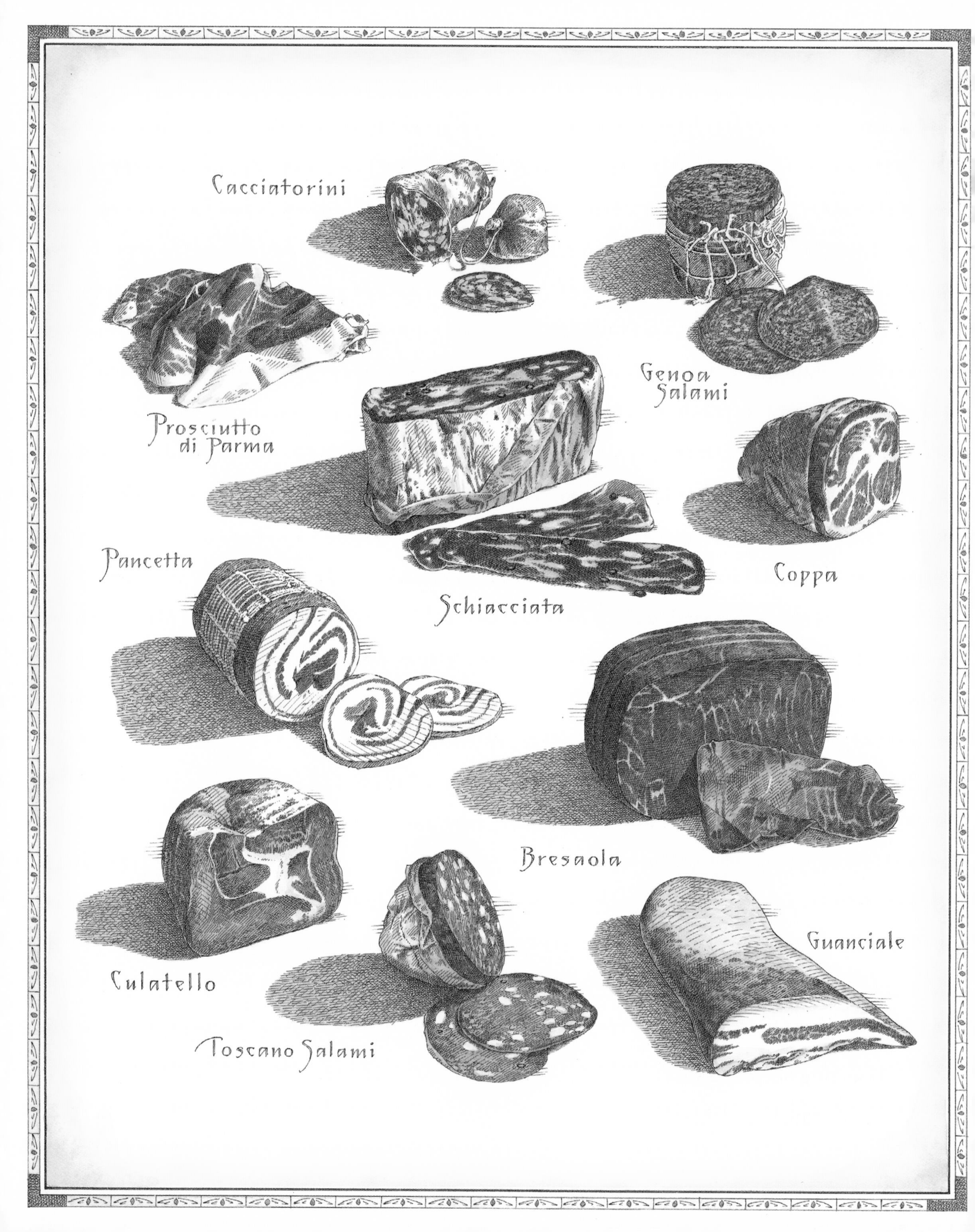
Cacciatorini
Genoa Salami
Prosciutto di Parma
Coppa
Pancetta
Schiacciata
Bresaola
Guanciale
Culatello
Toscano Salami

BEEF, PORK, AND LAMB

REVIVING THE ORIGINAL DRIVE-IN BURGER

J. KENJI LOPEZ-ALT, *July/August 2008*

Americans love hamburgers and, in spite of the myriad gourmet options featuring inch-thick patties with artisanal cheeses and dizzying arrays of toppings, fast-food burgers—as in billions served—remain the most popular choice. Our love affair with burgers began in the 1940s when a slew of drive-in hamburger restaurants sprang up in California. The best of these restaurants made their patties from freshly ground beef cooked to order. But as the biggest chains spread across the country, fresh-ground, high-quality beef gave way to preformed, deep-frozen patties made from scraps of meat you'd rather not think about.

These days, those of us outside of driving range from the few burger joints that continue to use the original methods have to be content with rubbery gray patties of questionable provenance and little beef flavor. But East Coasters got a break a couple of years ago when the Shake Shack opened in New York City. This humble stand, the brainchild of restaurateur Danny Meyer, offers burgers modeled after the drive-in original.

One taste of this burger opened my eyes to just how great the real deal could be. Like the California originals, these thin, quarter-pound burgers are made from freshly ground beef and cooked on a flat griddle. Fat rendering out of the meat collects on the griddle, frying the patty in its own grease and delivering a substantial crust. Crisp nooks and crannies riddle the patty's surface, while the interior is very loosely packed. The craggy, porous texture of this ultracrisp, ultrabrowned, ultrabeefy burger is perfect for catching the dripping juices, melted cheese, and tangy sauce that tops it.

Smitten by the experience, I returned to the test kitchen in Boston determined to develop my own recipe for drive-in burgers.

CHUCKING OUT THE CHUCK

A quick test using ordinary preground chuck from the supermarket fashioned into thin patties proved disappointing. Prepackaged hamburger is ground very fine and packaged tightly, compacting it before it even comes out of the container. The result is dense, rubbery, and dry patties with little beef flavor or crisp crust, specifically lacking in the pitted surface and loose texture I wanted. To improve my burgers, I'd need freshly ground meat. But with the dearth of good butchers in the neighborhood, I was going to have to grind it myself.

Two types of beef, ground at home in a food processor, make for burgers with craggy surfaces and beefy flavor.

I put chuck roasts through a meat grinder for my next batch of burgers. These patties were certainly less dense, but my other problems—rubberiness, dryness, and lack of beef flavor—remained. By trying over a dozen different cuts of meat and having tasters rate each sample on flavor and juiciness, I discovered that beefiness was dependent on cut, while juiciness corresponded to fat. I decided to grind my burgers from sirloin steak tips (also known as flap meat), the winner for beefiness, and to introduce an outside source of fat to increase juiciness. Butter diluted the flavor of the burger, while smoky bacon overshadowed its beefiness. On a whim, I tried mixing oil from a tin of anchovies into the beef, which added a great savory (not fishy) flavor. Unfortunately, as the meat cooked, the anchovy oil wept out, and my dryness problem persisted. What about more beef fat? Suet would be the logical choice, but it's not widely available. In the end, I found that well-marbled short ribs added the perfect amount of fat without diminishing beef flavor. The combination was more complicated than buying a single cut, I admit it. But why knock something that works?

That left me with rubberiness to deal with. After looking through my food science books, I discovered the culprit: collagen. As collagen proteins get heated past 130 degrees, they start to squeeze the meat, causing it to become dense and rubbery. (At 140 degrees, the collagen will begin to unravel, turning the meat from tough to tender, but this process takes hours—far longer than the mere minutes my burger would spend on the griddle.) The more that these proteins come in contact with each other, the more shrinkage and tightening will take place. So the key to a tender burger is to keep it as loosely packed as possible.

I knew that the meat got compressed as I lifted it up and formed it into patties in my hands. What if I never picked up the meat at all? I ground up more meat, letting it fall directly from the grinding tube onto a baking sheet. Then, without lifting it, I separated it into four piles and gently pressed each one into a patty. Even as they were cooking in the pan, I could tell that these patties were going to be different. Their juices bubbled up through the meat's porous surface and dripped back down, basting the burgers as they cooked. Biting into one revealed meat so tender it virtually fell apart. Just to make sure this success really could be attributed to the loosely packed meat, I made a new batch and compared it with burgers I had molded into a tight shape. The compressed burgers were rubbery and uninspiring, whereas the loose burgers were once again an unqualified success.

A QUESTION OF PROCESS

One more problem: Most home cooks don't own a meat grinder. Unless I could get around this roadblock, it made no difference how

good the burgers were. I decided to give the food processor a shot. Almost immediately after I turned the processor on, long stringy bits of fat and meat got caught up in the blade, causing the machine to jam. I patiently cleaned and recleaned the blade as I ground until I had what looked like a passable texture. But when I cooked the meat, the rubberiness was back. Clearly, the rough action of the food processor was mashing the meat together and reviving my old enemy, collagen.

I knew from making sausages that when meat gets too warm, it ends up being smeared instead of cleanly chopped. The same thing happened to my burger meat as it got battered in the food processor. The solution? I cut my meat into chunks and chilled them in the freezer before placing them in the food processor. This time the chunks were chopped, not pulverized, and the burgers cooked up just as perfectly tender and with as crisp a crust as those I had chopped in the meat grinder.

TOPPING IT OFF

As for the sauce, this style of burger is commonly served with a tangy and sweet Thousand Island–style dressing, and I found no reason to change that. Adding relish, sugar, and white vinegar to a mayo and ketchup base proved to be the best foil for the juicy, salty burger. Although cheddar and Swiss cheese had their proponents, most people preferred American. It filled the cracks and crevices in the patty with gooey cheese that didn't compete with the other flavors. A few thin slices of onion were preferred in lieu of "the works"—they allowed the flavor of the beef to take center stage unchallenged.

With my tender patty and toppings sandwiched by a soft toasted bun, I'd finally recaptured the flavor and texture that started a nationwide craze.

Best Old-Fashioned Burgers

SERVES 4

Sirloin steak tips are also sold as flap meat. Flank steak can also be used. If doubling the recipe, process the meat in three batches in step 2. Fry four burgers and serve them immediately before frying more, or cook them in two pans. Freeze extra patties, stacked, separated by parchment paper, and wrapped in three layers of plastic wrap, for up to two weeks. Thaw the patties in a single layer on a baking sheet at room temperature for 30 minutes before cooking.

10 ounces sirloin steak tips, trimmed and cut into 1-inch chunks
6 ounces boneless beef short ribs, trimmed and cut into 1-inch chunks
Salt and pepper
1 tablespoon unsalted butter
4 hamburger buns
½ teaspoon vegetable oil
4 slices deli American cheese (4 ounces)
Thinly sliced onion
1 recipe Classic Burger Sauce (recipe follows)

1. Place beef chunks on baking sheet in single layer, leaving ½ inch of space around each chunk. Freeze beef until very firm and starting to harden around edges but still pliable, 15 to 25 minutes.

2. Pulse half of beef in food processor until coarsely ground, 10 to 15 pulses, stopping and redistributing beef around bowl as necessary to ensure beef is evenly ground. Transfer beef to baking sheet by overturning workbowl, without directly touching beef. Repeat with remaining beef. Spread beef over sheet and inspect carefully, discarding any long strands of gristle or large chunks of hard meat or fat.

3. Gently separate beef into 4 equal mounds. Without picking beef up, use your fingers to gently shape each mound into loose patty ½ inch thick and 4 inches in diameter, leaving edges and surface ragged. Season top of each patty with salt and pepper. Using spatula, flip patties and season other side. Refrigerate patties while toasting buns.

4. Melt ½ tablespoon butter in 12-inch skillet over medium heat. Add bun tops, cut side down, and toast until light golden brown, about 2 minutes. Repeat with remaining ½ tablespoon butter and bun bottoms. Set buns aside and wipe skillet clean with paper towels.

5. Return skillet to high heat; add oil and heat until just smoking. Using spatula, transfer patties to skillet and cook, without moving them, for 3 minutes. Flip patties and cook for 1 minute. Top each patty with 1 slice American cheese and cook until cheese is melted, about 1 minute.

6. Transfer burgers to bun bottoms and top with onion. Spread about 1 tablespoon burger sauce on each bun top. Cover burgers and serve immediately.

accompaniment

Classic Burger Sauce

MAKES ABOUT ¼ CUP

2 tablespoons mayonnaise
1 tablespoon ketchup
½ teaspoon sweet pickle relish
½ teaspoon sugar
½ teaspoon distilled white vinegar
¼ teaspoon pepper

Whisk all ingredients together in bowl.

BETTER BEEF FOR A BETTER BURGER

Chuck is the usual choice for burgers. For the best flavor and tender juicy texture, we opted for two better cuts of beef: sirloin steak tips (right), which contribute big meaty taste, and well-marbled boneless short ribs (left), which lend the fat that keeps the burgers juicy. For best results, buy ribs with at least as much fat as the rib in the photo.

BONELESS SHORT RIBS

SIRLOIN STEAK TIPS

CRISPY ORANGE BEEF

LAN LAM, *January/February 2013*

When I hear the words "crispy orange beef," I expect just that: a dish of shatteringly crisp strips of battered beef coated in a sweet, savory, and tangy citrus sauce. Unfortunately, this is a dish that rarely lives up to its name, especially in the home kitchen. All too often it has neither crispiness nor any kind of orange flavor. That's because genuinely crispy results usually involve deep-frying in copious amounts of oil—something I think we'd all rather leave to the restaurant world. And who has dried tangerine peels, which give authentic versions their bright "orange" taste, just lying around the kitchen? My goal: to successfully bring this traditionally Sichuan, vibrantly flavored dish into my own kitchen without all that oily mess.

A quick search brought up dozens of recipes based on the Americanized version of the dish, first popularized by Manhattan's Shun Lee Palace in the early 1970s. These recipes call for coating the beef in a mixture of cornstarch and egg whites before cooking and then tossing it with a sweet orange sauce. Many, I noticed, were more stir-fry than anything else—not a lot of oil there. But not a lot of crispiness either, I discovered after a few tests. I would have to start at square one.

FEAR OF FRYING

I began the testing process with the simplest step: the cut of beef. I tried both flank and flap steak, cutting them into thin, wide strips and using a basic recipe I cobbled together from the Web. Each cut was plenty beefy, but my tasters unanimously preferred the looser-grained flap meat to the flank, which wasn't as tender. This easy decision out of the way, I turned to the more difficult matter at hand: frying.

Traditionally, crispy orange beef is made by deep-frying the strips of lightly battered beef in a full pot of oil—as much as 8 cups. During frying, water in the starchy crust turns to steam, leaving little crispy pockets in its wake. In the name of research, I tried a version cooked in this abundant amount of oil. Not surprisingly, it worked, producing crispy strips of perfectly cooked beef. But these traditional recipes call for painstakingly placing each piece of meat in the oil, one by one, and then removing each piece individually when fully cooked. All of that? A pain. I tried throwing in all of the beef together, but that yielded a sticky mess. The egg white and cornstarch batter acted as a glue, fusing the strips of meat together as soon as they hit the oil—and no amount of stirring could separate them. Between the large amount of oil and the persnickety frying technique, this method was out of the question.

Genuinely crispy beef without a full pot of oil is possible—as long as you treat the beef correctly.

I already knew that the few tablespoons of oil used in the stir-fry methods also didn't work, but what if I struck a compromise? I decided to try frying in 3 cups of oil—an amount that seemed manageable for the home kitchen and yet was still enough volume (I hoped) to produce truly crispy beef. This lesser amount of oil would certainly mean frying in batches, since dropping all the beef into the pot at once would cause the oil temperature to plunge dramatically, and if the oil wasn't hot enough, a crisp crust wouldn't have time to form before the beef overcooked. Fortunately, I found that three batches did the trick, allowing me to fry up nicely crisp pieces. But my problems weren't over. Even in these relatively small batches, the strips of beef still stuck together.

I had to try something new. I thought about other ways to create a crispy crust, and a classic bread-crumb coating jumped to mind. True, this type of coating is more typical of pan- or oven-fried foods, but why not give it a shot? I dipped the beef in flour, then egg wash, and then bread crumbs (panko, in this case) before frying. Sticking was not a problem with these strips of beef, and they looked bronzed and beautiful when they came out of the pot—I was ready to celebrate. But when we tasted them, we found that the large size of the crumbs relative to the size of the beef meant that the breading was actually thicker than the strips of meat themselves. To add insult to injury, this substantial crust contained deep crevices that sucked up the sauce, turning it soggy. Failure again.

I was feeling dejected and, for lack of any better ideas, decided to try simply dredging the meat in cornstarch alone. I was delighted to find that the cornstarch, which absorbed some of the juices at the surface of the beef, crisped up delicately in the hot oil, batch after batch. But I couldn't do a victory dance just yet. The beef pieces were still sticking together here and there. Plus, with this new, delicate coating, the thin but wide pieces of beef were folding over on themselves as they hit the oil, so that some of the cornstarch coating never fully cooked, leaving a pasty residue. Stirring did not help this situation; I had to tediously pick through the beef and unfold individual pieces. It was clear: I'd have to change the shape. Instead of flat little rectangles, I began slicing the beef into matchsticks. And when I dropped them in the oil, these pieces didn't fold up on themselves at all. They also had more surface area and more pointy edges and crags, further increasing crispiness. Even better, my tasters also raved at how remarkably ungreasy the meat seemed. Curious, I fried up a new batch, measuring the oil before and after cooking, and found that all of that beef had absorbed a total of just 2 tablespoons from the 3 cups of oil.

As good as my results were, I couldn't resist one more tweak, which I borrowed from our Argentine grilled steak recipe: I spread out the pieces of beef on a rack set in a rimmed baking sheet and placed the

sheet in the freezer for 45 minutes. The very cold, very dry air of the freezer removed moisture from the surface of the meat, further boosting crispiness and eliminating any residual sticking.

BETTER (BITTER) FLAVOR

Now that I was satisfied with the cooking method, I went back to flavor. I decided to keep things very simple and began by seasoning the beef in a tablespoon of soy sauce before dredging it in cornstarch.

I had been tossing my crispy beef in a sauce made with a few difficult-to-find ingredients including Chinese rice wine and sweet dark soy sauce. I looked for more-common pantry ingredients to replace these two. A combination of dry sherry, regular soy sauce, and molasses did the trick. But I had more trouble when it came to the orange flavor.

American versions of crispy orange beef call for orange zest, but traditional recipes use rehydrated tangerine peel. When I experimented with leaving fresh tangerine peel to dry for a few days in a sunny window, my tasters were wowed by the pungent depth it brought to the sauce—but this method took way too long. Dried orange peel is easy to find in the supermarket but has barely any flavor. This left me experimenting with fresh oranges. Instead of zesting the oranges, I used my vegetable peeler to pare away the peel as well as a portion of the bitter pith, which I sliced into slivers and tossed in the microwave to dry. While the pith added a subtle bitterness, the stint in the microwave robbed the peel of its volatile aromatic oils, diminishing its flavor. I decided to throw the strips of peel into a sauté pan. Letting the orange peel brown slightly introduced deeper, caramelized notes that came closer to the complex flavors of dried tangerine peel. Jalapeño added to the pan at the same time brought extra brightness.

After weeks of experimenting with crusts and sauce, here at last was a bright and flavorful, truly crispy orange beef worthy of the name.

Crispy Orange Beef

SERVES 4

We prefer to buy flap meat and cut our own steak tips. Use a vegetable peeler on the oranges and make sure that your strips contain some pith. Do not use low-sodium soy sauce. Serve this dish with steamed rice.

1½ pounds sirloin steak tips, trimmed
3 tablespoons soy sauce
6 tablespoons cornstarch
10 (3-inch) strips orange peel, sliced thin lengthwise (¼ cup), plus ¼ cup juice (2 oranges)
3 tablespoons molasses
2 tablespoons dry sherry
1 tablespoon rice vinegar
1½ teaspoons toasted sesame oil
3 cups vegetable oil
1 jalapeño chile, stemmed, seeded, and sliced thin lengthwise
2 tablespoons grated fresh ginger
3 garlic cloves, minced
½ teaspoon red pepper flakes
2 scallions, sliced thin on bias

1. Cut beef with grain into 2½- to 3-inch-wide lengths. Slice each piece against grain ½ inch thick. Cut each slice lengthwise into ½-inch-wide strips. Toss beef with 1 tablespoon soy sauce in bowl. Add cornstarch and toss until evenly coated. Spread beef in single layer on wire rack set in rimmed baking sheet and freeze until beef is very firm but not completely frozen, about 45 minutes.
2. Whisk orange juice, molasses, sherry, vinegar, sesame oil, and remaining 2 tablespoons soy sauce together in bowl.
3. Line second rimmed baking sheet with triple layer of paper towels. Heat vegetable oil in large Dutch oven over medium heat to 375 degrees. Carefully add one-third of beef and fry, stirring occasionally to keep beef from sticking together, until golden brown, about 1½ minutes. Using spider skimmer, transfer beef to paper towel–lined sheet. Return oil to 375 degrees and repeat with remaining beef in 2 batches. After frying, set aside 2 tablespoons frying oil.
4. Heat reserved oil in 12-inch skillet over medium-high heat until shimmering. Add orange peel and jalapeño and cook, stirring occasionally, until about half of orange peel is golden brown, 1½ to 2 minutes. Add ginger, garlic, and pepper flakes; cook, stirring frequently, until garlic is beginning to brown, about 45 seconds. Add soy sauce mixture and cook, scraping up any browned bits, until slightly thickened, about 45 seconds. Add beef and scallions and toss to coat. Transfer to platter and serve immediately.

TURNING ORANGE INTO TANGERINE

Traditionally, crispy orange beef is made with dried tangerine peels, which have a pungent and complex flavor but can be tricky to find. We mimic this flavor by leaving some bitter pith on orange peel that we brown in oil.

PURPOSELY PITHY
Leaving some pith on fresh orange peel helps to mimic the flavor of dried tangerine peel.

A BETTER CUT FOR FRYING

To prevent beef from folding over on itself while frying, cut flap meat steaks into 3-inch-wide lengths, then into ½-inch-thick slices, and the slices into ½-inch-wide strips.

PERFECT CAST IRON STEAK

RUSSELL SELANDER, *November/December 2016*

I have long been a fan of cooking in cast iron. So when I set out to develop a recipe for a great steak—one with a perfectly seared exterior and an interior that was evenly cooked from edge to edge—of course I turned to my great-grandmother's well-worn Wagner cast-iron skillet.

After an initial round of testing, though, I had found out a little secret: Despite cast iron's many virtues, you can't just plunk a steak into the pan and expect success. The recipes that I tried produced varied results, but none of them were encouraging. There were steaks with burnt exteriors and raw interiors and steaks with pale exteriors and overcooked interiors, and the browning was uneven across the board.

I decided to take a step back and investigate the cast-iron skillet a little more. It's said to produce a great seared steak because it retains heat well, but I suspected there was more to it than that. I knew from previous test kitchen testing that cast iron does not heat up evenly, and that seemed likely to be the root of the problem with the recipes I tried. I wanted to know just how unevenly cast iron heats and whether there was a way I could fix that.

GOING TOE TO TOE

I started by pitting cast-iron skillets against stainless steel–clad skillets to see how the heat was distributed in each. I lightly dusted both types of skillet with flour—since I wanted to be sure that the evenness of heating was not due to any inherent quality of the heat source—and, without any preheating, set the skillets over gas, electric, and induction burners at both medium and medium-high heat. The results were consistent for all three types of heat: evenly toasted, nicely golden-brown flour in the steel-clad skillets, and in the cast-iron skillets, pale flour with black splotches marking the places where the heat source actually came into contact with the pan.

But, I thought, since the dark spots were more well defined over medium-high heat than medium heat, maybe the heat level was the problem. To find out, I heated a cast-iron skillet over small and large gas flames, as well as over electric and induction burners. I took the temperature at the center, 3 inches off center, and at the inside edge of the skillet every 30 seconds for about 10 minutes during each test. The results confirmed what I was seeing with the flour test: No matter the level of heat or its source, the skillet had hot and cool spots.

Our science editor explained that most stainless steel–clad cookware is made up of layers of stainless steel around a core of aluminum, which conducts heat about 2½ times better than cast iron. Therefore, the heat moves across the skillet very easily. Since heat doesn't move as easily across cast iron, the skillet initially develops hot spots where it is directly touching the heat source.

For the ultimate sear in cast iron, how you preheat the pan matters as much as how you cook the steaks.

OVEN TO THE RESCUE

But I realized there was a change that could provide a solution: heating the pan in the oven. It would take a little longer, but because the oven's heat is not concentrated on a single part of the pan but rather comes at the pan more or less evenly from all directions, it guaranteed an evenly heated pan. An added advantage was that the oven could be set to a specific temperature, no matter what the heat source, whereas when using the stovetop I had found it difficult to accurately specify a single burner setting that worked across all types of heat sources.

But what was the best oven temperature? My goal was to get the skillet hot enough so that vegetable oil, which has a smoke point of between 400 and 450 degrees, would start to smoke as soon as I added it to the skillet. I put the skillet in the cold oven, as there was no sense in waiting for the oven to heat before adding the skillet, and set the oven temperature to 400 degrees. However, when I added the oil after heating the skillet, it took some time to start smoking. I continued to test temperatures at 25-degree intervals, pulling the skillet out and searing steaks, and eventually worked my way up to 500 degrees, which I found to be the ideal setting.

Now for the steak itself. I chose thick boneless strip steaks because they have big, beefy flavor and are easy to find. Salting the steaks and letting them sit while my pan heated in the oven would not only season the meat throughout but also help keep it moist and juicy. Patting them dry before searing helped them brown even more.

My next question was how much oil to use—and it turned out that I needed more than I thought I would. As meat cooks, it contracts; any ridges or divots get bigger, and without oil, they don't touch a heat source, resulting in a spotty brown steak rather than a gorgeously browned one. I settled on 2 tablespoons of oil, a hefty but necessary amount.

FLIPPING OUT

Two problems remained: I was still getting a rather large gray band, the area between the crust and interior that dries out and turns chalky. And my beautifully preheated pan was so hot that the crust it produced was actually too good—it was too thick and almost unpleasantly crunchy. To eliminate the gray band, one of my coworkers suggested that I try flipping the steak more often (I had been flipping it only once). The idea made sense, since each time a steak is flipped, the side not touching the skillet cooks with residual heat, which penetrates the meat more slowly, resulting in a smaller gray band. I wondered if flipping might also help prevent an overly thick crust. I found that flipping once every 2 minutes was just the right amount to ensure a perfectly rosy interior, but the crust was still thicker than I liked.

Then I did something I never thought I would do when searing: I turned down the heat. Because the cast iron retained the heat so well once it got up to the proper temperature, turning down the heat actually maintained the temperature I wanted, whereas keeping the heat high increased the skillet's temperature as time went on. So I got a great initial sear over medium-high heat and then reduced the heat until I found a sweet spot: about 8 minutes over medium-low heat. Combined with flipping every 2 minutes, this produced a perfect, gorgeously browned crust and a rosy interior from edge to edge.

The steak was now fantastic on its own, but a simple accompaniment would make it that much more special. Mixing up a compound butter to melt over the resting steaks was easier than making a pan sauce and was just as flavorful.

HOW CAST IRON HEATS

Cast iron doesn't heat as quickly as stainless steel–clad cookware because its thermal conductivity—the ability to transfer heat from one part of the metal to another—is lower. But it holds heat much more effectively; even when a relatively cool steak is added, the pan's temperature drop is minimal and the steak browns better. The trick is to make sure that the pan preheats thoroughly and evenly, which we do in a very hot oven (not on the stovetop) because the convective heat minimizes hot spots. Once the pan is hot, we set it over a moderate flame to maintain the heat and to avoid creating an overly thick crust.

Toasting flour demonstrates the uneven heating of cast iron on the stovetop.

Cast Iron Steaks with Herb Butter

SERVES 4

Don't forget to take the butter out to soften at least 30 minutes before you start to cook.

2 (1-pound) boneless strip steaks, 1½ inches thick, trimmed
Salt and pepper
4 tablespoons unsalted butter, softened
2 tablespoons minced shallot
1 tablespoon minced fresh parsley
1 tablespoon minced fresh chives
1 garlic clove, minced
2 tablespoons vegetable oil

1. Adjust oven rack to middle position, place 12-inch cast-iron skillet on rack, and heat oven to 500 degrees. Meanwhile, season steaks with salt and let sit at room temperature. Combine butter, shallot, parsley, chives, garlic, and ¼ teaspoon pepper in bowl; set aside.
2. When oven reaches 500 degrees, pat steaks dry with paper towels and season with pepper. Using potholders, remove skillet from oven and place over medium-high heat; turn off oven. Being careful of hot skillet handle, add oil and heat until just smoking. Cook steaks, without moving them, until lightly browned on first side, about 2 minutes. Flip steaks and cook until lightly browned on second side, about 2 minutes.
3. Flip steaks, reduce heat to medium-low, and cook, flipping every 2 minutes, until steaks are well browned and meat registers 120 to 125 degrees (for medium-rare), 7 to 9 minutes. Transfer steaks to carving board, dollop 2 tablespoons herb butter on each steak, tent with aluminum foil, and let rest for 5 to 10 minutes. Slice steaks ½ inch thick and serve.

variation

Cast Iron Steaks with Blue Cheese–Chive Butter

Omit shallot and parsley. Increase chives to 2 tablespoons and add ⅓ cup crumbled mild blue cheese to butter with chives.

PERFECT STEAK, INSIDE AND OUT

Searing steak in cast iron can produce the ultimate crust—but often at the expense of a rosy, tender interior. Here's how to get both.

USE LOTS OF OIL A generous 2 tablespoons of oil keeps the steak (which contracts during cooking) in contact with the heat, for more even browning.

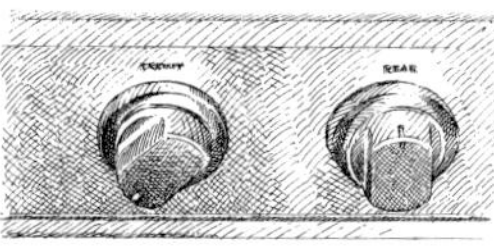

TURN THE HEAT DOWN After the initial sear, reduce the flame to medium-low; the pan will stay hot enough to sear the meat.

FLIP REPEATEDLY Turning the steak every 2 minutes prevents a gray, overcooked band from forming under the surface.

PEPPER-CRUSTED FILET MIGNON

SEAN LAWLER, *March/April 2006*

Filet mignon may be revered as the elite superstar of steaks, but it needs serious help in the kitchen to live up to that reputation on the palate. Chefs compensate for the relatively mild flavor of beef tenderloin by wrapping it in bacon or puff pastry, searing it to develop a dark, flavorful crust, and serving it with rich wine sauces or flavored butters.

Another popular way to dress up a filet is with a crust of cracked black peppercorns. I envisioned the pleasing contrast of a thick center of pink, soft-as-butter beef and a crunchy, spicy coating—a peppery hit with every bite. The daydreaming ended as I recalled the test kitchen's prior frustrations with peppercorn crusts. Peppercorns fall off in the pan, interfere with the meat's browning, and—used in sufficient quantity to create a real crust—deliver punishing pungency.

Simmering the peppercorns in oil tames their bite so they complement the buttery steak, not overpower it.

REMEMBRANCE OF STEAKS PAST

Our earlier recipe for Steak au Poivre solved these problems by coating only one side of each steak with the cracked peppercorns. The overall heat level was reduced by half, and the uncoated side got nicely browned, providing the necessary fond (browned bits in the pan) to create the classic brandy-cream sauce. A neat solution, but not one that could help me this time. That recipe used strip steaks that were, at most, an inch thick. Because the tenderloin muscle is small, filet steaks are usually cut almost twice as thick. I suspected a one-sided crust would not be sufficient, and a quick test proved it: Too many bites came with little or no crust, and when I did get a bite with peppercorns, peppercorns were all I tasted.

Thick, lean, tender, mild—how best to use peppercorns to complement these traits without overwhelming them? I started with the test kitchen's standard technique for cooking a filet mignon: searing it first in a hot pan with a small amount of oil, then finishing in the oven. Immediately, I encountered a problem. The cracked pepper kept the meat from making direct contact with the hot pan, so beneath the crust the steaks were unappealingly pale. I tried adding extra oil to the skillet, hoping it would bridge the gap between the pan and the meat. This was a partial success. On the downside, peppercorns were still falling off. Next, I made a thick paste of cracked peppercorns and oil, which I rubbed over the raw steaks. Before cooking, I pressed down on each peppercorn-adorned steak through a sheet of plastic wrap. Problem solved.

DOCTORING PEPPER

Now I had steaks that were well browned and coated in an attractive pepper crust, but the overall heat level was still intense. Inspired by an article on blooming spices in infused oils, I wondered how heating my peppercorn-oil paste might affect its flavor. I brought the mixture to a gentle simmer in a saucepan, and I was amazed at the change. In place of the stinging heat was a pleasant warmth that spread slowly across my palate. Now I could have a substantial peppercorn crust without the usual punishing heat.

FLAVOR ENHANCERS

To augment the flavor of the steaks' thick interior, I added a tablespoon of salt to the peppercorn paste and let the steaks sit, covered, for an hour before cooking. Sure enough, the meat became noticeably beefier—and flavorful enough to stand up to the assertive pepper crust.

As for accompaniments, the salting step bought me plenty of time to simmer a rich reduction sauce. Because it is so lean, filet mignon is also excellent with flavored butters.

Pepper-Crusted Filet Mignon

SERVES 4

For a milder pepper flavor, drain the cooled peppercorns in a fine-mesh strainer in step 1, toss them with 5 tablespoons of fresh oil, add the salt, and proceed. Serve with Port-Cherry Reduction or Blue Cheese–Chive Butter (page 88). If serving with Blue Cheese–Chive Butter, spoon 1 to 2 tablespoons of the butter over the steaks while they're resting.

5 tablespoons black peppercorns, cracked
5 tablespoons plus 2 teaspoons olive oil
1 tablespoon kosher salt
4 (7- to 8-ounce) center-cut filets mignons, 1½ to 2 inches thick, trimmed

1. Heat peppercorns and 5 tablespoons oil in small saucepan over low heat until faint bubbles appear. Continue to cook at bare simmer, swirling pan occasionally, until pepper is fragrant, 7 to 10 minutes. Remove from heat and set aside to cool. When mixture has cooled completely, add salt and stir to combine. Rub steaks with peppercorn mixture, thoroughly coating top and bottom of each steak. Cover steaks with plastic wrap and press gently to make sure peppercorns adhere; let stand at room temperature for 1 hour.
2. Meanwhile, adjust oven rack to middle position, place baking sheet on rack, and heat oven to 450 degrees. When oven reaches 450 degrees, heat remaining 2 teaspoons oil in 12-inch skillet over medium-high heat until just smoking. Place steaks in skillet and cook, without moving them, until dark brown crust has formed, 3 to 4 minutes. Using tongs, turn steaks and cook until well browned on second side, about 3 minutes.
3. Off heat, transfer steaks to hot sheet in oven. Roast until meat registers 115 to 120 degrees (for rare), 120 to 125 degrees (for medium-rare), or 130 to 135 degrees (for medium), 3 to 7 minutes. Transfer steaks to wire rack, tent with aluminum foil, and let rest for 5 minutes before serving.

accompaniments

Port-Cherry Reduction

MAKES ABOUT 1 CUP

1½ cups port
½ cup balsamic vinegar
½ cup dried tart cherries
1 shallot, minced
2 sprigs fresh thyme
1 tablespoon unsalted butter
Salt

1. Combine port, vinegar, cherries, shallot, and thyme in medium saucepan; simmer over medium-low heat until liquid has reduced to about ⅓ cup, about 30 minutes. Set aside, covered.
2. While steaks are resting, reheat sauce. Off heat, discard thyme, then whisk in butter until melted. Season with salt to taste.

Blue Cheese–Chive Butter

MAKES ABOUT ½ CUP

1½ ounces mild blue cheese, crumbled (⅓ cup), room temperature
3 tablespoons unsalted butter, softened
⅛ teaspoon salt
2 tablespoons minced fresh chives

Combine blue cheese, butter, and salt in medium bowl and mix with stiff rubber spatula until smooth. Fold in chives.

DECODING TENDERLOIN STEAKS

Cut from the center of the back, the tenderloin is the most tender (and most expensive) cut of the cow. Depending on their thickness, tenderloin steaks may be labeled (from thickest to thinnest) Châteaubriand, filet mignon, or tournedos.

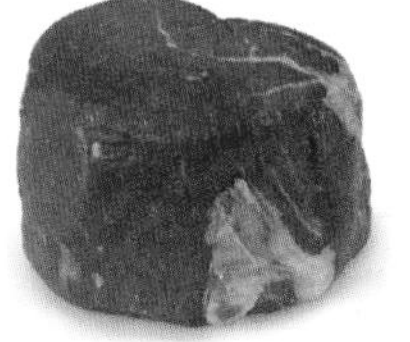

KEY STEPS FOR PEPPER-CRUSTED FILET MIGNON

Choking heat, gray exteriors, peppercorns that fall off with the slightest provocation—we encountered all these problems during recipe development. To avoid them, take these steps.

SIMMER Gently simmer the peppercorns in olive oil to mellow the heat.

COAT Coat the tops and bottoms of the steaks with the pepper mixture, pressing the excess into the sides.

REST Cover with plastic, pressing to make sure the peppercorns adhere. Let rest one hour.

BROWN AND ROAST Sear the steaks in a well-oiled skillet until browned beneath the peppercorn layer, then finish cooking in a hot oven to ensure browning on the sides of the steaks.

CRACKING PEPPERCORNS

Spread half of peppercorns on cutting board. Place skillet on top. Pressing down firmly with both hands, use rocking motion to crush peppercorns beneath "heel" of skillet. Move skillet back and forth, redistributing peppercorns as needed. Repeat with remaining peppercorns.

TAMING PEPPERCORN HEAT

We were relieved to learn that the pungent heat of black peppercorns can be mellowed by a brief simmer in oil. We were pleased with the effect but curious as to the cause. Research revealed that the natural irritant in peppercorns is called piperine. As peppercorns age, the piperine is converted into closely related molecules (called isomers) that have different flavor characteristics and that are less irritating to the nose and throat. Left sitting at room temperature in your cupboard, the peppercorns may take years to undergo this reaction, but the hot oil serves as a catalyst, driving the conversion at hundreds of times its natural speed, quickly tempering the pepper's pungency.

SPICE-RUBBED STEAK ON THE GRILL

ANDREA GEARY, *May/June 2012*

As a dedicated practitioner of the silk-purse-out-of-a-sow's-ear approach to cooking, I enjoy the challenge of transforming inexpensive ingredients into a memorable meal. But I've always conceded that when it comes to grilled steaks, there's no way around it: You get what you pay for.

With their tender texture and big-time beef flavor, pricey cuts from the middle of the steer (like rib eyes and T-bones) need little more than salt, pepper, and a few minutes over a hot fire to render them impressive. Try that minimalist technique on cheaper steaks from farther down the animal (the sirloin and the round) and you get meat that's chewy and dry, with flavors that veer toward liver-y and gamy. It's probably these flavor and texture challenges that inspire cooks to take a page from the barbecue manual and apply spice rubs to less expensive steaks. Unfortunately, in my experience that approach doesn't really work. Because cheap steaks exude little fat to bond with the spices, the rub tends to fall off in chunks. If by some stroke of luck the rub remains intact, it usually tastes dry and dusty; plus, nuances of flavor can vaporize over the fire.

Still, my skinflint tendencies aren't easily subdued. Surely there was a way to create a recipe for inexpensive grilled steak that was also tender and juicy, with a flavorful, crunchy crust that stayed in place.

CALLING ALL GLUTAMATES

First I had to find a steak that provided the best taste and texture for the money, so I looked to the sirloin and the round, settling on what we here in New England call the shell sirloin steak (variously called top butt, butt steak, top sirloin butt, top sirloin steak, and center-cut roast, depending on where you live). Tasters described the shell steak as having a relatively beefy taste, unlike cuts from the round, which were liver-y.

Salting the shell steaks before cooking was a given. Salt sprinkled liberally on the surface of the meat draws moisture from inside, which over time is then reabsorbed as the meat sits, seasoning it and changing the structure of the muscle fibers so that they hold on to more juices. But I'd have to do more than that to close the gap between a $6 steak and a $12 steak. Some recipes suggest that allowing a spice rub to sit on the meat for a period of time enables its flavors to be absorbed for more complex-tasting results. Science, however, refutes this: Most flavor compounds in spices are fat-soluble rather than water-soluble, so they can't penetrate below the surface of the steak. Furthermore, in tests of marinades, we've found that other than salt, the only water-soluble flavor compounds that can travel deep into the meat are glutamates.

So, what about glutamates? Scanning my pantry, I singled out two of the most potent sources of these compounds: tomato paste and—odd as it may sound—fish sauce, a condiment that we've called upon in other unlikely applications to amp up savory taste. I applied a rub made with kosher salt and a couple of teaspoons each of these two ingredients (to compensate for their extra sodium I cut back a little on the salt) and applied it to a set of steaks an hour before grilling. The difference in these steaks was remarkable: They boasted a much deeper flavor without any trace of my secret enhancements. Spurred by this success, I decided to add ½ teaspoon each of garlic powder and onion powder to the rub. Though neither substance contains significant levels of glutamates, their water-soluble flavors are potent enough (especially in concentrated powdered form) that even if they penetrated only ¼ inch into the meat, they might make a difference in the overall flavor. Tasters confirmed that my hunch was correct: The steaks treated with the powdered alliums along with salt, tomato paste, and fish sauce had noticeably richer flavor. On to the spice rub.

SPICING THINGS UP

My plan was to treat the steak with the salt-and-glutamate-packed paste first, wait an hour, and then apply a second, more conventional dry rub right before grilling. I tried a variety of rubs, but I found that those made mostly with dried herbs lost their flavor, while those based on spices fared better. It turns out that the flavors in herbs such as rosemary, sage, and thyme fade in the intense heat of the grill, but the compounds in certain spices do much better, particularly those containing capsaicin—namely, peppers, chiles, and paprika. Thus, rubs made predominantly from chile or pepper were clearly the way to go.

Scoring inexpensive shell sirloin steaks gives our potent spice rub serious sticking power.

First I tried rubs made with preground spices, but these formed a coating that was more pasty than crunchy. Since I had some time to spare between applying the salty glutamate rub and firing up the grill, I tried toasting some whole spices (cumin, coriander, red pepper flakes, and black peppercorns) in a skillet along with some earthy-tasting dried New Mexican chiles, and then I ground them coarsely in a coffee grinder. To round out the flavors, I also incorporated sugar, paprika, and ground cloves before pressing the rub onto the surface of the steak.

Tasters pronounced these steaks juicy, tender, and flavorful, and they greatly preferred the more robust texture of this home-ground rub. Still, there were two problems to be solved. First, despite the toasting step, the spices retained a slightly raw taste, the result of being cooked with very little fat, so the flavors couldn't "bloom." Second, tasters requested a more substantial crust. I sheepishly informed them that there had been more rub when I started grilling, but half of it had been left on the cooking grate. Clearly, I needed to find a way to help the spices stick to the steak and not to the grate.

I remembered when a coworker who was developing a recipe for pan-fried pork chops had difficulty persuading the breading to adhere to the meat. He eventually came up with the clever solution of making shallow cuts into the meat to give the breading more purchase. Doing the same with my steaks before adding the first rub seemed likely to be doubly advantageous: It would increase the surface area, which could give that first rub more opportunity to really get into the meat; plus, it could help the spice rub stick to the meat.

As I liberally greased the cooking grate in preparation for grilling my newly cross-hatched steaks, I wished that there were some way to put a layer of oil on the steaks themselves without disturbing their spice crust (which—I was pleased to see—was sticking quite nicely). The easy solution: A light spritz of vegetable oil spray or oil from a mister helped the steaks keep their rub intact through the grilling process.

These steaks were crusty and crunchy on the outside, with just enough heat and spice to complement the meat's rich flavor, and that little bit of added fat imparted by the spray gave the spices that fully developed "bloomed" flavor that tasters were after. The tender and juicy meat belied its $5.99-per-pound price tag. My inner cheapskate quietly rejoiced.

GETTING THE RUB TO STICK

Scoring the meat with shallow slits helps the salt paste and spice rub adhere to the meat and penetrate more deeply.

Grilled Steak with New Mexican Chile Rub

SERVES 6 TO 8

Shell sirloin steak is also known as top butt, butt steak, top sirloin butt, top sirloin steak, and center-cut roast. Spraying the rubbed steaks with oil helps the spices bloom, preventing a raw flavor.

Steak

2 teaspoons tomato paste
2 teaspoons fish sauce
1½ teaspoons kosher salt
½ teaspoon onion powder
½ teaspoon garlic powder
2 (1½- to 1¾-pound) boneless shell sirloin steaks, 1 to 1¼ inches thick, trimmed

Spice Rub

2 dried New Mexican chiles, stemmed, seeded, and flesh torn into ½-inch pieces
4 teaspoons cumin seeds
4 teaspoons coriander seeds
½ teaspoon red pepper flakes
½ teaspoon black peppercorns
1 tablespoon sugar
1 tablespoon paprika
¼ teaspoon ground cloves
Vegetable oil spray

1. *For the steak:* Combine tomato paste, fish sauce, salt, onion powder, and garlic powder in bowl. Pat steaks dry with paper towels. With sharp knife, cut 1⁄16-inch-deep slits on both sides of steaks, spaced ½ inch apart, in crosshatch pattern. Rub salt mixture evenly on both sides of steaks. Place steaks on wire rack set in rimmed baking sheet; let stand at room temperature for at least 1 hour. After 30 minutes, prepare grill.

2. *For the spice rub:* Toast chiles, cumin, coriander, pepper flakes, and peppercorns in 10-inch skillet over medium-low heat, stirring frequently, until just beginning to smoke, 3 to 4 minutes. Transfer to plate to cool, about 5 minutes. Grind spices in spice grinder or in mortar with pestle until coarsely ground. Transfer spices to bowl and stir in sugar, paprika, and cloves.

3A. *For a charcoal grill:* Open bottom vent completely. Light large chimney starter mounded with charcoal briquettes (7 quarts). When top coals are partially covered with ash, pour two-thirds evenly over grill, then pour remaining coals over half of grill. Set cooking grate in place, cover, and open lid vent completely. Heat grill until hot, about 5 minutes.

3B. *For a gas grill:* Turn all burners to high, cover, and heat grill until hot, about 15 minutes. Leave primary burner on high and turn other burner(s) to medium.

4. Clean and oil cooking grate. Sprinkle half of spice rub evenly over 1 side of steaks and press to adhere until spice rub is fully moistened. Lightly spray rubbed side of steak with oil spray, about 3 seconds. Flip steaks and repeat sprinkling with spice rub and coating with oil spray on second side.

5. Place steaks over hotter part of grill and cook until browned and charred on both sides and center registers 120 to 125 degrees (for medium-rare) or 130 to 135 degrees (for medium), 3 to 4 minutes per side. If steaks have not reached desired temperature, move to cooler side of grill and continue to cook. Transfer steaks to clean wire rack set in rimmed baking sheet, tent with aluminum foil, and let rest for 10 minutes. Slice meat thin against grain and serve.

variations

Grilled Steak with Ancho Chile–Coffee Rub

Substitute 1 dried ancho chile for New Mexican chiles, 2 teaspoons ground coffee for paprika, and 1 teaspoon cocoa powder for ground cloves.

Grilled Steak with Spicy Chipotle Chile Rub

Substitute 2 dried chipotle chiles for New Mexican chiles, 1 teaspoon dried oregano for paprika, and ½ teaspoon ground cinnamon for ground cloves.

INVESTIGATING STEAK TIPS

ELIZABETH GERMAIN, *May/June 2003*

Steak tips have never been on my list of favorite meats. It's not that I am a premium steak snob, but I was skeptical about a cut of meat that has long been the darling of all-you-can-eat restaurant chains where quantity takes precedence over quality. There is also some confusion about what constitutes a steak tip. Some steak tips are sautéed and served with a sauce (these are often called pub-style steak tips), some are marinated and grilled (known as tailgate tips). I was drawn to grilling and so began by testing five such recipes.

The recipes differed in the ingredients used to marinate the meat and the marinating time. The simplest recipe marinated the tips in a bottled Italian-style salad dressing for 24 hours. The most complex one marinated the meat for three days in a mixture that included aromatics and herbs. Despite such variations in time and ingredients, none of these grilled tips was very good. Some were mushy, but most were tough and dry. At this point, steak tips still seemed like a cheap cut of meat with promising beefy flavor but poor texture.

A soy sauce–based marinade acts like a brine, improving the flavor and juiciness of steak tips.

CHOOSING A CUT AND A MARINADE

Thinking that the problem might be the cut of meat, I went to the supermarket only to discover a confusing array of meats—cubes, strips, and steaks—labeled "steak tips." Still more confusing, these cubes, strips, and steaks could be cut from a half dozen different parts of the cow.

After grilling more than 50 pounds of tips, it became clear that the only cut worth grilling is one referred to by butchers as flap meat. When I grilled whole flap meat steaks and then sliced them on the bias before serving, tasters were impressed. Although the meat was still a bit chewy, choosing the right cut was a start.

I now turned to marinades. Given the long-held belief that acidic marinades tenderize tough meat, I created four recipes using four popular acids: yogurt, wine, vinegar, and fruit juice. To determine the best timing, I let the meat sit in each marinade for 4 hours and for 24 hours. Curious about marinades' other claim to fame—flavoring—I added aromatics, spices, and herbs.

The yogurt marinade was the least favorite, producing dry meat that was chewy and tough. Tasters also panned the wine-based marinade. The meat was tough and dry, the flavors harsh and bland. Some tasters liked the complex flavor of the vinegar marinade, but everyone found the tips to be "overly chewy." The marinade prepared with pineapple juice was the favorite. Both the four-hour and 24-hour versions yielded juicy, tender, and flavorful meat.

Why did pineapple juice make the best marinade? My first thought was proteases, enzymes that help to break down proteins. Proteases are found in pineapple, papaya, and other fruits. One of them, papain from papayas, is the active component of some meat tenderizers. But the juice I had been using was pasteurized, and the heat of pasteurization can disable such enzymes. To see if proteases were in fact at work, I devised three tests in which I made three more marinades: one with pasteurized pineapple juice from the supermarket; a second with pasteurized pineapple juice heated to the boiling point and then cooled; and a third with fresh pineapple pureed in a food processor.

The result? The fresh juice was a much more aggressive "tenderizer," so much so that it turned the meat mushy on the inside and slimy on the outside. I had learned three things: proteases do break down meat, but they don't make it any better (tasters universally disapproved of these tenderized tips); pasteurization does kill this enzyme (the fresh juice was much more powerful than the supermarket variety); and proteases were not responsible for the strong showing made by the original pineapple marinade. Why, then, did tasters prefer the pineapple marinade to those made with yogurt, wine, and vinegar?

After rereading the ingredient list in my pineapple marinade, I devised a new theory. The pineapple marinade included soy sauce, an ingredient that is packed with salt and that was not used in any of the other marinades. Was the soy sauce tenderizing the meat by acting like a brine? In the past, the test kitchen has demonstrated the beneficial effects of brining on lean poultry and pork.

To answer these questions, I ran another series of tests without any pineapple, trying various oil-based marinades made with salt or soy sauce (in earlier tests, I had determined that oil helped to keep the meat moist and promoted better searing). To use salt in a marinade, I first had to dissolve it. Because salt doesn't dissolve in oil, I used water, but the liquid prevented the meat from browning properly. That said, brining did make these steak tips tender and juicy.

I concluded that soy sauce, not pineapple juice, was the secret ingredient in tasters' favorite marinade. The salt in soy sauce was responsible for the improved texture of the steak tips, and the soy sauce also promoted browning. After experimenting with brining times, I determined that an hour was optimal. It allowed for the thicker parts of the meat to become tender while preventing the thinner sections from becoming too salty.

I then went to work on flavor variations: an Asian marinade with garlic, ginger, and orange zest; a Southwest-inspired marinade that included garlic, chili powder, and cumin; and a simple garlic-herb version with thyme and rosemary. I found that a squeeze of fresh citrus served with the steak provided a bright acidic counterpoint.

GRILLING DETAILS

Because this relatively thin cut cooks quickly, high heat is necessary to achieve a perfect crust. The uneven thickness of many tips presented a problem, though. The exterior would scorch by the time the thick portions were cooked, and the thin parts would be overcooked. A two-level fire, with more coals on one side of the grill to create hotter and cooler areas, solved the problem. I started the tips over high heat to sear them and then moved them to the cooler area to finish cooking.

I prefer my steaks grilled rare, so I was surprised to find that when cooked rare the meat was rubbery, whereas longer cooking gave it a tender chew—without drying out the meat. Even when cooked until well done, these tips were exceptionally juicy. I had the brine to thank again: The salty soy marinade helped the meat hold on to its moisture.

Conventional wisdom prompted one more test. As a chef in a restaurant, I learned that letting meat rest before slicing gives the fibers time to reabsorb the juices that have been dispersed during cooking. I grilled two more batches of tips and sliced one immediately after it came off the grill and the other five minutes later. Sure enough, the rested tips were both more juicy and more tender. Finally, a recipe for steak tips as pleasing to my palate as they are to my pocketbook.

BUYING STEAK TIPS

Steak tips can come from two areas of the cow. One kind comes from tender, expensive cuts in the middle of the cow, such as the tenderloin. But true steak tips come from various muscles in the sirloin and round. After tasting 50 pounds of cheap steak tips, tasters had a clear favorite: a single muscle that butchers call flap meat and that is typically labeled "sirloin tips." Flap meat may be sold as cubes, strips, or small steaks. It has a rich, beefy flavor and a distinctive longitudinal grain.

It's best to buy flap meat in steak form rather than cubes or strips, which are often cut from nearby muscles that are neither as tasty nor as tender. Because meat labeling is so haphazard, you must visually identify this cut; buying it in steak form makes this easy.

Grilled Sirloin Steak Tips

SERVES 4 TO 6

Sirloin steak tips, also known as flap meat, are sold as whole steaks, strips, and cubes. We prefer to buy whole steaks for this dish. A two-level fire allows you to brown the steak over the hotter side of the grill and then move it to the cooler side if it is not yet cooked through. If your steak is thin, however, you may not need to use the cooler side of the grill.

1 recipe marinade (recipes follow)
2 pounds sirloin steak tips, trimmed
Lime wedges

1. Combine marinade and beef in 1-gallon zipper-lock bag and toss to coat; press out as much air as possible and seal bag. Refrigerate for 1 hour, flipping bag halfway through marinating.

2A. ***For a charcoal grill:*** Open bottom vent completely. Light large chimney starter filled with charcoal briquettes (6 quarts). When top coals are partially covered with ash, pour two-thirds evenly over half of grill, then pour remaining coals over other half of grill. Set cooking grate in place, cover, and open lid vent completely. Heat grill until hot, about 5 minutes.

2B. ***For a gas grill:*** Turn all burners to high, cover, and heat grill until hot, about 15 minutes. Leave all burners on high.

3. Clean and oil cooking grate. Remove beef from bag and pat dry with paper towels. Place steak tips on grill (on hotter side if using charcoal) and cook (covered if using gas) until well browned on first side, about 4 minutes. Flip steak tips and continue to cook (covered if using gas) until meat registers 120 to 125 degrees (for medium-rare) or 130 to 135 degrees (for medium), 6 to 10 minutes longer. If exterior of meat is browned but steak is not yet cooked through, move to cooler side of grill (if using charcoal) or turn down burners to medium (if using gas) and continue to cook to desired doneness.

4. Transfer steak tips to carving board, tent with aluminum foil, and let rest for 5 to 10 minutes. Slice steak tips very thin against grain on bias and serve with lime wedges.

marinades

Southwestern Marinade

MAKES ABOUT ¾ CUP

⅓ cup soy sauce
⅓ cup vegetable oil
3 garlic cloves, minced
1 tablespoon packed dark brown sugar
1 tablespoon tomato paste
1 tablespoon chili powder
2 teaspoons ground cumin
¼ teaspoon cayenne pepper

Combine all ingredients in bowl.

Garlic, Ginger, and Soy Marinade

MAKES ABOUT ¾ CUP

Serve the steak tips with orange wedges instead of lime wedges if you use this marinade.

⅓ cup soy sauce
3 tablespoons vegetable oil
3 tablespoons toasted sesame oil
2 tablespoons packed dark brown sugar
1 tablespoon grated fresh ginger
2 teaspoons grated orange zest
1 scallion, sliced thin
3 garlic cloves, minced
½ teaspoon red pepper flakes

Combine all ingredients in bowl.

Garlic and Herb Marinade

MAKES ABOUT ¾ CUP

⅓ cup soy sauce
⅓ cup olive oil
3 garlic cloves, minced
1 tablespoon minced fresh rosemary
1 tablespoon minced fresh thyme
1 tablespoon packed dark brown sugar
1 tablespoon tomato paste
1 teaspoon pepper

Combine all ingredients in bowl.

"OVEN-GRILLED" LONDON BROIL

MARK BITTMAN, *May/June 1998*

First things first: London broil is a recipe, not a cut of meat. You take a thick steak, grill, broil, or pan-grill it, then slice it thin, on the bias across the grain. It's essentially a convenience food, a 20-minute protein blast that can form the backbone of any dinner.

The traditional cut for London broil is flank steak, a long, thin, boneless muscle that weighs a couple of pounds and comes from the flank section of the cow. Since it has some marbling—a key to flavor in meat—and is not a super-tough cut, it's really the perfect choice. And, historically, it has been inexpensive. But these days, flank steak is one of the more expensive cuts, which is how inexpensive round and shoulder steak have come to be labeled London broil, along with the required part-of-cow designation. You might see, for example, "top round steak for London broil." These cheaper cuts seemed worth a try.

For London broil that is both flavorful and inexpensive, choose the shoulder cut.

Before narrowing down the cuts, I decided to settle on a cooking technique. When the goal is simply a broiled steak, cooking is simple. All you want, after all, is a crisp crust and a rare-to-medium-rare interior. (Because they are so lean, rareness is especially important for these cuts.) Ideally, the dry crunch of the crust contrasts with the tender, juicy interior in every single slice. But my broiler doesn't generate enough heat to brown the exterior of even a 1½-inch thick steak before the interior becomes overcooked. Grilling worked fine, but I needed an alternative for indoor cooking. Pan-grilling was the most obvious solution, but there was also an obvious problem: smoke. When I got a cast-iron skillet blazing hot and threw the steak in there, it browned beautifully on both sides, and took about the same amount of time as grilling. But within a minute, the entire house—not just the kitchen—was filled with blue haze.

I decided to try the oven. Roasting couldn't possibly work; the oven wasn't going to produce the sudden "shock" that is so necessary for good searing. I thought about preheating my pan in the oven, but then I realized I could employ the same technique many restaurant chefs use—start the meat in a hot skillet on the stovetop, then transfer it to the hottest possible oven.

After some experimentation, I got this to work perfectly and the total cooking time was less than 10 minutes. I set the oven rack at the lowest position and preheated the oven to 500 degrees. When it was ready, I preheated a skillet for a few minutes, then added the steak and immediately moved the skillet into the oven. After 3 or 4 minutes, I turned the steak and finished the cooking. Now, I had a fairly crusty rare steak without having to light the grill. Eventually I made one further refinement to this technique: I used a pizza stone and preheated my oven for at least 30 minutes. The stone transferred more heat to the bottom of the skillet and produced a better crust, but I wouldn't consider it essential.

Timing varied according to the thickness of the steak. A 1-inch-thick flank steak could be done in 5 minutes. A thicker shoulder or round steak—say, 1½ inches or more—might take 8 minutes, or even a little longer. I learned to rely on my instant-read thermometer, and yanked the steak off the heat the second it read 120 degrees.

COMPARING THE CUTS

Having settled on a cooking method, I began comparing the different cuts. To work as London broil, a cut must be made up of one muscle; otherwise it simply falls apart when you slice it. There are only a few cuts of beef that meet this criterion. I eliminated one of them, the tri-tip cut, because it is too difficult for most consumers to find, and top sirloin along with the flank because it is too expensive. Eye of round has the wrong shape for steaks, while bottom round is almost always used for roasts.

That left me with two cuts: the top round and the shoulder. I quickly made an important discovery: Although supermarkets tend to market top round and shoulder the same way, the differences are enormous.

If you treat a 1- or 1½-inch-thick cut of shoulder exactly like flank you'll get decent results, a chewy but fairly flavorful steak at a substantial savings. Not only is shoulder the least expensive steak you can buy, it also has a little bit of fat, which you want. If, however, you cook a thick cut of top round that way, you're going to be disappointed. Round is lean and tight-grained, with a liver-like flavor that's almost disgusting in quickly cooked muscle meat. Having experimented with top round alongside shoulder during the early stages of my work (and including it in my final tests), I would say that shoulder is the best inexpensive substitute for flank steak. My tasters confirmed this. When they sampled London broil made from flank, shoulder, blade steak, and bottom and top round, they all preferred shoulder for its robust beef flavor and reasonably tender texture.

Now that I had the right cut and had learned how to cook it, I thought I'd see what help I could give it. With a properly cooked shoulder steak, both flavor and texture were good, but the first could be stronger and the second had a somewhat flaccid quality I could do without. I tried marinades and spice rubs, but both simply added their flavors, creating a different critter from the plain, simple steak I wanted. There was another problem with these treatments: Instead of improving the texture of the steak, they detracted from the quality of its crust. Even after I carefully dried the surface of the meat with paper towels, the wet marinades inhibited the formation of a good crust during the relatively short cooking times. And the dry rubs tended to burn or give the crust a

completely foreign flavor. I moved one step closer to my goal when I began to serve the plain broiled steaks with a huge lump of compound butter. Its flavors complemented rather than overwhelmed the meat, but the taste of the butter still remained more distinctive than I wanted.

At that point my quest forked, and I pursued two roads at once. I began "aging" the meat in my refrigerator, both with salt and without. I knew the salt was a gamble because it would draw out moisture, which would leave the meat with even less juice and make cooking times more critical. But I hoped that salt would intensify the flavor, and I knew enzymatic action would tenderize the meat some. The aging worked, although much better with salt than without. The meat gained flavor and a certain firmness. And the drier surface formed a better, crunchier crust than the untreated or wet-marinated steaks.

But there were considerable disadvantages to this process, not the least of which was that it required the kind of plan-ahead thinking that virtually destroyed the convenience of a simple steak. Furthermore, it became too salty for many people. Yet aging small pieces of meat like these without salting didn't do much at all. By the time the unsalted meat became tender and flavorful, it was so dried out that when I sliced it thin and left it raw, it resembled aged, air-dryed beef like *bresaola*. To me, the results were clear: No salting or aging was needed.

When I was finished, I compared a well-cooked, untreated shoulder steak to a flank steak, the traditional cut for London broil. The flank steak had better texture and flavor, but the differences were not that great. And the fact that I can buy the shoulder steak more cheaply and in a thicker cut will make it my London broil of choice in summers to come.

SINGLE-MUSCLE CUTS FOR LONDON BROIL

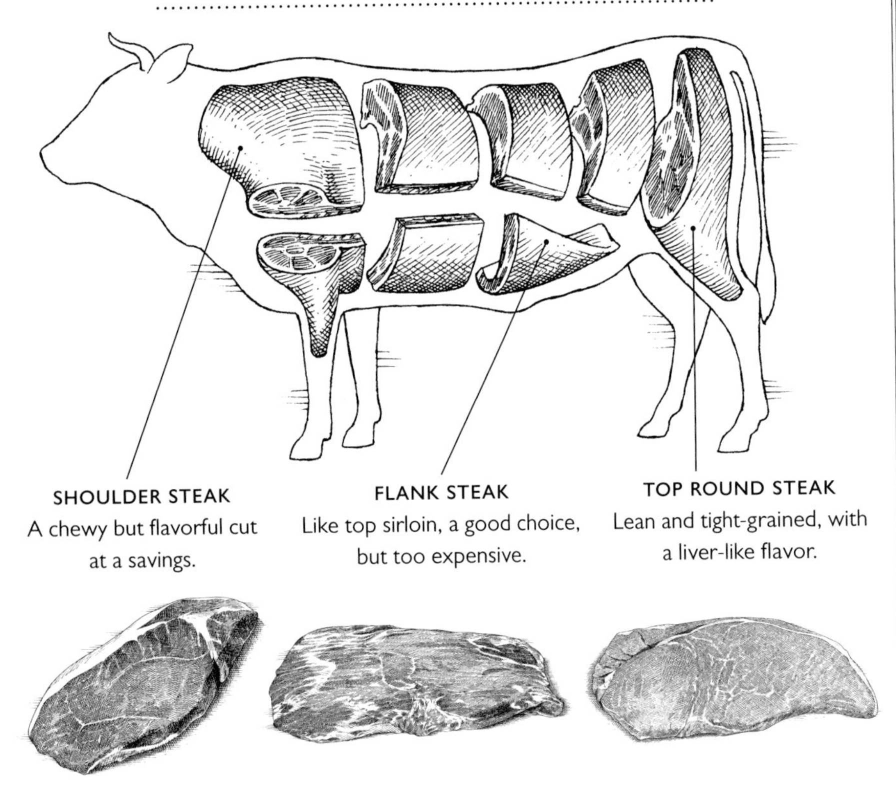

"Oven-Grilled" London Broil

SERVES 4

Using a pizza stone in the oven helps superheat the pan bottom, but this method works well without the stone, too. You will need an ovensafe skillet for this recipe; cast iron or stainless steel with an aluminum core work well.

1½–2 pounds boneless shoulder steak, about 1½ inches thick, patted dry
Salt and pepper

1. Adjust oven rack to lowest position; place pizza stone, if using, on rack and heat oven to 500 degrees for at least 30 minutes.
2. Meanwhile, heat 12-inch skillet for at least 3 minutes over high heat. Generously sprinkle both sides of steak with salt and pepper; add to pan. As soon as steak smokes, about 5 seconds, carefully transfer pan to oven; cook 3½ to 4 minutes, then flip steak and cook until well-seared and meat registers 120 to 125 degrees (for medium-rare), 3½ to 4 minutes longer. Transfer steak to cutting board; let rest for 5 minutes. Slice meat very thin against grain on bias. Season with salt and pepper to taste, and serve immediately with meat juices.

OVEN GRILLING

To achieve the high heat necessary for a good crust, preheat a pizza stone on an oven rack set in the lowest position.

ULTIMATE CHAR-GRILLED STEAK

DAN SOUZA, *July/August 2015*

While it's hard to beat the smoky char of a grilled thick-cut steak, since I started using the test kitchen method for pan-searing steaks, the indoor version more often approaches perfection. The technique calls for first baking a thick steak in a low oven and then searing it in a smoking-hot preheated skillet. The initial baking not only evenly cooks the meat but also dries and warms the steak's surface, resulting in lightning-fast searing—just a minute or so per side. The result is the platonic ideal of a steak: a crisp, well-browned crust and medium-rare meat from edge to edge. The time is so fast that, unlike with most methods, only a sliver of meat below the crust overcooks and loses its rosy hue.

But with grilling, though I've created some pretty hot grill setups over the years, it takes so long to evenly brown the steak that I overcook a fair amount of meat below the surface. This summer I decided to hold grilled steak to a higher standard: perfectly cooked meat, a well-browned and crisp crust, and great charcoal-grilled flavor.

SEARING QUESTION

To reach perfection, I suspected that I'd need to think outside the box—or as it turned out, the grill. In my research I came across a novel technique that relied on a charcoal chimney starter to not just light the coals but actually do the cooking. To produce an amazing sear, celebrity chef and food science guru Alton Brown mimics the intensity of a steakhouse-caliber broiler by placing a porterhouse steak on the grill grate and then putting a lit chimney of coals right over it. Other sources took a similar approach but flipped the setup, placing the chimney on the grill's charcoal grate and then arranging the steak, set on the cooking grate, on top.

I gave both methods a try (I settled on strip over rib-eye steaks since the former don't have as much internal fat and would thus cause fewer flare-ups) and one thing was for certain: Searing over a chimney was faster than any traditional grill setup I'd ever used, browning one side of the steak in about 2 minutes. Why? For much the same reason that a chimney is so effective at lighting a pile of coals: access to oxygen. In a chimney, the coals rest on a grate surrounded by big slits that let in lots of air, the sides of the chimney are perforated for additional airflow, and both the top and bottom of the chimney have wide openings. Together, these features allow a huge supply of oxygen to access the coals, which makes them burn hot. Plus, the cylindrical shape is ideal for focusing intense radiant heat toward the open ends.

But there was a downside to the chimney-based recipes. They all cooked the steaks start to finish over high heat, which inevitably led to an overcooked interior. To address this, I decided I would cook the interior of my steaks using our low-temperature oven method for pan-seared steaks and then move outside to sear them and give them that charcoal-grilled flavor.

After cooking a few steaks in a 275-degree oven for 30 minutes until they reached 105 degrees, I tried searing them both under and on top of a chimney. I quickly developed a preference for the latter. While putting the steak under the chimney avoided any chance of flare-ups because the fat dripped away from the heat source, ashes fell on the steak as it cooked and monitoring the browning required picking up the blazing-hot chimney. Putting the steak on top avoided both of these problems.

That said, the technique still had its issues. Placing a grill grate that measured more than 20 inches in diameter, on top of a glowing-hot 6-quart chimney starter that was a mere 7½ inches in diameter was precarious to say the least. In addition, the grate itself posed a problem: The hot bars of the grill grate seared the parts of the steak touching it faster than the radiant heat from the coals could brown the rest of the steak's surface. The result was blackened grill marks over an unappealing background of gray meat. And finally, flare-ups were a problem, even with strip steaks. Cutting off the fat cap was a simple way to extinguish the flare-up issue, but I didn't have a simple solution for the grill grate. Or maybe I did. Could I ditch the cooking grate entirely?

Keeping the coals in the chimney delivers steaks with a killer crust and rosy meat from edge to edge.

BETTER THAN GRATE

Cooking over a live fire without a grate isn't a new concept—think of a pig on a spit. But even with this precedent in mind, it felt a little odd as I ran two metal skewers, parallel to each other, lengthwise through the center of a 1¾-inch-thick strip steak. (One steak would easily serve two, so I figured that once I had my method down I could double the recipe.) After cooking my skewered steak through indoors, I moved outside and lit a chimney starter filled halfway with charcoal. As soon as the coals were ready, I set the skewered steak on top with the protruding ends of the skewers resting directly on the rim. I was finally onto something. In about 2 minutes the entire surface of the steak facing the coals turned a rich mahogany color and the edges charred beautifully. The gray band of overcooked meat was pretty small and the flavor was good. I just needed to make a few tweaks to reach perfection.

I noticed that the steak charred best at the edges, which made sense because the edges have more exposed surface area. With that in mind, I sliced the steak in half crosswise to create two more edges and thus more browning. This worked well, with the added benefit of making serving a breeze—I simply slid the cooked steaks off the skewers.

Scoring the surface of the steaks in a crosshatch pattern before cooking provided additional edges to brown and char.

Many tasters complained that the interiors of the steaks were bland, so I salted the meat and let it sit for an hour before putting it in the oven. This made a big flavor difference, but I saw a chance for improvement. I salted some more steaks and immediately popped them into a superlow 200-degree oven to cook for about an hour and a half (I cooked them to 120 degrees since carryover cooking would be minimal). The steaks were now well seasoned and cooked internally to perfection. And because the exterior had more time to dehydrate, these steaks browned and charred in just 60 seconds per side.

All that was left was to double the recipe to make four steaks on two sets of skewers. Since I was cutting each strip steak in half crosswise, I paired up the narrower ends on one set of skewers and the wider ends on another to ensure even cooking. I could only sear one pair at a time given the chimney's diameter, but it happened so fast that this didn't pose a problem.

With that, I had grilled steaks that lived up to the highest standards.

GRILLING STEAK OVER A CHIMNEY STARTER?

Coals are at their hottest in the chimney, not in the grill, where airflow is far more restricted. So leaving the coals in the chimney produces deep browning fast. Here's how it works.

CHIMNEY DESIGN
The cylindrical shape concentrates the heat. The open ends maximize airflow, keeping the fire burning intensely. A 7½-inch diameter is ideal for two steaks.

STEAK
We remove the fat cap and divide a strip steak in half. We crosshatch the surface for maximum browned crust. We salt, as always. We precook in the oven, low and slow.

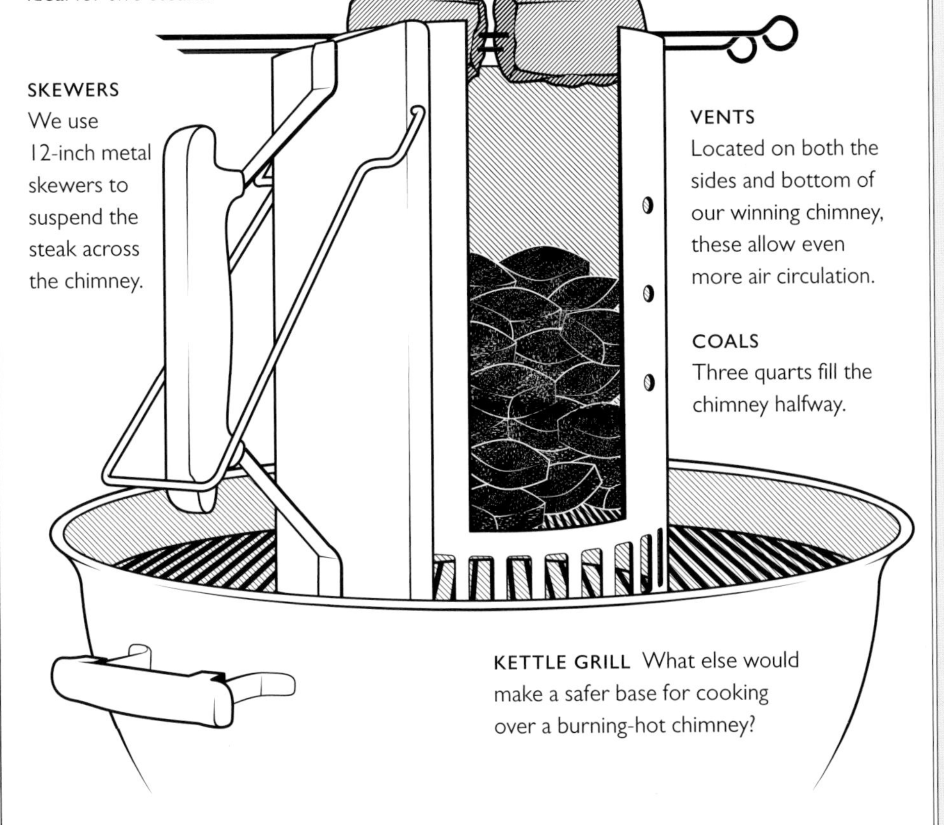

Ultimate Charcoal-Grilled Steaks

SERVES 4

Rib-eye steaks of a similar thickness can be substituted for strip steaks, although they may produce more flare-ups. You will need a charcoal chimney starter with a 7½-inch diameter and four 12-inch metal skewers for this recipe. If your chimney starter has a smaller diameter, skewer each steak individually and cook in four batches. It is important to remove the fat caps on the steaks to limit flare-ups during grilling.

2 (1-pound) boneless strip steaks, 1¾ inches thick, fat caps removed
Kosher salt and pepper

1. Adjust oven rack to middle position and heat oven to 200 degrees. Cut each steak in half crosswise to create four 8-ounce steaks. Cut 1/16-inch-deep slits on both sides of steaks, spaced ¼ inch apart, in crosshatch pattern. Sprinkle both sides of each steak with ½ teaspoon salt (2 teaspoons total). Lay steak halves with tapered ends flat on counter and pass two 12-inch metal skewers, spaced 1½ inches apart, horizontally through steaks, making sure to keep ¼-inch space between steak halves. Repeat skewering with remaining steak halves.
2. Place skewered steaks on wire rack set in rimmed baking sheet, transfer to oven, and cook until centers of steaks register 120 degrees, flipping steaks over halfway through cooking and removing them as they come to temperature, 1½ hours to 1 hour 50 minutes. Tent skewered steaks (still on rack) with aluminum foil.
3. Light large chimney starter filled halfway with charcoal briquettes (3 quarts). When top coals are completely covered in ash, uncover steaks (reserving foil) and pat dry with paper towels. Using tongs, place 1 set of steaks directly over chimney so skewers rest on rim of chimney (meat will be suspended over coals). Cook until both sides are well browned and charred, about 1 minute per side. Using tongs, return first set of steaks to wire rack in sheet, season with pepper, and tent with reserved foil. Repeat with second set of skewered steaks. Remove skewers from steaks and serve.

THE BEST BEEF TENDERLOIN

CHARLES KELSEY, *March/April 2009*

Nothing beats the extravagantly buttery texture of beef tenderloin. It may not be the most intensely flavored cut, but that is easily overcome by a rich sauce or accompaniment. The challenge is in expertly cooking the meat. The moist, delicate texture of tenderloin can easily be compromised by the oven's harsh heat. And considering its steep price, overcooking this special-occasion roast is not an option (my preferred cut rings up at about $18 per pound).

Yet when I tried a handful of recipes and techniques, all of which gave fairly vague instructions, the tenderloins emerged from the oven with one of two problems. Some cooked evenly but didn't have the dark, caramelized crust that gives meat a deep roasted flavor. Others had optimal flavor and an appealing brown crust, but were marred by a thick, gray band of overdone meat near the edge. I wanted a technique that produced perfectly cooked and deeply flavored meat—ideally without too much fuss.

To do justice to this luxurious cut, sear last, not first, and rub it with flavored butter.

GETTING EVEN

With only two options, whole and center-cut, choosing the style of tenderloin roast was straightforward but critical to my success. Whole tenderloin is huge—the typical roast is 5 or 6 pounds, serving up to 16 people. It often comes covered in a thick layer of fat and sinew that is time-consuming to trim and peel. Plus, its long, tapered shape is a challenge to cook evenly. Over the years, we've become fond of the smaller center-cut roast, known in industry argot as the Châteaubriand, after the 19th century French author and statesman François-René de Châteaubriand (who is said to have particularly enjoyed this prized meat). Some butchers charge significantly more for center-cut versus whole tenderloin, but it comes already trimmed (so there's no waste) and its cylindrical shape practically guarantees that both ends cook to the same degree of doneness. What you're getting is the best of the best—the centerpiece of the most exquisitely tender part of the cow.

To achieve a good crust on the meat, I could either sear it first in a skillet or simply crank up the oven as high as it would go, at the beginning or end of cooking. As oven-searing wouldn't require splattering grease on my stovetop or dirtying an extra pan, I started there. I tied the meat crosswise with twine at intervals to make it more compact and help form an even crust, and then placed the meat in a roasting pan that I'd preheated to further encourage browning. But no matter what I tried—starting out high (at 500 degrees) and dropping down much lower (400 degrees), or the reverse—the meat would not brown adequately. My best results came from simply cooking the tenderloin at 425 degrees for half an hour and turning it after 15 minutes. The roast that emerged from the oven looked promising, with a somewhat dark crust. But any hopes I had were dashed when I cut into the meat: The slices were a nice deep pink at the center but marred by a pesky band of gray, overcooked meat at the edge.

Pan searing it would have to be. I heated a few tablespoons of vegetable oil over medium-high heat in a large skillet and then added my roast, browning it on all sides before transferring it to the oven. This time, with browning already done, I placed it on a rack set in a rimmed baking sheet to promote air circulation and more even cooking. I prepared several roasts this way, and experimented with different oven temperatures, from 500 degrees on down to 350. Naturally, each of these roasts had a good-looking crust, but each also had an overdone "ring around the collar." The best of the bunch was the tenderloin roasted at 350, but there was still plenty of room for improvement. Tinkering around, I decided to try reversing the cooking order, roasting first, then searing, a technique we've used successfully in other meat recipes. The switch worked wonders here as well. Because the roast started out warm and dry, it could reach the 310 degrees necessary for browning to occur a lot faster than searing when it was raw, cold, and wet. (Until the moisture burns off, the surface of the meat can't rise above 212 degrees, the boiling point of water.) Less searing time, in turn, minimized the overcooked layer of gray.

Could I get rid of the gray band altogether by taking the oven temperature down further? In the past, the test kitchen has roasted meat at even lower temperatures with great success, transforming tough, inexpensive cuts into meltingly tender meat (see "Slow-Roasted Beef" on page 106). I hadn't initially thought to try slow roasting because tenderloin is so soft to begin with. Now I reconsidered. After tying several more roasts, I put them in the oven and began dialing back the temperature from 350 degrees. As it turned out, I didn't have that far to go: 300 degrees proved the magic temperature for yielding consistent ruby coloring from edge to edge.

BEEFING UP FLAVOR

Despite decent progress, I still hadn't coaxed deep beefy flavor from my mild-mannered tenderloin. The issue was the meat itself: With so little fat, it was lacking ideal flavor, even after searing to create a crust and carefully calibrating the cooking. I knew I could lean on a rich sauce like a béarnaise or an intense wine reduction—indeed, I was planning to add an accompaniment of some sort—but I was also set on intensifying the flavor of the meat itself.

First I was curious to explore some of the offbeat techniques I'd come across in my research. The most appealing involved roasting the meat wrapped in a couple slices

of bacon, which then get discarded and the meat seared. I had high hopes; after all, what doesn't taste better with bacon? Tenderloin, as it turned out; the bacon caused the meat to steam and didn't really add flavor. Shrouding the tenderloin in butter-soaked cheesecloth produced similarly uninspiring results. Soaking the meat in a soy-Worcestershire mix—ingredients often used to accentuate beef flavor—was just plain overpowering, more teriyaki than tenderloin.

In the end, a tried-and-true test kitchen method proved best—sprinkling all sides of the meat with salt, covering it with plastic wrap, and then letting it sit at room temperature. After sitting for an hour, the roast cooked up with significantly more flavor. Here's why: The salt draws juices out of the meat and then the reverse happens and the salt and moisture flow back in, drawing flavor deep into the meat.

I got the best results when, after salting the meat, I rubbed it with a couple of tablespoons of softened butter before cooking, which added satisfying richness. In fact, this technique was so effective that I decided against a rich sauce and instead created some easy compound butters, combining shallot with parsley, rosemary with Parmesan cheese, and chipotle chile with garlic and cilantro. The aroma of the flavored butter melting into the crevices of the meat proved irresistible to tasters. I had spent $1,200 on more than 25 tenderloins, but that satisfaction made it worth every penny.

TENDERLOIN TROUBLES

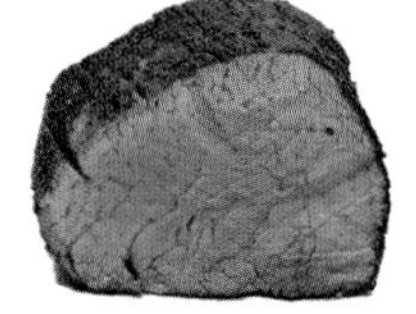

CRUSTY BUT OVERCOOKED
Tenderloin with a good flavorful crust is often marred by a band of gray, overcooked meat near the edge.

EVENLY COOKED BUT NO CRUST
Tenderloin that is rosy from edge to edge typically lacks a good crust and meaty flavor.

Roast Beef Tenderloin

SERVES 4 TO 6

Ask your butcher to prepare a trimmed center-cut Châteaubriand from the whole tenderloin, as this cut is not usually available without special ordering. If you are cooking for a crowd, this recipe can be doubled to make two roasts. Sear the roasts one after the other, wiping out the pan and adding new oil after searing the first roast. Both pieces of meat can be roasted on the same rack.

1 (2-pound) beef tenderloin center-cut Châteaubriand, trimmed
2 teaspoons kosher salt
1 teaspoon coarsely ground pepper
2 tablespoons unsalted butter, softened
1 tablespoon vegetable oil
1 recipe flavored butter (recipes follow)

1. Using 12-inch lengths of kitchen twine, tie roast crosswise at 1½-inch intervals. Sprinkle roast evenly with salt, cover loosely with plastic wrap, and let stand at room temperature for 1 hour. Meanwhile, adjust oven rack to middle position and heat oven to 300 degrees.
2. Pat roast dry with paper towels. Sprinkle roast evenly with pepper and spread butter evenly over surface. Transfer roast to wire rack set in rimmed baking sheet. Roast until center of roast registers 120 to 125 degrees (for medium-rare), 40 to 55 minutes, or 130 to 135 degrees (for medium), 55 minutes to 1 hour 10 minutes, flipping roast halfway through cooking.
3. Heat oil in 12-inch skillet over medium-high heat until just smoking. Place roast in skillet and sear until well browned on all sides, 1 to 2 minutes per side. Transfer roast to carving board and spread 2 tablespoons flavored butter evenly over top of roast; let rest for 15 minutes. Remove twine and cut meat crosswise into ½-inch-thick slices. Serve, passing remaining flavored butter separately.

accompaniments

Shallot and Parsley Butter

MAKES ABOUT ½ CUP

4 tablespoons unsalted butter, softened
½ shallot, minced
1 tablespoon minced fresh parsley
1 garlic clove, minced
¼ teaspoon salt
¼ teaspoon pepper

Combine all ingredients in bowl.

Chipotle and Garlic Butter with Lime and Cilantro

MAKES ABOUT ½ CUP

5 tablespoons unsalted butter, softened
1 tablespoon minced canned chipotle chile in adobo sauce plus 1 teaspoon adobo sauce
1 tablespoon minced fresh cilantro
1 garlic clove, minced
1 teaspoon honey
1 teaspoon grated lime zest
½ teaspoon salt

Combine all ingredients in bowl.

Rosemary and Parmesan Butter

MAKES ABOUT ½ CUP

4 tablespoons unsalted butter, softened
3 tablespoons grated Parmesan cheese
2 teaspoons minced fresh rosemary or ½ teaspoon dried
1 garlic clove, minced
Pinch red pepper flakes

Combine all ingredients in bowl.

IMPROVING CHEAP ROAST BEEF

DAVID PAZMIÑO, *January/February 2008*

For most families, Sunday roast beef isn't prime rib; it's a lesser cut that's sometimes good, sometimes not. The roasts my parents prepared throughout my childhood were typically tough and dried-out and better suited for sandwiches the next day. But when my grandfather was at the stove, he could take the same inexpensive cut and turn it into something special—tender, rosy, beefy-tasting meat that had everyone asking for seconds. I wanted to work the same kind of wizardry on my own Sunday roast.

First I needed to zero in on the most promising beef. After a week in the kitchen testing a slew of low-cost cuts, I had a clear winner: the eye-round roast. Though less flavorful than fattier cuts from the shoulder (the chuck) and less tender than other meat from the back leg (the round), my eye roast had one key attribute the others lacked: a uniform shape from front to back. This was a roast that would not only cook evenly but look good on the plate as well.

THE SHOWDOWN: HIGH OR LOW HEAT?

My next challenge was choosing between the two classic methods for roasting meat—high and fast or low and slow. I began with the more common high-heat approach, quickly searing the meat on the stovetop and then transferring it to a 450-degree oven for roasting. The technique works great with more upscale rib and loin cuts but showed its flaws with the leaner eye round, yielding meat that was overcooked and dried-out.

But before heading down the low-temperature path, which normally involves roasting meat in an oven set between 250 and 325 degrees, I wanted to try something more extreme. To extract maximum tenderness from meat, the popular 1960s nutritionist Adelle Davis advocated cooking it at the temperature desired when it was done. For a roast to reach an end temperature of 130 degrees for medium-rare, this process could involve 20 to 30 hours of cooking.

Tossing aside practical considerations like food safety and the gas bill, I decided I had to replicate this expert's findings. I set the one oven in the test kitchen capable of maintaining such a low temperature to 130 degrees and popped in an eye round. Twenty-four hours later, I pulled out a roast with juicy, meltingly tender meat that tasters likened to beef tenderloin. What special beef magic was going on here?

THE LOWDOWN

When I thought back to the test kitchen's discoveries when cooking thick-cut steaks, I had my answer: Beef contains enzymes that break down its connective tissues and act as natural tenderizers. These enzymes work faster as the temperature of the meat rises—but just until it reaches 122 degrees, at which point all action stops. Roasting the eye round in an oven set to 130 degrees allowed it to stay below 122 degrees far longer than when cooked in the typical low-temperature roasting range, transforming this lean, unassuming cut into something great.

But given that most ovens don't heat below 200 degrees—and that most home cooks don't want to run their ovens for a full day—how could I expect others to re-create my results? I would have to go as low as I could and see what happened. To accommodate the widest possible range of ovens, I settled on 225 degrees as my lowest starting point. I also decided I would brown the meat first to give it nice color and a crusty exterior. (While tender, my 130-degree roast had an unappetizing gray exterior.) Searing would also help to ensure food safety, since bacteria on roasts are generally confined to the outside.

When I took the roast out of the oven, however, I was disappointed. It was tender, but nothing like the texture of the eye round cooked at 130 degrees. What could I do to keep the meat below 122 degrees longer? A new idea occurred to me: Why not shut off the oven just before the roast reached 122 degrees? As the oven cooled, the roast would continue to cook even more slowly.

Using a meat-probe thermometer to track the internal temperature of the roast, I shut off the oven when the meat reached 115 degrees. Sure enough, the meat stayed below 122 degrees 30 minutes longer, allowing its enzymes to continue the work of tenderizing, before creeping to 130 degrees for medium-rare. Tasters were certainly happy with this roast. It was remarkably tender and juicy for a roast that cost so little.

To transform an eye-round roast into an impressive centerpiece, cook it in a low oven—then turn off the heat.

THE HOME STRETCH

With the tenderness problem solved, it was time to tackle taste. So far I'd simply sprinkled salt and pepper on the roast just before searing it. Perhaps the flavor would improve if the meat were salted overnight or even brined. Brining—normally reserved for less fatty pork and poultry—certainly pumped more water into the beef and made it very juicy, but it also made it taste bland, watery, and less beefy. Next I tried salting the meat for first four, then 12, and finally 24 hours. As might be expected, the roast benefited most from the longest salting. Because the process of osmosis causes salt to travel from areas of higher to lower concentration, the full 24 hours gave it the most time to penetrate deep into the meat. There was another benefit: Salt, like the enzymes in meat, breaks down proteins to further improve texture.

At last I had tender, flavorful beef for a Sunday roast that even my grandfather would have been proud to serve to his family.

Slow-Roasted Beef

SERVES 6 TO 8

Open the oven door as little as possible, and remove the roast from the oven while taking its temperature. If the roast has not reached the desired temperature in the time specified in step 4, reheat the oven to 225 degrees for 5 minutes, then shut it off and continue to cook the roast to the desired temperature. We don't recommend cooking this roast past medium. For a smaller (2½- to 3½-pound) roast, reduce the amount of kosher salt to 1 tablespoon and pepper to 1½ teaspoons. For a larger (4½- to 6-pound) roast, cut the meat in half crosswise before cooking to create two smaller roasts. Slice the roast as thin as possible and serve with Horseradish Cream Sauce, if desired (recipe follows).

1 (3½- to 4½-pound) boneless eye-round roast, trimmed
4 teaspoons kosher salt
2 teaspoons plus 1 tablespoon vegetable oil
2 teaspoons pepper

1. Rub roast thoroughly with salt, wrap in plastic wrap, and refrigerate for 18 to 24 hours.
2. Adjust oven rack to middle position and heat oven to 225 degrees. Pat roast dry with paper towels, rub with 2 teaspoons oil, and sprinkle with pepper.
3. Heat remaining 1 tablespoon oil in 12-inch skillet over medium-high heat until just smoking. Brown roast well on all sides, 12 to 16 minutes; reduce heat if pan begins to scorch. Transfer roast to wire rack set in rimmed baking sheet and roast until meat registers 115 degrees (for medium-rare), 1¼ to 1¾ hours, or 125 degrees (for medium), 1¾ to 2¼ hours.
4. Turn oven off and leave roast in oven, without opening door, until meat registers 130 degrees (for medium-rare) or 140 degrees (for medium), 30 to 50 minutes.
5. Transfer roast to carving board and let rest for 15 minutes. Slice meat crosswise as thin as possible and serve.

accompaniment

Horseradish Cream Sauce

MAKES ABOUT 1 CUP

Buy refrigerated prepared horseradish, not the shelf-stable kind.

½ cup heavy cream
½ cup prepared horseradish
1 teaspoon salt
⅛ teaspoon pepper

1. Whisk cream in bowl until thickened but not yet holding soft peaks, 1 to 2 minutes. Gently fold in horseradish, salt, and pepper.
2. Transfer cream sauce to serving bowl and refrigerate for at least 30 minutes or up to 1 hour before serving.

THE TRANSFORMATION FROM TOUGH TO TENDER

Along with salting and searing, the key to our eye round's makeover into a tender, juicy roast is keeping its internal temperature below 122 degrees for as long as possible.

1. **SALT** Salt the roast and allow it to rest for 18 to 24 hours. Salt breaks down proteins to improve texture.
2. **SEAR** Sear the meat in a hot pan before roasting. While this won't affect tenderness, it will boost flavor.

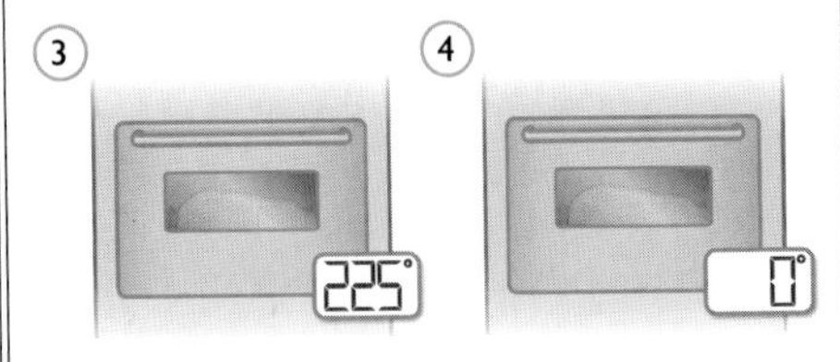

3. **OVEN ON** Cook the meat in an oven set to 225 degrees and open the door as infrequently as possible.
4. **OVEN OFF** When the roast reaches 115 degrees, turn off the oven and continue to cook the roast as the oven cools.

LOW-COST LINEUP

Not all bargain cuts have the potential to taste like a million bucks—or look like it when carved and served on a plate.

OUR FAVORITE EYE-ROUND ROAST
We singled out this cut not only for its good flavor and relative tenderness but also for its uniform shape that guarantees even cooking and yields slices that look good on the plate.

TOO FATTY CHUCK EYE
While undeniably tender and flavorful, its fat and gristle make this meat better for stew and pot roast than roast beef.

ODD SHAPE TOP ROUND
A deli staple for sandwiches, this cut comes in irregular shapes that can cook unevenly.

TOUGH TO CARVE BOTTOM ROUND RUMP
We ruled out this roast for being both tough and hard to carve against the grain.

ELEVATION IS IMPORTANT

Rather than placing our eye-round roast directly in a roasting pan, we first sear it in a hot skillet to develop a flavorful crust on the meat. But when we transfer the roast to the oven, we elevate it on a rack set inside a rimmed baking sheet. The rack allows the oven heat to circulate evenly around the meat and prevents the bottom crust from steaming in the oven (which would happen if the roast was set directly in a pan).

MODERNIZING FRENCH-STYLE POT ROAST

SANDRA WU, *November/December 2007*

Boeuf à la mode—"beef in the latest fashion"—is a classic French recipe that dates to a time when a multiday recipe was the rule rather than the exception. The earliest reference I found to this dish appeared in *Le Cuisinier François* (1651), an encyclopedic book that systematically catalogued French cuisine. Larding (inserting strips of marinated fat) and braising (searing the roast and simmering it partially submerged in liquid in a sealed pot) could transform an otherwise dry and chewy cut into a tender, moist, and flavorful roast. An added bonus of this cooking technique is that the braising liquid itself—red wine and beef stock—reduces into a thick, rich sauce to accompany the meat.

Although boeuf à la mode bears some similarity to American pot roast, this elegant French dish relies heavily on wine for flavor, adds collagen-rich veal and pork parts for body, and has a separately prepared mushroom-onion garnish. After spending days making five classic renditions of this old-fashioned recipe, I understood its allure—and its challenges. It is to pot roast what croissants are to refrigerated crescent rolls and, as such, required up to four days of preparation. To bring boeuf à la mode up to date for the modern home cook, some of the fussy techniques and hard-to-find ingredients would have to go.

Streamlining this old-world classic doesn't mean sacrificing complexity, thanks to a rich chuck-eye roast and a wine reduction.

BYE, BYE MARINADE

Traditionally, this recipe starts with threading strips of seasoned, brandy-soaked salt pork or fatback through the beef roast using a long needle, or *lardoir*. In addition to making up for the lack of marbling in the meat, larding adds flavor. I cut some fatback into thin strips, marinated them in brandy and seasonings, and struggled to pull them through the roast. For the amount of effort these steps took, I was disappointed when tasters felt the payoff wasn't that great. Today's grain-fed beef gets little exercise and has much more marbling than the leaner, grass-fed beef eaten in France when this recipe was created. As long as I chose the right cut (tasters liked a boneless chuck-eye roast best), there was plenty of fat in the meat and larding was just overkill. I was happy to ax this step from my recipe.

In all of the classic recipes I uncovered, the meat was marinated in a mixture of red wine and large-cut *mirepoix* (carrots, onions, and celery) for a significant period of time, up to three days in several cases. Testing various lengths of time, I found the effect superficial unless I was willing to invest at least two full days. Even then, the wine flavor penetrated only the outer part of the meat, and the vegetables didn't really add much. Frankly, the meat picked up so much wine flavor during the hours-long braising time that marinating didn't seem worth the effort.

In fact, some tasters actually complained that the meat was picking up too much wine flavor as it cooked; the beef tasted a bit sour and harsh. I reviewed a Julia Child recipe that called for marinating the roast in a mixture of wine and vegetables and then reducing that marinade by half before adding beef broth and beginning the braising process. Would cooking the wine before braising the beef in it tame its unpleasant alcoholic punch? I put the wine in a saucepan and reduced it to 2 cups. When I combined the reduced wine with the beef broth and used this mixture as the braising liquid, tasters were much happier. The wine tasted complex and fruity, not sour and astringent.

Most of the vegetable flavor in this dish comes from the garnish of glazed pearl onions and white mushrooms, which is traditionally cooked separately and added just before serving. To speed up the process, I used frozen rather than fresh pearl onions. But the sauce needed some vegetables to balance the wine and meat flavors. Sautéed onion and garlic helped build depth in the early stages of cooking, and tasters liked the sweetness contributed by large chunks of carrots added to the braising liquid later in the cooking process.

THE SAUCE MATTERS

I had the wine and vegetables under control, but my recipe didn't seem as rich and meaty as some of the test recipes I had prepared. My first thought was to salt the meat, something we do in the test kitchen to improve the beefy flavor in thick-cut steaks. It works by drawing moisture out of the meat and forming a shallow brine. Over time, the salt migrates back into the meat, seasoning it throughout rather than just on the exterior. Eventually, I discovered that salting the meat for just an hour was worth the minimal effort. The roast was nicely seasoned and tasted beefier.

Salt pork is traditionally added to the sauce for richness, but tasters preferred the smoky flavor of bacon. I decided to brown the meat in the bacon drippings and then add the bacon bits back to the braising liquid. My sauce was improving.

Compared with regular pot roast braising liquid, which is flavorful but relatively thin and brothy, the sauce that accompanies boeuf à la mode is richer and more akin to a sauce that might be found on a steak at a fine restaurant. Adding some flour to the sautéed onion and garlic helped with the overall consistency, but the sauce still lacked body. I tried adding pork rind, split calves' feet, and veal bones and liked the effect they had on the sauce—the collagen in these animal parts breaks down in the long cooking process and releases plenty of gelatin. But what if I went directly to the source instead?

I tried adding a tablespoon of powdered gelatin rehydrated in ¼ cup of cold water at the beginning of the recipe, but to no effect. The lengthy cooking time and high heat rendered the gelatin ineffective. I decided to try again, adding the gelatin during the sauce reduction stage. This helped, but not enough. It wasn't until I'd added the gelatin after the sauce had finished reducing that I got the results I had been looking for. Finally, it became rich and velvety, on par with the best classic recipe I'd tried at the beginning of my journey. Drizzled with this intense sauce and surrounded by the well-browned mushroom-onion garnish and tender carrots, this old-fashioned pot roast was the best I'd ever tasted.

ONE ROAST BECOMES TWO

The chuck-eye roast has great flavor, but we found that the interior fat is best trimmed before cooking. Simply pull the roast apart at the natural seam and trim away large knobs of fat from each half.

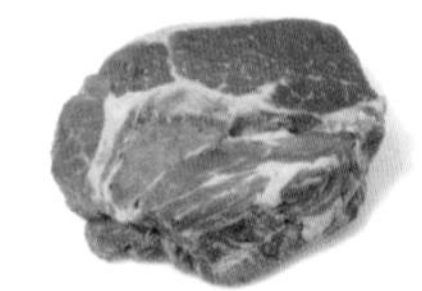

TOO FATTY **GOOD TO GO**

French-Style Pot Roast

SERVES 6 TO 8

Use a medium-bodied, fruity red wine, such as a Côtes du Rhône or Pinot Noir, for this recipe. The gelatin lends richness and body to the finished sauce; don't omit it. To prepare this dish in advance, follow the recipe through step 7, skipping the step of softening and adding the gelatin. Place the meat back in the reduced sauce, cool it to room temperature, cover it, and refrigerate it for up to two days. To serve, slice the beef and arrange it in a 13 by 9-inch baking dish. Bring the sauce to a simmer and stir in the gelatin until completely dissolved. Pour the warm sauce over the meat, cover it with aluminum foil, and bake it in a 350-degree oven until heated through, about 30 minutes. Serve this dish with boiled potatoes, buttered noodles, or steamed rice.

- 1 (4- to 5-pound) boneless beef chuck-eye roast, pulled apart at seams and trimmed
- Kosher salt and pepper
- 1 (750-ml) bottle red wine
- 10 sprigs fresh parsley, plus 2 tablespoons minced
- 2 sprigs fresh thyme
- 2 bay leaves
- 3 slices thick-cut bacon, cut into ¼-inch pieces
- 1 onion, chopped fine
- 3 garlic cloves, minced
- 1 tablespoon all-purpose flour
- 2 cups beef broth
- 4 carrots, peeled and cut on bias into 1½-inch pieces
- 3 tablespoons unsalted butter
- 2 cups frozen pearl onions, thawed
- 2 teaspoons sugar
- 10 ounces white mushrooms, trimmed and halved if small or quartered if large
- 1 tablespoon unflavored gelatin

1. Season beef with 2 teaspoons salt, place on wire rack set in rimmed baking sheet, and let stand at room temperature for 1 hour.
2. Meanwhile, bring wine to simmer in large saucepan over medium-high heat. Cook until reduced to 2 cups, about 15 minutes. Using kitchen twine, tie parsley sprigs, thyme sprigs, and bay leaves into bundle.
3. Pat beef dry with paper towels and season generously with pepper. Tie 3 pieces of kitchen twine around each piece of meat to keep it from falling apart.
4. Adjust oven rack to lower-middle position and heat oven to 300 degrees. Cook bacon in Dutch oven over medium-high heat, stirring occasionally, until crispy, 6 to 8 minutes. Using slotted spoon, transfer bacon to paper towel–lined plate and reserve. Pour off all but 2 tablespoons fat from pot; heat fat over medium-high heat until just smoking. Add beef to pot and brown on all sides, 8 to 10 minutes total. Transfer beef to large plate and set aside.
5. Reduce heat to medium; add onion and cook, stirring occasionally, until beginning to soften, 2 to 4 minutes. Add garlic, flour, and reserved bacon; cook, stirring constantly, until fragrant, about 30 seconds. Add broth, reduced wine, and herb bundle, scraping up any browned bits. Return beef and any accumulated juices to pot; increase heat to high and bring to simmer, then place large sheet of aluminum foil over pot and cover tightly with lid. Transfer pot to oven and cook, using tongs to turn beef every hour, until fork slips easily in and out of meat, 2½ to 3 hours, adding carrots to pot after 2 hours.
6. While beef cooks, bring butter, pearl onions, ½ cup water, and sugar to boil in 12-inch skillet over medium-high heat. Reduce heat to medium, cover, and cook until onions are tender, 5 to 8 minutes. Uncover, increase heat to medium-high, and cook until all liquid evaporates, 3 to 4 minutes. Add mushrooms and ¼ teaspoon salt; cook, stirring occasionally, until vegetables are browned and glazed, 8 to 12 minutes. Remove from heat and set aside. Sprinkle gelatin over ¼ cup water in bowl and let sit until gelatin softens, about 5 minutes.
7. Transfer beef to carving board and tent with foil. Let braising liquid settle, about 5 minutes; using large spoon, skim fat from surface. Discard herb bundle and stir in onion-mushroom mixture. Bring liquid to simmer over medium-high heat and cook until mixture is slightly thickened and reduced to 3¼ cups, 20 to 30 minutes. Season sauce with salt and pepper to taste. Add softened gelatin and stir until completely dissolved.
8. Remove twine and slice beef against grain into ½-inch-thick slices. Divide meat among warmed bowls or transfer to platter; arrange vegetables around meat, pour sauce over top, and sprinkle with minced parsley. Serve immediately.

IMPROVING PAN-FRIED PORK CHOPS

BRYAN ROOF, *November/December 2010*

Back when pork was fat-streaked and flavorful, great pan-fried pork chops came together from nothing more than a coating of seasoned flour and a quick turn in shimmering oil. The finished product—succulent meat encased in a delicate, crisp crust—was utterly simple and on the table in a matter of minutes, making this dish an ideal candidate for a weeknight supper.

But now that the fat, and the flavor, have been all but bred out of pigs, a fried pork chop needs more than a scant, spiced-up shell to give it appeal. Most recipes address that problem by simply packing on a more substantial crust—usually a triple layer of flour, eggs, and bread crumbs called a bound breading. It's a technique that works well enough, though I often find the coating a tad leathery and marred by gummy spots. Plus, this thick type of breading almost never clings tightly to the chop; it tends to flake off with the prick of a fork. My goal? A bound-breading makeover that would result in a lighter, crispier, flavorful sheath that stayed where it was put.

No gummy coatings here: Cornflakes, cornstarch, and buttermilk are the secrets to better breading.

PROTEIN PROBLEMS

I had one decision made before I even pulled out my frying pan: To keep this dish fast and easy, I'd forget bone-in chops and go with boneless center-cut loin chops. Shallow-frying these thin, tender chops takes just 2 to 5 minutes per side. Plus, four of them fit snugly in a large skillet, so I'd need to fry only two batches to feed four people.

As for the coating, I would put each component under the microscope and see what I learned. First up: the flour. A light dusting is meant to absorb moisture from both the meat and the eggs, creating a tacky base coat that acts as glue for the breading. But flour contains 10 to 12 percent protein—and when these proteins mix with the water (from the meat and the egg wash), they build structure that ultimately contributes to a heavier, tougher coating. In addition, pork exudes far more liquid than, say, chicken, and this can create gummy spots in the flour. If my goals were to lighten up the breading and get rid of any gumminess, this ingredient would have to go.

Fortunately, the only other option I could think of was a good bet: cornstarch. When cornstarch absorbs water, its starch granules swell and release sticky starch that forms an ultracrisp sheath when exposed to heat and fat, and we've used this powder to create just such a delicate, brittle layer on everything from oven fries to roast chicken. When I swapped the two ingredients, the chops boasted a casing that was indeed lighter and crispier.

But to my chagrin, I now had a new problem—the breading was barely holding on to the meat at all, with shards falling away like chipped paint as soon as I cut into it. After some research, I understood why: When it comes to creating sticky glue, cornstarch and egg wash are not the best pairing. First, cornstarch absorbs liquid less readily than flour. Second, the moisture in raw egg is bound up in its proteins, making it less available to be soaked up—an effect that not even the juicy pork could compensate for. Clearly, a wetter type of wash was in order. I tried heavy cream and buttermilk and noticed an immediate improvement in how the crust stuck to the chops. Tasters liked the subtle tang that buttermilk brought to the breading, so I settled on it, adding a dollop of mustard and a little minced garlic to perk up its flavor even more.

This wasn't the only good news to come out of switching liquids: The coating was now markedly lighter. When I thought about it, this effect made sense. Even a small amount of egg coagulates and puffs up when it cooks, so of course it would lead to a heavier coating than a dip in buttermilk.

STICKING POINTS

Up to this point, I'd been using bread crumbs as the final coat. But with buttermilk as my wash, they were absorbing too much liquid and weren't staying as crunchy. Fortunately, breading choices abound. I rolled the chops in Ritz crackers (too tender), Melba toast (too bland), cornmeal (too gritty), and Cream of Wheat (too fine). The best option turned out to be crushed cornflakes. These crisp flakes are a popular way to add craggy texture to oven-fried chicken, so I wasn't surprised when they worked here, too. On a whim, I added cornstarch to them before dredging the meat. Once swollen, the starch granules again worked their magic, turning the flakes even crispier in the hot fat.

With all three elements of my breading recalibrated, I prepped one last batch to fry. But just as I was about to put the chops in the pan, I was called away from the kitchen. When I returned about 10 minutes later, I threw them into a hot skillet as usual. To my surprise, the breading on these chops seemed practically soldered to the meat. Could the stronger grip have something to do with the resting period? To check, I fried up two batches of chops: one fried immediately after coating, and the other rested for 10 minutes first. Sure enough, the coating on the rested chops had a noticeably firmer grasp on the meat. Why? According to our science editor, the brief rest gave the cornstarch layer extra time to absorb moisture to form an even stickier paste. He also suggested a final step to ensure that the crust stayed put: lightly scoring the chops. Etching a shallow crosshatch pattern onto the meat's surface released moisture and tacky proteins that gave the coating an exceptionally solid footing.

With a crispy, flavorful coating that stayed glued to the meat, my pan-fried pork chops were just about perfect. To add a little pizzazz I also created a spiced-up variation. With or without the spice rub, this approach has banished bland pork chops from my table for good.

Crispy Pan-Fried Pork Chops

SERVES 4

We prefer natural to enhanced pork (pork that has been injected with a salt solution to increase moistness and flavor). Don't let the chops drain on the paper towels for longer than 30 seconds per side, or the heat will steam the crust and make it soggy.

⅔ cup cornstarch
1 cup buttermilk
2 tablespoons Dijon mustard
1 garlic clove, minced
3 cups cornflakes
Salt and pepper
8 (3- to 4-ounce) boneless pork chops, ½ to ¾ inch thick, trimmed
⅔ cup vegetable oil
Lemon wedges

1. Place ⅓ cup cornstarch in shallow dish. In second shallow dish, whisk buttermilk, mustard, and garlic until combined. Process cornflakes, ½ teaspoon salt, ½ teaspoon pepper, and remaining ⅓ cup cornstarch in food processor until cornflakes are finely ground, about 10 seconds. Transfer cornflake mixture to third shallow dish.

2. Adjust oven rack to middle position and heat oven to 200 degrees. Cut 1⁄16-inch-deep slits on both sides of chops, spaced ½ inch apart, in crosshatch pattern. Season chops with salt and pepper. Dredge 1 chop in cornstarch; shake off excess. Using tongs, coat with buttermilk mixture; let excess drip off. Coat with cornflake mixture; gently pat off excess. Transfer coated chop to wire rack set in rimmed baking sheet and repeat with remaining chops. Let coated chops stand for 10 minutes.

3. Heat ⅓ cup oil in 12-inch nonstick skillet over medium-high heat until shimmering. Place 4 chops in skillet and cook until golden brown and crispy, 2 to 5 minutes. Carefully flip chops and continue to cook until second side is golden brown and crispy and chops register 145 degrees, 2 to 5 minutes longer. Transfer chops to paper towel–lined plate and let drain for 30 seconds on each side. Transfer to clean wire rack set in rimmed baking sheet, then transfer to oven to keep warm. Discard oil in skillet and wipe clean with paper towels. Repeat process with remaining ⅓ cup oil and remaining 4 chops. Serve with lemon wedges.

WHERE BREADED COATINGS GO WRONG

The components of a traditional breading—flour, beaten egg, and bread crumbs—present special challenges when applied to juicy pork chops. Here's how we ensured a crust that stays put and packs plenty of crunch.

PROBLEM Gummy patches under the coating
SOLUTION We swap flour—the usual breading base coat—for cornstarch. Unlike flour, cornstarch contains no protein, so it cooks up lighter and crispier.

PROBLEM Breading pulls away
SOLUTION Instead of the typical egg wash, which puffs up when cooked and contributes to a heavier coating that can pull away from the meat, we use buttermilk as the second layer. It makes for a lighter shell that clings nicely to the chops.

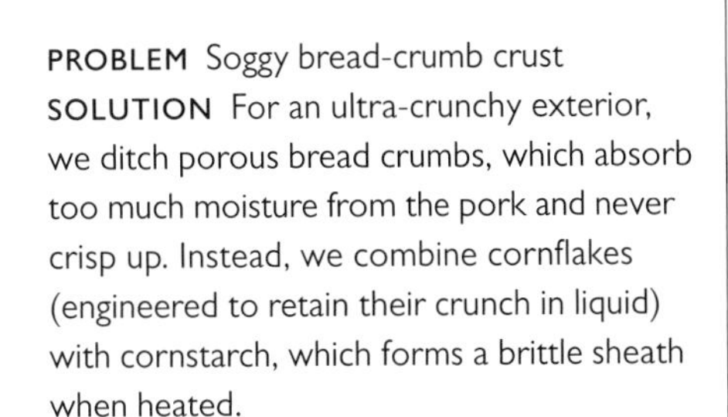

PROBLEM Soggy bread-crumb crust
SOLUTION For an ultra-crunchy exterior, we ditch porous bread crumbs, which absorb too much moisture from the pork and never crisp up. Instead, we combine cornflakes (engineered to retain their crunch in liquid) with cornstarch, which forms a brittle sheath when heated.

variation

Crispy Pan-Fried Pork Chops with Latin Spice Rub

Combine 1½ teaspoons ground cumin, 1½ teaspoons chili powder, ¾ teaspoon ground coriander, ⅛ teaspoon ground cinnamon, and ⅛ teaspoon red pepper flakes in bowl. Omit pepper; coat chops with spice rub after seasoning with salt in step 2.

GETTING A BETTER GRIP

Besides rethinking the ingredients in our coating, we came up with two other quick tricks to make sure the breading stays glued to the chop.

SCORE Making shallow cuts in the chops' surface releases juices and sticky meat proteins that dampen the cornstarch and help the coating adhere.

REST Letting the chops sit for 10 minutes after coating gives the cornstarch more time to absorb liquid and turn into an adhesive paste.

GRILLED GLAZED PORK TENDERLOIN ROAST

DAN SOUZA, *July/August 2013*

Pork tenderloin is wonderfully tender and versatile, it doesn't require much prep, and it's relatively inexpensive. But alas, this cut also comes with a certain set of challenges. Because tenderloin is so incredibly lean, it's highly susceptible to drying out during cooking. Then there's its ungainly tapered shape: By the time the large end hits a perfect medium (140 degrees), the skinnier tail is guaranteed to be overdone. And while my favorite way to prepare mild meats like tenderloin is grilling (to develop a rich, meaty crust), extreme heat and natural fluctuations in temperature make this hard to do well. I wanted to find a way to make grilled pork tenderloin a bit more foolproof and at the same time elevate this cut above its "casual supper" status to something more special and elegant.

A JUICY STORY

Keeping meat of any kind juicy on the grill is a perennial challenge. In the test kitchen, we have a couple of tricks for addressing the problem, namely salting or brining. Both techniques introduce salt into the flesh, where it tenderizes the meat and increases water retention. Using our preferred type of pork, unenhanced (or natural)—meaning that it has not been injected with a solution of water, salt, and sodium phosphate—I ran a side-by-side test in which I salted and brined a few tenderloins, slicked them with oil, and grilled them. Tasters reported that while both options proved juicier and more evenly seasoned than an untreated control, the brined samples were the most succulent. Settling on brining, I moved on to another variable that affects juiciness: grill setup.

When it comes to grilling delicate pork tenderloin, two roasts are better than one.

Many pork tenderloin recipes call for grilling the meat directly over a hot fire the entire time. The result? A well-browned exterior with a thick band of dry, overcooked meat below its surface—no thanks. A better approach, we've found, is to employ a combination high-low method: High heat provides great browning, which means great flavor, and low heat cooks meat evenly. And recently, we've favored cooking first over low heat followed by searing over high heat. During its initial stay on the cooler side of the grill, the meat's surface warms and dries, making for fast, efficient browning (and therefore precluding overcooking) when it hits the hotter part of the grate. Sure enough, when I gave this approach a try, I produced meat with rosy interiors surrounded by thin, flavorful crusts—at least at the thick ends. Unsurprisingly, the thin, tapered ends of the tenderloins (I was cooking two in order to serve six guests) were terribly overdone.

IT TAKES TWO

There was nothing I could do to the grill setup to make the unevenly shaped meat cook evenly, so what about altering the tenderloins themselves? Assuming the role of mad butcher, I pounded and portioned untold samples in search of a more uniform shape. Flattening the thicker end of the roast certainly made for more even cooking, but it also turned the cut into what looked like a gigantic, malformed pork chop. Slicing the tenderloin into medallions produced an awkward group of scallop-size pieces that were fussy to grill.

After a long, unsuccessful afternoon, I stood before the last two raw tenderloins on my cutting board. A light bulb went on: Why not tie them together? If I stacked the tenderloins the way that shoes come packed in a box—with the thick end of one nestled against the thin end of the other—I'd produce a single, evenly shaped roast. I gave it a shot, fastening together my brined double-wide roast with lengths of kitchen twine and brushing it with oil before heading out to the hot grill. About 35 minutes later, I had a piece of meat that was perfectly cooked from one end to the other. This larger roast took longer to come up to temperature, but the added grill time was a boon to taste: More time over the fire meant more smoky grill flavor.

These successes aside, there was still an obstacle in my way. When I carved my impressive-looking roast, each slice inevitably flopped apart into two pieces. While this wasn't a deal breaker, I was eager to see if I could establish a more permanent bond between the tenderloins.

THE GLUE THAT BINDS

Trying to get meat to stick together might sound unorthodox, but it's something that happens naturally all the time, at least with ground meat. In sausages, burgers, meatballs, and meatloaf, tiny individual pieces of protein fuse together to form a cohesive whole. I wasn't working with ground meat, but maybe I could use it as inspiration.

It turns out that anytime meat is damaged (such as during grinding, slicing, or even pounding), sticky proteins are released. The proteins' gluey texture is what makes it possible to form a cohesive burger from nothing but ground beef. If salt is added—as it is to make sausage—the proteins become even tackier. When heated, the protein sets into a solid structure, effectively binding the meat together. To see if I could use this information for my tenderloins, I tried roughing up their surfaces in a variety of ways: lightly whacking them with a meat mallet, scraping them with a fork, and rubbing them vigorously with coarse salt. I tested these methods before

brining, after brining, and both before and after brining. In the end, I found my solution.

The key to getting two tenderloins to bind together? A few simple scrapes of a fork along the length of each one before brining, followed by a very thorough drying after brining. The scrapes, acting much like grinding, released plenty of sticky proteins, which the salty brine made even stickier. Finally, thorough drying ensured that moisture wouldn't interfere with this bond during cooking (the sticky mixture continued to exude from the meat even after I blotted off moisture). The technique is simple and, while not perfect (some slices had better cling than others), it provided me with a platter of attractive, mostly intact slices. Hurdle cleared, I turned my attention to flavoring the roast.

GLAZED AND INFUSED

I wanted to dress up my beautifully browned pork tenderloin roast, and a bold, burnished glaze seemed like the ideal choice. Most glazes contain sugar, which caramelizes when exposed to heat, deepening flavor. But I wanted to add still more complexity. And I knew how to do it: by including glutamate-rich ingredients that enhance savory flavor. With this in mind, I combined glutamate-rich miso with sugar, mustard, mirin, and ginger. For my next version, I created a sweet and spicy glaze that benefited from the glutamates found in sweet and tangy hoisin sauce. When I tried out these new glazes on the pork, I was surprised by how much more flavor they contributed. It turns out that pork has a high concentration of nucleotides. When glutamates and nucleotides are combined, they have a synergistic effect that magnifies savory flavor significantly more than glutamates alone do.

The only thing left was to refine how I applied the glaze. After slowly grilling my roast on the cooler side of the grill, I slid it to the hotter side to brown. I then glazed one side at a time, allowing the glaze to char before repeating the process with the other three sides. I also reserved some glaze to add an extra blast of flavor at the table. Time to get the party started.

Grilled Glazed Pork Tenderloin Roast

SERVES 6

Since brining is a key step in having the two tenderloins stick together, we don't recommend using enhanced pork in this recipe.

2 (1-pound) pork tenderloins, trimmed
Salt and pepper
Vegetable oil
1 recipe glaze (recipes follow)

1. Lay tenderloins on cutting board, flat side (side opposite where silverskin was) up. Holding thick end of 1 tenderloin with paper towels and using dinner fork, scrape flat side lengthwise from end to end 5 times, until surface is completely covered with shallow grooves. Repeat with second tenderloin. Dissolve 3 tablespoons salt in 1½ quarts cold water in large container. Submerge tenderloins in brine and let stand at room temperature for 1 hour.

2. Remove tenderloins from brine and pat completely dry with paper towels. Lay 1 tenderloin, scraped side up, on cutting board and lay second tenderloin, scraped side down, on top so that thick end of 1 tenderloin matches up with thin end of other. Spray five 14-inch lengths of kitchen twine thoroughly with vegetable oil spray; evenly space twine underneath tenderloins and tie. Brush roast with vegetable oil and season with pepper. Transfer ⅓ cup glaze to bowl for grilling; reserve remaining glaze for serving.

3A. *For a charcoal grill:* Open bottom vent completely. Light large chimney starter filled with charcoal briquettes (6 quarts). When top coals are partially covered with ash, pour into steeply banked pile against side of grill. Set cooking grate in place, cover, and open lid vent completely. Heat grill until hot, about 5 minutes.

3B. *For a gas grill:* Turn all burners to high, cover, and heat grill until hot, about 15 minutes. Leave primary burner on high and turn off other burner(s).

4. Clean and oil cooking grate. Place roast on cooler side of grill, cover, and cook until meat registers 115 degrees, 22 to 28 minutes, flipping and rotating halfway through cooking.

5. Slide roast to hotter side of grill and cook until lightly browned on all sides, 4 to 6 minutes. Brush top of roast with about 1 tablespoon glaze and grill, glaze side down, until glaze begins to char, 2 to 3 minutes; repeat glazing and grilling with remaining 3 sides of roast, until meat registers 140 degrees.

6. Transfer roast to carving board, tent with aluminum foil, and let rest for 10 minutes. Remove twine and slice into ½-inch-thick slices. Serve with remaining glaze.

glazes

Miso Glaze

MAKES ABOUT ¾ CUP

3 tablespoons sake
3 tablespoons mirin
⅓ cup white miso paste
¼ cup sugar
2 teaspoons Dijon mustard
1 teaspoon rice vinegar
¼ teaspoon grated fresh ginger
¼ teaspoon toasted sesame oil

Bring sake and mirin to boil in small saucepan over medium heat. Whisk in miso and sugar until smooth, about 30 seconds. Remove pan from heat and continue to whisk until sugar is dissolved, about 1 minute. Whisk in mustard, vinegar, ginger, and sesame oil until smooth.

Sweet and Spicy Hoisin Glaze

MAKES ABOUT ¾ CUP

1 teaspoon vegetable oil
3 garlic cloves, minced
1 teaspoon grated fresh ginger
½ teaspoon red pepper flakes
½ cup hoisin sauce
2 tablespoons soy sauce
1 tablespoon rice vinegar

Heat oil in small saucepan over medium heat until shimmering. Add garlic, ginger, and pepper flakes; cook until fragrant, about 30 seconds. Whisk in hoisin and soy sauce until smooth. Remove pan from heat and stir in vinegar.

INTRODUCING MEXICAN PULLED PORK

CHARLES KELSEY, *May/June 2008*

For pork lovers, few things can top the rich flavor and supple texture of Southern-style barbecued pulled pork. But to cook it, you have to sit outside by your smoker all day. So I was intrigued when I learned that carnitas, Mexico's version of shredded pork, is cooked indoors. Spanish for "little meats," this taquería staple is used as a filling in tacos and burritos and boasts tender chunks of pork with a lightly crisped, caramelized exterior. Unlike barbecued pulled pork, where the spice rub and tangy sauce are prominent, in carnitas, the flavor of the pork, subtly accented by earthy oregano and sour orange, takes center stage.

Most Mexican restaurants prepare carnitas by gently frying well-marbled chunks of pork in gallons of lard or oil. But home cooks often forgo all the lard in favor of a more manageable method: simmering the meat in a seasoned broth in the oven and then sautéing it in some of the rendered fat. The latter method definitely sounded more appealing, but I wondered if simmering and sautéing could possibly yield the same results. I tried it anyway, gently cooking the meat in a couple quarts of water spiked with citrus and other typical carnitas flavorings, and pulling the pork out after it was softened. I then fried the meat in fat I'd skimmed from the cooking liquid.

To my surprise, the pork turned out tender, with a browned exterior and reasonably good flavor. If I'd gotten these results without even trying, surely with a little work I could do even better. But I wouldn't consider myself successful unless I could create carnitas with the addictive taste and texture of the deep-fried versions I've enjoyed in Mexican restaurants.

POWERS OF REDUCTION

I was using a boneless Boston butt, the cut most carnitas recipes call for and the same cut American cooks use for barbecued pulled pork. Though this shoulder roast contains a good amount of fat, which can translate to deep flavor, all the liquid in the pot washed out the taste. Over the course of several tests, I went from 8 cups of liquid down to 2, the bare minimum for cooking a 3- to 4-pound roast. It was better, but tasters still thought the pork flavor was not concentrated enough. Swapping out the water for chicken broth made little difference. And browning the meat before braising it also failed to intensify its taste. So where was the pork flavor going?

Down the drain, that's where. I'd been discarding the leftover cooking liquid after removing the meat and skimming off the fat. To capture that lost flavor, I would need to figure out how to reincorporate the liquid into the dish. Perhaps I could reduce the liquid, as the French do in their intensely flavored sauces. Back in the kitchen, I braised another batch of meat in the oven. This time, instead of pouring off the broth after I removed the pork, I left it in the pot, reducing it on the stovetop until it had the consistency of a thick, syrupy glaze.

FROM BRAISING TO BROILING

With the glaze at hand, I was left wondering what my next step should be. If I added the pork back to the pot, I was afraid the glaze would burn and stick to the bottom. Because I needed to get the exterior of the pork to crisp, more cooking was a must. What about tossing the pork with the glaze and putting it into the oven? I spread the coated meat on a rimmed baking sheet and turned on the broiler. To ensure that neither glaze nor meat would burn, I placed the sheet on the lower-middle rack. Minutes later, the carnitas emerged from the broiler beautifully caramelized, the shredded parts of the meat transformed into crisp wisps with wonderfully rich flavor. The only problem: super-greasy meat.

The greasiness was my fault; I had not defatted the cooking liquid before reducing it. But when I did skim away some of the fat, I ended up with a reduction that was thin and sticky and didn't flavor the meat as well. Going straight to the source, I trimmed as much fat as possible from the pork butt before cooking. This got rid of the greasiness, but it also left the carnitas too dry. Finally, I landed on the solution: Instead of spreading the carnitas directly on a baking sheet, I placed the meat on a rack set inside of it. The rack elevated the pieces of pork, allowing excess fat to drip down while the glaze stuck to the meat. The better air circulation under and around the pork also made for crispier shreds of meat.

A combination of braising and broiling produces tender pork with crisp, caramelized edges.

All that was left was to refine the flavors in the braising liquid. In traditional versions, other flavors take a back seat to the pork, and my recipe followed suit. Instead of garlic, I stuck with the mellow sweetness of onion. To emulate Mexican sour oranges, I used a mix of fresh lime and orange juices, adding the spent orange halves to the pot to impart floral notes. Bay leaves and oregano gave the meat aromatic accents. Cumin, though not a typical ingredient in carnitas, brought an earthy dimension that complemented the other flavors.

Tucked into warm corn tortillas, the mouth-watering taste and texture of my carnitas kept tasters coming back for more. And I hadn't needed to use a speck of lard.

Mexican Pulled Pork (Carnitas)

SERVES 6

We like serving carnitas spooned into small corn tortillas, taco-style, but it can also be used as a filling for tamales, enchiladas, and burritos. In addition to the traditional toppings—finely chopped white or red onion, fresh cilantro, thinly sliced radishes, sour cream, and lime wedges—we recommend serving the pork with guacamole. Pork butt roast is often labeled Boston butt in the supermarket.

1 (3½- to 4-pound) boneless pork butt roast, fat trimmed to ⅛ inch, cut into 2-inch pieces
2 cups water
1 onion, peeled and halved
2 tablespoons lime juice
1 teaspoon dried oregano
1 teaspoon ground cumin
2 bay leaves
Salt and pepper
1 orange, halved
18 (6-inch) corn tortillas, warmed

1. Adjust oven rack to lower-middle position and heat oven to 300 degrees. Combine pork, water, onion, lime juice, oregano, cumin, bay leaves, 1 teaspoon salt, and ½ teaspoon pepper in Dutch oven (liquid should just barely cover meat). Juice orange into bowl and remove any seeds (you should have about ⅓ cup juice). Add juice and spent orange halves to pot.

2. Bring mixture to simmer over medium-high heat, stirring occasionally. Cover pot and transfer to oven; cook until meat is soft and falls apart when prodded with fork, about 2 hours, flipping pieces of meat once during cooking.

3. Remove pot from oven and heat broiler. Using slotted spoon, transfer pork to bowl; discard onion, orange halves, and bay leaves from cooking liquid (do not skim fat from liquid). Carefully place pot over high heat (handles will be hot) and simmer liquid, stirring frequently, until thick and syrupy (spatula should leave wide trail when dragged through glaze), 8 to 12 minutes. (You should have about 1 cup reduced liquid.)

4. Using 2 forks, pull each piece of pork in half. Fold in reduced liquid; season with salt and pepper to taste. Spread pork in even layer on wire rack set in rimmed baking sheet or on broiler pan (meat should cover almost entire surface of rack or broiler pan). Place baking sheet on lower-middle rack and broil until top of meat is well browned (but not charred) and edges are slightly crispy, 5 to 8 minutes. Using wide metal spatula, flip pieces of meat and continue to broil until top is well browned and edges are slightly crispy, 5 to 8 minutes longer. (Finished pork can be refrigerated for up to 2 days.) Serve with tortillas.

SOUTH VERSUS SOUTH OF THE BORDER

Southern-style barbecued pulled pork (at left) is cooked outdoors in a smoker to create uniformly tender meat that's served drenched in barbecue sauce. The pork in our carnitas recipe (at right) is cooked in the oven and features a soft interior and a crisp, caramelized exterior complemented by garnishes, not sauce.

TENDER AND SAUCY

CRISP AND CARAMELIZED

MAKING INDOOR PULLED PORK

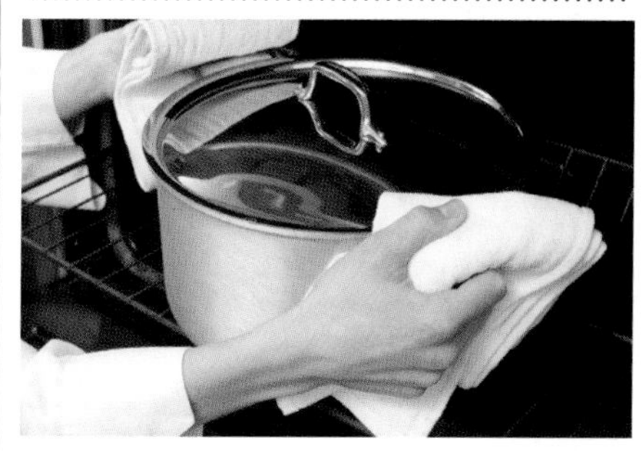

1. **OVEN-BRAISE** For fall-apart tender meat, oven-braise the pork at a low temperature in a covered Dutch oven for about 2 hours.

2. **REDUCE** Remove the pork and reduce the braising liquid to a glaze thick enough for a spatula to leave a trail when pulled through it.

3. **BROIL** Toss the pork with the glaze and broil it on the lower-middle rack in the oven to yield well-browned meat with crisp edges.

DON'T CUT THE FAT

Leaving a ⅛-inch layer of fat on the pork is critical to imparting the best flavor and texture to the final dish. Overtrimming the meat will lead to dry, bland carnitas.

TOO LEAN

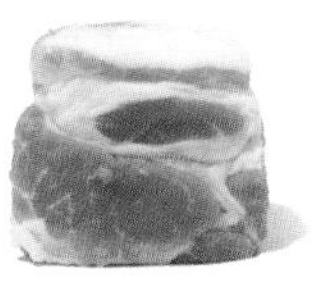

A PERFECT 10

SMOKY PULLED PORK ON A GAS GRILL

LAN LAM, *July/August 2014*

When it comes to making pulled pork on the grill, as barbecue purists will tell you, it's hard—if not impossible—to produce the same quality of smoke on a gas grill as you can over charcoal. That said, a gas grill is infinitely more convenient. There's no messy setup or cleanup, and you can cook a large pork roast on the grill the whole time instead of finishing it in the oven or dealing with refueling charcoal.

On behalf of those who embrace convenience (or don't have a charcoal grill), I set out to nail down a method for smoking over gas, delivering pulled pork that would rival that made with a charcoal grill. The only rule I set for myself: I would not cheat by using liquid smoke or any presmoked material (such as smoked tea leaves).

PRIMING THE PORK

I knew I would use pork butt because it's collagen-rich and has the right amount of intramuscular fat. During cooking, that fat renders while the collagen transforms into gelatin, together giving pulled pork its tender texture. Cutting the roast into thirds not only lessened the cooking time (which is usually about 7 hours) but also increased the surface area that smoke could cling to. I would add a spice rub later, but for now I decided to sprinkle on just salt to make it easier to assess smoke flavor. I wrapped the salted pieces tightly in plastic wrap and left them to sit overnight in the refrigerator, which would season the meat and change its protein structure so that it could retain more of its juices during cooking.

The next day, I moved out to the grill. I knew from experience that I would need to cook the pork until it reached an internal temperature of 195 degrees: If cooked any less, the meat would be chewy and tough, but if it went too much above 200 degrees, it would start to dry out. For the bulk of the cooking time, though, I wanted to keep the meat between 160 and 180 degrees, the range in which the connective tissue will slowly break down. To do this, a low-and-slow cooking method—using indirect heat and maintaining a grill temperature of around 300 degrees—would be key. A couple of water-filled pie plates under the grate would catch any juices and prevent them from burning. The plates would also create a moist environment that would keep the exterior of the pork from drying out and help smoke stick to the meat. A few quick tests (without smoke at this point) established a cooking time of 4 to 5 hours. With the framework of my recipe settled, I was ready to perfect the smoke.

Soaking just half of the wood chips and folding them into careful packets maximizes smoky flavor in the pork.

IN SEARCH OF SMOKE

I started by taking a close look at our procedures for using wood chips on a gas grill. The goal is to get chips to smolder slowly and consistently; if they ignite and burn up quickly, they can give the food a sooty, acrid flavor. We usually address this concern by soaking the chips in water for 15 minutes and then wrapping the soaked chips in a foil packet and poking a few holes in it to let out the smoke. The packet is placed on the primary burner, below the cooking grate. Starting with the flame on high gets the smoke going (and preheats the grill); we then adjust the heat to low to maintain the appropriate barbecuing temperature.

While these directions have always delivered acceptable results, they are also open to interpretation. Different size packets punctured with different-size openings can produce smoke flavor that ranges from decent to basically nonexistent. Obviously, I would need to come up with a very specific set of instructions for making the packets that would produce a consistent amount of smoke. The first step was to be as precise as possible about the quantity of chips, which, as persnickety as it might sound, means weighing them, not measuring them by volume. When barbecuing meat over a long period of time, we have typically called for 4 cups of chips, so I started with 4 cups of chips weighing 9½ ounces.

Next I experimented with the size of the foil packets. Wrapping all the chips in a single packet was unwieldy. I landed on dividing the chips between two 8 by 4½-inch packets, each of which sat nicely over the burner. I then tried cutting a number of openings of various sizes and shapes into the foil. I poked holes in some packets and cut slits in others. The openings control how much smoke goes out as well as how much oxygen comes in. When the oxygen was too plentiful (i.e., the openings were too large), the chips quickly burned up instead of smoldering. But if the openings were too small or too few, the chips didn't get enough oxygen to even smolder. Two evenly spaced 2-inch slits were best, producing a consistent stream of smoke. I also realized that I needed to be careful about how I arranged the packets on the burner, since the bars of the cooking grate could block the slits and prevent smoke from escaping.

I realized that soaking the chips wasn't preventing them from igniting; it was simply delaying the onset of smoke. Because I was so carefully controlling the oxygen availability, soaked or not, the chips in my packets weren't going up in flames, and in either case a packet filled with 2 cups of chips always produced about 45 to 60 minutes of smoke.

Since I had a set amount of smoke to work with, would it be better to use two packets of unsoaked chips, which would allow me to inundate the meat with smoke at the beginning of cooking, or would producing a

smaller stream of smoke over a longer period by using one packet of soaked chips and one packet of unsoaked chips be better? Our recipe for Smoked Chicken held a few answers. First, more smoke flavor gets absorbed early in the cooking process, since smoke contains mostly water-soluble compounds, and meat contains more water at the beginning of cooking. Second, a piece of food can absorb only so much smoke flavor at any given point. Finally, when the meat is at its smoke-absorption capacity, some smoke drifts away through the grill vents, but some of it can break down on the food's surface, giving it a harsh, acrid taste.

I ran two tests: I cooked one batch over two packets of dry chips, and another batch over one packet of soaked chips and one dry. While it was a close call, a handful of tasters felt that the batch in which both packets were dry and thus inundated with smoke was acrid-tasting. Stretching out the smoke over a longer period of time ensured that the pork could absorb maximum smoke gradually without off-flavors.

I wanted to boost the smokiness just a little more, but since I couldn't fit more wood on the grill, I needed to find a way to get more of the existing smoke into the meat. As it cooked, the pork was releasing smoke-infused juices into the water-filled pan below. Why should that flavor go to waste? When the smoke petered out after the first 1½ hours of cooking, I transferred the meat to a disposable aluminum roasting pan so any juices that released during the remaining cooking time would be collected and I could stir some back into the meat after shredding it. (Using all the juices made the final consistency too liquidy.)

I also wondered if there was a way to get more smoke to cling to the meat, instead of letting it escape through the vents. A coworker noted that my clothes smelled smokier on cold days: Since the surface of my coat was cold, when the smoke particles came in contact with it, they quickly changed from gas to solid, thus clinging to my coat rather than drifting off into the air. Could the same logic be applied to the pork? For my next test, I waited to pull the pork from the fridge until I was ready to start cooking. With these last tweaks, I'd really nailed a deep smoke flavor.

It was time to focus on the dry rub and the sauce. A simple mixture of paprika, brown sugar, and pepper rubbed onto the pork along with the salt added depth without taking over; it also provided color and helped create an appealing bark-like crust. For the sauce, a combination of cider vinegar, ketchup, brown sugar, and red pepper flakes cut cleanly through the pork's richness and helped amplify the smoky flavor.

Finally, in a blind side-by-side tasting of my gas-grilled pulled pork and pulled pork made on a charcoal grill, tasters unanimously agreed that my gas-grilled version boasted not just as much smoke flavor but, in fact, more. With this method, gas grill owners—or at least those who are willing to be very precise in their method—never have to feel sheepish about making pulled pork.

Smoky Pulled Pork on a Gas Grill

SERVES 8 TO 10

Pork butt roast is often labeled Boston butt in the supermarket. We developed this recipe with hickory chips, though other varieties of hardwood can be used. (We do not recommend mesquite chips.) Before beginning, check your propane tank to make sure that you have at least a half-tank of fuel. If you happen to run out of fuel, you can move the pork to a preheated 300-degree oven to finish cooking. Serve the pulled pork on white bread or hamburger buns with pickles and coleslaw.

Pork

Kosher salt and pepper
2 teaspoons paprika
2 teaspoons packed light brown sugar
1 (5-pound) boneless pork butt roast, trimmed
9½ ounces wood chips (4 cups)
2 (9-inch) disposable aluminum pie plates
1 (13 by 9-inch) disposable aluminum roasting pan

Vinegar Sauce

2 cups cider vinegar
2 tablespoons ketchup
2 teaspoons packed light brown sugar
1 teaspoon red pepper flakes
1 teaspoon kosher salt

1. ***For the pork:*** Combine 5 teaspoons salt, 2½ teaspoons pepper, paprika, and sugar in small bowl. Cut pork against grain into 3 equal slabs. Rub salt mixture into pork, making sure meat is evenly coated. Wrap pork tightly in plastic wrap and refrigerate for at least 6 hours or up to 24 hours.
2. Just before grilling, soak 2 cups wood chips in water for 15 minutes, then drain. Using large piece of heavy-duty aluminum foil, wrap soaked chips in 8 by 4½-inch foil packet. (Make sure chips do not poke holes in sides or bottom of packet.) Repeat with remaining 2 cups unsoaked chips. Cut 2 evenly spaced 2-inch slits in top of each packet.
3. Remove cooking grate and place wood chip packets directly on primary burner. Place disposable pie plates, each filled with 3 cups water, directly on other burner(s). Set grate in place, turn all burners to high, cover, and heat grill until hot and wood chips are smoking, about 15 minutes. Turn primary burner to medium and turn off other burner(s). (Adjust primary burner as needed to maintain grill temperature of 300 degrees.)
4. Clean and oil cooking grate. Place pork on cooler side of grill, directly over water pans; cover; and smoke for 1½ hours.
5. Transfer pork to disposable pan. Return disposable pan to cooler side of grill and continue to cook until meat registers 200 degrees, 2½ to 3 hours.
6. Transfer pork to carving board and let rest for 20 minutes. Pour juices from disposable pan into fat separator and let stand for 5 minutes.
7. ***For the vinegar sauce:*** While pork rests, whisk all ingredients together in bowl. Using 2 forks, shred pork into bite-size pieces. Stir ⅓ cup defatted juices and ½ cup sauce into pork. Serve, passing remaining sauce separately.

OVEN-BARBECUED RIBS WORTH MAKING

MATTHEW CARD, *January/February 2006*

The barbecue season for much of the country is cruelly short. When the temperature plunges as fall drifts into winter, it's virtually impossible to maintain the modest grill temperatures required to turn tough cuts of meat tender. When the craving strikes for crisp-crusted, smoky spareribs in midwinter, many of us have just two options: Head to the local BBQ shack or attempt them in the oven. But is it really possible to replicate outdoor ribs inside?

Barbecue is as much cooking method as flavoring agent. The low temperature and steady blanket of hardwood smoke work almost like braising, rendering the collagen to rich-tasting, silky gelatin. The low temperatures and moist environment are easy to replicate in the oven; the smoke, by contrast, is not.

The indoor barbecued-rib recipes I found were a dubious lot. Most smothered racks in smoke-flavored sauce and baked them slowly. Sure, the ribs tasted OK—slather an old shoe in smoky sauce and it will taste good—but none possessed the deep, rich flavor of true barbecue. Others slicked the ribs with liquid smoke, smearing on a dry rub just before baking—not much better. There's a fundamental difference between ribs that taste of smoke and ribs that are smoked.

SMOKE GETS IN MY EYES

There was a third option: indoor smoking. Indoor smokers are essentially roasting pans fitted with a wire rack and a tight-fitting lid. Shredded wood chips are dusted across the pan bottom, the food is set on the rack, and the pan is sealed. The pan is heated on the stovetop to ignite the chips, after which it enters the oven to finish cooking. Some indoor smokers work fairly well, but the designs are so basic that I opted to rig one up from equipment I had on hand.

Before I got ahead of myself, I had to choose the ribs. For outdoor barbecue, I favor St. Louis–style spareribs—pork spareribs (located near the belly) trimmed of skirt meat and excess cartilage—and saw no reason to change.

Squeezing the ribs onto a wire rack in the kitchen's biggest roasting pan, I tossed in a handful of hickory chips and sealed it with foil. I slid the pan over a burner set on high and waited. And waited. Smoke finally began seeping out from the foil long after I was afraid the pan would melt from such heat. Once the alarm sounded, I guessed the ribs were smoky enough and transferred the pan to a 250-degree oven to finish.

Lapsang Souchong tea leaves imbue the ribs with smoky flavor—no grill necessary.

The ribs tasted smoky alright, but this method certainly had flaws: It was hard finding a pan large enough to fit the ribs, it took me three trips to find wood chips (during off-season, most hardware stores switch out grilling paraphernalia for snow shovels), and the billowing smoke made the test kitchen reek of hickory for days.

Could I move the entire process to the oven, thereby containing the smoke? With no direct high heat, I could also switch to a rimmed baking sheet, which had enough room for the ribs to lie flat. I cranked the oven to 400 degrees, slid the ribs inside, and, once again, waited for smoke. An hour passed without the faintest whiff. After 1½ hours, I pulled the pan out and found gray, greasy, gristly-looking ribs without a hint of smoke flavor.

Higher heat? After turning up the temperature in 25-degree increments, I finally smelled smoke at 500 degrees. Where there's smoke, there should be flavor, but no such luck. The oven still wasn't hot enough to ignite the wood.

TEATIME

Desperate, I had a bottle of liquid smoke in hand when a colleague suggested another option: tea smoking. Chinese cooks smoke a variety of foodstuffs over smoldering black tea. So I replaced the wood chips with loose tea, closed the oven door, and—while the leaves didn't burn—the distinct aroma of tea that filled the kitchen surprised me. The ribs tasted faintly of it, too. Perhaps outright combustion wasn't necessary—"roasting" was enough to unlock the tea's flavor. Smoky-tasting Lapsang Souchong tea leaves, cured over smoldering pine or cypress boughs, seemed like the perfect candidate.

With the oven set to high heat (the leaves scattered across the bottom of the baking sheet), I could smell smoke in minutes. After 30 minutes, the ribs tasted decidedly smoky. Grinding the leaves to a fine powder (thereby maximizing the tea-to-baking-surface ratio) imbued the ribs with an even deeper flavor. Neither as sweet as hickory nor as sharp as mesquite, the tea perfumed the ribs with a rich smokiness far deeper than that lent by barbecue sauce or liquid smoke.

FULL STEAM AHEAD

The ribs were smoky, but the high heat required to "roast" the tea had also made them inedibly tough. The solution lay in the freezer. Chilling the rib racks as the oven preheated cooled them enough that they could withstand a very high heat and quickly absorb "smoke" without toughening. After just half an hour at 500 degrees, my prechilled ribs had absorbed as much of the smoky flavor as possible, and I could decrease the oven temperature dramatically.

To cook the ribs, I experimented with temperatures ranging between 200 and 300 degrees; 250 degrees proved the best compromise between texture and time. Within 2 hours—including the "smoking" time—the ribs were fork-tender, though moist and gummy. A pass under the high

heat of the broiler quickly turned the wet exterior into a chewy, crispy crust.

Following the lead of several recipes, I tried adding liquid to the pan (and resealing the foil to contain the steam) to see if an even moister environment could improve things. The ribs were ready in half the time. The moister the heat, the faster the heat transfer—right in line with the mechanics of braising. Water worked fine but added no flavor; apple juice—a common "mop" used to keep meat moist in outdoor barbecue—added welcome sweet depth.

WET OR DRY?

Smoky and tender but slightly bland, the ribs were ready for some spice. Barbecued ribs can be cooked "dry"—coated with spices and served as is—or "wet," brushed with sauce shortly before serving. I've always had a weakness for the latter, but tasters argued that the big-flavored sauce masked the tea's smokiness.

I knew I wanted to keep the rub simple to make way for the ribs' smoky, porky flavor so I opted for a combination of salt, pepper, paprika, cayenne, chili powder, and brown sugar. A thin slathering of mustard brought just the right tangy, sharp kick to the pork and, as an added bonus, helped the spices stick. For extra flavor, I added some minced garlic and a spoonful of ketchup.

Smoky-tasting to the bone, tender to a fault, and judiciously spicy, these ribs are so good I might even make them in midsummer.

Oven-Barbecued Spareribs

SERVES 4

To make this recipe, you will need a baking stone. It's fine if the ribs overlap slightly on the wire rack. Removing the surface fat keeps the ribs from being too greasy, and removing the membrane from the ribs allows the smoke to penetrate both sides of the racks and also makes the ribs easier to eat. Note that the ribs must be coated with the rub and refrigerated for at least 8 hours or up to 24 hours before cooking. Be careful when opening the crimped foil to add the juice, as hot steam and smoke will billow out. Serve these ribs with your favorite barbecue sauce, if desired.

6 tablespoons yellow mustard
2 tablespoons ketchup
3 garlic cloves, minced
3 tablespoons packed brown sugar
1½ tablespoons kosher salt
1 tablespoon paprika
1 tablespoon chili powder
2 teaspoons pepper
½ teaspoon cayenne pepper
2 (2½- to 3-pound) racks St. Louis–style spareribs, trimmed, membrane removed, and each rack cut in half
¼ cup finely ground Lapsang Souchong tea leaves (from about 10 tea bags, or ½ cup loose tea leaves ground to a powder in a spice grinder)
½ cup apple juice

1. Combine mustard, ketchup, and garlic in bowl; combine sugar, salt, paprika, chili powder, pepper, and cayenne in separate bowl. Spread mustard mixture in thin, even layer over both sides of ribs; coat both sides with spice mixture, then wrap ribs in plastic wrap and refrigerate for at least 8 or up to 24 hours.
2. Transfer ribs from refrigerator to freezer for 45 minutes. Adjust oven racks to lowest and upper-middle positions (at least 5 inches below broiler element). Place baking stone on lower rack and heat oven to 500 degrees. Sprinkle tea evenly over bottom of rimmed baking sheet; set wire rack in sheet. Place ribs meat side up on wire rack and cover with heavy-duty aluminum foil, crimping edges tightly to seal. Place sheet on stone and roast ribs for 30 minutes, then reduce oven temperature to 250 degrees, leaving oven door open for 1 minute to cool. While oven is open, carefully open 1 corner of foil and pour apple juice into bottom of sheet; reseal foil. Continue to roast until meat is very tender and begins to pull away from bones, about 1½ hours. (Begin to check ribs after 1 hour; leave loosely covered with foil for remaining cooking time.)
3. Remove foil and carefully flip racks bone side up; place baking sheet on upper rack. Heat broiler; cook ribs until well browned and crisp in spots, 5 to 10 minutes. Flip ribs meat side up and cook until browned and crisp, 5 to 7 minutes longer. Let cool for at least 10 minutes before cutting racks into individual ribs. Serve.

CHOOSING PORK RIBS

There are several types of ribs available, but for our indoor recipe, the choice was clear.

SPARERIBS
Ribs from near the pig's fatty belly. An acceptable choice, but needs a fair amount of home trimming.

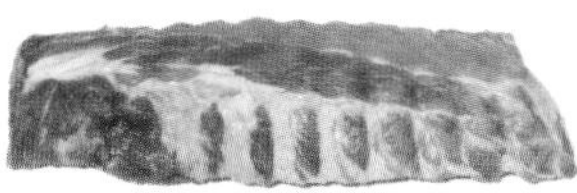

BABY BACK
Smaller, leaner ribs from the (adult) pig's back. Tender, but the meat dries out too quickly for our recipe.

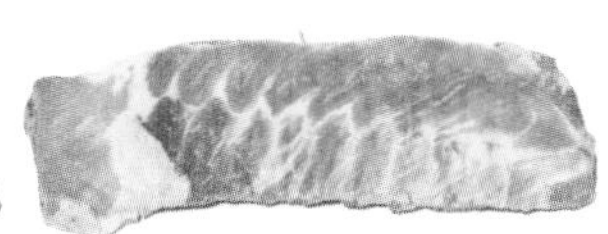

ST. LOUIS STYLE
Spareribs that have been trimmed of skirt meat and excess cartilage. Minimal fuss, and our top choice.

WHERE THERE'S SMOKE

Cured over smoldering pine or cypress, Lapsang Souchong tea brews up so smoky that, as a beverage, it's an acquired taste. But as a flavoring agent, it provides the smokiness missing in most indoor rib recipes. Loose tea leaves and tea bags work equally well. (Twining's Lapsang Souchong tea bags are widely available at supermarkets.)

JUST DON'T ADD WATER

MEMPHIS-STYLE DRY-RUB RIBS

ANDREA GEARY, *July/August 2010*

The sweet, sticky, fall-off-the-bone pork sparerib is the pride of many U.S. cities, but only one—Memphis, Tennessee—can take credit for the dry-rub rib. Unlike the wetter version, dry-rub ribs should be cooked to the precise stage at which they are fully tender and their fat has completely rendered but the meat still clings lightly to the bone and boasts a slightly resilient chew. There's no sauce; instead, a thin cider- or vinegar-based "mop" is brushed across the ribs intermittently during cooking to cool down the meat and prevent the interior moisture from evaporating. In collaboration with long, slow pit smoking, the rub—a mixture of salt, sugar, and spices applied to the rack up to a day before cooking—forms a deeply flavored "bark," or crust, that is the hallmark of Memphis barbecue.

Most rib joints outside the River City don't even attempt to replicate them—and those that have seldom do them justice. To get my fix, I mail-ordered a few racks from beloved landmarks like Charlie Vergos' Rendezvous and Central BBQ. But ribs that have suffered the indignity of being cooked, frozen, packaged, shipped, thawed, and warmed are hardly the same. I was determined to re-create Memphis barbecue on my own turf. That left me with my kettle grill and a tall stack of barbecue cookbooks.

Of the many backyard-friendly recipes I tried, cookbook author David Rosengarten's sweet-spicy, slow-'cued (read: 7-hour) ribs were the clear favorite. Tasters raved about these ribs: They were smoky and tender, encrusted in a thick bark with gentle heat. As for me, I was too tired to eat after nearly a full day tending the grill. There had to be a faster, less fussy route to Memphis.

OUTSIDE IN

First, I needed a proper barbecue setup. For a fire that would maintain the key amount of indirect heat (roughly 250 to 275 degrees) long enough to break down the connective tissue in the ribs, I piled the coals on one side of the grill in what's known as a half-grill fire. To avoid the constant dance of lifting the lid to add more charcoal to keep the heat stabilized, I mounded coals I'd burned for 15 minutes in a chimney starter on top of unlit coals, which would allow me to extend the life of the flame without opening the grill. I also stowed a pan of water underneath the cooking grate on the cooler side of the grill, where it would absorb heat and work to keep the temperature stable, as well as help keep the meat moister.

This relatively hands-off technique kept the grill in the 250-degree range for a full hour and a half—but still nowhere near long enough for the meat to fully tenderize. What about moving the operation indoors? We've often had success combining the smoke of the grill with the steady heat and convenience of the oven to streamline slow-cooked barbecue recipes. The question was the order of operations: grill to oven or oven to grill?

Since a crusty bark was one of the main goals, it made sense to start the ribs in the oven and finish them on the grill, where their exterior could dry out just before serving. I applied my rub—a slight variation on Rosengarten's original, containing a sweet-hot mix of powdered spices, brown sugar, salt, and dried thyme—the day before cooking (standard procedure for these ribs). I then wrapped the rubbed ribs in foil (easier than mopping them, since they could baste in their own juices) and threw them into a 275-degree oven. In the meantime, I set up my grill with the same half-grill fire.

Three hours later, I pulled the ribs from the oven and unwrapped them. They were undeniably tender, but we all agreed they looked a bit sweaty and steamy, too. Hoping the fire would correct this, I transferred them to the cooler side of my kettle, placed some soaked hickory chunks on the live coals to generate smoke, and replaced the lid, opening and closing vents as necessary to maintain the 250-degree temperature and occasionally mopping the ribs with a mixture of apple juice and cider vinegar. An hour later, the ribs showed no sign of a bark. In desperation, I dragged the racks to the hot side of the grill to finish, hoping that the extra heat would crisp up their exterior.

My tasters were not fooled. The wet, soft-textured ribs screamed "braise," not "barbecue" and still had no bark to speak of. Much of the rub had also washed away during their oven time, leaving only a hint of spice. Tasters found the smoke flavor acrid and superficial. Where had I gone wrong?

For unbeatable barbecued ribs that don't take all day, we take the racks inside to finish cooking in the oven.

SMOKE WITHOUT FIRE

Research revealed the first serious misstep: exposing the ribs to smoke after they cooked. Smoke contains both water-soluble and fat-soluble flavor compounds. As traditional dry-rub ribs cook, the water-soluble compounds dissolve in the meat's surface moisture and get left behind as it evaporates. Fat-soluble compounds, on the other hand, dissolve in the rendering fat, which then spreads through the meat, lubricating the muscle fibers and depositing smoke flavor as it goes. The problem is, if the ribs start cooking in the oven, much of the fat renders and drips out of the meat before it even gets to the grill. Once on the coals, the parcooked ribs have less fat for the smoke compounds to dissolve in, resulting in a one-dimensional, ashtray-like essence, not the full-on smokiness I was after.

I reversed the cooking order in the next batch, placing the raw, spice-rubbed rib racks over the cooler side of the grill while two hickory chunks smoldered over the coals.

After 45 minutes I rotated and mopped the slabs, let them cook another 45 minutes, and finally transferred them to a wire rack set over a rimmed baking sheet to bring them indoors. The ribs then got a second vinegar-juice coat on their way into a 300-degree oven—cranking up the heat just a bit, I hoped, would expedite the cooking without compromising the meat's texture—where they stayed until tender and thick-crusted. I even mimicked my grill setup by pouring 1½ cups water into the rimmed baking sheet, which gently humidified the cooking environment. But I'd overcompensated: The texture was fine, but now my ribs were so smoky that their flavor verged on burnt kindling. To curb the fume flavor, I downsized from wood chunks to a mere ¾ cup of soaked wood chips, which smoldered just long enough (30 minutes) to give the ribs a clean, subtly wood-smoked flavor.

RUBBED THE RIGHT WAY

Up to this point, I'd been following the advice of many recipes, applying my rub to the ribs a full day before cooking them for maximum flavor. On first inspection, this made sense: More time means more penetration, which means a more flavorful result, right? But the thinness of the meat on the bones meant that the rub didn't have very far to travel. Did I really need to keep the rub on the ribs for such a long time? I set up a time check: I rubbed the spice mixture onto one batch of ribs and let them sit overnight before cooking. I then applied rub on a second batch and threw these ribs on the grill as soon as I had the fire ready, about 30 minutes later. One taste revealed that applying the rub right before cooking gave me all the flavor I needed.

The last puzzle piece was figuring out when the ribs were done. Wet ribs are nearly impossible to overcook. But dry-rub ribs are have a very small window during which they are perfectly cooked. The foolproof solution? A thermometer. As long as I pulled my ribs out of the oven when the thickest section reached 195 degrees, the meat turned out consistently tender with satisfying chew. Next time I'm craving smoky, porky, complex barbecue, I'll leave the sweet sauce—and the mail-order forms—on the shelf.

Memphis-Style Barbecued Spareribs

SERVES 4 TO 6

Be sure not to remove the membrane that runs along the bone side of the ribs; this membrane prevents some of the fat from rendering out and is authentic to this style of ribs.

1 recipe Spice Rub (recipe follows)
2 (2½- to 3-pound) racks St. Louis–style spareribs, trimmed
½ cup apple juice
3 tablespoons cider vinegar
1 (13 by 9-inch) disposable aluminum roasting pan (if using charcoal) or 2 (9-inch) disposable aluminum pie plates (if using gas)
¾ cup wood chips, soaked in water for 15 minutes and drained

1. Rub 2 tablespoons spice rub on each side of each rack of ribs. Let ribs sit at room temperature while preparing grill.
2. Combine apple juice and vinegar in small bowl and set aside.
3A. *For a charcoal grill:* Open bottom vent halfway and evenly space 15 unlit charcoal briquettes on 1 side of grill. Place disposable pan filled with 2 cups water on other side of grill. Light large chimney starter one-third filled with charcoal briquettes (2 quarts). When top coals are partially covered with ash, pour evenly over unlit coals. Sprinkle soaked wood chips over lit coals. Set cooking grate in place, cover, and open lid vent halfway. Heat grill until hot and wood chips are smoking, about 5 minutes.
3B. *For a gas grill:* Place soaked wood chips in pie plate with ¼ cup water and set over primary burner. Place second pie plate filled with 2 cups water on other burner(s). Turn all burners to high, cover, and heat grill until hot and wood chips are smoking, about 15 minutes. Turn primary burner to medium-high and turn off other burner(s). (Adjust primary burner as needed to maintain grill temperature of 250 to 275 degrees.)
4. Clean and oil cooking grate. Place ribs meat side down on cooler side of grill, over water-filled pan. Cover (position lid vent over meat if using charcoal) and cook until ribs are deep red and smoky, about 1½ hours, brushing with apple juice mixture and flipping and rotating racks halfway through cooking. About 20 minutes before removing ribs from grill, adjust oven rack to lower-middle position and heat oven to 300 degrees.
5. Set wire rack in rimmed baking sheet and transfer ribs to prepared rack. Brush top of each rack of ribs with 2 tablespoons apple juice mixture. Pour 1½ cups water into sheet; roast for 1 hour. Brush ribs with remaining apple juice mixture and continue to cook until meat is tender and registers 195 degrees, 1 to 2 hours longer. Transfer ribs to cutting board, tent with aluminum foil, and let rest for 15 minutes. Slice ribs between bones and serve.

spice rub

Spice Rub

MAKES ABOUT ½ CUP

For a less spicy rub, you can reduce the cayenne to ½ teaspoon.

2 tablespoons paprika
2 tablespoons packed light brown sugar
1 tablespoon salt
2 teaspoons chili powder
1½ teaspoons pepper
1½ teaspoons garlic powder
1½ teaspoons onion powder
1½ teaspoons cayenne pepper
½ teaspoon dried thyme

Combine all ingredients in bowl.

A NEW WAY WITH KEBABS

ANDREW JANJIGIAN, *July/August 2013*

When I was growing up, my Armenian family had two basic meat-grilling modes for warm-weather events: skewered leg of lamb—shish kebab—or spiced ground lamb patties. Armenians call these *losh* kebabs, but they are known nearly everywhere else in the Middle East as *kofte*.

My family's version of kofte falls in line with some of the more common versions served in the Middle East, so when I set out to develop my own recipe, I used my father's as a baseline. He uses a mixture of hand-ground lamb, bread crumbs, grated onion, cumin, chiles, and whatever fresh herbs are available, kneading the ingredients together to disperse the fat and flavor and form an almost sausage-like springiness. His boldly spiced patties are quickly grilled over high heat on long metal skewers, making them tender and juicy on the inside and encased in a smoky, crunchy coating of char. To serve, he stuffs the kofte in pita and drizzles on a tangy yogurt-garlic sauce.

But it had always been my father who actually made this dish at our house, and when I began my testing I quickly learned that the problem with kofte is that it's finicky. Because the patties are small, the meat easily overcooks and becomes dry. And since kofte is kneaded by hand in order to get the meat proteins to cross-link and take on a resilient texture, I found that it's easy to make it too springy—or not springy enough. I rounded up a handful of existing kofte recipes using a range of binders, spices, and kneading times, but I found that most of the results turned out dry and crumbly or were simply tough. I wanted my kofte to be warm and flavorful, with a cooling sauce; tender yet intact; and easy to boot. And I wanted to achieve this without needing years of practice.

FROM THE GROUND (MEAT) UP

Kofte is traditionally made by mincing meat—usually lamb—by hand with a cleaver. Unlike machine grinding, which roughs up the meat fibers to the point that they can't easily hold on to moisture upon cooking, hand mincing is far gentler and leads to kofte that is juicy and tender. But hand mincing is a lot of work—and therefore, for me, a nonstarter. Even using the food processor to grind my own meat seemed like too much. I would stick with preground meat from the grocery store. And though I decided to go with lamb—its rich flavor pairs so well with earthy spices and smoky grill char—I wanted to develop a recipe that worked with ground beef, too.

This Middle-Eastern specialty gets its sausage-like texture from gelatin and pine nuts.

After cobbling together a working recipe of ground lamb and grated onion, along with a little cumin, chile, and fresh parsley, I began trying to solve the moisture issue. In the test kitchen we usually turn to panades made from soaked bread or bread crumbs to keep ground meat patties moist when cooked through, since their starches help hold on to moisture released by the meat as it cooks. Many kofte recipes also use some form of binder, but when I tried bread crumbs, standard sandwich bread, torn-up pita bread, and all-purpose flour, these add-ins introduced other problems. While they all helped retain a bit of moisture and kept the kofte together, when enough was used to prevent drying out on the grill, the panades gave the kofte an unwelcome pastiness, and they muted the flavor of the lamb. But what other options did I have?

I thought about meatballs, and one recipe in particular: our Classic Spaghetti and Meatballs for a Crowd. For this recipe, we used a panade along with powdered gelatin. Gelatin holds up to 10 times its weight in water, and the gel that forms when it hydrates is highly viscous (which is why sauces made from gelatin-rich reduced meat stocks are so silky smooth). And unlike starches, you need very tiny amounts of gelatin to see benefits, so it doesn't usually have negative effects on texture or flavor. Could gelatin work solo in my kofte? I tried adding a mere teaspoon per pound of lamb and then refrigerated the kofte to help the meat firm up and hold fast to the skewer, and I was pleased by the results: I now had nice, juicy kofte.

But I was still left with a problem. With the preground meat plus a solid 2 minutes of kneading, which was not only traditional but also necessary to help keep the kofte together on the grill, many of my finished products were so springy that they could practically bounce. I remembered a recipe I'd seen that had included bulgur. This coarse cracked wheat most likely wouldn't melt into the meat like bread crumbs but would instead keep the meat a bit separated and therefore less springy and more tender when cooked. I had high hopes. But when I tried bulgur, adding a couple of tablespoons to the mix, I found that it only made the kofte gritty. I tried it again in smaller quantities, but the unpleasant texture remained.

GOING NUTS

The bulgur gave me an idea, though: What about incorporating something of a similar size but of a softer consistency? I'd seen a few kofte recipes containing ground pine nuts or pistachios, and I'd assumed that the nuts were used for flavor rather than texture. For my next test, I added a few tablespoons of ground pine nuts to the mixture. The results were even better than I'd hoped. The nuts helped prevent toughness in the kofte without adding their own texture. And best of all, thanks to the oil they contained, they gave the kofte a subtle but noticeable boost in richness.

Now all that remained was to sort out the flavorings and a sauce. Many kofte recipes contain *baharat*, a Middle Eastern spice blend that is a common seasoning for meat dishes.

Recipes vary widely, but the common denominators are usually black pepper, cumin, coriander, and chile pepper. I came up with my own combination of these, with cumin as the dominant player and hot smoked paprika as the chile. To these I also added smaller amounts of ground cinnamon, nutmeg, and cloves. As for herbs, equal amounts of fresh parsley and mint did the trick. For the sauce, I borrowed an idea from a recipe I'd found in *Jerusalem* (2012), a cookbook from British chefs Yotam Ottolenghi and Sami Tamimi: I added a small amount of tahini to the traditional mixture of crushed garlic, lemon juice, and yogurt usually served with kofte; it gave the sauce a depth to match that of the kofte itself.

With that, there was one last test to perform: Serve the kofte to my family. The result? My kofte was a big hit. Even my dad asked for the recipe.

SKIP THE BURGER AND TRY THIS

These kebabs take only a little longer to throw together than burgers but boast far more complex flavors and textures. For sandwiches, serve in warm pita bread.

TASTY SAUCE Ours features traditional garlicky yogurt, plus a little tahini for added complexity.

SPRINGY YET TENDER TEXTURE Kneading the ground meat gives the kofte a sausage-like spring, while incorporating ground pine nuts ensures that it also stays tender.

WARM SPICES Spices added to the meat, including hot smoked paprika, cumin, and cloves, contribute heat and depth.

FRESH HERBS The bright, grassy flavors of two other mix-ins, parsley and mint, complement the kofte's richness.

Grilled Lamb Kofte

SERVES 4 TO 6

Serve with rice pilaf or make sandwiches with warm pita bread, sliced red onion, and chopped fresh mint. You will need eight 12-inch metal skewers for this recipe.

Yogurt-Garlic Sauce

1 cup plain whole-milk yogurt
2 tablespoons lemon juice
2 tablespoons tahini
1 garlic clove, minced
½ teaspoon salt

Kofte

½ cup pine nuts
4 garlic cloves, peeled
1½ teaspoons hot smoked paprika
1 teaspoon salt
1 teaspoon ground cumin
½ teaspoon pepper
¼ teaspoon ground coriander
¼ teaspoon ground cloves
⅛ teaspoon ground nutmeg
⅛ teaspoon ground cinnamon
1½ pounds ground lamb
½ cup grated onion, drained
⅓ cup minced fresh parsley
⅓ cup minced fresh mint
1½ teaspoons unflavored gelatin
1 large disposable aluminum roasting pan (if using charcoal)

1. *For the yogurt-garlic sauce:* Whisk all ingredients together in bowl. Set aside.

2. *For the kofte:* Process pine nuts, garlic, paprika, salt, cumin, pepper, coriander, cloves, nutmeg, and cinnamon in food processor until coarse paste forms, 30 to 45 seconds. Transfer mixture to large bowl. Add lamb, onion, parsley, mint, and gelatin; knead with your hands until thoroughly combined and mixture feels slightly sticky, about 2 minutes. Divide mixture into 8 equal portions. Shape each portion into 5-inch-long cylinder about 1 inch in diameter. Using eight 12-inch metal skewers, thread 1 cylinder onto each skewer, pressing gently to adhere. Transfer skewers to lightly greased baking sheet, cover with plastic wrap, and refrigerate for at least 1 hour or up to 24 hours.

3A. *For a charcoal grill:* Using skewer, poke 12 holes in bottom of disposable pan. Open bottom vent completely and place pan in center of grill. Light large chimney starter filled two-thirds with charcoal briquettes (4 quarts). When top coals are partially covered with ash, pour into pan. Set cooking grate in place, cover, and open lid vent completely. Heat grill until hot, about 5 minutes.

3B. *For a gas grill:* Turn all burners to high, cover, and heat grill until hot, about 15 minutes. Leave all burners on high.

4. Clean and oil cooking grate. Place skewers on grill (directly over coals if using charcoal) at 45-degree angle to grate. Cook (covered if using gas) until browned and meat easily releases from grill, 4 to 7 minutes. Flip skewers and continue to cook until browned on second side and meat registers 160 degrees, about 6 minutes longer. Transfer skewers to platter and serve, passing yogurt-garlic sauce separately.

variation

Grilled Beef Kofte

Substitute 80 percent lean ground beef for lamb. Increase garlic to 5 cloves, paprika to 2 teaspoons, and cumin to 2 teaspoons.

GRASS-FED VERSUS GRAIN-FED LAMB

Grass-fed and grain-fed lamb taste different. This is because when lambs eat grain—even just for a short period before slaughter—it impacts the composition of the animal's fat, where most of its unique flavor resides. A grain-based diet reduces the concentration of the medium-length branched fatty acids, the ones that give lamb its distinctive flavor. This means that grain-fed lamb has a less intense "lamb" flavor, and can taste slightly sweeter.

UPDATING SHEPHERD'S PIE

ANDREA GEARY, *November/December 2012*

I once made a fabulous shepherd's pie. It was the very antithesis of those watery, gray, flavorless pies pushed by frozen food companies and school cafeterias. But this story is not about that shepherd's pie, because I will never make that particular recipe again.

The reason is simple: It took most of a day to produce. After boning, trimming, and cutting up lamb shoulder, I seared the meat in batches (making a greasy mess of the stovetop in the process) and braised it with vegetables and homemade stock for a couple of hours. From there, I reduced the cooking liquid to make a sauce, chopped the cooked meat, replaced the spent vegetables with fresh, and transferred the filling to a baking dish. Finally, I prepared the mashed potatoes (boiling, mashing, mixing) and piped them over the filling. While the top crisped in the oven, I cleaned up the kitchen—no small feat because I had used almost every piece of cooking equipment I owned. I loved that pie—but only a blissfully uninformed diner would call that dish comfort food; an honest cook would likely describe it as marathon food.

Another thing: Though it made a very satisfying meal, the pie was heavy. Shepherd's pie may be a holdover from a time when physical laborers needed robust sustenance, but as someone who enjoys a 21st-century urban lifestyle, I can't really justify eating like a preindustrial farmer. But I admit: The classic combination of meat, gravy, and potatoes is undeniably attractive on chilly winter nights. Maybe I could make a modernized shepherd's pie—a bit lighter, much less messy, and a lot quicker to prepare.

MAKE IT GROUND, PLEASE

I'm not the first to think shepherd's pie needs an overhaul, and the most common shortcut is to use ground meat. Ground lamb seemed the obvious choice until I learned in *Irish Traditional Cooking* (1995) by Darina Allen, godmother of the cuisine, that modern-day shepherd's pie in Ireland is almost always made with beef. Since beef is more popular in the United States, ground beef it would be.

But it took me only one test to realize that I couldn't simply swap out chunks of meat for the ground kind; the two don't cook the same way. Searing chunks produces tender meat with a lovely brown crust. Ground beef, on the other hand, presents so much surface area to the pan that it gives up considerably more moisture as it cooks. The result: nubbly, dry crumbles that don't brown well. No thanks.

So, my meat left unbrowned, I nonetheless persevered. I added onions and carrots and let them soften a bit, and then I introduced some flour to thicken the eventual sauce. I stirred in herbs along with some beef broth and let the whole thing simmer and reduce while I cooked and mashed the potatoes. I transferred the filling to a baking dish and—thinking I was simplifying things—ditched my piping bag and spread the potatoes on top with a rubber spatula, which turned out to be messy and difficult because the soupy filling conspired against me. Finally, I placed the pie in the oven to crisp the top.

Had my aim been to re-create the shepherd's pie served on budget airlines and in hospitals, I could have called this a success. The meat, even unbrowned, was chewy; the carrots were cooked to mush; and the "gravy" tasted pretty much like what it was: thickened canned beef broth.

FOND OF FLAVOR

Fortunately, I had a good lead on how to improve the meat's texture. We recently discovered that treating pork with baking soda tenderizes the meat by raising its pH. Hoping to achieve the same effect here, I stirred ½ teaspoon of baking soda and 2 tablespoons of water (to ensure that it would distribute evenly) into the raw ground meat and let the mixture rest while I prepared the mashed potatoes. That did the trick, rendering the meat soft and tender, even after several minutes of simmering. On to beefing up the filling's lackluster flavor.

Since my gravy would not be based on browned meat flavors, I looked to other options. An approach to vegetarian gravy looked promising: Cook onions and mushrooms in a skillet with a little bit of fat over fairly high heat until they're deep brown and a fond starts to form in the pan; then stir in tomato paste and garlic and allow the fond to get quite dark. I went ahead with this method, deglazing the pan with some fortified wine (ordinary red wine required me to use so much it left the sauce boozy) after a good layer of fond had developed. Then I added flour and, when the mixture was very deeply browned, fresh thyme and bay leaves, followed by beef broth and Worcestershire sauce to liberate that valuable crust from the bottom of the skillet. I was rewarded with a sauce that boasted rich color and savory depth.

A streamlined ground beef filling and a sturdy, scallion-laced mashed potato topping make for a truly comforting shepherd's pie.

With my sauce bubbling and thick, I added 1½ pounds of ground beef broken into chunks and covered the skillet for roughly 10 minutes, lifting the lid once during cooking to stir. That's when I noticed the small pools of grease exuded by the meat. One downside of not browning the meat was that I had no opportunity to pour off its fat. Switching from 85 percent lean ground beef (the test kitchen's usual choice) to 93 percent lean beef helped. The leaner beef stayed moist and tender, thanks to the baking soda treatment, and only a few tiny pools of fat remained. To get rid of these, I first tried adding more flour, but mixed in so late in the process, it tasted raw and starchy. Instead, I turned to the Asian trick of stirring in a slurry of cornstarch and water, which took care of the problem very nicely.

As for the spuds, the recipe I'd been using calls for a full stick of butter and 1 cup of half-and-half—not exactly the lighter approach I was going for. I cut the amount of butter in half and subbed milk for the half-and-half. Because soft, moist mashed potatoes would merge with the gravy rather than form a crust, I also decreased the dairy by 50 percent and added an egg yolk for extra structure.

For convenience's sake, I elected to leave the cooked filling in the skillet—except that I still had to resolve the issue of spreading the solid potatoes over the soupy mixture. I decided to give piping another go, but this time, I eschewed my fancy pastry bag and star tip for a zipper-lock bag with a corner cut off. Depositing the potatoes onto the filling from above was far easier than trying to spread them over a wet base. Once they were in place, I smoothed them with the back of a spoon and traced ridges in them with a fork; that way they'd get really crusty under the broiler.

One problem remained: The browned, crispy potato topping certainly looked appealing, but its flavor paled in comparison with the robust filling. Looking to add some pizzazz, I reviewed the British Isles' various regional potato dishes, and a recipe for champ, Ireland's simple mixture of mashed potatoes and chopped scallions, caught my attention. Stirring a handful of chopped scallion greens into my own mash freshened the whole dish without adding heft.

With its simmered lean ground beef, rich but not heavy gravy, and lighter, fresher mash, my updated shepherd's pie was not just faster to make than the traditional version but also less guilt-inducing—and still every bit as delicious. At last, comfort food that even the cook could enjoy.

Shepherd's Pie

SERVES 4 TO 6

Don't use ground beef that's fattier than 93 percent or the dish will be greasy.

1½ pounds 93 percent lean ground beef
Salt and pepper
½ teaspoon baking soda
2½ pounds russet potatoes, peeled and cut into 1-inch chunks
4 tablespoons unsalted butter, melted
½ cup milk
1 large egg yolk
8 scallions, green parts only, sliced thin
2 teaspoons vegetable oil
1 onion, chopped
4 ounces white mushrooms, trimmed and chopped
1 tablespoon tomato paste
2 garlic cloves, minced
2 tablespoons Madeira or ruby port
2 tablespoons all-purpose flour
1¼ cups beef broth
2 carrots, peeled and chopped
2 teaspoons Worcestershire sauce
2 sprigs fresh thyme
1 bay leaf
2 teaspoons cornstarch

1. Toss beef with 2 tablespoons water, 1 teaspoon salt, baking soda, and ¼ teaspoon pepper in bowl until thoroughly combined. Set aside for 20 minutes.

2. Meanwhile, place potatoes and 1 tablespoon salt in medium saucepan and add water to cover by 1 inch. Bring to boil over high heat. Reduce heat to medium-low and simmer until potatoes are soft and paring knife can be slipped in and out of potatoes with little resistance, 8 to 10 minutes. Drain potatoes and return them to saucepan. Return saucepan to low heat and cook, shaking saucepan occasionally, until any surface moisture on potatoes has evaporated, about 1 minute. Off heat, mash potatoes or press potatoes through ricer set over saucepan. Stir in melted butter. Whisk milk and egg yolk together in small bowl, then stir into potatoes. Stir in scallion greens and season with salt and pepper. Cover and set aside.

3. Heat oil in broiler-safe 10-inch skillet over medium heat until shimmering. Add onion, mushrooms, ½ teaspoon salt, and ¼ teaspoon pepper; cook, stirring occasionally, until vegetables are just starting to soften and dark bits form on bottom of skillet, 4 to 6 minutes.

4. Stir in tomato paste and garlic; cook until bottom of skillet is dark brown, about 2 minutes. Add Madeira and cook, scraping up any browned bits, until evaporated, about 1 minute. Stir in flour and cook for 1 minute. Add broth, carrots, Worcestershire, thyme sprigs, and bay leaf; bring to boil, scraping up any browned bits.

5. Reduce heat to medium-low, add beef in 2-inch chunks to broth, and bring to gentle simmer. Cover and cook until beef is cooked through, 10 to 12 minutes, stirring and breaking up meat chunks with 2 forks halfway through cooking. Stir cornstarch and 2 teaspoons water together in bowl. Stir cornstarch mixture into filling and continue to simmer for 30 seconds. Discard thyme sprigs and bay leaf. Season with salt and pepper to taste.

6. Adjust oven rack 5 inches from broiler element and heat broiler. Place mashed potatoes in large zipper-lock bag and snip off 1 corner to create 1-inch opening. Pipe potatoes in even layer over filling, making sure to cover entire surface. Smooth potatoes with back of spoon, then use tines of fork to make ridges over surface. Place skillet on rimmed baking sheet and broil until potatoes are golden brown and crusty and filling is bubbly, 10 to 15 minutes. Let cool for 10 minutes before serving.

RETHINKING LEG OF LAMB

DAN SOUZA, *March/April 2013*

Who cooks lamb? Not many people. Not often. Not in America, anyway. I know. Not even I cook it, and it's not because I don't enjoy eating it. Lamb has a richness of flavor unmatched by beef or pork, with a meaty texture that can be as supple as that of tenderloin. It pairs well with a wide range of robust spices, and my favorite cut, the leg, can single-handedly elevate a holiday meal from ordinary to refined. The real reason I avoid leg of lamb is that my past experiences cooking it were undermined by the many challenges it can pose.

Roasting a bone-in leg of lamb invariably delivers meat of different degrees of doneness; the super-thin sections of muscle near the shank go beyond well-done while you wait for the meat closest to the bone to come up to temperature. And even when I've successfully roasted this cut, carving it off the bone into presentable pieces proved humbling. Opting for a boneless, tied leg of lamb partly alleviates these issues—the meat cooks more evenly and carving is simplified. But this approach presents problems of its own, the biggest being the poor ratio of well-browned crust to tender meat and the unavoidable pockets of sinew and fat that hide in the mosaic of muscles.

Maybe it would be easiest to just pick up a user-friendly rack of lamb next time I'm in the ovine mood, but that smacks of defeat, and I love a challenge. I wanted a roast leg of lamb with a good ratio of crispy crust to evenly cooked meat and one that was simple to carve and serve, all the while providing me with a ready-made sauce. I was after a lazy man's roast leg of lamb.

A CUT ABOVE

I immediately decided to forgo bone-in and tied boneless roasts in favor of a different preparation: a butterflied leg of lamb. Essentially a boneless leg in which the thicker portions have been sliced and opened up to yield a relatively even slab of meat, this cut is most often chopped up for kebabs or tossed onto a hot grill. But its uniformity and large expanse of exterior made me think it might do well as a roast, too. My first move was to ensure an even thickness by pounding any thicker areas to roughly 1 inch. Examining this large slab of lamb on my cutting board, I realized an unexpected benefit of this preparation: access to big pockets of intermuscular fat and connective tissue. These chewy bits, which aren't accessible even in boneless roasts, don't render or soften enough during cooking. Now I was able to carve out and remove them easily. Another benefit was the ability to season this roast far more efficiently than either a bone-in or a boneless leg.

Roasting a butterflied leg of lamb on a bed of whole, bloomed spices guarantees bold, aromatic flavor.

Though many people brine lamb, I noticed that the profile of this butterflied leg resembled that of a very large, thick-cut steak. I decided to treat it like one: I seasoned both sides with kosher salt and let it sit for an hour. Treating the lamb this way provided many of the benefits of a brine: It was better seasoned, juicier, and more tender than untreated samples. Unlike brining, however, salting left my lamb with a relatively dry surface—one that could brown and crisp far better during roasting. To ensure that the salt would cover more of the meat, I crosshatched the fat cap on the top surface of the leg by scoring just down to the meat. Roasted to 130 degrees on a baking sheet in a moderate oven, the lamb was well seasoned and featured a decent crust, but still the exterior portions were overcooked by the time the center came up to temperature. I knew I could do better.

TWICE-COOKED LEG OF LAMB

Years of roasting meat have helped us figure out how to do it well. One thing we know is that roasting low and slow ensures good moisture retention and even cooking. The exterior and interior temperatures will be much closer in a roast cooked at 300 degrees than in one blasted at 500 degrees. With this in mind, I tried roasting my salted lamb at a range of relatively low oven temperatures, from 225 degrees on up to 325 degrees. Sure enough, going lower resulted in juicier, more evenly cooked meat. I struck a balance between time and temperature at 250 degrees. So far so good: I was turning out tender, juicy leg of lamb in only 40 minutes of roasting.

But now I ran up against a second tenet of good roasting: High heat develops the rich, meaty flavors associated with the Maillard reaction. It's a paradox we commonly address by cooking at two different heat levels—sear in a skillet over high heat and then gently roast. But my roast was too large for stovetop searing. It was clear that I'd need to sear it in the oven, where my options for high heat were 500 degrees or the broiler. I tested both options and found that beginning in a 500-degree oven was too slow for my thin roast. By the time I rendered and crisped the exterior, I'd overcooked the meat below the≈surface. Broiling was markedly better. I achieved the best results by slow-roasting the lamb first and then finishing it under the broiler, which allowed me to further dry the meat's surface and promote faster browning. Just 5 minutes under the broiler produced a burnished, crisped crust but left the meat below the surface largely unaffected. Now it was time to address the spices.

SPICE WORLD

Lamb's bold flavor is complemented, rather than overpowered, by a liberal use of spices. I wanted to find the ideal way to incorporate a blend of them, and my first thought was to include them from the outset. I toasted equal parts cumin, coriander, and mustard seeds and rubbed the mixture over both sides of the lamb along with the salt. Things looked (and smelled) quite good while the lamb gently cooked at 250 degrees, but they took a turn for the worse once I transitioned to broiling. The broiler's intense heat turned the top layer of spices into a blackened, bitter landscape in a matter of minutes.

Luckily it wasn't all bad news—the spices under the lamb had started to bloom and soften during their stay in the oven, adding texture and bursts of flavor where they clung to the meat. What if I ditched the top layer of spices and focused on getting the most out of what was underneath? After salting my next lamb, I placed whole coriander, cumin, and mustard seeds, as well as smashed garlic and sliced ginger, on a baking sheet along with a glug of vegetable oil and popped it in the oven. This would take full advantage of the concept of blooming—a process by which, through the application of heat, fat-soluble flavor compounds in a spice are released from a solid state into a solution, where they mix together, therefore gaining even more complexity. When the lamb was ready to be cooked, I simply removed the baking sheet, placed the lamb (fat side up) on top of the spice-oil mixture, and returned it to the oven to roast.

I had hit the roast-lamb jackpot. Without a layer of spices to absorb the heat, the top of the roast once again turned a handsome golden brown under the broiler, while the aromatics and infused oil clung to the bottom and provided rich flavor. Tasters were pleased but wanted more complexity, so I added shallots, strips of lemon zest, and bay leaves (which I removed before adding the lamb) to the pan oil. This lamb was close to my ideal: a browned crust encasing medium-rare meat, perfumed with pockets of spice and caramelized alliums. The last step was to put all of that infused oil to good use.

While the lamb rested, I strained the infused oil and pan juices into a bowl and whisked in some lemon juice, shallot, and cilantro and mint. This vinaigrette was meaty, aromatic, and fresh-tasting. The time had come to carve, and it proved as simple as slicing up a steak. I transferred the meat to a platter, dressed it with some of the sauce, and—in less than 2 hours—was ready to eat. Lazy man's leg of lamb, indeed.

Roast Butterflied Leg of Lamb with Coriander, Cumin, and Mustard Seeds

SERVES 8 TO 10

We prefer the subtler flavor and larger size of lamb labeled "domestic" or "American" for this recipe. The amount of salt (2 tablespoons) in step 1 is for a 6-pound leg. If using a larger leg (7 to 8 pounds), add an additional teaspoon of salt for every pound.

Lamb

1 (6- to 8-pound) butterflied leg of lamb
Kosher salt
⅓ cup vegetable oil
3 shallots, sliced thin
4 garlic cloves, peeled and smashed
1 (1-inch) piece ginger, sliced into ½-inch-thick rounds and smashed
1 tablespoon coriander seeds
1 tablespoon cumin seeds
1 tablespoon mustard seeds
3 bay leaves
2 (2-inch) strips lemon zest

Sauce

⅓ cup chopped fresh mint
⅓ cup chopped fresh cilantro
1 shallot, minced
2 tablespoons lemon juice
Salt and pepper

1. ***For the lamb:*** Place lamb on cutting board with fat cap facing down. Using sharp knife, trim any pockets of fat and connective tissue from underside of lamb. Flip lamb over, trim fat cap so it's between ⅛ and ¼ inch thick, and pound roast to even 1-inch thickness. Cut slits, spaced ½ inch apart, in fat cap in crosshatch pattern, being careful to cut down to but not into meat. Rub 2 tablespoons salt over entire roast and into slits. Let stand, uncovered, at room temperature for 1 hour.

2. Meanwhile, adjust oven racks 4 to 5 inches from broiler element and to lower-middle position and heat oven to 250 degrees. Stir together oil, shallots, garlic, ginger, coriander seeds, cumin seeds, mustard seeds, bay leaves, and lemon zest on rimmed baking sheet and bake on lower-middle rack until spices are softened and fragrant and shallots and garlic turn golden, about 1 hour. Remove sheet from oven and discard bay leaves.

3. Thoroughly pat lamb dry with paper towels and transfer, fat side up, to sheet (directly on top of spices). Roast on lower-middle rack until lamb registers 120 degrees, 30 to 40 minutes. Remove sheet from oven and heat broiler. Broil lamb on upper rack until surface is well browned and charred in spots and lamb registers 125 degrees, 3 to 8 minutes for medium-rare.

4. Remove sheet from oven and, using 2 pairs of tongs, transfer lamb to carving board (some spices will cling to bottom of roast); tent with aluminum foil and let rest for 20 minutes.

5. ***For the sauce:*** Meanwhile, carefully pour pan juices through fine-mesh strainer into medium bowl, pressing on solids to extract as much liquid as possible; discard solids. Stir in mint, cilantro, shallot, and lemon juice. Add any accumulated lamb juices to sauce and season with salt and pepper to taste.

6. With long side facing you, slice lamb with grain into 3 equal pieces. Turn each piece and slice across grain into ¼-inch-thick slices. Serve with sauce. (Briefly warm sauce in microwave if it has cooled and thickened.)

variations

Roast Butterflied Leg of Lamb with Coriander, Rosemary, and Red Pepper

Omit cumin and mustard seeds. Toss 6 sprigs fresh rosemary and ½ teaspoon red pepper flakes with oil mixture in step 2. Substitute parsley for cilantro in sauce.

Roast Butterflied Leg of Lamb with Coriander, Fennel, and Black Pepper

Substitute 1 tablespoon fennel seeds for cumin seeds and 1 tablespoon black peppercorns for mustard seeds in step 2. Substitute parsley for mint in sauce.

Mint
Rosemary
Dill
Basil
Thyme
Oregano
Sage
Tarragon
Chives
Flat-Leaf Parsley
Chervil
Curly Parsley

POULTRY

KOREAN FRIED CHICKEN WINGS

ANDREA GEARY, *July/August 2016*

I crave fried chicken as much as the next person, but I have never been partial to fried wings. To me, they're bar snacks—fine for occasionally sharing with friends but not substantial or satisfying enough to make a meal out of—and certainly not worth the trouble to make at home.

At least, that's how I felt until I tasted the fried wings at a Korean restaurant. The biggest selling point of this style is its thin, crackly exterior that gives way to juicy meat with an audible crunch—an especially impressive trait considering that the surface of the chicken is doused with a wet sauce. And unlike many styles of wings that are just sweet, salty, or fiery, these delivered a perfect balance of all those flavors.

That profile has made this style of fried chicken wildly popular as an accompaniment to beer and the pickled side dishes known as *banchan* in South Korean bars and restaurants. In fact, the fried chicken–beer combination is now a multibillion-dollar industry that has spawned the term *chimaek* (*chi* for "chicken" and *maek* for "maekju," the Korean word for beer), a South Korean festival, and (in the past decade or so) worldwide restaurant chains like Bon Chon that are centered on this particular dish.

A brief rest after twice-frying allows these wings to stay exceptionally crispy, even beneath a layer of sweet-spicy sauce.

Needless to say, I was hooked and was determined to make Korean fried chicken for myself. Once I started to research the recipe, I also learned a practical explanation for using wings: In Korea, where chickens are smaller, restaurants often cut up and fry the whole bird, but because the larger breasts and thighs on American birds are harder to cook evenly, wings are the easier choice. The more I thought about it, I didn't see why I couldn't make a meal out of Korean fried chicken wings; their bold flavors would surely pair well with a bowl of rice and (in place of the banchan) a bright, fresh slaw.

THE CRUST OF THE MATTER

Replicating the sauce would be easy enough once I figured out the ingredients. So I first focused on nailing the wings' delicate but substantial crunch, reviewing the coatings and frying methods I found in a handful of recipes. The coatings varied considerably—from a simple cornstarch dredge to a thick batter made with eggs, flour, and cornstarch—and I found methods for both single frying and double frying. Figuring I'd start with a minimalist approach, I tossed 3 pounds of wings (which would feed at least four people) in cornstarch before frying them once, for about 10 minutes, in a Dutch oven filled with 2 quarts of 350-degree oil.

The meat on these wings was a tad dry, but their worst flaw was the coating—or lack thereof. Most of the cornstarch fell off as soon as the wings hit the oil, so the crust was wimpy—nothing that could stand up to a sauce—and only lightly browned.

Thinking that the starch needed some moisture to help it cling to the chicken, I next tried a series of batter coatings. Not surprisingly, the shaggy mixture of flour, cornstarch, and egg fried up thick and craggy, more like the coating on American fried chicken. I also tried a combination of just cornstarch and water, but it was another bust: Adding enough liquid to make the mixture loose enough to coat the chicken also made it too runny to cling, but without enough water the mixture thickened up like liquid cement. Coating the wings with a creamy, loose slurry of flour and water yielded a nicely thin crust, though it was a bit tough and lacked the elusive shattery texture I was after. From there, I tried various ratios of cornstarch to flour and found that supplementing a flour-based batter with just 3 tablespoons of cornstarch helped the coating crisp up nicely. I understood why once I learned that flour and cornstarch play different but complementary roles in frying: The proteins in wheat flour help the batter bond to the meat and also brown deeply; cornstarch (a pure starch) doesn't cling or brown as well as flour, but it crisps up nicely. Why? Because pure starch releases more amylose, a starch molecule that fries up supercrispy. Cornstarch also can't form gluten, so it doesn't turn tough.

I dunked the wings in the batter and let the excess drip back into the bowl before adding them to the hot oil. When they emerged, I thought I'd finally nailed the crust, which was gorgeously crispy and brown. But when I slathered the wings with my placeholder sauce (a mixture of the spicy-sweet Korean chile-soybean paste *gochujang*, sugar, garlic, ginger, sesame oil, soy sauce, and a little water) and took a bite, I paused. They'd gone from supercrispy to soggy in minutes.

ON THE DOUBLE

It was a setback that made me wonder if double frying might be worth a try, so I ran the obvious head-to-head test: one batch of wings fried continuously until done versus another fried partway, removed from the oil and allowed to rest briefly, and then fried again until cooked through. After draining them, I would toss both batches in the same amount of sauce to see which one stayed crispier.

It wasn't even a contest: Whereas the wings that had been fried once and then sauced started to soften up almost instantly, the double-fried batch still delivered real crunch after being doused with the sauce. What's more, the double-fried wings were juicier than any batch I'd made before. Why? Chicken skin contains a lot of moisture, so producing crispy wings (which have a higher ratio of skin to meat than any other part of the chicken) means removing as much moisture as possible from the chicken skin before the meat overcooks. When you fry just once, the meat finishes cooking before all of the moisture is driven out of the chicken skin, and the remaining moisture migrates to the crust and turns it soggy. Covering the wings with sauce makes the sogginess even worse. But when you fry twice, the interruption of the cooking and the brief cooldown period slow the cooking of the meat; as a result, you can extend the overall cooking time and expel all the moisture from the skin without overcooking the chicken.

There was my proof that double frying was worth the time—and, frankly, it wasn't the tediously long cooking process I thought it would be. Yes, I had to do the first fry in two batches, for two reasons: The oil temperature would drop too much if I put all the chicken in at once because there would be so much moisture from the skin to cook off; plus, the wet coating would cause the wings to stick together if they were crowded in the pot. But the frying took only about 7 minutes per batch. As the parcooked wings rested on a wire rack, I brought the oil temperature up to 375 degrees. Then, following the lead of one of the more prominent Korean fried chicken recipes I'd found, I dumped all the wings back into the pot at once for the second stage. After another 7 minutes, they were deeply golden and shatteringly crispy. All told, I'd produced 3 pounds of perfectly crispy wings in roughly half an hour. Not bad.

SAVORY, SPICY, SWEET

Back to my placeholder sauce, which was close but a tad sharp from the raw minced garlic and ginger. Instead, I placed the ginger and garlic in a large bowl with a tablespoon of sesame oil and microwaved the mixture for 1 minute, just long enough to take the edge off. Then I whisked in the remaining sauce ingredients. The sweet-savory-spicy balance was pitch-perfect.

Before tossing them in the sauce, I let the wings rest for 2 minutes so the coating could cool and set. When I did add them to the sauce, they were still so crispy that they clunked encouragingly against the sides of the bowl. In fact, the crust's apparent staying power made me curious to see how long the crunch would last, so I set some wings aside and found that they stayed truly crispy for 2 hours. Impressive—even though I knew they'd be gobbled up long before that.

Korean Fried Chicken Wings

SERVES 4 TO 6 AS A MAIN DISH

A rasp-style grater makes quick work of turning the garlic into a paste. Gochujang, a Korean chile-soybean paste, can be found in Asian markets and in some supermarkets. Tailor the heat level of your wings by adjusting its amount. If you can't find gochujang, substitute an equal amount of Sriracha sauce and add only 2 tablespoons of water to the sauce. Use a Dutch oven that holds 6 quarts or more. For a complete meal, serve with steamed white rice and a slaw.

1 tablespoon toasted sesame oil
1 teaspoon garlic, minced to paste
1 teaspoon grated fresh ginger
1¾ cups water
3 tablespoons sugar
2–3 tablespoons gochujang
1 tablespoon soy sauce
2 quarts vegetable oil
1 cup all-purpose flour
3 tablespoons cornstarch
3 pounds chicken wings, cut at joints, wingtips discarded

1. Combine sesame oil, garlic, and ginger in large bowl and microwave until mixture is bubbly and garlic and ginger are fragrant but not browned, 40 to 60 seconds. Whisk in ¼ cup water, sugar, gochujang, and soy sauce until smooth; set aside.
2. Heat vegetable oil in large Dutch oven over medium-high heat to 350 degrees. While oil heats, whisk flour, cornstarch, and remaining 1½ cups water in second large bowl until smooth. Set wire rack in rimmed baking sheet and set aside.
3. Place half of wings in batter and stir to coat. Using tongs, remove wings from batter one at a time, allowing any excess batter to drip back into bowl, and add to hot oil. Increase heat to high and cook, stirring occasionally to prevent wings from sticking, until coating is light golden and beginning to crisp, about 7 minutes. (Oil temperature will drop sharply after adding wings.) Transfer wings to prepared rack. Return oil to 350 degrees and repeat with remaining wings. Reduce heat to medium and let second batch of wings rest for 5 minutes.
4. Heat oil to 375 degrees. Carefully return all wings to oil and cook, stirring occasionally, until deep golden brown and very crispy, about 7 minutes. Return wings to rack and let stand for 2 minutes. Transfer wings to reserved sauce and toss until coated. Return wings to rack and let stand for 2 minutes to allow coating to set. Transfer to platter and serve.

HOW TO CUT UP CHICKEN WINGS

Our recipe for Korean Fried Chicken Wings calls for cutting the wings into three parts: drumettes, midsections, and wingtips. Here's how to do it.

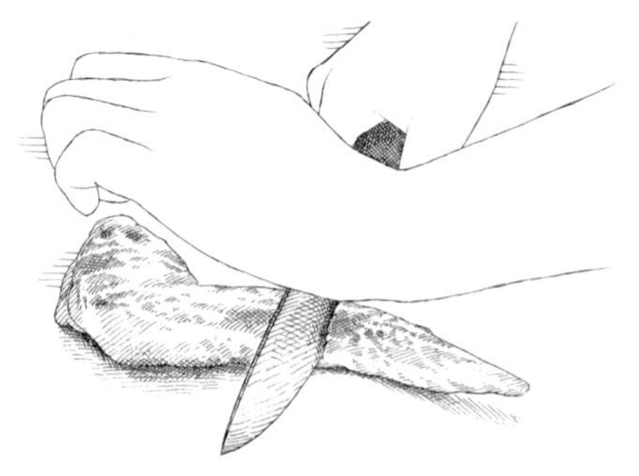

1. Using your fingertip, locate joint between wingtip and midsection. Place blade of chef's knife on joint, between bones, and using palm of your nonknife hand, press down on blade to cut through skin and tendon, as shown.

2. Find joint between midsection and drumette and repeat process to cut through skin and joint. Discard wingtip.

THE IMPORTANCE OF COOKING IN BATCHES

When preparing to fry our wings, we heat the oil to 350 degrees and then cook the wings in batches. We do this because trying to cook the wings all at once (at least for the first fry) would cause the freshly battered wings to stick together; plus, the temperature of the oil would drop too much. Although the temperature will still drop when you add half of the wings, as long as it stays above 250 degrees (where there is enough energy to evaporate water and brown the exterior), the results will be fine.

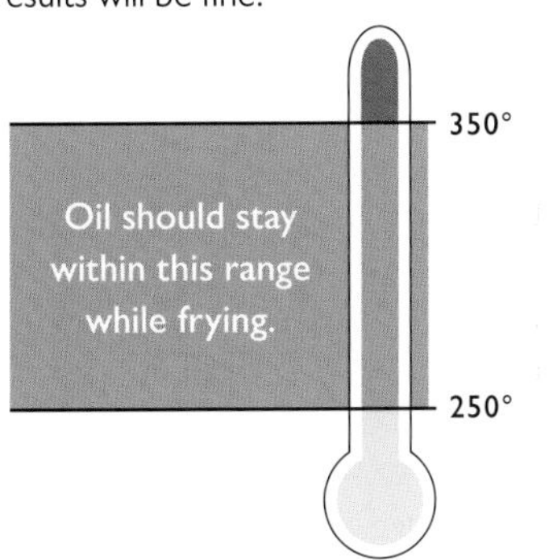

WINGING IT, KOREAN-STYLE

Korean fried chicken wings boast a big crunch and a complex sauce that make them appealing to eat, but they also employ a relatively quick and easy cooking method that makes them more appealing to prepare than many other styles of fried chicken.

DOUBLE FRYING ISN'T DOUBLE THE WORK

Double frying is crucial for the crunchy texture of our wings because it drives more moisture from the skin—but it's not as onerous as you might think. Each batch of wings takes just 7 minutes, and the second fry can be done in one large batch.

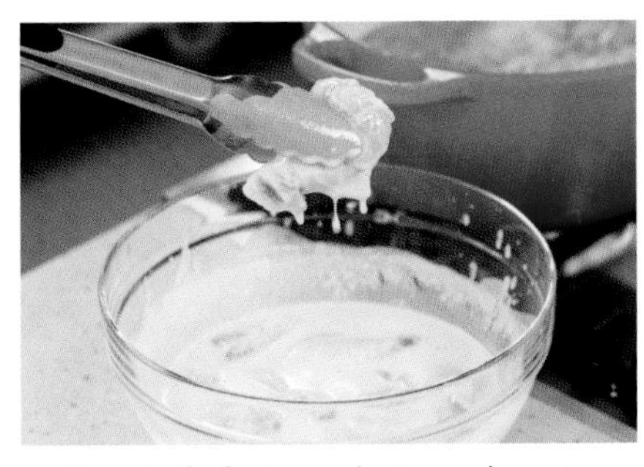

1. Place half of wings in batter and toss to coat. Remove wings from batter one at a time, allowing excess batter to drip back into bowl, and add to hot oil.

2. Increase heat to high and cook, stirring occasionally, until coating is light golden and beginning to crisp, about 7 minutes. Transfer wings to prepared rack and repeat with second batch of wings.

3. Heat oil to 375 degrees, carefully return all wings to oil, and cook, stirring occasionally, until deep golden-brown and very crispy, about 7 minutes. Return to wire rack and let rest for 2 minutes before tossing with sauce.

A NEW WAY TO PAN-SEAR CHICKEN BREASTS

KEITH DRESSER, *March/April 2010*

What cook desperate for a quick dinner hasn't thrown a boneless, skinless chicken breast into a hot pan, keeping fingers crossed for edible results? The fact is, pan-searing is a surefire way to ruin this cut. Unlike a split chicken breast, which has the bone and skin to help keep the meat moist and juicy, a boneless, skinless breast is fully exposed to the intensity of the hot pan. Inevitably, it emerges moist in the middle and dry at the edges, with an exterior that's leathery and tough. But there's no denying the appeal of a cut that requires no butchering. What would it take to get a pan-seared boneless, skinless breast every bit as flavorful, moist, and tender as its skin-on counterpart?

SLOW COOKER

I wasn't the only one to think that the typical sear-cover-and-cook approach needed an overhaul. The problem is that the center of a thick chicken breast takes a long time to reach 165 degrees. Meanwhile, the outer layers are busy overcooking, losing moisture, and turning stringy and tough. One unconventional recipe called for parcooking the chicken in water before searing. In theory, the idea was sound: Poaching would cook the breasts gently and evenly, and the parcooked, warm chicken should take much less time to develop a flavorful brown crust than straight-from-the-fridge meat. Less time in a hot skillet equals less moisture lost. The chicken was juicy and brown, all right—but also flavorless, since much of the chicken's juices seeped into the cooking liquid and subsequently got poured down the drain.

Moving on, I tried ditching the water bath in lieu of the oven, still keeping the same gently-parcook-then-sear order. I placed four chicken breasts in a baking pan, cooked them in a 275-degree oven until they hit 150 degrees, and then seared them. They browned quickly and beautifully, but while the meat was moist enough on the inside, the exterior had so dehydrated that I practically needed a steak knife to saw through it.

What about salting? Like brining, salting changes the structure of meat proteins, helping them to retain more moisture as they cook. Ideally, chicken should be salted for at least 6 hours to ensure full penetration and juiciness. But boneless, skinless breasts are supposed to be quick and easy, so I wasn't willing to commit more than 30 extra minutes to the process. I found that poking holes into the meat with a fork created channels for the salt to reach the interior of the chicken, maximizing the short salting time. This made the interior even juicier, but the exterior was still too dried out.

How could I protect the chicken's exterior from the oven's dry heat? I tried the exact same method, this time wrapping the baking dish tightly in foil before heating. Bingo! In this enclosed environment, any moisture released by the chicken stayed trapped under the foil, keeping the exterior from drying out without becoming so overtly wet that it couldn't brown quickly. In fact, this cover-and-cook method proved so effective that I could combine the 30-minute salting step with the roasting step.

TAKE COVER

I now had breasts that were supremely moist and tender on the inside with a flavorful, browned exterior—a big improvement. With a little more effort, could I do better still? To protect thin cutlets from the heat of the pan and encourage faster browning, many recipes dredge them in flour. Raw breasts are malleable, so they make good contact with the pan. The parcooked breasts, on the other hand, had already firmed up slightly, so only some of the flour was able to come in contact with the hot oil in the pan, leading to spotty browning.

Simple dredging was out, and I definitely didn't want to go the full breading route. The only other thing I could think of was a technique from Chinese cooking called velveting. Here the meat is dipped in a mixture of oil and cornstarch, which provides a thin, protective layer that keeps the protein moist and tender even when exposed to the ultrahigh heat of stir-frying. Though I'd never heard of using this method on large pieces of meat like breasts, I saw no reason it wouldn't work here. I brushed my parcooked chicken with a mixture of 2 tablespoons melted butter (which would contribute more flavor than oil) and a heaping tablespoon of cornstarch before searing it.

We start cooking boneless chicken breasts in the oven so they need only a brief stint in a hot pan to brown.

As soon as I put the breasts in the pan, I noticed that the slurry helped the chicken make better contact with the hot skillet, and as I flipped the pieces, I was happy to see an even, golden crust. However, tasters reported that the cornstarch was leaving a slightly pasty residue. Replacing it with flour didn't work; the protein in flour produced a crust that was tough and bready instead of light and crisp. It turned out that achieving the right balance of protein and starch was the key. A mixture of 3 parts flour to 1 part cornstarch created a thin, browned, crisp coating that kept the breast's exterior as moist as the interior—some tasters thought it was even better than real chicken skin itself.

Served on its own or with a simple pan sauce, this tender, crisp-coated chicken far surpassed any other pan-seared breasts I've ever made.

Pan-Seared Chicken Breasts

SERVES 4

For the best results, buy similarly sized chicken breasts. If the breasts have the tenderloin attached, leave it in place and follow the upper range of baking time in step 1. For optimal texture, sear the chicken immediately after removing it from the oven. Serve with Lemon and Chive Pan Sauce (recipe follows), if desired.

- 4 (6- to 8-ounce) boneless, skinless chicken breasts, trimmed
- 2 teaspoons kosher salt
- 1 tablespoon vegetable oil
- 2 tablespoons unsalted butter, melted
- 1 tablespoon all-purpose flour
- 1 teaspoon cornstarch
- ½ teaspoon pepper

1. Adjust oven rack to lower-middle position and heat oven to 275 degrees. Using fork, poke thickest half of breasts 5 or 6 times and sprinkle each with ½ teaspoon salt. Transfer breasts, skinned side down, to 13 by 9-inch baking dish and cover tightly with aluminum foil. Bake until breasts register 145 to 150 degrees, 30 to 40 minutes.
2. Remove chicken from oven; transfer, skinned side up, to paper towel–lined plate; and pat dry with paper towels. Heat oil in 12-inch skillet over medium-high heat until just smoking. While skillet is heating, whisk melted butter, flour, cornstarch, and pepper together in bowl. Lightly brush top of chicken with half of butter mixture. Place chicken in skillet, coated side down, and cook until browned, about 4 minutes. While chicken browns, brush with remaining butter mixture. Flip breasts, reduce heat to medium, and cook until second side is browned and breasts register 160 degrees, 3 to 4 minutes. Transfer breasts to large plate and let rest for 5 minutes before serving.

accompaniment

Lemon and Chive Pan Sauce

MAKES ABOUT ¾ CUP

- 1 shallot, minced
- 1 teaspoon all-purpose flour
- 1 cup chicken broth
- 1 tablespoon lemon juice
- 1 tablespoon minced fresh chives
- 1 tablespoon unsalted butter, chilled
- Salt and pepper

Add shallot to now-empty skillet and cook over medium heat until softened, about 2 minutes. Add flour and cook, stirring constantly, for 30 seconds. Slowly whisk in broth, scraping up any browned bits. Bring to vigorous simmer and cook until reduced to ¾ cup, 3 to 5 minutes. Stir in any accumulated chicken juices; return to simmer and cook for 30 seconds. Off heat, whisk in lemon juice, chives, and butter. Season with salt and pepper to taste. Pour sauce over chicken and serve immediately.

A PERFECT COATING COMBO

To end up with moist exteriors, our pan-seared boneless, skinless breasts needed light protection. But slurries made with melted butter and the usual suspects—cornstarch and flour—each had issues. Cornstarch is a pure starch prone to forming a gel that left pasty spots on the meat. The proteins in flour, on the other hand, link together to form gluten, leading to an overly tough, bready coating. Using a combination of cornstarch and flour, however, created the perfect light, crisp, evenly browned coating.

The explanation is simple: Each ingredient tempers the effect of the other. With flour in the mix, the cornstarch is sufficiently diluted by protein to prevent it from forming a paste, whereas the protein is diluted enough that it doesn't cause the crust to become bready.

BETTER BONELESS BREASTS

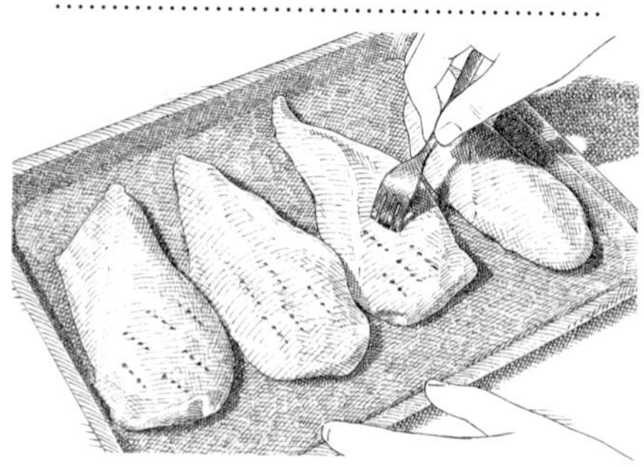

1. **POKE AND SALT** Salting chicken seasons meat, keeping it moist. Poking thicker part of breasts ensures even seasoning.

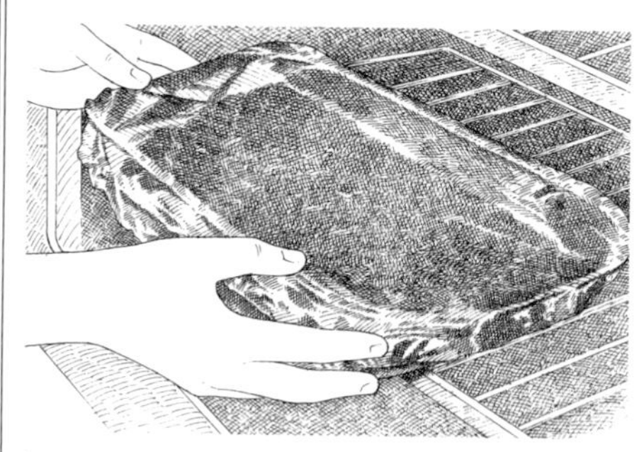

2. **COVER AND BAKE** Baking at low temperature in foil-covered dish cooks chicken evenly and keeps exterior from drying out.

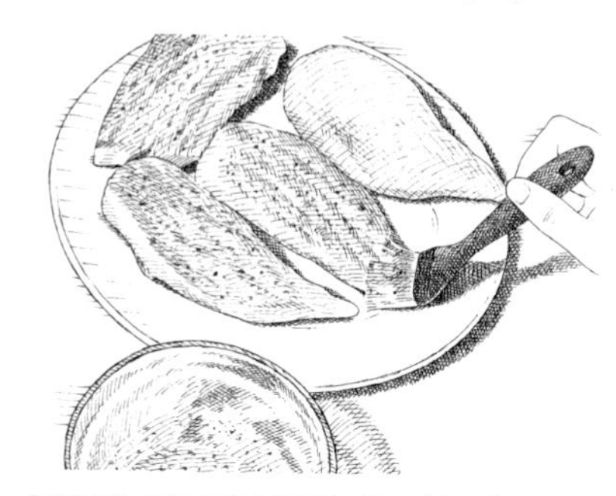

3. **BRUSH ON COATING** Brushing butter, flour, and cornstarch onto breasts creates "skin" to protect meat during searing.

4. **SEAR QUICKLY** Briefly searing parcooked coated breasts keeps them moist and creates crisp exteriors.

ULTIMATE PAN-SEARED SKIN-ON CHICKEN BREASTS

ANDREW JANJIGIAN, *January/February 2014*

I'm always on the lookout for ways to get great skin on chicken. By that I mean skin that's paper-thin, deep golden brown, and so well crisped that it crackles when you take a bite. Such perfectly cooked skin, however, is actually a rarity. A good roast chicken may have patches of it, but the rotund shape of the bird means that uneven cooking is inevitable and that some of the skin will also cook up flabby and pale. And even on relatively flat chicken parts, there's the layer of fat beneath the skin to contend with: By the time it melts away during searing, the exterior often chars and the meat itself overcooks.

When I recently came across one of the best specimens of chicken I'd ever tasted, I had to figure out how to recreate it myself. The restaurant was Maialino (a Danny Meyer venture) in New York City, and the dish was Pollo alla Diavola. The tender meat and the tangy, spicy pickled cherry pepper sauce that was served with it had their own charms, but the chicken skin was incredible—a sheath so gorgeously bronzed and shatteringly crunchy that I'd swear it was deep-fried.

Starting skin-on chicken breasts in a cold pan and weighing them down for part of the cooking time gives them shatteringly crisp skin.

STARTING SMALL(ER)

There were a number of hurdles to achieving the same chicken-skin nirvana at home, not the least of which was the cut of meat itself. At Maialino, the kitchen serves half of a chicken per person, removing all but the wing bones from the meat before searing it.

The point of all that butchery is to flatten out the bird so that its entire surface makes direct, even contact with the pan—a must for producing thoroughly rendered, deeply crisped skin. But since few home cooks can do that kind of knife work confidently and quickly, I decided to keep things simple and work with only breast meat. Removing the breast bones required just a few quick strokes of a sharp knife. Moreover, switching from half chickens to split breasts made for more reasonable portions. I would serve a pair of breasts—enough for two people—and keep things simple so that the dish would work as a weeknight meal.

Of course, the drawback to working with breast meat would be its tendency to overcook, particularly once I'd removed the bones—poor conductors of heat and, therefore, good insulators. My very basic initial cooking technique was placing the boned breasts skin side down in a hot, oiled skillet to crisp up their surface and then flipping the meat to let it color briefly on the other side. This gave me fairly crispy skin but meat that was dry and chalky. When I tried a slightly gentler approach, briefly pan-searing the chicken skin side down and then transferring the pan to the more even heat of a 450-degree oven until the breasts were cooked through, the meat was only somewhat more moist and tender. Clearly, some form of pretreatment was essential if I wanted the meat to be as succulent as the skin was crispy.

Brining was out, since it introduces additional water to the meat and inevitably leaves the skin slightly waterlogged. Salting would be the way to go. Besides seasoning the meat deeply and helping it retain moisture as it cooks, salt would assist in drying out the skin. To further encourage the skin's dehydration (as well as the salt's penetration), I poked holes in both the skin and meat with a sharp knife before applying the salt.

WORTH THE WEIGHT

Salting and slashing helped, but they got me only so far with the skin, which indicated that my simple searing technique needed tweaking. Thus far, the best I'd accomplished was unevenly cooked skin: patches that were gorgeously crispy and brown and adjacent patches that were inedibly pale and flabby. What's more, the skin tended to shrink away from the edges of the breast as it cooked, which, apart from the unsightly appearance, caused the now-exposed meat to turn dry and leathery. Finally, the thin end of the breast still cooked up a bit dry by the time the thick end had fully cooked.

Evening out the thickness of the meat was easy: I simply pounded the thick end of the breast gently so that the entire piece cooked at the same rate. As for evening out the browning of the skin, I adapted a classic Italian technique that the chef at Maialino also uses: pinning the bird to the cooking surface with bricks. I mimicked that technique by weighing down the chicken breasts with a heavy Dutch oven. (Since I had no interest in transferring the weighty duo of pans to the oven, I'd switch to cooking the breasts entirely on the stovetop.) After cooking the breasts for 10 minutes over medium heat, I removed the pot and surveyed the skin, which, for the most part, was far crispier than ever before and not at all shrunken. But pockets of fat persisted under the surface at the center and along the edges. And the meat? It was way overcooked now that it was pressed hard against the hot surface.

Amid my frustration, I had noticed that when I removed the Dutch oven, a puff of steam arose from the pan—moisture from the chicken that had been trapped beneath the pot. That moisture was thwarting my skin-crisping efforts, so I wondered if the weight was necessary for the entire cooking time or if I could remove it partway through to prevent moisture buildup.

I prepared another batch, this time letting the breasts cook in the preheated oiled skillet under the pot for just 5 minutes before uncovering them. At this stage the skin was only just beginning to brown, but as it continued to cook for another 2 to 4 minutes, the skin remained anchored to the pan, crisping up nicely without contracting in the least. Removing the pot early also allowed the meat to cook a bit more gently. But it wasn't quite gentle enough; dry meat still persisted.

The core problem—that it takes longer to render and crisp chicken skin than it does to cook the meat—had me feeling defeated until I realized a way to give the skin a head start: a "cold" pan. It's a classic French technique for cooking duck breasts—the ultimate example of delicate meat covered with a layer of fatty skin. Putting the meat skin side down in the oiled pan before turning on the heat allows more time for the skin to render out its fat before the temperature of the meat reaches its doneness point. I hoped this approach would apply to chicken.

Initially, I thought I'd hit a roadblock: The breasts were sticking to the skillet—a nonissue when adding proteins to a hot pan, which usually prevents sticking. Fortunately, by the time the skin had rendered and fully crisped up, the breasts came away from the surface with just a gentle tug. Once the skin had achieved shattering crispiness, all it took was a few short minutes on the second side to finish cooking the meat.

TRY A LITTLE TANGINESS

The chicken was tasty enough as is, but to dress things up a bit, I set my sights on developing a few sauces.

My own rendition of Maialino's alla diavola sauce was a reduction of pickled-pepper vinegar and chicken broth, thickened with a little flour and butter and garnished with a few chopped pickled peppers. I also came up with a pair of variations on the same acid-based theme: lemon-rosemary and maple–sherry vinegar.

Satisfying my inner chicken skin perfectionist was gratifying in and of itself. But coming up with a quick and elegant way to dress up ordinary old chicken breasts? That was even better.

Crispy-Skinned Chicken Breasts with Vinegar-Pepper Pan Sauce

SERVES 2

This recipe requires refrigerating the salted meat for at least 1 hour before cooking. Two 10- to 12-ounce chicken breasts are ideal, but three smaller ones can fit in the same pan; the skin will be slightly less crispy. A boning knife or sharp paring knife works best to remove the bones from the breasts. To maintain the crispy skin, spoon the sauce around, not over, the breasts when serving.

Chicken

2 (10- to 12-ounce) bone-in split chicken breasts
Kosher salt and pepper
2 tablespoons vegetable oil

Pan Sauce

1 shallot, minced
1 teaspoon all-purpose flour
½ cup chicken broth
¼ cup chopped pickled hot cherry peppers, plus ¼ cup brine
1 tablespoon unsalted butter, chilled
1 teaspoon minced fresh thyme
Salt and pepper

1. *For the chicken:* Place 1 chicken breast, skin side down, on cutting board, with ribs facing away from knife hand. Run tip of knife between breastbone and meat, working from thick end of breast toward thin end. Angling blade slightly and following rib cage, repeat cutting motion several times to remove ribs and breastbone from breast. Find short remnant of wishbone along top edge of breast and run tip of knife along both sides of bone to separate it from meat. Remove tenderloin (reserve for another use) and trim excess fat, taking care not to cut into skin. Repeat with second breast.
2. Using tip of paring knife, poke skin on each breast evenly 30 to 40 times. Turn breasts over and poke thickest half of each breast 5 or 6 times. Cover breasts with plastic wrap and pound thick ends gently with meat pounder until ½ inch thick. Evenly sprinkle each breast with ½ teaspoon kosher salt. Place breasts, skin side up, on wire rack set in rimmed baking sheet, cover loosely with plastic, and refrigerate for at least 1 hour or up to 8 hours.
3. Pat breasts dry with paper towels and sprinkle each breast with ¼ teaspoon pepper. Pour oil in 12-inch skillet and swirl to coat. Place breasts, skin side down, in oil and place skillet over medium heat. Place heavy skillet or Dutch oven on top of breasts. Cook breasts until skin is beginning to brown and meat is beginning to turn opaque along edges, 7 to 9 minutes.
4. Remove weight and continue to cook until skin is well browned and very crispy, 6 to 8 minutes. Flip breasts, reduce heat to medium-low, and cook until second side is lightly browned and meat registers 160 to 165 degrees, 2 to 3 minutes. Transfer breasts to individual plates and let rest while preparing pan sauce.
5. *For the pan sauce:* Pour off all but 2 teaspoons oil from skillet. Return skillet to medium heat and add shallot; cook, stirring occasionally, until shallot is softened, about 2 minutes. Add flour and cook, stirring constantly, for 30 seconds. Increase heat to medium-high, add broth and brine, and bring to simmer, scraping up any browned bits. Simmer until thickened, 2 to 3 minutes. Stir in any accumulated chicken juices; return to simmer and cook for 30 seconds. Remove skillet from heat and whisk in peppers, butter, and thyme; season with salt and pepper to taste. Spoon sauce around breasts and serve.

variations

Crispy-Skinned Chicken Breasts with Maple–Sherry Vinegar Pan Sauce

In step 5, substitute 2 tablespoons sherry vinegar for brine, 1 tablespoon maple syrup for peppers, and sage for thyme.

Crispy-Skinned Chicken Breasts with Lemon-Rosemary Pan Sauce

In step 5, increase broth to ¾ cup and substitute 2 tablespoons lemon juice for brine. Omit peppers and substitute rosemary for thyme.

THE PROBLEM WITH CHICKEN STIR-FRIES

KERI FISHER, *May/June 2004*

The most common, and probably most appealing, stir-fry is made with chicken. Sounds easy, right? Well, it turns out that a good chicken stir-fry is more difficult to prepare than a beef or pork stir-fry because chicken, which has less fat, inevitably becomes dry and stringy when cooked over high heat. I was after a stir-fry that featured tender, juicy, bite-size pieces of chicken paired with just the right combination of vegetables in a simple yet complex-flavored sauce. And because this was a stir-fry, it had to be fairly quick.

In the past, we've used a marinade to impart flavor to meat destined for stir-fries. Chicken was no exception. Tossing the pieces of chicken into a simple soy-sherry mixture for 10 minutes before cooking added much-needed flavor, but it did nothing to improve the texture of the meat.

The obvious solution to dry chicken was brining, our favorite method of adding moisture to poultry. A test of brined boneless breasts (preferred over thighs) did in fact confirm that this method solved the problem of dry chicken. However, a half hour or more of brining time followed by 10 minutes of marinating was out of the question for a quick midweek stir-fry. It seemed redundant to soak the chicken first in one salty solution (brine) and then another (marinade), so I decided to combine the two, using the soy sauce to provide the high salt level in my brine. This turned out to be a key secret of a great chicken stir-fry. Now I was turning out highly flavored, juicy pieces of chicken—most of the time. Given the finicky nature of high-heat cooking, some batches of chicken still occasionally turned out tough because of overcooking.

THE VELVET GLOVE

I next turned to a traditional Chinese technique called velveting, which involves coating chicken pieces in a thin cornstarch and egg white or oil mixture, then parcooking in moderately heated oil. The coating holds precious moisture inside; that extra juiciness makes the chicken seem more tender. Cornstarch mixed with egg white yielded a cakey coating; tasters preferred the more subtle coating provided by cornstarch mixed with oil. This velveted chicken was supple, but it was also pale, and, again, this method seemed far too involved for a quick weeknight dinner.

A hybrid brine/marinade gives lean chicken breasts flavor and moisture in minutes, guaranteeing that the pieces cook up tender and supple.

I wondered if the same method—coating in a cornstarch mixture—would work if I eliminated the parcooking step. It did. This chicken was not only juicy and tender, but it also developed an attractive golden brown coating. Best of all, the entire process took less than 5 minutes. The only problem was that the coating, which was more of an invisible barrier than a crust, became bloated and slimy when cooked in the sauce.

Our science editor explained that the cornstarch was absorbing liquid from the sauce, causing the slippery finish. He suggested cutting the cornstarch with flour, which created a negligible coating—not too thick, not too slimy—that still managed to keep juices inside the chicken. Substituting sesame oil for peanut oil added a rich depth of flavor.

After trying everything from pounded to cubed chicken, tasters voted for simple flat ¼-inch slices, which were all the more easy to cut after freezing the breasts for 15 minutes. These wide, flat slices of chicken browned easily. I cooked them in two batches, first browning one side and then turning them over to quickly brown the second side rather than constantly stirring (or "stir"-frying) as so many other recipes suggest. Although choosing not to stir-fry seemed counterintuitive, I found that the constant motion of that method detracted from the browning of the chicken.

THE FINISH

As for the vegetables in my recipe, a combination of bok choy and red bell pepper worked well with the chicken. For the sauce, the test kitchen has found that chicken broth, rather than soy sauce, makes the best base because it is not overpowering. Oyster sauce works nicely as a flavoring ingredient. We have also tested the addition of cornstarch to help the sauce coat the meat and vegetables and have found that a small amount is necessary. Otherwise, the sauce is too thin and does not adhere properly.

The basic stir-fry method was previously developed in the test kitchen. After the protein (in this case, the chicken) is cooked and removed from the pan, the vegetables are stir-fried in batches, garlic and ginger (the classic stir-fry combination) are quickly cooked in the center of the pan, and then the protein is returned to the pan along with the sauce. This final mixture is cooked over medium heat for 30 seconds to finish.

In the end, a great chicken stir-fry doesn't really take more time to prepare than a bad one. It does, however, require more attention to detail and knowledge of a few quick tricks.

Gingery Stir-Fried Chicken and Bok Choy

SERVES 4

To make slicing the chicken easier, freeze it for 15 minutes. Serve with white rice.

Sauce
¼ cup chicken broth
2 tablespoons dry sherry
1 tablespoon soy sauce
1 tablespoon oyster sauce
2 teaspoons grated fresh ginger
1 teaspoon cornstarch
1 teaspoon sugar
½ teaspoon toasted sesame oil
¼ teaspoon red pepper flakes

Stir-Fry
2 teaspoons grated fresh ginger
1 garlic clove, minced
2 tablespoons plus 2 teaspoons vegetable oil
1 cup water
¼ cup soy sauce
¼ cup dry sherry
1 pound boneless, skinless chicken breasts, trimmed and cut crosswise into ¼-inch-thick strips
2 tablespoons toasted sesame oil
1 tablespoon cornstarch
1 tablespoon all-purpose flour
1 pound bok choy, stalks cut on bias into ¼-inch slices, greens cut into ½-inch-wide strips
1 small red bell pepper, stemmed, seeded, and cut into ¼-inch-wide strips

1. *For the sauce:* Whisk all ingredients together in bowl and set aside.
2. *For the stir-fry:* Combine ginger, garlic, and 1 teaspoon vegetable oil in small bowl and set aside. Combine water, soy sauce, and sherry in medium bowl. Add chicken and stir to break up clumps. Cover with plastic wrap and refrigerate for at least 20 minutes or up to 1 hour. Pour off liquid from chicken.
3. Mix sesame oil, cornstarch, and flour in medium bowl until smooth. Transfer chicken to bowl and toss with cornstarch mixture until evenly coated.
4. Heat 2 teaspoons vegetable oil in 12-inch nonstick skillet over high heat until just smoking. Add half of chicken to skillet in single layer and cook until golden brown, about 1 minute. Using tongs, flip chicken and lightly brown second side, about 30 seconds. Transfer chicken to clean bowl. Repeat with 2 teaspoons vegetable oil and remaining chicken.
5. Add remaining 1 tablespoon vegetable oil to now-empty skillet and heat until just smoking. Add bok choy stalks and bell pepper and cook, stirring, until beginning to brown, about 1 minute. Push vegetables to sides of skillet. Add ginger mixture to center and cook, mashing mixture into pan, until fragrant, about 30 seconds. Stir mixture into vegetables and continue to cook until stalks are crisp-tender, about 30 seconds longer. Stir in bok choy greens and cook until beginning to wilt, about 30 seconds.
6. Return chicken to skillet. Whisk sauce to recombine and add to skillet; reduce heat to medium and cook, stirring constantly, until sauce is thickened and chicken is cooked through, about 30 seconds. Transfer to platter and serve.

CHOOSING THE RIGHT PAN

When stir-frying, a 12-inch nonstick skillet is best: It's large enough to accommodate food without any steaming or sticking. A flat-bottomed wok has less surface area in contact with the stovetop than the nonstick skillet. In conventional skillets, the chicken sticks, burns, or steams.

THE BEST CHOICE
Nonstick Skillet

A MEDIOCRE CHOICE
Flat-Bottomed Wok

A BAD CHOICE
Traditional Skillet

THE WORST CHOICE
Small Skillet

PREPPING BOK CHOY

1. Trim bottom inch from head of bok choy. Cut leafy green portion away from either side of white stalk.

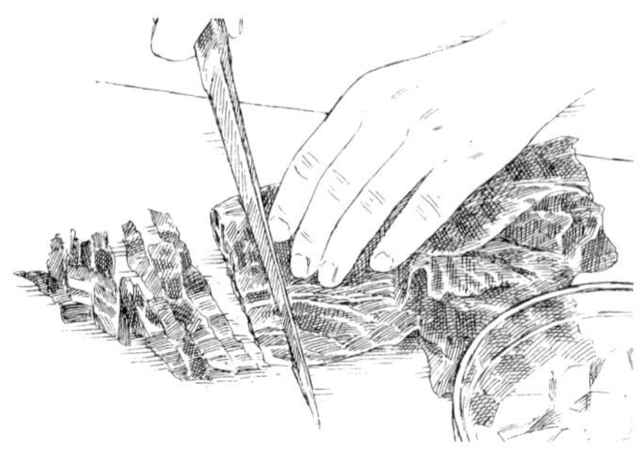

2. Cut each stalk in half lengthwise and then crosswise on bias into ¼-inch-wide pieces. Stack leafy greens and then slice crosswise into ½-inch-wide strips.

SLICING CHICKEN THIN

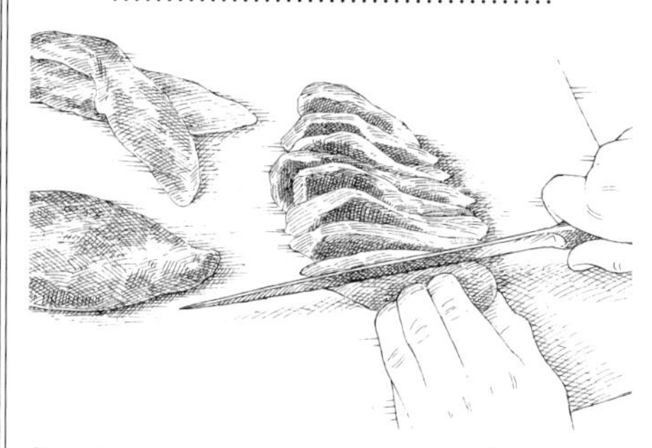

Slice breasts across grain into ¼-inch-wide strips. Cut center pieces in half so they are same length as end pieces. Cut tenderloins on diagonal to produce pieces similar in size to strips of breast meat.

FOOLPROOF BARBECUED CHICKEN

LAN LAM, *July/August 2013*

I have fond memories of eating barbecued chicken when I was growing up, but not because the chicken was any good. My family's version of this summertime staple, one of the few American dishes that my immigrant parents made, involved my father dousing chicken parts with bottled sauce and dumping the pieces over a ripping-hot fire. He would then spend the next 45 minutes shuffling them around on the grate in a vain effort to get the pieces to cook evenly. Some of the pieces always cooked up dry, while others were raw at the bone. Worse, flare-ups caused by fat dripping onto the coals carbonized the skin well before it had a chance to fully render. But it was summer, it was fun to eat outside, and if we poured enough of the (inevitably) ultrasweet sauce on the chicken, we could mask its shortcomings.

I've eaten enough subpar barbecued chicken to realize that my dad is not the only one who doesn't know how to produce juicy, deeply seasoned, evenly cooked chicken parts on the grill. With decades of test kitchen barbecuing experience on my side, I set out to foolproof this American classic.

MAKING ARRANGEMENTS

There were a few basic barbecue tenets I put in place from the get-go. First, I ditched the single-level fire recommended by a surprising number of recipes and built an indirect one: I corralled all the coals on one side of the kettle, enabling me to sear the chicken over the hotter side and then pull it over to the cooler side, where the meat would cook gently and the skin could render slowly. Cooking the chicken opposite from (rather than on top of) the coals for most of the time would also cut back on flare-ups. Second, I salted the meat and let it sit for several hours before grilling it, since this pretreatment would change the meat's protein structure so that it would hold on to more moisture as it cooked—added insurance against overcooking. Finally, I would wait to apply barbecue sauce (which usually contains sugary ingredients) until after searing; this would prevent the sauce from burning and give the skin a chance to develop color.

I proceeded to sear 6 pounds of breasts and leg quarters on the hotter part of the grill. Once both sides of the meat were brown, I dragged the pieces to the cooler part of the kettle, painted on some placeholder bottled sauce, and considered my core challenge: how to ensure that both the white and dark pieces cooked at an even pace.

Since food that sits closest to the fire cooks faster, I lined up the fattier, more heat-resistant leg quarters closest to the coals and the leaner, more delicate breasts farther away and covered the grill. About an hour later, the breast meat was just about done, the skin was nicely rendered and thin, and the sauce was concentrated and set. The problem was that several leg quarters were chewy and dry. Salting clearly wasn't enough to protect them from the heat, even when positioned next to the coals instead of on top of them.

Brushing the sauce on in stages keeps its flavor bright and prevents it from burning on the grill.

GETTING EVEN

I needed a way to even out and lower the heat without using less charcoal (when I used 25 percent less charcoal, the heat dwindled before the meat finished cooking).Instead, I set a disposable aluminum pan opposite the coals and partially filled it with water. Both the pan and the water absorb heat, lowering the owverall temperature inside the kettle and eliminating hot spots.

I cooked another batch using the water pan and finally made some headway. The ambient temperature inside the grill had dropped by about 50 degrees—a good sign. I checked the pieces midway through grilling and was pleased to see that the dark meat was cooking at a slower, steadier pace. By the end of the hour, both the white and dark pieces were hitting their target temperatures (160 and 175 degrees, respectively).

FLAVOR MAKERS

My cooking method had come a long way, but I could hardly call my results "barbecued." For one thing, I needed a homemade alternative for the characterless bottled sauce. My tasters also reminded me that, although the chicken was nicely seasoned after salting, the flavor of the meat itself was unremarkable once you got past the skin.

But salting the chicken reminded me that I could easily apply bolder flavor in the same way—with a rub. I kept the blend basic: In addition to the kosher salt, I mixed together equal amounts of onion and garlic powders and paprika; a touch of cayenne for subtle heat; and a generous 2 tablespoons of brown sugar, which would caramelize during cooking.

For the sauce, I fell back on the test kitchen's go-to recipe, which smartens the typical ketchup-based concoction. Molasses adds depth, while cider vinegar, Worcestershire sauce, and Dijon mustard keep sweetness in check. Grated onion, minced garlic, chili powder, cayenne, and pepper round out the flavors.

But there was a downside to applying the sauce just after searing: Namely, after cooking for an hour, it lost a measure of its bright tanginess. Instead, I applied the sauce in stages, brushing on the first coat just after searing and then applying a second midway through grilling. That minor adjustment made a surprisingly big difference. I also reserved some of the sauce for passing at the table.

This was perfectly cooked, seriously good chicken. Now all I have to do is convince my dad to let me handle the cooking at our next family barbecue.

Sweet and Tangy Barbecued Chicken

SERVES 6 TO 8

When browning the chicken over the hotter side of the grill, move it away from any flare-ups.

Chicken

2 tablespoons packed dark brown sugar
1½ tablespoons kosher salt
1½ teaspoons onion powder
1½ teaspoons garlic powder
1½ teaspoons paprika
¼ teaspoon cayenne pepper
6 pounds bone-in chicken pieces (split breasts and/or leg quarters), trimmed

Sauce

1 cup ketchup
5 tablespoons molasses
3 tablespoons cider vinegar
2 tablespoons Worcestershire sauce
2 tablespoons Dijon mustard
¼ teaspoon pepper
2 tablespoons vegetable oil
⅓ cup grated onion
1 garlic clove, minced
1 teaspoon chili powder
¼ teaspoon cayenne pepper
1 large disposable aluminum roasting pan (if using charcoal) or 2 disposable aluminum pie plates (if using gas)

1. *For the chicken:* Combine sugar, salt, onion powder, garlic powder, paprika, and cayenne in bowl. Arrange chicken on rimmed baking sheet and sprinkle both sides evenly with spice rub. Cover with plastic wrap and refrigerate for at least 6 hours or up to 24 hours.

2. *For the sauce:* Whisk ketchup, molasses, vinegar, Worcestershire, mustard, and pepper together in bowl. Heat oil in medium saucepan over medium heat until shimmering. Add onion and garlic; cook until onion is softened, 2 to 4 minutes. Add chili powder and cayenne and cook until fragrant, about 30 seconds. Whisk in ketchup mixture and bring to boil. Reduce heat to medium-low and simmer gently for 5 minutes. Set aside ⅔ cup sauce to baste chicken and reserve remaining sauce for serving. (Sauce can be refrigerated for up to 1 week.)

3A. *For a charcoal grill:* Open bottom vent halfway and place disposable pan filled with 3 cups water on 1 side of grill. Light large chimney starter filled with charcoal briquettes (6 quarts). When top coals are partially covered with ash, pour evenly over other half of grill (opposite disposable pan). Set cooking grate in place, cover, and open lid vent halfway. Heat grill until hot, about 5 minutes.

3B. *For a gas grill:* Place 2 disposable pie plates, each filled with 1½ cups water, directly on 1 burner of gas grill (opposite primary burner). Turn all burners to high, cover, and heat grill until hot, about 15 minutes. Turn primary burner to medium-high and turn off other burner(s). (Adjust primary burner as needed to maintain grill temperature of 325 to 350 degrees.)

4. Clean and oil cooking grate. Place chicken, skin side down, over hotter side of grill and cook until browned and blistered in spots, 2 to 5 minutes. Flip chicken and cook until second side is browned, 4 to 6 minutes. Move chicken to cooler side and brush both sides with ⅓ cup sauce. Arrange chicken, skin side up, with leg quarters closest to fire and breasts farthest away. Cover (positioning lid vent over chicken if using charcoal) and cook for 25 minutes.

5. Brush both sides of chicken with remaining ⅓ cup sauce and continue to cook, covered, until breasts register 160 degrees and leg quarters register 175 degrees, 25 to 35 minutes longer.

6. Transfer chicken to serving platter, tent with aluminum foil, and let rest for 10 minutes. Serve, passing reserved sauce separately.

DOES YOUR LEG QUARTER NEED A TRIM?

Some leg quarters come with the backbone still attached. Here's an easy way to remove it.

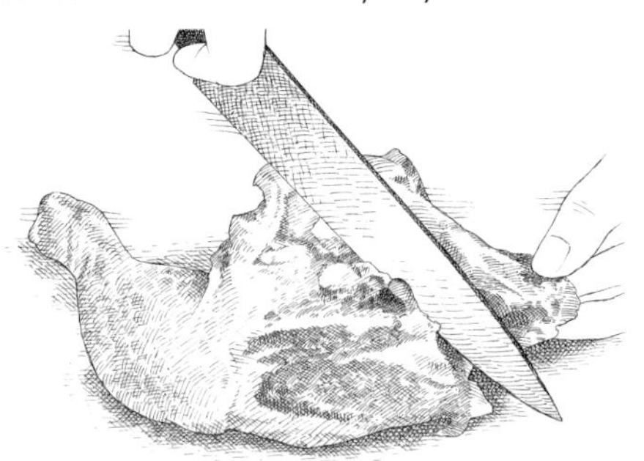

Holding the leg quarter skin side down, grasp the backbone and bend it back to pop the thigh bone out of its socket. Place the leg on a cutting board and cut through the joint and any attached skin.

PACKAGED PARTS HAVE A WEIGHT PROBLEM

Grabbing a package of chicken parts is usually a lot faster than standing in line at the meat counter to buy them individually. But that convenience may come at a cost. The same chicken parts aren't required to be the same weight and their size can vary dramatically. For example, the U.S. Department of Agriculture permits leg quarters sold together to weigh between 8.5 and 24 ounces. Breasts can come from chickens that weigh between 3 and 5.5 pounds—a difference that translates to the breasts themselves. Such a disparity can be a problem when you're trying to get food to cook at the same rate. This lack of standardization showed up in our own shopping. We bought 26 packages of split breasts and leg quarters (representing five brands) from five different supermarkets. When we weighed each piece and calculated the maximum weight variation within each package, the differences were startling: The largest pieces were twice the size of the smallest. Worse, some leg quarters came with attached backbone pieces that had to be cut off and discarded (which means throwing away money). Lesson learned: Whenever possible, buy chicken parts individually from a butcher, who can select similar-size pieces.

RESCUING BARBECUED CHICKEN KEBABS

MATTHEW CARD, *May/June 2011*

In theory, barbecued chicken kebabs sound pretty great: char-streaked chunks of juicy meat lacquered with sweet-sharp barbecue sauce. Using skewers sounds easy, too—a fast-and-loose sort of way to capture the charms of barbecued chicken without the time and patience needed to cook a whole bird or the focus essential to tending a host of mixed parts. Ah, but if only the kebabs lived up to that promise. The quandary is that without an insulating layer of skin, even the fattiest thigh meat can dry out and toughen when exposed to the blazing heat of the grill. And forget about ultralean skinless breast meat: It's a lost cause. Simply slathering barbecue sauce onto skewered chicken chunks—the approach embraced by most recipes—does little to address this fundamental problem. In fact, it's often one of the ruining factors: If applied too early or in too great a volume, the sauce drips off the meat, burns, and fixes the chicken fast to the grill.

RUBBED THE RIGHT WAY

My goal was simple: juicy, tender chicken with plenty of sticky-sweet, smoke-tinged flavor. I wanted an everyday sort of recipe, one that would work equally well with white or dark meat (skewered separately since they cook at different rates) and brushed with a no-nonsense homemade barbecue sauce. But before I got to the sauce (I would use a simple ketchup-based placeholder for now), I had to ensure that the meat was as moist and tender as possible. Brining was the natural next step.

The secret to the best smoky, richly flavored chicken kebabs is rubbing them with a spiced bacon paste.

When meat soaks in salty water, the salt helps pull the liquid into the meat, plumping the chicken and thoroughly seasoning it. The salt also denatures the meat proteins, creating gaps that trap water and guard against drying out. But brining isn't a cure-all: When I made kebabs with chicken breasts and thighs that I brined after cutting them into pieces (1-inch chunks cooked through relatively quickly yet required enough time on the grill to pick up smoky flavor), the brine made the meat so slick and wet that any barbecue sauce I brushed on toward the end of cooking dribbled off.

Would a dry method work better? Sure enough, a heavily salted dry spice mixture (I let the rubbed chicken sit for 30 minutes before grilling) was just the ticket. As the mixture sat, the salt drew the juices to the surface of the chicken pieces, where they mixed with the seasonings and then flowed back into the chicken. The rub also crisped up on the chicken's exterior as it cooked, forming a craggy surface that the sauce could really cling to. To avoid overpowering the chicken, I steered clear of outspoken spices, settling on both sweet and smoked paprika, the former contributing depth and the latter helping to boost the overall smokiness of the dish. A few teaspoons of sugar added to the rub aided in browning, pleasantly complicating flavor.

WHEN CHICKEN MEETS PIG

With its ruddy exterior, my chicken now looked the part, but the meat was still not quite moist enough and, despite the improvements made by the spices, lacked sufficient depth of flavor. In a hunt for a solution, I read up on Middle Eastern kebab cookery. I learned that Turkish chefs skewer slices of pure lamb fat between lamb chunks before grilling. The fat melts during cooking, continually basting the lean meat.

Using musky lamb fat in a chicken recipe seemed too weird, but what about another fatty yet more complementary meat: smoky bacon? I cut several strips into 1-inch pieces and spliced the chicken pieces with the fatty squares before putting the kebabs on the grill. Unfortunately, by the time the chicken was cooked through, the bacon—tightly wedged as it was between the chicken chunks—had failed to crisp. For my next attempt, I tried wrapping strips of bacon around the kebabs in a spiral-like helix. This time, the bacon turned crunchy, but its flavor overwhelmed the chicken's more delicate taste.

If strips didn't work, how about rendered bacon fat? I liberally coated the prepared kebabs with drippings from freshly cooked bacon and set them on the grill grate. Within minutes, the fat trickled into the coals and prompted flare-ups, blackening most of the chicken. What wasn't burnt, however, was moist and tasted addictively smoky.

If raw strips were too much of a good thing and rendered fat dripped off too quickly, was there an in-between solution? This time around, I finely diced a few slices of bacon and mixed them with the chicken chunks, salt, and spices. After giving the kebabs a 30-minute rest in the refrigerator, I grilled them over a moderately hot half-grill fire. (I had piled all of the coals on one side of the grill and left the other half empty to create a cooler "safety zone" on which to momentarily set the kebabs in the event of a flare-up.) Once the chicken was browned on one side (this took about 2 minutes), I flipped it a quarter turn, giving me nearly done meat in about eight minutes. At this point, I brushed barbecue sauce onto the kebabs, leaving them on the grill for just a minute or two longer to give the sauce a chance to caramelize. (Adding the sauce any earlier is a surefire route to scorched chicken.) The bacon bits clung

tenaciously to the chicken, producing the best results yet.

But I wasn't finished. The bacon hadn't cooked evenly: Some bits were overly crisp and others still a little limp. I had an idea that would take care of the problem: grinding the bacon into a spreadable paste. Admittedly, the concept was a bit wacky, but I'd come this far with bacon, so why not? I tossed a couple of strips of raw bacon into a food processor and ground them down to a paste, which I then mixed with the chicken chunks and dry rub. As before, I rested the coated chicken in the refrigerator for half an hour before putting it on the grill. The chicken looked beautiful when it came off the fire: deeply browned and covered in a thick, shiny glaze, with no burnt bacon bits in sight. But to my great disappointment, not to mention puzzlement, the chicken was now dry and had lost flavor. I repeated the test to make sure this batch wasn't a fluke and got the same results.

What could be going on? The only thing I was doing differently was coating the chicken in paste rather than simply mixing it with small pieces of the smoked meat combined with the salt, sugar, and spices. Then it occurred to me: Maybe the fatty ground-up bacon was adhering so well to the chicken that it was acting as a barrier to the salt, which now couldn't penetrate the meat. What if I first salted the meat for 30 minutes, then tossed it with the sugar, spices, and bacon paste right before I put it on the grill? This simple change was the answer: The chicken was juicy, tender, and full-flavored, with a smoky depth that complemented the barbecue sauce. Now about that sauce . . . To enliven my classic ketchup, mustard, and cider vinegar mixture, I stirred in some grated onion and Worcestershire sauce. A spoonful of brown sugar and a little molasses added just enough bittersweet flavor to counter the sauce's tanginess. Simmered for a few minutes, the mixture tasted bright and balanced and boasted a thick, smooth texture that clung well to the chicken. As I watched this final batch of supremely moist, smoky, perfectly cooked kebabs disappear as fast as I could pull them off the grill, I knew that this recipe had realized its full potential.

Barbecued Chicken Kebabs

SERVES 6

Use the large holes of a box grater to grate the onion. We prefer dark thigh meat for these kebabs, but white meat can be used. Don't mix white and dark meat on the same skewer, since they cook at different rates. If you have thin pieces of chicken, cut them larger than 1 inch and roll or fold them into approximate 1-inch cubes. Turbinado sugar is commonly sold as Sugar in the Raw. Demerara sugar can be substituted. You will need four 12-inch metal skewers for this recipe.

Sauce

½ cup ketchup
¼ cup molasses
2 tablespoons grated onion
2 tablespoons Worcestershire sauce
2 tablespoons Dijon mustard
2 tablespoons cider vinegar
1 tablespoon packed light brown sugar

Kebabs

2 pounds boneless, skinless chicken breasts or thighs, trimmed and cut into 1-inch chunks
2 teaspoons kosher salt
2 tablespoons paprika
4 teaspoons turbinado sugar
2 teaspoons smoked paprika
2 slices bacon, cut into ½-inch pieces

1. *For the sauce:* Bring all ingredients to simmer in small saucepan over medium heat and cook, stirring occasionally, until reduced to about 1 cup, 5 to 7 minutes. Transfer ½ cup sauce to small bowl and set aside for cooking; set aside remaining sauce for serving.

2. *For the kebabs:* Toss chicken and salt together in large bowl; cover with plastic wrap and refrigerate for at least 30 minutes or up to 1 hour.

3. Pat chicken dry with paper towels. Combine paprika, sugar, and smoked paprika in small bowl. Process bacon in food processor until smooth paste forms, 30 to 45 seconds, scraping down sides of bowl as needed. Add bacon paste and spice mixture to chicken and mix until chicken is completely coated. Thread chicken tightly onto four 12-inch metal skewers.

4A. *For a charcoal grill:* Open bottom vent completely. Light large chimney starter three-quarters filled with charcoal briquettes (4½ quarts). When top coals are partially covered with ash, pour evenly over half of grill. Set cooking grate in place, cover, and open lid vent completely. Heat grill until hot, about 5 minutes.

4B. *For a gas grill:* Turn all burners to high, cover, and heat grill until hot, about 15 minutes. Turn all burners to medium-high.

5. Clean and oil cooking grate. Place kebabs on grill (on hotter side if using charcoal) and cook (covered if using gas), turning kebabs every 2 to 2½ minutes, until well browned and slightly charred, about 8 minutes. Brush top surface of kebabs with ¼ cup reserved sauce for cooking, flip, and cook until sauce is sizzling and browning in spots, about 1 minute. Brush second side of kebabs with remaining ¼ cup reserved sauce for cooking, flip, and continue to cook until sizzling and browning in spots, about 1 minute longer.

6. Transfer kebabs to large platter, tent with aluminum foil, and let rest for 5 to 10 minutes. Serve, passing reserved sauce for serving separately.

BACON PASTE—WEIRD BUT IT WORKS

To create a protective coating that keeps the chicken moist on the grill, we chop two slices of bacon, pulse them in a food processor until smooth, and then toss the resulting paste (along with sugar and spices) with the raw chicken chunks.

GRILLED GLAZED CHICKEN BREASTS

KEITH DRESSER, *September/October 2013*

Throwing a few boneless, skinless chicken breasts on the grill and painting them with barbecue sauce always sounds like a good idea. This lean cut is available everywhere, it cooks fast, and it makes a light, simple meal. The trouble is that the results are usually flawed. Because these disrobed specimens cook in a flash over coals, it's hard to get chicken that not only tastes grilled but also has a good glaze without overcooking it. Here's the dilemma: If you wait to apply the glaze until the meat is browned well, it's usually dry and leathery by the time you've lacquered on a few layers. (And you need a few layers to build anything more than a superficial skim of sauce.) But if you apply the glaze too soon, you don't give the chicken a chance to brown, a flavor boost that this bland cut badly needs. Plus, the sugary glaze is prone to burning before the chicken cooks through.

But the ease of throwing boneless, skinless breasts on the grill is too enticing to pass up. I decided to fiddle with the approach until I got it right: tender, juicy chicken with the smoky taste of the grill, glistening with a thick coating of glaze. While I was at it, I wanted to create glazes specifically designed to accentuate, not overwhelm, this lean cut's delicate flavors.

BETTER BROWNING IN A HURRY

My first step was to brine the meat. I knew that a 30-minute saltwater soak would help keep the chicken juicy and well seasoned and could be accomplished while the grill was heating. I also opted for a two-level fire, which means that I piled two-thirds of the coals on one side of the kettle and just one-third on the other side. This would allow me to sear the breasts over the coals and then move them to the cooler side to avoid burning when I applied the glaze.

My real challenge was to figure out how to speed up browning, also known as the Maillard reaction, and the consequent formation of all those new flavor compounds that help meat taste rich and complex. If the chicken browned faster, it would leave me more time to build a thick glaze that would add even more flavor. My first thought was to enlist the aid of starch in absorbing some of the moisture on the exterior of the meat that normally would need to burn off before much browning could occur. First I tried dredging the breasts in flour, but this made them bready. Next I tried cornstarch, but this approach turned the breasts gummy. A technique we have employed when pan-searing chicken breasts—creating an artificial "skin" using a paste of cornstarch, flour, and melted butter—gave us better results. The starches (which break down into sugars) and the butter proteins helped achieve a browned surface more quickly, and the porous surface readily held a glaze. Unfortunately, the chicken still tasted more breaded than grilled.

Switching gears, I tried rubbing the surface of the chicken with baking soda. Baking soda increases the pH of the chicken, making it more alkaline, which in turn speeds up the Maillard reaction. Alas, while this did speed up browning, even small amounts left behind a mild soapy aftertaste.

I was unsure of what to do next. But then I remembered a really unlikely sounding test that one of my colleagues tried when attempting to expedite the browning of pork chops: dredging the meat in nonfat dry milk powder. While this strange coating did brown the meat more quickly, it made the chops taste too sweet. But might it be better suited for browning chicken? It was worth a try. After lightly dusting the breasts with milk powder (½ teaspoon per breast) and lightly spraying them with vegetable oil spray to help ensure that the powder stuck, I threw them on the grill. I was thrilled when the chicken was lightly browned and had nice grill marks in less than 2 minutes, or about half of the time of my most successful previous tests. Why was milk powder so effective? It turns out that dry milk contains about 36 percent protein. But it also contains about 50 percent lactose, a so-called reducing sugar. And the Maillard reaction takes place only after large proteins break down into amino acids and react with certain types of sugars—reducing sugars like glucose, fructose, and lactose. In sum, milk powder contained just the two components that I needed to speed things up.

Milk powder encourages browning and creates a tacky surface for the flavorful glaze to cling to.

But that wasn't the only reason milk powder was so successful in quickly triggering browning. Like starch, it's a dry substance that absorbs the excess moisture on the meat. This is helpful because moisture keeps the temperature too low for significant browning to take place until the wetness evaporates. There was yet one more benefit to using the milk powder: It created a thin, tacky surface that was perfect for holding on to the glaze. And now, with expedited browning in place, I had time to thoroughly lacquer my chicken with glaze by applying four solid coats before it finished cooking.

GREAT GLAZE

Next it was time to focus on perfecting the glaze itself. I started with flavor. Since I knew that I wanted to limit the amount of sweetness so as not to overpower the mild flavor of the chicken, I began by testing a host of ingredients that would be thick enough to serve as a clingy base but weren't sugary. It was a diverse group, but I settled on mustard and hoisin sauce. Then, in order to add balance and complexity, I introduced acidity in the form of vinegar, as well as a healthy dose of spices and aromatics, such as ground fennel seeds, fresh ginger, and spicy Sriracha sauce.

My next step was to add a sweet (but not too sweet) element, which would provide further balance, promote browning, and give even more of a sticky cling to the glaze. Sweeteners like maple syrup, brown sugar, and fruit jams made the glazes saccharine. Corn syrup, which is about half as sweet as the other sweeteners, worked far better, giving the glaze just a goodly amount of stickiness while keeping the sweetness level under control. Two tablespoons was just the right amount.

But all was not perfect: The glazes still had a tendency to become too loose when applied to the hot chicken after it browned. Whisking in a teaspoon of cornstarch helped.

At this point I was feeling pretty good. But many tasters wanted an even thicker glaze. This time I looked to adjust my cooking technique. My fix? I switched up the point at which I applied the glaze. Instead of brushing it on right before flipping the chicken, I began to apply the glaze immediately after it was flipped. This meant that less glaze stuck to the grill—and the glaze applied to the top of the chicken had time to dry out and cling. The result? Chicken breasts robed in a thick, lacquered glaze. My dinner was ready.

Grilled Glazed Boneless, Skinless Chicken Breasts

SERVES 4

¼ cup salt
¼ cup sugar
4 (6- to 8-ounce) boneless, skinless chicken breasts, trimmed
2 teaspoons nonfat dry milk powder
¼ teaspoon pepper
Vegetable oil spray
1 recipe glaze (recipes follow)

1. Dissolve salt and sugar in 1½ quarts cold water. Submerge chicken in brine, cover, and refrigerate for at least 30 minutes or up to 1 hour. Remove chicken from brine and pat dry with paper towels. Combine milk powder and pepper in bowl.

2A. *For a charcoal grill:* Open bottom vent completely. Light large chimney starter mounded with charcoal briquettes (7 quarts). When top coals are partially covered with ash, pour two-thirds evenly over half of grill, then pour remaining coals over other half of grill. Set cooking grate in place, cover, and open lid vent completely. Heat grill until hot, about 5 minutes.

2B. *For a gas grill:* Turn all burners to high, cover, and heat grill until hot, about 15 minutes. Leave primary burner on high and turn other burner(s) to medium-high.

3. Clean and oil cooking grate. Sprinkle half of milk powder mixture over 1 side of chicken. Lightly spray coated side of chicken with oil spray until milk powder is moistened. Flip chicken and sprinkle remaining milk powder mixture over second side. Lightly spray with oil spray.

4. Place chicken, skinned side down, over hotter part of grill and cook until browned on first side, 2 to 2½ minutes. Flip chicken, brush with 2 tablespoons glaze, and cook until browned on second side, 2 to 2½ minutes. Flip chicken, move to cooler side of grill, brush with 2 tablespoons glaze, and cook for 2 minutes. Repeat flipping and brushing 2 more times, cooking for 2 minutes on each side. Flip chicken, brush with remaining glaze, and cook until chicken registers 160 degrees, 1 to 3 minutes. Transfer chicken to plate and let rest for 5 minutes before serving.

THE POWER OF MILK POWDER

To make sure that our chicken breasts could be both browned and glazed in the time it took the chicken to cook, we had to accelerate browning. A surprising ingredient—milk powder—was the solution. Milk powder contains both protein and so-called reducing sugar (in this case, lactose), the keys to the Maillard reaction, the chemical process that causes browning. Faster browning gave us more time to layer on the glaze.

BROWNING BOOSTER

glazes

Honey Mustard Glaze

MAKES ABOUT ⅔ CUP

2 tablespoons cider vinegar
1 teaspoon cornstarch
3 tablespoons Dijon mustard
3 tablespoons honey
2 tablespoons light corn syrup
1 garlic clove, minced
¼ teaspoon ground fennel seeds

Whisk vinegar and cornstarch in small saucepan until cornstarch has dissolved. Whisk in mustard, honey, corn syrup, garlic, and fennel seeds. Bring mixture to boil over high heat. Cook, stirring constantly, until thickened, about 1 minute. Transfer glaze to bowl.

Spicy Hoisin Glaze

MAKES ABOUT ⅔ CUP

For a spicier glaze, use the larger amount of Sriracha sauce.

2 tablespoons rice vinegar
1 teaspoon cornstarch
⅓ cup hoisin sauce
2 tablespoons light corn syrup
1–2 tablespoons Sriracha sauce
1 teaspoon grated fresh ginger
¼ teaspoon five-spice powder

Whisk vinegar and cornstarch in small saucepan until cornstarch has dissolved. Whisk in hoisin, corn syrup, Sriracha, ginger, and five-spice powder. Bring mixture to boil over high heat. Cook, stirring constantly, until thickened, about 1 minute. Transfer glaze to bowl.

GRILLED LEMON CHICKEN

PAM ANDERSON, *May/June 1998*

I've been watching my father grill for almost 40 years now. He's at least fifth generation Deep South—not the kind of man who would fire up his grill for some wimpy pizza, mahi-mahi, or basket of vegetables. For as long as I can remember, he's been grilling the same four things—steak, spareribs, barbecued pork butt, and finally, his signature dish, lemon chicken.

My father is a pretty confident griller, but that lemon chicken turned him into a nervous Nelly. Every time he made it he was obsessed with the same goal: to make sure that it absorbed as much lemon flavor as possible. After he'd arranged the chicken parts neatly over the hot coals, he would brush each one with a mixture of lemon, oil, and garlic salt. He basted meticulously throughout the entire grilling process, carefully moving the chicken around and over to make sure each piece cooked evenly.

Achieving bold citrus flavor in grilled chicken is all about timing.

Dad almost dreaded taking that first bite for fear the lemon had not penetrated. Though we sometimes had to stretch the truth, Mom and I always assured him that it had. When the chicken was at its best, we marveled: "The lemon flavor's gone right into the bone!"

Because Dad felt his odds on whether the lemon would take or not were about fifty-fifty, he'd have me taste-test the chicken before he took it off the grill. About halfway through cooking, he'd start breaking off and feeding me the wings. Even though I always told him they tasted lemony enough, he could read the truth in my eyes. (You can never trust a hungry 10-year-old who's been sitting still with her father for over an hour.) The grill lid would fly open, and he'd begin his basting again, hoping his fire would stay alive long enough to get a few more drops of lemon sauce onto the chicken.

Dipping the chicken in the leftover lemon basting sauce was always one of my favorite ways of ensuring good lemon flavor (salmonella was just a twinkle in the chicken's eye back then), but to Dad it meant failure. When he saw me sneak the leftover sauce to the table and slip a piece of my breast meat into the bowl, he'd start mentally kicking himself.

He tried a number of experiments over the years, but it wasn't until long after I'd left home that he called, his voice veering high with excitement. "I've finally discovered the secret to lemon chicken!" he exclaimed. It turned out that one day while frying fish, his oil cooled off and was absorbed by the fish. At this point, it suddenly occurred to him that over lower heat his cooked chicken might better absorb his lemon sauce. What was bad for the fish in oil, might be good for the chicken in lemon sauce.

This time, rather than baste the chicken from start to finish, he threw the salt-and-peppered chicken parts on the grill and cooked them until they were virtually done. At this point, he took the fire down really low and started brushing them. This, he said, consistently gave him the intense lemon flavor he was after. After 40 years, he had finally come up with a foolproof method.

HE WAS RIGHT

I gave Dad's technique a try and realized he was onto something. I liked the fresh, perky lemon flavor of the chicken sauced at the end, but I couldn't really be sure that it was better than his many lemon chicken experiments over the years. Which lemon chicken was best? Was it the one where the lemon mixture was applied before, during, or after cooking? So I grilled three chickens—one that was marinated in lemon juice, garlic, and oil for two hours, a second that was basted with the same mixture throughout grilling, and a third that was grilled by my father's method, rolling the cooked chicken around in the lemon mixture, returning it to the grill, and basting it for a few minutes longer. With each chicken, I used a two-level fire, with most of the coals under half of the cooking grate and fewer coals under the remaining half. This allowed me to sear the chicken well over the coals but also to regulate its cooking, moving it to the cooler area if it was cooking too quickly or if flare-ups occurred.

If you weren't comparing them with my father's newly discovered secret, you'd say the marinated and basted chickens were just fine. The chicken flavored at the end, however, stole the show. Not only did it have a fresher flavor, its juices had mingled with the lemon, garlic, and oil to make a wonderful sauce. The basted chicken, on the other hand, had lost much of its lemon juice to the fire, requiring more lemon mixture to complete the job, and even with more sauce, it turned out drier than the other two.

My dad's technique became my favorite, especially after I made a few personal adjustments. First, I almost always brine poultry before cooking it, and brined lemon chicken was always preferred to unbrined in side-by-side tasting. Since brining made garlic salt out of the question, I tried using minced garlic, but because the chicken was on the grill for such a relatively short time after the marinade was applied, it tasted raw. I eventually found that mincing the garlic to almost a paste and warming it in a small saucepan until it began to sizzle improved the garlic flavor immensely.

Although my father would never consider doctoring up his chicken, I thought herbs such as thyme, cilantro, rosemary, and oregano and spices such as cumin, coriander, and fennel might be nice additions. Herbs were easy. They could be stirred directly into the lemon mixture. But spices were questionable. Would they, like the garlic, taste raw with so little cooking time and over so low a heat?

Once again, I made three batches of chicken—one that was rubbed with crushed coriander seeds before cooking; a second

that was brushed at the end with a marinade containing crushed coriander seeds; and a third that was brushed with a marinade containing toasted, then crushed coriander seeds. My tasters and I much preferred the last, where toasted seeds were crushed, stirred into the marinade, and applied at the end. The spices that cooked on the chicken the entire time were less flavorful and tended to char. And besides, toasted seeds, like toasted nuts, just taste better.

Since the lemon flavor was so much cleaner and brighter when the sauce was applied at the end of cooking, I thought other acids might work equally well. Lime, certainly, was good, but low-acid vinegar sauces, such as rice wine and balsamic vinegars, were less impressive primarily, I think, because there wasn't a fresh flavor to preserve.

Whether lemon chicken that's been brushed at the end of cooking is better because the lemon flavor actually permeates the meat, or because the flavors are brighter and fresher, or because there's an intensely flavored dipping sauce from the intermingled lemon, garlic, olive oil, and chicken juices, I don't know. What I do know is that after 40 years of guesswork, my father definitely got it right.

Grilled Lemon Chicken

SERVES 6 TO 8

The 1½-hour brining time is recommended but not essential; skip it if you're in a hurry or using a kosher chicken. It's fine to use chicken parts, such as drumsticks and thighs, separated or not, or breasts and wings, separated at the joint connecting wing to breast. Grilling whole chickens is also an option, but only if you remove the backbones and butterfly each chicken before brining. If flare-ups occur, temporarily move the pieces to the cooler side of the grill. If you have it on hand, 1 tablespoon of minced fresh rosemary makes a nice addition to the lemon sauce.

Salt and pepper
2 (3½- to 4-pound) whole chickens, each cut into 10 pieces (4 breast pieces, 2 drumsticks, 2 thighs, 2 wings), giblets discarded
6 garlic cloves
¼ cup extra-virgin olive oil
1 cup lemon juice (6 lemons)
1 tablespoon minced fresh thyme or 1½ teaspoons dried

1. Dissolve ½ cup salt in 2 quarts cold water in large container. Submerge chicken in brine, cover, and refrigerate for 1½ hours. Remove chicken from brine and pat dry with paper towels. Season chicken with pepper.

2A. *For a charcoal grill:* Open bottom vent completely. Light large chimney starter filled with charcoal briquettes (6 quarts). When top coals are partially covered with ash, pour two-thirds evenly over half of grill, then pour remaining coals over other half of grill. Set cooking grate in place, cover, and open lid vent completely. Heat grill until hot, about 5 minutes.

2B. *For a gas grill:* Turn all burners to high, cover, and heat grill until hot, about 15 minutes. Leave all burners on high.

3. While grill heats, mince garlic and sprinkle lightly with salt. Drag flat side of chef's knife over garlic-salt mixture to form paste. Heat oil and garlic mixture in small saucepan over low heat until garlic sizzles, 1 to 2 minutes. Stir in lemon juice. Transfer half of lemon mixture to small bowl and set aside. Transfer remaining half of lemon mixture to 13 by 9-inch baking dish.

4. Clean and oil cooking grate. Place chicken on grill (hotter side if using charcoal), skin side down. Cook (covered if using gas) until well browned on both sides, 15 to 20 minutes, flipping halfway through cooking. Stir thyme into lemon mixture in baking dish, then place chicken pieces in baking dish and turn to coat.

5. Return chicken pieces to cooler side of grill (if using charcoal), skin side up, or turn burners to medium-low (if using gas). Continue to cook (covered if using gas) until breasts register 160 degrees and thighs/drumsticks register 175 degrees, about 5 minutes longer, brushing twice with reserved lemon mixture.

6. Transfer chicken to serving platter, tent with aluminum foil, and let rest for 5 to 10 minutes before serving.

MINCING GARLIC TO A PASTE

1. Mince garlic and then sprinkle it lightly with salt.

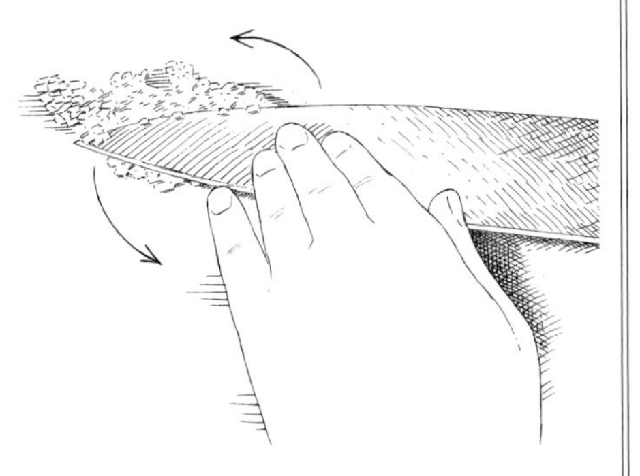

2. Drag flat side of chef's knife over garlic-salt mixture to form paste.

variation

Grilled Lime Chicken with Jalapeño and Coriander

An equal amount of toasted and crushed cumin seeds may be substituted for the coriander seeds.

Add 2 teaspoons minced jalapeño chiles and 2 teaspoons toasted and crushed coriander seeds with garlic mixture. Substitute lime juice (8 limes) for lemon juice and 2 tablespoons minced fresh cilantro for thyme.

THE ULTIMATE CRISPY FRIED CHICKEN

KAY RENTSCHLER AND BRIDGET LANCASTER, *May/June 2001*

Fried chicken is patently American, but what makes it so great? First, the crust. Crisp and crackling with flavor, the crust must cleave to the chicken itself, not flake off in chips, and it should be a deep, uniform mahogany with no evidence of greasiness. As for the chicken, it should be tender, seasoned, and flavorful.

But frying chicken at home is a daunting task—a messy tableau of buttermilk dip and breading, hot fat, and splatters. The results are often not worth the mess: greasy, peeling chicken skin and dry, unseasoned meat.

BOOSTING THE BRINE

For our recipe, we decided against poorly butchered packaged chicken in favor of a whole bird cut at home into manageable pieces. Our first decision was what type of pretreatment to give the chicken. In our first stove-side excursion, we fried up several batches of chicken, half of which had been brined for 2 hours while the other half had not. The tasting results were unequivocal: Unbrined chicken earned marks far below those of its well-seasoned, juicy, brined competition.

We also knew, however, that soaking chicken pieces in some kind of liquid before breading is traditional. We examined a number of soaking solutions and found that the bright, acidic flavor and clinging viscosity of buttermilk produced the best flavor accents and the richest browning during cooking. Appreciating the tang of a buttermilk soak but unwilling to forgo the succulence of brined chicken, we decided to add the saline blast of a brine to the buttermilk, doubling the rewards and minimizing the number of steps. We boosted the buttermilk brine's flavor by adding crushed garlic, crumbled bay leaves, and sweet paprika. This remarkable "twofer" won high marks indeed—well above those garnered by a soak or brine alone. We also spiked the brine with ¼ cup of sugar—not enough to sweeten it but enough to bring other flavors out of hiding.

DOUBLE DIPPING

To find out what kind of coating was best, we tested straight flour against a panoply of options: matzo crumbs, ground saltines, cornflakes, ground Melba toasts, cornmeal, and panko. In the end, plain flour—requiring in this instance no seasoning whatsoever since the chicken had been brined—won out thanks to the integrity and lightness of the crust it produced.

Many fried chicken recipes use a single breading process in which the chicken is dipped first into beaten egg and then into flour or crumbs. A double, or bound, breading requires dipping the chicken first into flour, then egg, and finally flour or crumbs. We were surprised to discover that single breading is actually messier than double breading; the latter's dry first flouring maintains tidiness and establishes control before the egg dip. The double breading offered a superior base coat without being overly thick or tough.

AIR PLAY

Another practice that has made its way into many fried chicken recipes is air-drying breaded chicken before frying, which supposedly crisps up the skin. We tested the effects of air-drying the chicken before and after breading and compared the results with chicken that had undergone no air drying. The air-dried-first chicken proved best, with a lighter, crispier, and flakier texture.

While this version initially seemed ideal, we noticed that its delicate crispness succumbed to sandiness and porosity over the course of a few hours. The memory of a particularly light but resilient crust of a chicken-fried steak recipe persuaded us to add baking soda and baking powder to an egg wash bolstered with buttermilk. Stirred into the wash, ½ teaspoon of soda and 1 teaspoon of powder produced just enough carbon dioxide to lighten the breading to perfection—and also keep it crisp as it cooled.

FRY TIME

We ruled out deep frying in favor of pan frying, which is much more manageable for home cooks. With this method, only half the chicken is submerged in the fat at any point and must be flipped. The oil stays hotter and, theoretically, produces less of a mess. After judging several different oils for smoke point, flavor, and crust crispness, we preferred peanut oil.

A buttermilk brine and a rest in the fridge before breading work wonders to create a perfect crackling crust.

While a cast-iron skillet seemed the obvious choice for pan frying, splatters were dramatically reduced when we used a Dutch oven. In fact, a Dutch oven maintained temperature significantly better than anything else we tried. Covering the Dutch oven during the first half of frying did one better: It reduced splatters to a fine spray, maintained oil temperature impeccably, and fried the chicken through in about 15 minutes total, versus the 20 minutes per side recommended in many recipes. This time-efficient frying method made up for the fact that the chicken needed to be fried in two batches. As much as we would have liked to find a way to fit 10 pieces into a 12-inch Dutch oven all at once, success eluded us. But it was really no big deal. It simply meant that by the time the second batch was fried up, the first batch was cool enough to eat.

The Ultimate Crispy Fried Chicken

SERVES 4 TO 6

Note that the chicken needs to brine for at least 2 hours and then air-dry for at least 2 hours before frying. Avoid using kosher chicken in this recipe or it will be too salty. Use a Dutch oven that holds 6 quarts or more. Maintaining an even oil temperature is key here.

8 cups buttermilk
3 garlic heads, cloves separated, peeled, and smashed
½ cup plus 2 tablespoons salt
¼ cup sugar
2 tablespoons paprika
3 bay leaves, crumbled
1 (3½-pound) whole chicken, cut into 8 pieces (4 breast pieces, 2 drumsticks, 2 thighs), wings and giblets discarded
3–4 cups peanut oil or vegetable shortening
4 cups all-purpose flour
1 large egg
1 teaspoon baking powder
½ teaspoon baking soda

1. Whisk 7 cups buttermilk, garlic, salt, sugar, paprika, and bay leaves together in large container. Add chicken and turn to coat. Cover and refrigerate for at least 2 hours or up to 3 hours.
2. Set wire rack in rimmed baking sheet. Rinse chicken, place on prepared wire rack, and refrigerate, uncovered, for 2 hours. (Chicken can be covered with plastic wrap and refrigerated for up to 6 hours.)
3. Adjust oven rack to middle position and heat oven to 200 degrees. Line large plate with triple layer of paper towels. Set second wire rack in second rimmed baking sheet. Add oil to large Dutch oven until it measures about ¾ inch deep and heat over medium-high heat to 375 degrees.
4. Meanwhile, spread flour in shallow dish. Lightly beat egg, baking powder, and baking soda together in medium bowl, then whisk in remaining 1 cup buttermilk (mixture will bubble and foam). Working with 1 piece at a time, dredge chicken in flour, shaking off excess, then dip in buttermilk mixture, letting excess drip off. Dredge chicken in flour again, shaking off excess, and return to wire rack.
5. When oil is hot, carefully transfer half of chicken to pot, skin side down. Cover and fry, adjusting burner, if necessary, to maintain oil temperature of 325 degrees, until deep golden brown, 7 to 11 minutes. (After 4 minutes, check chicken for even browning and rearrange if some pieces are browning faster than others.) Flip chicken and continue to cook until breasts register 160 degrees and drumsticks/thighs register 175 degrees, 6 to 8 minutes longer. (Smaller pieces may cook faster than larger pieces. Remove pieces from pot as they reach correct temperature.) Let chicken drain briefly on prepared plate, then transfer to second prepared wire rack and place in oven to keep warm.
6. Return oil to 375 degrees and repeat with remaining chicken. Serve.

CUTTING UP A WHOLE CHICKEN FOR FRYING

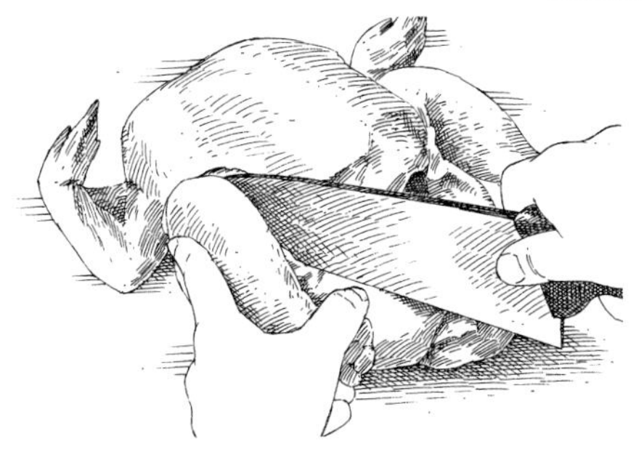

1. With sharp chef's knife, cut through skin around leg where it attaches to breast.

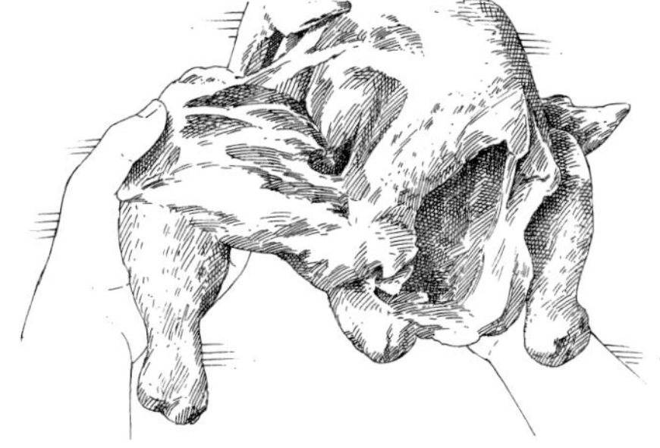

2. Pop leg joint out of its socket. Use chef's knife to cut through flesh and skin to detach leg from body.

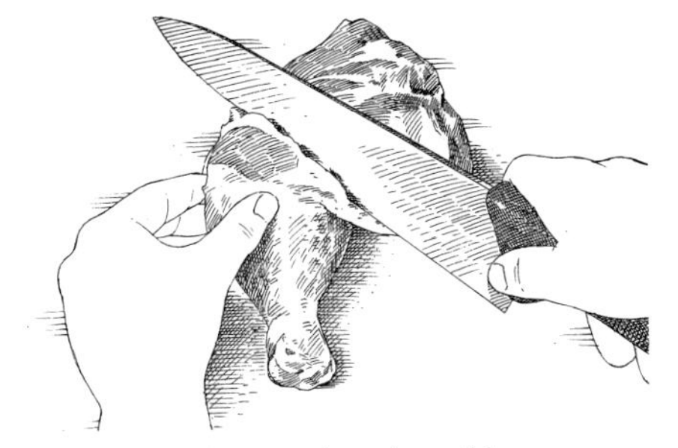

3. Cut through joint where line of fat separates thigh and drumstick. Repeat steps 1 through 3 with other leg.

4. Bend wing out from breast and cut through joint. Cut through cartilage to remove wing. Cut through joint to split. Repeat with other wing.

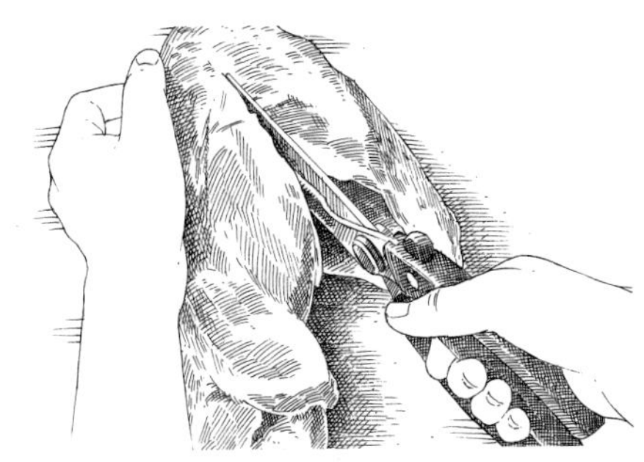

5. Using poultry shears, cut along ribs to completely separate back from breast. Discard backbone.

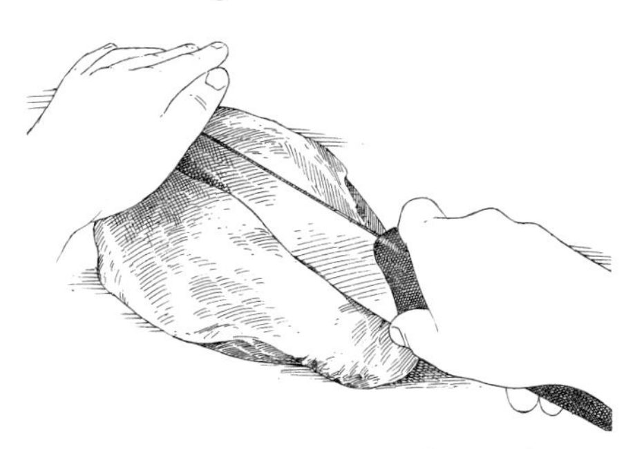

6. Place knife on breastbone, then apply pressure to cut through and separate breast into halves. Cut each breast in half crosswise.

FASTEST WEEKNIGHT CHICKEN

LAN LAM, *March/April 2017*

A juicy, crisp-skinned roast chicken is always welcome in my house, but achieving it on a weeknight can seem like wishful thinking. A few years back, we made this goal more manageable with our Weeknight Roast Chicken, which cut a good 50 minutes off the usual 2½-hour preparation time. That recipe eliminates brining (and salting, which must be done overnight) and calls for starting the bird in a preheated skillet in a very hot oven and then turning off the heat midway through cooking. The hot skillet jump-starts the cooking of the thighs, while finishing the bird in a cooling oven ensures that the breast stays moist and tender. Though a roast chicken that clocks in at 1 hour and 40 minutes from start to finish is impressive, I wondered if I could speed things up even more.

RACKING UP SOLUTIONS

Out of the gate I knew that, as in our previous recipe, I would skip salting and brining to save as much time as possible. Next, I made a big decision: I wouldn't roast my chicken. Instead, I would broil it. An oven takes 20 minutes to preheat, while a broiler requires just 5 minutes. Beyond that, roasting relies on the air in the oven to transfer heat to the chicken, and air is a poor conductor. A broiler heats the chicken directly via waves of radiant heat, which transfer heat much more efficiently.

We harness the intense heat of the broiler to produce juicy meat and crisp skin.

Flattening the bird by butterflying it was the essential first step. If I didn't do this, the skin on the breast, which would be situated close to the heat, would burn before the thighs, located farther away, would cook through. With a good pair of kitchen shears, the task took just a few minutes. After applying a thin coat of oil, I generously seasoned both sides with salt and pepper. But before I could start broiling, I needed to settle on a rack position. While one might reflexively use the top rack for broiling, it's not always the best option. Think of the broiler element in an electric oven as a collection of hot lights affixed to the top of the oven. The farther the food is from the "lights," the more diffuse and uniform the illuminated area, while placing food closer to the element will create concentrated spots of "light." To cook the chicken evenly and efficiently, I needed to set the oven rack far enough from the element to minimize the number of hot spots but not so far away that the chicken cooked too slowly.

I broiled a few birds, placing the rack about 6 inches from the element and moving it progressively farther away. As I expected, the farther away I placed the rack, the more even the cooking and browning became—but too far and the chicken cooked through before I got enough browning on the skin. Twelve to 13 inches from the broiler was the sweet spot. I preheated the broiler, placed my butterflied chicken on a baking sheet, and slid the sheet into the oven, rotating it once halfway through the cooking time.

The results were promising but not perfect. I'd shaved off about 30 minutes (it took me 1 hour and 20 minutes start to finish), and after the prep, it was totally hands-off except for the quick rotation. But though I'd stopped cooking at our usual target doneness temperature of 160 degrees, the breast was dry and overcooked, while the leg quarters were undercooked. Plus, there were problems with the skin. Despite the fact that I'd flattened the bird and rotated it during cooking, the skin had blistered and blackened in spots, particularly on the legs, which had contracted due to the intense heat and drawn up away from the sheet, closer to the heat source. The fat also hadn't rendered away completely, leaving the skin rubbery in places. I wanted to fix these problems, and I wanted to shave off even more time.

THE HEAT IS ON (AND OFF)

To help the fat deposits under the skin render better, I used a paring knife to pierce the skin in multiple spots, which would allow the fat to escape. As for getting the dark and white meat to reach the right doneness temperatures at the same time, I needed to slow down the rate at which the white meat cooked while speeding up the dark meat. My solution was two-pronged. First, I swapped out the baking sheet for a skillet and preheated the skillet on the stovetop before adding the chicken. Second, I didn't preheat the broiler but rather put the chicken in a cold oven and then turned on the broiler. This allowed the legs to begin cooking as soon as the chicken went into the hot pan, while the breast side, held slightly away from the pan by the ribs, would cook from above at a slower rate. To further ensure that the legs wouldn't scorch, I tied them together with kitchen twine to keep them from drawing up toward the heat source.

As yet another safeguard against overcooking, I decided to remove the chicken from the oven a little sooner. A chicken roasted until the breast meat reaches an internal temperature of 160 degrees carries over about 5 to 7 degrees, but because of the broiler's more intense, direct heat, the meat was carrying over more—an extra 10 to 15 degrees. This left the lean breast meat dried out and chalky. Removing the chicken from the oven when the breast reached 155 degrees allowed it to carry over to just the right temperature and helped keep it moist. The thighs reached about 180 degrees, above our usual target of 175 degrees, but with their extra fat for protection, they could handle it. As a bonus, pulling the chicken out earlier shaved off a couple more minutes.

POKING HOLES

Now my chicken was much more tender and juicy. But the skin wasn't what I had imagined—it was still too dark in spots. Upon closer inspection I saw that the portions of skin that I had pierced had stayed flush against the meat and were perfectly browned. But the remaining unpierced areas were blistered and blackened. Here's why: Water exuded by the meat was turning into steam. In areas where that steam couldn't escape, it inflated the skin away from the flesh. The closer the skin was to the broiler element, the more it charred. The fix was simple. When I pierced the skin at ¾-inch intervals all over, sure enough, the chicken emerged from the broiler with deeply and evenly browned, well-rendered skin.

After transferring the bird to a carving board, I contemplated the drippings left in the skillet. They were nicely seasoned and had an intense chicken flavor. Could I turn them into a pan sauce with minimal work? I stirred in a smashed garlic clove and some thyme sprigs and let them infuse while the chicken rested; then I skimmed the fat from the surface with a spoon. The impact was impressive; I had a simple but surprisingly full-flavored sauce to serve alongside the chicken.

When I glanced up at the clock, I saw that I had cut the cooking time down to 45 minutes and the total time to 1 hour and 5 minutes. Here was a golden-brown, juicy, tender, hands-off broiled chicken and sauce fit for any night of the week.

One-Hour Broiled Chicken and Pan Sauce

SERVES 4

If your broiler has multiple settings, choose the highest one. This recipe requires a broiler-safe skillet. In step 3, if the skin is dark golden brown but the breast has not yet reached 155 degrees, cover the chicken with aluminum foil and continue to broil. Monitor the temperature of the chicken carefully during the final 10 minutes of cooking, because it can quickly overcook. Do not attempt this recipe with a drawer broiler.

1 (4-pound) whole chicken, giblets discarded
1½ teaspoons vegetable oil
Kosher salt and pepper
4 sprigs fresh thyme
1 garlic clove, peeled and crushed
Lemon wedges

1. Adjust oven rack 12 to 13 inches from broiler element (do not preheat broiler). Place chicken breast side down on cutting board. Using kitchen shears, cut through bones on either side of backbone. Trim off any excess fat and skin and discard backbone. Flip chicken over and press on breastbone to flatten. Using tip of paring knife, poke holes through skin over entire surface of chicken, spacing them approximately ¾ inch apart.

2. Rub ½ teaspoon oil over skin and sprinkle with 1 teaspoon salt and ½ teaspoon pepper. Flip chicken over, sprinkle bone side with ½ teaspoon salt, and season with pepper. Tie legs together with kitchen twine and tuck wings under breasts.

3. Heat remaining 1 teaspoon oil in broiler-safe 12-inch skillet over high heat until just smoking. Place chicken in skillet, skin side up, and transfer to oven, positioning skillet as close to center of oven as handle allows (turn handle so it points toward one of oven's front corners). Turn on broiler and broil chicken for 25 minutes. Rotate skillet by moving handle to opposite front corner of oven and continue to broil until skin is dark golden brown and thickest part of breast registers 155 degrees, 20 to 30 minutes longer.

4. Transfer chicken to carving board and let rest, uncovered, for 15 minutes. While chicken rests, stir thyme sprigs and garlic into juices in pan and let stand for 10 minutes.

5. Using spoon, skim fat from surface of pan juices. Carve chicken and transfer any accumulated juices to pan. Strain sauce through fine-mesh strainer and season with salt and pepper to taste. Serve chicken, passing pan sauce and lemon wedges separately.

PREVENT BLACKENED SKIN

In our early tests, the chicken's skin bubbled up from the meat, which put it closer to the broiler and caused it to burn. Our solution? Pierce the skin at ¾-inch intervals all over the bird, which provides enough vents for steam to escape.

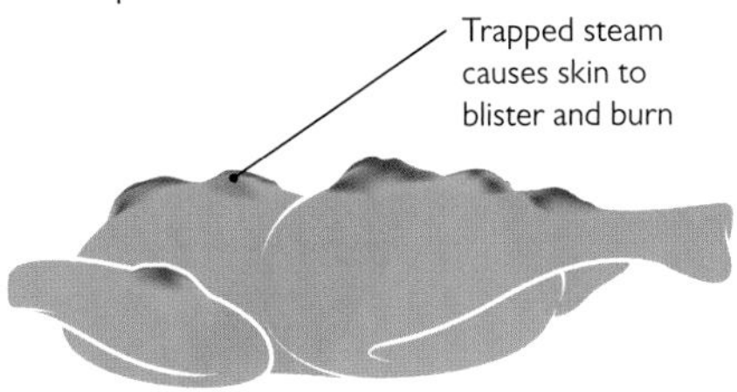

FOR PERFECT BROILED CHICKEN, KEEP IT OUT OF THE SPOTLIGHT

For even cooking and browning, the butterflied chicken must be placed at the right distance from the broiler element. Though electric and gas broilers are designed differently, both work the same way: The radiant heat is more focused and intense near the element and becomes more diffuse the farther away it gets.

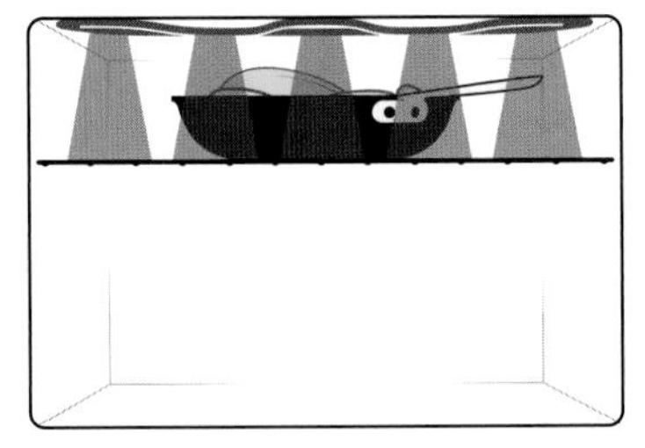

SPOTTY COVERAGE

When the oven rack is placed too close to the broiler element, the heat radiating from the "spotlights" is concentrated, resulting in burnt skin and uneven cooking.

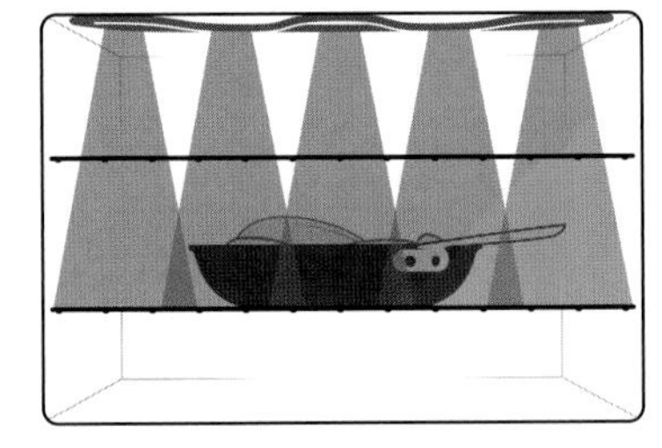

UNIFORM COVERAGE

When the oven rack is placed farther from the broiler element, the heat radiating from the "spotlights" is diffused, which results in browned skin and even cooking.

BETTER GLAZED ROAST CHICKEN

DAVID PAZMIÑO, *March/April 2009*

Most glazed roast chicken recipes offer some variation on these instructions: Roast a chicken as you would normally, painting on a sweet glaze 15 to 30 minutes before the bird is done. It sounds simple, but following these recipes actually turns up a host of troubles, as the problems inherent in roasting chicken (dry breast meat, flabby skin, big deposits of fat under the skin) are compounded by the problems of a glaze (won't stick to the meat, burns in patches, introduces moisture to already flabby skin).

Yet I know that great glazed chicken is possible. Barbecued rotisserie chicken turns slowly as it cooks, making it a cinch to apply sauce to every nook and cranny while also ensuring even cooking. Likewise, Chinese chefs glaze whole ducks that roast while suspended from hooks, turning out perfectly lacquered, crisp-skinned birds. With these techniques as my inspiration, I set out to develop a method for evenly glazed roast chicken with crisp skin and moist, tender meat.

CHICKEN ON A RACK

I chose a large roaster chicken (6 to 7 pounds), enough to feed four to six people, and started with an approach we developed for Crisp Roast Chicken. I separated the skin from the meat and pricked holes in the fat deposits (to allow rendering fat to escape, resulting in crisper skin), then rubbed it with salt and baking soda (to dehydrate the skin and help it to crisp) and let the chicken rest. I then roasted the chicken breast-side down on a V-rack at 450 degrees for 30 minutes, flipped it over, and roasted it another 30 minutes. Then, with the chicken nearly done, I brushed it with a simple glaze of maple syrup, marmalade, vinegar, and Dijon mustard, and finished it with a blast of 500-degree heat.

While the meat was moist and evenly cooked, the glaze was disappointing. The top of the bird was a lacquered mahogany, while the bottom was merely golden brown—a good color for roast chicken, but not the deep, even tone I expected with a glaze. And although the precautions I'd taken helped the fat render from beneath the skin, 15 minutes of steaming under a moist glaze left the skin woefully soggy.

CHICKEN ON A CAN

With one side of the chicken facing down during the entire glazing process, I could never hope to glaze the whole bird evenly. Short of installing meat hooks or a rotisserie in my oven, what could I do? A vertical roaster, which cooks chicken standing up, was possible, but did I really want yet another gadget in the kitchen? Then I remembered a simpler alternative, found right in my fridge: a beer can. We've had great success placing a beer can in the chicken cavity and standing it upright on the grill, which allows heat to circulate freely so that the bird cooks evenly from all sides. Why not bring this popular technique from the barbecue circuit into my oven?

I prepared the chicken and applied a rub as before. After allowing the chicken to rest for an hour, I grabbed a 16-ounce can of beer (the large bird didn't fit on anything smaller), took a few sips to prevent spills, and straddled the chicken on top. I then placed it in a roasting pan (the helper handles on the pan make it the best choice for transporting the bird), and slid it into the oven. The technique seemed like a winner—no awkward flipping, glazing every nook and cranny was easy, and fat dripped freely out of the bird. But cutting into the chicken revealed that the breast, now exposed to the high oven heat for the entire cooking time, was dry and tough. Scaling back the oven temperature to a gentler 325 degrees resolved this issue, but even without steaming under a glaze, the skin was far from crisp.

A GLAZE OF GLORY

To develop a crisp skin, the chicken needs to finish roasting at a very high heat (around 500 degrees) for about 30 minutes. But in the time it takes the oven to heat from 325 to 500 degrees, the delicate breast meat overcooks. With regular roast chicken, we've solved this problem by letting it rest at room temperature for about 20 minutes while the oven heats up for its final blast. Would that work with a vertically roasted chicken? Though the rested-before-blasted chicken came out much crisper than before and the breast meat was perfectly cooked, the glaze was still robbing my chicken of optimum skin quality.

For glazed roast chicken that has it all, don't apply the glaze until the end of cooking.

This was the problem: Most recipes call for a watery glaze that slowly reduces and thickens as the bird cooks—a hindrance when you're trying to crisp the skin. What if I reduced the glaze on the stovetop before I applied it? That way, I could wait to brush on the glaze only at the very end, when it wouldn't ruin the texture of the skin. I made another glaze, this time thickening it with cornstarch. I reduced it to a syrupy consistency and applied it before the final 5 minutes of roasting. This chicken emerged from the oven with a burnished sheen of deep brown, and its rendered skin crackled as I cut into it, revealing moist, tender meat. For good measure, I brushed more glaze on the chicken and made extra to pass tableside. Now when I hanker for perfect glazed chicken, I'll forget about the rotisserie—all I need is a beer can to get the job done right.

Glazed Roast Chicken

SERVES 4 TO 6

For best results, use a 16-ounce can of beer. A larger can will work, but do not use a 12-ounce can, as it will not support the chicken's weight. A vertical poultry roaster can be used in place of the beer can, but we recommend using only a model that can be placed in a roasting pan. Taste your marmalade before using it; if it is overly sweet, reduce the amount of maple syrup by 2 tablespoons.

Chicken

- 1 (6- to 7-pound) whole chicken, giblets discarded
- 2½ teaspoons salt
- 1 teaspoon pepper
- 1 teaspoon baking powder
- 1 (16-ounce) can beer

Glaze

- 1 teaspoon cornstarch
- ½ cup maple syrup
- ½ cup orange marmalade
- ¼ cup cider vinegar
- 2 tablespoons unsalted butter
- 2 tablespoons Dijon mustard
- 1 teaspoon pepper

1. *For the chicken:* Place chicken, breast side down, on cutting board. Using tip of sharp knife, make four 1-inch incisions along back of chicken. Using your fingers, gently loosen skin covering breast and thighs. Using metal skewer, poke 15 to 20 holes in fat deposits on top of breast and thighs. Tuck wings behind back.
2. Combine salt, pepper, and baking powder in bowl. Pat chicken dry with paper towels. Sprinkle salt mixture evenly all over chicken. Rub mixture in with your hands, coating entire surface evenly. Transfer chicken, breast side up, to wire rack set in rimmed baking sheet and refrigerate, uncovered, for at least 30 minutes or up to 1 hour. Meanwhile, adjust oven rack to lowest position and heat oven to 325 degrees.
3. Open beer can and pour out (or drink) about half of liquid. Place can in middle of roasting pan and spray lightly with vegetable oil spray. Slide chicken over can so drumsticks reach down to bottom of can, chicken stands upright, and breast is perpendicular to bottom of pan. Roast chicken until skin starts to turn golden and breast registers 140 degrees, 1¼ to 1½ hours. Carefully remove pan from oven and increase oven temperature to 500 degrees.
4. *For the glaze:* While chicken cooks, stir cornstarch and 1 tablespoon water in bowl until no lumps remain. Bring maple syrup, marmalade, vinegar, butter, mustard, and pepper to simmer in medium saucepan over medium-low heat and cook, stirring occasionally, until reduced to ¾ cup, 6 to 8 minutes. Slowly whisk in cornstarch mixture; return to simmer and cook for 1 minute. Remove saucepan from heat.
5. When oven temperature reaches 500 degrees, pour 1½ cups water into roasting pan and return pan to oven. Roast until chicken skin is evenly browned and crispy, breast registers 160 degrees, and thighs register 175 degrees, 24 to 30 minutes. (Check chicken halfway through roasting; if top is becoming too dark, place 7-inch square piece of aluminum foil over neck and wingtips of chicken and continue to roast. If pan begins to smoke and sizzle, add additional ½ cup water to pan.)
6. Brush chicken with ¼ cup glaze and continue to roast until browned and sticky, about 5 minutes longer. (If glaze starts to stiffen, return to low heat to soften.) Carefully remove pan from oven; transfer chicken, still on can, to carving board; and brush with ¼ cup glaze. Let chicken rest for 20 minutes.
7. While chicken rests, strain juices from pan through fine-mesh strainer into fat separator; let liquid settle for 5 minutes. Whisk ½ cup defatted juices into remaining ¼ cup glaze in saucepan and set over low heat. Using 2 large wads of paper towels, carefully transfer chicken from can to carving board. Carve chicken, adding any accumulated juices to sauce. Serve, passing sauce separately.

PRIMING CHICKEN FOR CRISPER SKIN

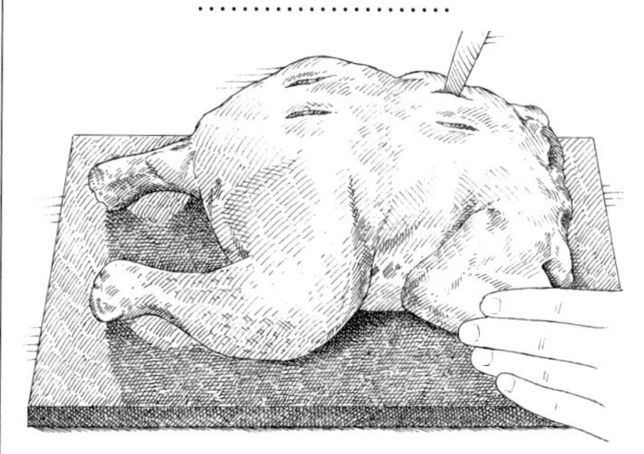

1. **CUT CHANNELS** in the skin along the chicken's back to create openings for fat to escape.

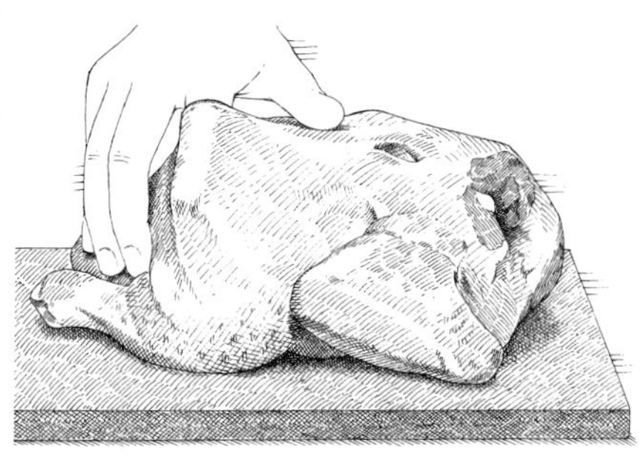

2. **LOOSEN THE SKIN** from the thighs and breast to allow rendering fat to trickle out.

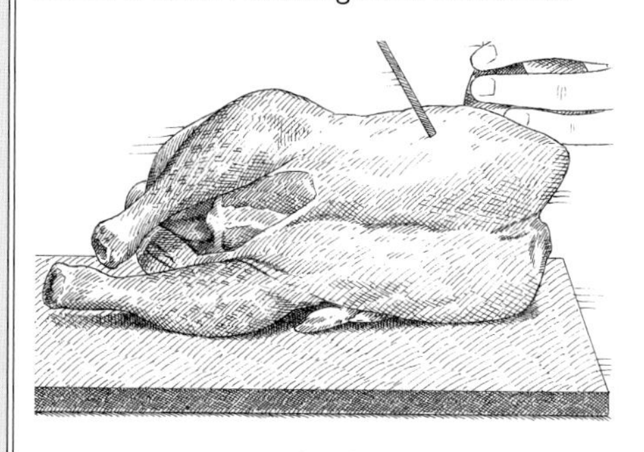

3. **POKE HOLES** in the skin of the breast and thighs to create additional channels for fat and juices to escape.

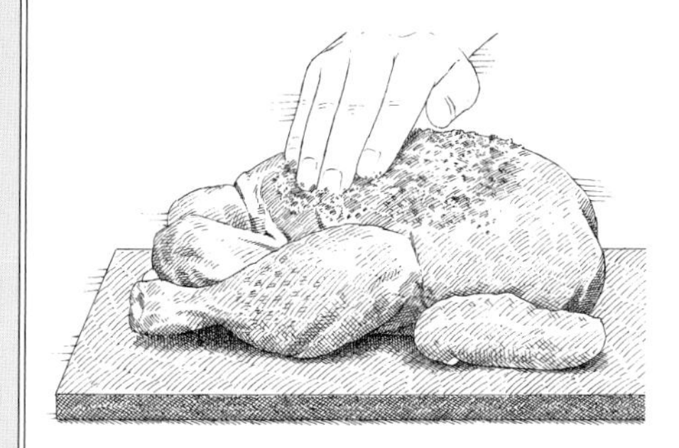

4. **APPLY A RUB** of salt and baking powder; air-dry in the refrigerator before roasting for crisper skin.

BEST ROAST CHICKEN AND VEGETABLES

ANDREW JANJIGIAN, *January/February 2016*

The idea of roasting a whole chicken with an abundance of root vegetables—think potatoes, carrots, parsnips—has a lot of appeal. Not only do you get a twofer of entrée and side dish from a single pan, but the result promises to turn everyday ingredients into something greater: a delicious, bronzed centerpiece and a side of vegetables that are beautifully caramelized and infused with deep, savory chicken flavor.

That said, I've always found it challenging to roast both components in the same pan without compromising the results. Surrounding the chicken with vegetables slows down the cooking of the thighs, the part of the bird you actually want to cook more quickly (it's the delicate breast meat that needs to cook slowly). This arrangement also prevents the skin on the lower portion of the bird from browning. Meanwhile, the crowded vegetables steam in their juices rather than brown, and because a whole chicken sheds quite a bit of fat, the vegetables also wind up greasy.

The secret to a perfect marriage of roast chicken and root vegetables is to keep them apart until the last second.

While there are ways around these issues, I wondered if it would be easier to achieve presentation-worthy chicken and perfectly roasted vegetables by cooking the two components separately. I'd just have to find another way to infuse the vegetables with rich chicken flavor.

SKILLET SOLUTION

It was essential to use the drippings from the chicken to flavor the vegetables, so I needed to find a way to produce evenly cooked dark and white meat and nicely browned skin and a good amount of drippings. I settled on a 12-inch skillet. Its low sides let air circulate around the skin for even browning, and its narrow diameter ensured that the drippings would pool and brown rather than burn as they would in a wide roasting pan. I also decided to preheat the skillet so that the thighs, which were in contact with the pan, would get a jump start, helping them finish cooking at the same time as the white meat.

When the chicken had finished roasting, I set it aside on a carving board to rest and admired the thick, dark golden deposit of flavorful proteins, or fond, on the bottom of the skillet—just the stuff the vegetables were waiting for. I poured a little bit of water into the skillet to loosen the fond and give me more liquid to work with, then poured the liquid into a fat separator to create two types of flavor bases—fat and concentrated juices. I tossed the potatoes with a few tablespoons of the fat, which would help them brown and crisp, and then placed them on a baking sheet in a hot oven.

Once they were tender and nicely browned, I tossed them with the concentrated juices and returned them to the oven for a few minutes. The result? In a word, spectacular. The potatoes were coated with a deeply savory glaze that tasted of pure chicken.

But it took about 40 minutes to cook the vegetables; I wanted a faster method. First, however, there were a few minor improvements to the chicken to attend to. One: The meat was a bit dry—it required some pretreatment. Because I was after a streamlined recipe, I opted to brine rather than salt, since salting can take significantly longer. I also added sugar to my brine, which would boost the meat's flavor and help the coated vegetables caramelize. Two: The skin was nicely browned but unevenly crisp because some pockets of fat didn't fully render. Pricking the fat deposits before cooking solved this problem, and also helped the brine season the meat more quickly. I also rubbed the skin with olive oil before cooking to keep it from turning leathery and to enhance browning.

UNCOVERING THE BEST APPROACH

My new plan was to cook the vegetables most of the way through in the oven on a rack below the chicken and then finish them while the chicken rested. The problem was that the vegetables' exteriors dried out before their interiors had turned tender, leaving them shriveled and tough. Parboiling them before finishing them in the oven had potential but seemed fussy—and I knew of a better way. In the past we've roasted root vegetables by arranging the pieces in a single layer on a baking sheet and then covering the sheet with foil to trap moisture so that they can steam and cook through evenly. We then remove the foil to let moisture evaporate and return the vegetables to a very hot oven to brown.

After a few tests, I had my method: Cook the vegetables on a baking sheet, covered, beneath the chicken for 30 minutes. Then remove the foil and let them sit while the chicken finished up (another 20 minutes, give or take). In this time, the excess moisture evaporated from residual heat. Once the chicken was finished, I set it aside, deglazed the pan and separated the fat as before, and tossed the potatoes with a few tablespoons of the fat before returning them to the oven to brown. Once they were nicely browned, I poured the chicken-y liquid from the pan over the potatoes and cooked them until the liquid had reduced to a glazy coating. I found that they browned most evenly and quickly with the oven turned up to 500 degrees. With a perfectly cooked, beautifully browned chicken and plenty of richly flavorful root vegetables, this was a recipe that finally delivered on the promise of this old-fashioned classic.

Best Roast Chicken with Root Vegetables

SERVES 4 TO 6

Cooking the chicken in a preheated skillet will ensure that the breast and thigh meat finish cooking at the same time. This recipe requires brining the chicken for 1 hour before cooking. If using a kosher chicken, do not brine in step 1, but season with ½ teaspoon salt in step 3.

- 1 (3½- to 4-pound) whole chicken, giblets discarded
- Salt and pepper
- ½ cup sugar
- 1½ pounds Yukon Gold potatoes, peeled and cut into 2-inch pieces
- 12 ounces carrots, peeled, halved crosswise, thick halves halved lengthwise
- 12 ounces parsnips, peeled, halved crosswise, thick halves halved lengthwise
- 4 teaspoons extra-virgin olive oil
- ¼ cup water
- 1 teaspoon minced fresh thyme
- 1 tablespoon chopped fresh parsley

1. With chicken breast side down, use tip of sharp knife to make four 1-inch incisions along back. Using your fingers, gently loosen skin covering breast and thighs. Use metal skewer to poke 15 to 20 holes in fat deposits on top of breast halves and thighs. Dissolve ½ cup salt and sugar in 2 quarts cold water in large container. Submerge chicken in brine, cover, and refrigerate for 1 hour.
2. Adjust oven racks to upper-middle and lower-middle positions and heat oven to 450 degrees. Place 12-inch ovensafe skillet on upper rack and heat for 15 minutes. Spray rimmed baking sheet with vegetable oil spray. Arrange potatoes, carrots, and parsnips with cut surfaces down in single layer on baking sheet and cover sheet tightly with aluminum foil.
3. Remove chicken from brine and pat dry with paper towels. Combine 1 tablespoon oil and ½ teaspoon pepper in small bowl. Rub entire surface of chicken with oil-pepper mixture. Tie legs together with twine and tuck wingtips behind back.
4. Carefully remove skillet from oven (handle will be hot). Add remaining 1 teaspoon oil to skillet and swirl to coat. Place chicken, breast side up, in skillet. Return skillet to upper rack and place sheet of vegetables on lower rack. Cook for 30 minutes.
5. Remove vegetables from oven, remove foil, and set aside. Rotate skillet and continue to cook chicken until breast registers 160 degrees and thighs register 175 degrees, 15 to 25 minutes longer.
6. Transfer chicken to carving board and let rest, uncovered, for 20 minutes. Increase oven temperature to 500 degrees. Add water to skillet. Using whisk, stir until brown bits have dissolved. Strain sauce through fine-mesh strainer into fat separator, pressing on solids to remove any remaining liquid. Let liquid settle for 5 minutes. Pour off liquid from fat separator and reserve. Reserve 3 tablespoons fat, discarding remaining fat.
7. Drizzle vegetables with reserved fat. Sprinkle vegetables with thyme, 1 teaspoon salt, and ½ teaspoon pepper and toss to coat. Place sheet on upper rack and roast for 5 minutes. Remove sheet from oven. Using thin, sharp metal spatula, turn vegetables. Continue to roast until browned at edges, 8 to 10 minutes longer.
8. Pour reserved liquid over vegetables. Continue to roast until liquid is thick and syrupy and vegetables are tender, 3 to 5 minutes. Toss vegetables to coat, then transfer to serving platter and sprinkle with parsley. Carve chicken and transfer to platter with vegetables. Serve.

FLAVORING THE VEGETABLES

Half the allure of a roast chicken and vegetable dinner is having vegetables that are infused with rich, savory chicken flavor. So if it isn't ideal to cook the vegetables in the same pan with the chicken, how do you get chicken-y vegetables? Here's what we do.

SEPARATE Create two flavor bases by separating the chicken fat from the juices.

TOSS WITH FAT Coat the parcooked vegetables with some of the fat to help them brown.

TOSS WITH JUICES Add the juices near the end of cooking so they reduce to a savory glaze.

MIXING UP THE MEDLEY

We recommend sticking with 1½ pounds of potatoes for half the vegetable mixture, but to switch things up, you can substitute 1½ pounds of the following vegetables for the carrots and parsnips.

Vegetable	Preparation
Turnips	Peel and cut into 1-inch pieces.
Beets/Celery Root	Peel and cut into ½-inch pieces.
Shallots	Peel and halve lengthwise, leaving root end attached. Place on sheet cut side down.
Leeks	Using white and light green parts only, halve pieces lengthwise, leaving root end attached. Place on sheet cut side down.

IF YOU DON'T HAVE A FAT SEPARATOR . . .

PAPER CUP/FREEZER

1. Pour pan drippings into paper cup. Freeze until fat has begun to solidify on top, about 10 minutes.
2. Over small bowl, poke hole in bottom of cup with skewer. Let drippings run out through hole.

COOKING SPOON

Let liquid settle for about 10 minutes. Use wide, shallow spoon to skim fat from surface.

BULB BASTER

Let liquid settle for about 10 minutes. Plunge baster into liquid beneath fat and draw into baster, then deposit in another container.

RECONSTRUCTING STUFFED ROAST CHICKEN

SANDRA WU, *March/April 2005*

Stuffed roast chicken should be the culinary equivalent of a power couple. Each partner brings a lot to the table, and this marriage represents the ultimate symbiotic relationship—at least in theory. The stuffing elevates the roast chicken beyond common everyday fare, while the chicken lends flavor and moisture to what would otherwise be dry bread crumbs. And, unlike roast turkey, its bigger and more complicated cousin, stuffed roast chicken should be simple. But stuffed roast chicken often doesn't deliver. What you get instead is either a perfectly cooked bird filled with lukewarm stuffing (hello, salmonella!) or safe-to-eat stuffing packed in parched poultry. I also wanted more than a few tablespoons of stuffing per person, a problem given the small cavity of a roasting chicken, even one weighing in at more than 5 pounds. No wonder most home cooks ask for a trial separation when it comes to this everyday recipe.

We've roasted literally thousands of chickens in the test kitchen and made more than our fair share of stuffing. It will come as no surprise, then, that I immediately decided to brine the bird before stuffing and roasting it. This was the only way to ensure moist, flavorful white meat. Next I was on to the stuffing, and my initial tests revolved around the traditional stuff-and-truss method used in turkey preparation. This technique was an abject failure. When I packed the chicken loosely with stuffing, I ended up with a miserly 1½ cups. I then packed the chicken until it nearly burst (about 3 cups), first heating the stuffing to 145 degrees in a microwave to give it a head start. But the stuffing still did not reach the safe temperature of 165 degrees by the time the meat was done. Apparently, fully cooked stuffing meant overcooked breast meat.

SWITCHING GEARS

A few years back, the test kitchen developed a method for high-roast chicken that started with a butterflied bird. (The backbone is removed and the bird is flattened and then roasted at 500 degrees.) I figured it was worth a try. I began with a flattened, brined bird and placed it on top of a broiler pan with 3 cups of stuffing directly beneath the chicken and another 5 cups in the bottom of the pan. After an hour, the skin on the chicken was crisp and evenly browned and the meat mostly moist. Finally, I had enough stuffing (at a safe 165 degrees) to feed a crowd, but now it suffered from a dual identity. The stuffing underneath the cavity was cohesive, while its counterpart in the bottom of the pan was dry and crunchy. When I tried placing all of the stuffing in the bottom of the pan (not directly beneath the chicken), it became greasy. In addition, the chicken (technically speaking) was not stuffed.

For my next test, I replaced the broiler pan with a traditional roasting pan and piled a mound of stuffing into it before placing a splayed butterflied chicken on top. After about an hour at 500 degrees, the chicken was slightly dry and the stuffing had many burnt bits. At 425 degrees, the chicken skin browned less evenly, but the stuffing was moist and cohesive. Tasters agreed that 450 degrees yielded the best results, although the stuffing was still charred in some areas and was greasy from the rendered fat.

To solve these two problems, I began a series of tests that eventually culminated in a strange version of culinary origami. First, I placed the stuffing inside an 8-inch square baking dish upon which the butterflied chicken perched; the whole thing then went into a roasting pan. Because the splayed chicken extended partially over the top of the baking dish, I hoped most of the fat from the skin would drip into the roasting pan rather than into the stuffing, but this was not the case. Next, I turned to aluminum foil, creating a packet around the stuffing that I poked with holes so the chicken juices could irrigate the dry contents. Sure, this stuffing was moist, but it lacked color and texture because it was shielded from the oven's dry heat. Finally, I made an aluminum foil bowl, mounded the stuffing into it, and placed the chicken on top, snugly encasing the stuffing. After about an hour of roasting, with a single pan rotation in between, the stuffing was browned and chewy on the bottom as well as moist and flavorful throughout from the juices. The fat from the skin was deposited directly into the roasting pan, never even touching the stuffing. Even though the roasting pan was hot, I could easily grab the foil bowl with my bare hands and dump the stuffing in one fell swoop into a serving bowl. Good technique and cleanup, all in one!

Kitchen shears and aluminum foil are all you need to achieve perfect chicken and stuffing.

THE RIGHT STUFF

It was time to get serious about stuffing. An informal poll in the test kitchen revealed that most people wanted a jazzed-up version of a traditional bread stuffing. I obliged by replacing the typical onion with thinly sliced leek, adding the requisite celery, and throwing in some chopped mushrooms for additional texture and substance. A dose of minced garlic, fresh sage and parsley, and chicken broth finished my recipe.

With a roasting technique and stuffing recipes now in place, I had finally managed to turn stuffed roast chicken into a successful marriage.

"Stuffed" Roast Butterflied Chicken

SERVES 4 TO 6

While the chicken brines, prepare the stuffing and set it aside until you're ready to cook the chicken. Use a traditional (not nonstick) roasting pan to prepare this recipe; the dark finish of a nonstick pan may cause the stuffing to overbrown.

Salt and pepper
1 (5- to 6-pound) whole chicken, giblets discarded
1 teaspoon olive oil
1 recipe Mushroom-Leek Bread Stuffing with Herbs (recipe follows)

1. Dissolve ½ cup salt in 2 quarts cold water in large container. Submerge chicken in brine, cover, and refrigerate for 1 hour.
2. Adjust oven rack to lower-middle position and heat oven to 450 degrees. Remove chicken from brine and pat dry, inside and out, with paper towels. With chicken breast side down, using kitchen shears, cut through bones on either side of backbone; discard backbone. Flip chicken over and press on breastbone to flatten. Rub skin with oil and season with pepper.
3. Stack two 12-inch squares of aluminum foil on top of each other. Fold edges to construct 8 by 6-inch bowl. Spray inside of bowl with vegetable oil spray and place bowl in roasting pan. Gently mound and pack stuffing into foil bowl and position chicken skin side up over stuffing (chicken should extend past edges of bowl so that most of fat renders into roasting pan, not into foil bowl; adjust edges of foil as necessary to fit shape of chicken cavity). Roast until chicken is just beginning to brown, about 30 minutes. Rotate pan and continue to roast until skin is crispy and deep golden brown and breast registers 160 degrees, thighs register 175 degrees, and stuffing registers 165 degrees, 25 to 35 minutes longer. Transfer chicken to carving board and let rest, uncovered, for 10 minutes.
4. While chicken rests, transfer stuffing from foil bowl to serving bowl and fluff with spoon. Carve chicken and serve with stuffing.

stuffing

Mushroom-Leek Bread Stuffing with Herbs

The dried bread cubes for this stuffing can be made in advance and stored in an airtight container or zipper-lock bag for up to one week.

6 slices hearty white sandwich bread, cut into ¼-inch cubes
2 tablespoons unsalted butter
8 ounces white mushrooms, trimmed and chopped
1 small leek, white and light green parts only, halved lengthwise, sliced ⅛ inch thick, and washed thoroughly
1 small celery rib, chopped fine
1 large garlic clove, minced
¼ cup minced fresh parsley
½ teaspoon minced fresh sage or ¼ teaspoon dried
½ teaspoon minced fresh thyme or ¼ teaspoon dried
½ cup plus 2 tablespoons chicken broth
1 large egg
½ teaspoon salt
½ teaspoon pepper

1. Adjust oven rack to middle position and heat oven to 250 degrees. Spread bread in single layer on rimmed baking sheet. Bake until thoroughly dried but not browned, about 30 minutes, stirring once halfway through baking.
2. Meanwhile, melt butter in 12-inch skillet over medium-high heat. Add mushrooms, leek, and celery and cook, stirring occasionally, until beginning to soften, about 4 minutes. Add garlic and continue to cook, stirring frequently, until vegetables begin to brown, 2 to 3 minutes. Stir in parsley, sage, and thyme and cook until fragrant, about 1 minute. Remove skillet from heat; set aside.
3. Whisk broth, egg, salt, and pepper in large bowl until combined. Add bread and mushroom mixture and toss gently until evenly moistened and combined. Set aside until ready to use.

BUTTERFLYING AND STUFFING THE CHICKEN

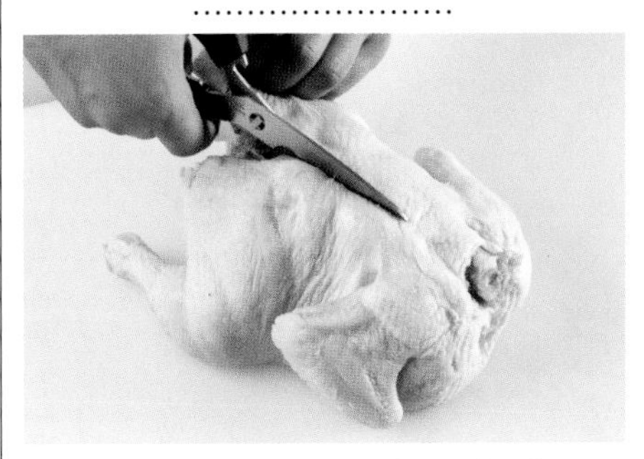

1. Cut through bones on either side of backbone; discard backbone.

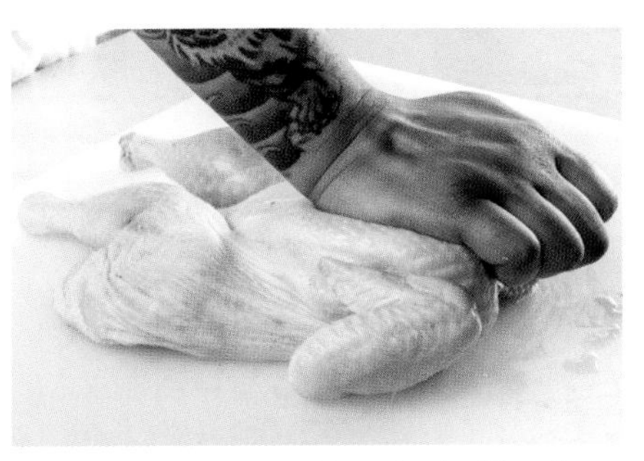

2. Flip chicken over and use heel of hand to flatten breastbone.

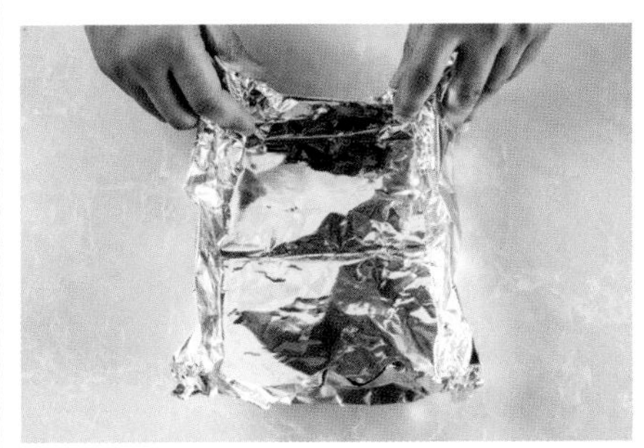

3. Stack two 12-inch squares of foil on top of each other. Fold edges to construct 8 by 6-inch bowl. Coat bowl with foil and pack stuffing into bowl.

4. Position chicken over stuffing. Adjust edges of foil bowl to fit shape of chicken cavity.

UPDATING CHICKEN AND DUMPLINGS

FRANCISCO J. ROBERT, *September/October 2009*

Chicken and dumplings is as classic as American food gets: Cooks in this country have been making the dish since the colonists arrived at Jamestown in the early 17th century. Over time, the dish has taken on distinct regional differences: Northerners typically like their broth thick and their dumplings fluffy, while down South the broth is usually more soup-like, with flat, square dumplings. Regional variances aside, a general rule applies to the chicken: The more mature the bird, the better the flavor. Generations ago, an egg hen or rooster several years old would be simmered for 4 or even 6 hours until falling off the bone, producing a rich broth. The simple addition of dumplings turned the broth into a flavorful, thrifty meal.

Chickens sold in supermarkets today are usually no more than seven weeks old. By comparing these young fowl in traditional recipes calling for hours of stewing with modern ones that simmer the birds for under an hour, I proved conventional wisdom right: No matter how long you cook them, whole young chickens yield unimpressive broth. To coax old-fashioned, full flavor from supermarket birds—and create dumplings that would please both Northern and Southern palates—it was time for some modern adjustments.

STOCK ANSWERS

Great chicken broth needs two things: flavor and body. Without a mature chicken for my broth, my first task was figuring out if a particular part of a younger bird would produce a flavorful broth. To this end, I made a series of broths with thighs, drumsticks, and breasts, both skin-on and skin-off, simmering a pound of each in a quart of water for 45 minutes. With or without skin, the stock made with just white meat was thin and flavorless, the meat dry and bland. Drumsticks produced richer broth with meat that was less dried out, but the skin-on thighs were a clear winner, with the most deeply flavored broth of the lot and meat that stayed tender.

To further boost flavor, I implemented a few tricks the test kitchen has used with success. First trick: Replace water with canned broth. Though canned broth can taste thin and metallic on its own, when cooked with real chicken parts, it turns decidedly richer, and its tinny flavor is no longer detectable. Second trick: Brown the meat before adding the liquid. As the skin crisps, the Maillard reaction kicks in, creating hundreds of new, complex flavors. Finally, trick three: Finesse the flavor by browning aromatic vegetables in the browned bits from the seared chicken and adding alcohol. Browning chopped carrots, celery, and onions until caramelized introduces sweetness, while ¼ cup of dry sherry—preferred by tasters over white wine and vermouth—adds acidity and depth.

Enhancing store-bought broth by simmering chicken thighs and wings gives our soup deep flavor, fast.

I had the flavor of the broth where I wanted it, but I still had to resolve the North-South debate about body. Northerners turn to flour as a thickener, while Southerners tend to leave well enough alone. I prepared two versions: The first batch I left plain, the other I thickened with ½ cup of flour (the amount typical in many Yankee versions of the dish) just before deglazing with the sherry. Tasters rejected the sludgy consistency of this broth outright as "heavy" and akin to "chicken pot pie filling." Knocking the flour down to ¼ cup produced broth with just the right amount of body (my colleagues deemed the straight broth too thin), but all agreed it muted the chicken flavor. Cutting the flour to 2 tablespoons still masked chicken essence. Switching to cornstarch had the same effect.

Looking for an alternative, I recalled that extended boiling (at least a couple of hours) converts the connective tissue in a chicken carcass to gelatin and thickens the broth. I didn't want my broth cooking for hours, but then I realized I'd left something out of my initial broth testing: wings. Because of their multiple joints, wings contain far more connective tissue than legs or breasts. If I added plenty of wings (a package of six seemed right) with the thighs, could I extract enough gelatin to thicken the broth? This turned out to be just what I needed to create a full-bodied liquid with potent chicken flavor that was rich without being in any way heavy. Time to move on to the dumplings.

DUMPLING DIVIDE

In the South, dumplings are made of dough rolled out to about ¼ inch thick and cut into squares that are then added to the pot. It's a tedious and messy process that yields dense, doughy dumplings. The Yankee approach is far simpler, resulting in fluffier dumplings made just like drop biscuits. Here you simply mix flour and leavener in one bowl and fat and a liquid in another, combine the two mixtures rapidly, and scoop out biscuit-size balls that you drop into the broth.

Given the differences in technique, I wasn't disappointed when (except for two holdouts from Kentucky and Alabama) my colleagues preferred the lighter Yankee dumplings. The problem was, they weren't actually all that light.

Since the Yankee dumplings are so closely related to oven-baked drop biscuits, I tried using our standard drop biscuit recipe (flour, salt, sugar, baking powder and soda, butter, and buttermilk) in the soup to see if it would produce more pillowy results. These

dumplings had great tangy buttermilk flavor. And because they had more leavener and butter than the earlier recipes I had tried, they were far from leaden. In fact, they had the opposite problem: They were so fragile, they disintegrated into the broth as they cooked.

The ideal dumpling should have all the lightness of our drop biscuits, but enough structure to hold together in the broth. Knowing that fat coats flour and weakens its structure, I tried gradually cutting down on the 8 tablespoons of butter in the recipe. At 4 tablespoons, their structure improved somewhat; removing any more compromised flavor. Since I was cooking my dumplings in a moist environment instead of a dry oven, my next thought was cutting back the liquid. Reducing the amount of buttermilk from a full cup to ¾ cup was another improvement—but the dumplings were still far too delicate.

Perhaps the problem was too much leavener, which can lead to over-rising and poor structure. Completely eliminating the baking powder (only baking soda remained) gave them just the right density in the center, but they were still mushy around the edges. While eggs are not traditional biscuit ingredients, I tried adding one, hoping that the extra protein would help the dumpling hold together. A whole egg was too much: Tasters didn't like the eggy flavor. A single egg white whisked into the buttermilk added just the right amount of structure without affecting flavor. Another useful tweak was waiting to add the dumplings until the broth was simmering, reducing their time in the broth to help keep them whole.

One last problem remained: Steam was condensing on the inside of the lid of the Dutch oven and dripping onto the dumplings, turning their tops soggy. Could I somehow catch the moisture before it dripped back down? I tried wrapping a kitchen towel around the lid of the Dutch oven. It worked like a charm, trapping the moisture before it had a chance to drip down and saturate my light-as-air dumplings and flavor-packed broth.

Lighter Chicken and Dumplings

SERVES 6

You can substitute ½ cup of plain yogurt thinned with ¼ cup of milk for the buttermilk, if desired. To include white meat (and lose a bit of flavor in the process), replace two chicken thighs with two 6-ounce boneless, skinless chicken breasts; brown the breasts along with the thighs and remove them from the stew once they register 160 degrees, 20 to 30 minutes. The collagen in the wings helps thicken the stew; do not omit them.

Stew

2½ pounds bone-in chicken thighs, trimmed
Salt and pepper
2 teaspoons vegetable oil
2 small onions, chopped fine
2 carrots, peeled and cut into ¾-inch pieces
1 celery rib, minced
¼ cup dry sherry
6 cups chicken broth
1 teaspoon minced fresh thyme
1 pound chicken wings, trimmed
¼ cup chopped fresh parsley

Dumplings

2 cups all-purpose flour
1 teaspoon sugar
1 teaspoon salt
½ teaspoon baking soda
¾ cup buttermilk, chilled
4 tablespoons unsalted butter, melted and hot
1 large egg white

1. *For the stew:* Pat thighs dry with paper towels and sprinkle with 1 teaspoon salt and ¼ teaspoon pepper. Heat oil in Dutch oven over medium-high heat until shimmering. Add thighs, skin side down, and cook until skin is well browned, 5 to 7 minutes. Using tongs, flip thighs and brown second side, 5 to 7 minutes longer; transfer to large plate. Pour off all but 1 teaspoon fat from pot.

2. Add onions, carrots, and celery to pot and cook, stirring occasionally, until caramelized, 7 to 9 minutes. Stir in sherry, scraping up any browned bits. Stir in broth and thyme. Return thighs and any accumulated juices to pot and add wings. Bring to simmer, cover, and cook until thigh meat offers no resistance when poked with tip of paring knife but still clings to bones, 45 to 55 minutes.

3. Remove pot from heat and transfer chicken to cutting board. Let broth settle for 5 minutes, then skim fat from surface. When chicken is cool enough to handle, remove skin. Using your fingers, pull meat from thighs and, if desired, wings and cut into 1-inch pieces. Return meat to pot and bring stew to simmer over low heat.

4. *For the dumplings:* Whisk flour, sugar, salt, and baking soda together in large bowl. Combine buttermilk and melted butter in medium bowl, stirring until butter forms small clumps; whisk in egg white. Add buttermilk mixture to flour mixture and stir with rubber spatula until just incorporated and batter pulls away from sides of bowl.

5. Stir parsley into stew and season with salt and pepper to taste. Using greased 1-tablespoon measure or #60 scoop, drop level scoops of batter over top of stew, spacing them about ¼ inch apart (you should have about 24 dumplings). Wrap lid of pot with clean dish towel (keeping towel away from heat source) and cover pot. Simmer gently until dumplings have doubled in size and toothpick inserted in center comes out clean, 13 to 16 minutes. Serve immediately.

BEST PARTS FOR BROTH

WINGS NATURAL THICKENER
The multiple joints in chicken wings contain lots of collagen that converts into gelatin during cooking—a better broth thickener than flour, which masks chicken flavor.

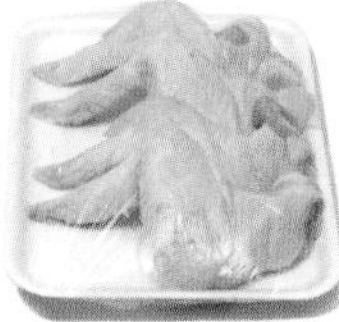

THIGHS FULL O' FLAVOR
Pound for pound, chicken thighs impart richer flavor to broth than any other part of the bird. Plus, they require far less cooking time than a whole bird or carcass.

BEEFING UP TURKEY BURGERS

PAM ANDERSON WITH MELISSA HAMILTON, *July/August 1998*

One summer vacation my 15-year-old daughter decided to become a vegetarian. After a week-long debate, we finally compromised on white meat. In other words, she was excused from lamb, beef, and pork as long as she would eat fish and fowl. Since hamburgers were one of her weaknesses, I thought she'd cave in pretty quickly. But what seemed like a teen fad has evolved into a way of life.

Since hamburgers are a regular summer supper for us, I needed to find a substitute sandwich for her. Ground turkey was the obvious first choice, but we found out pretty quickly that a lean, fully cooked turkey burger, seasoned simply with salt and pepper, was a weak stand-in for an all-beef burger. Simply put, it was dry, tasteless, and colorless. At the time, believing this was just a passing phase, I had very little energy for turkey burger exploration and simply switched to breaded chicken cutlets.

Now, three years later, finding my daughter's red-meat resolve still rock solid, I set out to develop a turkey burger that would not only please her, but would also be a desirable, healthier option for the rest of the family. I wanted a turkey burger with beef burger qualities—dark and crusty on the outside, full-flavored and juicy inside.

THE MEAT CASE

Finding the right meat was crucial to developing the best turkey burger. According to the National Turkey Federation, I had three options—white meat (with 1 to 2 percent fat), dark meat (over 15 percent fat), and a blend of the two (ranging from 7 to 15 percent fat).

At the grocery store, I found multiple variations on the white meat/dark meat theme, including preformed lean patties, higher-fat ground fresh turkey on Styrofoam trays or frozen in tubes like bulk sausage, lower-fat ground turkey breasts, and of course individual turkey parts I could grind up myself. I bought them all, took them home, and fired up a skillet.

I first tested the preformed lean patties—refrigerated and frozen—and found them mediocre. To varying degrees, the frozen ones had a week-old-roast-turkey taste. A few bites from one of the refrigerated varieties turned up significant turkey debris—tendon, ground up gristle, and bone-like chips. I moved on to bulk ground turkey.

The higher-fat (15 percent) ground turkey turned out to be flavorful and reasonably juicy with a decent, burger-like crust. Frankly, these burgers didn't need too much help. On the other hand, I didn't see much point in eating them either. Given that a great beef burger contains only 20 percent fat, a mere 5 percent fat savings didn't seem worth it.

For turkey burgers that please like their all-beef cousins, grind your own turkey in the food processor.

At the other extreme with only 1 or 2 percent fat was ground turkey breast. As I was mixing and forming these patties, I knew I had about as much chance of making them look, taste, and feel like real burgers as I did of making vanilla wafers taste like chocolate chip cookies. They needed a binder to keep them from falling apart. They needed extra fat to keep them from parching and extra fat in the pan to keep them from sticking. And they needed flavor to save them from blandness.

With 7 percent fat, lean ground turkey was the most popular style at all the grocery stores I checked. Burgers made from this mix were dry, rubbery-textured, and mild-flavored. With a little help, however, these leaner patties were meaty enough to have real burger potential.

Most flavorful of all and only about 10 percent fat were the boned and skinless turkey thighs I ground myself in the food processor. I first tried grinding the skin with the meat but found that it ground inconsistently and I had to pick it out. In the next batch I left it out and found the meat was equally flavorful and lower in calories (my butcher declared my home-ground skinless turkey almost 90-percent lean when he tested it in his Univex Fat Analyzer).

For all the obvious reasons, I had sworn that even if I liked the outcome I wasn't going to make grind-your-own-turkey part of the recipe, but these burgers—meaty-flavored with a beef-like chew—were far superior to any I made with the commercially ground turkey. Of course, I had suspected as much, given my liking for grind-your-own-chuck beef burgers. If you are willing to take the time, food-processor-ground turkey thighs cook up into low-fat turkey burgers with great flavor and texture.

I CAN'T BELIEVE IT'S NOT BURGER

For those with little time or energy for this process, I decided to see what I could do to improve the lean commercially ground turkey. To improve texture and juiciness, I started with the obvious—milk-soaked bread. For comparison I also made burgers with buttermilk- and yogurt-soaked bread. All these additions made the burgers feel too much like meatloaf and destroyed whatever meaty flavor there had been, since turkey is mild to start with. The bread and milk lightened the meat's color unpleasantly, while the sugar in both ingredients caused the burgers to burn easily and made it impossible to develop a good thick crust.

I tried dozens of other fillers to improve the texture, and the real winner—for flavor, texture, and easy availability—was ricotta cheese. Moist and chewy, it gave the burger the texture boost it needed and required very little effort.

Finally, I decided to experiment a bit with added flavorings, and found that some Worcestershire and Dijon mustard enhanced the burgers' taste without drawing attention to themselves.

The Best Grilled Turkey Burgers

SERVES 4

1 (2-pound) bone-in turkey thigh, skinned and boned, cut into 1-inch chunks
2 teaspoons Worcestershire sauce
2 teaspoons Dijon mustard
½ teaspoon salt
½ teaspoon pepper
1 tablespoon vegetable oil
4 hamburger buns, toasted

1. Arrange turkey chunks on baking sheet and freeze until semifirm, about 30 minutes.
2. Working in 3 batches, pulse semifrozen turkey chunks in food processor until largest pieces are no bigger than ⅛ inch, 12 to 14 pulses. Transfer ground turkey to bowl and stir in Worcestershire, mustard, salt, and pepper. Divide meat into 4 portions and lightly toss 1 portion from hand to hand to form ball, then lightly flatten ball with your fingertips into 1-inch-thick patty. Press center of patty down with your fingertips until it is about ½ inch thick, creating a slight depression. Repeat with remaining portions.

3A. *For a charcoal grill:* Open bottom vent completely. Light large chimney starter three-quarters filled with charcoal briquettes (4½ quarts). When top coals are partially covered with ash, pour two-thirds evenly over half of grill, then pour remaining coals over other half of grill. Set cooking grate in place, cover, and open lid vent completely. Heat grill until hot, about 5 minutes.

3B. *For a gas grill:* Turn all burners to high, cover, and heat grill until hot, about 15 minutes.

4. Clean and oil cooking grate. Place burgers on grill (hotter side if using charcoal) and cook, without pressing on them, until well browned on both sides, 5 to 7 minutes, flipping halfway through cooking.
5. Move burgers to cooler side of grill (if using charcoal), or turn all burners to medium (if using gas). Cover and continue to cook until burgers are cooked through, 5 to 7 minutes longer, flipping halfway through cooking.
6. Transfer burgers to serving platter, tent with aluminum foil, and let rest for 5 to 10 minutes before serving on buns.

variations

Quicker Turkey Burgers

This recipe will enrich store-bought ground lean turkey so that it makes excellent burgers. Ricotta cheese can burn easily, so keep a close watch on the burgers as they cook.

Substitute 1¼ pounds 93 percent lean ground turkey for turkey thighs and add ½ cup whole-milk ricotta cheese to turkey with seasonings.

Miso Turkey Burgers

Japanese miso, a paste made from fermenting rice, barley, or soybeans, gives the turkey burgers a particularly savory, beefy flavor.

Stir 2 teaspoons white miso together with 2 teaspoons water. Omit Worcestershire and mustard and add miso mixture with seasonings.

Indoor Turkey Burgers

Pan-frying develops an especially nice crust on the burgers when grilling isn't an option.

Heat 2 teaspoons vegetable oil in 12-inch skillet over medium heat until just smoking. Add burgers to pan and cook over medium heat without moving burgers until bottom side of each is dark brown and crusted, 3 to 4 minutes. Flip burgers and continue to cook until bottom side is light brown but not yet crusted, 3 to 4 minutes longer. Reduce heat to low, position skillet lid slightly ajar on pan to allow steam to escape, and continue to cook 8 to 10 minutes longer, flipping burgers if necessary to promote deep browning, until burgers register 160 degrees. Serve.

PREPPING TURKEY THIGHS FOR BURGERS

We found that the extra step of grinding fresh turkey thighs ourselves made the most flavorful, best-textured burgers.

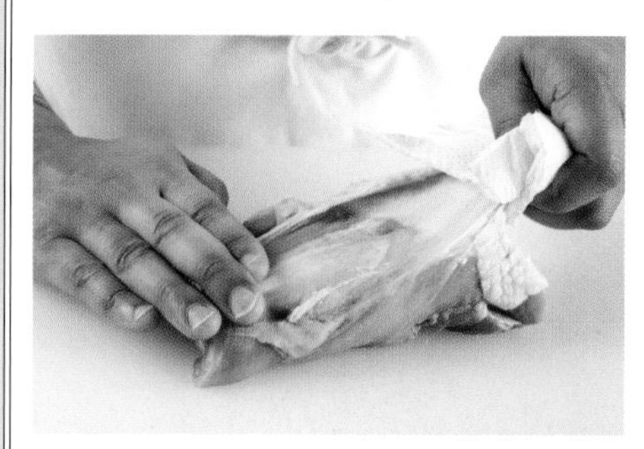

1. To remove skin from turkey thigh, grasp it with paper towel for better traction and pull.

2. With boning knife, cut along top of thigh bone, scrape meat away on both sides and underneath, and discard bone.

3. Cut thigh meat into 1-inch strips and then cut each strip into 1-inch cubes. Freeze until semifrozen.

THE PROBLEM WITH ROAST TURKEY

J. KENJI LOPEZ-ALT, *November/December 2008*

For most of us, juicy, perfectly cooked roast turkey shrouded in crisp, burnished skin is like a desert mirage: a beautiful idea, yes, but one that always seems just out of reach. Here's the crux of the problem: getting the dark meat up to temperature and the skin crisp without overcooking the white meat. Breast meat needs to reach about 160 degrees and not much more or its muscle proteins will tighten up, squeezing out juices. At the same time, dark meat must be cooked to 175 degrees. Another problem is that dark meat cooks especially slowly, particularly the thighs, which, due to the anatomy of a turkey, are shielded from direct oven heat.

Enter two safeguards we've long advocated in the test kitchen: salting the turkey or brining it in saltwater. Both measures change the structure of the bird's muscles, allowing it to retain more moisture, especially at the exterior of the breast, the area most prone to overcooking. But neither measure is foolproof, and each takes the better part of a day. I wanted to cut out at least one kitchen task this Thanksgiving and skip that extra step. My goal was no less than the perfect turkey recipe, an approach that would get my fowl from supermarket to table in just a few hours, with meat as moist as prime rib and crisp, crackling skin. And since this would be the ideal recipe, I wanted to end up with great and easy gravy, too.

TAKING TURKEY'S TEMPERATURE

To find out exactly how much of the turkey was hitting the 160-degree mark, I roasted a turkey using our standard method (start in a 400-degree oven breast-down and finish breast-up at 325 degrees). I took the temperature of the breast meat at ¼-inch intervals all the way from the coolest point (which registered 160 degrees) to the very exterior. This test showed that more than 50 percent of the turkey breast was reaching temperatures above 180 degrees, with some parts reaching nearly 200 degrees. No wonder brining is usually necessary to ensure meat that isn't completely dried out!

This problem was nearly identical to a dilemma I had encountered last year when developing a recipe for thick-cut steaks, when I found that high-heat cooking caused the outer layers to overcook. The solution? Lower the heat. I baked the steaks in a gentle 275-degree oven before finishing them in a hot pan, resulting in perfectly and evenly cooked meat. Maybe, I reasoned, a slow-roasted turkey might also be the key to juicy meat.

I roasted my next turkey at 275 degrees, again taking its temperature at ¼-inch intervals once the center had reached 160 degrees. This time, the majority of the meat stayed reasonably close to the 160-degree mark, with only the outermost layers reaching between 170 and 180 degrees—a marked improvement that was verified by correspondingly juicier breast meat. But three problems had emerged. The most obvious was the pale and flabby skin, which failed to brown at the lower temperature. Second was the extremely long cooking time (more than 5 hours), which not only tied up the oven but left the meat in the 40- to 140-degree "danger zone" (the temperature range at which bacteria flourish) for too long. Finally, with the lower temperature, while the breast meat stayed closer to 160 degrees, so, unfortunately, did the legs and thighs. By the time the breast was done cooking, the thighs were still a disquieting pale pink.

SEPARATION ANXIETY

I knew from past chicken recipes that spreading the legs out from the breast helps them to cook faster. Could separating them completely help even more? Even the most sentimental cook would surely give up their Norman Rockwell dream of a whole golden brown bird emerging from the oven in exchange for the juiciest turkey with the simplest preparation.

Rather than go through the hassle of breaking down a whole turkey, I bought a turkey breast along with two leg quarters (thighs and drumsticks). I roasted them elevated on a rack over a baking sheet to promote air circulation. This time, after just under three hours in the oven, the breast had reached 160 degrees. And without the insulating effect of the turkey's backbone and breast meat, the thighs and drumsticks serendipitously reached 175 degrees just as the breast finished cooking! Cutting into the breast revealed tender, juicy meat.

Swapping out a whole turkey for parts and roasting at a low temperature guarantees the juiciest meat.

The only remaining problem was the skin. Most turkey recipes achieve crisp skin by starting the bird in a hot oven to brown it, then lowering the heat to finish cooking. But a higher starting temperature meant a higher oven temperature the whole way through, which led to dried-out meat. Increasing the heat near the end seemed more promising, but ultimately proved untenable; leaving the turkey in the oven as it heated up slowly also caused it to overcook. But what if I allowed the turkey to cool before popping it back in the oven to crisp the skin? I roasted more parts, this time removing them from the oven before raising the temperature as high as it would go—500 degrees. I allowed the turkey to rest for a full half hour until the temperature of the meat had dropped to around 130 degrees. After the turkey was in the oven for 15 minutes, I hesitantly poked my instant-read thermometer into the skin, which made an encouraging crack. The thermometer revealed what one taste soon confirmed—the turkey was perfectly cooked from center to edge and surrounded by flawlessly rendered, crisp skin.

THE GRAVY TRAIN

My remaining task was to find a simple way to create rich gravy. For a foundation, I placed a mixture of carrots, celery, onions, and flavorings under the turkey with some chicken broth. After a couple hours in the oven, the savory roasted vegetables were further seasoned by turkey drippings. Once the meat was cooked (but before crisping the skin), I strained the liquid and added more canned broth. The turkey's resting period gave me plenty of time to cook up a dark golden roux from flour and butter that I whisked into the broth. Barely 20 minutes later, the roux and broth had thickened into an intense gravy.

I'll still brine a turkey whenever I get the urge to provide a picture-perfect Thanksgiving centerpiece. But I have a feeling most times I won't even start worrying about the bird until the afternoon of the big day, knowing that I can easily produce juicy turkey with crisp skin—and a rich gravy—all in time for dinner.

DON'T LEAVE YOUR TURKEY HIGH AND DRY

EXPERIMENT We roasted two non-brined turkeys, one using our standard high-heat approach (start in a 400-degree oven and finish at 325 degrees), the other roasted at 275 degrees the entire time. Once the center of each breast hit 160 degrees (the ideal temperature for moist, tender white meat), we recorded its temperature at ¼-inch intervals to the very exterior.

RESULTS The outermost layers of the high-heat breast topped a moisture-obliterating 210 degrees. The exterior of the slow-roasted breast reached a much more moderate 176 degrees—proving that if you can roast at low heat, the meat will still be moist, even without a brine.

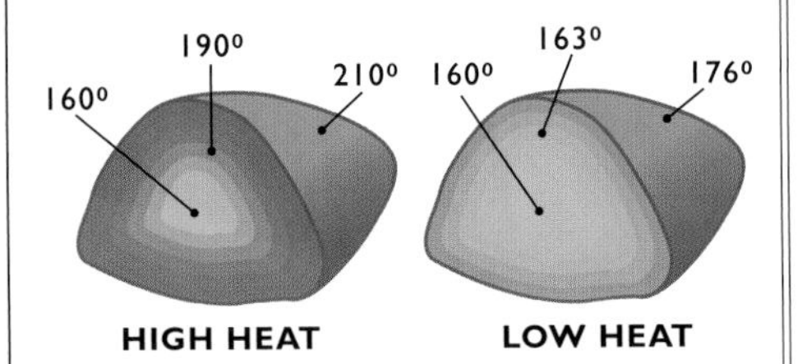

Slow-Roasted Turkey with Gravy

SERVES 10 TO 12

Instead of drumsticks and thighs, you may use two (1½- to 2-pound) whole leg quarters. The recipe will also work with a turkey breast alone; in step 2, reduce the butter to 1½ tablespoons, the salt to 1½ teaspoons, and the pepper to 1 teaspoon. Many supermarkets carry "hotel-style" turkey breasts, which still have the wings and rib cage attached. If this is the only type of breast you can find, you will need to remove the wings and cut away the rib cage with kitchen shears before proceeding with the recipe.

Turkey
3 onions, chopped
3 celery ribs, chopped
2 carrots, peeled and chopped
5 sprigs fresh thyme
5 garlic cloves, peeled and halved
1 cup chicken broth
1 (5- to 7-pound) whole bone-in turkey breast, trimmed
4 pounds turkey drumsticks and thighs, trimmed
3 tablespoons unsalted butter, melted
1 tablespoon salt
2 teaspoons pepper

Gravy
2 cups chicken broth
3 tablespoons unsalted butter
3 tablespoons all-purpose flour
2 bay leaves
Salt and pepper

1. *For the turkey:* Adjust oven rack to lower-middle position and heat oven to 275 degrees. Arrange onions, celery, carrots, thyme sprigs, and garlic in even layer on rimmed baking sheet. Pour broth into sheet. Place wire rack on top of vegetables.
2. Pat turkey parts dry with paper towels. Brush turkey parts on all sides with melted butter and sprinkle with salt and pepper. Place breast skin side down and drumsticks and thighs skin side up on wire rack in vegetable-filled sheet, leaving at least ¼ inch between pieces.
3. Roast turkey parts for 1 hour. Using 2 large wads of paper towels, turn turkey breast skin side up. Continue to roast until breast registers 160 degrees and drumsticks/thighs register 175 degrees, 1 to 2 hours longer. Remove sheet from oven and transfer wire rack with turkey to second rimmed baking sheet. Let turkey parts rest for at least 30 minutes or up to 1½ hours.
4. *For the gravy:* Strain vegetables and liquid from sheet through fine-mesh strainer set in 4-cup liquid measuring cup, pressing on solids to extract as much liquid as possible; discard solids. Add broth to measuring cup (you should have about 3 cups liquid).
5. Melt butter in medium saucepan over medium-high heat. Add flour and cook, stirring constantly, until flour is dark golden brown and fragrant, about 5 minutes. Slowly whisk in bay leaves and broth mixture and gradually bring to boil. Reduce heat to low and simmer, stirring occasionally, until gravy is thick and measures 2 cups, 15 to 20 minutes. Discard bay leaves. Off heat, season gravy with salt and pepper to taste. Cover and keep warm.
6. Heat oven to 500 degrees. Place sheet with turkey in oven. Roast until skin is golden brown and crispy, about 15 minutes. Transfer turkey to carving board and let rest, uncovered, for 20 minutes. Carve and serve with gravy.

SHOPPING FOR TURKEY PARTS

Most supermarkets carry whole bone-in turkey breasts as well as leg quarters and individually packaged thighs and drumsticks. Try to avoid breasts that have been injected with a saline solution (often called "self-basters"), as we find it masks the natural flavor of the turkey. Also, ignore any pop-up timer that may come with the breast; the meat will be long overcooked by the time the popper pops.

REINVENTING BREAD STUFFING

DAVID PAZMIÑO, *November/December 2010*

Stuffing fans generally fall into two camps: those who favor the crusty version baked in a dish, and those who love their stuffing cooked in the turkey's cavity, where it can absorb the bird's flavorful juices. I envy the households where the plentiful baking-dish version is in high demand. At my house, everyone wants a helping of the ultrasavory, supermoist stuffing from inside the bird, but there's never enough to go around. This year I was determined to revamp the stuffing cooked outside the bird to give it the rich flavor and soft texture of stuffing from the turkey cavity. Then everyone who loved this style could come back for seconds, even thirds.

BASIC BEGINNINGS

I would start with the easy stuff: nailing down a basic recipe. The usual suspects in stuffing are canned chicken broth, celery and onion cooked in butter, eggs, fresh herbs—I chose time-honored thyme and sage—and, of course, dried cubes of bread. Many recipes call for drying the bread cubes by simply leaving them out for a few days. I already knew this was not an option. As bread stales at room temperature, its starch molecules undergo a process called retrogradation, causing it to become hard but not necessarily dry. Instead, I would "stale" the bread cubes in a 200-degree oven for an hour. This method actually removes moisture, ultimately leading to a drier structure that allows the bread to soak up more liquid for a better-tasting stuffing.

We make our stuffing taste as though it was cooked inside the bird by topping it with turkey wings.

Normally, stuffing can be made with anything from cornbread to artisanal loaves, French baguettes, or Italian bread. But I wondered if one would prove better than another for achieving the moist texture I was shooting for. I didn't want to fool with making cornbread or hunting down a good ready-made batch, so I rounded up the other three candidates, along with sliced sandwich bread. I cut each bread into cubes and staled them in the oven. I was right to be concerned about the style of bread: Baguettes had too high a ratio of crust to interior, leading to a chewy stuffing. The superfine crumb of Italian loaves became overly soggy and blown out, while artisanal breads like ciabatta were simply too tough. The best choice turned out to be ordinary, easy-to-find sandwich bread, which baked up soft but still retained some shape.

TRICKLE-DOWN THEORY

It was time to get on with my real goal: infusing the dressing with meaty turkey flavor. Ground sausage is a great way to impart an extra meaty dimension to stuffing, so what about simply adding ground turkey to the recipe? I browned 1 pound in a skillet, combined it with the other stuffing ingredients, threw everything in a baking dish, and put the whole thing in the oven. This got me nowhere. Unlike ground sausage, which, when added to stuffing, brings to the mix lots of flavorful fat and often herbs and spices, ground turkey is both relatively lean and bland. All it did was produce lumps of none-too-flavorful meat amid the bread cubes.

Next, I flirted with the idea of swapping the canned broth with a rich homemade turkey stock that I could reduce for extra intensity. That fantasy lasted about a minute as I tried to imagine myself tending to a pot of stock, all the while juggling the dozens of other things I needed to get done for the big feast. There had to be an easier way to re-create the rich fatty juices that trickle down inside the bird. Then it occurred to me: I could actually get that same trickle-down effect by covering the stuffing in the baking dish with turkey parts—in essence, creating a makeshift turkey cavity.

First I tried meaty turkey legs and thighs, which had the obvious advantage of exuding lots of flavorful juices (and fat). These proved a bit cumbersome, so I turned to turkey wings. To get every last bit of turkey juice and fat to render, I split the wings into sections and poked holes in the skin with a paring knife. I arranged the perforated wing pieces on the stuffing and baked it in a moderate oven—375 degrees—for an hour, until the wings reached a safe 175 degrees. I was onto something. The flavorful juice and fat from the roasted wings had penetrated deep into the stuffing. The only problem? The top layer had dried out in the oven.

The next time around, I covered the wings and stuffing with foil. This kept the stuffing moist, but the wings didn't get a chance to brown. Without all the new flavor compounds created by browning, the stuffing didn't have the richness I had noted in my previous attempt. If I wanted browning, the only other option was to sear the wings before placing them on the stuffing. I was happy to find that the 3 pounds of wings I'd been using fit into a skillet in one batch. After searing, I removed them, then sautéed the aromatics and added the chicken broth. Another benefit of this approach was that I could scrape up the flavorful fond that had built up on the bottom of the pan and incorporate it into the savory liquid. I combined the liquid with the aromatics and the bread along with eggs and more chicken broth (to augment the juices from the wings) and placed the mixture in a baking dish, arranging the seared wings atop the stuffing. I covered the dish with foil, and to prevent the bottom of the stuffing from becoming crusty, I placed the baking dish on a baking sheet, which offered some protection against the oven's heat.

A little over an hour later, I had moist, tender stuffing that certainly looked the part—and my tasters declared it to be as rich and savory as any inside-the-bird stuffing

they'd sampled. Stuffing this good shouldn't be reserved for the holidays, I thought, so I tested my new recipe using chicken wings, which unlike turkey wings are easy to find year-round. Since chicken wings are less fatty and meaty than turkey wings, I discovered that I needed to increase the amount of chicken broth and decrease cooking time to get comparable results.

With so much turkey flavor, I needed only to add some sausage, tart dried cherries, and toasted pecans to give my stuffing true holiday pizzazz. I also created a couple of variations: one with bacon, sautéed apples, and leeks, and another with just a handful of parsley for fresh flavor.

Ultramoist, full of turkey flavor, and in a quantity that allowed my guests to have multiple helpings, these stuffings clearly showed that they didn't need to be stuffed at all.

TURKEY WINGS TO THE RESCUE

Baking stuffing with browned turkey wings on top creates the same rich savoriness of stuffing cooked inside the bird.

1. **BROWN WINGS** Sear turkey wings to give stuffing savory depth.

2. **TOP, COVER, BAKE** Top stuffing with browned wings, cover with aluminum foil to trap moisture, and bake.

Bread Stuffing with Sausage, Dried Cherries, and Pecans

SERVES 10 TO 12

Two pounds of chicken wings can be substituted for the turkey wings. If you're using chicken wings, separate them into two sections (it's not necessary to separate the tips) and poke each segment four or five times. Also, increase the amount of chicken broth to 3 cups, reduce the amount of butter to 2 tablespoons, and cook the stuffing for only 1 hour (the chicken wings should register above 175 degrees at the end of cooking). Use the meat from the cooked turkey or chicken wings to make salad or soup.

2 pounds hearty white sandwich bread, cut into ½-inch cubes (16 cups)
3 pounds turkey wings, cut at joints, trimmed
2 teaspoons vegetable oil
1 pound bulk pork sausage
4 tablespoons unsalted butter
1 large onion, chopped fine
3 celery ribs, minced
Salt and pepper
2 tablespoons minced fresh thyme
2 tablespoons minced fresh sage
2½ cups chicken broth
3 large eggs
1 cup dried cherries
1 cup pecans, toasted and chopped fine

1. Adjust oven racks to upper-middle and lower-middle positions and heat oven to 250 degrees. Divide bread cubes between 2 rimmed baking sheets and spread in even layer. Bake until edges have dried but centers are slightly moist (bread should yield to pressure), 45 minutes to 1 hour, stirring several times during baking. (Bread can be toasted up to 24 hours in advance.) Transfer bread to large bowl and increase oven temperature to 375 degrees.
2. While bread bakes, use paring knife to poke 10 to 15 holes in each turkey wing segment. Heat oil in 12-inch skillet over medium-high heat until shimmering. Add wings in single layer and cook until golden brown, 4 to 6 minutes per side. Transfer wings to separate bowl.
3. Return now-empty skillet to medium-high heat, add sausage, and cook, breaking into ½-inch pieces with wooden spoon, until browned, 5 to 7 minutes. Using slotted spoon, transfer sausage to paper towel–lined plate.
4. Add butter to fat left in skillet and melt over medium heat. Add onion, celery, and ½ teaspoon salt and cook, stirring occasionally, until vegetables are softened, 7 to 9 minutes. Stir in thyme, sage, and 1 teaspoon pepper and cook until fragrant, about 30 seconds. Stir in 1 cup broth, scraping up any browned bits, and bring to simmer. Add vegetable mixture to bowl with dried bread and toss to combine.
5. Grease 13 by 9-inch baking dish. Whisk eggs, 1½ teaspoons salt, remaining 1½ cups broth, and any accumulated juices from wings together in bowl. Add cherries, pecans, sausage, and egg mixture to bread mixture and toss to combine; transfer to prepared dish. Arrange wings on top of stuffing, cover tightly with aluminum foil, and place dish on rimmed baking sheet. Bake on lower oven rack until wings register 175 degrees, 1 to 1¼ hours. Remove foil and transfer wings to plate; reserve for another use. Using fork, gently fluff stuffing. Let rest for 5 minutes before serving.

variations

Bread Stuffing with Leeks, Bacon, and Apples

Omit pecans. Substitute 12 ounces bacon, cut into ½-inch pieces, for sausage. In step 3, cook bacon in skillet over medium heat until crisp, 5 to 7 minutes. Using slotted spoon, transfer bacon to paper towel–lined plate; pour off all but 2 tablespoons fat from skillet. Proceed with recipe from step 4, substituting 2 leeks, white and light green parts only, sliced thin, for onion and 3 Granny Smith apples, cored and cut into ¼-inch pieces, for cherries.

Bread Stuffing with Fresh Herbs

Omit sausage and increase butter to 6 tablespoons. After browned turkey wings have been removed in step 2, melt butter in skillet over medium heat. Proceed with recipe from step 4, substituting 3 tablespoons chopped fresh parsley for dried cherries and pecans.

Bluegill
Atlantic Salmon
Channel Catfish
American Shad
Walleye
Brook Trout
Striped Bass
Rainbow Trout

FISH AND SHELLFISH

FISH EN PAPILLOTE

KEITH DRESSER, *March/April 2009*

Cooking *en papillote*—where the food is baked in a tightly sealed, artfully folded parchment package to essentially steam in its own juices—may seem as outdated as Beef Wellington and Pheasant under Glass. But there's a reason the technique has held its own through countless culinary fads and fashions. It's an easy, mess-free way to enhance delicate flavor, particularly that of fish, leaving no odors to linger in the kitchen. The fish cooks quickly in such a moist environment, and because there's no water added to dilute flavors, it's a more flavorful method than ordinary poaching. It requires little additional fat and, if you throw in vegetables, adds up to a light but satisfying "one-pouch" meal.

When done correctly, that is. Without the right blend of flavorings, the fish can taste so lean and bland, you might as well be dining on diet food. Not all vegetables pair well with fish, and careful consideration must be given to their size and whether precooking is necessary, or you can wind up with overcooked fish surrounded by undercooked vegetables. I wanted to create an approach worthy of this technique's haute roots, with moist, flaky fish and tender-firm vegetables flavored by the rich, aromatic goodness of their mingled juices.

FOILED AGAIN

All the classic recipes call for cutting parchment paper into attractive shapes such as teardrops, hearts, and butterflies, then creasing the seams into painstakingly precise little folds. But just looking at the illustrations made my thumbs throb. I wanted to get dinner on the table as quickly as possible—not create origami. I went directly to aluminum foil, sandwiching the fish between two 12-inch squares and crimping the edges to create an airtight seal that would lock in steam. This was admittedly not as glamorous as an intricately folded parchment packet, but definitely serviceable.

My next step was to figure out what type of fish worked best in this dish and how long it would take to cook. After trying a variety of fish fillets, I quickly determined that tasters favored flaky, mild fish like haddock and cod over more assertively flavored fish like salmon or tuna. In the moist atmosphere of the foil pouch, these oilier fish had a tendency to overpower the flavors of the vegetables (for the moment I was simply placing the fish on a bed of sliced zucchini); better to save them for sautéing or searing.

We use foil, not parchment paper, and the right blend of vegetables and flavorings to create a satisfying one-pouch meal.

Since the goal of cooking en papillote is to create enough steam from the food's own juices, most recipes recommended cranking the heat way up, even as high as 500 degrees. Though a wet method like this one is more forgiving than a dry approach like roasting, 500 degrees seemed excessive. And it was. When I opened the foil after just 15 minutes for a "nick and peek," my 1-inch fillets were chalky white and well-done (and the zucchini was slightly underdone). Cooking at this temperature for less time didn't work either—the food was barely in the oven long enough for steam to form, leaving both fish and vegetable undercooked. After more experimentation, I arrived at 450 degrees for 15 minutes as the ideal temperature and cooking time—hot enough to produce steam relatively quickly but not so hot that the food overcooked. Placing the packets on the lower-middle rack of the oven, close to the heat source, helped concentrate the exuded liquid and deepen its flavor.

VEGGIN' OUT

With the cooking time and temperature nailed down, I could now turn my attention to selecting the vegetables. I quickly winnowed my options. Dense vegetables such as potatoes, even when parcooked, failed to cook evenly in the foil packets. Vegetables with an absorbent structure, like eggplant, simply cooked into mush in all the moisture. Others, such as broccoli, overpowered the delicate fish flavor. Beyond these considerations, the most important aspect was how the vegetables were prepared before they went into the packets. I found that carrots and leeks could be added to the packets raw, provided they were cut into matchsticks. The zucchini was much improved—and the juices in the packet less diluted—if I salted it first to get rid of excess moisture.

While tasters liked these fish and vegetable pairings, many felt that the components lacked harmony and overall the dish tasted a little too lean. A dash of vermouth, which was absorbed by the fish and vegetables, boosted flavor but not quite enough. What if I created a topping to flavor the fish as it cooked? A tomato, garlic, and olive oil "salsa" added kick to my zucchini variation, while a compound butter flavored with garlic, herbs, and zest enlivened the main recipe. These toppings basted the fish as it cooked and mingled with the wine and juices given off by the vegetables, leaving behind an aromatic, full-flavored sauce that perfectly complemented the fish. Each recipe was so light, fresh, and easy to prepare, it couldn't be more contemporary.

Cod Baked in Foil with Leeks and Carrots

SERVES 4

Haddock, red snapper, halibut, and sea bass also work well in this recipe as long as the fillets are 1 to 1¼ inches thick. Open each packet promptly after baking to prevent overcooking, and make sure to open packets away from you to avoid steam burns.

4 tablespoons unsalted butter, softened
2 garlic cloves, minced
1¼ teaspoons finely grated lemon zest, plus lemon wedges for serving
1 teaspoon minced fresh thyme
Salt and pepper
2 tablespoons minced fresh parsley
2 leeks, white and light green parts only, cut into 2-inch-long segments, halved lengthwise, washed thoroughly, and cut into ⅛-inch-thick matchsticks
2 carrots, peeled and cut into 2-inch-long matchsticks
¼ cup dry vermouth or dry white wine
4 (6- to 8-ounce) skinless cod fillets, 1 to 1¼ inches thick

1. Combine butter, 1 teaspoon garlic, ¼ teaspoon lemon zest, thyme, ¼ teaspoon salt, and ⅛ teaspoon pepper in small bowl. Combine parsley, remaining garlic, and remaining 1 teaspoon lemon zest in second small bowl and set aside. Place leeks and carrots in medium bowl, season with salt and pepper, and toss to combine.
2. Adjust oven rack to lower-middle position and heat oven to 450 degrees. Cut eight 12-inch sheets of aluminum foil; arrange 4 sheets flat on counter. Divide leek-carrot mixture in center of foil sheets and sprinkle with vermouth. Pat cod dry with paper towels, season with salt and pepper, and place on top of vegetables. Divide butter mixture among fillets, spreading over top of each fillet. Place second foil sheet on top of cod, crimp edges together in ½-inch fold, then fold over 3 more times to create packet about 7 inches square. Place packets on rimmed baking sheet, overlapping slightly if necessary. (Packets can be refrigerated for up to 6 hours before baking. If packets are refrigerated for more than 30 minutes, increase cooking time by 2 minutes.)
3. Bake packets for 15 minutes, then transfer to individual plates. Open carefully (steam will escape) and, using metal spatula, gently slide contents onto plates, along with any accumulated juices. Sprinkle with parsley mixture. Serve immediately, passing lemon wedges separately.

ASSEMBLING FOIL PACKETS

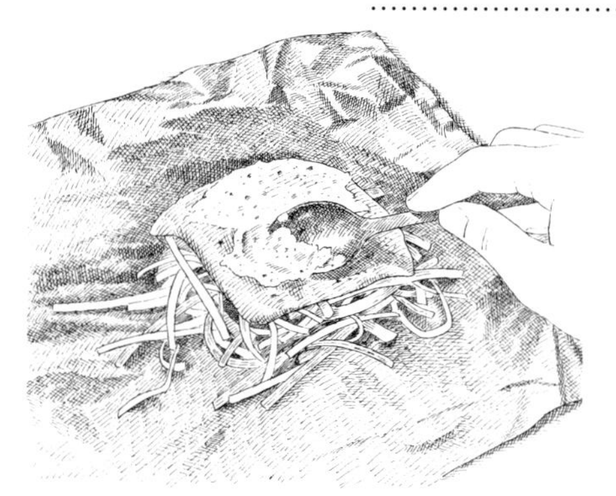

1. Arrange vegetables on foil first so they will be closest to heat source; drizzle with vermouth to deepen flavor. Top vegetables with fish and spread compound butter or topping over it for increased richness.

2. Top with second piece of foil and crimp edges together in ½-inch fold, then fold over 3 more times to create airtight packet about 7 inches square.

variation

Cod Baked in Foil with Zucchini and Tomatoes

SERVES 4

1 pound zucchini, sliced ¼ inch thick
Salt and pepper
2 plum tomatoes, cored, seeded, and chopped
2 tablespoons extra-virgin olive oil
2 garlic cloves, minced
1 teaspoon minced fresh oregano
⅛ teaspoon red pepper flakes
¼ cup dry vermouth or dry white wine
4 (6- to 8-ounce) skinless cod fillets, 1 to 1¼ inches thick
¼ cup chopped fresh basil
Lemon wedges

1. Toss zucchini with ½ teaspoon salt in bowl, transfer to colander, and let sit for 30 minutes. Pat zucchini dry thoroughly with paper towels, pressing firmly on each slice to remove as much liquid as possible. Meanwhile, combine tomatoes, oil, garlic, oregano, pepper flakes, ¼ teaspoon salt, and ⅛ teaspoon pepper in bowl.
2. Adjust oven rack to lower-middle position and heat oven to 450 degrees. Cut eight 12-inch sheets of aluminum foil; arrange 4 flat on counter. Shingle zucchini in center of foil sheets and sprinkle with vermouth. Pat cod dry with paper towels, season with salt and pepper, and place on top of zucchini. Spread tomato mixture over fish. Place second foil sheet on top of cod, crimp edges together in ½-inch fold, then fold over 3 more times to create packet about 7 inches square. Place packets on rimmed baking sheet, overlapping slightly if necessary.
3. Bake packets for 15 minutes, then transfer to individual plates. Open carefully (steam will escape) and, using metal spatula, gently slide contents onto plates, along with any accumulated juices. Sprinkle with basil and serve immediately, passing lemon wedges separately.

A BETTER WAY TO POACH FISH

DAN SOUZA, *March/April 2012*

If your experience with poached fish is limited to the lean, bland preparation you might be served at a wedding or a weight-loss spa, a technique popular at high-end restaurants will permanently change your perception—and serve as a reminder as to why poaching became a classic approach to cooking fish in the first place. The key perk: Submerging fish in liquid and gently cooking it at below simmer temperatures—anywhere from 130 to 180 degrees—renders the delicate flesh silky and supple. In this case, however, there is one major amendment to the technique that elevates it above the usual poached fish: Rather than the usual lean bath of water, wine, broth, or some combination thereof, the poaching liquid is olive oil.

On paper, cooking delicate fish fillets in a pot of fat sounds like a greasy recipe for disaster, but when I tried it the results were stunning—lighter, moister, and more fragrant than any traditionally poached fish I'd ever tasted—and they explained why this technique has become so popular in top restaurants. Another plus: The flavor-infused poaching oil can be whirred into a rich, glossy emulsion and drizzled over the fish as a sauce. The dish, I realized, would make elegant fare, provided I could get around one obvious challenge: the cost—and mess—of heating up a large amount of olive oil for just one meal. I would have to figure out how to scale the oil way back.

Oil-poaching delicate fish fillets in the oven makes this recipe hands-off and foolproof.

OIL EMBARGO

My first decision was to go with skinless fillets since the oil would never get hot enough to crisp the skin. I settled on cod for its firm, meaty flesh and clean flavor. As for the amount of oil, I reasoned that the smaller the surface area of the cooking vessel, the deeper the liquid would pool, so I reached past my trusty 12-inch nonstick skillet for its 10-inch sibling. Unfortunately, this setup still demanded about 1½ cups of oil to cover the four 6-ounce fillets. My only other idea was to displace some of the oil by placing half an onion in the skillet and arranging the fillets around it—a trick that worked but got me down only another ¼ cup. Clearly, I needed a more drastic solution.

That's when I started to wonder if completely immersing the fillets in oil was necessary. The alternative—pouring enough oil into the pan to come roughly halfway up the sides of the fish (about ¾ cup)—would mean flipping the fish partway through poaching to ensure that it cooked through. But that seemed a small price to pay for significantly cutting my oil dependence. I gave it a shot, basting the exposed half of each fillet with a few spoonfuls of oil (to prevent evaporation), popping a lid on the pan, and placing the skillet over the lowest burner setting. The good news was that the method worked; the fillets were supremely moist and tender—considerably more so than any water-poached fish, and not at all oily.

The bad news was that it was fussy. With relatively little oil in the pan, the temperature spiked quickly and required that I constantly fiddle with the burner knob to keep the oil in my target range (140 to 150 degrees), which would slowly bring my fish to an ideal internal temperature of 130 degrees, with little risk of going over. Placing a homemade heat diffuser fashioned from a ring of aluminum foil over the burner didn't reliably tame the flame. What I needed was a steadier, less-direct heat source, and for that I turned to the oven.

I figured that I could simply bring the oil to 140 degrees on the stovetop, slip in the fish, and then transfer the skillet into a low oven. But it wasn't quite that easy; the oil temperature immediately plummeted when I added the still-cold fillets, and the temperature recovery time in the oven was slow. But I had an idea: I'd heat the oil on the stovetop to well above my target temperature and then rely on the oven's more-even heat to keep it in the poaching sweet spot.

After a slew of tests, I hit upon a winning combination: Heat the oil to 180 degrees, nestle in the fillets (each sprinkled with kosher salt), and set the pan in a 250-degree oven. The oil temperature recovered within 15 minutes, by which point the lower half of the fish was cooked. I flipped the fillets, replaced the lid, and returned them to the oven. This batch emerged incredibly moist and velvety, and thanks to my oven method, the process was now largely hands-off. What I had was good—but I wanted to make it even better.

CRUNCH TIME

We often salt meat and allow it to rest before cooking, both to enhance juiciness and to bring seasoning deep into the interior. Why not try this with fish? For my next round of testing, I salted the fillets about 20 minutes before cooking. This technique worked beautifully: Moisture beaded on the surface of the fish, where it dissolved the salt and created a concentrated brine that was eventually absorbed back into the flesh to bolster flavor.

I also wanted something that could serve as a textural contrast to the silky fish. Restaurants often garnish their oil-poached fillets with lightly fried vegetables and fresh herbs, and I reasoned that I could approximate that by crisping something in the oil before cooking the fish. Fried artichoke hearts have always been a favorite of mine, so I defrosted a bag of them, patted them dry, and halved them lengthwise before tossing them with cornstarch (for extra crunch) and dropping them into the shimmering oil with some minced garlic.

Tasters loved the crisp garnish, but after cranking up the heat to fry, I then had to wait more than 10 minutes for the oil to cool to my target of 180 degrees before the pan went

into the oven. The solution proved easy: Rather than dump in all the oil at once, I'd fry the garnishes in ½ cup of oil, strain it, and add the remaining ¼ cup of room temperature oil to the pan to speed the cooling. The tweak made all the difference; about 5 minutes after frying, the oil was cool enough for poaching.

DRESSED TO IMPRESS

Frying up a garnish had also left me with an added bonus: flavor-infused oil to use for a sauce. I poured ½ cup into the blender and whirred it with whole cherry tomatoes (for bright sweetness), half a shallot, sherry vinegar, and salt and pepper. After a quick spin on high speed and a pass through a fine-mesh strainer, I had a silky-smooth vinaigrette.

Dressed up with the sauce, the crispy artichoke garnish, a few slices of fresh cherry tomato, and a sprinkle of chopped parsley, my elegant plate was complete—not to mention plenty simple to pull off at home.

WHY POACH IN OIL?

Poaching in oil allows fish to retain more of its juices than poaching in wine or broth, leading to remarkably moist, velvety results. This is because cooking in oil is inherently more gentle than cooking in water. And while you might expect that fish poached in fat would be greasy, it actually absorbs very little oil. Why? In order for oil to penetrate the fish, moisture must exit first. But because oil and water repel each other, it's very difficult for moisture inside the fish to readily enter the oil. Hence, more of the juices stay in the fish. In fact, in our tests, oil-poached fish lost just 14 percent of its weight during cooking, while water-poached fillets lost 24 percent.

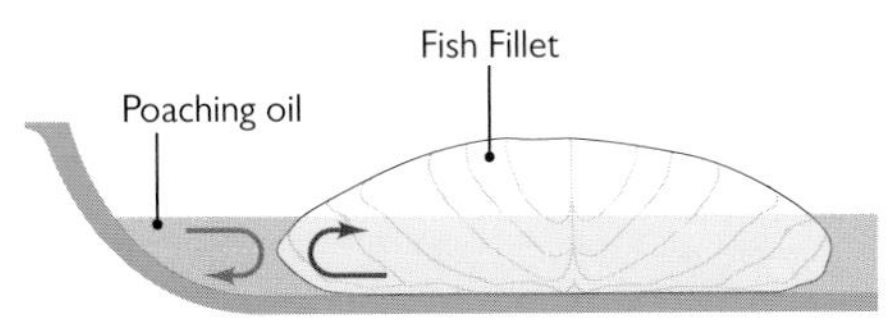

OIL AND WATER DON'T MIX

Poached Fish Fillets with Sherry-Tomato Vinaigrette

SERVES 4

Fillets of meaty white fish such as cod, halibut, sea bass, or snapper work best in this recipe. Make sure the fillets are at least 1 inch thick. A neutral oil such as canola can be substituted for the pure olive oil. A 4-ounce porcelain ramekin can be used in place of the onion half in step 3. Serve with couscous or steamed white rice.

Fish

4 (6-ounce) skinless white fish fillets, 1 inch thick
Kosher salt
4 ounces frozen artichoke hearts, thawed, patted dry, and sliced in half lengthwise
1 tablespoon cornstarch
¾ cup olive oil
3 garlic cloves, minced
½ onion, peeled

Vinaigrette

4 ounces cherry tomatoes
½ small shallot, peeled
4 teaspoons sherry vinegar
Kosher salt and pepper

1 tablespoon minced fresh parsley
2 ounces cherry tomatoes, cut into ⅛-inch-thick rounds

1. *For the fish:* Adjust oven racks to middle and lower-middle positions and heat oven to 250 degrees. Pat fish dry with paper towels and season each fillet with ¼ teaspoon salt. Let sit at room temperature for 20 minutes.
2. Meanwhile, toss artichokes with cornstarch in bowl to coat. Heat ½ cup oil in 10-inch nonstick ovensafe skillet over medium heat until shimmering. Shake excess cornstarch from artichokes and add to skillet; cook, stirring occasionally, until crisp and golden, 2 to 4 minutes. Add garlic and continue to cook until garlic is golden, 30 to 60 seconds. Strain oil through fine-mesh strainer into bowl. Transfer artichokes and garlic to ovensafe paper towel–lined plate and season with salt. Do not wash strainer.
3. Return strained oil to skillet and add remaining ¼ cup oil. Place onion half in center of pan. Let oil cool until it registers about 180 degrees, 5 to 8 minutes. Arrange fish fillets, skinned side up, around onion (oil should come roughly halfway up fillets). Spoon a little oil over each fillet, cover skillet, transfer to upper rack, and cook for 15 minutes.
4. Remove skillet from oven. Using 2 spatulas, carefully flip fillets. Cover skillet, return to upper rack, and place plate with artichokes and garlic on lower rack. Continue to cook fish until it registers 130 to 135 degrees, 9 to 14 minutes longer. Gently transfer fish to serving platter, reserving ½ cup oil, and tent fish with aluminum foil. Turn off oven, leaving plate of artichokes in oven.
5. *For the vinaigrette:* Process cherry tomatoes, shallot, vinegar, ¾ teaspoon salt, and ½ teaspoon pepper with reserved ½ cup fish cooking oil in blender until smooth, 1 to 2 minutes. Add any accumulated fish juices from platter, season with salt to taste, and blend for 10 seconds. Strain sauce through fine-mesh strainer; discard solids.
6. To serve, pour vinaigrette around and over fish. Garnish each fillet with warmed crisped artichokes and garlic, parsley, and tomato rounds. Serve immediately.

variation

Poached Fish Fillets with Miso-Ginger Vinaigrette

For fish, substitute 8 scallion whites, sliced ¼ inch thick, for artichoke hearts; omit garlic; and reduce amount of cornstarch to 2 teaspoons. For vinaigrette, process 6 scallion greens, 8 teaspoons lime juice, 2 tablespoons mirin, 4 teaspoons white miso paste, 2 teaspoons minced fresh ginger, and ½ teaspoon sugar with ½ cup fish cooking oil as directed in step 5. Garnish fish with 2 thinly sliced scallion greens and 2 halved and thinly sliced radishes.

POACHED SALMON FILLETS

J. KENJI LOPEZ-ALT, *May/June 2008*

Poached salmon seems like the ideal stovetop recipe: It's fast, it requires just one pot, and there's no splattering oil to burn yourself on or strong odors to permeate the house. And, when done right, the fish has an irresistibly supple, velvety texture delicately accented by the flavors of the poaching liquid. Add a simple sauce and the dish is even more flavorful. But when done wrong, which seems to be the usual case, the fish has a dry, chalky texture and washed-out taste that not even the richest sauce can redeem.

The classic method for poaching salmon is to gently simmer an entire side of fish in a highly flavored broth called a court-bouillon. The salmon is cooled and served cold, often as part of a buffet. But I wasn't looking for a make-ahead method for cold salmon to serve a crowd. I wanted to produce perfectly cooked, individual portions of hot salmon and a sauce to go with them—all in under half an hour.

FINESSING FLAVOR

My first objective was to achieve great texture and flavor in the salmon itself; after that I'd focus on the sauce. First consideration: the cooking liquid. A classic court-bouillon is made by filling a pot with water, wine, herbs, vegetables, and aromatics and boiling it all very briefly (*court-bouillon* is French for "short-boiled stock"). After straining the solids, you're left with an intensely flavored liquid in which to poach your fish. The broth's strong flavors are absorbed by the fish, which helps compensate for all the salmon flavor that leaches out into the liquid.

For velvety poached salmon, we use a small amount of liquid and elevate the fish on lemon slices.

This method certainly did produce flavorful results. However, there was just one annoying little problem: To cook dinner for four, I'd just prepped a slew of ingredients (onions, carrots, celery, leeks, parsley) and bought still others (bay leaves, tomato paste, peppercorns, and white wine), only to dump them and the stock down the drain at the end. This waste isn't bothersome when you're preparing a side of fish to feed a group, but it's hardly worth it for a simple Tuesday night supper at home.

What if I used less liquid? At the very least, this would mean I'd have to buy and prep (and waste) fewer ingredients; plus, using less liquid would likely mean less flavor leaching out of the salmon. I poached the salmon in just enough liquid to come half an inch up the side of the fillets. Flavor-wise, this was my most successful attempt yet. In fact, the salmon retained so much of its own natural flavor that I wondered if I could cut back even more on the quantity of vegetables and aromatics I was using in the liquid. A couple of shallots, a few herbs, and some wine proved to be all I needed. But nailing the flavor issue brought another problem into sharp relief—dry texture.

SEEKING SUPPLE TEXTURE

Like all animal flesh, salmon has a certain temperature range at which it is ideal to eat. The proteins in salmon begin coagulating at around 120 degrees, transforming it from translucent to opaque. At around 135 degrees, the flesh is completely firm and will start to force moisture out from between its protein fibers. Any higher, and the salmon becomes dry as cardboard (like a well-done steak). I had been using an instant-read thermometer to ensure that the centers of my salmon fillets were exactly 125 degrees (medium) before removing them from the poaching liquid. But testing the temperature of various parts of the fillet showed that by the time the center was 125 degrees, most of the other thinner sections registered higher temperatures. I was concerned that the texture of these thinner areas would be dry, but found their higher fat content kept them moist.

With high cooking temperatures, the exterior of a piece of meat will cook much faster than the interior. This is great when pan-searing the skin of a salmon fillet or a beef steak, when you want a browned exterior and rare interior, but it's no good for poaching, where the goal is to have an evenly cooked piece all the way through. The most obvious solution was to lower the cooking temperature. For the next batch, I placed the salmon in the cold pan with poaching liquid and brought the liquid barely up to a simmer, then reduced the heat to its lowest possible setting and covered the pan until the salmon cooked through. Then I realized a new problem that I'd unwittingly introduced when I reduced the amount of cooking liquid: Since the salmon wasn't totally submerged in liquid, it relied on steam to deliver heat and flavor. At such a low temperature, even with a lid on, not enough steam was being created to efficiently cook the parts of the fish sticking out above the liquid. Was there a way to create more steam without increasing the temperature?

Thinking back to high school chemistry, I remembered that adding alcohol to water lowers its boiling temperature: The higher the concentration of alcohol, the more vapor will be produced as the liquid is heated. More vapor, in turn, means better heat transfer, which leads to faster cooking, even at temperatures below a simmer. I also knew that alcohol could increase the rate at which proteins denature. Therefore, if I used more alcohol in the cooking liquid, it would theoretically be able to cook the fish faster and at a lower temperature. I increased the ratio of wine to water, going from a few tablespoons of wine to ½ cup. Acid also helps fish protein denature (in addition to improving flavor), so I squeezed a little lemon juice into the liquid before adding the salmon. My hopes were high as I opened the lid to a burst of steam and salmon that appeared perfectly cooked. Everything was fine until my fork got to the bottom of the fillet. Even though the top, sides, and center were now just right, the bottom, which had been in direct contact with the pan, was still overcooked.

I knew I wasn't the first person to ever have this problem—in fact, a solution already exists: a fish poacher. This specialized pan comes with a perforated insert that elevates the fish, allowing it to cook evenly on all sides. But I wasn't about to go out and buy an expensive new pan for a technique that I'd only use a few times a year. Then I realized that I had the solution literally in my hand. Instead of squeezing lemon juice into the poaching liquid, I sliced the fruit into thin disks and lined the pan with them. By resting the salmon fillets on top of the lemon slices, I was able to insulate the fish from the pan bottom while simultaneously flavoring it. This time the salmon came out evenly cooked all the way through.

SETTLING THE SAUCE

It was time to focus on the sauce. Ticking off the list of ingredients in my super-concentrated poaching liquid, I realized I had the foundation of a beurre blanc, so I didn't have to make a separate sauce. This classic French sauce is made by reducing wine flavored with vinegar, shallots, and herbs and then finishing it with butter. I would need only to reduce my poaching liquid and whisk in the butter. But since a few tablespoons of butter per serving would push this dish out of the "everyday" category, I developed a vinaigrette-style variation in which I used olive oil instead of butter; tasters liked the oil version as much as the original.

This salmon-poaching method guarantees moist and delicately flavored fish and produces just the right amount of poaching liquid for a great-tasting sauce—all without boiling away any flavor or pouring ingredients down the drain.

Poached Salmon with Herb and Caper Vinaigrette

SERVES 4

To ensure uniform pieces of salmon that cook at the same rate, buy a whole center-cut fillet and cut it into four pieces. If a skinless whole fillet is unavailable, remove the skin yourself or follow the recipe as directed with a skin-on fillet, adding 3 to 4 minutes to the cooking time in step 2. This recipe will yield salmon fillets cooked to medium-rare.

2 lemons
2 tablespoons chopped fresh parsley, stems reserved
2 tablespoons chopped fresh tarragon, stems reserved
1 large shallot, minced
½ cup dry white wine
½ cup water
1 (1¾- to 2-pound) skinless salmon fillet, about 1½ inches thick
2 tablespoons capers, rinsed and chopped
2 tablespoons extra-virgin olive oil
1 tablespoon honey
Salt and pepper

1. Line plate with paper towels. Cut top and bottom off 1 lemon, then cut into eight to ten ¼-inch-thick slices. Cut remaining lemon into 8 wedges and set aside. Arrange lemon slices in single layer across bottom of 12-inch skillet. Scatter herb stems and 2 tablespoons minced shallot evenly over lemon slices. Add wine and water to skillet.
2. Use sharp knife to remove any whitish fat from belly of salmon and cut fillet into 4 equal pieces. Place salmon fillets in skillet, skinned side down, on top of lemon slices. Set pan over high heat and bring liquid to simmer. Reduce heat to low, cover, and cook until sides are opaque but center of thickest part of fillet is still translucent when checked with tip of paring knife and registers 125 degrees (for medium-rare), 11 to 16 minutes. Off heat, use spatula to carefully transfer salmon and lemon slices to prepared plate and tent with aluminum foil.
3. Return pan to high heat and simmer cooking liquid until slightly thickened and reduced to 2 tablespoons, 4 to 5 minutes. Meanwhile, combine capers, oil, honey, chopped parsley and tarragon, and remaining minced shallot in medium bowl. Strain reduced cooking liquid through fine-mesh strainer into bowl with herb mixture, pressing on solids to extract as much liquid as possible. Whisk to combine and season with salt and pepper to taste.
4. Season salmon with salt and pepper to taste. Using spatula, carefully lift and tilt salmon fillets to remove lemon slices. Place salmon on serving platter or individual plates and spoon vinaigrette over top. Serve, passing lemon wedges separately.

A FISH (ALMOST) OUT OF WATER

Our improved poaching method produces salmon with better flavor and texture by using a lot less liquid.

STANDARD POACH
The classic poaching method calls for submerging salmon completely in liquid in a deep pan, which causes flavor to leach out and leads to dry, flavorless fish.

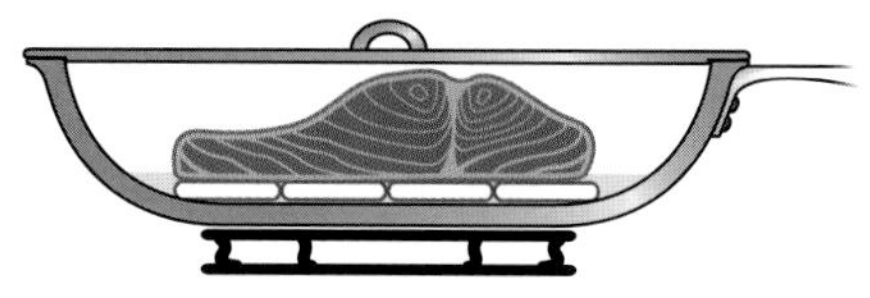

SHALLOW POACH
In our method, small amounts of liquid allow the salmon to cook at a lower temperature, preserving flavor. Lemon slices under the fillets keep their bottoms from overcooking.

HOW TO BROIL SALMON

ADAM RIED AND JULIA COLLIN DAVISON, *September/October 2000*

Salmon is a surefire crowd-pleaser, but it's not always easy to make for a crowd. Many cooks shy away from poaching, and our favorite indoor cooking method—pan-searing individual portions—can get cumbersome with too many pieces of fish. Our preferred outdoor cooking techniques—hot-smoking and straightforward grilling—can accommodate larger pieces of fish, but for denizens of the North, among whom we count ourselves, cooking outside is impractical, if not impossible, for almost half the year.

So we set out to beat the odds: to find the best way of cooking a whole side of salmon, enough to feed eight or more guests, in the oven. We wanted fish that was moist but not soggy, firm but not chalky, and nicely crusted, with golden, flavorful caramelization over its flesh. If we could work some interesting flavors and contrasting textures into the bargain, all the better.

CRUST IS KEY

Creating some flavorful caramelization on the flesh of the fish was a key goal, so we focused right away on high-heat cooking. Baking, though it seemed like a natural choice, was out because it implies cooking in a moderate, 350-degree oven, which would never brown the fish. Heating things up from there, we tested roasting at oven temperatures of 400, 450, and 500 degrees. To our surprise, none of them worked well. Even at 500 degrees on a preheated pan, the fish remained pale, owing to the necessarily short 16-minute cooking time (any more time in the oven and the fish would overcook). Another source of consternation was moisture—not the lack of it, as we might have expected, but an excess. The abundance of fat and collagen in the farmed Atlantic salmon we were using melted during cooking, giving the fish an overly wet, slippery texture and fatty mouthfeel.

Broiling was the next step up in heat, and here we met with some success. The salmon browned nicely under the intense broiler heat and, as a result, developed better flavor. Some of the copious moisture evaporated, leaving the fish with a much-improved texture, drier and firmer yet still juicy. None of the broiling and roasting combinations we went on to try topped broiling from start to finish. We were on the right track to be sure, but plain broiled salmon was not terribly inspiring. If we were going to serve this to a crowd of people at a weekend dinner party, a flavor boost and some textural interest would be absolutely necessary.

TOPPING ANTICS

The addition of an interesting topping for the fish could, we thought, achieve both goals. Dried bread crumbs came immediately to mind—and left almost as quickly once we tasted them. The flavor was lackluster and the texture akin to sawdust. Our favorite panko bread crumbs were judged too light in flavor and feathery in texture. Fresh bread crumbs were a crisp improvement, and toasted fresh bread crumbs laced with garlic, herbs, and butter were better still. But there were more avenues to explore. Dry spice rubs, similar to what we might apply to grilled fish, met with mixed results. Glazes and spice pastes won praise for their flavor, but since they were wet, they added little texture.

Potatoes were another topping possibility. Potato crusts on fish are typically engineered by laying paper-thin slices of potato on the fish and sautéing it on the stovetop. Testing proved that the slices would not form a cohesive crust without the direct heat of a hot pan. In addition, we couldn't slice them thin enough without the help of a mandoline. But because tasters loved the potato flavor, we tried some other methods. A crust of grated raw potatoes remained too loose and crunchy. Sautéing the grated potato before applying it to the fish helped some, but not enough, while completely precooking the potatoes robbed them of both flavor and texture.

We use crushed potato chips for an ultracrisp crust, and wait until partway through broiling to add them so they don't burn.

As we clung tenaciously to the notion of potato flavor while groping for another way to build a crisp, crunchy texture, a fellow test cook smirked and suggested, half in jest, that we try crushed potato chips. Everyone in the test kitchen at the time laughed, but after settling down, we looked at one another and said, practically in unison, "Let's try it." Imagine our astonishment, then, at the chips' overwhelming success. Though a bit greasy and heavy on their own, they offered just what we were looking for in a crust: great potato flavor and crunch that wouldn't quit. After lightening the chips by mixing in some fresh toasted bread crumbs and adding dill for complementary flavor, we found ourselves with an excellent, if unorthodox, topping. We also found that the chips made a rich foil for some of the other flavors we wanted to add.

Because the chips brown under the broiler in just a minute—literally—we broiled the fish until it was almost cooked through before adding the topping. This gave us just the texture we wanted. After adding a flavorful wet element (mustard) to help the crumbs adhere to the fish, we knew we had it: a quick, oven-cooked, well-flavored, texturally interesting—and rather surprising—salmon dinner for eight.

Broiled Salmon with Mustard and Crisp Dilled Crust

SERVES 8 TO 10

Heavy-duty aluminum foil measuring 18 inches wide is essential for creating a sling that aids in transferring the cooked side to a cutting board. Use a large baking sheet so that the salmon will lie flat. If you can't get the fish to lie flat, even when positioning it diagonally on the baking sheet, trim the tail end. If you prefer to cook a smaller (2-pound) fillet, ask to have it cut from the thick center of the fillet, not the thin tail end, and begin checking doneness a minute earlier. We prefer thick-cut and kettle-cooked potato chips in this recipe; ridged chips will work in a pinch.

3 slices hearty white sandwich bread, crusts removed
4 ounces high-quality potato chips, finely crushed (1 cup)
6 tablespoons minced fresh dill
1 (3½-pound) skin-on side of salmon, pinbones removed
1 teaspoon olive oil
Salt and pepper
3 tablespoons Dijon mustard
Lemon wedges

1. Adjust oven rack to middle position and heat oven to 400 degrees. Pulse bread in food processor to even ¼-inch pieces, about 10 pulses. Spread crumbs evenly on rimmed baking sheet and toast, stirring occasionally, until golden brown and crisp, 4 to 5 minutes. Combine toasted crumbs, crushed potato chips, and dill in bowl.

2. Adjust oven racks 3 inches and 6 inches from broiler element and heat broiler. Cut piece of heavy-duty aluminum foil to be 1 foot longer than side of salmon, then fold lengthwise in thirds. Lay foil diagonally across rimmed baking sheet. Lay salmon, skin side down, on foil, rub with oil, and season with salt and pepper. Broil salmon on upper rack until surface is spotty brown and center is still translucent when checked with tip of paring knife and registers 125 degrees (for medium-rare), 9 to 11 minutes.

3. Remove fish from oven. Working quickly, spread evenly with mustard, then press bread-crumb mixture onto fish. Return salmon to lower rack and broil until crust is deep golden brown, about 1 minute.

4. Using foil sling, transfer salmon to cutting board (or serving platter). Run spatula underneath salmon to loosen it from foil. Using spatula to hold salmon in place on cutting board, gently pull foil out from underneath salmon. Serve with lemon wedges.

variations

Broiled Salmon with Chutney and Crisp Spiced Crust

Use a smooth mango chutney for this recipe. If you can find only chunky mango chutney, puree it in a food processor until smooth before using.

Melt 2 tablespoons unsalted butter in 8-inch skillet over medium heat. Off heat, add 1 minced garlic clove, ½ teaspoon ground cumin, ½ teaspoon paprika, ¼ teaspoon ground cinnamon, ¼ teaspoon cayenne, and ¼ teaspoon salt. Set aside. Substitute 3 tablespoons chopped fresh parsley for dill, toss butter-spice mixture into bread crumbs along with potato chips, and substitute 3 tablespoons smooth mango chutney for Dijon mustard.

Broiled Salmon with Spicy Cilantro-Citrus Paste and Crisp Crust

Process 2 cups cilantro leaves, 3 shallots, 2 stemmed and seeded jalapeño chiles, one 1-inch piece peeled fresh ginger, 3 garlic cloves, 2 tablespoons honey, and 2 teaspoons grated lime zest plus 3 tablespoons juice (2 limes) in food processor until smooth, about 30 seconds, scraping down bowl as necessary. Omit dill and substitute ½ cup cilantro-citrus paste for Dijon mustard.

PREPARING THE SALMON

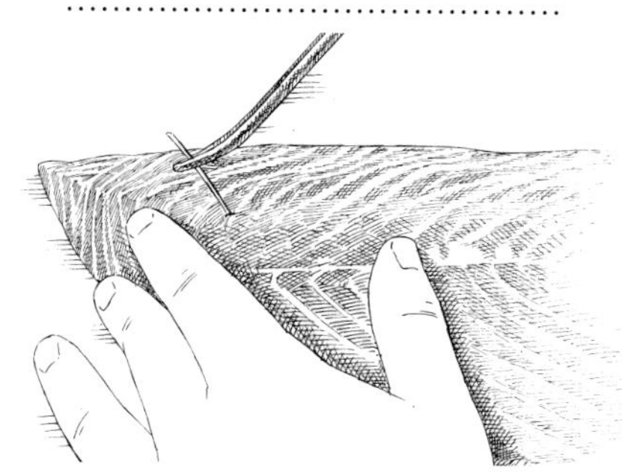

1. Run your fingers over surface to feel for pinbones, then remove them with tweezers or needle-nose pliers.

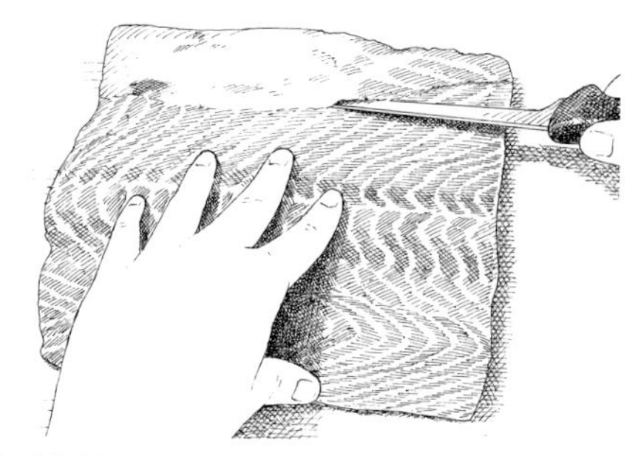

2. Hold sharp knife at slight downward angle to flesh and cut off whitish, fatty portion of belly.

SERVING THE SALMON

To ensure a beautiful presentation, we broil the salmon on a foil sling, which we use to transfer the finished salmon from the baking sheet to the cutting board. Here's how we get the salmon off the foil neatly and in one piece.

Using foil sling, transfer salmon to cutting board. Run spatula underneath fish to loosen. Use spatula to hold salmon in place and gently pull foil out.

THE BEST PAN-SEARED SALMON

ANDREW JANJIGIAN, *May/June 2016*

Pan-searing salmon sounds so straightforward that I've never given much thought to the technique. Normally, I'd add a little oil to a nonstick skillet, get it good and hot, sprinkle a few skinless fillets with salt and pepper, slide them into the pan, and cook them on both sides until the fish was cooked through and browned on the exterior but still pink on the inside.

But when I gave this approach a more critical look, I could see that it had two flaws. While the fish had a nice rosy interior at its thickest point, it was a bit overcooked and dry at the thinner end. Secondly, the exteriors of the fillets were more tough than crisp. I wanted to take advantage of the intense heat of the skillet to produce a golden-brown, ultracrisp crust on salmon fillets while keeping their interiors moist.

Brining the fish briefly and cooking the salmon with the skin on guarantees moist, not tough, flesh.

The solution to the dryness problem was relatively easy: salt. Either salting or brining would season the flesh and help keep it moist. This being a quick weeknight dinner, I didn't want to wait 2 hours for salting to do its job. Brining took about 15 minutes, and as long as I patted the fillets dry with paper towels before cooking, I found that the treatment didn't significantly inhibit browning.

I decided to focus on getting a really nice sear on only the flesh side since it would be facing up when the fillet was plated. Plus, browning both sides could lead to overcooking. Cooking the fish through with the flesh side down the entire time produced a wonderfully crisp crust, but it also left me with an unworkable dilemma: Either the face-up (skinned) side was nearly sushi-raw, or the rest of the fillet overcooked while I waited for the face-up side to cook through. Covering the pan with a lid toward the end helped cook the fish through more evenly, but this trapped moisture, softening the crust.

There was one piece left to tinker with: the heat level. What if I added the fish to a cold pan and then turned on the heat? This would allow the fish to cook through gently as the pan slowly came up to temperature. I'd then flip the fillets over after the skillet was good and hot so they could form a crust and finish cooking through.

I quickly discovered a problem starting with a not-so-hot skillet: No matter how gently I cooked the first side, it tended to dry out and turn tough on the very exterior. When I was skinning the salmon for my next test, I came up with the solution: Leave the skin on. It could serve to protect that first side as it cooked, and I could simply remove it after flipping the fish.

Sure enough, this worked perfectly. Even better, the skin shed enough fat as it cooked that I was able to cook the fish without needing to add a single drop of oil to the pan.

This salmon was excellent with just a squirt of lemon, but a mango-mint salsa was easy to make, and its bright flavor balanced the salmon's richness.

Pan-Seared Salmon

SERVES 4

To ensure uniform cooking, buy a 1½- to 2-pound center-cut salmon fillet and cut it into four pieces. Using skin-on salmon is important here, as we rely on the fat underneath the skin as the cooking medium (as opposed to adding extra oil). If using wild salmon, cook it until it registers 120 degrees. If you don't want to serve the fish with the skin, we recommend peeling it off the fish after cooking rather than before. Serve the salmon with lemon wedges or with our Mango-Mint Salsa (recipe follows), if desired.

Kosher salt and pepper
4 (6- to 8-ounce) skin-on salmon fillets
Lemon wedges

1. Dissolve ½ cup salt in 2 quarts cold water in large container. Submerge salmon in brine and let stand at room temperature for 15 minutes. Remove salmon from brine and pat dry with paper towels.
2. Sprinkle bottom of 12-inch nonstick skillet evenly with ½ teaspoon salt and ½ teaspoon pepper. Place fillets, skin side down, in skillet and sprinkle tops of fillets with ¼ teaspoon salt and ¼ teaspoon pepper. Heat skillet over medium-high heat and cook fillets without moving them until fat begins to render, skin begins to brown, and bottom ¼ inch of fillets turns opaque, 6 to 8 minutes.
3. Using tongs, flip fillets and continue to cook without moving them until centers are still translucent when checked with tip of paring knife and register 125 degrees, 6 to 8 minutes longer. Transfer fillets, skin side down, to serving platter and let rest for 5 minutes before serving with lemon wedges.

accompaniment

Mango-Mint Salsa

MAKES ABOUT 1 CUP

Adjust the salsa's heat level by reserving and adding the jalapeño seeds, if desired.

1 mango, peeled, pitted, and cut into ¼-inch pieces
1 shallot, minced
3 tablespoons lime juice (2 limes)
2 tablespoons chopped fresh mint
1 jalapeño chile, stemmed, seeded, and minced
1 tablespoon extra-virgin olive oil
1 garlic clove, minced
½ teaspoon salt

Combine all ingredients in bowl.

INTRODUCING GRILL-SMOKED SALMON

ANDREW JANJIGIAN, *July/August 2012*

The process of smoking fish over hardwood has a long tradition, and rich, fatty salmon is well suited to the technique. But smoked salmon's unique taste and texture don't come easy: The translucent, mildly smoky slices piled on bagels are produced by ever-so-slowly smoking (but not fully cooking) salt-cured fillets at roughly 60 to 90 degrees, a project that requires specialized equipment and loads of time (at least 24 hours and as long as five days). Then there is hot smoking, a procedure in which cured fillets are fully cooked at higher temperatures (100 to 250 degrees) for one to eight hours. The higher heat results in a drier texture and a more potent smokiness, so the fish is often flaked and mixed into dips and spreads.

Both approaches deliver terrific results—but are impractical (if not impossible) for a home cook to pull off. Sure, you can impart a touch of smokiness by tossing wood chips onto hot charcoal and quickly grilling fish fillets, but I had also heard of a lesser-known, more intriguing option that captures both the intense, smoky flavor of hot-smoked fish and the firm but silky texture of the cold-smoked type. It's easy because the fish is cooked via indirect heat on a grill—a familiar and uncomplicated technique. And although the resulting fillets have a distinctive taste, they are not overpoweringly salty or smoky, so they're suitable as an entrée either warm from the grill or at room temperature.

A salt-and-sugar rub before cooking over an indirect grill fire produces silky, smoky fillets.

To try out these smoky, succulent fillets, I scoured cookbooks for recipes. The typical first step in smoking fish is to cure the flesh with salt; some authors recommended brining, others directly salting the fillet. To keep the preparation time in check, I steered away from recommendations for curing the fish for longer than an hour or two.

The other criteria, smoking temperature and length of exposure–both crucial to the final result—were all over the map. One recipe called for smoking the fish at 350 degrees for a modest 20 minutes; another let it go twice as long at only 275 degrees.

IN TREATMENT

With so many factors at play, I decided to try a simple brine first, soaking a center-cut skin-on fillet (retaining the skin would make it easier to remove the fillet from the grill) in the test kitchen's usual 9 percent solution of salt and water for 2 hours. For the time being, I used a moderate amount of coals, dumping 4 quarts of lit charcoal on one side of the grill, along with a few soaked wood chips to provide the smoke. I placed the fish on the cooking grate opposite the coals, popped the cover on the grill, and smoked the fish until it was still a little translucent at the center, about 25 minutes.

The result was illuminating if not exactly spectacular. The long stay in the brine had the unfortunate effect of making the salmon terribly bloated; plus, it seemed to highlight the fish's natural oiliness in an unpleasant way—a far cry from the supple but firm texture I was after.

For my next try, I covered the salmon in a generous blanket of kosher salt—its coarse texture makes it cling to food better than table salt—and refrigerated it uncovered on a wire rack on a baking sheet. After an hour, a considerable amount of liquid had been drawn to the surface of the flesh. I knew that if I waited any longer, the fluid would start to migrate back into the salmon through the process of osmosis, leading to a bloated texture, so I promptly removed it from the refrigerator, blotted the moisture with a paper towel, and took it out to the grill for smoking. This sample was considerably better than the brined fish: incredibly moist yet still firm—and not at all soggy. It wasn't perfect, though, since most tasters found it too salty to be enjoyed as a main dish. I tried dialing down the amount of salt as well as salting for a shorter amount of time, but alas, the fish didn't achieve the proper texture.

Back at my desk, I looked for a solution in the recipes that I'd collected and came across a few that called for adding sugar to the cure. I knew that, like salt, sugar is hygroscopic, meaning it attracts water. Could sugar pull moisture from the salmon as effectively as salt? Not quite: Because individual molecules of sucrose are much larger than sodium and chloride ions, sugar is, pound for pound, about 12 times less effective than salt at attracting moisture. Still, it was a workable option; I just had to do some tinkering. Eventually, I determined that a ratio of 2 parts sugar to 1 part salt produced well-balanced taste and texture in the finished salmon. Using these proportions, the fish firmed up nicely; plus, it was far less salty and the sugar counterbalanced its richness.

SMOLDERING ISSUES

With a reliable curing method in hand, I could finally fine-tune my smoking technique. My current setup was far from ideal: By the time the fish was sufficiently smoky, it was dry and flaky. Conversely, when it was cooked perfectly—still silky and slightly pink in the interior, or about 125 degrees—the smoke flavor was faint. Adding more wood chips only gave the fillet a sooty flavor. Instead, I tried to cool down the temperature of the grill by reducing the amount of charcoal from 4 quarts to 3 quarts. This helped somewhat, since the fish cooked more slowly (a full 30 to 40 minutes) and had more time to absorb smoke.

But the smoke flavor still wasn't as bold as I wanted. Rather than manipulating the cooking time any further, I turned to the salmon itself, cutting the large fillet into individual serving-size portions. This seemingly minor tweak resulted in big payoffs: First, it ensured more thorough smoke exposure (in the same amount of time) by creating more surface area. Second, the delicate pieces were far easier to get off the grill in one piece than a single bulky fillet. (To that end, I also started placing the fillets on a piece of foil coated with vegetable oil spray.) Finally, I found that I could now use an even cooler fire (produced with a mere 2 quarts of charcoal): The smaller fillets still reached their ideal serving temperature in the same amount of time that the single, larger fillet had taken. Plus, the gentler fire rendered the fillets incomparably tender.

With a smoky, rich taste and a silky, supple texture, my quick smoked salmon recipe was, to put it plainly, smoking hot.

Grill-Smoked Salmon

SERVES 6

Use center-cut salmon fillets of similar thickness so that they cook at the same rate. If using wild salmon, cook until the thickest part of the fillet registers 120 degrees. The best way to ensure uniformity is to buy a 2½- to 3-pound whole center-cut fillet and cut it into six pieces. If you'd like to use wood chunks instead of wood chips when using a charcoal grill, substitute two wood chunks, soaked in water for 1 hour, for the wood chip packet. Avoid mesquite wood chunks for this recipe. Serve the salmon with lemon wedges or our "Smoked Salmon Platter" Sauce (recipe follows).

2 tablespoons sugar
1 tablespoon kosher salt
6 (6- to 8-ounce) center-cut skin-on salmon fillets
2 cups wood chips

1. Combine sugar and salt in bowl. Set wire rack in rimmed baking sheet, set salmon on rack, and sprinkle flesh side evenly with sugar mixture. Refrigerate, uncovered, for 1 hour. With paper towels, brush any excess salt and sugar from salmon and blot dry. Return salmon on wire rack to refrigerator, uncovered, while preparing grill.

2. Just before grilling, soak 1 cup wood chips in water for 15 minutes, then drain. Using large piece of heavy-duty aluminum foil, wrap soaked and unsoaked chips together in 8 by 4½-inch foil packet. (Make sure chips do not poke holes in sides or bottom of packet.) Cut 2 evenly spaced 2-inch slits in top of packet.

3A. ***For a charcoal grill:*** Open bottom vent halfway. Light large chimney starter one-third filled with charcoal briquettes (2 quarts). When top coals are partially covered with ash, pour into steeply banked pile against side of grill. Place wood chip packet on coals. Set cooking grate in place, cover, and open lid vent halfway. Heat grill until hot and wood chips are smoking, about 5 minutes.

3B. ***For a gas grill:*** Remove cooking grate and place wood chip packet directly on primary burner. Set grate in place, turn primary burner to high (leave other burners off), cover, and heat grill until hot and wood chips are smoking, 15 to 25 minutes. Turn primary burner to medium. (Adjust primary burner as needed to maintain grill temperature of 275 to 300 degrees.)

4. Fold piece of heavy-duty foil into 18 by 6-inch rectangle. Place foil rectangle on cooler side of grill and place salmon fillets on foil, spaced at least ½ inch apart. Cover (position lid vent over salmon if using charcoal) and cook until center of thickest part of fillet is still translucent when checked with tip of paring knife and registers 125 degrees (for medium-rare), 30 to 40 minutes. Transfer to platter and serve warm or at room temperature.

accompaniment

"Smoked Salmon Platter" Sauce

MAKES 1½ CUPS

1 large egg yolk, plus 1 hard-cooked large egg, chopped fine
2 teaspoons Dijon mustard
2 teaspoons sherry vinegar
½ cup vegetable oil
2 tablespoons capers, rinsed, plus 1 teaspoon brine
2 tablespoons minced shallot
2 tablespoons minced fresh dill

Whisk egg yolk, mustard, and vinegar together in medium bowl. Whisking constantly, slowly drizzle in oil until emulsified, about 1 minute. Gently fold in capers and brine, shallot, dill, and hard-cooked egg.

NOW WE'RE SMOKIN'

Typically, cold- or hot-smoking salmon requires special equipment and a serious time investment. Our recipe captures the best of both methods and cooks in only 30 to 40 minutes on a regular grill.

COLD-SMOKED
Slick and silky; mild smoke

HOT-SMOKED
Dry and firm; potent smoke

HYBRID GRILL-SMOKED
Ultramoist; rich, balanced smoke

BUILDING A BETTER SHRIMP COCKTAIL

MARK BITTMAN, *July/August 1997*

Nothing is more basic than shrimp cocktail, and given its simplicity, few dishes are more difficult to improve. Yet I set out to do just that this past winter and believe I succeeded.

Shrimp cocktail, as everyone must know, is "boiled" shrimp served cold with "cocktail" sauce, typically a blend of bottled ketchup or chili sauce spiked with horseradish. It's easy enough to change the basic pattern in order to produce a more contemporary cold shrimp dish; you could, for example, grill shrimp and serve them with a fresh tomato salsa (and many people have done just that). But there is something refreshing and utterly classic about traditional shrimp cocktail, and sometimes it fits the occasion better than anything else.

I saw three ways to challenge the traditional method of preparing shrimp cocktail in order to produce the best-tasting but recognizable version of this dish. One, work on the flavor of the shrimp; two, work on the cooking method for the shrimp; three, produce a great cocktail sauce.

FLAVORING THE SHRIMP

The shrimp in shrimp cocktail can be ice-cold strings of protein, chewy or mushy, or they can be tender, flavorful morsels that barely need sauce. To achieve the latter, you need to start with the best shrimp you can find and give them as much flavor as they can handle without overwhelming them.

If you start with good shrimp and follow a typical shrimp cocktail recipe—that is, simmer the shrimp in salted water until pink—the shrimp will have decent but rarely intense flavor. The easiest way to intensify the flavor of shrimp is to cook them in their shells. But, as I found out, this has an obvious drawback: It's far easier to peel shrimp when they are raw than once they are cooked.

It's better, then, to make shrimp stock, a simple enough process that takes only 5 minutes using just the shrimp shells, and a process that can be vastly improved if you make it gradually. To do so, every time you use shrimp for any purpose, place the peels in a pot with water to cover, then simmer them for 5 minutes. Cool, strain, and freeze the resultant stock. Use this stock as the cooking liquid for your next batch of shrimp peels. Naturally, this stock will become more and more intense each time you add to it. Even after one batch of peels, however, it's infinitely better than plain water for cooking shrimp.

For the best flavor and texture, we poach shrimp in a simple shrimp stock off the heat.

Next, I thought, it would be best to see what other flavors would complement the shrimp without overpowering it. My first attempt was to use beer and a spicy commercial seasoning, but this was a near disaster; the shrimp for cocktail should not taste like a New Orleans crab boil. Next I tried a court bouillon, the traditional herb-scented stock for poaching fish, but quickly discovered that the game wasn't worth the candle; I wanted a few quick additions to my shrimp stock that would add complexity without making a simple process complicated.

After trying about 20 different combinations, involving wine, vinegar, lemon juice, and a near-ludicrous number of herbs and spices, I settled on the mixture given in the recipe here. It contains about 25 percent white wine, a dash of lemon juice, and a more-or-less traditional herb combination. Variations are certainly possible, but I would caution you against adding more wine or lemon juice; both were good up to a point, but after that their pungency became overwhelming.

COOKING THE SHRIMP

Although I was pleased at this point with the quality of the shrimp's flavor, I still thought it could be more intense. I quickly learned, however, that the answer to this problem was not to keep pouring flavorings into the cooking liquid; that was self-defeating because I eventually lost the flavor of the shrimp. I decided to try to keep the shrimp in contact with the flavorings for a longer period of time.

I tried several methods to achieve this, including starting the shrimp in cold water with the seasonings and using a longer cooking time at a lower temperature. But shrimp cooks so quickly—this is part of its appeal, of course—that these methods only served to toughen the meat. What worked best, I found, was to bring the cooking liquid to a boil, turn it off, and add the shrimp. Depending on their size, I could leave them in contact with the liquid for up to 10 minutes (even a little longer for jumbo shrimp), during which time they would cook through without toughening, while taking on near perfect flavor.

THE COCKTAIL SAUCE

Here I felt I was treading a fine line. I wanted to make a better sauce, but I still wanted it to be recognizable as cocktail sauce. Starting with fresh or canned tomatoes, I discovered, just didn't work: The result was often terrific (some might say preferable), but it was not cocktail sauce. It was as if I had decided to make a better version of liver and onions by substituting foie gras for veal liver—it might be "better," but it would no longer be liver and onions.

I went so far as to make American-style ketchup from scratch, an interesting project but not especially profitable, in that the effect was to duplicate something sold in near-perfect form in the supermarket. Again, there are more interesting tomato-based sauces than ketchup, but they're not ketchup.

So I decided the best thing I could do was to find the bottled ketchup or chili sauce I liked best and season it myself. First I had to determine which made the better base, ketchup or chili sauce. The answer to this question was surprising but straightforward: ketchup. Bottled chili sauce is little more than vinegary ketchup with a host of seasonings added. The less expensive chili sauces have the acrid, bitter taste of garlic powder, monosodium glutamate, or other dried seasonings. The more expensive ones have more honest flavors but still did not compare to the cocktail sauce I whipped up in 3 minutes using basic store-bought ketchup. In addition, chili sauce can be four to eight times as expensive as ketchup.

My preference in cocktail sauce has always been to emphasize the horseradish. But ketchup and horseradish, I knew, were not enough. Cocktail sauce benefits from a variety of heat sources, none of which overpower the other, and the sum of which still allows the flavor of the shrimp to come through. I liked the addition of chili powder. I also liked a bit of bite from cayenne, but only a pinch. Black pepper plays a favorable role as well (as does salt, even though ketchup is already salty). Finally, after trying high-quality wine vinegar, balsamic vinegar, rice vinegar, sherry vinegar, and distilled vinegar, I went back to lemon, which is the gentlest and most fragrant acidic seasoning. In sum, the keys to good cocktail sauce include: ordinary ketchup, fresh lemon juice, horseradish (fresh is best—even month-old bottled horseradish is pathetic compared to a just-opened bottle), and fresh chili powder. Proportions can be varied to taste.

Herb-Poached Shrimp with Cocktail Sauce

SERVES 4

When using larger or smaller shrimp, increase or decrease cooking times for shrimp by 1 to 2 minutes, respectively.

Shrimp

1 pound jumbo shrimp (16 to 20 per pound), peeled and deveined, shells reserved
1 teaspoon salt
1 cup dry white wine
5 sprigs fresh parsley
1 sprig fresh tarragon
1 teaspoon lemon juice
5 coriander seeds
4 whole peppercorns
½ bay leaf

Cocktail Sauce

1 cup ketchup
1 tablespoon lemon juice
2½ teaspoons prepared horseradish
1 teaspoon ancho chili powder (or other mild chili powder)
¼ teaspoon salt
¼ teaspoon pepper
Pinch cayenne pepper

1. *For the shrimp:* Bring reserved shells, 3 cups water, and salt to boil in medium saucepan over medium-high heat; reduce heat to low, cover, and simmer until fragrant, about 5 minutes. Strain stock through sieve, pressing on shells to extract all liquid.
2. Bring stock, wine, parsley, tarragon, lemon juice, coriander seeds, peppercorns, and bay leaf to boil in large saucepan over high heat; boil 2 minutes. Turn off heat and stir in shrimp; cover and let stand until firm and pink, 8 to 10 minutes. Drain shrimp, reserving stock for another use. Plunge shrimp into ice water to stop cooking, then drain again. Transfer to bowl, cover with plastic wrap, and refrigerate until chilled, about 1 hour.
3. *For the cocktail sauce:* Stir all ingredients together in small bowl. Season with additional salt and pepper to taste. Serve with shrimp.

SHRIMP BASICS

BUYING SHRIMP Virtually all of the shrimp sold in supermarkets today have been previously frozen, either in large blocks of ice or by a method called "individually quick- frozen," or IQF for short. Supermarkets simply defrost the shrimp before displaying them on ice at the fish counter. We highly recommend purchasing bags of still-frozen shrimp and defrosting them as needed at home, since there is no telling how long "fresh" shrimp may have been kept on ice at the market. IQF shrimp have a better flavor and texture than shrimp frozen in blocks, and they are convenient because it's easy to defrost just the amount you need. Also, shrimp should be the only ingredient listed on the bag; some packagers add preservatives, but we find treated shrimp to have an unpleasant, rubbery texture.

SORTING OUT SHRIMP SIZES Shrimp are sold both by size (small, medium, etc.) and by the number needed to make 1 pound, usually given in a range. Choosing shrimp by the numerical rating is more accurate, because the size label varies from store to store. Here's how the two sizing systems generally compare:

SMALL	51 to 60 per pound
MEDIUM	41 to 50 per pound
MEDIUM-LARGE	31 to 40 per pound
LARGE	26 to 30 per pound
EXTRA-LARGE	21 to 25 per pound
JUMBO	16 to 20 per pound

DEFROSTING SHRIMP You can thaw frozen shrimp overnight in the refrigerator in a covered bowl. For a quicker thaw, place them in a colander under cold running water; they will be ready in a few minutes. Thoroughly dry the shrimp before cooking.

PERFECTING SHRIMP SCAMPI

ANDREW JANJIGIAN, *January/February 2016*

Shrimp scampi is rarely awful—it's unusual for things to go terribly wrong when garlic, wine, and butter are involved—but restaurant versions always make me wish I'd ordered differently. I have never been presented with the ultimate scampi, the one that I can almost taste when I peruse the menu: perfectly cooked, briny beauties in a garlicky, buttery (but not greasy) white wine sauce.

When I last made my way through a mediocre rendition, I decided it was time to realize this ideal scampi vision at home. Since shrimp are susceptible to overcooking, which can make them dry and tough, I gave my shrimp (1½ pounds, enough to serve four) a short dunk in a saltwater solution to season them and help preserve moisture. I then heated extra-virgin olive oil in a skillet, sautéed a few cloves of minced garlic and a dash of red pepper flakes, and added the shrimp. Once the shrimp turned opaque, I splashed in some dry white wine and followed it with a chunk of butter, a big squeeze of lemon juice, and a sprinkle of parsley.

My guests and I didn't go hungry that night, but the scampi was far from perfect. One problem was that the sauce separated into a butter-and-oil slick floating on top of the wine—not ideal in the looks department or for dunking bread into. (While some serve shrimp scampi over a pile of spaghetti, I think it's best with a crusty loaf.) Then there were the shrimp: Some were a little overdone, while others were still translucent. Finally, the overall dish was shy on both seafood and garlic flavors. For results that I'd be truly satisfied with, some adjustments were in order.

SHRIMP TALES

Back in the test kitchen, I thought about ways to improve the shrimp. Flavorful crustaceans are often thought of as sweet, so would adding sugar to the brine be beneficial? Sure enough, my colleagues agreed that when used judiciously (2 tablespoons of sugar along with 3 tablespoons of salt in 1 quart of water), the sugar subtly boosted the natural flavor of the shrimp. I also found that using untreated shrimp, with no added salt or preservatives, produced the best results.

Another detail to consider was the cooking method. The inconsistent doneness of my first batch had come from crowding the skillet, so I needed to sauté the shrimp in batches. Or did I? What if, instead of sautéing the shrimp and then adding the wine, I gently poached the shrimp in the wine? As it turned out, this approach cooked all of the shrimp just right and in unison, as long as the skillet was covered with a lid to trap steam.

Now that I had flavorful, properly cooked shrimp, it was time to tackle the sauce. I had three items on my to-do list. First: Seriously bump up the flavor. (I'd found that the 5 minutes or so that it took to cook the shrimp wasn't long enough to impart much of a seafood taste to the dish.) Second: Add extra garlic for a more robust punch. Third: Fix the separated consistency.

WASTE NOT, WANT NOT

A few ladles of stock made from trimmings, bones, or other ingredient scraps can be a great way to infuse flavor into a sauce. Here I could make a stock from the shrimp shells, so I started buying shell-on shrimp instead of the prepeeled type (to save time, I started using the jumbo size so I'd have fewer to peel). To coax out every bit of savoriness, I first browned the shells in a little olive oil and then simmered them in the wine for 30 minutes with a few sprigs of thyme for a little more complexity. But the stock didn't taste all that shrimpy. My incorrect assumption was that simmering the shells for a longer period of time would extract more flavor from them. A timing test conducted by a fellow test cook debunked that myth, finding that you get more flavor out of shrimp shells if you simmer them for only 5 minutes. This was an easy change I was happy to make.

Next, I doubled the amount of garlic. It worked to boost the garlic flavor but not without a cost: All of those minced pieces gave the sauce a gritty quality. To prevent this, I switched from mincing the cloves to slicing them into thin rounds. But since sliced garlic is milder in flavor than minced (garlic's bite is created in the act of damaging its cells; the finer it's cut, the stronger its flavor will be) the switch required that I double the number of cloves, to eight.

Poaching—rather than sautéing—the shrimp in wine enhanced with browned shrimp shells takes this dish from good to great.

All that remained was to bind the fats and wine together into a cohesive sauce. In other words, I needed a stabilizer. I considered my choices: Flour, gelatin, and even pectin would work, but cornstarch seemed like the best option since it would require virtually no cooking to get the job done. I could hydrate the cornstarch in some of the wine, but I decided that it would be more convenient to use the lemon juice I was adding to the sauce for brightness. A mere teaspoon of cornstarch worked like a charm. I stirred the mixture into the sauce before adding the butter, which easily whisked into the rest of the sauce and stayed there, giving it a creamy, silky texture. In fact, it was so rich and creamy that I was able to scale back the amount of butter to 4 tablespoons without anyone finding it too lean. And there it was: the scampi I'd been looking for all along.

Shrimp Scampi

SERVES 4

Extra-large shrimp (21 to 25 per pound) can be substituted for jumbo shrimp. If you use them, reduce the cooking time in step 3 by 1 to 2 minutes. We prefer untreated shrimp, but if your shrimp are treated with sodium or preservatives like sodium tripolyphosphate, skip the brining in step 1 and add ¼ teaspoon of salt to the sauce in step 4. Serve with crusty bread.

3 tablespoons salt
2 tablespoons sugar
1½ pounds jumbo shrimp (16 to 20 per pound), peeled, deveined, and tails removed, shells reserved
2 tablespoons extra-virgin olive oil
1 cup dry white wine
4 sprigs fresh thyme
3 tablespoons lemon juice, plus lemon wedges for serving
1 teaspoon cornstarch
8 garlic cloves, sliced thin
½ teaspoon red pepper flakes
¼ teaspoon pepper
4 tablespoons unsalted butter, cut into ½-inch pieces
1 tablespoon chopped fresh parsley

1. Dissolve salt and sugar in 1 quart cold water in large container. Submerge shrimp in brine, cover, and refrigerate for 15 minutes. Remove shrimp from brine and pat dry with paper towels.

2. Heat 1 tablespoon oil in 12-inch skillet over high heat until shimmering. Add shrimp shells and cook, stirring frequently, until they begin to turn spotty brown and skillet starts to brown, 2 to 4 minutes. Remove skillet from heat and carefully add wine and thyme sprigs. When bubbling subsides, return skillet to medium heat and simmer gently, stirring occasionally, for 5 minutes. Strain mixture through colander set over large bowl. Discard shells and reserve liquid (you should have about ⅔ cup). Wipe out skillet with paper towels.

3. Combine lemon juice and cornstarch in small bowl. Heat remaining 1 tablespoon oil, garlic, pepper flakes, and pepper in now-empty skillet over medium-low heat, stirring occasionally, until garlic is fragrant and just beginning to brown at edges, 3 to 5 minutes. Add reserved wine mixture, increase heat to high, and bring to simmer. Reduce heat to medium, add shrimp, cover, and cook, stirring occasionally, until shrimp are just opaque, 5 to 7 minutes. Remove skillet from heat and, using slotted spoon, transfer shrimp to bowl.

4. Return skillet to medium heat, add lemon juice–cornstarch mixture, and cook until slightly thickened, 1 minute. Remove from heat and whisk in butter and parsley until combined. Return shrimp and any accumulated juices to skillet and toss to combine. Serve, passing lemon wedges separately.

WHEN LESS TIME MEANS MORE FLAVOR

It's easy to view shrimp shells simply as an impediment to the sweet, briny flesh within, but the shells actually contain lots of flavorful compounds that can be extracted into a stock. We've always assumed that, as with beef bones, the longer shrimp stock simmered, the more intense its flavor would be. But was that really true? To find out, we designed a test to determine the optimal simmering time.

EXPERIMENT We simmered batches of shrimp shells in water, covered, for 5, 10, 15, and 30 minutes and then strained out the shells. We asked tasters to evaluate the flavor of each sample.

RESULTS Tasters almost unanimously chose the 5- and 10-minute simmered samples as "more potent," "shrimpier," and "more aromatic" than the 15- and 30-minute simmered samples.

EXPLANATION While some of the savory compounds found in shrimp shells are stable (i.e., they stay in the stock, rather than release into the atmosphere), the compounds that we associate with shrimp flavor are highly volatile. The longer a stock is simmered, the more of these molecules will release into the air, and the blander the stock will be.

TAKEAWAY For the most flavorful shrimp stock, simmer shells for just 5 minutes.

ALL ABOUT GARLIC

Garlic is an essential flavor component of our Shrimp Scampi. Here's everything you need to know about it.

BUYING GARLIC Pick heads without spots, mold, or sprouting. Squeeze them to make sure they are not rubbery or missing cloves. The garlic shouldn't have much of a scent. Of the various garlic varieties, your best bet is soft-neck garlic, since it stores well and is heat-tolerant. This variety features a circle of large cloves surrounding a small cluster at the center. Hard-neck garlic has a stiff center staff surrounded by large, uniform cloves and boasts a more intense flavor. But since it's easily damaged and doesn't store as well as soft-neck garlic, wait to buy it at the farmers' market.

STORING GARLIC Whole heads of garlic should last at least a few weeks if stored in a cool, dark place with plenty of air circulation to prevent spoiling and sprouting.

PREPARING GARLIC Keep in mind that garlic's pungency emerges only after its cell walls are ruptured, triggering the creation of a compound called allicin. The more a clove is broken down, the more allicin that is produced. In our Shrimp Scampi, we love a big hit of garlic flavor, but mincing the cloves gave the sauce a gritty texture. Switching to sliced garlic eliminated grittiness but also gave the sauce less garlic flavor, since the cloves were less broken down. Upping the number of cloves to eight gave us the best of both worlds. Also, it's best not to cut garlic in advance; the longer cut garlic sits, the harsher its flavor.

GREAT ROAST SHRIMP

ANDREW JANJIGIAN, *January/February 2013*

When I set out to find the best way to make roasted shrimp, I thought I'd hit the jackpot. Quick-cooking shrimp make an easy weeknight dinner, and the idea of roasting them until they develop deep, flavorful browning seemed so natural that I figured there were plenty of good recipes out there to learn from.

Imagine my surprise, then, when the handful I tried produced pale, insipid shrimp that looked as though they'd been baked, not roasted. Some of the missteps seemed obvious, such as crowding lots of small shrimp (tossed with oil and aromatics) on a sheet pan or in a baking dish, where their exuded moisture caused them to steam and prevented browning. Some of the oven temperatures were also strangely low—around 300 degrees. I was sure I could do better, while keeping the technique simple enough for an easy weeknight meal.

THE HEAT IS ON

My challenge was clear from the start: The goals of roasting—a juicy interior and a thoroughly browned exterior—were impeded by the fact that lean shrimp cook through very quickly. Knowing that, I made two immediate decisions: First, I would crank the oven temperature very high to get good browning on the exterior of the shrimp— 500 degrees seemed like a fine place to start. Second, I would use the biggest shrimp I could get. That meant skipping right past even the extra-large size and reaching for the jumbo (16 to 20 per pound) shrimp, which would be the least likely to dry out in the heat. Using larger shrimp would also mean that there would be fewer pieces crowding the pan, and their smaller total amount of surface area would mean that less steam would be created—therefore making browning possible. As a test run, I oiled and seasoned 2 pounds of peeled shrimp with nothing more than a little salt and pepper (I'd explore flavorings once I'd nailed down a cooking method) and slid them into the oven on a sheet pan.

I thought the 500-degree blast would get the shrimp good and brown in a hurry, so I hovered around the oven and checked on their color every couple of minutes. Trouble was, the color never came—and while I waited and waited for the browning to kick in, the shrimp turned from tender and slightly translucent to fully opaque. I knew before I plunged a fork into them that they were overcooked. Clearly, high heat alone wasn't going to cut it, so I started experimenting. "Searing" them by preheating the baking sheet in the 500-degree oven helped, but only a little, since the pan's temperature plummeted as soon as the shrimp hit. Blasting the next batch under the broiler finally delivered some decent browning to the topsides of the shrimp, but their undersides were still damp and utterly pale.

Butterflying shell-on shrimp allows the heady flavors of garlic and spices to thoroughly coat the flesh.

Part of the problem was air circulation. When we roast beef or pork, we often elevate them on a rack so that hot air can surround them, drying out and browning even the underside of the meat. With that in mind, I tried broiling my next batch of shrimp on a wire rack set in the baking sheet—and finally started to see some real progress.

But the approach wasn't perfect. The heat of my broiler, as with all broilers, was uneven, which meant that I had to rotate the baking sheet halfway through cooking to prevent the shrimp from scorching under the element's hot spots, and even then I got a few desiccated pieces. In addition to using jumbo shrimp, the situation demanded a foolproof buffer against the heat, and the obvious answer was to brine the shrimp. The extra moisture that gets pulled into the lean flesh with the salt helps it stay moist even in a hot oven. Thanks to the shrimp's relatively small size, just a 15-minute soak in brine ensured that inside they stayed nice and plump—not to mention well seasoned throughout. Outside, however, they still shriveled under the broiler's heat before they had a chance to develop deep "roasted" color and flavor.

AN A-PEELING SOLUTION

I hoped that a thorough coat of olive oil (I'd been lightly glossing my shrimp) might stave off evaporation, but while the extra fat did keep the shrimp a bit more moist, it did nothing to even out browning. The idea of giving the shrimp a protective layer inspired another idea, though: What if I took advantage of the shrimp's natural protective coating and roasted them in their shells? Surely their "jackets" would prevent the surface of the meat from shriveling and, being drier than the meat, would probably brown quickly, too. The downside would be that shell-on shrimp are messier to eat, but if the results were good, having to peel them at the table would be worth it.

To make deveining and (later) peeling the shrimp easier, I used a pair of kitchen shears to split their shells from end to end without removing them from the flesh, and then I proceeded with my brine-and-broil technique. The results were stunning: shrimp that were moist and plump inside and evenly browned outside. In fact, the depth of the shrimp's "roasted" flavor exceeded my expectations and prompted me to mention the results to our science editor, who replied with some surprising intel. Turns out that the shells were doing much more than protecting the crustaceans' flesh: They are loaded with sugars, proteins, and other flavor-boosting compounds that amplify the rich seafood flavor.

Juicy, deeply browned shrimp complete, I moved on to tackle flavorings. I was already splitting the shells across the back and deveining the shrimp, so I took the technique one step further and butterflied the exposed flesh, cutting through the meat just short of severing it into two pieces. Then, to jazz up the oil-salt-pepper base, I added spices (anise seeds and red pepper flakes), six cloves of garlic, parsley, and melted butter (a natural pairing with briny seafood) and worked the flavorful mixture deep into the meat before broiling. Just as brining had seasoned the shrimp throughout, butterflying the pieces and thoroughly coating them with the oil-spice mixture made for seriously bold flavor. And since my tasters instantly gobbled up the shrimp—some of them shell and all—I developed two equally quick, flavorful variations: a Peruvian-style version with cilantro and lime and an Asian-inspired one with cumin, ginger, and sesame.

A great-tasting dish that requires almost no prep work and goes from the oven to the table in fewer than 10 minutes? I knew I'd be making this one year-round.

BUTTERFLYING SHELL-ON SHRIMP

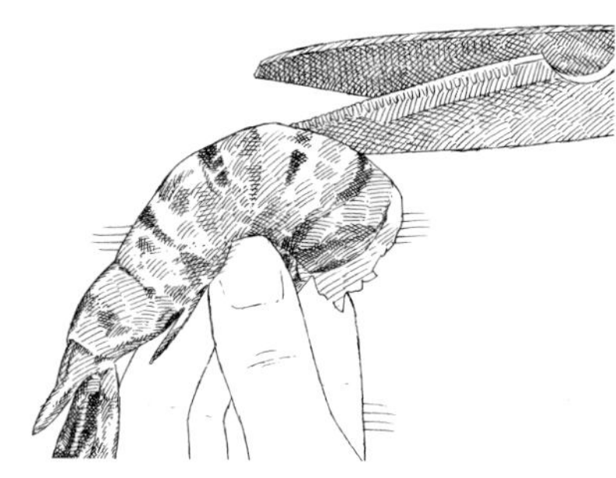

1. Starting at head of shrimp, snip through back of shell with kitchen shears. (This can also be done with very sharp paring knife: Cut from tail end of shell toward head.) Devein shrimp but do not remove shell.

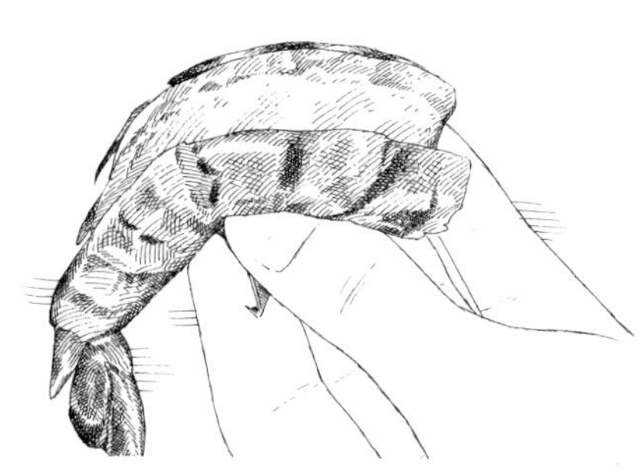

2. Using paring knife, carefully continue to cut ½-inch slit in shrimp, making sure not to split it in half completely.

Garlicky Roasted Shrimp with Parsley and Anise

SERVES 4 TO 6

Don't be tempted to use smaller shrimp with this cooking technique; they will be overseasoned and are prone to overcooking.

¼ cup salt
2 pounds shell-on jumbo shrimp (16 to 20 per pound)
4 tablespoons unsalted butter, melted
¼ cup vegetable oil
6 garlic cloves, minced
1 teaspoon anise seeds
½ teaspoon red pepper flakes
¼ teaspoon pepper
2 tablespoons minced fresh parsley
Lemon wedges

1. Dissolve salt in 1 quart cold water in large container. Using kitchen shears or sharp paring knife, cut through shells of shrimp and devein but do not remove shells. Using paring knife, continue to cut shrimp ½ inch deep, taking care not to cut in half completely. Submerge shrimp in brine, cover, and refrigerate for 15 minutes.
2. Adjust oven rack 4 inches from broiler element and heat broiler. Combine melted butter, oil, garlic, anise seeds, pepper flakes, and pepper in large bowl. Remove shrimp from brine and pat dry with paper towels. Add shrimp and parsley to butter mixture; toss well, making sure butter mixture gets into interiors of shrimp. Arrange shrimp in single layer on wire rack set in rimmed baking sheet.
3. Broil shrimp until opaque and shells are beginning to brown, 2 to 4 minutes, rotating sheet halfway through broiling. Flip shrimp and continue to broil until second side is opaque and shells are beginning to brown, 2 to 4 minutes longer, rotating sheet halfway through broiling. Transfer shrimp to serving platter and serve immediately, passing lemon wedges separately.

variations

Garlicky Roasted Shrimp with Cilantro and Lime

Annatto powder, also called achiote, *can be found with the Latin American foods at your supermarket. An equal amount of paprika can be substituted.*

Omit butter and increase vegetable oil to ½ cup. Omit anise seeds and pepper. Add 2 teaspoons lightly crushed coriander seeds, 2 teaspoons grated lime zest, and 1 teaspoon annatto powder to oil mixture in step 2. Substitute ¼ cup minced fresh cilantro for parsley and lime wedges for lemon wedges.

Garlicky Roasted Shrimp with Cumin, Ginger, and Sesame

Omit butter and increase vegetable oil to ½ cup. Decrease garlic to 2 cloves and omit anise seeds and pepper. Add 2 teaspoons toasted sesame oil, 1½ teaspoons grated fresh ginger, and 1 teaspoon cumin seeds to oil mixture in step 2. Substitute 2 thinly sliced scallion greens for parsley and omit lemon wedges.

THE SURPRISING POWER OF SHRIMP SHELLS

We found that cooking shrimp in their shells kept them juicier, but our shell-on roasted shrimp boast such savory depth that we wondered if there wasn't more to this outer layer than we thought. Our science editor confirmed our suspicions. First, shrimp shells contain water-soluble flavor compounds that will get absorbed by the shrimp flesh during cooking. Second, the shells are loaded with proteins and sugars—almost as much as the flesh itself. When they brown, they undergo the flavor-enhancing Maillard reaction just as roasted meats do, which gives the shells even more flavor to pass along to the flesh. Third, like the flesh, the shells contain healthy amounts of glutamates and nucleotides, compounds that dramatically enhance savory umami flavor when present together in food. These compounds also get transferred to the meat during cooking, amplifying the effect of its own glutamates and nucleotides.

AN EASIER WAY TO GRILL SHRIMP

REBECCA HAYS, *July/August 2006*

Shrimp can turn from moist and juicy to rubbery and dry in the blink of an eye, a consequence of their small size and lack of fat. Add the unpredictability of cooking over a live fire, and the challenge is magnified. Grilling shrimp in their shells to shield them from the coals' scorching heat works well, but I'm always disappointed when the seasonings get stripped off at the table along with the shells. I wanted tender, juicy, boldly seasoned grilled shrimp without having to lick my fingers.

PEEL OUT

I started by preparing the test kitchen's existing recipe for grilled shrimp, substituting peeled shrimp for shell-on. (I'd investigate flavorings later.) I followed every mandate, plumping the shrimp in a saltwater brine (which helps keep them moist), threading them onto skewers, brushing with oil, then quickly grilling over moderate heat. After a few minutes over the fire, the shrimp were tough and dehydrated—no surprise given their shell-free state. Also problematic was the absence of attractive (and flavorful) char marks.

Suspecting that brining was causing the shrimp to become waterlogged and, thus, hindering caramelization, I grilled a batch of unbrined samples. Sure enough, these shrimp began to pick up the flavor of the grill with a few faint, yet promising, marks.

Having discarded brining, I next built an especially hot fire by banking all the coals on one side of the grill. I seasoned a batch of shrimp with salt and pepper (plus a pinch of sugar to encourage caramelization), set them on the grate, and waited. And waited. Even with a screaming-hot fire, the only way to get sufficient charring was to leave the shrimp on the grill for 4 or 5 minutes, yet each passing minute brought me closer to shrimp jerky and farther from a decent dinner.

Shrimp cook so quickly because of their small size. Jumbo shrimp would afford me a few extra minutes, but with a cost of more than $25 per pound and spotty availability, there had to be a better way.

What if I crammed several normal-sized shrimp very tightly together on a skewer, creating a faux "jumbo" shrimp? Sure enough, this homemade giant shrimp cooked at a slightly slower pace, giving me the extra minutes of grilling time the shrimp needed for charring.

TRIAL BY FIRE

With a decent grilling method at hand, I could finally start investigating flavorings. I tried to add personality with ground spices, but this was a mistake. A flare-up torched the spice paste, turning it bitter. Minced garlic? Scorched. Fresh herbs? Scorched again.

As soon as each shrimp develops an attractive char, it goes into the pan of simmering sauce to finish cooking at a much gentler pace.

Scouring our library shelves, I reviewed every grilled seafood recipe I could find. I eventually happened upon a few recipes in which shellfish was given an initial sear over a hot fire and then transferred to a sauce waiting on the cooler side of the grill. Intrigued, I grilled a few shrimp and slid them into a sauce that simmered in a disposable aluminum pan. These shrimp were a tad overdone but soaked up plenty of the flavorful sauce.

I started transferring the shrimp to the sauce before they were fully cooked. This way, I could get char marks and then switch to a more forgiving cooking method (gentle simmering in the sauce) until the shrimp were done. I finally had an infallible recipe that delivered everything I wanted in grilled shrimp: tender flesh, attractive charring, tons of flavor—and no shells.

HOW TO PEEL AND DEVEIN SHRIMP

Many supermarkets carry easy-peel shrimp. The shells have been split open along the back for easy removal and the shrimp have already been deveined. If you can't find them, here is how to do the job yourself.

1. Break shell on underside of shrimp, under swimming legs. (The shell comes off the body of the shrimp very easily and the legs will come off as the shell is removed.)

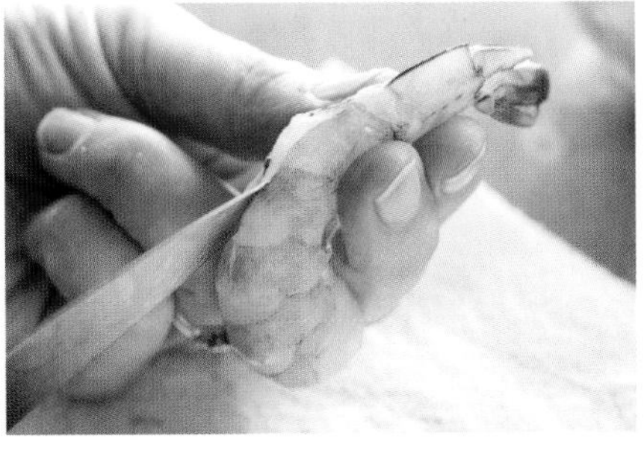

2. Use paring knife to make shallow cut along back of shrimp to expose vein. (Although this vein doesn't affect flavor, we remove it to improve the appearance of cooked shrimp.)

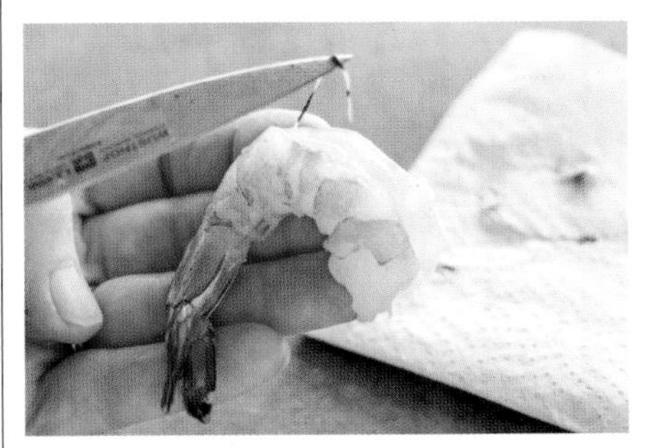

3. Use tip of knife to lift vein out. Discard vein by wiping knife blade against paper towel.

Grilled Shrimp Skewers with Chermoula Sauce

SERVES 4

The shrimp and sauce finish cooking together on the grill, so prepare the sauce ingredients while the grill is heating up. To fit all the shrimp on the cooking grate at once, you will need three 14-inch metal skewers. Serve with grilled bread.

Shrimp

- 1½ pounds extra-large shrimp (21 to 25 per pound), peeled and deveined
- 2 tablespoons olive oil
- Salt and pepper
- ¼ teaspoon sugar

Sauce

- 1 small red bell pepper, stemmed, seeded, and chopped fine
- ⅓ cup finely chopped red onion
- ¼ cup extra-virgin olive oil
- 3 garlic cloves, minced
- 1 teaspoon paprika
- ½ teaspoon ground cumin
- ¼ teaspoon cayenne pepper
- ⅛ teaspoon salt
- 1 (13 by 9-inch) disposable aluminum roasting pan
- ⅓ cup minced fresh cilantro
- 2 tablespoons lemon juice, plus lemon wedges for serving

1. *For the shrimp:* Pat shrimp dry with paper towels. Thread shrimp onto three 14-inch metal skewers, alternating direction of heads and tails. Brush both sides of shrimp with oil; season with salt and pepper. Sprinkle 1 side of each skewer evenly with sugar.

2A. *For a charcoal grill:* Open bottom vent completely. Light large chimney starter filled with charcoal briquettes (6 quarts). When top coals are partially covered with ash, pour evenly over half of grill. Set cooking grate in place, cover, and open lid vent completely. Heat grill until hot, about 5 minutes.

2B. *For a gas grill:* Turn all burners to high, cover, and heat grill until hot, about 15 minutes. Leave primary burner on high and turn other burner(s) to medium-low.

3. Clean cooking grate, then repeatedly brush grate with well-oiled paper towels until grate is black and glossy, 5 to 10 times.

4. *For the sauce:* Combine bell pepper, onion, oil, garlic, paprika, cumin, cayenne, and salt in disposable pan. Place disposable pan on hotter side of grill and cook, stirring occasionally, until hot, 1 to 3 minutes. Move disposable pan to cooler side of grill.

5. Place shrimp, sugared side down, on hotter side of grill and use tongs to push shrimp together on skewers if they have separated. Cook shrimp until lightly charred, 4 to 5 minutes. Using tongs, flip shrimp and continue to cook until second side is pink and slightly translucent, 1 to 2 minutes longer.

6. Carefully lift each skewer from grill and use tongs to slide shrimp off skewers into disposable pan with sauce. Toss shrimp with sauce to combine. Cook, stirring, until shrimp are opaque throughout, about 30 seconds. Remove disposable pan from grill, add cilantro and lemon juice, and toss to combine. Transfer to platter and serve with lemon wedges.

THE RIGHT SETUP

With grilled shrimp, timing can be tricky. We solved the problem by setting up two cooking zones. On the hotter side, we sear the shrimp over dry heat until almost done. On the cooler side, we keep a disposable pan of simmering sauce, where the shrimp finish cooking at a gentler pace. Crowding the shrimp on the skewers bought us a few extra minutes on the hotter side, giving the shrimp better charring.

variations

Grilled Shrimp Skewers with Spicy Lemon-Garlic Sauce

Omit sauce ingredients. Combine 4 tablespoons unsalted butter, cut into 4 pieces; ¼ cup lemon juice (2 lemons); 3 minced garlic cloves; ½ teaspoon red pepper flakes; and ⅛ teaspoon salt in 13 by 9-inch disposable aluminum pan. Just before cooking shrimp, place disposable pan on hotter side of grill and cook, stirring occasionally, until butter melts, about 1½ minutes. Move to cooler side of grill while cooking shrimp and substitute for sauce in step 6. Toss with ⅓ cup minced fresh parsley before serving.

Grilled Shrimp Skewers with Fresh Tomato Sauce with Feta and Olives

Omit sauce ingredients. Combine ¼ cup extra-virgin olive oil; 1 large tomato, cored, seeded, and minced; 1 tablespoon minced fresh oregano; and ⅛ teaspoon salt in 13 by 9-inch disposable aluminum pan. Just before cooking shrimp, place disposable pan on hotter side of grill and cook, stirring occasionally, until hot, about 1½ minutes. Move to cooler side of grill while cooking shrimp and substitute for sauce in step 6. Toss with 1 cup crumbled feta; ⅓ cup kalamata olives, chopped fine; 3 thinly sliced scallions; and 2 tablespoons lemon juice before serving.

CROWDING SHRIMP ONTO A SKEWER

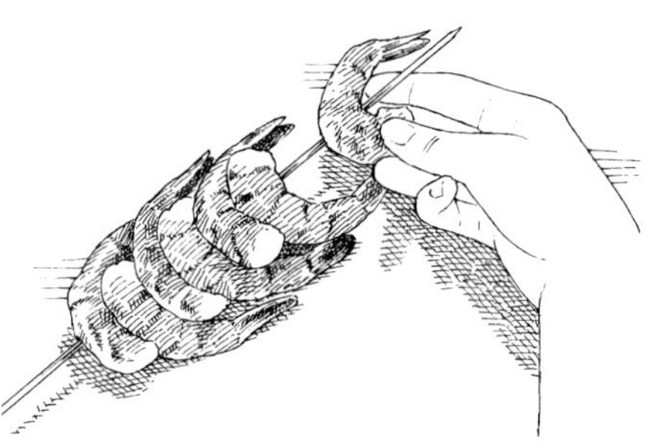

Pass the skewer through the center of each shrimp. As you add shrimp to the skewer, alternate the directions of the heads and tails for a compact arrangement of about 12 shrimp. The shrimp should be crowded and touching each other.

GREAT PAN-SEARED SCALLOPS

BRYAN ROOF, *November/December 2009*

For a restaurant chef, pan-seared scallops are as easy as it gets: Slick a superhot pan with oil, add the shellfish, flip them once, and serve. The whole process takes no more than a couple of minutes and produces golden-crusted beauties with tender, medium-rare interiors. But try the same technique at home and you're likely to run into trouble. The problem is that most home stovetops don't get nearly as hot as professional ranges, so it's difficult to properly brown the scallops without overcooking them. Moreover, restaurant chefs pay top dollar for scallops without chemical additives, which are known in the industry as "dry." The remainder, called "wet" scallops—the type available in most supermarkets—are treated with a solution of water and sodium tripolyphosphate (STPP) to increase shelf life and retain moisture. Unfortunately, STPP lends a soapy, off-flavor to the scallops, and the extra water only compounds the problem of poor browning.

To achieve superior pan-seared scallops, I had to find a solution to the browning conundrum. I also had to get rid of the chemical taste of STPP.

WATERSHED MOMENTS

My first stop was the supermarket fish counter. Scallops are available in a range of sizes: A pound of the hard-to-find large sea variety contains eight to 10 scallops, while a pound of the petite bay variety may have as many as 100 pencil eraser–size scallops. Since small scallops are more prone to overcooking than large, I opted for the biggest commonly available size: 10 to 20 per pound. I decided to work with wet scallops first. After all, if I could develop a good recipe for finicky wet scallops, it would surely work with premium dry scallops.

I started by seasoning 1½ pounds (the right amount for four people) with salt and pepper. I heated 1 tablespoon of vegetable oil in a 12-inch stainless-steel skillet, then added the scallops in a single layer and waited for them to brown. After 3 minutes, they were steaming away in a ¼-inch-deep pool of liquid. At the 5-minute mark, the moisture in the skillet evaporated and the flesh began to turn golden. But at this point it was too late: The scallops were already overcooked and tough, and I hadn't even flipped them.

To dry out the scallops, I tried pressing them between kitchen towels. When 10 minutes didn't work, I tried a full hour—even leaving a third batch overnight in the refrigerator. The results were disheartening. While slightly drier than unblotted scallops, the pressed batches still exuded copious amounts of liquid in the skillet (and they still tasted soapy; I'd focus on that later). My conclusion: Beyond a 10-minute blot, there's no point in trying to remove moisture from wet scallops before cooking.

For restaurant-quality scallops, we soak them in a lemon juice–enhanced brine and then baste them with butter after flipping.

It was becoming clear that to dry out the water-logged scallops for good browning, I'd have to get the pan as hot as possible. Without a high-output range, it was important to pay careful attention to technique. I started by waiting to add the scallops to the skillet until the oil was beginning to smoke, a clear indication of heat. I also cooked the scallops in two batches instead of one, since crowding would cool down the pan. Finally, switching to a nonstick skillet ensured that as the scallops cooked, the browned bits formed a crust on the meat instead of sticking to the skillet. These were steps in right direction, but the scallops were still overcooked and rubbery by the time they were fully browned.

BUTTER UP

Would switching from oil to butter help my cause? Butter contains milk proteins and sugars that brown rapidly when heated, so I hoped that it would help the scallops turn golden before they overcooked. But my hopes were dashed when in my next batch, the butter that I'd swapped for oil actually made matters worse: It burned before the scallops were cooked through.

Then I recalled a method I'd used when cooking steaks and chops in restaurants: butter-basting. I gave it a try with my scallops, searing them in oil on one side and adding a tablespoon of butter to the skillet after flipping them. I tilted the skillet to allow the butter to pool, then used a large spoon to ladle the foaming butter over the scallops. Waiting to add the butter ensured that it had just enough time to work its browning magic on the shellfish, but not enough time to burn. The scallops now achieved a deep golden brown crust in record time, and their moist interiors were preserved. They weren't quite as tender and juicy as dry scallops, but they were darn close.

LEMON AID

Only one problem remained, and it was a big one: the soapy flavor of STPP. I already knew from earlier tests that blotting removes neither excess water nor STPP, but what about the opposite approach: soaking in water to wash out the STPP? It was a flop. No matter how long or carefully I rinsed the scallops, the STPP still remained.

I thought things over and decided that if I couldn't remove the STPP, I would try to mask it. I thought maybe a saltwater brine was the answer because it would penetrate the scallops deeply. The brine did provide even seasoning, but not enough to mask the chemical flavor. I noted that the phosphate in STPP is alkaline. What if I covered it up by

putting acidic lemon juice in the brine? Problem solved. Only the most sensitive tasters now picked up on a hint of chemical off-flavors; most tasted only the sweet shellfish complemented by the bright flavor of citrus.

With my wet-scallop approach established, it was finally time to test my recipe on dry scallops. I skipped the soaking step, which was unnecessary in the absence of STPP, and proceeded with the recipe. The result? Scallops that rivaled those made on a powerful restaurant range, golden brown on the exterior and juicy and tender on the interior. I was happy to serve them with just a squeeze of lemon, but fancier occasions call for a sauce. For those instances, I developed a couple of recipes based on a classic accompaniment: browned butter.

GOING FOR A SOAK

So-called "wet" scallops have been treated with sodium tripolyphosphate (STPP), which lends a disagreeable flavor. Could we get rid of the STPP by soaking the scallops in water?

THE EXPERIMENT We prepared three batches of "wet" scallops, soaking the first in a quart of water for 30 minutes, soaking the second for an hour, and leaving the third untreated. We then cooked each batch according to our recipe and sent them to a lab to be analyzed for STPP content.

THE RESULTS The scallops soaked for 30 minutes only had about 10 percent less STPP than the untreated batch, and soaking for a full hour wasn't much better: Only about 11 percent of the STPP was removed. Tasters were still able to identify an unpleasant chemical flavor in both soaked samples.

THE EXPLANATION The phosphates in STPP form a chemical bond with the proteins in scallops, which prevent the STPP from being washed away.

THE SOLUTION Rather than try to remove the chemical taste from STPP-treated scallops, we masked it by soaking them in a solution of lemon juice, water, and salt.

Pan-Seared Scallops

SERVES 4

We recommend buying "dry" scallops, which don't have chemical additives and taste better than "wet." Dry scallops will look ivory or pinkish; wet scallops are bright white. If using wet scallops, soak them in a solution of 1 quart of cold water, ¼ cup of lemon juice, and 2 tablespoons of salt for 30 minutes before proceeding with step 1, and do not season with salt in step 2. If you are unsure whether your scallops are wet or dry, conduct this quick test: Place 1 scallop on a paper towel–lined plate and microwave on high power for 15 seconds. If the scallop is "dry," it will exude very little water. If it is "wet," there will be a sizable ring of moisture on the paper towel. (The microwaved scallop can be cooked as is.) If serving with a sauce (recipes follow), prepare it while the scallops dry (between steps 1 and 2).

1½ pounds large sea scallops, tendons removed
Salt and pepper
2 tablespoons vegetable oil
2 tablespoons unsalted butter
Lemon wedges

1. Place scallops on rimmed baking sheet lined with clean dish towel. Place second clean dish towel on top of scallops and press gently on towel to blot liquid. Let scallops sit at room temperature for 10 minutes while towels absorb moisture.
2. Season scallops on both sides with salt and pepper. Heat 1 tablespoon oil in 12-inch nonstick skillet over high heat until just smoking. Add half of scallops in single layer, flat side down, and cook, without moving them, until well browned, 1½ to 2 minutes.
3. Add 1 tablespoon butter to skillet. Using tongs, flip scallops and continue to cook, using large spoon to baste scallops with melted butter (tilt skillet so butter runs to 1 side) until sides of scallops are firm and centers are opaque, 30 to 90 seconds longer (remove smaller scallops as they finish cooking). Transfer scallops to large plate and tent with aluminum foil. Wipe skillet clean with paper towels and repeat cooking with remaining oil, scallops, and butter. Serve immediately with lemon wedges.

accompaniments

Lemon Brown Butter

MAKES ABOUT ¼ CUP

Watch the butter carefully, as it can go from brown to burnt quickly.

4 tablespoons unsalted butter, cut into 4 pieces
1 small shallot, minced
1 tablespoon minced fresh parsley
2 teaspoons lemon juice
½ teaspoon minced fresh thyme
Salt and pepper

Heat butter in small saucepan over medium heat and cook, swirling saucepan constantly, until butter turns dark golden brown and has nutty aroma, 4 to 5 minutes. Add shallot and cook until fragrant, about 30 seconds. Off heat, stir in parsley, lemon juice, and thyme. Season with salt and pepper to taste. Cover to keep warm.

Tomato-Ginger Sauce

MAKES ABOUT ½ CUP

Watch the butter carefully, as it can go from brown to burnt quickly.

6 tablespoons unsalted butter
1 plum tomato, cored, seeded, and chopped
1 tablespoon grated fresh ginger
1 tablespoon lemon juice
¼ teaspoon red pepper flakes
Salt

Heat butter in small saucepan over medium heat and cook, swirling pan constantly, until butter turns dark golden brown and has nutty aroma, 4 to 5 minutes. Add tomato, ginger, lemon juice, and pepper flakes and cook, stirring constantly, until fragrant, about 1 minute. Season with salt to taste. Cover to keep warm.

THE BEST WAY TO COOK MUSSELS

ANDREW JANJIGIAN, *September/October 2013*

I'm always amazed when I ask friends how often they make mussels—and their answer is "Never." I love cooking mussels. They're cheap and quick to prepare, with tender flesh and a briny-sweet built-in broth created by the merging of the mussels and their steaming liquid. Their flavor is distinct but still tame enough to pair with a wide variety of aromatic ingredients.

So why don't more people make them? My friends all cite the same reasons: Mussels are hard to clean, and it seems a little dicey trying to figure out if they're safe to eat. Fortunately, these misconceptions are easy to dispel. Most mussels these days need very little cleaning. The vast majority are farmed, which leads to less sand and grit and fewer of the stringy beards that cling to the shell. As for figuring out whether a mussel is safe to cook, this couldn't be more straightforward. Your first clue is smell: A dead mussel smells very bad, whereas a live mussel should smell pleasantly briny, and its shell (if open) should close when tapped. That's it. If a mussel is alive before you cook it, it will be safe to eat when it's done.

We steam mussels in the oven in a covered roasting pan to ensure even cooking.

The real problem with mussels, especially if you're a perfectionist like me, is that they come in all different sizes. They run from pinky-finger small to almost palm-size large, and buying them en masse—they're usually sold in multipound bags—makes it virtually impossible to select a group that's made up of mussels that are all the same size and, therefore, will all cook at the same rate. This means that when steamed, a solid number of mussels will turn out perfectly, with shells open and the meat within plump, juicy, and easy to extract. But inevitably some will remain closed (a sign that they're undercooked). If cooked until every last one has opened wide, however, an equal number of mussels will turn out overdone—shriveled, mealy, and tough. Could I figure out a way to get more of them to cook at the same rate?

First I needed a basic recipe. Most sources using the classic French method of steaming mussels, or *moules marinières*, follow this simple model: Sauté garlic and other aromatics in a Dutch oven, pour in wine and bring it to a boil, add the mussels, cover the pot, and cook for 10 minutes or so, until all the mussels have opened. Toss in a handful of herbs, stir, and serve with crusty bread to sop up the broth.

There were differences in the recipes I tried, of course. The more successful ones had you boil down the wine a bit before adding the mussels in order to take the edge off the alcohol and round out the flavors of the finished broth. Ditto for those recipes that added some sort of dairy as a thickener at the end of cooking to give the sauce body and help it cling to the mussels. Finally, although you don't want to overpower the mussels' own flavors, a little aromatic complexity is a plus. In the end, I decided that red pepper flakes, thyme sprigs, and bay leaves (along with a generous amount of parsley) were just the right combination.

FLEX MUSSELS

With a good basic recipe in hand, I moved on to the major mussel-cooking conundrum. I wondered if a more gentle approach would prevent those mussels that opened first from drying out before their fellow bivalves caught up. I cooked two batches of mussels in big pots on the stove—one at a simmer and the other at a rolling boil. Not surprisingly, those cooked at a simmer took longer, and tasters found them a bit more moist and tender, but overall there wasn't a huge difference between the two approaches. If I waited for virtually every mussel to open, I was left with a fair number of tough, overcooked specimens.

But it was during this test that I realized another problem inherent in the traditional method of cooking mussels: the use of a big pot on the stove. With a relatively large number of mussels (at least a pound per person), my pot was nearly full to the brim, which made stirring once or twice to redistribute the mussels unwieldy. Shaking the pot, as other recipes have you do, was not at all effective at moving the mussels around. And if the mussels stay put, this only exacerbates the problem of uneven cooking, since the mussels at the bottom of the pot, whether small or large, are exposed to more heat. I tried cutting the amount of mussels in half so I could stir them more easily to see if that made more of them cook at the same rate. And sure enough, far more mussels opened at the same time so that fewer were overcooked. But how could I mimic this result and still cook the quantity of mussels I wanted? A pot or pan with more surface area—or, better yet, a large roasting pan?

One way we've achieved more even cooking in recipes is by using the oven rather than the stove. In the oven, heat surrounds the food on all sides, leading to more even (and gentle) cooking than is possible on the stove, where the heat can't help but be more aggressive at the bottom of the pan. So for my next test, I preheated the oven to its highest setting. I placed 4 pounds of mussels in a large roasting pan, covered it tightly with foil, set it on the middle oven rack—and waited, fingers crossed. These mussels took a bit longer to cook (even at 500 degrees, the oven is more gentle than a direct flame), but when they were done, I breathed a sigh of relief: Only one or two hadn't opened and the others were moist and plump.

Now all that was left was convincing my friends to get past their objections to cooking mussels. Once they discovered how unfounded their fears were and tried my method for oven steaming, I knew they'd be as hooked as I am on cooking mussels at home.

Oven-Steamed Mussels

SERVES 2 TO 4

Discard any mussel with an unpleasant odor or with a cracked or broken shell or a shell that won't close. Serve with crusty bread.

- 1 tablespoon extra-virgin olive oil
- 3 garlic cloves, minced
- Pinch red pepper flakes
- 1 cup dry white wine
- 3 sprigs fresh thyme
- 2 bay leaves
- 4 pounds mussels, scrubbed and debearded
- ¼ teaspoon salt
- 2 tablespoons unsalted butter, cut into 4 pieces
- 2 tablespoons minced fresh parsley

1. Adjust oven rack to lowest position and heat oven to 500 degrees. Heat oil, garlic, and pepper flakes in large roasting pan over medium heat; cook, stirring constantly, until fragrant, about 30 seconds. Add wine, thyme sprigs, and bay leaves and bring to boil. Cook until wine is slightly reduced, about 1 minute. Add mussels and salt. Cover pan tightly with aluminum foil and transfer to oven. Cook until most mussels have opened (a few may remain closed), 15 to 18 minutes.

2. Remove pan from oven. Push mussels to sides of pan. Add butter to center and whisk until melted. Discard thyme sprigs and bay leaves, sprinkle parsley over mussels, and toss to combine. Serve immediately.

THE PROBLEM WITH THE POT

Because mussels steamed in a pot are crowded on top of one another, it's difficult to stir (or shake) them around—and cook them evenly. The mussels closest to the heat source cook faster than the ones on top.

CLOSE AND CROWDED

In a pot, mussels stuck on the bottom open more quickly.

variations

Oven-Steamed Mussels with Hard Cider and Bacon

Omit garlic and red pepper flakes. Heat oil and 4 slices thick-cut bacon, cut into ½-inch pieces, in roasting pan until bacon has rendered and is starting to crisp, about 5 minutes. Proceed with recipe as directed, substituting dry hard cider for wine and ¼ cup heavy cream for butter.

Oven-Steamed Mussels with Leeks and Pernod

Omit red pepper flakes and increase oil to 3 tablespoons. Heat oil; 1 pound leeks, white and light green parts only, halved lengthwise, sliced thin, and washed thoroughly; and garlic in roasting pan until leeks are wilted, about 3 minutes. Proceed with recipe as directed, omitting thyme sprigs and substituting ½ cup Pernod and ¼ cup water for wine, ¼ cup crème fraîche for butter, and chives for parsley.

Oven-Steamed Mussels with Tomato and Chorizo

Omit red pepper flakes and increase oil to 3 tablespoons. Heat oil and 12 ounces Spanish-style chorizo sausage, cut into ½-inch pieces, in roasting pan until chorizo starts to brown, about 5 minutes. Add garlic and cook until fragrant, about 30 seconds. Proceed with recipe as directed, adding 1 (28-ounce) can crushed tomatoes to roasting pan before adding mussels and increasing butter to 3 tablespoons.

SIX GOOD THINGS TO KNOW ABOUT MUSSELS

1 THEY'RE SAFE TO EAT. Mussels are routinely tested by state and local agencies for the presence of algae-derived toxins. The Monterey Bay Aquarium's Seafood Watch program calls them a "Best Choice" for environmental sustainability.

2 THEY NEED ALMOST NO CLEANING. Most mussels are cultivated on long ropes suspended from rafts, which leaves them free of sand and grit—and for the most part, beards. In general, all they need is a quick rinse under the tap.

3 IT'S EASY TO TELL WHEN THEY'RE FRESH. A live mussel will smell pleasantly briny. If open, its shell should close up when lightly tapped (but give it a moment; some mussels take longer than others to clam up).

4 IT'S EQUALLY EASY TO TELL WHEN THEY'RE NOT. A dead mussel deteriorates rapidly and will smell almost immediately. Also discard any mussel with a cracked or broken shell or a shell that won't close.

5 YOU CAN STORE MUSSELS FOR UP TO THREE DAYS. As soon as you bring them home, place them in a bowl, cover it with a wet paper towel, and store it in the fridge.

6 UNOPENED COOKED MUSSELS NEEDN'T BE DISCARDED. A mussel that's closed after cooking isn't unfit to eat. It's a sign that the mussel needs more cooking. To open a reluctant mussel, microwave it briefly (30 seconds or so).

"BEARDED"? DON'T WORRY.

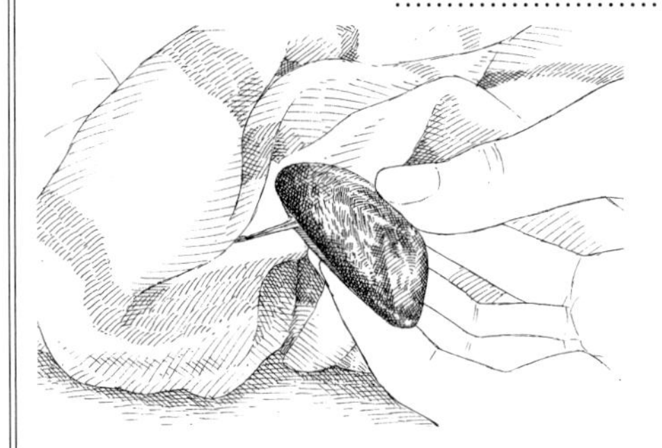

Because of the way they're cultivated, most mussels these days are free of the fibrous strands, or "beards," that wild mussels use to hold on to rocks and other surfaces. If your mussel has a beard, simply use a clean dish towel to grasp the beard and then pull it firmly to remove.

REALLY GOOD CRAB CAKES

LAN LAM, *May/June 2012*

It's a given that the best crab cakes are made with meat that's just been picked from the shell. But since fresh crabmeat is usually impossible to come by, I almost never make them at home. That's a shame, though, because crab cakes are relatively quick and easy to throw together: Most recipes call for simply mixing the shucked meat with aromatics, herbs, spices, and a binder such as mayo or beaten egg; forming cakes and dredging them in bread crumbs; and quickly pan-frying them until they're golden brown and crisp.

But is fresh-shucked meat really the only acceptable option? As we discovered in a recent crabmeat tasting, a couple of brands of pasteurized crabmeat (available either canned or in the refrigerated section of most supermarkets) are surprisingly good alternatives to the fresh stuff. I decided to make it my goal to come up with the best possible crab cakes—sweet, plump meat delicately seasoned and seamlessly held together with a binder that didn't detract from the seafood flavor—regardless of whether I was starting with fresh crabmeat.

MILKING IT

The obvious first step: figuring out what type of packaged crabmeat to use. Species aside, all crabmeat is graded both by size and by the part of the crab from which it's taken. Most crab cake recipes call for plump, pricey jumbo lump or lump, while some suggest finer, flakier backfin crabmeat.

I was pretty sure my colleagues would prefer the meatier texture of jumbo lump or lump, but I made crab cakes with all three grades just to double-check. I put together a bare-bones recipe, mixing 1 pound of meat with mayonnaise and eggs, forming the mixture into eight cakes, rolling them in panko (supercrisp Japanese bread crumbs), and pan-frying them. No contest: Tasters overwhelmingly preferred the cakes made with jumbo lump or lump crabmeat. Flavor was another matter. Not only were the binders dulling the sweet crabmeat flavor, but all three batches tasted and smelled inescapably fishy. When I mentioned the result to our science editor, he suggested soaking the meat in milk to rid it of its unpleasant fishiness. It was a great quick trick. When I submerged the crabmeat in 1 cup of milk, the fishiness washed away after just a 20-minute soak.

IN A BIND

Figuring I'd solved the toughest problem, I moved on to consider more conventional crab cake decisions like flavors and binders. Celery and onion (both briefly sautéed before joining the crabmeat) plus Old Bay seasoning were classic additions that nicely rounded out the rich flavor of the crabmeat. But the flavor-muting binders were a trickier issue. Reducing and/or leaving out the mayo or egg allowed the clean crabmeat flavor to come through. However, the unfortunate (if predictable) consequence was that the binder-free batches fell apart during cooking.

Putting aside the mayo and eggs for the moment, I tried the first two out-of-the-box ideas that came to mind: a béchamel and a panade. Unfortunately, both tests flopped. The former, a combination of milk, flour, and butter, rendered the crab mixture mushy. The latter, a thick paste made from milk and bread that's often used in meatballs, was sticky and difficult to incorporate without breaking apart the crabmeat. Even worse, the starches and dairy in both binders deadened the crab flavor just as much as the mayonnaise and eggs had.

I was feeling short on ideas when I remembered a product I had used when I worked in high-end restaurants: "Meat glue," as it's commonly referred to, is a powdered protein that some chefs use to help bind foods together. Buying this stuff was out of the question here, but what about cobbling together a hack version? I couldn't turn protein into powder, but I could puree it. More specifically, I could call on another idea from my restaurant days: a mousseline. This delicate, savory mousse is composed mainly of pureed meat or fish and just a little cream. To enhance the briny sweetness and plump bite of the crabmeat, I figured I'd use shrimp. I wouldn't need much of it, and since the shrimp would be pureed, I could use whatever size was cheapest.

A puree of shrimp and cream holds our crab cakes together without distracting from the seafood flavor.

To that end, I blitzed 6 ounces of shrimp in the food processor with 6 tablespoons of cream, plus the Old Bay, a little Dijon mustard, hot sauce, and fresh lemon juice for punchy flavor. As I'd hoped, the resulting mousse was a great stand-in; in fact, our science editor noted that this was a true meat glue. Pureeing the shrimp released fragments of sticky muscle proteins that delicately held the clumpy pieces of crabmeat together through the breading and cooking process. When tasters raved about the clean crab flavor that I had achieved, I knew this idea was a keeper. Their only quibble: The inside texture of the cakes was a bit too springy and bouncy, and a few stray clumps of crabmeat were falling off during cooking. Scaling back the mousse mixture by a third took care of the bounce, but pieces were still breaking off as I flipped the cakes.

GIVE IT A REST

I had one other, more subtle idea in mind to help make the crab cakes a bit more sturdy: briefly chilling them before cooking, which allows them to firm up, forming a less fragile cake. I ran a side-by-side test, refrigerating one batch for a half-hour before pan-frying, while immediately cooking the other. The chill paid off: These cakes not only felt noticeably sturdier than the unrested batch but also held up considerably better during cooking.

My tasters' one lingering request concerned the breading. The panko was definitely crispier than traditional bread crumbs, but the flakes soaked up moisture from the cakes, losing some of their crunch and falling off the sides. Color was also a problem, as the only surfaces that browned nicely were those that came in contact with the pan. My two quick fixes: crushing half of the panko to make smaller pieces that would adhere better to the cakes and toasting all of the crumbs before coating to deepen and even out their color and beef up their crunch.

By starting with readily available pasteurized crabmeat and devising a few easy tricks to clean up its flavor and keep the meat neatly bound, I'd created a recipe for crab cakes that I could make even without fresh crabmeat.

CRAB CAKE CLARITY

Most recipes resort to flavor-dulling binders such as mayonnaise and eggs. Instead, we employ a two-step approach that enhances the meat's delicate flavor while providing just as much structure.

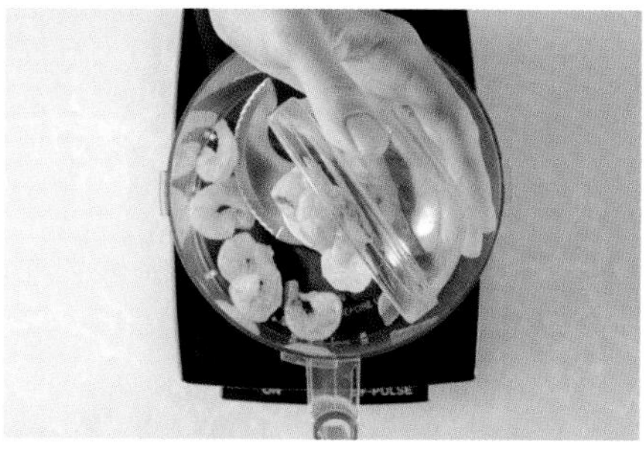

BIND WITH SHRIMP A puree of shrimp and cream holds the cakes together without dulling the meat's delicate flavor.

FIRM UP IN FRIDGE Resting the cakes in the refrigerator for 30 minutes helps them set.

Best Crab Cakes

SERVES 4

Either fresh or pasteurized crabmeat can be used in this recipe. With packaged crab, if the meat smells clean and fresh when you first open the package, skip steps 1 and 4 and blot away any excess liquid. Serve with Rémoulade Sauce (recipe follows).

1 pound lump crabmeat, picked over for shells
1 cup milk
1½ cups panko bread crumbs
Salt and pepper
2 celery ribs, chopped
½ cup chopped onion
1 garlic clove, peeled and smashed
1 tablespoon unsalted butter
4 ounces shrimp, peeled, deveined, and tails removed
¼ cup heavy cream
2 teaspoons Dijon mustard
1 teaspoon lemon juice
½ teaspoon hot sauce
½ teaspoon Old Bay seasoning
¼ cup vegetable oil

1. Place crabmeat and milk in bowl, making sure crab is totally submerged. Cover and refrigerate for 20 minutes.

2. Meanwhile, place ¾ cup panko in small zipper-lock bag and crush fine with rolling pin. Transfer crushed panko to 10-inch nonstick skillet and add remaining ¾ cup panko. Toast over medium-high heat until golden brown, about 5 minutes. Transfer panko to shallow dish, stir in ¼ teaspoon salt, and season with pepper to taste. Wipe out skillet.

3. Pulse celery, onion, and garlic in food processor until finely chopped, 5 to 8 pulses, scraping down sides of bowl as needed. Transfer vegetables to large bowl. Rinse processor bowl and blade. Melt butter in now-empty skillet over medium heat. Add vegetables, ½ teaspoon salt, and ⅛ teaspoon pepper; cook, stirring frequently, until vegetables are softened and all moisture has evaporated, 4 to 6 minutes. Return vegetables to large bowl and let cool completely. Rinse out skillet and wipe clean.

4. Drain crabmeat in fine-mesh strainer, pressing firmly to remove milk but being careful not to break up lumps of crabmeat.

5. Line rimmed baking sheet with parchment paper. Pulse shrimp in clean, dry processor until finely ground, 12 to 15 pulses, scraping down sides of bowl as needed. Add cream and pulse to combine, 2 to 4 pulses, scraping down sides of bowl as needed. Transfer shrimp puree to bowl with vegetables. Add mustard, lemon juice, hot sauce, and Old Bay; stir until well combined. Add crabmeat and fold gently with rubber spatula, being careful not to overmix and break up lumps of crabmeat. Divide mixture into 8 balls and firmly press into ½-inch-thick patties. Place patties on prepared sheet, cover tightly with plastic wrap, and refrigerate for 30 minutes.

6. Coat each patty with panko, pressing firmly to adhere crumbs to exterior. Heat 1 tablespoon oil in clean, dry skillet over medium heat until shimmering. Place 4 patties in skillet and cook, without moving them, until golden brown, 3 to 4 minutes. Using 2 spatulas, carefully flip patties. Add 1 tablespoon oil, reduce heat to medium-low, and continue to cook until second side is golden brown, 4 to 6 minutes longer. Transfer cakes to platter. Wipe out skillet and repeat with remaining 4 patties and remaining 2 tablespoons oil. Serve immediately.

accompaniment

Rémoulade Sauce

MAKES ABOUT ½ CUP

½ cup mayonnaise
½ teaspoon capers, drained and rinsed
½ teaspoon Dijon mustard
1 small garlic clove, chopped coarse
1½ teaspoons sweet pickle relish
1 teaspoon hot sauce
1 teaspoon lemon juice
1 teaspoon minced fresh parsley
Salt and pepper

Pulse all ingredients except salt and pepper in food processor until well combined but not smooth, about 10 pulses. Season with salt and pepper to taste. Transfer to serving bowl. (Rémoulade can be refrigerated for up to 3 days.)

PAELLA ON THE GRILL

LAN LAM, *July/August 2016*

If you've ever made paella, you probably know that no two versions of this famous Spanish rice dish are prepared the same way. The basic template consists of medium-grain rice cooked in a wide, shallow vessel (traditionally, a *paellera*) with a flavor base called *sofrito*, broth and maybe wine, and a jumble of meat and/or seafood. Within this framework, the proteins can be anything from poultry to pork to any species of shellfish; the seasonings may include garlic, saffron, smoked paprika—or all of the above; and the embellishments might be peas, bell peppers, or lemon. As the rice absorbs the liquid, the grains in contact with the pan form a caramelized crust known as *socarrat*—the most prized part of the dish. The final product is colorful and flavor-packed: a one-pot showpiece that's perfect for entertaining.

What you might not know is that while most modern recipes are cooked on the stove or in the oven, paella was originally made on the grill, and many Spanish cooks still make it that way today. The live fire gives the dish a subtle smokiness and provides an extra-large cooking surface that encourages even socarrat development—a distinct advantage over a stove's burners or the indirect heat of an oven, which often yield a spotty or pale crust.

Adding each ingredient at the right time—and in the right place—is key to perfect grilled paella.

But in my experience, grilling comes with challenges of its own. Besides the usual problem—the quicker-cooking proteins overcook while they wait for heartier items to cook through—keeping a charcoal fire alive can be tricky. Plus, most recipes call for a paella pan, which only enthusiasts keep on hand.

The grilled paella I had in mind would feature tender-chewy rice strewn with moist chicken, sausage, and shellfish; a uniformly golden, crisp crust; and an efficient, reliable cooking method.

GETTING SET UP

A paella pan alternative had to be grill-safe, deep enough to accommodate the food (I wanted a recipe that serves eight), and broad to maximize the amount of socarrat. A disposable aluminum pan was large enough, but its flimsy walls made it a nonstarter given the hefty amount of food I was cooking. But a sturdy stainless-steel roasting pan was easy to maneuver, and its surface area was generous—three times as spacious as a large Dutch oven. I worried that the pan's underside would darken on the grill, but during testing I quickly discovered that the exterior stayed remarkably clean on both charcoal and gas grills.

As for the fire setup, I needed a single layer of coals to expose the pan's base to even heat, but I also needed long-lasting heat output that wouldn't require refueling. So I lit 7 quarts (rather than our usual 6 quarts) of charcoal and poured them evenly across the kettle's surface, hoping that would be enough. (On a gas grill, I'd simply crank the burners to high.)

STAGGERING ALONG

Knowing I'd have to stagger the additions of the proteins to get them to finish cooking at the same time, I first set the roasting pan over the fire and browned boneless, skinless chicken thighs (richer in flavor than breasts) that I'd halved for easier portioning. From there, I pushed the meat to the side, sautéed the sofrito (finely chopped onion, bell pepper, and tomato) until it softened, and followed with minced garlic, smoked paprika, and saffron. Then came the rice. Traditional Bomba and Valencia have more bite than other medium-grain rices, but Arborio is easier to find and made a good substitute. I stirred it in with a mixture of chicken broth, clam juice, and dry sherry that I hoped would highlight the proteins. Once the rice had absorbed most of the liquid, I scattered chunks of slightly spicy, smoky, cured Spanish chorizo; shrimp (seasoned first with oil, garlic, smoked paprika, and salt); and littleneck clams over the top and let the paella cook until the grains were plump and the underside sizzled—the audible cue that a flavorful crust was forming.

My staggering strategy wasn't quite right. The chicken was a tad dry, while the sausage wasn't warmed through and the shellfish were just shy of done. Maybe part of the problem was not only when I was adding the proteins but also where I was placing them in the pan. Thinking that the thighs would stay moist if they cooked more gently, I arranged them around the cooler perimeter of the pan. As for the chorizo, shrimp, and clams, they merely sat on top of the rice and received relatively little heat when I added them after most of the liquid had been absorbed. Instead, I partially submerged the shrimp and clams (hinge side down so that their juices could be absorbed by the rice) in the center of the rice after the liquid came to a simmer and then scattered the chorizo over top. As the liquid reduced, all three components would stay warm without overcooking.

DIVIDE AND CONQUER

Back to the heat output: The larger fire almost held out until the rice was cooked. But to completely close the gap between the cooking time and the fuel output, I made adjustments to both.

First, I covered the lit coals with 20 fresh briquettes that would gradually ignite during cooking. Next, I seared the chicken thighs directly on the grates rather than in the roasting pan (they'd still finish cooking at the edges of the pan). They browned in half the time and picked up valuable grill flavor.

Then, I retooled the sofrito to make it quicker. Instead of waterlogged fresh peppers and tomato, I used roasted red peppers and

tomato paste—shortcuts to the caramelized sweetness achieved in a long-cooked sofrito. I also divided the sofrito into two parts, sautéing the peppers with the onions in the roasting pan but adding the tomato paste and aromatics (toasted first to deepen their flavor) to the cooking liquids. Finally, I brought the seasoned broth to a boil in a saucepan so that it would quickly simmer when I poured it into the roasting pan.

Finally, the proteins were spot-on, but I took a couple of extra steps to ensure that the rice cooked evenly from top to bottom, periodically shuffling the pan around over the fire to avoid any hot spots and scraping a corner of the rice with a spoon to track the socarrat development. When the grains were almost cooked through, I scattered thawed frozen peas over the surface (they would add sweet pop and color) and covered the grill so that the trapped steam would heat them through and finish cooking any underdone grains at the surface.

The finished paella was a stunner—as impressive to eat as it was to behold. And now that I had the blueprint for making it successfully on the grill, I wasn't sure I'd ever go back to the indoor version.

SCRUBBING CLAMS

After being dug, clams are often held on flats submerged in salt water for several days. During this time they expel grit; scrubbing is only necessary to remove exterior sand and grit before cooking.

Use soft brush (sometimes sold as vegetable brush) to scrub away any bits of sand trapped in shells.

Paella on the Grill

SERVES 8

This recipe was developed using a light-colored 16 by 13.5-inch tri-ply roasting pan; however, it can be made in any heavy roasting pan that measures at least 14 by 11 inches. If your roasting pan is dark in color, the cooking times will be on the lower end of the ranges given. The recipe can also be made in a 15- to 17-inch paella pan. If littlenecks are unavailable, use 1½ pounds of shrimp in step 1 and season them with ½ teaspoon salt.

1½ pounds boneless, skinless chicken thighs, trimmed and halved crosswise
Salt and pepper
12 ounces jumbo shrimp (16 to 20 per pound), peeled and deveined
6 tablespoons extra-virgin olive oil
6 garlic cloves, minced
1¾ teaspoons hot smoked paprika
3 tablespoons tomato paste
4 cups chicken broth
1 (8-ounce) bottle clam juice
⅔ cup dry sherry
Pinch saffron threads (optional)
1 onion, chopped fine
½ cup jarred roasted red peppers, chopped fine
3 cups Arborio rice
1 pound littleneck clams, scrubbed
1 pound Spanish-style chorizo, cut into ½-inch pieces
1 cup frozen peas, thawed
Lemon wedges

1. Place chicken on large plate and sprinkle both sides with 1 teaspoon salt and 1 teaspoon pepper. Toss shrimp with 1 tablespoon oil, ½ teaspoon garlic, ¼ teaspoon paprika, and ¼ teaspoon salt in bowl until evenly coated. Set aside.

2. Heat 1 tablespoon oil in medium saucepan over medium heat until shimmering. Add remaining garlic and cook, stirring constantly, until garlic sticks to bottom of saucepan and begins to brown, about 1 minute. Add tomato paste and remaining 1½ teaspoons paprika and continue to cook, stirring constantly, until dark brown bits form on bottom of saucepan, about 1 minute. Add broth, clam juice, sherry, and saffron, if using. Increase heat to high and bring to boil. Remove saucepan from heat and set aside.

3A. ***For a charcoal grill:*** Open bottom vent completely. Light large chimney starter mounded with charcoal briquettes (7 quarts). When top coals are partially covered with ash, pour evenly over grill. Using tongs, arrange 20 unlit briquettes evenly over coals. Set cooking grate in place, cover, and open lid vent completely. Heat grill until hot, about 5 minutes.

3B. ***For a gas grill:*** Turn all burners to high, cover, and heat grill until hot, about 15 minutes. Leave all burners on high.

4. Clean and oil cooking grate. Place chicken on grill and cook until both sides are lightly browned, 5 to 7 minutes total. Return chicken to plate. Clean cooking grate.

5. Place roasting pan on grill (turning burners to medium-high if using gas) and add remaining ¼ cup oil. When oil begins to shimmer, add onion, red peppers, and ½ teaspoon salt. Cook, stirring frequently, until onion begins to brown, 4 to 7 minutes. Add rice (turning burners to medium if using gas) and stir until grains are well coated with oil.

6. Arrange chicken around perimeter of pan. Pour broth mixture and any accumulated juices from chicken over rice. Smooth rice into even layer, making sure nothing sticks to sides of pan and no rice rests atop chicken. When liquid reaches gentle simmer, place shrimp in center of pan in single layer. Arrange clams in center of pan, evenly distributing with shrimp and pushing hinge sides of clams into rice slightly so they stand up. Distribute chorizo evenly over surface of rice. Cook (covered if using gas), moving and rotating pan to maintain gentle simmer across entire surface of pan, until rice is almost cooked through, 12 to 18 minutes. (If using gas, heat can also be adjusted to maintain simmer.)

7. Sprinkle peas evenly over paella, cover grill, and cook until liquid is fully absorbed and rice on bottom of pan sizzles, 5 to 8 minutes. Continue to cook, uncovered, checking bottom of pan frequently with metal spoon, until uniform golden-brown crust forms, 8 to 15 minutes longer. (Rotate and slide pan around grill as necessary to ensure even crust formation.) Remove pan from grill, cover with aluminum foil, and let stand for 10 minutes. Serve with lemon wedges.

A BLUEPRINT FOR PAELLA ON THE GRILL

Producing perfectly cooked paella on the grill isn't hard; it just takes some planning as to exactly where and when to add each element.

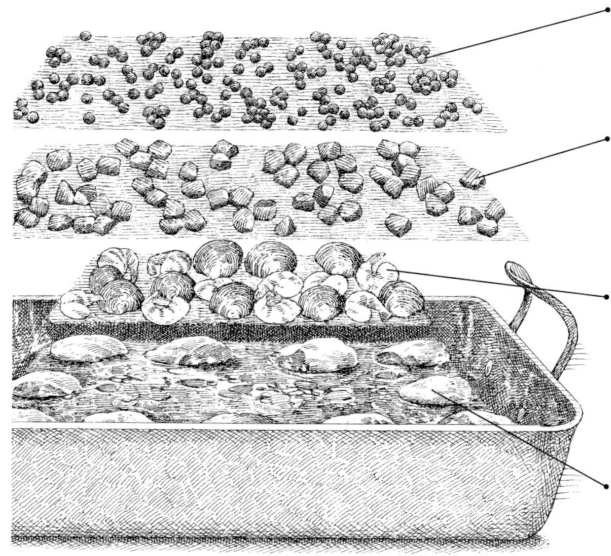

PEAS Scattered across the surface at the end of cooking, the peas stay plump.

CHORIZO Added before the liquid is absorbed, the pre-cooked cured sausage warms through without drying out.

SHRIMP & CLAMS Partially submerging the shellfish in the simmering liquid in the center of the pan ensures that they stay warm without overcooking.

CHICKEN After being seared on the grill, the thighs are arranged around the pan's cooler perimeter, where they cook through slowly and gently.

LARGE ROASTING PAN Thanks to the roasting pan's generous surface area—nearly triple that of a Dutch oven—the rice develops lots of the prized crust called *socarrat*. (Don't worry; the pan won't burn.)

WHY START ON THE STOVE?

Most of the cooking for our Paella on the Grill is done outside, but starting on the stove helps to streamline and speed up the recipe.

SIMPLIFY THE SOFRITO Tomatoes are an essential part of the *sofrito*, or flavor base, of paella, but fresh tomatoes contain a lot of liquid that must be cooked off. Instead, we use tomato paste and bloom it on the stove along with the garlic and paprika.

MAKE A WARM, FLAVORFUL BROTH We build a flavor-packed broth by adding chicken broth, clam juice, sherry, and saffron to our tomato paste base. Bringing this mixture to a boil before grilling warms it up so that it simmers quickly once added to the roasting pan.

SETTING UP THE GRILL FOR PAELLA

Our typical single-level fire wasn't cutting it for our Paella on the Grill. Here's how we solved the problem.

When using a charcoal grill, we add 7 quarts of lit coals (rather than the usual 6) to the grill, then top the coals with 20 unlit briquettes to keep the fire burning long enough to complete the recipe.

GETTING TO KNOW SAFFRON

A key flavor component in dishes like paella, saffron is sometimes called "red gold," and is the world's most expensive spice. It's made from the dried stigmas of *Crocus sativus* flowers; the stigmas are so delicate they must be harvested by hand in a painstaking process. (It takes about 200 hours to pick enough stigmas to produce just 1 pound of saffron, which typically sells for thousands of dollars.)

Luckily, a little saffron goes a long way, adding a distinct reddish-gold color, notes of honey and grass, and a slight hint of bitterness. You can find it as powder or threads, but we've found threads are more common. The major producers are Iran and Spain; the saffron you find in the supermarket is usually Spanish. Look for bottles that contain dark red threads—saffron is graded, and the richly hued, high-grade threads from the top of the stigma yield more flavor than the lighter, lesser-grade threads from the base.

Bambino
Udmalbet
White Round
Apple Green
Rosa Bianca
Bianca Oval
Kermit
Auberaine du Burkina-Faso
Santana
Lilac Bride
Comprido
Louisiana Long Green

VEGETARIAN MAINS

HOW TO COOK EGGPLANT

STEPHEN SCHMIDT, *July/August 1993*

Many people complain that their eggplant dishes are either tough, pithy, and astringently bitter, or oil-soaked, slimy, and tasteless. This is not inevitable. Eggplant can (and should) be firm and meaty, with a rich, sweet, nut-like flavor. As many cookbooks tell you, this effect can only be achieved if the eggplant is macerated in salt, rinsed, and then pressed nearly dry before cooking. Now that I have experimented with eggplant in a formal and systematic way, I better understand why this procedure works and how best to do it.

DEALING WITH EXCESSIVE LIQUID

I always thought that the reason you had to rid eggplant of much of its liquid before cooking is because the liquid is bitter. It turns out, however, that this is not the case. The real problem is that eggplant is packed with water. When I dried inch-thick slices in the oven, for example, they lost two-thirds of their weight long before they were dry.

Eggplant is extremely porous. When not first salted and pressed, it drinks up oil like a sponge, presenting cooks with two equally bad options: To keep the eggplant from sticking and burning, he or she can simply quit frying it long before it is cooked through. Unfortunately, this leaves the eggplant tough and bitter. Alternatively, the cook can continue to pour more oil into the pan and keep cooking the eggplant until tender. But, with all that juice turning to steam inside it, the eggplant dissolves into a soupy, oil-soaked mush by the time it is cooked.

The solution is salting. Salt draws water out of cells by creating such a high concentration of dissolved ions outside the cell walls that water inside is drawn out. Salting alone, however, is not sufficient. The flesh of the eggplant must also be firmly pressed between sheets of paper towels; pressing extrudes the juice and compacts the flesh.

To confirm this, I generously salted ¾-inch eggplant slices and let them sit for a full 5 hours. I then divided the slices into two equal portions. The first portion I just rinsed and patted lightly with paper towels; the second portion I pressed until the flesh had shrunk in both weight and volume by roughly half and had become a translucent brownish-green. I then sautéed each batch separately in a 9-inch nonstick skillet over medium-low heat, using 1½ tablespoons of olive oil each time.

Salting and then pressing eggplant rids it of excess moisture, producing a firm, meaty texture that takes well to caramelization.

The slices that had been only patted dry drank up every drop of oil almost at once, and ended up tasting greasy and bland. Furthermore, they become so mushy that they all but fell apart on the spatula when I removed them from the pan. The pressed slices, by contrast, absorbed just a teaspoon of the olive oil, and they turned out delicious—firm, sweet, and covered on both sides with a lovely crisp, chewy, caramelized glaze.

Finally, to make sure that salting actually was a prerequisite to pressing, I attempted to press some unsalted eggplant slices. As I had expected, they were too punky to bear the pressure and simply crumbled when pressed; sautéed, they turned to mush.

For the salt to do its job, eggplant must macerate for at least 1½ hours, preferably for two to three. But I found that steaming is an acceptable last-minute alternative. If short on time, steam the eggplant over rapidly boiling water for 3 to 5 minutes, or just until a firm pinch will dent it rather than causing it to break apart. Turn the eggplant out onto a triple thickness of paper towels and let it cool until it's comfortable to handle. Next, cover it with additional towels and press to release the moisture, exerting rather gentle pressure lest you mash it to a pulp. Steaming makes for a softer and less flavorful final result than salting, but it is far better than no preliminary attention at all.

PARTICULARS OF THE PROCESS

One bit of advice that I had sometimes ignored and sometimes heeded was to salt eggplant in a colander. My experiments indicate that this is indeed a good idea. Even after a thorough rinsing, eggplant that was macerated in a bowl was markedly saltier than that which had been drained in a colander, perhaps because it had been actually sitting in a salt water solution. Conscientious rinsing is also important: it not only floods away excess salt but softens the eggplant, facilitating pressing.

Then there is the matter of the skin. I have almost always peeled eggplant, believing that the skin would not soften sufficiently during cooking. But, when salted and pressed, whether broiled, baked, or fried, eggplant was delicious with the skin left on. When I simmered the sautéed eggplant in crushed tomatoes or in some other liquid, the peel was even further softened. Since the skin is not only pretty but also helps the pieces to hold their shape, it usually should be left on. Finally, no matter what the cooking method, eggplant always comes out firmer, browner, and sweeter when cooked slowly rather than quickly.

Broiled Eggplant Slices

SERVES 4 TO 6

As an alternative to broiling, you can bake the eggplant on the upper-middle rack of a 375-degree oven for 20 to 25 minutes, turning it once. You can substitute finely shredded fresh basil for the parsley, if desired.

- 2 pounds eggplant, cut crosswise into ¾-inch-thick rounds
- Kosher salt and pepper
- 2 tablespoons extra-virgin olive oil
- 4 teaspoons balsamic vinegar
- 2 garlic cloves, minced
- 2 tablespoons minced fresh parsley

1. Line baking sheet with triple layer of paper towels and set aside. Toss eggplant with 1 tablespoon salt in large bowl, transfer to colander, and let sit for at least 1½ hours or up to 3 hours, stirring periodically.
2. Wipe excess salt from eggplant. Lay eggplant slices about 1 inch apart on prepared baking sheet, then cover with another triple layer of paper towels. Using your palms, press each eggplant slice very firmly until it looks green and translucent and feels firm and leathery when pressed between your fingertips. (Repeat pressing on fresh towels if eggplant has not yet reached this stage.)
3. Adjust oven rack 8 inches from broiler element and heat broiler. Whisk together oil, vinegar, and garlic. Arrange eggplant slices on rimmed baking sheet and brush both sides with oil mixture. Broil eggplant until mahogany brown, 6 to 8 minutes per side. Sprinkle eggplant with parsley, season with salt and pepper to taste, and serve.

Sauteéd Eggplant

SERVES 4 TO 6

You can substitute finely shredded fresh basil for the parsley, if desired. Serve with rice.

- 2 pounds eggplant, cut crosswise into ¾-inch-thick rounds, then cut into ¾-inch strips
- Kosher salt and pepper
- 3 tablespoons extra-virgin olive oil
- 3 garlic cloves, minced
- 2 tablespoons minced fresh parsley

1. Line baking sheet with triple layer of paper towels and set aside. Toss eggplant with 1 tablespoon salt in large bowl, transfer to colander, and let sit for at least 1½ hours and up to 3 hours, stirring periodically.
2. Wipe excess salt from eggplant. Lay eggplant strips about 1 inch apart on prepared baking sheet, then cover with another triple layer of paper towels. Using your palms, press each eggplant strip very firmly until it looks green and translucent and feels firm and leathery when pressed between your fingertips. (Repeat pressing on fresh towels if eggplant has not yet reached this stage.)
3. Heat oil in 12-inch skillet over medium-high heat until shimmering. Add eggplant strips and cook until they begin to brown, about 3 minutes. Reduce heat to medium-low and cook, stirring occasionally, until eggplant is fully tender and lightly browned, 15 to 20 minutes. Stir in garlic and cook for 2 minutes. Off heat, stir in parsley, season with salt and pepper to taste, and serve.

variations

Sautéed Eggplant with Crisped Bread Crumbs

Pulse 1 slice hearty white sandwich bread, torn into quarters, in food processor to coarse crumbs, about 10 pulses. Add bread crumbs with garlic in step 3 and toss lightly to coat strips. Turn heat to high and cook until crumbs begin to brown, about 1 minute. Toss and continue to cook until crumbs are fully browned, about 1 minute longer. Substitute finely shredded fresh basil for parsley.

Sautéed Eggplant in Spicy Garlic Sauce

Any type of vinegar works in this recipe.

Combine 2 tablespoons dry sherry, 2 tablespoons soy sauce, 2 tablespoons vinegar, and 1 teaspoon sugar in small bowl; set aside. Substitute 2 tablespoons toasted sesame oil and 1 tablespoon peanut or vegetable oil for olive oil. Increase garlic to 6 cloves and add 2 teaspoons grated fresh ginger and ¼ teaspoon red pepper flakes with garlic in step 3. Cook 1 minute, add sherry mixture, and simmer until eggplant absorbs liquid, about 1 minute. Substitute 2 tablespoons minced fresh cilantro plus 2 tablespoons thinly sliced scallions for parsley.

Sautéed Eggplant in Tomato Sauce with Basil

Stir in 1¼ cups crushed tomatoes after garlic has cooked for 1 minute. Simmer until tomatoes thicken slightly, 2 to 3 minutes. Substitute ⅓ cup finely shredded fresh basil for parsley.

PRESSING EGGPLANT

Press eggplant firmly to give it a drier, more compact structure for easier cooking.

EGGPLANT VARIETIES

Four of the most common varieties of eggplant are large globe, small Italian, slender Chinese, and apple-shaped Thai. We've found the globe eggplant to be the most versatile. Globe eggplants contain fewer seeds than their sister varieties, and their firm flesh retains its shape after cooking, making them an ideal choice for most cooking applications. When shopping, look for eggplants that are firm, with smooth skin and no soft or brown spots. They should feel heavy for their size. Eggplants are very perishable and will get bitter if they overripen, so aim to use them within a day or two. They can be stored in a cool, dry place short-term, but for more than one or two days, refrigeration is best.

GLOBAL FAVORITE

MAIN-DISH VEGETABLE STIR-FRIES

DAVID PAZMIÑO, *May/June 2006*

For a fast and easy weeknight dinner, it's hard to beat a stir-fry: Sliced meat and chopped vegetables are cooked quickly over high heat, then tossed with a bold-flavored sauce and served. Take out the meat, however, and this one-dish meal devolves into a side dish. The all-vegetable stir-fry has plenty of pleasing contrasts of flavor and texture but nothing substantial enough to anchor the dish firmly in entrée territory.

Unlike many of my colleagues, I was convinced there was a way to make a satisfying meal out of nothing but stir-fried vegetables. It wasn't the meat they were missing from these all-veggie stir-fries, I reasoned, but the meatiness. And with a few strategically chosen vegetables, I thought I could change the mind of even the most unapologetic carnivore in the test kitchen.

MEATY MUSHROOMS

Scanning the produce aisle of my supermarket, it wasn't hard to figure out where to start. If it was meaty heft and texture I was after, mushrooms were the obvious choice—specifically, hearty portobellos. To capitalize on their bulk and meatiness, I cut them into wedges large enough to stand out from the other vegetables.

The only problem now was the gills, which often broke off and muddied the sauce. I tried cooking the mushrooms on the tops only (to keep the gills intact), but this technique left the mushrooms leathery and raw-tasting. Scraping the gills off with a spoon before cooking solved the problem.

Meaty, hearty portobello mushrooms create a satisfying meatless stir-fry when seared and coated with a glossy glaze.

Now that I had settled on a cooking technique for my starring vegetable, it was time to move on to the supporting cast. Using the kitchen's tried-and-true procedure for stir-fries, I simply plugged in the portobellos where the sliced meat usually went: Cook the portobellos in batches and set them aside; steam-sauté the longer-cooking vegetables (such as carrots and broccoli) and set them aside; stir-fry the softer vegetables (such as celery and bell pepper), greens (napa cabbage or bok choy), and aromatics (garlic and ginger); then add all of the vegetables back to the pan along with a flavorful sauce.

The technique worked without a hitch, but I thought the portobellos could still be more distinct from the other vegetables. Taking another cue from meat stir-fries, I experimented with marinades and coatings, but to no avail. Soaking the mushrooms in a soy-based marinade left them soggy, slimy, and difficult to sear. Dipping them in different combinations of egg and cornstarch created a distinct crust initially, but the mushrooms' high moisture content eventually made the crust unappetizingly chewy and wet. A simple sear proved best after all, but I wondered if a glaze (made from my existing sauce ingredients) might help. Adding soy sauce, chicken broth, and sugar as the mushrooms finished cooking yielded a shiny, flavorful glaze that provided just the boost they had been lacking.

OTHER MEAT STAND-INS?

While not exactly a vegetable, firm tofu seemed promising as an easy stand-in for the mushrooms. Because it's packaged in water, tofu has a significant amount of moisture, so I first dredged it in cornstarch to give it some textural contrast. Not only was this method simple (no pressing or freezing, as so many other recipes required), but the results pleased even the skeptics who claimed they didn't like tofu.

My stir-fries are proof that I don't need meat to assemble a quick and substantial main course.

CHOOSING AND PREPARING VEGETABLES FOR A STIR-FRY

Portobello mushrooms and tofu are the mainstays in our stir-fries. As for the other vegetables, you can use those called for in the recipe or swap them with another vegetable from the same category below. We recommend using one longer-cooking vegetable, one quicker-cooking vegetable, and a leafy green.

LONGER-COOKING VEGETABLES (TO YIELD 2 CUPS)

CARROTS 4 small	Peeled, sliced on bias ¼ inch thick
BROCCOLI 8 ounces	Stalks discarded, florets cut into 1¼-inch pieces
CAULIFLOWER 8 ounces	Core removed, florets cut into 1¼-inch pieces
ASPARAGUS 1 pound medium	Bottoms trimmed, cut on bias into 1½-inch lengths
GREEN BEANS 8 ounces	Ends trimmed, cut on bias into 1½-inch lengths

QUICKER-COOKING VEGETABLES (TO YIELD 1 CUP)

BELL PEPPER 1 medium	Stemmed, seeded, and cut into ½-inch dice
SNOW PEAS 3 ounces	Strings and tough ends trimmed
CELERY 3 medium ribs	Ends trimmed, cut on bias ½ inch thick
ZUCCHINI OR SUMMER SQUASH 1 small	Seeded, quartered lengthwise, and cut on bias ¼ inch thick

LEAFY GREENS (TO YIELD 2 CUPS STEMS AND 4 CUPS GREENS)

BOK CHOY OR NAPA CABBAGE 1 small (about 1 pound)	Stems/cores and greens separated, Stems/cores cut into ¼-inch strips, greens into ¾-inch strips

Stir-Fried Portobellos with Ginger-Oyster Sauce

SERVES 3 TO 4

This stir-fry cooks quickly, so have everything chopped and ready before you begin to cook. Toast the sesame seeds (if using) in a dry skillet over medium heat until fragrant (about 1 minute), and then remove the pan from the heat so that the seeds won't scorch. Serve with rice.

Glaze
¼ cup chicken broth or vegetable broth
2 tablespoons soy sauce
2 tablespoons sugar

Sauce
1 cup chicken broth or vegetable broth
3 tablespoons oyster sauce
1 tablespoon soy sauce
1 tablespoon cornstarch
2 teaspoons toasted sesame oil

Vegetables
¼ cup vegetable oil
4 teaspoons grated fresh ginger
2 garlic cloves, minced
1½ pounds portobello mushroom caps, gills removed, caps cut into 2-inch wedges
3 carrots, peeled and sliced on bias ¼ inch thick
½ cup chicken broth or vegetable broth
1 pound bok choy, stalks sliced on bias into ¼-inch-wide strips, greens sliced into ¾-inch-wide strips
2 ounces snow peas, strings removed
1 tablespoon sesame seeds, toasted (optional)

1. *For the glaze:* Whisk broth, soy sauce, and sugar together in small bowl.
2. *For the sauce:* Whisk all ingredients together in second small bowl.
3. *For the vegetables:* Combine 1 teaspoon oil, ginger, and garlic in third small bowl and set aside. Heat 3 tablespoons oil in 12-inch nonstick skillet over medium-high heat until just smoking. Add mushrooms and cook, without stirring, until browned on 1 side, 2 to 3 minutes. (Skillet will be crowded at first; arrange mushrooms in single layer as they shrink.) Flip mushrooms, reduce heat to medium, and cook until second side is browned and mushrooms are tender, about 5 minutes. Increase heat to medium-high, add glaze, and cook, stirring constantly, until glaze is thickened and mushrooms are coated, 1 to 2 minutes. Transfer mushrooms to plate.
4. Heat 1 teaspoon oil in clean, dry skillet over medium-high heat until just smoking. Add carrots and cook, stirring occasionally, until beginning to brown, 1 to 2 minutes. Add broth, cover, and cook until carrots are just tender, 2 to 3 minutes. Uncover and cook until liquid evaporates, about 30 seconds. Transfer carrots to plate with mushrooms.
5. Heat remaining 1 teaspoon oil in now-empty skillet over medium-high heat until just smoking. Add bok choy stalks and snow peas and cook, stirring occasionally, until beginning to brown and soften, 1 to 2 minutes. Add bok choy greens and cook, stirring frequently, until wilted, about 1 minute.
6. Push vegetables to sides of skillet. Add ginger mixture to center and cook, mashing mixture into skillet, until fragrant, 15 to 20 seconds. Stir ginger mixture into vegetables.
7. Return mushrooms and carrots to skillet, add sauce, and cook, stirring constantly, until sauce is thickened and vegetables are coated, 2 to 3 minutes. Transfer to platter; sprinkle with sesame seeds, if using; and serve immediately.

USE A GENTLE TOUCH WHEN WASHING MUSHROOMS

Contrary to popular belief, you *can* wash mushrooms—you just want to avoid overdoing it. In the test kitchen, we place whole mushrooms in a colander, rinse them gently under cool running water, and then immediately pat them dry with paper towels. Keep in mind that this only applies to whole mushrooms: The exposed flesh of cut mushrooms will soak up water like a sponge, so clean mushrooms before slicing them.

variations

Stir-Fried Portobellos with Sweet Chili-Garlic Sauce

Substitute honey for sugar in glaze. For sauce, reduce broth to ¾ cup, increase soy sauce to 3 tablespoons, and substitute 2 tablespoons honey, 1 tablespoon rice vinegar, and 1 teaspoon Asian chili-garlic sauce for oyster sauce and sesame oil. In step 3, increase garlic to 4 cloves.

Stir-Fried Tofu with Ginger-Oyster Sauce

Cut 14 ounces extra-firm tofu into 24 triangles by holding chef's knife parallel to cutting board and cutting block in half horizontally to form 2 rectangular planks, cutting each plank into 6 squares, then cutting each square diagonally into 2 triangles. Spread ⅓ cup cornstarch in baking dish; dredge tofu in cornstarch to evenly coat. Heat 3 tablespoons vegetable oil in 12-inch nonstick skillet over medium-high heat until shimmering, add tofu in single layer, and cook until golden brown, 4 to 6 minutes. Gently flip tofu; cook until second sides are golden brown, 4 to 6 minutes. Add glaze to skillet and cook, stirring, until glaze is thick and tofu is coated, 1 to 2 minutes. Transfer tofu to plate. Substitute tofu for portobellos.

PREPARING PORTOBELLO MUSHROOMS FOR STIR-FRY

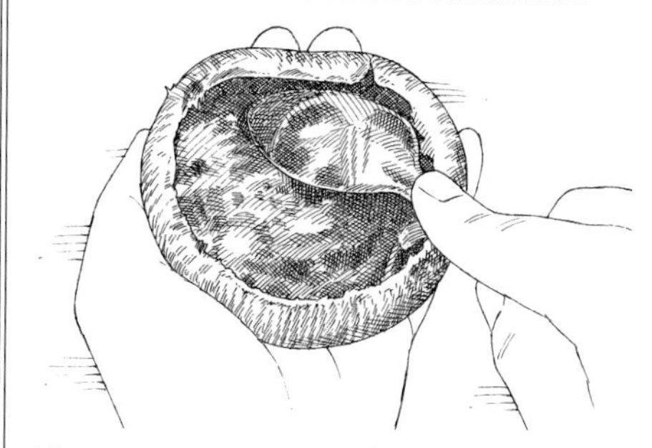

After removing stem, gently scrape underside of mushroom with dinner spoon to remove feathery gills.

EGGPLANT INVOLTINI

ANDREA GEARY, *July/August 2014*

The first recipe I made for eggplant *involtini* ("little bundles" in Italian) was so complicated and messy that I wondered if it was the malicious invention of someone who wanted cooks to suffer.

It started innocently enough with a homemade tomato sauce. While that simmered, I cut two eggplants lengthwise into ½-inch-thick planks and fried them. Frying sounds like one step, but in this case it was actually several: Before frying, I had to salt the planks for 45 minutes to remove excess moisture, pat them dry, and coat them in flour, eggs, and bread crumbs. After doing that with four batches, I was still only halfway done.

I mixed up a ricotta filling, spread a dollop of it on each slice, rolled up the slices, and arranged them in a baking dish. I poured the sauce over the bundles, topped the assembly with mozzarella and Parmesan, and baked it for 30 minutes—barely enough time to clear up the devastation my project had left in its wake.

The resulting dish was rich and hefty, similar to classic eggplant Parmesan, though the process had been slightly more arduous, thanks to that rolling-rather-than-layering step. While eggplant Parmesan is justifiably popular, both the making and the eating are a bit heavy going for the height of summer.

But I was charmed by those tidy little involtini, and the combination of eggplant, tomato sauce, and cheese has timeless appeal. My goal: Come up with a version of involtini that would emphasize the eggplant and minimize the fuss.

THE (NOT SO) BITTER TRUTH

Many eggplant recipes begin by treating the cut fruit with a heavy dose of salt to draw out excess moisture. It supposedly pulls out bitterness, too.

Let's start with the second claim: It's true that unsalted eggplant can taste a tad bitter from compounds called alkaloids that are found under the skin and in the seeds, but salt doesn't really draw many of those compounds out. As we've found with other bitter-tasting foods, such as coffee and grapefruit, salt merely masks bitter flavors; it doesn't eliminate them. And though eggplants were once very bitter indeed, as food scientist Harold McGee points out in *On Food and Cooking* (2004), this trait has been reduced through selective breeding methods. In short, bitterness is less of an issue than it once was. But the excess water problem? That's real.

We streamline this Italian classic by baking instead of frying eggplant and making the sauce in a skillet.

The flesh of an eggplant is made up of millions of tiny air-filled compartments enclosed by water-fortified walls. If you fry eggplant without removing some of that water beforehand, two things happen: First, those air sacs flood with oil, turning the eggplant greasy. Second, when heat turns the water to steam, some of it will become trapped in the eggplant's flesh. And as the steam forcibly tries to escape, it will damage the structure of the fruit. The result? Mushy, oily, and entirely unappetizing eggplant.

When you salt eggplant, some of that water is removed, so the walls of the air sacs weaken and collapse. That sounds bad, but it's actually good: The end result is eggplant with a more compact, meatier consistency. And a denser texture means that there are fewer places for oil to get trapped.

But I didn't want to devote 45 minutes to drying out the eggplant if I didn't have to. Instead, I tried a test kitchen shortcut: microwaving the planks in a single layer for about 6 minutes. Unfortunately, the microwave's limited capacity meant that I could work with only one-quarter of the eggplant at a time, so 12 slices of eggplant required almost half an hour of intermittent engagement. It wasn't ideal.

BAKE IT BETTER

By this time there was a rebellious thought lurking in the back of my mind: Maybe I wouldn't fry the eggplant. True, most recipes I found required frying the planks, either breaded or plain, but I was after a simpler, lighter, cleaner-tasting dish. And if I didn't fry, maybe I wouldn't have to salt.

Recipes for grilled eggplant rarely call for preliminary salting. That's because there's little oil on the grill for the flesh to soak up, and the eggplant's excess water quickly evaporates. I wasn't about to fire up the grill, but I wondered if other dry-heat cooking methods might offer the same benefits.

I peeled two eggplants and cut them into ½-inch-thick planks. I then brushed the planks with oil, seasoned them with salt and pepper, and baked them on two greased parchment-lined baking sheets in a 375-degree oven for about 30 minutes. Happily, they emerged light brown and tender, with a compact texture that was neither mushy nor sodden. Though the tops and sides of the slices had dried out nicely, there was still a bit of residual moisture on the undersides, so I let the planks cool and firm up on the baking sheet for 5 minutes and then flipped them to allow the remaining steam to escape. These slices were meaty and tender, but not at all squishy, and I didn't miss frying. It was time to move on to the filling.

LESS CHEESE, MORE FLAVOR

Ricotta, which forms the base for most involtini fillings, is subtle, so you have to use a lot of it if you want it to stand up to the tomato sauce. But for these lighter involtini, I wanted to decrease the overall amount of cheese. Swapping some of the ricotta for a lesser amount of a more assertive cheese seemed like the way to go.

I limited myself to 1 cup of ricotta, which was half the amount required by that initial recipe. Adding ½ cup of grated Pecorino, a ¼ cup of chopped basil, and some lemon juice bumped up the flavor, but the texture was unexpectedly tight and bouncy.

I realized that the Pecorino, which is a dry, aged cheese, was the source of that tight, granular texture. Just a small handful was fine, but when I added a full ½ cup to 1 cup of ricotta, the texture of the filling deteriorated from creamy to firm. In fact, it reminded me of ground meat that had been overcooked, and I wondered if it was indeed the same problem: an excessive linking of proteins. And that thought led me to the solution: bread crumbs.

When you add a paste of bread crumbs and milk (called a panade) to ground meat, it interferes with the linking of the meat proteins so that the cooked meat stays loose and soft. Bingo. When I incorporated just one slice of bread, whizzed to crumbs in the food processor, into the ricotta-Pecorino combo (no milk required), the filling remained creamy.

STREAMLINING THE SAUCE

It was time to circle back to the beginning: the tomato sauce. The placeholder recipe I had been working with called for sautéing onions and garlic, adding canned diced tomatoes and seasonings, and simmering the sauce for at least an hour. It wasn't all that onerous, but my success with the eggplant and the filling had raised the bar, and now I demanded a sauce that could be made from start to finish while the eggplant had its 30-minute stint in the oven.

Diced tomatoes don't break down easily because they're treated with calcium chloride during processing to help them keep their chunky shape, hence the lengthy cooking time. I swapped the diced tomatoes for more-tender canned whole tomatoes (where the calcium chloride works only on the exterior of the tomato) that I chopped roughly, and the sauce came together in about half the time. To trim a few more minutes, I stripped the sauce down to the bare bones: just garlic, oregano, tomatoes, and a pinch of red pepper flakes. This simpler sauce fit perfectly into my more streamlined dish.

Between ditching the salting, trading frying for baking, and making a quick—rather than long-simmered—sauce, I had saved loads of time on prep, but it occurred to me that I could save a bit more time on cleanup, too. I made the sauce in a 12-inch skillet instead of a saucepan, and I nestled the filled eggplant rolls directly in the simmering sauce. When the rolls had begun to warm through, I moved the whole skillet to the broiler instead of the oven.

After about 5 minutes, the eggplant was nicely browned and the sauce was bubbly and hot. I let my creation cool slightly and then crowned it with an additional dusting of Pecorino and a sprinkling of basil before serving directly from the skillet.

No one would mistake this light, fresh skillet supper for rich and heavy eggplant Parmesan. The eggplant truly shines, and the cheese and sauce complement it rather than weigh it down. And the best part might just be how easy it is to make—no one will ever blame me for taking advantage of a cook's precious time.

Eggplant Involtini

SERVES 4 TO 6

Select shorter, wider eggplants for this recipe. Part-skim ricotta may be used, but do not use fat-free ricotta. Serve the eggplant with crusty bread and a salad.

2 large eggplants (1½ pounds each), peeled and sliced lengthwise into ½-inch-thick planks (12 planks), end pieces trimmed to lie flat
6 tablespoons vegetable oil
Kosher salt and pepper
2 garlic cloves, minced
¼ teaspoon dried oregano
Pinch red pepper flakes
1 (28-ounce) can whole peeled tomatoes, drained, juice reserved, and tomatoes chopped coarse
1 slice hearty white sandwich bread, torn into 1-inch pieces
8 ounces (1 cup) whole-milk ricotta cheese
1½ ounces Pecorino Romano cheese, grated (¾ cup)
¼ cup plus 1 tablespoon chopped fresh basil
1 tablespoon lemon juice

1. Adjust 1 oven rack to lower-middle position and second rack 8 inches from broiler element. Heat oven to 375 degrees. Line 2 rimmed baking sheets with parchment paper and spray generously with vegetable oil spray. Brush both sides of eggplant slices with 2½ tablespoons oil, then season with ½ teaspoon salt and ¼ teaspoon pepper. Flip slices over and repeat on second side with another 2½ tablespoons oil, ½ teaspoon salt, and ¼ teaspoon pepper. Arrange eggplant slices in single layer on prepared baking sheets. Bake until tender and lightly browned, 30 to 35 minutes, switching and rotating sheets halfway through baking. Let eggplant cool for 5 minutes, then flip each slice over using thin spatula.
2. Meanwhile, heat remaining 1 tablespoon oil in 12-inch broiler-safe skillet over medium-low heat until shimmering. Add garlic, oregano, pepper flakes, and ½ teaspoon salt and cook until fragrant, about 30 seconds. Stir in tomatoes and their juice, increase heat to high, and bring to simmer. Reduce heat to medium-low and simmer until thickened, about 15 minutes. Remove from heat and cover to keep warm.
3. Pulse bread in food processor until finely ground, 10 to 15 pulses. Combine bread crumbs, ricotta, ½ cup Pecorino, ¼ cup basil, lemon juice, and ½ teaspoon salt in bowl.
4. With widest short side of eggplant facing you, spoon about 3 tablespoons ricotta mixture over bottom third of each eggplant slice (use slightly more filling for larger slices and slightly less for smaller slices). Gently roll up each eggplant slice.
5. Heat broiler. Place eggplant rolls seam side down in tomato sauce in skillet. Bring sauce to simmer over medium heat and cook for 5 minutes. Transfer skillet to oven and broil until eggplant is well browned and cheese is heated through, 5 to 10 minutes. Remove from broiler. Sprinkle with remaining ¼ cup Pecorino and let stand 5 minutes. Sprinkle with remaining 1 tablespoon basil and serve.

BEST VEGETABLE CURRY

REBECCA HAYS, *May/June 2007*

The term "curry" is derived from the Tamil word *kari*, which simply means "sauce" or "gravy." There are thousands of ways to make curry. When flavorful beef or lamb is the main ingredient, even a mediocre recipe usually yields a decent outcome. But vegetable curry is a different story: It's all too easy to turn out a second-rate, if not awful, dish. Delicate vegetables are often watery carriers for the sauce, offering little personality of their own.

Vegetable curries can be complicated affairs, with lengthy ingredient lists and fussy techniques meant to compensate for the lack of meat. But I wanted something simpler—a curry I could make on a weeknight in less than an hour. Most streamlined recipes I tried, however, were uninspired. A few attempted to make up for the flavor deficit by overloading the dish with spices, and the results were harsh and overpowering. I had my work cut out for me.

While some curries are made with exotic whole and ground spices (fenugreek, asafetida, dried rose petals, and so on), I decided to limit myself to everyday ground spices such as cumin, cloves, cardamom, cinnamon, and coriander. My testing dragged on for days, and it was hard to reach consensus in the test kitchen. Frankly, most of the homemade spice mixtures I tried were fine.

Blooming store-bought curry powder and garam masala makes a potent flavor base for our curry.

I had been reluctant to use store-bought curry powder, assuming its flavor would be inferior to a homemade blend, but it seemed worth a try. I was surprised when tasters liked the curry powder nearly as well as a homemade mixture made with seven spices. It turns out that store-bought curry powder contains some of the exotic spices I had dismissed at the outset. As long as I used enough, my recipe had decent flavor.

Looking for ways to improve the flavor of the curry powder, I tried toasting the spices in a skillet until their seductive aroma emerged. This simple step took just 1 minute and turned commercial curry powder into a flavor powerhouse. Why was toasting so beneficial? When added to a simmering sauce, spices can be heated to only 212 degrees. In a dry skillet, temperatures can exceed 500 degrees, causing flavors to explode.

With the spices settled, I turned to building the rest of my flavor base. Many classic recipes begin with a generous amount of sautéed onion, which adds depth and body to the sauce, and I followed suit. Ghee (clarified butter) is traditionally used to sauté the onions. It adds terrific richness, though I found that vegetable oil was a fine substitute. Almost all curry recipes—meat and vegetable alike—add equal amounts of garlic and ginger to the onions, and I found no reason to stray from this well-balanced tradition. Wanting to take my meatless sauce to the next level, I stirred in a minced fresh chile for heat and a spoonful of tomato paste for sweetness. The latter ingredient was decidedly inauthentic, but I found it really helped. As the onions caramelized with the other ingredients, fond (flavorful dark bits) developed in the bottom of the pan, mimicking the phenomenon that occurs when browning meat. I then added the toasted curry powder to the pan and let it dissolve. Creating a supercharged base for my curry took just 15 minutes.

VEGETABLE PICKING

I decided to include chickpeas and potatoes for heartiness, along with one firm and one soft vegetable. Eventually, I settled on a classic pairing of cauliflower and peas. Although the combination of textures and colors was good, the vegetables were a bit bland. For meat curries, the beef or lamb is often added to the sauce without any prior flavor development, but I figured my vegetables should bring something to the dish. Oven roasting them definitely helped but took too much time. Instead, I tried browning the potatoes along with the onions. This unconventional move was an unqualified success, substantially boosting the flavor of the potatoes.

Could other vegetables come up in flavor, too? An Indian cooking method called *bhuna* involves sautéing the spices and main ingredients together to enhance and meld flavors. I tried this technique with cauliflower, as well as eggplant and green beans (used in a recipe variation), and they all developed a richer, more complex flavor. Next, I determined that a combination of water and pureed canned tomatoes, along with a splash of cream or coconut milk, allowed the delicate vegetables and fragrant spices to shine.

Lastly, I experimented with garam masala, a spice blend often sprinkled onto Indian dishes before serving. Like curry powder, garam masala varies among cooks but usually includes warm spices such as black pepper, cinnamon, coriander, and cardamom (its name means "hot spice" in Hindi). Following my success with the curry powder, I decided to buy a jar of commercial garam masala. But when I added a few pinches to the curry postcooking, the result was raw and harsh-tasting. What if I toasted the garam masala in a skillet along with the curry powder? Lightning did strike twice, as the garam masala mellowed into a second wave of flavor that helped the curry reach an even more layered complexity. Here was a robust, satisfying vegetable curry that relied on supermarket staples.

Indian-Style Curry with Potatoes, Cauliflower, Peas, and Chickpeas

SERVES 4 TO 6

Be sure to gather and prepare all of your ingredients before you begin cooking the curry. For a spicier curry, include the chile seeds and ribs. You can substitute 2 teaspoons ground coriander, ½ teaspoon ground black pepper, ¼ teaspoon ground cardamom, and ¼ teaspoon ground cinnamon for the garam masala. Serve the curry with rice, yogurt, and Cilantro-Mint Chutney and/or Onion Relish (recipes follow), if desired.

2 tablespoons sweet or mild curry powder
1½ teaspoons garam masala
¼ cup vegetable oil
3 garlic cloves, minced
1 tablespoon grated fresh ginger
1 serrano chile, stemmed, seeds and ribs removed, and minced
1 tablespoon tomato paste
1 (14.5-ounce) can diced tomatoes
2 onions, chopped fine
12 ounces red potatoes, unpeeled, cut into ½-inch chunks
1¼ pounds cauliflower florets, cut into 1-inch pieces
1 (15-ounce) can chickpeas, rinsed
1¼ cups water
Salt
1½ cups frozen peas
¼ cup heavy cream or coconut milk

1. Toast curry powder and garam masala in 8-inch skillet over medium-high heat, stirring occasionally, until spices darken slightly and become fragrant, about 1 minute. Transfer spices to small bowl; set aside. In separate small bowl, stir 1 tablespoon oil, garlic, ginger, serrano, and tomato paste together; set aside. Pulse tomatoes and their juice in food processor until coarsely chopped, 3 to 4 pulses; set aside.
2. Heat remaining 3 tablespoons oil in Dutch oven over medium-high heat until shimmering. Add onions and potatoes and cook, stirring occasionally, until onions are caramelized and potatoes are golden brown around edges, about 10 minutes. (Reduce heat to medium if onions darken too quickly.)
3. Reduce heat to medium. Clear center of pot, add garlic mixture, and cook, mashing mixture into pan, until fragrant, 15 to 20 seconds. Stir garlic mixture into vegetables. Add toasted spices and cook, stirring constantly, for 1 minute longer. Add cauliflower and cook, stirring constantly, until spices coat florets, about 2 minutes longer.
4. Add tomatoes, chickpeas, water, and 1 teaspoon salt, scraping up any browned bits. Bring to boil over medium-high heat. Cover, reduce heat to medium, and cook, stirring occasionally, until vegetables are tender, 10 to 15 minutes. Stir in peas and cream and continue to cook until heated through, about 2 minutes longer. Season with salt to taste, and serve.

KEYS TO BUILDING FLAVOR

We create big flavors in our vegetable curry using supermarket staples.

1. Toast the curry powder and garam masala in a dry skillet.

2. Add tomato paste to the traditional garlic, ginger, and chiles for sweetness and depth.

variation

Indian-Style Curry with Sweet Potatoes, Eggplant, Green Beans, and Chickpeas

Substitute 12 ounces sweet potato, peeled and cut into ½-inch pieces, for red potatoes. Substitute 8 ounces green beans, trimmed and cut into 1-inch pieces, and 1 pound eggplant, cut into ½-inch pieces, for cauliflower. Omit peas.

accompaniments

Cilantro-Mint Chutney

MAKES ABOUT 1 CUP

2 cups fresh cilantro leaves
1 cup fresh mint leaves
⅓ cup plain whole-milk yogurt
¼ cup finely chopped onion
1 tablespoon lime juice
1½ teaspoons sugar
½ teaspoon ground cumin
¼ teaspoon salt

Process all ingredients in food processor until smooth, about 20 seconds, scraping down sides of bowl halfway through processing. (Chutney can be refrigerated for up to 24 hours.)

Onion Relish

MAKES ABOUT 1 CUP

If using a regular yellow onion, increase the amount of sugar to 1 teaspoon.

1 Vidalia onion, chopped fine
1 tablespoon lime juice
½ teaspoon paprika
½ teaspoon sugar
⅛ teaspoon salt
Pinch cayenne pepper

Combine all ingredients in medium bowl. (Relish can be refrigerated for up to 24 hours.)

INDIAN-STYLE SPINACH WITH FRESH CHEESE

MATTHEW CARD, *September/October 2012*

As Indian restaurant classics go, *saag paneer* is right up there with wildly popular chicken tikka masala and crispy fried samosa triangles, and for good reason. The paneer—lightly firm, milky cubes of fresh homemade cheese—is simmered in a creamy spinach sauce that's heady with garlic, ginger, chiles, and warm spices. Served with a scoop of fragrant basmati rice, it's one of the most satisfying main dishes I know of—in any cuisine.

But as much as I love ordering the dish at restaurants, I've never tried making it. Why? Well, for one thing, you have to make your own cheese and I'd always assumed that would be a lot of trouble. But then I paged through a couple of Indian cookbooks and discovered that the method is dead simple. In fact, the whole dish looked surprisingly approachable, the familiar vegetables and spices erasing my preconceived notion that this entrée would require a slew of specialty purchases. Feeling confident (and hungry), I decided to give it a whirl.

THE WHEY TO CURDS

I wasn't kidding when I said the cheese-making process was simple. According to most Indian cookbooks I consulted, all you need to do is heat some milk (about 3 quarts to make enough cheese for four to six people), add acid to curdle it, strain off the whey, and press the remaining curds into a sliceable "cake." The result looks and tastes a bit like cottage cheese, but it's drier and firmer because much more of the water is pressed out. That said, there were some details to iron out—specifically, what kind of milk and acid to use. A dozen or so batches later I had my answers. First (and not surprisingly), whole milk made the creamiest, most full-flavored paneer by far. (Low-fat versions were passable.)

The other half of the equation—the acid—yielded a less predictable result. Plain old white vinegar and lemon juice are the most common coagulants used to curdle the milk, while some recipes called for buttermilk. The first two got the job done, but paneer made with buttermilk stood out as strikingly complex. One cup of buttermilk per quart of regular milk resulted in a cheese that was tender and creamy but still firm enough to hold its shape when simmered.

As for forming the curds into a cake, the method couldn't have been simpler: Drawing up the ends of the cheesecloth pouch, I squeezed the curds to wring out as much moisture as possible and then sandwiched the pouch between a pair of dinner plates and weighted the top with a Dutch oven. Forty-five minutes later—about the time that I guessed it would take me to put together the spinach sauce—I had a tender-firm block, which I sliced into tidy half-inch cubes. (In subsequent tests, I discovered that the cheese could be made up to three days ahead.)

We boost the flavor of the spinach sauce by adding mustard greens, buttermilk, and cashews.

MASALA MATTERS

On to the sauce. According to most recipes, this is simply a thick puree of sautéed spinach (bunched mature spinach for now—I'd test other varieties later), aromatics, and spices, plus a little milk or cream. Exactly which aromatics and spices went into the pan distinguished one regional variation from another, but I started with a typical combination of minced onion, chiles, generous spoonfuls of both garlic and ginger, whole cumin seeds, and ground coriander and cardamom, all sautéed in butter. My tasters deemed the heady mixture bold and complex but just a bit unbalanced, with the pungent aromatics overshadowing the warm spices. I saw to their complaint with a dash of cinnamon and an unusual (but not unheard-of) hit of sweet, earthy paprika.

I also followed the lead of the recipes that I came across that called for brightening the sauce with tomatoes. Fresh (and almost always out-of-season) tomatoes were dull and watery, while tomato paste deadened the sauté with its overly sweet, "cooked" flavors. I had better results with drained, diced canned tomatoes, which I added to the pan after the aromatics were brown and fragrant.

GOING GREEN

With the cheese and spices settled, I moved on to the meat—or, rather, vegetable—of the matter: the spinach. Because greens cook down a great deal, I needed nearly 2 pounds to make the sauce—but cleaning and stemming all that spinach was a pain. I'd hoped that frozen spinach would fit the bill, but no such luck. The defrosted leaves lacked the sweetness and depth of the fresh stuff. But bagged fresh curly spinach (which has been prewashed and stemmed) held its own against bunched spinach, so at least I could do away with all the cleaning.

That was one fussy spinach cookery step gone, but I had another to address: tediously sautéing the piles of spinach leaves in batches to drive off moisture and create a more manageable mass for pureeing. Hoping to streamline the process, I loaded the leaves into a large microwave-safe bowl and gave them a 3-minute zap. Sure enough, the once-fluffy pile had shrunk to a small flattened mound by the time the buzzer went off. I roughly chopped the wilted greens, which released more water, and into the blender they went with the sautéed aromatics.

Nobody disagreed that the recipe was getting close, but there was something missing—assertiveness, according to one taster, and maybe some texture to the sauce. I paged through some of the Indian cookbooks again and came across an intriguing idea. Apparently, some versions of saag paneer include a secondary, stronger-flavored green (saag, in fact, is a generic term for any leafy green), like kale, collards, or mustard greens. Intrigued, I paired each of these greens (also microwaved until wilted) with the spinach and was encouraged by the improved results. But it was the peppery bite of the mustard greens that magnified the flavors of both the spinach and the spices. To create texture in the sauce, I chopped and reserved ⅓ cup of each green (along with some of the aromatics and tomatoes) to add directly to the skillet.

As for the dairy component, I tried yogurt and cream, but buttermilk won out with its moderate richness and tang; plus, it was convenient, since I had leftovers from making the paneer. A brief simmer before adding the cheese tied all of the flavors together and tightened up the now-velvety sauce.

The texture of the sauce was just where I wanted it, but it didn't seem rich enough. As I was casting about for ideas, I noticed that the final dish is sometimes garnished with buttery cashews. Thinking that perhaps cashews were just what my recipe needed, I stirred a handful of finely chopped nuts into the sauce. They added richness without dulling the flavors one bit, but the gritty texture was objectionable. The solution proved as simple as pureeing the cashews into the sauce along with the other ingredients so that they added creaminess but went undetected. To finish the dish, I topped it with coarsely chopped cashews and chopped fresh cilantro.

With my final recipe, I can have an authentic-tasting rendition of my favorite Indian entrée within an hour—using supermarket staples. I've never been happier to have my assumptions proved wrong.

Indian-Style Spinach with Fresh Cheese (Saag Paneer)

SERVES 4 TO 6

To ensure that the cheese is firm, wring it tightly in step 2 and be sure to use two plates that nestle together snugly. Use commercially produced cultured buttermilk in this recipe. We found that some locally produced buttermilks didn't sufficiently coagulate the milk. Serve with basmati rice.

Cheese

3 quarts whole milk
3 cups buttermilk
1 tablespoon salt

Spinach Sauce

1 (10-ounce) bag curly-leaf spinach, rinsed
12 ounces mustard greens, stemmed and rinsed
3 tablespoons unsalted butter
1 teaspoon cumin seeds
1 teaspoon ground coriander
1 teaspoon paprika
½ teaspoon ground cardamom
¼ teaspoon ground cinnamon
1 onion, chopped fine
Salt and pepper
3 garlic cloves, minced
1 tablespoon grated fresh ginger
1 jalapeño chile, stemmed, seeded, and minced
1 (14.5-ounce) can diced tomatoes, drained and chopped coarse
½ cup roasted cashews, chopped coarse
1 cup water
1 cup buttermilk
3 tablespoons minced fresh cilantro

1. *For the cheese:* Line colander with triple layer of cheesecloth and set in sink. Bring milk to boil in Dutch oven over medium-high heat. Whisk in buttermilk and salt, turn off heat, and let stand for 1 minute. Pour milk mixture through cheesecloth and let curds drain for 15 minutes.

2. Pull edges of cheesecloth together to form pouch. Twist edges of cheesecloth together, firmly squeezing out as much liquid as possible from cheese curds. Place taut, twisted cheese pouch between 2 large plates and weigh down top plate with heavy Dutch oven. Set aside at room temperature until cheese is firm and set, about 45 minutes, then remove cheesecloth. (Cheese can be wrapped in plastic wrap and refrigerated for up to 3 days.) Cut cheese into ½-inch pieces.

3. *For the spinach sauce:* Microwave spinach in covered bowl until wilted, about 3 minutes. Let cool slightly, then chop enough spinach to measure ⅓ cup. Transfer remaining spinach to blender. Microwave mustard greens in covered bowl until wilted, about 4 minutes. Let cool slightly, then chop enough mustard greens to measure ⅓ cup; combine with chopped spinach. Transfer remaining mustard greens to blender with remaining spinach.

4. Meanwhile, melt butter in 12-inch skillet over medium-high heat. Add cumin seeds, coriander, paprika, cardamom, and cinnamon and cook until fragrant, about 30 seconds. Add onion and ¾ teaspoon salt and cook, stirring frequently, until softened, about 3 minutes. Stir in garlic, ginger, and jalapeño and cook, stirring frequently, until lightly browned and just beginning to stick to pan, 2 to 3 minutes. Stir in tomatoes and cook mixture until pan is dry and tomatoes are beginning to brown, 3 to 4 minutes. Remove skillet from heat.

5. Transfer half of onion mixture, ¼ cup cashews, and water to blender with greens and process until smooth, about 1 minute. Stir puree, chopped greens, and buttermilk into skillet with remaining onion mixture and bring to simmer over medium-high heat. Reduce heat to low, cover, and cook until flavors have blended, 5 minutes. Season with salt and pepper to taste. Gently fold in cheese cubes and cook until just heated through, 1 to 2 minutes. Transfer to serving dish, sprinkle with remaining ¼ cup cashews and cilantro, and serve.

RICE AND LENTILS WITH CRISPY ONIONS

ANDREW JANJIGIAN, *September/October 2014*

Whenever I eat the Levantine rice and lentil pilaf known as *mujaddara* (pronounced "MOO-ha-druh"), I think of an anecdote that cookbook author Claudia Roden recounts in *A Book of Middle Eastern Food* (1972). When her Egyptian aunt presented guests with this dish (which she called *megadarra*), she would ask them to excuse this food of the poor, to which they would reply: "Keep your food of kings and give us megadarra every day!"

That perfectly sums up my affection for the dish. Essentially the "rice and beans" of the Middle East, this might be the most spectacular example of how a few humble ingredients can add up to a dish that's satisfying, complex, and deeply savory. Though every household and restaurant differs in its approach, it's simple to throw together. Basically: Boil basmati rice and lentils together until each component is tender but intact, then work in warm spices such as coriander, cumin, cinnamon, all-spice, and pepper, as well as a good measure of minced garlic. But the real showpiece of the dish is the onions—either fried or caramelized—which get stirred into and sprinkled over the pilaf just before serving. Their flavor is as deep as their mahogany color suggests, and they break up the starchy components. Finished with a bracing garlicky yogurt sauce, this pilaf is comfort food at its best.

I had every intention of making this dish a regular weeknight main course in my house but, frankly, had been disappointed with the recipes I'd tried. They all could do a better job cooking the lentils and rice, which I've found either too firm or overcooked and mushy. And while the onions should be the best part, the ones I made were either leathery, cloyingly sweet, or too crunchy. I could—and would—do better.

A STAGGERED START

For any other lentil recipe, my first test might be to figure out which variety was best for the job, but in this case I knew that ordinary brown or green lentils were the way to go. When cooked properly, they become tender while just holding their shape—a consistency that ensures that they meld well with the tender-chewy rice. The other option, French *lentilles du Puy*, would remain too firm and distinct.

To streamline this comforting dish, we cook the rice and lentils together and parcook the onions before frying.

So I moved on to the cooking method. Lentil cookery is simple: Bring water to a boil with lentils (use a 4:1¼ ratio) and a dash of salt, reduce the heat to low and simmer until they're just tender, and drain.

But cooking lentils with rice was another matter, since I needed both components, which cook at different rates, to emerge evenly tender and also form a cohesive pilaf. I had two options: cook the rice and lentils in separate pots and fold them together or simmer them together in one pot, staggering their start times by parcooking the lentils until they are just tender, draining them, combining them with raw rice and a measured amount of water, and simmering until the liquid is absorbed. Or I could try a variation on the absorption approach, in which the rice and parcooked lentils are cooked pilaf-style—that is, toasted in fat before liquid is added.

After a battery of tests, it was clear that a combination of staggered and pilaf-style cooking was the way to go. Giving the lentils a 15-minute head start ensured that they finished cooking on pace with the rice. This step also allowed me to drain away their muddy cooking liquid before combining them with the rice, which made for a cleaner-looking dish. Toasting the rice in oil brought out the grain's nutty flavor and let me deepen the flavor of the spices and garlic by cooking them in the fat, too.

The one snag: Even after I parcooked the lentils, they still absorbed quite a bit of water, robbing the rice of the liquid it needed to cook through. Adding more water didn't help; the lentils soaked it up faster than the rice and turned mushy. Fortunately, I had solved a similar problem for Rice and Pasta Pilaf (page 327) when the pasta was absorbing too much liquid and leaving the rice dry. I soaked the raw rice in hot water for 15 minutes (while the lentils simmered), which softened the grains' exteriors so that they could absorb water more easily. Plus, this step loosened and washed away some of the starches, helping the rice cook up fluffy, not sticky.

OIL AND WATER

On to those onions. I wanted to go the deep-fried route, as the onions' crispy-chewy texture would be the perfect contrast to the soft pilaf. And given that I'd be both stirring the fried onions into the dish and using them as a garnish, I'd start with a generous 2 pounds so I'd have plenty even after the onions shrank way down during cooking.

The downsides of frying are the time it takes (multiple batches cooked for upwards of 30 minutes apiece) and the large amount of oil, so I made it my goal to cut down on both. Most of the cooking time is spent waiting for the water in the onions to boil away, so I thought about ways to rid the onions of some liquid before they hit the oil. The obvious answer: salt, the thirsty mineral we regularly use to pull water from vegetables.

So after cutting the onions into thin half-moons, I coated them with a couple of teaspoons of salt and let them sit. After 10 minutes, they'd shed a few tablespoons of water—encouraging results. I rinsed them to remove excess salt, dried them thoroughly, and fried them in two batches in a Dutch oven.

Frankly, the time savings were disappointing—just 5 minutes from each batch—so I took more drastic draining measures. After tossing the onions with the salt, I popped the bowl into the microwave for 5 minutes. Now I was getting somewhere: This two-step approach pulled more moisture from the slices and jump-started the cooking process. Still, batch frying was fussy and long; I was hovering over that pot of oil for more than 40 minutes, waiting for the heaps of onions to shrink and crisp.

That's when a thought occurred to me. The onions were initially piled high in the pot, but there was room to spare once they really started to cook down. Did I even need to bother with batch frying?

I sliced, salted, and microwaved another batch, this time piling all the onions into the pot at once, and turned the burner to high. Most of the onion slices started out well above the surface of the oil, but sure enough, they collapsed quickly and everything was soon fully submerged. About 25 minutes later, every last morsel was deeply golden and crispy with just a hint of chew. Not only that, but they were so far below the oil's surface that I felt bold and made another batch with just 1½ cups of oil—half the amount I'd been using. Happily, these were every bit as crispy and golden as the onions cooked in 3 cups of oil. I strained them and packed the onion-infused oil into a container to save, as it adds savory depth to salad dressings, sautés, and sauces.

In fact, why not swap the 3 tablespoons of oil that I was using for the pilaf for an equal amount of the reserved onion oil, boosting the savory flavor of the pilaf right from the start? I also added a touch of sugar to the rice and lentils to complement the warmth of the spices—a tweak I'd seen in a few mujaddara recipes. Many versions also suggested stirring in fresh herbs; I chose cilantro for its fresh, faintly citrusy flavor and bright color.

As I scooped myself a bowl of the fragrant pilaf; scattered a handful of crispy, supersavory onions on top; and dolloped on a quick-to-make garlicky yogurt sauce, I couldn't help thinking that this was in fact food fit for a king.

Rice and Lentils with Crispy Onions (Mujaddara)

SERVES 4 TO 6

Do not substitute smaller French lentils for the green or brown lentils. When preparing the Crispy Onions, be sure to reserve 3 tablespoons of the onion cooking oil for cooking the rice and lentils.

Yogurt Sauce

1 cup plain whole-milk yogurt
2 tablespoons lemon juice
½ teaspoon minced garlic
½ teaspoon salt

Rice and Lentils

8½ ounces (1¼ cups) green or brown lentils, picked over and rinsed
Salt and pepper
1¼ cups basmati rice
1 recipe Crispy Onions (recipe follows), plus 3 tablespoons reserved oil
3 garlic cloves, minced
1 teaspoon ground coriander
1 teaspoon ground cumin
½ teaspoon ground cinnamon
½ teaspoon ground allspice
⅛ teaspoon cayenne pepper
1 teaspoon sugar
3 tablespoons minced fresh cilantro

1. *For the yogurt sauce:* Whisk all ingredients together in bowl. Refrigerate while preparing rice and lentils.
2. *For the rice and lentils:* Bring lentils, 4 cups water, and 1 teaspoon salt to boil in medium saucepan over high heat. Reduce heat to low and cook until lentils are tender, 15 to 17 minutes. Drain and set aside. While lentils cook, place rice in medium bowl and cover by 2 inches with hot tap water; let stand for 15 minutes.
3. Using your hands, gently swish rice grains to release excess starch. Carefully pour off water, leaving rice in bowl. Add cold tap water to rice and pour off water. Repeat adding and pouring off cold tap water 4 or 5 times, until water runs almost clear. Drain rice in fine-mesh strainer.
4. Heat reserved onion oil, garlic, coriander, cumin, cinnamon, allspice, cayenne, and ¼ teaspoon pepper in Dutch oven over medium heat until fragrant, about 2 minutes. Add rice and cook, stirring occasionally, until edges of rice begin to turn translucent, about 3 minutes. Add 2¼ cups water, sugar, and 1 teaspoon salt and bring to boil. Stir in lentils, reduce heat to low, cover, and cook until all liquid is absorbed, about 12 minutes.
5. Off heat, remove lid, fold dish towel in half, and place over pot; replace lid. Let stand for 10 minutes. Fluff rice and lentils with fork and stir in cilantro and half of crispy onions. Transfer to serving platter, top with remaining crispy onions, and serve, passing yogurt sauce separately.

accompaniment

Crispy Onions

MAKES 1½ CUPS

It is crucial to thoroughly dry the microwaved onions after rinsing. The best way to accomplish this is to use a salad spinner. Reserve 3 tablespoons of oil when draining the onions to use in Rice and Lentils with Crispy Onions. The remaining oil may be stored in an airtight container and refrigerated for up to four weeks.

2 pounds onions, halved and sliced crosswise into ¼-inch-thick pieces
2 teaspoons salt
1½ cups vegetable oil

1. Toss onions and salt together in large bowl. Microwave for 5 minutes. Rinse thoroughly, transfer to paper towel–lined baking sheet, and dry well.
2. Heat onions and oil in Dutch oven over high heat, stirring frequently, until onions are golden brown, 25 to 30 minutes. Drain onions in colander set in large bowl. Transfer onions to paper towel–lined baking sheet to drain.

KOREAN RICE BOWL

ANDREA GEARY, *May/June 2016*

At its most basic, a rice bowl is not so much a recipe as it is a practical style of eating popular across Asia: Top warm rice with an array of seasoned vegetables, a fried egg, maybe a small amount of meat, and a piquant sauce, and stir it up for a complete meal that's true comfort food: nourishing, flavorful, texturally interesting, and healthy.

To me, the ultimate interpretation of a rice bowl is Korean *dolsot* bibimbap, where the rice takes on a brown, crisp crust that makes the dish very satisfying. *Bibim* means "mixed," *bap* means "rice," and a dolsot is the heavy single-serving stone bowl in which the bibimbap is traditionally assembled. The vessel is heated and then coated with sesame oil so the soft rice sizzles when it's piled in. While the garnishes are arranged on top, the heat retained in the stone crisps the bottom layer of rice, which gets combined with the softer rice and other components when the dish is mixed together.

I don't own a set of the stone bowls, so I usually go to a Korean restaurant for bibimbap. But since many of the ingredients are staples, I wanted to try simulating stone-bowl bibimbap at home. And why stop at the traditional single-serving size? The assembled dish is so impressive that I knew I'd want to show off for guests and make a family-style dish that would serve at least four.

BIBIMBAP BASICS

First I'd make the rice and the sauce, which could sit while I prepared the garnishes. Korean cooks use soft, slightly resilient short-grain white rice for bibimbap because its clingy surface helps it form a more cohesive crust than smooth long-grain rice would. I rinsed the grains in several changes of cool water to wash away excess starch that makes the rice too sticky. I then simmered equal parts rice and water, plus a bit of salt, in a covered saucepan while I turned my attention to the sauce. The primary component would be *gochujang*, a thick Korean chile paste that's sweet, savory, and spicy. The rest of the sauce, which I based on a Korean recipe, was toasted sesame oil and a bit of sugar along with enough water to make the mixture just runny enough for drizzling.

Part of what makes bibimbap so impressive to serve—the tidy piles of colorful and texturally varied garnishes—is also what makes it a bit of a marathon to prepare. One shortcut would be to cut back on the number of garnishes, starting with the meat. Authentic but hard-to-find dried ferns and daikon radishes were next to go, and I slimmed the rest of the list to a mix of chopped spinach, shredded carrots, and sliced shiitake mushrooms. I sautéed them sequentially in a skillet for even cooking, seasoning each batch with soy sauce, sugar, garlic, and scallions before returning them to individual bowls. To build a substantial crust of rice, I'd need something that, like a dolsot, held heat for a long time. It occurred to me that my cast-iron skillet behaves the same way. I set it over high heat, added vegetable oil and a little sesame oil for a flavor boost, carefully added the rice, and patted it into an even layer. I let the rice cook for 2 minutes to get the crust going and then arranged the garnishes on top before frying the eggs in a separate skillet I had warmed. I placed the finished eggs in the center of the vegetables, drizzled on the sauce, removed the pan from the heat, and stopped briefly to admire the lovely sight. Later I would be glad I had paused, because things were about to get ugly.

ALL MIXED UP

Stirring transforms the orderly bibimbap into a jumble of colors and textures. It's an impressive sight, but it was especially dramatic this time because my skillet was too shallow to contain everything; rice, vegetables, eggs, and sauce went everywhere. Plus, the crust had broken into very small pieces that quickly lost their crunch in the soft rice.

The first change was obvious: Switch to a deeper Dutch oven to better accommodate the mixing step. I'd still have to cook the three vegetables separately, but since they were all seasoned similarly, I made a mixture of soy sauce, sugar, scallions, and garlic (and a little bit of water to help things cook) that I could add in measured amounts to each batch. Both stainless-steel and cast-iron Dutch ovens worked, but the heftier enameled cast-iron pot yielded a more substantial crust, so I went with that.

To serve a crowd without losing the authentic tastes and textures of this Korean dish, we use a Dutch oven.

Finally, I was tempted to try a controversial step: not rinsing the rice. I made two batches—one with rinsed rice and one with unrinsed—and, frankly, the shortcut was worth it. There's so much going on in this dish that my tasters didn't notice much of a difference. To make sure everyone got substantial pieces of crust, I mixed the bibimbap in two stages, first combining the vegetables, eggs, and soft rice and then digging deep and scraping up the crust in big pieces that stayed crunchy.

I was delighted with my family-style bibimbap, but it was missing a crisp, pungent element. In a Korean household or restaurant, a dish of the spicy fermented cabbage known as kimchi would fill that role—and if you can get it (kimchi is available in many supermarkets and Asian markets), it's a great addition. As a stand-in, I quickly pickled a mixture of bean sprouts and sliced cucumbers. It made for a bright, fresh accompaniment that could also be prepared ahead of time—and it completed my version of this hearty, savory one-pot meal.

Korean Rice Bowl (Dolsot Bibimbap)

SERVES 6

For a quick dinner, prepare the pickles, chile sauce, and vegetables a day ahead (warm the vegetables to room temperature in the microwave before adding them to the rice). You can also substitute store-bought kimchi for the pickles to save time. The Korean chile paste gochujang *is sold in Asian markets and some supermarkets. If you can't find it, an equal amount of Sriracha can be substituted. Because Sriracha is more watery than gochujang, omit the water from the chile sauce and stir just 1 tablespoon of sauce into the rice in step 9. For a true bibimbap experience, bring the pot to the table before stirring the vegetables into the rice in step 9.*

Pickles
1 cup cider vinegar
2 tablespoons sugar
1½ teaspoons salt
1 cucumber, peeled, quartered lengthwise, seeded, and sliced thin on bias
4 ounces (2 cups) bean sprouts

Chile Sauce
¼ cup gochujang
3 tablespoons water
2 tablespoons toasted sesame oil
1 teaspoon sugar

Rice
2½ cups short-grain white rice
2½ cups water
¾ teaspoon salt

Vegetables
½ cup water
3 scallions, minced
3 tablespoons soy sauce
3 garlic cloves, minced
1 tablespoon sugar
1 tablespoon vegetable oil
3 carrots, peeled and shredded (2 cups)
8 ounces shiitake mushrooms, stemmed, caps sliced thin
1 (10-ounce) bag curly-leaf spinach, stemmed and chopped coarse

Bibimbap
2 tablespoons plus 2 teaspoons vegetable oil
1 tablespoon toasted sesame oil
4 large eggs

1. ***For the pickles:*** Whisk vinegar, sugar, and salt together in medium bowl. Add cucumber and bean sprouts and toss to combine. Gently press on vegetables to submerge. Cover and refrigerate for at least 30 minutes or up to 24 hours.
2. ***For the chile sauce:*** Whisk gochujang, water, oil, and sugar together in small bowl. Cover and set aside.
3. ***For the rice:*** Bring rice, water, and salt to boil in medium saucepan over high heat. Cover, reduce heat to low, and cook for 7 minutes. Remove rice from heat and let sit, covered, until tender, about 15 minutes.
4. ***For the vegetables:*** While rice cooks, stir together water, scallions, soy sauce, garlic, and sugar. Heat 1 teaspoon oil in Dutch oven over high heat until shimmering. Add carrots and stir until coated. Add ⅓ cup scallion mixture and cook, stirring frequently, until carrots are slightly softened and moisture has evaporated, 1 to 2 minutes. Using slotted spoon, transfer carrots to small bowl.
5. Heat 1 teaspoon oil in now-empty pot until shimmering. Add mushrooms and stir until coated with oil. Add ⅓ cup scallion mixture and cook, stirring frequently, until mushrooms are tender and moisture has evaporated, 3 to 4 minutes. Using slotted spoon, transfer mushrooms to second small bowl.
6. Heat remaining 1 teaspoon oil in now-empty pot until shimmering. Add spinach and remaining scallion mixture and stir to coat spinach. Cook, stirring frequently, until spinach is completely wilted but still bright green, 1 to 2 minutes. Using slotted spoon, transfer spinach to third small bowl. Discard any remaining liquid and wipe out pot with paper towel.
7. ***For the bibimbap:*** Heat 2 tablespoons vegetable oil and sesame oil in now-empty pot over high heat until shimmering. Carefully add cooked rice and gently press into even layer. Cook, without stirring, until rice begins to form crust on bottom of pot, about 2 minutes. Using slotted spoon, transfer carrots, spinach, and mushrooms to pot and arrange in piles that cover surface of rice. Reduce heat to low.
8. While crust forms, heat remaining 2 teaspoons vegetable oil in 10-inch nonstick skillet over low heat for 5 minutes. Crack eggs into small bowl. Pour eggs into skillet; cover and cook (about 2 minutes for runny yolks, 2½ minutes for soft but set yolks, and 3 minutes for firmly set yolks). Slide eggs onto vegetables in pot.
9. Drizzle 2 tablespoons chile sauce over eggs. Without disturbing crust, use wooden spoon to stir rice, vegetables, and eggs until combined. Just before serving, scrape large pieces of crust from bottom of pot and stir into rice. Serve in individual bowls, passing pickles and extra chile sauce separately.

EASY TO MAKE—AND MAKE AHEAD

Don't let the lengthy recipe intimidate you. The pickles, chile sauce, and vegetables can all be prepared ahead, so all that's left to do on the day of is cook the rice and eggs. Plus, leftover pickles and chile sauce make great condiments for other applications like sandwiches, burgers, noodles, and eggs.

A BOWL THAT HOLDS THE HEAT

Traditionally, *dolsot* bibimbap is served in individual stone bowls that retain heat. The bowl is coated with sesame oil, so that when the rice is added, the bottom layer of rice crisps and gives the dish great textural contrast when everything is stirred together. Because most home cooks don't have stone bowls, we make a family-size portion in a heavy Dutch oven by heating oil in the pot and cooking the rice until a crusty bottom layer forms.

REALLY GOOD VEGETABLE TART

ANDREW JANJIGIAN, *January/February 2012*

Compared with more formal tarts baked in fluted pans, a free-form tart's beauty lies in its rustic simplicity. You roll out the dough, add the filling, and then draw in the edges to form a pleated packet. This method requires far less effort than precisely fitting pastry into a molded pan, and it looks just as attractive.

But when it comes to savory applications, free-form tarts can have their flaws. Many recipes simply borrow a pastry dough intended for fruit and swap in vegetables. After trying a few such versions, I realized that for vegetables, not just any crust would do. Vegetables have far less of the pectin that holds on to moisture and binds a fruit filling together, so they are prone to leaking liquid into the crust or falling apart when the tart is sliced. What's more, vegetables don't pack the concentrated, bright flavors of fruit. To make up for these deficits, I needed a crust that was extra-sturdy and boasted a complex flavor of its own. I also wanted a robust-tasting filling with enough sticking power to hold together when cut.

Adding whole-wheat flour and giving our tart dough a few simple folds yields a flaky yet sturdy crust with great nutty flavor.

STRUCTURAL ANALYSIS

I started by putting together an all-butter pie dough, trading half of the white flour for whole-wheat. Its earthy flavor, I hoped, would complement the savory filling, and its coarser consistency would turn out a pleasantly hearty crumb. I pulsed the dry ingredients and butter in the food processor a few times and then dumped the mixture into a bowl, added a little water, and stirred it until thoroughly combined. To ensure that the butter stayed firm enough to leave air pockets when it melted in the oven, creating flakiness, I chilled the dough for about an hour before rolling it out.

The good news: The crust tasted great. The bad news: It had a crumbly, dense texture. And I was pretty sure I knew why.

All standard doughs, pastry or otherwise, get their structure from gluten, the network of proteins that forms when flour is mixed with water. The challenge when working with whole-wheat flour is that it contains the bran and germ. (These are stripped away in white flour, leaving only the starchy endosperm.) Since the bran and germ contain none of the gluten-forming proteins found in the endosperm, the more whole-wheat flour in a dough, the heavier and more likely it will be to fall apart.

To strengthen the dough, I'd need to cut back on the whole-wheat flour, but 25 percent was as low as I could go before I lost too much of its nutty taste. And there was another problem: As the proportion of white flour, and therefore gluten, increased, the dough became tough. I wasn't overworking the dough—a typical cause. Could the problem be water? Because the bran and germ need more water than the endosperm does to become fully hydrated, I'd added a little more than I would have in an all-white-flour dough. The extra liquid was being taken up by the white flour's gluten-forming proteins, thus creating more gluten and making the dough more susceptible to overworking. To reduce toughness, then, I'd need to either cut back on the water or find an even gentler way to handle the dough.

LIQUID ASSETS

Our previous solution to tough pastry calls for replacing some of the water with vodka, but that dough is too soft to work as a free-form crust. Acids can weaken the bonds that form between gluten strands, so tried adding vinegar. A teaspoon—the most I could add before the dough tasted too vinegary—did tenderize it a little, but not enough.

What if I took a hands-off approach to mixing and let the flour absorb the water on its own? I hoped that partially mixing the dough and then letting it rest before rolling it out might allow the water to migrate to drier parts and produce pastry that was workable—but not overworked.

I gave it a shot, just barely mixing the dry and wet ingredients together and then chilling the dough briefly. When I pulled out the dough about 45 minutes later, most of the dry flour had disappeared and the dough was remarkably supple but not floppy. I nudged it together and then rolled it out and baked it. The result: a tender, moist, and decently flaky crust without any toughness. But I wouldn't settle for decently flaky. I wanted a crust with the long, striated layers in puff pastry; such large horizontal sheets would also make the crust more resistant to splitting when sliced. The layers in puff pastry are created through the painstaking process of rolling and folding the dough many times and chilling it in between. To see if I could mimic this approach in a more modest way, I dumped the rested shaggy mass onto the counter, rolled it into a rectangle, and folded it into thirds, like a business letter. I repeated the process just twice more. The results were even better than I'd hoped: The increase in layers rendered the crust wonderfully flaky and less apt to shatter when cut.

FILL'ER UP

Working with a sturdy crust, however, didn't mean that I could throw in my shiitake mushrooms and leeks raw, since they'd leach moisture and render the crust soggy. Sautéing the leeks took only a few minutes and concentrated their flavor. And I hastened the evaporation process by heating the mushrooms in the microwave. To introduce rich, complex flavor and not too much moisture, I worked in a hefty dollop of crème fraîche and some Dijon mustard as well as some crumbled Gorgonzola. This rustic tart amounted to a perfect vegetarian meal.

Mushroom and Leek Galette

SERVES 6

Cutting a few small holes in the dough prevents it from lifting off the pan as it bakes. An overturned baking sheet can be used in place of the baking stone. This dough will require a generous amount of flour (up to ¼ cup) to roll out.

Dough

- 1¼ cups (6¼ ounces) all-purpose flour
- ½ cup (2¾ ounces) whole-wheat flour
- 1 tablespoon sugar
- ¾ teaspoon salt
- 10 tablespoons unsalted butter, cut into ½-inch pieces and chilled
- 7 tablespoons ice water
- 1 teaspoon distilled white vinegar

Filling

- 1¼ pounds shiitake mushrooms, stemmed and sliced thin
- 5 teaspoons olive oil
- 1 pound leeks, white and light green parts only, halved lengthwise, sliced ½ inch thick, and washed thoroughly (3 cups)
- 1 teaspoon minced fresh thyme
- 2 tablespoons crème fraîche
- 1 tablespoon Dijon mustard
- Salt and pepper
- 3 ounces Gorgonzola cheese, crumbled (¾ cup)
- 1 large egg, lightly beaten
- Kosher salt
- 2 tablespoons minced fresh parsley

1. *For the dough:* Process all-purpose flour, whole-wheat flour, sugar, and salt in food processor until combined, about 5 seconds. Scatter butter over top and pulse until it forms pea-size pieces, about 10 pulses. Transfer mixture to medium bowl.
2. Sprinkle ice water and vinegar over mixture. With rubber spatula, use folding motion to mix until loose, shaggy mass forms with some dry flour remaining (do not overwork). Transfer mixture to center of large sheet of plastic wrap, press gently into rough 4-inch square, and wrap tightly. Refrigerate for 45 minutes.
3. Transfer dough to floured counter. Roll into 11 by 8-inch rectangle with short side of rectangle parallel to edge of counter. Using bench scraper, bring bottom third of dough up, then fold upper third over it, folding like business letter into 8 by 4-inch rectangle. Turn dough 90 degrees counterclockwise. Roll dough again into 11 by 8-inch rectangle and fold into thirds again. Turn dough 90 degrees counterclockwise and repeat rolling and folding into thirds. After last fold, fold dough in half to create 4-inch square. Press top of dough gently to seal. Wrap in plastic and refrigerate for at least 45 minutes or up to 2 days.
4. *For the filling:* Microwave mushrooms in covered bowl until just tender, 3 to 5 minutes. Transfer to colander and let drain; return to bowl. Meanwhile, heat 1 tablespoon oil in 12-inch skillet over medium heat until shimmering. Add leeks and thyme, cover, and cook, stirring occasionally, until leeks are tender and beginning to brown, 5 to 7 minutes. Transfer to bowl with mushrooms. Stir in crème fraîche and mustard. Season with salt and pepper to taste; set aside.
5. Adjust oven rack to lower-middle position, set baking stone on rack, and heat oven to 400 degrees. Line rimmed baking sheet with parchment paper. Remove dough from refrigerator and let stand at room temperature for 15 to 20 minutes. Roll dough into 14-inch circle about ⅛ inch thick on floured counter. (Trim edges as needed to form rough circle.) Transfer dough to prepared sheet. Using straw or tip of paring knife, cut five ¼-inch circles in dough (one at center and four evenly spaced halfway from center to edge of dough). Brush top of dough with 1 teaspoon oil.
6. Spread half of filling evenly over dough, leaving 2-inch border around edge. Sprinkle half of Gorgonzola over filling, cover with remaining filling, and top with remaining Gorgonzola. Drizzle remaining 1 teaspoon oil over filling. Grasp 1 edge of dough and fold outer 2 inches over filling. Repeat around circumference of tart, overlapping dough every 2 to 3 inches; gently pinch pleated dough to secure but do not press dough into filling. Brush dough with egg and sprinkle evenly with kosher salt.
7. Lower oven temperature to 375 degrees. Set sheet on stone and bake until crust is deep golden brown and filling is beginning to brown, 35 to 45 minutes. Let tart cool on sheet on wire rack for 10 minutes. Using offset or wide metal spatula, loosen tart from parchment and carefully slide tart onto cutting board. Sprinkle parsley over filling, cut into wedges, and serve.

PLEATING A FREE-FORM TART

1. Gently grasp 1 edge of dough round and make 2-inch-wide fold over filling.

2. Lift and fold another segment of dough over first fold to form pleat. Repeat every 2 to 3 inches.

DON'T DOUBT YOUR DOUGH

Barely mixing the dough and then letting it rest in the refrigerator hydrates the flour while minimizing gluten development, creating a more tender crust. Don't worry if the dough looks loose and shaggy—it's supposed to.

SHAGGY DOUGH

REALLY GOOD BLACK BEAN BURGERS

ERIKA BRUCE, *September/October 2015*

When it comes to vegetarian recipes, veggie burgers have never been high on my list. Most rely on such a hodgepodge of ingredients, with multiple grains and vegetables that need to be individually prepared before they go into the burger, that they are a lot of work to put together. Black bean burgers seem more approachable. The earthy beans promise a hearty, satisfying meal, and because the beans themselves provide plenty of substance, ideally the process wouldn't be much more complicated than making an everyday beef burger—just mash up a couple of cans of beans, add a few complementary ingredients, shape into patties, and cook.

When I reviewed recipes, I found that there were a couple of approaches to handling the beans: They could be coarsely chopped, lightly mashed with a fork, or pureed until smooth. To bind the beans together, almost all recipes relied on eggs, and many also loaded up on starchy ingredients like bread crumbs or oats. Unfortunately, I wasn't impressed when I tried them. Lots of starch made it easy to shape chopped beans and eggs into patties, but these burgers turned into dry, tasteless hockey pucks once cooked. At the other end of the spectrum were the recipes that called for mashed or pureed beans. The cohesive, hummus-like texture held together nicely even with minimal binders, but it also produced a burger with a gluey, pasty consistency.

Tortilla chips help to bind our black bean burgers without interfering with the earthy flavor.

As for add-ins, recipes tended to follow the lead of veggie burgers by throwing in everything from porcini mushrooms and soy sauce to poblano peppers and cashew nuts. I was after burgers that featured earthy bean flavor at their heart with just enough seasoning and mix-ins to give them a little zest and intrigue. I also wanted patties that weren't wet or gluey but rather just cohesive enough to hold together when flipped in the pan, with a little textural contrast from chunks of beans and a nice crust.

A HILL OF BEANS

After draining and rinsing a couple of cans of beans, I spread the beans on paper towels to rid them of moisture. My thinking was the drier they were, the less starchy binder they might require. And to avoid a smooth, mushy texture, the beans would have to retain some of their shape. But they still needed to be broken down enough to incorporate well, so I pulled out the food processor. A couple of pulses produced nicely chopped pieces that would offer a bit of texture.

To transform the chopped beans into a cohesive burger mix, I tried stirring in a beaten egg along with a handful of panko bread crumbs. (I used only a small amount so as to let the bean flavor come to the fore.) Like tiny sponges, the bread crumbs did an excellent job of absorbing the egg's moisture, but even a little bit made the burgers taste bready. What's more, one egg seemed insufficient since each and every burger broke apart into crumbles as I flipped it.

Many recipes call for some sort of precooked grains, such as rice or bulgur, to bind the beans, but in the interest of simplicity, I opted to avoid that path. Instead, I experimented with a different sort of starch that would complement the Latin American provenance of black beans: tortilla chips. Since I already had the food processor out, I quickly blitzed a few chips before pulsing in the beans. Then I added two beaten eggs to help hold the burgers together. Everything seemed great—that is, until I tried to pack the burgers into patties. The mixture was so wet and sticky that shaping them was nearly impossible.

BOUND FOR GLORY

Adding more ground chips would only mute the flavor of the beans, so I took a lunch break, hoping that an hour of hands-off time would allow the starches in the beans and the tortilla chips to absorb the liquid from the egg. Just as I had hoped, the mixture was much easier to handle after it sat in the fridge for an hour. These patties were easy to form, held their shape fairly well, and developed a crisp, golden brown crust when I fried them in a little bit of oil. Unfortunately, they still occasionally broke apart as I flipped them.

To glue the burgers together more effectively, I took the unorthodox step of adding a good sprinkling of flour. After all, we often use flour in combination with beaten egg to get a breading to cling to meat. Sure enough, since wheat contains sticky amylopectin starches, a mere 2 tablespoons all but guaranteed that the burger would stay together, without negatively affecting flavor.

Now the burgers just needed some personality. Avoiding additions that were high in moisture or that needed to be cooked down ahead of time (such as onions and peppers), I landed on minced garlic and scallions and chopped fresh cilantro. They were quick and easy and fit my Latin American theme. For even more complexity, I spiked the mixture with citrusy coriander and smoky cumin. Finally, a dash of hot sauce added zip.

These burgers were ready to be topped with the usual fixings—gooey melted cheese, thinly sliced onion, lettuce leaves, and tomato slices—or more deluxe toppings like a creamy avocado-feta spread, spicy chipotle mayonnaise, or a tangy roasted tomato-orange jam.

Black Bean Burgers

SERVES 6

The black bean mixture needs to be refrigerated for at least 1 hour or up to 24 hours prior to cooking. When forming the patties, it is important to pack them firmly together. Serve the burgers with your favorite toppings or with one of our spreads (recipes follow).

2 (15-ounce) cans black beans, rinsed
2 large eggs
2 tablespoons all-purpose flour
4 scallions, minced
3 tablespoons minced fresh cilantro
2 garlic cloves, minced
1 teaspoon ground cumin
1 teaspoon hot sauce (optional)
½ teaspoon ground coriander
¼ teaspoon salt
¼ teaspoon pepper
1 ounce tortilla chips, crushed coarse (½ cup)
2 tablespoons plus 2 teaspoons vegetable oil
6 hamburger buns

1. Line rimmed baking sheet with triple layer of paper towels and spread beans over towels. Let stand for 15 minutes.

2. Whisk eggs and flour in large bowl until uniform paste forms. Stir in scallions; cilantro; garlic; cumin; hot sauce, if using; coriander; salt; and pepper until well combined.

3. Process tortilla chips in food processor until finely ground, about 30 seconds. Add beans and pulse until beans are roughly broken down, about 5 pulses. Transfer bean mixture to bowl with egg mixture and mix until well combined. Cover and refrigerate for at least 1 hour or up to 24 hours.

4. Adjust oven rack to middle position and heat oven to 200 degrees. Divide bean mixture into 6 equal portions. Firmly pack each portion into tight ball, then flatten into 3½-inch-diameter patty. (Patties can be wrapped individually in plastic wrap, placed in a zipper-lock bag, and frozen for up to 2 weeks. Thaw patties before cooking.)

5. Heat 2 teaspoons oil in 10-inch nonstick skillet over medium heat until shimmering. Carefully place 3 patties in skillet and cook until bottoms are well browned and crispy, about 5 minutes. Flip patties, add 2 teaspoons oil, and cook second side until well browned and crispy, 3 to 5 minutes. Transfer burgers to wire rack set in rimmed baking sheet and place in oven to keep warm. Repeat with remaining 3 patties and 4 teaspoons oil. Transfer burgers to buns and serve.

KEYS TO AN IDEAL BLACK BEAN BURGER

Here's what we did to create a burger full of earthy bean flavor that wasn't muted by too much starchy binder.

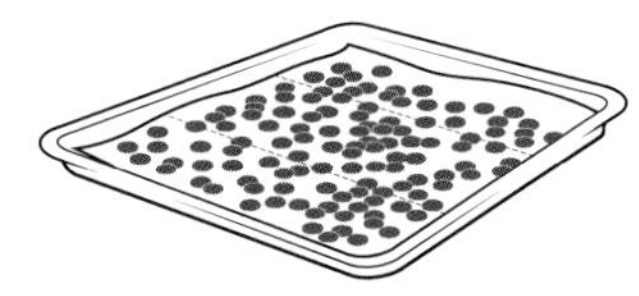

DRY BEANS Removing excess moisture by draining on paper towels helps cut down on the need for absorbent binders.

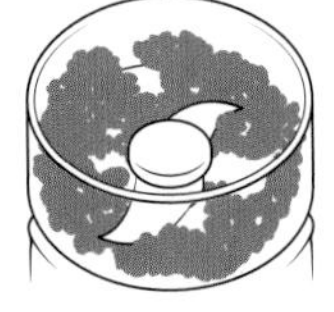

PULSE, DON'T PUREE Pulsing the beans with tortilla chips (we processed them first) keeps the beans chunky for textural contrast.

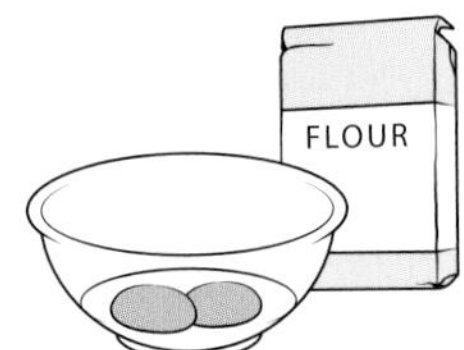

GIVE IT EXTRA CLING In addition to eggs and starchy tortilla chips, we add flour to hold the mix together.

LET IT REST Letting the mixture sit gives the starches time to soak up the eggs so the burgers are easier to handle.

accompaniments

Avocado-Feta Spread

MAKES ABOUT 1¼ CUPS

1 ripe avocado, cut into ½-inch pieces
1 ounce feta cheese, crumbled (¼ cup)
1 tablespoon extra-virgin olive oil
1 teaspoon lime juice
⅛ teaspoon salt
⅛ teaspoon pepper

Using fork, mash all ingredients in bowl until mostly smooth.

Chipotle Mayonnaise

MAKES ABOUT 1 CUP

3 tablespoons mayonnaise
3 tablespoons sour cream
2 teaspoons minced canned chipotle chile in adobo sauce
1 garlic clove, minced
⅛ teaspoon salt

Combine all ingredients in bowl. Cover and refrigerate for at least 1 hour.

Roasted Tomato–Orange Jam

MAKES ABOUT 1 CUP

12 ounces cherry tomatoes, halved
1 shallot, sliced thin
1 tablespoon extra-virgin olive oil
¼ teaspoon salt
⅛ teaspoon ground cinnamon
2 tablespoons orange marmalade

Adjust oven rack to middle position and heat oven to 425 degrees. Toss tomatoes, shallot, oil, salt, and cinnamon together in bowl. Transfer to aluminum foil–lined rimmed baking sheet and roast until edges of tomatoes are well browned, 15 to 20 minutes. Let cool slightly, then transfer tomato mixture to food processor. Add marmalade and process until smooth, about 10 seconds.

THE BEST VEGETARIAN CHILI

LAN LAM, *November/December 2012*

I love chili, but I admit that vegetarian versions are usually the last kind I'd think to make. Most lack depth and complexity, so while they may taste lively and bright initially, their flavor fades. They rely on beans and chunky veggies for heartiness—but in truth that heartiness is just an illusion. Neither ingredient offers any real replacement for the flavor, texture, and unctuous richness that meat provides. It doesn't help matters that such chilis are typically made with canned beans and lackluster commercial chili powder.

But do vegetarian chilis really have to be this way? I set out to build a version as rich, savory, and deeply satisfying as any meat chili out there—one that even meat lovers would make on its own merits, not just to serve to vegetarian friends.

HEAT AND BEANS

The first ingredient to tackle was the seasoning that gives the dish its name. Though we've found premade chili powders we like, even the best can't compete with a powder that you grind yourself from dried chiles. Plus, the commercial products tend to have a gritty, dusty texture that comes from grinding chiles whole—including the stems and seeds, which never fully break down. For my homemade blend, I opted for two widely available dried chiles: mild, sweet ancho and earthy New Mexican. I toasted them to bring out their flavor and then, after removing the stems and seeds, pulverized the peppers to a fine powder in a spice grinder with some dried oregano.

Bulgur and walnuts give our vegetarian chili the appealing texture and savory flavor of meat versions.

Next up: beans. For greater complexity, I wanted to use a mix of beans with different characteristics, singling out sweet, nutty cannellinis and meaty, earthy pintos. Canned beans are certainly convenient, but they also tend to be bland and mushy, so I opted for dried, calling on our quick-brining method. This entails bringing the beans to a boil in a pot of salted water and then letting them sit, covered, for an hour. The brine ensures soft, creamy beans (sodium ions from salt weaken the pectin in the bean skins, for a softer texture) that are well seasoned and evenly cooked.

Meanwhile, the beans' hour-long rest gave me plenty of time to prep the remaining ingredients. I started out with my dried chile and oregano powder, cumin for earthy depth, and finely chopped onions for sweetness. I sautéed the onions just until they began to brown and then added the spices to bloom in the hot oil. In went my brined, rinsed beans and water; I then covered the pot and placed it in a 300-degree oven. (If they were on the stovetop, I'd have to stir the beans to prevent scorching, but in the more even, gentle heat of the oven they could simmer unattended.) I checked the beans periodically as they cooked. After 45 minutes, they were just tender. This was a great time to introduce a can of diced tomatoes, which I whizzed up in a food processor with lots of garlic and some fresh jalapeños to kick up the heat. The tomatoes would keep the beans from falling apart during the remainder of cooking, since the basic building blocks of legumes—polysaccharides—do not readily dissolve in acidic conditions. Another 2 hours and the beans were perfectly cooked: creamy and tender but not blown out.

But I still had just a pot of flavored beans. Now to turn it into a real chili…

"BEEFING" IT UP

Besides the beans, most vegetarian chilis replace the bulk that meat contributes with some combination of diced vegetables. But these recipes miss a major point: In addition to adding volume and flavor, meat gives chili its distinctive texture. Properly made meat chili is a homogeneous mixture of ground or diced meat napped in a thick, spicy sauce. No matter how you slice or dice them, cut vegetables can't deliver that same sturdy texture. They also tend to water down the dish.

In my research I'd come across vegetarian chilis that called for nuts, seeds, or grains, and with nothing to lose I decided to try a few of these more unusual add-ins. Chopped pumpkin seeds were a failure: They didn't break down during cooking, leaving sharp, crunchy bits that tasters found distracting. Long-grain rice, meanwhile, turned to mush by the time the beans were cooked through, and large, round grains of pearl barley were too chewy and gummy. Finally, I hit the jackpot: I stirred in some nutty little granules of bulgur when I added the tomatoes to the pot. Even after the long simmer, these precooked wheat kernels (which are normally plumped up by a quick soak in water) retained their shape, giving the chili the textural dimension that it had been missing.

My recipe was progressing nicely, but it still didn't have the rich depth of flavor that could help turn what was a good chili into something great. I knew that the canned tomatoes were introducing some savory flavor, but I needed a more potent source, so I added a few dollops of umami-packed tomato paste as well as a few tablespoons of soy sauce.

But the flavor was still too one-dimensional. While developing a vegetable soup recently, I'd learned that umami boosters fall into two categories—glutamates and nucleotides—and that they have a synergistic effect when used together. Dried mushrooms are rich in nucleotides and could amplify the effect of the glutamate-rich soy sauce and tomatoes. Since I was already grinding my chile peppers, I simply tossed in some chopped, dried shiitake mushrooms at the same time, in order to take advantage of their flavor-boosting qualities without adding distinct chunks of mushroom.

Sure enough, this batch was the meatiest yet. But could I take things even further? I reviewed a list of umami-rich foods and was surprised to see that walnuts contain more than twice as many glutamates as do tomatoes. For my next batch I toasted some walnuts, ground them in a food processor, and then stirred them into the chili along with the tomatoes and bulgur. In terms of savory depth, tasters unanimously deemed this batch the winner to date, and there were added bonuses: The fat from the nuts offered some richness, and the tannins in the skins contributed a slightly bitter note that balanced the other flavors.

Now my chili had complexity, but it still didn't have the lingering depth of a meat chili. I took a step back and thought about what meat really brings to chili. Its fat not only contributes flavor but also boosts that of the other ingredients and affects how you taste them. The flavor compounds in spices (chile peppers and cumin, in particular) are far more soluble in fat than in water, so a watery sauce dulls their flavor, whereas oils and fats allow them to bloom. What's more, fat coats the surface of your mouth, giving flavors staying power on the palate. I began slowly increasing the amount of vegetable oil that I was using to sauté the aromatics and found that ¼ cup brought the flavors into focus and allowed them to linger pleasantly instead of disappearing after a few seconds.

Everything was perfect but for one issue: When I took the chili out of the oven, I found that some of the fat had separated out, leaving a slick on top. A quick stir helped, but at the suggestion of our science editor, I tried a more vigorous stir followed by a 20-minute rest. This led to a thick, velvety chili that you could stand a spoon in. Here's why: Stirring released starches from the beans and bulgur, which absorbed the water in the sauce, allowing the sauce to stabilize around the fat droplets and prevent the oil from separating out again—in a sense creating a kind of emulsion.

There was nothing left to do but stir in some cilantro for a touch of freshness. Whether garnished with a little of everything or just a dollop of sour cream, each bite of chili was hearty and full-flavored—and no one missed the meat.

Best Vegetarian Chili

SERVES 6 TO 8

We prefer to use whole dried chiles, but the chili can be prepared with jarred chili powder. If using chili powder, grind the shiitakes and oregano and add them to the pot with ¼ cup of chili powder in step 4. Pinto, black, red kidney, small red, cannellini, or navy beans can be used in this recipe, either a single variety or a combination of beans. For a spicier chili use both jalapeños. Serve with diced avocado, chopped red onion, lime wedges, sour cream, and shredded Monterey Jack or cheddar cheese.

Salt
1 pound (2½ cups) dried beans, rinsed and picked over
2 dried ancho chiles
2 dried New Mexican chiles
½ ounce dried shiitake mushrooms, chopped coarse
4 teaspoons dried oregano
½ cup walnuts, toasted
1 (28-ounce) can diced tomatoes, drained with juice reserved
3 tablespoons tomato paste
3 tablespoons soy sauce
1–2 jalapeño chiles, stemmed and chopped coarse
6 garlic cloves, minced
¼ cup vegetable oil
2 pounds onions, chopped fine
1 tablespoon ground cumin
⅔ cup medium-grain bulgur
¼ cup chopped fresh cilantro

1. Bring 4 quarts water, 3 tablespoons salt, and beans to boil in Dutch oven over high heat. Remove pot from heat, cover, and let stand for 1 hour. Drain beans and rinse well.
2. Adjust oven rack to middle position and heat oven to 300 degrees. Arrange ancho and New Mexican chiles on rimmed baking sheet and toast until fragrant and puffed, about 8 minutes. Transfer to plate and let cool, about 5 minutes. Stem and seed toasted chiles. Working in batches, grind toasted chiles, shiitakes, and oregano in spice grinder or with mortar and pestle until finely ground.
3. Process walnuts in food processor until finely ground, about 30 seconds. Transfer to bowl. Process drained tomatoes, tomato paste, soy sauce, jalapeño(s), and garlic in food processor until tomatoes are finely chopped, about 45 seconds, scraping down bowl as needed.
4. Heat oil in Dutch oven over medium-high heat until shimmering. Add onions and 1¼ teaspoons salt; cook, stirring occasionally until onions begin to brown, 8 to 10 minutes. Lower heat to medium, add ground chile mixture and cumin, and cook, stirring constantly, until fragrant, about 1 minute. Add rinsed beans and 7 cups water and bring to boil. Cover pot, transfer to oven, and cook for 45 minutes.
5. Remove pot from oven. Stir in bulgur, ground walnuts, tomato mixture, and reserved tomato juice. Return to oven and cook until beans are fully tender, about 2 hours.
6. Remove pot from oven, stir chili well, and let stand, uncovered, for 20 minutes. Stir in cilantro and serve. (Chili can be made up to 3 days in advance.)

GIVE IT A STIR (AND A REST)

To capitalize on the ability of the fat in the chili to create body in the sauce, we gave the chili a vigorous stir and a 20-minute rest after we took it out of the oven. Stirring helped to release starch from the beans and the bulgur. The starch then clustered around the fat droplets in the chili, preventing them from coalescing and helping to create a thick, velvety emulsion that never left a slick of oil on top of the chili, no matter how many times we reheated it.

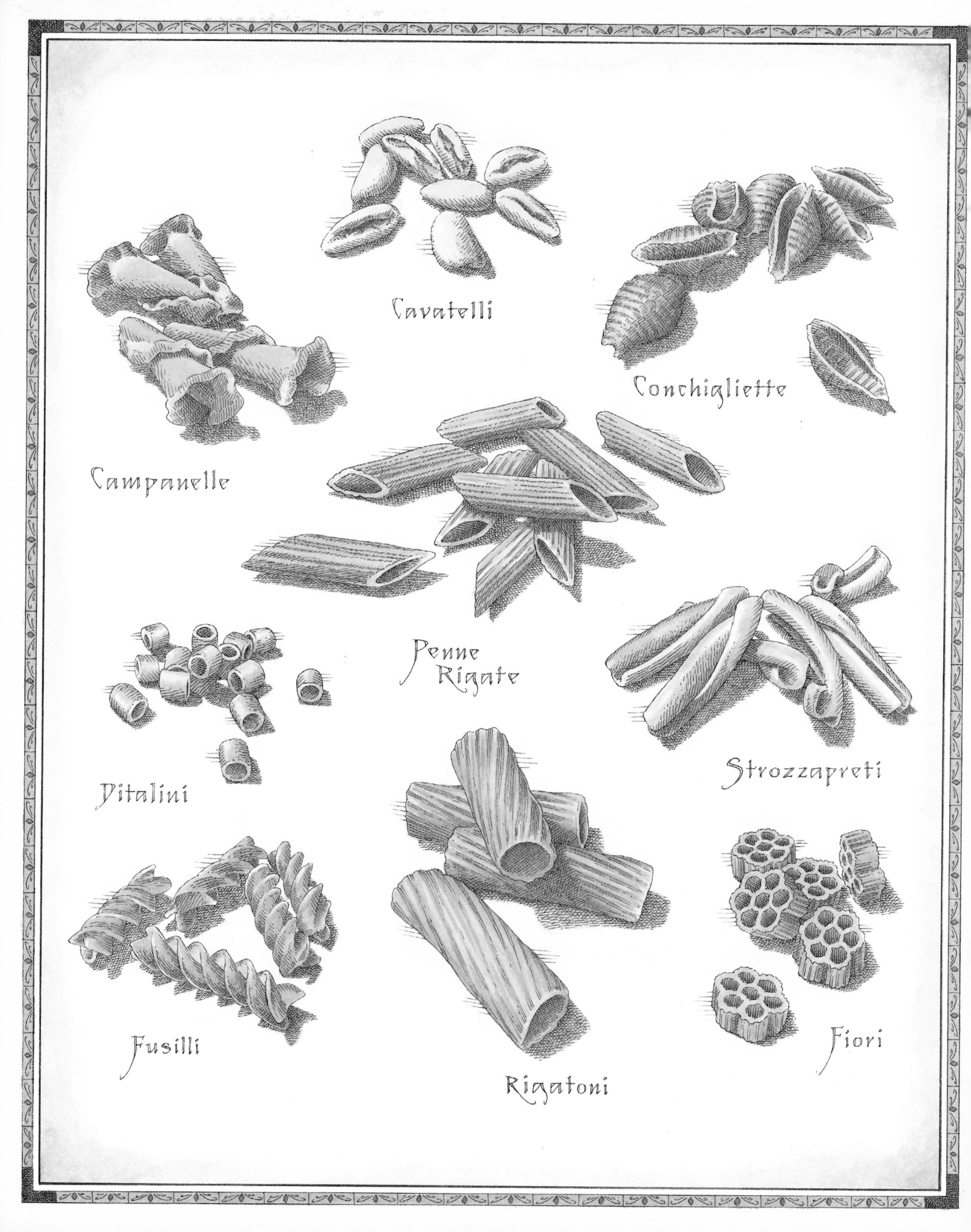

Cavatelli
Conchigliette
Campanelle
Penne Rigate
Strozzapreti
Ditalini
Fusilli
Rigatoni
Fiori

PASTA AND NOODLES

FRESH PASTA WITHOUT A MACHINE

DAN SOUZA, *May/June 2012*

One challenge I've always wanted to set for myself is figuring out how to make pasta with nothing more than the dough, a rolling pin, and some elbow grease. While mechanical pasta rollers aren't all that expensive, many home cooks don't own them. But as anyone who has ever attempted to roll out a block of hard pasta dough by hand knows, it's no easy task. The dough has a tendency to spring back—and if it isn't rolled out gossamer thin, the pasta will never achieve the right al dente texture when cooked. So how do Italian cooks manage to pull off this feat? One answer: years of perseverance.

In her *Essentials of Classic Italian Cooking* (1992), Marcella Hazan devotes no fewer than six pages to the classic hand-rolling technique perfected in the Emilia-Romagna region of Italy. Employing extra-thin, super-long rolling pins measuring 1½ inches in diameter and 32 inches in length, Italians in this part of the country have developed a series of stretching movements that can transform a lump of firm dough into a thin, delicate sheet. Besides the obvious drawback of needing a generous work surface to accommodate the pin, Hazan is the first to admit that this traditional technique must be exhaustively practiced "until the motions are performed through intuition rather than deliberation."

While I'm typically game for a hard-won lesson in authenticity, even I have limits. I wanted a dough that any cook could roll out with ease on the first try and that would cook up to that incomparably tender, silky yet slightly firm texture that makes fresh pasta so worth making.

ZERO LUCK

In addition to centuries of experience, Italians have another hand-rolling advantage—the best kind of flour for the job: *doppio zero*, or 00. The name denotes the fine talcum-like grind that gives pasta and baked goods made with the flour an almost creamy mouthfeel. To see what I was missing, I mail-ordered some and mixed up a batch of dough following a typical approach: I put the usual ratio of 2 cups of flour to three whole eggs in a food processor and processed until they formed a cohesive ball. I then turned the dough out on the counter, kneaded it for several minutes, and set it aside to relax for about 20 minutes. Sure enough, the 00 (which has a protein content of 9 percent) produced a malleable dough that was far easier to work with than dough made from all-purpose flour.

Adding extra egg yolks and a little bit of olive oil to our pasta dough makes it silky, supple, and easy to roll out by hand.

To achieve similarly soft dough, my first inclination was to dilute the protein content of all-purpose flour (which boasts 10 to 12 percent protein) by cutting it with cake flour (which has 6 to 8 percent protein). I substituted increasing amounts of cake flour for all-purpose and noted that swapping even a quarter of the all-purpose flour for cake flour had a dramatic impact on both the raw dough and the cooked noodles. With 25 percent cake flour in the mix, my dough was much softer, less elastic, and easier to roll out. Unfortunately, what I had gained in convenience I lost in the texture of the cooked strands, which released a lot of starch into the cooking water and emerged with a pitted, pebbly surface. Our science editor explained why: For noodles to remain intact and leach only a little starch into the cooking water, the starch granules in the flour need to be fully surrounded by a strong network of proteins. But the bleach in cake flour not only weakens the proteins but also makes the starch more absorbent and prone to bursting—a good thing when you want a tender cake but not when you're making pasta. Clearly, I needed a different strategy for producing softer, more malleable dough, so I turned my attention to the amount of liquid in the recipe.

IS WETTER BETTER?

Traditional pasta dough is about 30 percent water (compared with around 55 percent hydration for a basic sandwich loaf), all of which comes from the eggs. I figured that simply upping the hydration level would create a softer dough that would be easier to roll out, so I experimented with adding plain water to a batch of dough and an extra egg white (the white accounts for 80 percent of an egg's moisture) to another. Just as I'd hoped, these more hydrated doughs were more extensible—at least initially. But they had their downsides: First, the wetter surface of the dough caused considerable sticking, which required the heavy use of bench flour during rolling and led to cooked pasta with a starchy, gummy surface. Second, by adding more water, I'd allowed for too much gluten development, creating dough that, although easier to roll out at first, developed a greater tendency to snap back to its original shape once stretched out; this also meant pasta that cooked up tough and chewy. Still, I felt I was on to something by increasing the liquid in my recipe. Olive oil is a common addition to many fresh pasta recipes. What if I introduced it instead of water?

I mixed up a few more batches of dough, adding increasing amounts of olive oil. As the oil amount increased, the dough became more supple and easier to roll out. But because fat coats the proteins, inhibiting gluten formation, too much oil once again weakened the dough's structure, leading to excess starch loss in the water and a compromised texture. I found my upper limit at 2 tablespoons of oil.

I was finally getting somewhere, but this dough was still far from user-friendly.

THAT'S ALL, YOLKS

Up to this point I had tried adding water, protein (from egg whites), and fat to my dough, but I hadn't experimented with the one ingredient that contains all three: yolks. Many pasta doughs substitute yolks for some of the whole eggs, because while they still contain about 50 percent water, they are also loaded with fat and emulsifiers, both of which limit gluten development. Unlike doughs made with cake flour or excessive amounts of oil, dough made with extra yolks still has plenty of structure thanks to the coagulation of the egg proteins. To 2 cups of flour, two whole eggs (I ditched one whole egg from the traditional formula), and 2 tablespoons of olive oil, I kept adding yolks until I had a truly soft, easy-to-work dough that boiled up nice and tender. The magic number proved to be six extra yolks.

This dough took on a beautiful yellow hue, yielded to gentle pressure with a rolling pin, and cooked up into delicate ribbons with a springy bite. While tasters had been concerned that the pasta would taste too eggy, they needn't have feared. The sulfurous compounds responsible for the flavor we associate with eggs reside primarily in the whites, not the yolks.

Finally, I turned my attention to finding the best way to rest, roll, and cut the pasta.

A LITTLE R&R

After being mixed, pasta dough is often rested for 20 to 30 minutes to allow the flour to hydrate and the gluten to cross-link into a network and then relax. Would a longer rest be even better? To find out, I let the next batch sit at room temperature for an extended period of time, cutting and rolling out pieces every 30 minutes. After an hour, my dough was significantly more malleable—and it continued to soften over the next three hours (four hours of resting time was ideal, though not critical for success).

This dough was worlds away from the dense blocks I'd struggled with in the past, but it still required a bit of technique to roll out. I knew I needed to avoid using too much bench flour: A little cling is a good thing, as it prevents the dough from springing back too easily. Plus, as I'd already learned, excess flour doesn't get incorporated into the dough and turns the surface of the pasta coarse and gummy. With all that in mind, I first cut the dough into six manageable pieces. Working with one at a time, I used my hands in combination with a rolling pin to make the dough into a 6 by 20-inch rectangle.

From here, the possibilities were limitless. For ribbon-style pasta, I allowed the sheets to dry on kitchen towels until firm around the edges (a step that enabled me to avoid dusting with more flour) before folding them up in 2-inch intervals and slicing crosswise to the desired thickness.

With dough that's this easy to roll out and that cooks up into wonderfully springy, delicate noodles, I'd wager that even cooks with pasta machines might be tempted to leave them in the cabinet.

Fresh Pasta without a Machine

MAKES 1 POUND; SERVES 4 TO 6

If using a high-protein all-purpose flour such as King Arthur, increase the number of egg yolks to seven. The longer the dough rests in step 2, the easier it will be to roll out. When rolling out the dough, avoid adding too much flour, which may result in excessive snapback. To make the pasta ahead, follow the recipe through step 5, transfer the baking sheet of pasta to the freezer, and freeze until the pasta is firm. Transfer to a zipper-lock bag and store for up to two weeks. Cook frozen pasta straight from the freezer as directed in step 6.

2 cups (10 ounces) all-purpose flour, plus extra as needed
2 large eggs plus 6 large yolks
2 tablespoons olive oil
1 tablespoon salt
1 recipe sauce (recipes follow)

1. Process flour, eggs and yolks, and oil in food processor until mixture forms cohesive dough that feels soft and is barely tacky to touch, about 45 seconds. (If dough sticks to fingers, add up to ¼ cup flour, 1 tablespoon at a time, until barely tacky. If dough doesn't become cohesive, add up to 1 tablespoon water, 1 teaspoon at a time, until it just comes together; process 30 seconds longer.)
2. Turn dough ball onto dry counter and knead until smooth, 1 to 2 minutes. Shape dough into 6-inch-long cylinder. Wrap in plastic wrap and let rest at room temperature for at least 1 hour or up to 4 hours.
3. Cut cylinder crosswise into 6 equal pieces. Working with 1 piece of dough at a time (rewrap remaining dough), dust both sides with flour, place cut side down on clean counter, and press into 3-inch square. Using heavy rolling pin, roll into 6-inch square. Dust both sides of dough lightly with flour. Starting at center of square, roll dough away from you in 1 motion. Return rolling pin to center of dough and roll toward you in 1 motion. Repeat rolling steps until dough sticks to counter and measures roughly 12 inches long. Lightly dust both sides of dough with flour and continue to roll until dough measures roughly 20 inches long and 6 inches wide, frequently lifting dough to release it from counter. (You should be able to easily see outline of your fingers through dough.) If dough firmly sticks to counter and wrinkles when rolled out, dust dough lightly with flour.
4. Transfer pasta sheet to clean dish towel and let stand, uncovered, until firm around edges, about 15 minutes; meanwhile, roll out remaining dough.
5. Starting with 1 short end, gently fold pasta sheet at 2-inch intervals until sheet has been folded into flat, rectangular roll. Using sharp chef's knife, slice crosswise into 3⁄16-inch-thick noodles. Use your fingers to unfurl pasta and transfer to baking sheet. Repeat folding and cutting remaining sheets of dough. Cook noodles within 1 hour or freeze.
6. Bring 4 quarts water to boil in large pot. Add pasta and salt and cook until tender but still al dente, about 3 minutes. Reserve 1 cup cooking water, then drain pasta and return it to pot. Toss with sauce and serve immediately.

Olive Oil Sauce with Anchovies and Parsley

MAKES 1 CUP;
ENOUGH FOR 1 POUND PASTA

⅓ cup extra-virgin olive oil
2 garlic cloves, minced
2 anchovy fillets, rinsed, patted dry, and minced
Salt and pepper
2 tablespoons chopped fresh parsley
4 teaspoons lemon juice

1. Heat oil in 12-inch skillet over medium-low heat until shimmering. Add garlic, anchovies, ½ teaspoon pepper, and ⅛ teaspoon salt; cook until fragrant, about 30 seconds. Remove pan from heat and cover to keep warm while cooking pasta.
2. To serve, return pan to medium heat. Add cooked pasta, ½ cup reserved cooking water, parsley, and lemon juice; toss to combine, adjusting consistency with remaining reserved cooking water as needed. Season with salt and pepper to taste, and serve immediately.

Tomato–Browned Butter Sauce

MAKES 3 CUPS;
ENOUGH FOR 1 POUND PASTA

Watch the butter closely so that the solids don't burn.

1 (28-ounce) can whole peeled tomatoes
4 tablespoons unsalted butter, cut into 4 pieces
2 garlic cloves, minced
½ teaspoon sugar
Salt and pepper
2 teaspoons sherry vinegar
3 tablespoons chopped fresh basil
Grated Parmesan cheese

1. Process tomatoes and their juice in food processor until smooth, about 30 seconds. Melt 3 tablespoons butter in 12-inch skillet over medium-high heat, swirling occasionally, until butter is dark brown and releases nutty aroma, about 1½ minutes. Stir in garlic and cook for 10 seconds. Stir in processed tomatoes, sugar, and ½ teaspoon salt and simmer until sauce is slightly reduced, about 8 minutes. Remove pan from heat; whisk in vinegar and remaining 1 tablespoon butter. Season with salt and pepper to taste; cover to keep warm while cooking pasta.
2. To serve, return pan to medium heat. Add cooked pasta, ¼ cup reserved cooking water, and basil; toss to combine, adjusting consistency with remaining reserved cooking water as needed. Season with salt and pepper to taste, and serve immediately with Parmesan.

Walnut Cream Sauce

MAKES 2 CUPS;
ENOUGH FOR 1 POUND PASTA

1½ cups walnuts
¾ cup dry white wine
½ cup heavy cream
1 ounce Parmesan cheese, grated (½ cup)
Salt and pepper
¼ cup minced fresh chives

1. Toast walnuts in 12-inch skillet over medium heat until golden and fragrant, 2 to 4 minutes. Process 1 cup walnuts in food processor until finely ground, about 10 seconds. Transfer to small bowl. Pulse remaining ½ cup walnuts in food processor until coarsely chopped, 3 to 5 pulses. Bring wine to simmer in now-empty skillet over medium-high heat; cook until reduced to ¼ cup, about 3 minutes. Whisk in cream, walnuts, Parmesan, ¼ teaspoon salt, and ½ teaspoon pepper. Remove pan from heat and cover to keep warm.
2. To serve, return pan to medium heat. Add pasta, ½ cup reserved cooking water, and chives; toss to combine, adding remaining cooking water as needed to adjust consistency. Season with salt and pepper to taste; serve immediately.

ROLLING AND CUTTING PASTA DOUGH BY HAND

To roll pasta by hand, we start with a soft, malleable dough and work with one small, manageable piece at a time.

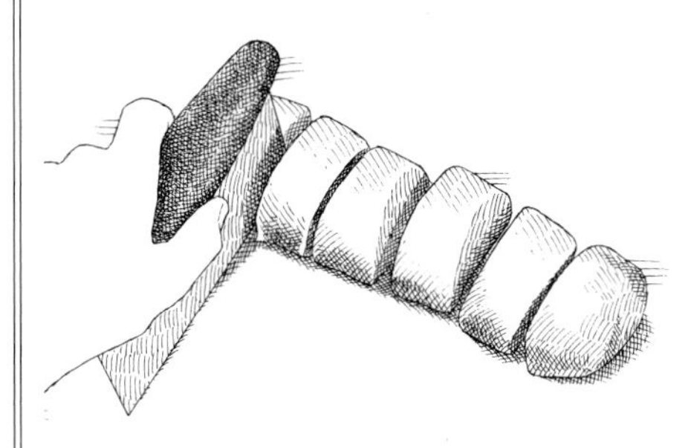

1. WORK WITH SMALL PIECES Divide rested dough into 6 equal pieces. Working with 1 piece at a time (keeping other dough pieces covered), dust with flour, then press cut side down into 3-inch square. With rolling pin, roll into 6-inch square and dust with flour.

2. ROLL FROM CENTER Roll dough to 6 by 12 inches, rolling from center of dough one way at a time; dust with flour. Continue rolling to 6 by 20 inches, lifting frequently to release from counter. Transfer dough to kitchen towel and air-dry for 15 minutes.

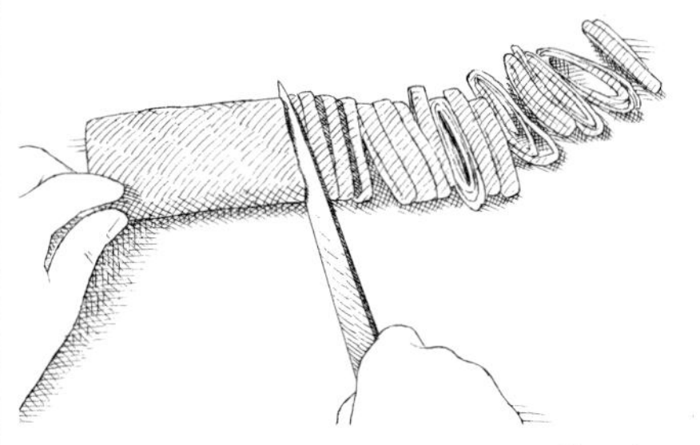

3. FOLD AND CUT INTRO STRIPS Starting with short end, gently fold dried sheet at 2-inch intervals to create flat roll. Slice into 3⁄16-inch-thick noodles. Use your fingers to unfurl pasta; transfer to baking sheet.

REINVENTING MACARONI AND CHEESE

PAM ANDERSON WITH KAREN TACK, *January/February 1997*

Macaroni and cheese has always been on my "must-explore" list. It's just eaten too often in this country for us to ignore it. Kids in particular say yes to macaroni and cheese when they turn up their noses at everything else. Unfortunately, it's the boxed version, complete with orange cheese powder, that's made most often.

There are two distinct styles of macaroni and cheese: béchamel-based, in which macaroni is blanketed with a cheesy white sauce, usually topped with crumbs, and baked. The other variety, the kind my mother always made, is custard-based. In this style, a mixture of egg and milk is poured over layers of grated cheese and noodles. As the dish bakes, the eggs, milk, and cheese set into a custard. It can also be topped with bread crumbs, although my mom always sprinkled crushed saltine crackers over hers.

Evaporated milk creates a perfect creamy base for a macaroni and cheese that is almost as quick to make as boxed versions.

This should be a wonderful, satisfying dish, but many of the recipes I looked at seemed tired, leaden, and uninspired. After compiling a bunch of test recipes, I began to wonder if I really did still love this simple dish. Then I read the chapter on macaroni and cheese in John Thorne's *Simple Cooking* (1989). "As it happens," he begins, "I'm very fond of macaroni and cheese, and keep a special spot in my heart for cooks who genuinely love it: they are not that many." After reading his four-page essay, I suspected that his recipe for macaroni and cheese was the real one, the others mere shadows.

NO COMPARISON

Making the dish confirmed that John Thorne's macaroni and cheese was the best. I could do our usual in-depth testing, but I knew up front I wouldn't come up with anything better.

Thorne's recipe starts with macaroni cooked just shy of al dente and then tossed with butter. Evaporated milk, hot sauce, dry mustard, eggs, and lots of cheese are stirred into the noodles. The combination is baked for 20 minutes, with cheese and milk additions and a thorough stir every 5 minutes. Frequent stirring allows the eggs to thicken without setting, which results in an incredibly silky sauce. During cooking, the sauce settles into the tubular openings, offering a burst of cheese with each new bite. I was delighted. Never had I gotten a dish right on the first try. For once, someone else had done the homework.

Just to confirm my belief, I baked the two styles of macaroni and cheese defined earlier: one with a cheese-flavored béchamel sauce, the other thickened with eggs, milk, and cheese. Neither compared to Thorne's dish. The béchamel-based version was grainy and tasted exactly as Thorne predicted: not like macaroni and cheese, but "macaroni with cheese sauce."

Of the two macaroni and cheeses, I preferred the cheesier-flavored custard version. Because this custard-based macaroni and cheese was simply a variant of Thorne's recipe, I thought I might offer it as an alternative to stirring. A side-by-side tasting proved the two macaroni and cheese dishes to be very different, however, and the stirred version remained superior in my mind. Compared to the luxuriously silky cheese sauce of the stirred macaroni, the baked egg, milk, and cheese formed a dry custard that set around the noodles. Thorne's recipe was clearly still the best.

PUTTING IT TO THE TEST

The competition ruled out, I moved forward to study Thorne's recipe a little more closely. Did the dish really require evaporated milk or was this an idiosyncrasy of the late '30s when the recipe was first published in *The Home Comfort Cook Book* (1937). Wouldn't regular milk or half-and-half work equally well? What other cheeses, besides sharp cheddar, would taste good?

I had also thought of a few possible refinements. First, I found that at the end of the 20 minutes of baking, the dish was hot, but hardly piping. By the time a person had consumed his or her portion, the cheese sauce had cooled and set a bit. I also missed the contrasting textures of crunchy bread crumbs and soft noodles and sauce. Thorne's advice to sprinkle the macaroni and cheese with crumbled common crackers was one possibility, but I was looking for something a little more finished. Although I liked the rich, full cheese flavor Thorne achieved with a whole pound of cheese, I found myself full after only a few bites. I wanted to find out if the dish was just as good with less cheese.

After testing the recipe with whole and low-fat milks and half-and-half, I realized that evaporated milk was not an ingredient thoughtlessly left in. All the macaroni and cheese dishes made with fresh milk curdled a bit, resulting in a chalky, grainy texture. The one made with evaporated milk remained silky-smooth. The evaporation and sterilization process stabilizes the milk, which in turn, stabilizes the macaroni and cheese.

After making the dish with Vermont, New York, and Wisconsin cheddars, I preferred the less sharp Wisconsin variety. Because the recipe calls for such a large quantity, a slightly milder cheese is preferable. Further testing confirmed this point. Macaroni and cheese made with Gruyère was so strong I couldn't even eat it. To my surprise, highly processed cheeses such as American performed quite

well in this dish. Much like evaporated milk, the more processing, the more stable the cheese and the more creamy the dish. For flavor, use cheddar; for texture, buy American. I also found the dish did not suffer with only 12 ounces of cheese compared to the 1 pound called for in the original recipe.

I found that I could not remedy the dish's lukewarm temperature problem by leaving it in the oven much longer than the suggested 20 minutes. Doing so ran the risk of curdling the eggs, and the dish started to develop a subtle grainy texture. So I tried two solutions, both of which worked. To avoid pouring hot macaroni into a cold dish, I stuck the pan in the preheating oven. By the time the macaroni was ready to drain, the pan emerged from the oven pot-holder hot. Warming the milk a bit before mixing it with the pasta also gave the dish a warm head start.

As suggested by Thorne, crisp common crackers sprinkled over the macaroni and cheese offer a much-needed foil to the rich, unctuous sauce. For a further refinement, I toasted some fresh buttered bread crumbs.

After I shared this recipe with friend and cooking colleague Stephen Schmidt, he reported back his finding that if one used a heavy-bottomed pot and cooked it over low heat, it was possible to forgo the baking step altogether and make the macaroni and cheese on top of the stove in less than 15 minutes. I tried his suggestion and found the stovetop macaroni and cheese to be as good as the baked one. By following his method, it was possible to complete this dish in virtually the same amount of time it would take to make the boxed stuff. And considering the same preparation time and a few dollars more buy you the difference between an institutional experience and the real McCoy, I would call this recipe a no-brainer.

Stovetop Macaroni and Cheese

SERVES 4

You can skip the bread crumbs and sprinkle the dish with crumbled common crackers or saltines, if desired.

Bread Crumbs

3 slices hearty white sandwich bread, torn into quarters
2 tablespoons unsalted butter, melted
Salt

Macaroni and Cheese

2 large eggs
1 (12-ounce) can evaporated milk
1 teaspoon dry mustard, dissolved in 1 teaspoon water
Salt
¼ teaspoon pepper
¼ teaspoon hot sauce
8 ounces elbow macaroni (2 cups)
4 tablespoons unsalted butter
12 ounces sharp cheddar, American, or Monterey Jack cheese, shredded (3 cups)

1. *For the bread crumbs:* Pulse bread in food processor to coarse crumbs, about 10 pulses. Melt butter in 12-inch skillet over medium heat. Add bread crumbs and cook, stirring often, until beginning to brown, 4 to 6 minutes. Season with salt to taste; set aside.
2. *For the macaroni and cheese:* Mix eggs, 1 cup evaporated milk, mustard mixture, ½ teaspoon salt, pepper, and hot sauce in bowl.
3. Meanwhile, bring 2 quarts water to boil in Dutch oven. Add pasta and 1½ teaspoons salt and cook, stirring often, until al dente. Drain pasta and return to pot over low heat. Add butter and toss to melt.
4. Add egg mixture and three-quarters of cheese to pasta and toss until thoroughly combined and cheese starts to melt. Gradually add remaining evaporated milk and remaining cheese, stirring constantly, until mixture is hot and creamy, about 5 minutes. Serve immediately, sprinkling individual portions with toasted bread crumbs.

variation

"Baked" Macaroni and Cheese

Add ¼ cup grated Parmesan cheese to toasted bread crumbs. Adjust oven rack 6 inches from broiler element and heat broiler. Transfer macaroni and cheese mixture to 13 by 9-inch broiler-safe baking dish and sprinkle with bread-crumb mixture. Broil until topping turns deep golden brown, 1 to 2 minutes. Let casserole cool for 5 minutes before serving.

WHAT IS EVAPORATED MILK?

Evaporated milk is merely milk that is gently heated in a vacuum (a process called forewarming) so that 60 percent or more of the water evaporates. The resulting thick liquid is then sterilized and canned. Evaporated milk has about twice the concentration of fat and protein as regular whole milk.

Since evaporated milk is impervious to curdling, it guarantees a silky, smooth texture in our Stovetop Macaroni and Cheese recipe. The reason for this is the process by which this product is made. In regular milk, the main proteins, namely large casein molecules, tend to clump together when exposed to heat. The forewarming process makes the proteins more resistant to curdling. During forewarming, the big casein molecules are surrounded by smaller molecules of whey protein, and the whey proteins get in the way of the clumping of the casein molecules. Salts and other additives also interfere with the clumping of the casein molecules. Salts (disodium phosphate and/or sodium citrate) improve the ability of the proteins in the mix to retain water (the release of water is another symptom of curdling). Carrageenan gum may also be added to the finished product to prevent fat separation during storage.

STREAMLINING MARINARA

DAVID PAZMIÑO, *March/April 2006*

There's something great about a quick tomato sauce: fast, furious, and fresh. But what a quick sauce offers in convenience it lacks in the complexity of a slowly simmered tomato sauce, the best known of which may be marinara.

Unfortunately, complexity of flavor means lots of time in the kitchen, which is in short supply on a Tuesday night. My goal was to produce a multidimensional sauce in less than an hour, starting the clock the moment I entered the kitchen and stopping it when dinner was on the table. Weeding through hundreds of marinara recipes, I settled on testing not only a variety of "quick" versions but also some that were cooked for longer than an hour. The differences were readily apparent. The quick sauces were generally thin and lacked depth of flavor. The long-cooked sauces got the complexity right, but most relied on an ambitious laundry list of ingredients to achieve it—not to mention a lot of time. The sauce I was after had to capture some of these robust flavors within the confines of fairly quick cooking.

A TRICK WITH TOMATOES

Because prime fresh tomatoes are available for such a limited time during the year, I opted for canned. But which variety should I choose?

Crushed, pureed, and diced tomatoes offered the ultimate ease in sauce making: Open can, dump contents into pan. But all three options have downsides. Pureed tomatoes go into the can already cooked, which imparts a stale, flat flavor to the final sauce. Crushed tomatoes are generally packed in tomato puree: same problem. With these, my sauces came out tasting like unremarkable homemade versions of the jarred spaghetti sauces sold at the supermarket. With canned diced tomatoes, the problem was texture, not flavor. In the past, we've learned that manufacturers treat diced tomatoes with calcium chloride to keep them from turning to mush and losing their shape. That's fine for many dishes, but for recipes in which a smooth consistency is desired, calcium chloride does its job too well, making the tomatoes harder to break down—and the resulting sauces oddly granular.

The only choice left, then, was canned whole tomatoes. (While whole tomatoes are also treated with calcium chloride, the chemical has direct contact with a much smaller percentage of the tomato.) The big drawback of using whole tomatoes in a sauce is that they have to be cut up. Chopping them on a cutting board was a mess. The solution was to dump the tomatoes into a strainer over a bowl and then hand-crush them, removing the hard core and any stray bits of skin.

That's when I made the first of several decisions that would enable me to get long-simmered complexity in a short time. Most marinara recipes call for simply adding a can (or two) of tomatoes to the pot, juice and all—and some even call for throwing in a can of water. Now that I was separating the solids from the juice anyway, why not experiment with adding less of the reserved liquid? The trick worked: By adding only 2½ cups of the drained juice from two cans of whole tomatoes (rather than the full 3½ cups I had collected) and omitting the extra water, I managed to cut the simmering time by almost 20 minutes.

Up until now I had been following the standard marinara procedure of sautéing aromatics (onions and garlic) in olive oil in a saucepan before adding the tomatoes, liquid, and flavorings, then simmering. That's fine if you have all day, but I had only an hour. So I switched from a saucepan to a skillet, hoping the greater surface area would encourage faster evaporation and, thus, faster concentration of flavors.

It was faster, all right—down to just under an hour—but I felt that the sauce could use gutsier tomato flavor. Not only was the solution simple, but it was the key step in giving my quick sauce the complexity of a long-simmered one. Before adding the liquids and simmering, I sautéed the tomato meats until they glazed the bottom of the pan. Only then did I add the liquids, a normally routine step that, by essentially deglazing the pan, added crucial flavor to my sauce.

BALANCING ACTS

It was time to develop more depth of flavor. Onions added a pleasant sweetness, but carrots added an earthy flavor that diminished that of the tomatoes. Sugar, added at the end of cooking, proved to be the working solution to balance the flavors: too much and my sauce began to taste like it came out of a jar; too little and the acidity overwhelmed the other flavors. Tasters loved the robust, complex flavor of red wine, and a mere ⅓ cup was just the right amount. But not just any bottle: Wines with a heavy oak flavor rated lower than those with little to no oak presence.

We use canned whole tomatoes in our quick marinara, reserving a few to add at the end for brightness.

I now had a good marinara ready to serve in less than an hour—about half the time of many recipes. Could I further bolster the complexity without adding minutes? On a hunch, I tried reserving a few of the uncooked canned tomatoes and adding them near the end of cooking. When I served this sauce alongside the earlier version, tasters were unanimous in their preference for the new sauce; just six tomatoes pureed into the sauce at the end added enough brightness to complement the deeper profile of the cooked sauce.

So far the sauce had little flavor from herbs beyond oregano. Fresh basil, also added at the end, contributed a floral aroma that complemented the sauce's careful balance of sweet and acid.

Marinara Sauce

MAKES 4 CUPS;
ENOUGH FOR 1 POUND PASTA

Because canned tomatoes vary in acidity and saltiness, it's best to add sugar, salt, and pepper to taste just before serving. Chianti or Merlot works well for the dry red wine. We like a smoother marinara, but if you prefer a chunkier sauce, give it just three or four pulses in the food processor in step 4.

2 (28-ounce) cans whole peeled tomatoes
3 tablespoons extra-virgin olive oil
1 onion, chopped fine
2 garlic cloves, minced
2 teaspoons minced fresh oregano or ½ teaspoon dried
⅓ cup dry red wine
3 tablespoons chopped fresh basil
Sugar
Salt and pepper

1. Pour tomatoes and their juice into strainer set over large bowl. Open tomatoes with your hands and remove seeds and fibrous cores; let tomatoes drain excess liquid, about 5 minutes. Remove ¾ cup tomatoes from strainer and set aside. Set aside 2½ cups tomato juice and discard remainder.
2. Heat 2 tablespoons oil in 12-inch skillet over medium heat until shimmering. Add onion and cook until softened and lightly browned, 5 to 7 minutes. Stir in garlic and oregano and cook until fragrant, about 30 seconds.
3. Stir in strained tomatoes and increase heat to medium-high. Cook, stirring often, until liquid has evaporated, tomatoes begin to stick to bottom of skillet, and brown fond forms around pan edges, 10 to 12 minutes. Stir in wine and cook until thick and syrupy, about 1 minute. Stir in reserved tomato juice, scraping up any browned bits. Bring to simmer and cook, stirring occasionally, until sauce is thick, 8 to 10 minutes.
4. Pulse sauce and reserved tomatoes in food processor until slightly chunky, about 8 pulses. Return sauce to now-empty skillet and stir in basil and remaining 1 tablespoon oil. Season with sugar, salt, and pepper to taste before serving.

GETTING SLOW-SIMMERED FLAVOR FAST

The best marinaras have lots of complexity—and demand lots of cooking time. Here's how we speed up the process.

DRAIN JUICE A can of tomatoes has more juice than solids. We jump-start flavor concentration by draining off almost a cup of juice beforehand.

CARAMELIZE SOLIDS Caramelizing the tomato solids briskly in a large skillet before deglazing with liquid ingredients further deepens the flavor profile.

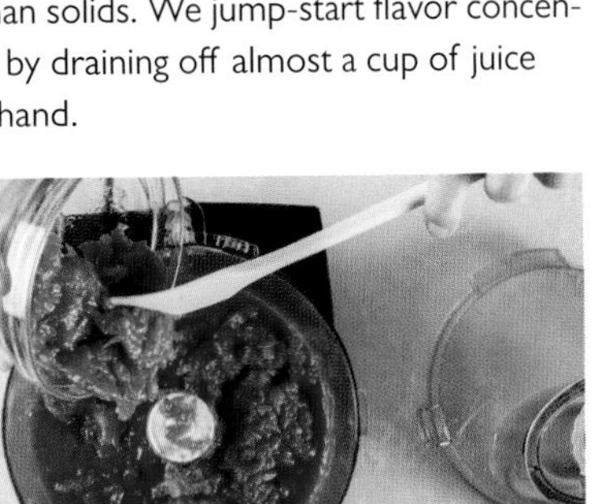

ADD RAW TOMATOES Reserving a few uncooked tomatoes to add at the end contributes an extra note of freshness to the cooked sauce.

ADD SUGAR Seasoning the finished sauce with sugar in addition to the usual salt and pepper brings out the complexity of the wine and balances the acidity of the tomatoes.

MATCHING PASTA SHAPES WITH SAUCE

In Italy there is a fine art to matching pasta shapes and sauces, but in the test kitchen, we are a bit freer with the pairing and endorse just one general rule: you should be able to eat the pasta and sauce easily in each mouthful. This means that the texture and consistency of the sauce should work with the pasta shape.

Long strands are best with smooth sauces or pestos or light sauces, such as oil and garlic. In general, wider long noodles, such as fettuccine, can more easily support slightly chunkier sauces than can very thin noodles like spaghetti. Wide pastas like fettuccine or tagliatelle are also well suited to creamy sauces like Alfredo. Short tubular or molded pasta shapes do an excellent job of trapping chunkier sauces. Sauces with very large chunks are best with shells, rigatoni, or other large tubes. Sauces with small to medium chunks pair well with fusilli or penne. Since our Marinara Sauce can be as smooth or chunky as you choose (depending on how many times you pulse it in the food processor), be sure to pair your final sauce with an appropriate pasta shape. If pulsing the sauce eight times as called for in the recipe, we like to use a long-strand pasta like spaghetti.

BETTER PASTA SALAD WITH PESTO

SANDRA WU, *July/August 2006*

More light and refreshing than a cream-based sauce or a chunky ragù, pesto makes a top-notch accompaniment to pasta during the sultry summer months. There's nothing complicated about this uncooked Ligurian sauce, which consists of processed fresh basil, garlic, pine nuts, Parmigiano-Reggiano cheese, and olive oil. And tossing it with hot, just-cooked pasta couldn't be easier. But numerous issues arise once pesto is added to a pasta salad. The refrigerator dulls the color and flavor of the pesto, which turns greasy and clumpy as the pasta cools.

PERFECTING THE PESTO

I began by trying varying ratios of the five integral ingredients: basil, garlic (blanched briefly to tame its harsh bite), Parmesan cheese, olive oil (extra-virgin), and pine nuts (toasted to enhance their nutty flavor). I had to use a lot of basil (between 3 and 4 packed cups) to achieve decent herbal flavor and enough bulk. But when made even a few hours ahead of time, the basil turned dark and muddy. Adding another green element seemed the obvious solution. Parsley is a common trick, but I needed to use so much that it began to compete with the basil flavor. I'd seen frozen chopped spinach used, but while it turned the pesto a nice, bright green, it also made the texture stringy. The easy solution was to add a small amount of fresh baby spinach, which provided a lovely bright green color and smooth texture without interfering with the basil flavor.

Fresh baby spinach keeps our pesto bright green, and a small amount of mayonnaise provides a luscious texture.

While the relatively thin consistency of traditional pesto might be fine for hot noodles, a thicker, creamier pesto was in order for room-temperature pasta. But no matter how much I fiddled with ingredient amounts, the pesto was always less than optimally creamy. Upping the quantity of cheese and pine nuts thickened the pesto, but also made it salty, gritty, and pasty. Adding more oil to smooth out the mixture only made the pesto greasy.

Since this dish wasn't exactly an Italian classic, I decided to borrow a standard ingredient used in many American pasta salads: mayonnaise. The creamy condiment served as the perfect binder—so long as it was used in moderation. Six tablespoons was enough to provide a luscious texture.

PREPARING THE PASTA

The best pasta shapes for this dish have a textured surface with a concave nook or two that can trap the pesto and keep it from sliding off. With its indented center and jagged edges, farfalle made an excellent partner. Unlike hot pasta, which should generally be cooked until al dente, the pasta used in salads should cook slightly longer, until tender.

When the pesto was added straight to just-cooked pasta, it took an hour to reach room temperature. The hot pasta also "cooked" the basil, deadening its impact. Rinsing the pasta in cold water cooled it down quickly but made the surface of the pasta too slick to hold on to the pesto. The solution was to let the pasta cool in a single layer on a rimmed baking sheet, tossing it in a splash of oil to prevent sticking.

Finally, I added lemon juice to cut through the richness. An extra ½ cup of toasted pine nuts folded into the pesto-coated pasta added a sweet, nutty note and textural contrast. Small cherry or grape tomatoes contributed color and bursts of freshness. Finally, I had translated a Ligurian mainstay into an American picnic classic.

Pasta Salad with Pesto

SERVES 8 TO 10

Other pasta shapes can be substituted for the farfalle.

2 garlic cloves, unpeeled
1 pound farfalle
Salt and pepper
5 tablespoons extra-virgin olive oil
3 cups fresh basil leaves, lightly bruised
1 cup baby spinach
¾ cup pine nuts, toasted
2 tablespoons lemon juice
1½ ounces Parmesan cheese, grated (¾ cup), plus extra for serving
6 tablespoons mayonnaise
12 ounces cherry tomatoes, quartered

1. Bring 4 quarts water to boil in large pot. Add garlic and cook for 1 minute. Remove garlic with slotted spoon and rinse under cold water to stop cooking. Let garlic cool slightly, then peel and chop fine; set aside.
2. Add pasta and 1 tablespoon salt to boiling water and cook, stirring often, until tender. Reserve ¼ cup cooking water. Drain pasta, toss with 1 tablespoon oil, and spread in single layer on rimmed baking sheet. Let pasta and cooking water cool to room temperature, about 30 minutes.
3. Process basil, spinach, ¼ cup pine nuts, lemon juice, garlic, and 1 teaspoon salt in food processor until smooth, about 30 seconds, scraping down sides of bowl as needed. Add Parmesan, mayonnaise, and remaining ¼ cup oil and process until thoroughly combined; transfer to large bowl.
4. Toss cooled pasta with pesto, adding reserved cooking water, 1 tablespoon at a time, until pesto evenly coats pasta.
5. Fold in remaining ½ cup pine nuts and tomatoes. Season with salt and pepper to taste. Serve.

SPAGHETTI AL VINO BIANCO

ANDREA GEARY, *March/April 2012*

A plate of pasta and a glass of wine are a natural pairing. But I'd long heard references to a dish called *spaghetti al vino rosso* that exploits their affinity: You cook the pasta in wine instead of water and then top it off with olive oil, a bit of butter, and a sprinkling of cheese. The concept is not without precedent: Cooking rice in a wine-spiked broth transforms it from a blank slate into a complex and wonderful risotto. I figured the same could be true of pasta if I could just pin down a reliable recipe.

Easier said than done. Recipes were hard to track down, and the ones I found were all over the map. One called for boiling the spaghetti in a 50/50 mix of water and red wine that was then (wastefully) poured down the drain. In another, a whole bottle of wine was reduced to a glaze (eliminating all of its pleasant booziness) and used to coat spaghetti cooked separately in water. A third approach resembled risotto-making and seemed the most promising: the pasta was parcooked in water and then transferred to a skillet where about 2 cups of wine were added in increments so that the pasta could absorb the wine as it finished cooking.

Reducing some white wine into a glaze and adding the rest slowly to the pasta as it finishes cooking makes for a balanced dish.

But the dish wasn't perfect. While tasters liked the pasta's lively wine kick, they also found the dish tannic. The real deal breaker, though? Its unappetizing purple-gray color.

My research indicated that this was a dish almost always made with red wine. Nevertheless, I wondered what would happen if I swapped the red wine for white, which would get rid of the hideous mauve color. I tried it and found that the switch also solved the tannin problem, since such flavors come from the grape skins, which are removed early in the process of making white wine. But now I had a new issue: The spaghetti wasn't as robustly flavored.

I thought back to the method that reduced a full bottle of wine in a skillet. I experimented with reducing about a third of a bottle of white wine to a glaze while the spaghetti parcooked in water. Then I introduced the partially cooked spaghetti to the glaze and added the remainder of the bottle gradually, stirring as the spaghetti finished cooking. The glaze provided subtle complexity, but we agreed that this spaghetti was going to need more than just olive oil, butter, and Pecorino Romano to hold its own.

Garlic and red pepper flakes were easily incorporated into the glaze. Crisp, salty pancetta sprinkled over the pasta before serving was also a shoo-in. Arugula's peppery notes complemented the other flavors perfectly. Pine nuts added textural contrast.

My spaghetti was almost complete, but it seemed a tad dry. I had been stirring in some cold butter along with reserved pasta water at the end, but the resulting sauce was too insubstantial. A little bit of cream was just the thing to bulk it up.

Spaghetti al Vino Bianco

SERVES 4

Use a good-quality dry white wine but avoid a heavily oaked white such as Chardonnay. If the wine reduction is too sharp in step 2, season it to taste with up to 1 tablespoon of sugar, adding it in 1-teaspoon increments.

1 tablespoon extra-virgin olive oil
4 ounces pancetta, cut into ¼-inch pieces
2 garlic cloves, minced
Pinch red pepper flakes
1 (750-ml) bottle dry white wine
Salt and pepper
Sugar
1 pound spaghetti
5 ounces (5 cups) baby arugula
1 ounce Pecorino Romano cheese, grated (½ cup), plus extra for serving
⅓ cup heavy cream
¼ cup pine nuts, toasted and chopped coarse

1. Heat oil and pancetta in 12-inch skillet over medium-high heat; cook until pancetta is browned and crispy, 4 to 5 minutes. Using slotted spoon, transfer pancetta to paper towel–lined plate. Pour off all but 2 tablespoons fat from skillet.
2. Reduce heat to medium-low and add garlic and pepper flakes to skillet. Cook, stirring frequently, until garlic begins to turn golden, 1 to 2 minutes. Carefully add 1½ cups wine and increase heat to medium-high. Cook until wine is reduced to ½ cup, 8 to 10 minutes. Add ½ teaspoon salt. Season with up to 1 tablespoon sugar to taste if needed.
3. Bring 4 quarts water to boil in large pot. Add pasta and 1 tablespoon salt and cook, stirring often, until pasta is flexible but not fully cooked, about 4 minutes. Reserve 2 cups cooking water, then drain pasta.
4. Transfer pasta to skillet with reduced wine. Place skillet over medium heat; add ½ cup unreduced wine and cook, tossing constantly, until wine is fully absorbed. Continue to add remaining wine, ½ cup at a time, tossing constantly, until pasta is al dente, about 8 minutes. (If wine is absorbed before spaghetti is fully cooked, add ½ cup reserved cooking water at a time to skillet and continue to cook.)
5. Remove skillet from heat. Place arugula on top of pasta; pour ¼ cup reserved cooking water over arugula, cover, and let stand for 1 minute. Add ¼ cup Pecorino and cream; toss until sauce lightly coats pasta and arugula is evenly distributed. Season with salt and pepper to taste. Transfer to platter and sprinkle with pine nuts, pancetta, and remaining ¼ cup Pecorino. Serve immediately, passing extra Pecorino separately.

FRESH TOMATO PUTTANESCA

ANDREW JANJIGIAN, *September/October 2013*

At the end of summer, I inevitably find myself with a glut of beautiful garden tomatoes, both small and large. As a result, I'm always searching for ways to use them beyond salads. Puttanesca, that most boisterous of classic Italian sauces (legend has it that it was invented by Neapolitan prostitutes on break between customers), is one of my favorite tomato-based sauces.

I love the clash of flavors that this sauce presents: Spicy pepper flakes, pungent garlic, and salty anchovies, olives, and capers meet up with clean-tasting fresh herbs and tangy-sweet tomatoes. Putting my harvest to use in this quick sauce would address the generic "cooked" quality that stems from using canned tomatoes, the usual choice for this dish. I wasn't aiming for a no-cook sauce, but I did want a fresher puttanesca—one that retained the fruits' clean-tasting sweetness alongside the richer, more assertive flavors that are the essence of this dish.

A FRESH START

My first step was trying several varieties of tomato in a basic puttanesca: minced garlic and anchovies (anchovy paste, for convenience), red pepper flakes, chopped black olives, and capers, all sautéed in olive oil. Juicy larger tomatoes required me to reduce the sauce to avoid a watery consistency, but when I did, its fresh flavor all but disappeared. But low-moisture grape (or cherry) tomatoes, once halved, need very little simmering time to reduce to a sauce-like consistency. Availability was on my side, too: Not only is my garden full of these tomatoes by summer's end but they're also consistently decent in supermarkets year-round.

There was a downside: The larger ratio of skin to flesh meant that my sauce was full of chewy skins. Since I wasn't about to skin dozens of tiny tomatoes, I gave them a quick blitz in a blender, which pulverized the skins completely.

Unfortunately, doing so also caused them to shed more moisture—not as much as big tomatoes but enough that it seemed I would have to revert to a longer simmering time. What if I drained the pureed tomatoes in a strainer before adding them to the sauce? That way, I could discard the exuded liquid.

But I quickly realized my faulty thinking. The majority of tomato flavor resides in the juice, jelly, and seeds, so I'd essentially be throwing away the best part. The better approach was to briefly simmer the juice to concentrate its flavor. Once it had reduced to ⅓ cup, I added the uncooked pulp along with the olives and capers. When the sauce was heated through, the bulk of the tomatoes had softened but still tasted fresh.

To give our sauce lots of fresh tomato flavor without a watery texture, we reduce the tomatoes' juice and then add the pulp.

SALTY AND SOUR

Now to tame the rowdier ingredients: the olives and the capers. I tested common varieties of high-quality black olives. Salt-cured were too salty, but brine-cured kalamata and Gaeta, both of which were fruity and pleasantly crisp-tender, were equally excellent choices. I chopped them coarsely—any finer and the sauce turned a muddy brown. I did finely chop the capers, however, so that their briny punch hit every bite. A smidgen of dried oregano introduced complexity; ½ cup of minced fresh parsley offered freshness.

One final adjustment: Finding myself out of the standard spaghetti or linguine, I reached for campanelle. Tasters preferred the compact size and convoluted twists of this pasta, since it did a better job of trapping the coarse sauce. Plus, aesthetically it hinted at a summertime pasta salad, giving the dish an overall fresher appeal.

Summer Pasta Puttanesca

SERVES 4

We prefer to make this dish with campanelle, but fusilli and orecchiette also work. Very finely mashed anchovy fillets (rinsed and dried before mashing) can be used instead of anchovy paste.

3 tablespoons extra-virgin olive oil
4 garlic cloves, minced
1 tablespoon anchovy paste
¼ teaspoon red pepper flakes
¼ teaspoon dried oregano
1½ pounds grape or cherry tomatoes
1 pound campanelle
Salt
½ cup pitted kalamata olives, chopped coarse
3 tablespoons capers, rinsed and minced
½ cup minced fresh parsley

1. Combine oil, garlic, anchovy paste, pepper flakes, and oregano in small bowl. Process tomatoes in blender until finely chopped but not pureed, 15 to 45 seconds. Transfer to fine-mesh strainer set in large bowl and let drain for 5 minutes, occasionally pressing gently on solids with rubber spatula to extract liquid (this should yield about ¾ cup). Reserve tomato liquid and pulp.
2. Bring 4 quarts water to boil in large pot. Add pasta and 1 tablespoon salt and cook, stirring often, until al dente. Reserve 1 cup cooking water, then drain pasta and return it to pot.
3. While pasta is cooking, cook garlic-anchovy mixture in 12-inch skillet over medium heat, stirring frequently, until garlic is fragrant but not browned, 2 to 3 minutes. Add tomato liquid and simmer until reduced to ⅓ cup, 2 to 3 minutes. Add olives, capers, and tomato pulp and cook until just heated through, 2 to 3 minutes. Stir in parsley.
4. Add sauce to pasta and toss to combine, adjusting consistency with reserved cooking water as needed. Season with salt to taste, and serve immediately.

SPRING VEGETABLE PASTA

ANDREW JANJIGIAN, *May/June 2011*

You'd never know that pasta primavera, a pseudo-Italian dish that appears on virtually every chain restaurant menu, actually has roots in French haute cuisine. The usual reproduction—a random jumble of produce tossed with noodles in a heavy, flavor-deadening cream sauce—tastes nothing like spring. Surprisingly, when I dug up the original recipe from New York's famed Le Cirque restaurant, my colleagues found it wasn't all that inspiring either, despite taking about 2 hours to prepare and dirtying five pans. First, the vegetables (which had been painstakingly blanched one by one) were bland. Second, the cream-, butter-, and cheese-enriched sauce dulled flavor and didn't really unify the dish. If I wanted a true spring-vegetable pasta—with a few thoughtfully chosen vegetables and a light, but full-bodied sauce that clung well to the noodles and brought the dish together—I'd have to start from the beginning.

GROWING VEGETABLE FLAVOR

Before I began cooking, I had some produce shopping to do. Freely testing my way through various spring staples, I landed on a pair of classics—asparagus and green peas—plus garlic and leeks for their aromatic depth and sweetness, chives for their fresh bite and onion-y overtones, and mint, a natural match for peas.

Simmering broth with the vegetable scraps and then using the enhanced broth to cook the pasta infuses this dish with flavor.

I also decided at the outset to do away with the tedious blanching step. I found that by sautéing the vegetables in stages in a large Dutch oven, I was able to ensure that each one maintained its crisp-tender texture while taking on a touch of flavorful browning. First went the leeks, followed by the chopped asparagus, the minced garlic, and finally the frozen baby peas, which needed only a minute over the heat to lend sweetness to the mix.

But as I'd learned from the original recipe, simply tossing sautéed vegetables with the pasta didn't add up to a dish any greater than the sum of its parts. What I needed was a way to tie the dish together and give it depth of flavor—a job that's usually reserved for the sauce. The chicken broth used in the original recipe didn't seem like the best way to enhance the vegetable flavor, so I swapped it for vegetable broth. To give it depth, I simmered the broth with the pile of scraps I'd peeled and trimmed away from the vegetables (the green parts of the leeks and the woody ends of the asparagus), along with some extra garlic and peas. But once I'd strained the broth and added the cream and butter—necessary to give the sauce body—any flavor advantage I had gained was lost. I tried cutting back on the dairy, but the result was so thin that it just slid off the pasta. The bottom line: The vegetables alone weren't enough to give the dish flavor.

THE POT THICKENS

I was thinking of calling it quits when a colleague reminded me that Italian cookery has a tradition of parboiling pasta in water and then letting it finish cooking for a minute or two in whatever sauce is being served. The technique has a twofold benefit: As the pasta cooks, it absorbs some of the sauce and takes on its flavors. In exchange, the noodles release some of their starches into the sauce, which helps build body. It wouldn't hurt to try this approach. I prepared another batch, this time boiling the pasta (spaghetti, for now) for a couple of minutes in the water, draining it, and then allowing it to finish cooking in my enhanced vegetable broth. Everyone agreed that while this was a step in the right direction, the results were still too subtle.

Then a thought occurred to me: If I was going to add the pasta to the broth eventually, why not get the full benefit of the broth's flavor and use it to cook the pasta from the start? The concept was nothing new, of course: It's a classic risotto technique, in which the rice and broth work together to produce a glossy, full-bodied "sauce" that thoroughly flavors and coats each grain. When I tried the approach with pasta, the results weren't quite perfect, but they were promising: The noodles, which I had boiled in a modest 5 cups of liquid (4 cups of broth, 1 cup of water) until they were al dente and the Dutch oven was almost dry, emerged more flavorful and lightly coated with the silky, starchy pot liquor. In fact, the sauce was thick enough that I didn't even need to add any cream or butter to give it body.

Now that I was on a roll, I wondered if I couldn't stretch the risotto technique even farther. Traditionally, the raw rice grains "toast" for a few minutes in some hot fat before the liquid is added, taking on a nutty richness. Adapting this technique for my pasta recipe seemed like a natural move, except for the problem of the long spaghetti strands, which I'd need to break up first. It seemed easier to just change the shape of the noodle. After testing half a dozen shorter shapes, I opted for bell-shaped campanelle: They held on to the sauce nicely, without clinging to one another or compressing into a mass. (Bow tie–shaped farfalle and penne quills made fine substitutes.)

Now that I had the right pasta shape, I went back to the cooking technique. After sautéing the vegetables, I wiped out the pot, added a splash of extra-virgin olive oil, and toasted the pasta until it started to color. Continuing with the classic risotto method, I poured in some dry white wine (its crisp acidity would brighten the sauce), stirring the mixture until most of the liquid had cooked

off, and added the hot broth and cranked up the heat to a boil. When I stuck in my fork about 10 minutes later, the results were remarkably improved: tender pasta pieces coated with a light but lustrous and creamy sauce that more than hinted at the sweet, grassy flavors of the vegetables.

Once the sautéed vegetables were incorporated, all the dish needed was a little flavor tweaking here and there. Along with the minced garlic, I added a dash of hot pepper flakes and, just before serving, a handful of grated Parmesan. Finally, I brightened the whole lot with a splash of lemon juice plus a handful of combined fresh chopped mint, chives, and lemon zest.

Nothing against the folks at Le Cirque, mind you, but unlike their original primavera, my recipe—a match-up of grassy, bright-tasting vegetables and nutty pasta in a complex, richly flavored sauce—truly tasted like spring, and came together in a fraction of the time.

Spring Vegetable Pasta

SERVES 4 TO 6

Campanelle is our pasta of choice in this dish, but farfalle and penne are acceptable substitutes.

- **1½ pounds leeks, white and light green parts halved lengthwise, sliced ½ inch thick, and washed thoroughly, plus 3 cups coarsely chopped dark green parts, washed thoroughly**
- **1 pound asparagus, tough ends trimmed, chopped coarse, and reserved; spears cut on bias into ½-inch lengths**
- **2 cups frozen peas, thawed**
- **4 cups vegetable broth**
- **1 cup water**
- **4 garlic cloves, minced**
- **2 tablespoons minced fresh mint**
- **2 tablespoons minced fresh chives**
- **½ teaspoon grated lemon zest plus 2 tablespoons juice**
- **6 tablespoons extra-virgin olive oil**
- **Salt and pepper**
- **¼ teaspoon red pepper flakes**
- **1 pound campanelle**
- **1 cup dry white wine**
- **1 ounce Parmesan cheese, grated (½ cup), plus extra for serving**

1. Bring leek greens, asparagus trimmings, 1 cup peas, broth, water, and half of garlic to boil in large saucepan. Reduce heat to medium-low and simmer gently for 10 minutes. While broth simmers, combine mint, chives, and lemon zest in bowl; set aside.
2. Strain broth through fine-mesh strainer into 8-cup liquid measuring cup, pressing on solids to extract as much liquid as possible (you should have 5 cups broth; add water as needed to equal 5 cups). Discard solids and return broth to saucepan. Cover and keep warm.
3. Heat 2 tablespoons oil in Dutch oven over medium heat until shimmering. Add leeks and pinch salt and cook, covered, stirring occasionally, until leeks begin to brown, about 5 minutes. Add asparagus spears and cook until asparagus is crisp-tender, 4 to 6 minutes. Add pepper flakes and remaining garlic and cook until fragrant, about 30 seconds. Add remaining 1 cup peas and continue to cook for 1 minute longer. Transfer vegetables to bowl and set aside. Wipe out pot with paper towels.
4. Heat remaining ¼ cup oil in now-empty pot over medium heat until shimmering. Add pasta and cook, stirring often, until just beginning to brown, about 5 minutes. Add wine and cook, stirring constantly, until absorbed, about 2 minutes.
5. When wine is fully absorbed, add warm broth and bring to boil. Cook, stirring frequently, until most of liquid is absorbed and pasta is al dente, 8 to 10 minutes. Off heat, stir in Parmesan, lemon juice, vegetables, and half of herb mixture. Season with salt and pepper to taste, and serve immediately, passing extra Parmesan and remaining herb mixture separately.

FOR BETTER FLAVOR, COOK PASTA LIKE RISOTTO

To deepen the overall flavor of our Spring Vegetable Pasta and add body to the sauce, we cook the pasta like rice.

1. **TOAST PASTA** Sautéing the raw pasta in oil gives it a nutty, rich flavor.

2. **ADD WINE AND BROTH** A cup of white wine gets absorbed by the pasta, contributing brightness; boiling the pasta in enhanced vegetable broth boosts flavor.

3. **COOK UNTIL CREAMY** As the pasta cooks, it gets coated in the creamy, starch-thickened broth—no cream needed.

RESCUING PASTA ALLA NORMA

DAWN YANAGIHARA, *July/August 2009*

Sicilian *pasta alla Norma* is a lively combination of tender eggplant and robust tomato sauce, seasoned with herbs, mixed with al dente pasta, and finished with shreds of salty, milky ricotta salata (salted and pressed ricotta cheese made from sheep's milk). The textures and flavors have much more nuance than the typical pasta with tomato sauce, and the eggplant lends pasta alla Norma a heartiness—a virtual meatiness—that makes it superbly satisfying.

Although not widely known outside Italy, this pasta is a classic in Sicily, where it was named for a 19th-century opera in which a druid priestess, Norma, perishes alongside her Roman lover. As the story goes, the opera was such a sensation, it inspired a Sicilian chef to create this dish in tribute to the opera and its composer, Vincenzo Bellini, a native son.

Microwaving the eggplant streamlines prep and allows it to caramelize, boosting flavor.

But even a classic faces pitfalls. After cooking a slew of different pasta alla Norma versions, I began to know them all too well. The eggplant is a big production to prepare, usually requiring salting before frying, and often ends up soggy and slick with oil. The tomatoes tend to coagulate into a heavy, overwhelming sauce, or they're so few they don't form an adequate foundation. The flavors in the dish can easily drown out the subtle essence of the eggplant.

Determined to do better, I set out to develop a bold, complex pasta. I wanted a weeknight meal with rich tomato and eggplant flavors and smooth, silky texture—without an excessive amount of work.

A STEAMY SETUP

Most pasta alla Norma recipes advise salting cubed eggplant to draw out its excess moisture, usually for about an hour. Since I was keen to streamline at every opportunity, this was the place to start. To determine if I could skip or at least shorten salting, I prepared batches with eggplant I had salted for an hour, a half hour, 15 minutes, and not at all. After tasting these different versions side by side, I had to conclude that salting for an hour was best: It drew out the most moisture, which helped the eggplant brown better and cook faster.

Next, I considered how to cook the eggplant. One of the first recipes I tried called for frying two eggplants, cut into strips, in 3 inches of oil. The eggplant soaked up about half its weight in oil, turning silky and very rich. But it made for a heavy, greasy sauce—not to mention the fact that frying splattered my stovetop with oil and required almost 40 minutes of watchful cooking in batches. Frying, I decided, was out. I briefly considered roasting the eggplant, but this method also seemed slow for a weeknight meal. The remaining option was sautéing in a lesser amount of oil. Unfortunately, when I tried this approach, the eggplant was almost always underdone and still required cooking in batches. Hoping to cook the eggplant more deeply, I peeled the skin before cubing and sautéing—but the difference was barely discernible, so the peel stayed on.

Looking for new ideas, I recalled an ingenious method for removing moisture from eggplant developed by a test kitchen colleague working on a recipe for caponata, another Sicilian eggplant dish. Instead of salting the eggplant and then leaving it to drain on paper towels on the countertop, he zapped the salted cubes in the microwave for 10 minutes. The salt draws out moisture that microwaving turns into steam, all the while causing the eggplant to collapse and compress its air pockets. The collapsed air pockets, in turn, soak up less oil in the pan. Put into practice for pasta alla Norma, this method was a resounding success. It was much faster than traditional salting and achieved even better results; the eggplant pieces came out of the microwave quite dry (a good start for browning). Furthermore, microwaving shrank the cubes to a size that could handily be cooked in just one batch in a 12-inch skillet.

Now I could try sautéing again, and this time it worked perfectly, browning the eggplant and adding rich flavor. I cooked a few batches, browning them to various degrees. Not surprisingly, the deeply caramelized eggplant tasted the roundest and fullest, with toasty notes accenting the vegetable's elusive sweetness. It was so flavorful that there really was nothing to be missed about frying.

Finally, I tried different types of eggplant: portly globe eggplants; smaller, more svelte Italian eggplants; and slender, lavender-colored Chinese eggplants. All worked, but in the end, I preferred globe eggplants, which have a tender yet resilient texture and far fewer seeds than other varieties, including Italian eggplants. Cut into cubes, they retained their shape even after sautéing.

A SAVORY SURPRISE

The base for pasta alla Norma is a simple tomato sauce to which the eggplant is added. I was sure that in-season tomatoes would give the dish fresh flavor, but after a couple rounds of testing, I concluded that the trouble of peeling and then salting them (to avoid a stringy, watery sauce) was more effort than I wanted for a midweek meal. It would be far better to develop a simple year-round option.

Diced canned tomatoes yielded a bright-tasting sauce with a coarse texture, but since the eggplant was already cut into cubes, the sauce was too chunky. My tasters preferred a sauce made with canned crushed tomatoes—a full 28-ounce can—for its thick consistency, which added cohesion.

To season the sauce, I started with a modest amount of garlic—two cloves, minced—but ended up using twice that amount to add some pungency. A small measure of red pepper flakes added a suggestion of heat, a generous dose of chopped basil brought fresh flavor, and a tablespoon of extra-virgin olive oil stirred in at the end with the basil gave the sauce rich, round, fruity notes.

The sauce tasted fine tossed with the pasta, especially when sprinkled with a generous dose of ricotta salata cheese, yet something was missing. It seemed to lack backbone. I was considering a break with tradition by adding pancetta or prosciutto when a test kitchen colleague offered a novel suggestion: anchovies. Of course! Cooked in oil with garlic and red pepper flakes, one minced fillet was good, but two were even better, giving the sauce a deep, savory flavor without any trace of fishiness.

A SIMMERING FINALE

So far, I had well-browned eggplant and a flavorful tomato sauce. To determine how best to bring these elements together, I made a couple more batches. For the first, I browned the eggplant, set it aside, made the sauce in the same skillet, and then added the eggplant to the sauce and simmered them together only long enough to heat through, no more than five minutes. For the second, I built the tomato sauce right on top of the browned eggplant so that they simmered together for about 10 minutes. The latter wound up a bit mushy and somewhat muddled, with some of the eggplant soggy and tattered. But the former had crisp, clear qualities—the eggplant's caramelization could still be tasted, and its tender texture had integrity. Even with only a few minutes of simmering, the eggplant had a tendency to soak up tomato juices, causing the sauce to become rather thick, so the final adjustment was adding a little reserved pasta cooking water when tossing the sauce with the pasta. Now all the components—the pasta, the tomato sauce, and the eggplant—were perfectly in tune. No longer a tragedy, my pasta alla Norma was on the table in well under an hour, without theatrics but with bold and balanced flavors.

Pasta alla Norma

SERVES 4

Ricotta salata is traditional, but French feta, Pecorino Romano, and Cotija (a firm, crumbly Mexican cheese) are acceptable substitutes. We prefer kosher salt because it clings best to the eggplant. If using table salt, reduce salt amounts by half. For a spicier sauce, use the larger amount of red pepper flakes.

1½ pounds eggplant, cut into ½-inch pieces
Kosher salt
¼ cup extra-virgin olive oil
4 garlic cloves, minced
2 anchovy fillets, rinsed, patted dry, and minced
¼–½ teaspoon red pepper flakes
1 (28-ounce) can crushed tomatoes
6 tablespoons chopped fresh basil
1 pound ziti, rigatoni, or penne
3 ounces ricotta salata, shredded (1½ cups)

1. Toss eggplant with 1 teaspoon salt in large bowl. Line large plate with double layer of coffee filters and lightly spray with vegetable oil spray. Spread eggplant in even layer over coffee filters; wipe out bowl with paper towels and set aside. Microwave eggplant until dry to touch and slightly shriveled, about 10 minutes, tossing halfway through cooking. Let cool slightly.

2. Transfer eggplant to now-empty bowl, drizzle with 1 tablespoon oil, and toss gently to coat; discard coffee filters and reserve plate. Heat 1 tablespoon oil in 12-inch nonstick skillet over medium-high heat until shimmering. Add eggplant and cook, stirring every 1½ to 2 minutes (more frequent stirring may cause eggplant pieces to break apart), until well browned and fully tender, about 10 minutes. Transfer eggplant to now-empty plate and set aside. Let skillet cool slightly, about 3 minutes.

3. Heat 1 tablespoon oil, garlic, anchovies, and pepper flakes in now-empty skillet over medium heat. Cook, stirring often, until garlic turns golden but not brown, about 3 minutes. Stir in tomatoes, bring to simmer, and cook, stirring occasionally, until slightly thickened, 8 to 10 minutes. Add eggplant and continue to cook, stirring occasionally, until eggplant is heated through and flavors meld, 3 to 5 minutes longer. Stir in basil and remaining 1 tablespoon oil and season with salt to taste.

4. Meanwhile, bring 4 quarts water to boil in large pot. Add pasta and 2 tablespoons salt and cook, stirring often, until al dente. Reserve ½ cup cooking water, then drain pasta and return it to pot. Add sauce to pasta and toss to combine. Adjust consistency with reserved cooking water as needed. Serve immediately with ricotta salata.

RICOTTA SALATA'S UNDERSTUDIES

Ricotta salata, a firm, tangy Italian sheep's-milk cheese that bears little resemblance to the moist ricotta sold in tubs, is an essential component of traditional pasta alla Norma. If you can't find it, consider these options instead.

FRENCH FETA Milder but tangy, this is a close cousin to ricotta salata in flavor and texture.

PECORINO ROMANO Hard and dry, with a slightly more assertive aroma and flavor than ricotta salata.

COTIJA Made with cow's milk, this Mexican cheese has a firm yet crumbly texture, but is less complex than ricotta salata.

PASTA WITH GREENS AND BEANS

REBECCA HAYS, *November/December 2005*

Italians have a knack for transforming humble ingredients into remarkable meals, and the rustic trio of pasta, hearty greens, and beans is no exception: When carefully prepared, the combination is sublime. But making something out of almost nothing takes time. In this case, dried cannellini beans are gently simmered until tender and greens are cleaned, cooked, and seasoned. Tossed with al dente pasta and a sprinkling of Parmesan, the result is rich and satisfying. If I could find a few shortcuts yet retain the complex flavors of the original, this dinner could become a regular in my midweek repertoire.

A BITTER BEGINNING

The hearty greens that Italians usually mix with pasta and beans include turnip, dandelion, chicory, mustard, broccoli rabe, collards, and kale. To reduce bitterness, many recipes call for blanching, shocking (dunking in ice water), squeezing dry, chopping, and sautéing them. The resulting greens are robust but not overpowering, but the whole process demands time and multiple pieces of kitchen equipment.

We streamline this classic Italian dish by using a hybrid sauté/braise technique to wilt the greens.

Two of the choices, kale and collard greens, were standouts: Tasters noted their appealing qualities but made not one mention of bitterness, giving me hope for a straightforward cooking method. Sure enough, a simple sauté tasted great, but the quantity of raw greens necessary meant that I would have to cook them in three or four batches. The solution was a sauté/braise combination. I quickly wilted half of the greens in a hot pan with olive oil, aromatic onions and garlic, and spicy red pepper flakes and then squeezed in the remainder of the raw greens. I poured in broth to serve as the braising liquid, and, 15 minutes later, tender, flavorful greens were mine.

FINISHING TOUCHES

As for the pasta, I'd run across a few references to whole-wheat spaghetti and decided to try it—despite some skepticism among a few health-food-fearing colleagues. I prepared a batch, served it up, and braced myself for the reactions. Surprise: Tasters unanimously preferred the nutty flavor of whole-wheat pasta to traditional semolina pasta for this dish. In fact, the more potent dimension of flavor provided by the whole-wheat pasta was the missing link, adding complexity that brought the beans and greens into a pleasing harmony.

To finish, I worked in some heavy-hitting ingredients to compensate for the flavor deficiency of the canned beans (the shortcut alternative to cooking them myself): tomatoes, olives, and Parmesan cheese. Still more garlic, in the form of chips, contributed welcome crunch.

One last note: I knew from experience that draining the pasta and finishing it in the sauce helps to integrate the components of a dish, and this one was no exception. Just a few minutes of simmering went a long way toward joining the gutsy flavors. Now I can have classic Italian comfort food, even when time isn't on my side.

Whole-Wheat Pasta with Greens and Beans

SERVES 4 TO 6

3 tablespoons olive oil, plus extra for drizzling
8 garlic cloves (5 sliced thin lengthwise, 3 minced)
Salt and pepper
1 onion, chopped fine
½ teaspoon red pepper flakes
1½ pounds kale or collard greens, stemmed and cut into 1-inch pieces
1 (14.5-ounce) can diced tomatoes, drained
¾ cup chicken or vegetable broth
1 (15-ounce) can cannellini beans, rinsed
¾ cup pitted kalamata olives, chopped coarse
1 pound whole-wheat spaghetti
2 ounces Parmesan cheese, grated fine (1 cup), plus extra for serving

1. Heat oil and sliced garlic in 12-inch straight-sided sauté pan over medium heat. Cook, stirring often, until garlic turns golden but not brown, about 3 minutes. Using slotted spoon, transfer garlic to paper towel–lined plate and sprinkle garlic lightly with salt.
2. Add onion to oil left in pan and cook over medium heat until softened and lightly browned, 5 to 7 minutes. Stir in minced garlic and pepper flakes and cook until fragrant, about 30 seconds. Add half of kale and cook, tossing occasionally, until starting to wilt, about 2 minutes. Add tomatoes, broth, ¾ teaspoon salt, and remaining kale and bring to simmer. Reduce heat to medium, cover (pan will be very full), and cook, tossing occasionally, until kale is tender, about 15 minutes (mixture will be somewhat soupy). Stir in beans and olives.
3. Meanwhile, bring 4 quarts water to boil in large pot. Add pasta and 1 tablespoon salt and cook, stirring often, until just shy of al dente. Reserve ½ cup cooking water, then drain pasta and return it to pot. Add kale mixture to pasta and cook over medium heat, tossing to combine, until pasta absorbs most of liquid, about 2 minutes.
4. Off heat, stir in Parmesan. Adjust consistency with reserved cooking water as needed. Season with salt and pepper to taste, and serve immediately, drizzling individual portions with extra oil and passing garlic chips and extra Parmesan separately.

TAMING GARLIC SHRIMP PASTA

FRANCISCO J. ROBERT, *November/December 2008*

In theory, garlic shrimp pasta has all the makings of an ideal weeknight meal. Toss a few quick-cooking ingredients—shrimp, garlic, oil, wine—with boiled dried pasta, and only the salad's left holding up dinner.

But there are challenges. Delicate shrimp overcooks in a matter of seconds. Volatile garlic can easily become overbearing or bitter (or simply disappear). Add to that the feat of getting a brothy sauce to coat the pasta, and this simple recipe turns into a precarious balancing act. But I still wanted it all: al dente pasta and moist shrimp bound by a supple sauce infused with a deep garlic flavor.

Before facing the garlic problem, I tackled the shrimp. I ruled out fast-cooking medium shrimp, as well as expensive extra-large and jumbo, landing on midpriced-but-meaty large shrimp (26 to 30 per pound). Searing them quickly over high heat yielded an overcooked texture. Poaching kept the shrimp moist but didn't contribute much flavor. I tentatively settled on sautéing them gently in garlic and oil while building the sauce.

To build layers of garlic flavor, we use it in the marinade for the shrimp, to infuse the cooking oil, and as an element of the dish.

Starting with a basic working recipe, I sautéed the shrimp with three cloves of minced garlic in a modest amount of olive oil. Removing the shrimp, I added a pinch of red pepper flakes and a cup of white wine, reduced the sauce, then tossed it with the shrimp and linguine. The results were just OK: weak garlic, moist but lackluster shrimp, and a thinnish sauce.

Upping the garlic to six cloves gave me indisputably garlicky pasta. But now I had a new problem: All that garlic cooked unevenly. Sautéed too little, and the garlic tastes raw and harsh; too long, and random burnt granules impart a bitter taste. Turning the heat to the lowest setting and simmering the garlic longer yielded a sweet, nutty taste, but my tasters missed the brasher notes.

Borrowing tricks from our Spanish-Style Garlic Shrimp recipe, I split the difference. First, I slowly simmered the oil with smashed garlic cloves (more effective in this task than minced) over low heat, discarded the toasted cloves, and built the sauce using the infused oil. Just before adding the wine, I quickly sautéed a smaller amount of minced garlic (just long enough to bloom the flavor). Marinating the shrimp for 20 minutes with additional minced garlic gave the dish just the balanced, deeply layered garlic flavor I wanted.

Next, I tinkered with the sauce. Bottled clam broth added after the vermouth contributed complexity, bolstering the shrimp flavor. To get the sauce to cling to the pasta, I stirred a little flour into the oil as a thickener and added some cold butter to finish.

I was close, but tasters remarked that the shrimp stayed hidden in the tangle of linguine, and there simply weren't enough bites. Swapping out the linguine for a chunky tubular pasta made it easy to find the shrimp, and cutting each shrimp into thirds before cooking ensured that nearly every bite boasted a tasty morsel.

Garlicky Shrimp Pasta

SERVES 4 TO 6

Marinate the shrimp while you prepare the remaining ingredients. Use the smaller amount of red pepper flakes for a milder sauce.

1 pound large shrimp (26 to 30 per pound), peeled, deveined, and each shrimp cut into 3 pieces
3 tablespoons olive oil
9 garlic cloves, peeled (5 cloves minced and 4 cloves smashed)
Salt and pepper
1 pound penne, ziti, or other short, tubular pasta
¼–½ teaspoon red pepper flakes
2 teaspoons all-purpose flour
½ cup dry vermouth or white wine
¾ cup bottled clam juice
½ cup chopped fresh parsley
3 tablespoons unsalted butter
1 teaspoon lemon juice, plus lemon wedges for serving

1. Combine shrimp, 1 tablespoon oil, one-third of minced garlic, and ¼ teaspoon salt in bowl. Let shrimp marinate at room temperature for 20 minutes.
2. Heat smashed garlic and remaining 2 tablespoons oil in 12-inch skillet over medium-low heat, stirring often, until garlic turns golden but not brown, 4 to 7 minutes. Off heat, remove garlic with slotted spoon and discard. Set skillet with oil aside.
3. Bring 4 quarts water to boil in large pot. Add pasta and 1 tablespoon salt and cook, stirring often, until al dente. Reserve ½ cup cooking water, then drain pasta and return it to pot.
4. While pasta cooks, return skillet to medium heat. Add shrimp along with marinade, spread into even layer, and cook, without stirring, until oil starts to bubble gently, 1 to 2 minutes. Stir shrimp and continue to cook until almost cooked through, about 1 minute longer. Remove shrimp with slotted spoon and transfer to clean bowl. Add remaining minced garlic and pepper flakes to skillet and cook over medium heat until fragrant, about 30 seconds. Add flour and cook, stirring constantly, for 1 minute. Slowly whisk in vermouth and cook for 1 minute. Stir in clam juice and parsley and cook until mixture starts to thicken, 1 to 2 minutes. Off heat, whisk in butter until melted, then stir in lemon juice.
5. Add shrimp and sauce to pasta and toss to combine. Add reserved cooking water as needed to adjust consistency. Season with pepper to taste. Serve immediately, passing lemon wedges separately.

MEATLESS "MEAT" SAUCE

LAN LAM, *May/June 2017*

Though I didn't grow up in an Italian family, I can still appreciate the appeal of a bowl of pasta dressed with tomatoey meat sauce. The sauce is rich and savory, clings well to just about any noodle shape, and can be thrown together quickly with basic ingredients such as ground beef, canned tomatoes, onion, garlic, and seasonings. That's why I make it so often.

The thing is, sometimes I want a meatless version instead, either because I'm hosting vegetarian guests or, increasingly, because I'm trying to eat less meat. And the more I think about it, the more I realize that what I crave most about a quick meat sauce like this isn't the flavor of the meat itself, since this type of sauce doesn't taste particularly beefy. It's the rich, savory flavor and hearty, unctuous body that I want. Do you really need meat to achieve the look and feel—and even the savoriness—of a good meat sauce? I decided to find out.

BUILD THE BASE

The typical Italian American meat sauce gets most of its savory depth from browning the ground beef. As the beef cooks, it releases juices that reduce and form a flavor-packed fond on the bottom of the pot. From there, you remove and reserve the beef and cook the onion, garlic, and seasonings (such as oregano and red pepper flakes) in the rendered fat, which adds to the flavor base. You then add canned tomatoes and the browned beef to the pot and simmer the sauce long enough to tenderize the meat a bit and allow the flavors to meld.

Finding a savory stand-in for the ground beef was an obvious place to start, and mushrooms were my first instinct. They're a popular meat alternative because they're an excellent source of both glutamic acid and nucleotides, molecules packed with savory umami flavor. Plus, their cell walls are made of a heat-stable substance called chitin, so instead of breaking down and turning to mush when cooked, they retain some satisfying meat-like chew.

That explained why so many of the vegetarian "meat" sauce recipes I tried called for mushrooms, but in most cases I found their earthy flavor too dominant; I wasn't trying to make a mushroom sauce, after all. However, a modest amount of mushroom presence would be a good thing as long as I balanced it with other components.

Mushrooms and chickpeas, chopped quickly in a food processor, give this meatless sauce a hearty texture and savory flavor.

I ruled out more assertively flavored varieties, including porcini and shiitake, in favor of earthy but more neutral-tasting cremini, and I kept the amount to a judicious 10 ounces. To quickly chop them into ground meat–size bits, I blitzed them in a food processor. From there, I sautéed them in extra-virgin olive oil with a bit of salt; the oil would mimic the richness of rendered beef fat, and the salt would both season the mushrooms and pull water from them so that it could evaporate for faster browning. Once the mushrooms had developed some color, I added an onion (also chopped in the food processor) and a healthy scoop of tomato paste, another umami booster. When the onions were translucent and the paste had darkened to a deep rust red (a sign that its sugar had caramelized and its flavor had intensified), I added garlic, dried oregano, and red pepper flakes; stirred in the tomatoes; and simmered the sauce for about 20 minutes.

Tossed with some pasta, this early batch looked thin and tasted one-dimensional, but it was undeniably savory. What I needed was a partner for the mushrooms that would provide the sauce with some bulk and flavor balance.

FILL 'ER UP

I began to scour cookbooks and blogs for other ingredient ideas, steering clear of meat fakers such as tempeh and seitan. Instead, I compiled a list of vegetables, grains, and nuts that might mimic the hearty, lush consistency of ground beef without revealing themselves too obviously: cauliflower, eggplant, walnuts, cashews, lentils, and bulgur.

But the list quickly shortened. The nuts took the better part of an hour to become fully tender, even after I broke them up in the food processor. And the bulgur grains absorbed so much water that the sauce looked and tasted like a wheaty porridge. Lentils didn't look or taste right in an Italian American–style sauce, eggplant had to be roasted to break down, and chopped cauliflower lost votes for its sulfurous aroma.

Chickpeas were the most promising candidate. Canned ones would be just fine for this quick sauce; they softened nicely after a few pulses in the food processor and just 15 minutes of cooking. The only drawback was that they overthickened the sauce, so I tried rinsing them after chopping to remove as much of their excess starch as possible. When that didn't help enough, I tried adding another can of crushed tomatoes, but it contained too much pulp and not enough liquid and made the sauce too tomatoey. Ultimately, I added a couple of cups of vegetable broth along with the crushed tomatoes, which loosened the sauce without diluting the flavor. For an authentic finish, I stirred in chopped fresh basil.

The pantry staples made it quick. The food processor made it easy. And when my colleagues asked if they could take home the leftovers, I suspected that this sauce might become just as popular as the meat kind.

Meatless "Meat" Sauce with Chickpeas and Mushrooms

MAKES 6 CUPS;
ENOUGH FOR 2 POUNDS PASTA

Make sure to rinse the chickpeas after pulsing them in the food processor or the sauce will be too thick.

10 ounces cremini mushrooms, trimmed
6 tablespoons extra-virgin olive oil
Salt and pepper
1 onion, chopped
5 garlic cloves, minced
1¼ teaspoons dried oregano
¼ teaspoon red pepper flakes
¼ cup tomato paste
1 (28-ounce) can crushed tomatoes
2 cups vegetable broth
1 (15-ounce) can chickpeas, rinsed
2 tablespoons chopped fresh basil

1. Pulse mushrooms in 2 batches in food processor until chopped into ⅛- to ¼-inch pieces, 7 to 10 pulses, scraping down sides of bowl as needed. (Do not clean workbowl.)
2. Heat 5 tablespoons oil in Dutch oven over medium-high heat until shimmering. Add mushrooms and 1 teaspoon salt and cook, stirring occasionally, until mushrooms are browned and fond has formed on bottom of pot, about 8 minutes.
3. While mushrooms cook, pulse onion in food processor until finely chopped, 7 to 10 pulses, scraping down sides of bowl as needed. (Do not clean workbowl.) Transfer onion to pot with mushrooms and cook, stirring occasionally, until onion is soft and translucent, about 5 minutes. Combine remaining 1 tablespoon oil, garlic, oregano, and pepper flakes in bowl.
4. Add tomato paste to pot and cook, stirring constantly, until mixture is rust-colored, 1 to 2 minutes. Reduce heat to medium and push vegetables to sides of pot. Add garlic mixture to center and cook, stirring constantly, until fragrant, about 30 seconds. Stir in tomatoes and broth; bring to simmer over high heat. Reduce heat to low and simmer sauce for 5 minutes, stirring occasionally.
5. While sauce simmers, pulse chickpeas in food processor until chopped into ¼-inch pieces, 7 to 10 pulses. Transfer chickpeas to fine-mesh strainer and rinse under cold running water until water runs clear; drain well. Add chickpeas to pot and simmer until sauce is slightly thickened, about 15 minutes. Stir in basil and season with salt and pepper to taste. Serve. (Sauce can be refrigerated for up to 2 days or frozen for up to 1 month.)

A SPEEDY PROCESS

To make this recipe as quick as possible, most of the "knife work" takes place in a food processor. Even better, you don't have to wash the processor bowl between uses.

GETTING TO "MEATY" WITHOUT MEAT

By zeroing in on the specific qualities meat brings to a meat sauce, we were able to replicate them in our meatless version.

SAVORY DEPTH from well-browned cremini mushrooms and tomato paste
HEARTY TEXTURE from drained, chopped chickpeas
RICHNESS from 6 tablespoons of extra-virgin olive oil

PASTA POINTERS

Boiling pasta in salted water is a straightforward kitchen task, but you can improve your results with these simple tricks.

1 USE PLENTY OF WATER—OR STIR OFTEN As pasta boils, it leaches starches into the cooking water, which can cause the noodles to stick together. The easiest way to cut down on sticking is to boil pasta in a generous amount of water—4 quarts per pound of dried pasta—to dilute the starches. However, if you don't have a pot large enough for all the water, you can reduce the water by half and stir the pasta frequently during cooking.

2 SALT THE WATER Salting the cooking water ensures that seasoning gets into the pasta, not just on it. Add 1 tablespoon of salt to 4 quarts of water (or 1½ teaspoons to 2 quarts), making sure to stir well so that the salt will dissolve.

3 SKIP THE OIL Since it merely sits on top of the cooking water, adding a splash of olive oil to the pot before adding the pasta doesn't prevent the pasta from sticking together as it cooks—though it may help keep the water from boiling over. To prevent the pasta from sticking together, simply stir it for a minute or two after adding it to the boiling water.

4 CHECK FOR DONENESS OFTEN We recommend ignoring the cooking times listed on packaging, which are almost always too long and result in mushy, overcooked pasta. Tasting the pasta is the best way to check for doneness. We prefer pasta cooked al dente, meaning that it has a bit of resistance in the center when bitten.

5 RESERVE SOME WATER Before draining the pasta, reserve about ½ cup of the cooking water, which is flavorful, somewhat salty, and starchy. It can be used to loosen a thick sauce without diluting the sauce's body or flavor as much as plain water would.

ITALIAN-STYLE MEAT SAUCE

CHARLES KELSEY, *March/April 2008*

In Italy, cooking a meaty pasta sauce is an all-day affair. Whether they use ground meat for a *ragù alla bolognese* or chunks of meat for a rustic sauce, one thing is for sure: These sauces slowly simmer for 3 or 4 hours—or even longer. This long simmer develops concentrated flavor and, more important, breaks down the meat, giving it a soft, lush texture.

In America, "Italian meat sauce" has typically come to mean a shortcut version in which ground beef, onions, garlic, and canned tomatoes are thrown together in a pot and cooked for half an hour. While such a sauce may be quick, its lackluster flavor and rubbery meat bear no resemblance to its Italian cousins. But the trouble is, when I crave pasta with meat sauce, I don't always have hours to spend on a Bolognese. Could I develop a meat sauce to make on a weeknight that tasted like it had been simmering for, if not all day, at least a good part of it?

MEAT OF THE MATTER

My search started with analyzing Bolognese recipes and I discovered right away that the best ones don't brown the meat. Instead, they call for cooking the ground meat until it loses its raw color and then adding the liquid ingredients one by one, slowly reducing each and building flavor before adding the next. One of the first liquids in the pot is usually some form of dairy, a Bolognese sauce's signature ingredient that imparts a sweet creaminess to the dish. Most American meat sauces, on the other hand, brown the beef first—a step that adds flavor but toughens the meat. They also skip the dairy in favor of tomato sauce, which doesn't provide the milk fat or the same layers of complex flavor.

Would eliminating the browning step and adding milk work better? I headed to the test kitchen to find out. After sautéing onion and garlic, I stirred in a pound of ground beef, breaking it up with a wooden spoon. As soon as it started to lose its raw color, I immediately added ½ cup of milk along with the tomatoes, and then simmered the sauce for 30 minutes or so. The results were disappointing: Some of the meat was tender and moist, but most of it was tough and mealy. And despite the milk, the sauce lacked flavor overall. If anything, without sufficient time to reduce, the milk actually overpowered the meat flavor in the sauce. It occurred to me that in order for the milk to develop the new flavor compounds that are its key contribution to a Bolognese sauce, a lengthy simmer was necessary. Would cooking the sauce a little longer—45 minutes instead of 30—help? Not enough to notice. Furthermore, the extra 15 minutes of simmering had little impact on the meat, which was still more rubbery than not.

It was time to look beyond Bolognese for ways to improve my simple weeknight sauce. Meat tenderizer seemed like an obvious place to start. A few teaspoons did soften the beef, but it also made it spongy. Would soy sauce work? Soy sauce is a base ingredient in many of our steak marinades, where it acts much like a brine, tenderizing meat by helping it retain moisture. But I quickly discovered that while soy minimizes moisture loss in large pieces of meat, such as steak, it has virtually no impact on tiny bits of ground beef. After a little research I found out why: Bigger pieces of meat contain more water, which takes a longer time to evaporate during cooking. The water in small pieces of ground meat, on the other hand, evaporates almost immediately, and not even soy sauce can help prevent this.

A colleague suggested a trick that hadn't occurred to me: mixing in a panade. This paste of bread and milk is often blended into meatballs and meatloaf to help them hold their shape and retain moisture during cooking. It was worth a try. Using a fork, I mashed up a piece of bread with some milk until I had a smooth paste and mixed it into the ground beef until well combined. I then proceeded as usual with the rest of the recipe: stirring the beef mixture into the sautéed onions and garlic, adding the tomatoes, and simmering. I noticed a difference in the sauce even before I ladled it over pasta for tasters. The meat looked moister and, sure enough, tasters confirmed that it was. It turns out that starches from the bread absorb liquid from the milk to form a gel that coats and lubricates the meat, much in the same way as fat. But all was not perfect: Tasters were pleased with the meat's tenderness but complained that the sauce was too chunky and resembled chili. No problem. I pulsed the meat and panade together in a food processor to create finer pieces of supple, juicy meat.

A panade gives our quick-cooked beef a lush texture; browned mushrooms deepen the sauce's flavor.

BEEFING UP FLAVOR

With the meat issue solved, it was time to turn my attention to flavor. Without browning or a lengthy simmer to concentrate and build new layers of flavor, complexity and depth were noticeably lacking from my sauce. Could the type of ground beef I used enhance flavor? I bought four different kinds—ground round, chuck, and sirloin, as well as meat labeled "ground beef" (a mix of various beef cuts and trimmings)—and made four sauces. The ground round was bland and spongy, but tasters liked the other three equally well. Eighty-five percent lean beef proved to have just the right degree of leanness, adding richness without making the sauce greasy. Still, tasters were pressing, "Where's the beef [flavor]?"

Next, I tested a range of ingredients that are often used to boost meaty flavor. Beef broth ended up imparting a tinny taste to the sauce. Worcestershire and steak sauce overwhelmed it with their potent flavorings, and red wine lent a sour taste. Finally, I tried mushrooms—and at last I had a winner. The mushrooms brought a real beefiness to the sauce. After experimenting with different types, I discovered that plain white mushrooms worked just fine. The key was browning them. I minced a modest amount (about 4 ounces) and added them to the pan with the onions. Browning concentrated their flavor but left them tender and supple, allowing them to add complexity without otherwise letting their presence be known.

When it came to other components of the sauce, tasters liked a mix of diced and crushed tomatoes. The diced tomatoes brought a chunky texture, and the crushed provided a smooth foundation. I reserved a small amount of juice from the drained diced tomatoes to deglaze the pan after browning the mushrooms. This little trick gave the sauce's tomato flavor a boost, as did a tablespoon of tomato paste. Earlier, I had ruled against milk in the sauce (except for the couple of tablespoons in the panade), but I reinstated dairy in the form of a handful of grated Parmesan, which brought a welcome tanginess. With a dash of red pepper flakes and some fresh oregano, I was done.

I now had a sauce with meltingly tender meat that was as complex and full-bodied as any sauce simmered for under an hour could be. True, no one would mistake it for a Bolognese—but no one would ever believe I hadn't rushed home early to put it on the stove, either.

Simple Italian-Style Meat Sauce

MAKES ABOUT 6 CUPS; ENOUGH FOR 2 POUNDS PASTA

Except for ground round, this recipe will work with most types of ground beef, as long as it is 85 percent lean. (Eighty percent lean beef will turn the sauce greasy; 90 percent will make it fibrous.) If using dried oregano, add the entire amount with the reserved tomato juice in step 2. Serve over pasta with extra grated Parmesan; we like to use rigatoni or penne.

4 ounces white mushrooms, trimmed and halved if small or quartered if large
1 slice hearty white sandwich bread, torn into quarters
2 tablespoons whole milk
Salt and pepper
1 pound 85 percent lean ground beef
1 tablespoon olive oil
1 large onion, chopped fine
6 garlic cloves, minced
1 tablespoon tomato paste
¼ teaspoon red pepper flakes
1 (14.5-ounce) can diced tomatoes, drained with ¼ cup juice reserved
1 tablespoon minced fresh oregano or 1 teaspoon dried
1 (28-ounce) can crushed tomatoes
¼ cup grated Parmesan cheese

1. Pulse mushrooms in food processor until finely chopped, about 8 pulses, scraping down sides of bowl as needed; transfer to bowl. Add bread, milk, ½ teaspoon salt, and ½ teaspoon pepper to now-empty processor and pulse until paste forms, about 8 pulses. Add beef and pulse until mixture is well combined, about 6 pulses.
2. Heat oil in large saucepan over medium-high heat until just smoking. Add onion and mushrooms and cook until vegetables are softened and well browned, 6 to 12 minutes. Stir in garlic, tomato paste, and pepper flakes and cook until fragrant and tomato paste starts to brown, about 1 minute. Stir in reserved tomato juice and 2 teaspoons oregano, scraping up any browned bits. Stir in beef mixture and cook, breaking up any large pieces with wooden spoon, until no longer pink, about 3 minutes, making sure that beef does not brown.
3. Stir in diced tomatoes and crushed tomatoes and bring mixture to simmer. Reduce heat to low and cook until sauce has thickened and flavors meld, about 30 minutes. Stir in Parmesan and remaining 1 teaspoon oregano and season with salt and pepper to taste. Serve. (Sauce can be refrigerated for up to 2 days or frozen for up to 1 month.)

SHOPPING: GROUND BEEF

Ground beef can be made from a variety of cuts, and fat levels vary from 70 to 95 percent lean. Our meat sauce recipe calls for any 85 percent lean ground beef other than ground round. But when a recipe doesn't specify, how do you know what to buy? Here's a guide:

GROUND CHUCK Cut from the shoulder, ground chuck is distinguished by its rich, beefy flavor and tender texture.

GROUND SIRLOIN This cut from the cow's midsection near the hip offers good beefy flavor, but it can be on the dry side. Generally fairly lean.

GROUND BEEF A mystery meat of sorts, ground beef can be any cut or combination of cuts, which means flavor and texture are rarely consistent.

GROUND ROUND Lean, tough, and often gristly, ground round comes from the rear upper leg and rump of the cow.

PANADE TO THE RESCUE

A paste of milk and bread, called a panade, is responsible for keeping the ground beef in our meat sauce moist and tender. Panades are typically used to help foods such as meatballs and meatloaf hold their shape (and moisture), so we were surprised that our panade didn't just dissolve into a meat sauce where the beef is crumbled. Our science editor told us that starches from the bread absorb liquid from the milk to form a gel that coats and lubricates the protein molecules in the meat, keeping them moist and preventing them from linking together to form a tough matrix. Mixing the beef and panade in a food processor ensures that the starch is well dispersed.

ULTIMATE RAGU ALLA BOLOGNESE

BRYAN ROOF, *November/December 2011*

R*agù alla bolognese*, the hearty meat sauce native to the northern Italian city for which it is named, has always been a simple concept—but with a lot of complications to hamper its simplicity. Despite its undisputed Bolognese pedigree, there are countless "authentic" interpretations on record. While ground beef is the common starting point, many versions add ground pork and often veal as well. Others supplement the ground meat with finely chopped *salumi*, usually pancetta or prosciutto. Some recipes call for brightening the ragu with crushed tomatoes; others lean toward the drier, more concentrated depth of tomato paste. One version may call for white wine, another for red—some may call for no wine at all. Cooking times range from 90 minutes to 3 hours.

But the most controversial point of all? Dairy. Depending on which source you consult, milk and/or cream is either an essential component, lending further richness and supposedly tenderizing the long-cooked meat, or it has no place in the sauce whatsoever. In other words, what constitutes "real" ragu Bolognese is largely a matter of interpretation.

The only thing that all Italian cooks seem to agree on is this: The end product should be hearty and rich but not cloying, with a velvety texture that lightly clings to the noodles, and tomatoes should be a bit player in this show. The true star is the meat.

A little gelatin gives this sauce a silky, glossy texture, and six types of meat offer complex depth of flavor.

I'd never felt strongly about the dairy issue myself, until recently, when I sampled a Bolognese sauce made by Dante de Magistris, an Italian chef in Boston with a big following. His version was by far the meatiest, most complex version I'd ever had. I was so taken with it that I asked him for a breakdown of the recipe. Two points stood out. First, he used a whopping six meats: ground beef, pork, and veal; pancetta; mortadella (bologna-like Italian deli meat); and, to my surprise, chicken livers. Second, de Magistris stood squarely in the no-dairy camp, claiming that when he learned to make the dish in Bologna, milk and cream were definitely not included.

Those clues—plus the test kitchen's library of Italian cookbooks—were enough to get me started on my own dairy-free Bolognese. I was determined to make my version home cook–friendly and yet satisfying to even the most discriminating Italian palate.

THE MEAT OF THE MATTER

I started with a test batch that I based on de Magistris's version, loading up the pot with the components of the flavor base, or *soffritto* (chopped carrot, celery, and onion), followed by five different meats. (I wasn't sure I really needed the chicken livers, so I left them out for the time being.) I then stirred in crushed tomatoes.

I let it all simmer, covered, for a couple of hours. The result was acceptably rich and flavorful, but I still had a good bit of tweaking to do, to both the ingredient list and the technique.

I made several more batches, adding a fistful of minced sage to the meat—considered an essential component by some sources—and trying various proportions of all five meats until I landed on 12 ounces each for the ground beef, pork, and veal and 4 ounces each of pancetta and mortadella. Some of the other classic Bolognese recipes I'd consulted specified that the ground meat should be cooked only until it loses its pink color, lest the browning lead to toughness. But I found the textural compromise to be far subtler than the flavor benefit of a good sear.

I also decided to ignore tradition and add the meat to the pot before the soffritto. Without the interference of moisture from the vegetables, I could get a much better sear on the meat; plus, sautéing the veggies in the meats' rendered fat built up even richer flavor.

What gave me pause was a more minor complaint: finely chopping the pancetta and mortadella. It was tedious work, so I called on my food processor to take over. The job was literally done with the push of a button. In fact, the appliance worked so efficiently that I also pulsed the soffritto components before sautéing them in the meats' rendered fat.

I moved on to the next major decision: the best kind of tomato product to use. The recipes I'd read didn't help narrow things down—I'd seen everything from the crushed tomatoes I had been using up until now to sauce to paste. One source I consulted even suggested that tomatoes were not originally part of the sauce. That idea reminded me that I liked the unobtrusive texture of tomato paste in de Magistris's version, so I added a healthy dollop to the pot, and then let the mixture go. Once the fond had taken on a deep rust tone, I poured in a few big glugs of red wine, deglazed the pan by scraping up the browned bits with a wooden spoon, and let the sauce simmer gently for the better part of 2 hours. When the sauce was nearly done, I boiled some pasta and tossed the noodles with the ragu.

Flavorwise, the sauce was in good shape: rich and complex and, thanks to the wine and tomato paste, balanced with just enough acidity. But as my tasters noted, this ragu had a textural flaw: Its consistency was pebbly, dry, and not particularly sauce-like.

VELVET UNDERGROUND

There was one element of de Magistris's recipe that I had overlooked in my earlier attempts: Just before the long simmering step, he ladled some homemade *brodo* (or broth) into the ragu, repeating the step twice more during cooking to moisten the reduced sauce. I suspected that the brodo—and the technique of adding the brodo in stages—had an important effect on the texture of Bolognese. Besides boosting the meaty flavor, the bones used to make the broth give up lots of gelatin as they simmer, which renders the liquid glossy and viscous. The more the broth reduced in the Bolognese, the more savory and satiny it became. But homemade broth was out of the question for me. Simmering bones for hours on top of making the ragu was just too much fuss; I'd have to make do with commercial broth.

No surprise here: The ragus I made with store-bought broth didn't measure up to the Bolognese made with homemade broth—especially in regard to texture. I started brainstorming other ways to mimic the velvetiness contributed by the gelatin in real brodo—and realized that the answer was right in front of me: powdered gelatin. It's a trick we've used to lend suppleness to all-beef meatloaf and viscosity to beef stew—two qualities that I was looking for in my ragu. I prepped multiple batches of the sauce, blooming varying amounts of gelatin—from 1 teaspoon all the way up to a whopping 8—in a combination of canned beef and chicken broth (1 cup each) before proceeding with the recipe. Every batch was an improvement over the gelatin-free ragus, but the powder's effect was relatively subtle until I got up into the higher amounts, which rendered the sauce ultrasilky. That settled it: Eight teaspoons it was.

I had one more thought about the canned broth: Since the flavor and body of the canned stuff hardly equaled that of a real brodo, I wondered if the reduction step was really doing that much for the sauce. One side-by-side test gave me my answer: The batch into which I'd added all the broth at once boasted just as much meatiness and body as the one with the staggered additions. It also finished cooking in about 90 minutes.

And yet while canned broth plus gelatin nicely solved the texture problem, the sauce still lacked a certain depth and roundness of flavor. Fortunately, I still had one card left to play: chicken livers. They'd seemed superfluous to me at first, but I wondered if finely chopping them and tossing them in at the end might get at the complexity I was after. That they did—but according to my tasters, their effect was a bit too strong. Pureeing them in the food processor worked much better; this way, their rich, gamy flavor incorporated seamlessly into the sauce.

Though my sauce could hardly get any more perfect, I just couldn't push away the thought that kept sneaking into my head: What would happen if the sauce included a little dairy? I made one last batch, adding 1 cup of milk along with the broth. But when my tasters sampled this latest version, the consensus was unanimous: Dairy muted its meaty flavor, and they liked it better without.

Without dairy, I knew that some Italian cooks out there would not consider my recipe authentic. But no matter: The sauce was undeniably complex, rich-tasting, and lusciously silky. And besides, how could any version be Bolognese without a little controversy?

Pasta with Ragù alla Bolognese

SERVES 4

This recipe makes enough sauce to coat 2 pounds of pasta. Leftover sauce may be refrigerated for up to three days or frozen for up to one month. Eight teaspoons of gelatin is equivalent to 1 ounce. If you can't find ground veal, use an additional 12 ounces of ground beef.

1 cup chicken broth
1 cup beef broth
8 teaspoons unflavored gelatin
1 onion, chopped coarse
1 large carrot, peeled and chopped coarse
1 celery rib, chopped coarse
4 ounces pancetta, chopped
4 ounces mortadella, chopped
6 ounces chicken livers, trimmed
3 tablespoons extra-virgin olive oil
12 ounces 85 percent lean ground beef
12 ounces ground pork
12 ounces ground veal
3 tablespoons minced fresh sage
1 (6-ounce) can tomato paste
2 cups dry red wine
Salt and pepper
1 pound pappardelle or tagliatelle
Grated Parmesan cheese

1. Combine chicken broth and beef broth in bowl; sprinkle gelatin over top and set aside. Pulse onion, carrot, and celery in food processor until finely chopped, about 10 pulses, scraping down sides of bowl as needed; transfer to second bowl. Pulse pancetta and mortadella in now-empty processor until finely chopped, about 25 pulses, scraping down sides of bowl as needed; transfer to third bowl. Process chicken livers in now-empty processor until pureed, about 5 seconds; transfer to fourth bowl.
2. Heat oil in Dutch oven over medium-high heat until shimmering. Add beef, pork, and veal and cook, breaking up meat with wooden spoon, until all liquid has evaporated and meat begins to sizzle, 10 to 15 minutes. Add sage and pancetta mixture and cook, stirring frequently, until pancetta is translucent, 5 to 7 minutes, adjusting heat as needed to keep fond from burning. Add chopped vegetables and cook, stirring frequently, until softened, 5 to 7 minutes. Add tomato paste and cook, stirring constantly, until rust-colored and fragrant, about 3 minutes.
3. Stir in wine, scraping up any browned bits. Simmer until sauce has thickened, about 5 minutes. Stir in broth mixture and return to simmer. Reduce heat to low and cook at bare simmer until thickened (wooden spoon should leave trail when dragged through sauce), about 1½ hours.
4. Stir in pureed chicken livers, increase heat to medium-high, bring to boil, and immediately remove from heat. Season with salt and pepper to taste; cover and keep warm.
5. Bring 4 quarts water to boil in large pot. Add pasta and 1 tablespoon salt and cook, stirring often, until al dente. Reserve ¾ cup cooking water, then drain pasta and return it to pot. Add half of sauce and reserved cooking water to pasta and toss to combine. Serve with Parmesan.

ITALIAN BEEF AND ONION RAGU

ANDREA GEARY, *November/December 2013*

There are those who have the best of everything, and there are those who make the best of everything. The residents of 16th-century Naples fell into the latter category. Faced with a population explosion that caused severe food shortages, they created a thrifty yet supremely satisfying gravy of beef and aromatic vegetables known, ironically, as *la Genovese*. (The provenance of the name is unclear: Some theorize that Genovese cooks brought it to Naples; others believe that the name references the reputed frugality of the people of Genoa.)

Later, in the 19th century, onions took center stage, and the dish became one of the region's most beloved. The classic preparation is straightforward: A piece of beef, usually from the round, is placed in a pot and covered with approximately twice its weight in sliced onions, along with chopped aromatic vegetables, salt, and perhaps some herbs. Then several cups of water and a bit of wine go into the pot, and the mixture is simmered for anywhere from 3 to 6 hours, until the liquid has evaporated, the beef is tender, and the onions have cooked down into a soft, pulpy mass.

Traditionally, frugal cooks served the beef-flavored onion gravy (notice that I didn't mention tomatoes; the dish predates the introduction of tomatoes to European kitchens) as a sauce for sturdy tubular pasta like rigatoni. (Incidentally, the sauce doesn't include garlic either.) The meat itself was typically reserved for a second meal, or at least a second course, with a vegetable. But in these comparatively prosperous times, the beef is more likely to be shredded and incorporated into the sauce for a substantial single dish—exactly the kind of pasta sauce I love to make in cold-weather months.

HUMBLE BEGINNINGS

I started with a very traditional recipe, but since I was making just one meal, not two, I immediately cut down the amount of beef and onions to a more practical size—1 pound of trimmed beef round and 2½ pounds of thinly sliced onions, which I hoped would produce six to eight servings. To those key players I added a finely chopped carrot and celery stalk, plus some chopped marjoram and salt, all of which I put in a Dutch oven with 8 cups of water and 1 cup of white wine (the meat is not usually seared). I let the pot bubble away for a good 2½ hours, giving it an occasional stir to keep the contents cooking evenly. By that point, the beef was fully cooked; I removed it to let it cool before chopping it (its texture was too tight to shred) and adding it back to the sauce. In the meantime I reduced the oniony cooking liquid.

Cooking the beef and onions with a small amount of water creates an ultrasavory ragu.

Perhaps not surprisingly, this early version did not produce the succulent, deeply flavorful ragu I had envisioned. The lean round was not the best cut to be using in a moist-heat environment; it lacks fat and collagen, which keep meat tasting tender and juicy, so it cooked up dry and tight. Also, reducing the sauce itself took too long—almost 40 minutes. Lastly, the color of the sauce was an unappealing beige.

What did impress me was the deeply savory flavor of the onions. They weren't sharp and sulfurous like fresh onions, nor did they have the sweetness of the caramelized kind. They were just plain beefy-tasting. In fact, one taster observed that the onions tasted beefier than the actual beef. I would come back to this discovery once I'd nailed down the basics of the sauce—for starters, the meat.

TESTING THE WATER

Beef round's tight grain makes this cut a good candidate for slicing, but since I was in pursuit of more tender meat that I could shred and return to the sauce, I moved to our favorite braising cuts: short ribs, blade steaks, and chuck-eye roast. The latter won for its beefy flavor, tenderness, and (in homage to the thrifty nature of this dish) relatively low price tag. The only glitch? Cooked whole, it took upwards of 3½ hours to turn tender. Cutting it into four chunks reduced the cooking time to 2½ hours and allowed me to trim away intramuscular fat pockets. I also seasoned the roast with salt and pepper before cooking and moved the braising to a low (300-degree) oven, where the meat would cook more evenly.

And I cut way back on the water—down to 3 cups—hoping to drastically shorten the reduction time. But even with that little amount, it still took about a half-hour of stovetop reduction to turn the onions and cooking liquid saucy. I wondered: Did I have to add water at all?

In the next batch I omitted the water and simply nestled the beef in the onion mixture and sealed the pot tightly with foil (to lock in steam) and then the lid. This worked well; the meat braised to perfect tenderness in the released juices, and the sauce required less stovetop reduction time—just 10 minutes. But strangely, this version tasted less savory.

To ramp up meatiness, I turned to innovations that started to show up in later Genovese recipes: pancetta and salami (which I finely chopped in the food processor) and tomato paste. They all made the ragu more savory, particularly the umami-rich tomato paste when I browned it in the pot before adding the onions. The tomato paste also warmed up the color of the formerly drab-looking finished sauce. But while this batch tasted meatier than the previous one, it still was not as savory as the first version. I was baffled. I had not only added meaty ingredients but also taken away the world's most neutral ingredient: water.

SAVORY SECRET

A consultation with our science editor solved the mystery. Astonishingly, it was the water that was the key to extracting the meaty flavor that was locked inside the onions. That meatiness is due to a water-soluble compound known as 3-mercapto-2-methylpentan-1-ol (MMP), the byproduct of a reaction that occurs when onions are cut and then heated in water.

By eliminating the water, I was severely limiting the development of savory flavors, so I added back 2 cups—just enough to cover the onions but not so much that the sauce's reduction time would be lengthy. I also switched from slicing the onions to chopping them in the food processor—a timesaving technique that would also lead to the creation of more MMP. This time the sauce regained the meatiness of the original batch, and then some, with the pancetta, salami, and tomato paste. Even better, I found that I could cook it in the oven with the lid off, which encouraged evaporation and saved me some reducing time at the end. The sauce was a bit sweet, so I reserved half of the wine for adding at the end for extra brightness.

One last tweak: I found that when I vigorously mixed—instead of just lightly tossed—together the cooked pasta and sauce and a bit of cheese, the starch on the surface of the pasta pulled the components together, helping keep the liquid from separating out from the solids.

I had to hand it to those thrifty 16th-century Neapolitans. This was a true ragu—humble at its roots but as savory and satisfying as the meat-and-tomato-heavy versions that would follow. My 21st-century tweaks would make it a staple in my wintertime pasta sauce rotation.

Rigatoni with Beef and Onion Ragu

SERVES 6 TO 8

If marjoram is unavailable, substitute an equal amount of oregano. Pair this dish with a lightly dressed salad of assertively flavored greens.

1 (1- to 1¼-pound) boneless beef chuck-eye roast, cut into 4 pieces and trimmed of large pieces of fat
Kosher salt and pepper
2 ounces pancetta, cut into ½-inch pieces
2 ounces salami, cut into ½-inch pieces
1 small carrot, peeled and cut into ½-inch pieces
1 small celery rib, cut into ½-inch pieces
2½ pounds onions, halved and cut into 1-inch pieces
2 tablespoons tomato paste
1 cup dry white wine
2 tablespoons minced fresh marjoram
1 pound rigatoni
1 ounce Pecorino Romano cheese, grated (½ cup), plus extra for serving

1. Sprinkle beef with 1 teaspoon salt and ½ teaspoon pepper and set aside. Adjust oven rack to lower-middle position and heat oven to 300 degrees.

2. Process pancetta and salami in food processor until ground to paste, about 30 seconds, scraping down sides of bowl as needed. Add carrot and celery and process 30 seconds longer, scraping down sides of bowl as needed. Transfer paste to Dutch oven and set aside; do not clean out processor bowl. Pulse onions in processor in 2 batches, until ⅛- to ¼-inch pieces form, 8 to 10 pulses per batch.

3. Cook pancetta mixture over medium heat, stirring frequently, until fat is rendered and fond begins to form on bottom of pot, about 5 minutes. Add tomato paste and cook, stirring constantly, until browned, about 90 seconds. Stir in 2 cups water, scraping up any browned bits. Stir in onions and bring to boil. Stir in ½ cup wine and 1 tablespoon marjoram. Add beef and push into onions to ensure that it is submerged. Transfer to oven and cook, uncovered, until beef is fully tender, 2 to 2½ hours.

4. Transfer beef to carving board. Place pot over medium heat and cook, stirring frequently, until mixture is almost completely dry. Stir in remaining ½ cup wine and cook for 2 minutes, stirring occasionally. Using 2 forks, shred beef into bite-size pieces. Stir beef and remaining 1 tablespoon marjoram into sauce and season with salt and pepper to taste. Remove from heat, cover, and keep warm.

5. Bring 4 quarts water to boil in large pot. Add rigatoni and 2 tablespoons salt and cook, stirring often, until just al dente. Drain rigatoni and add to warm sauce. Add Pecorino and stir vigorously over low heat until sauce is slightly thickened and rigatoni is fully tender, 1 to 2 minutes. Serve, passing extra Pecorino separately.

A SURPRISING FORMULA FOR MEATY FLAVOR

Much of the meaty flavor in our Genovese ragu actually comes from the onions, which contain a compound called 3-mercapto-2-methylpentan-1-ol, or MMP for short. When an onion is cut, some of its sulfur compounds combine to form a new compound: propanethial-S-oxide—the stuff that makes your eyes tear. When heated, this compound turns into MMP. MMP's flavor is water-soluble, which means that to create it, water must be present. So to harness MMP's full savory power, we chop the onions in a food processor (thereby releasing more compounds that can be transformed into MMP) and cook the onions and meat in 2 cups of water.

LOTS OF ONIONS

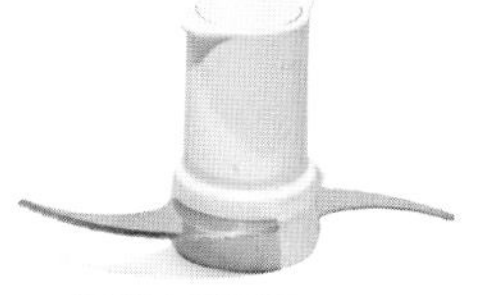
PROCESSED FINE

WATER

SPAGHETTI AND (GREAT) MEATBALLS

JACK BISHOP, *January/February 1998*

Like most Italian Americans, I have fond memories of my grandmother's Sunday dinner. As a main course, she served two kinds of sausage, braciole (rolled flank steak stuffed with cheeses, herbs, and garlic), and meatballs, all simmered in tomato sauce and all designed to be eaten over spaghetti. It was delicious and decadent.

Although my grandmother is a fabulous cook, her meatballs were never the best part of the meal. (My siblings and I fought over the braciole or spicy sausage.) However, it's the meatball part of this traditional Italian American feast that most other Americans are familiar with as part of the now-classic spaghetti and meatballs.

For this story, I wanted to make great meatballs (something the kids in my family would fight over) and try to streamline the recipe in the process. My grandmother would spend the better part of the weekend cooking Sunday dinner. I wanted to develop a spaghetti and meatball recipe that could be on the table in less than an hour—a breeze for weekend cooking and doable on weeknights when pressed for time.

RIGHT TEXTURE, RIGHT BINDER

The problem with most meatballs is that they are too dense and heavy. Serving meatballs over thin, long noodles is already a bit awkward. If the meatballs are compact, overcooked little hamburgers, the dish can be so leaden that Alka-Seltzer is the only dessert that makes sense.

Many cooks think of meatballs as hamburgers with seasonings (cheese, herbs, garlic, etc.) and a round shape. This is partly true. However, unlike hamburgers, which are best cooked rare or medium-rare, meatballs are cooked through until well-done. At this point, ground beef and seasonings will form dry, tough hockey pucks. Meatballs require additional ingredients to keep them moist and lighten their texture. My testing first focused on ingredients that would give meatballs a moister, softer consistency.

I started out with a simple recipe (ground beef plus a little cheese, parsley, salt, and pepper) and tested the various binders—eggs, dried bread crumbs, fresh bread crumbs, ground crackers, and bread soaked in milk—that were common in the recipes uncovered during my research.

A panade made with soft bread and buttermilk keeps our meatballs moist, tender, and cohesive.

I started with a whole egg and decided that it was a welcome addition. Meatballs made without egg were heavier and drier.

Next I added dried supermarket bread crumbs (the choice of my grandmother and most meatball recipe writers) to one batch and crustless bread soaked in milk (the second most popular bread binder) to another. The differences were quite clear. The crumbs soaked up any available moisture and compounded the problems caused by cooking meatballs to the well-done stage. Adding bread crumbs might be a way to extend the meat—an idea with appeal in less prosperous times—but hardly necessary in an age where the meat for this recipe cost $2. In comparison, the meatballs made with the soaked bread were moister, creamier, richer, and even more pâté-like in consistency. Clearly, milk was an important part of the equation.

There were a few problems with my first test using torn bread and milk. I soaked the crustless bread and then squeezed it dry as directed in many recipes but was still having trouble getting the bread to meld seamlessly into the meatball mixture. I saw a recipe where the crustless, torn bread cubes were cooked with milk into a paste. Although this method worked fine, I found myself waiting around for the mixture to cool before adding it to the meat.

The idea of mashing the bread and milk into a paste was good; I just wondered if I could do it without cooking. After several attempts, I devised this scheme: I starting by tearing the bread into small cubes. I placed the bread in a small bowl, drizzled the milk over it, and then mashed them together with a fork. I let the mixture sit for 10 minutes as the bread absorbed the liquid and eventually formed a smooth, thick paste. (In the meantime, I prepared the other ingredients for the meatballs.) By the time the bread was ready, so were the rest of the ingredients and I just added the entire bread-milk mixture to the bowl with the meat and seasonings.

Besides solving the problem of bread chunks being recognizable in my meatballs, this method has an added benefit. With more milk, the meatballs were even creamier and moister than versions made with bread that had been soaked and squeezed. Of course, there is a limit to how much milk can be added before the meatball mixture is too hard to handle. But ½ cup milk per pound of ground beef was clearly the winner in this first round of testing.

In the past, my colleague Pam Anderson found that yogurt adds a delicious flavor to meatloaf. Yogurt is too thick to properly soften bread by my method so I tried thinning it with some milk. Meatballs made with thinned yogurt were even richer, creamier, and more flavorful than those made with plain milk. I also tried buttermilk and the results were equally delicious, and there was no need to thin the liquid before adding it to the bread.

I went back to the issue of the egg one more time and tried the yolk only. As I suspected, the fats and emulsifiers in the yolk added moistness and richness. The white was only making the mixture sticky and harder to handle, so I eliminated it.

MEATS AND SEASONINGS

I next experimented with various meats. Until this point, I had been using all ground chuck. Leaner ground round made the meatballs dry. Ground veal was too bland. But a little ground pork, when added in a ratio of 3 parts chuck to 1 part pork, gave the meatballs another flavor dimension.

Freshly grated Parmesan cheese was needed for flavor, as was a little fresh parsley. Basil's delicate flavor was better showcased in the tomato sauce. Raw garlic improved the flavor of the meatballs but raw onions were problematic because they tended to shrink during cooking and caused little pockets to form in the meatballs. I tried cooking the onions first, which was an improvement, but in the end the meatballs were delicious without them and I wanted to avoid precooking ingredients if possible.

I then tested three cooking techniques—roasting, broiling, and traditional pan-frying. After roasting for 25 minutes at 450 degrees the meatballs emerged nicely browned, but dry and crumbly. Broiling proved messier than pan-frying and also dried out the meatballs. Pan-frying was my method of choice.

When pan-frying, I found it important to wait until the oil was hot before adding the meatballs. I made sure to turn the meatballs several times to create a dark brown crust on all sides. This prevented them from getting soggy when placed in the tomato sauce.

I wondered if I could save cleanup time and add flavor by building the tomato sauce in the same pan used to fry the meatballs. I emptied the vegetable oil, leaving behind the browned bits on the bottom of the pan. I then added a little fresh olive oil and started my tomato sauce. Not only did this method prove convenient, but it gave depth to my quick-cooking sauce.

Meatballs need a thick, smooth sauce—the kind produced by canned crushed tomatoes. I added a little garlic and basil to the tomatoes, but otherwise kept the flavorings simple so that the focus would remain on the meatballs. Once the tomato sauce thickened, I added the browned meatballs and simmered them just until heated through. With a pot of spaghetti on the stove, dinner was ready to go.

Classic Spaghetti and Meatballs

SERVES 4 TO 6

If you don't have buttermilk, you can substitute 6 tablespoons of plain yogurt thinned with 2 tablespoons of milk. When forming the meatballs, use a light touch; if compacted, they will be dense and hard.

Meatballs

2 slices hearty white sandwich bread, crusts removed, torn into small pieces
½ cup buttermilk
12 ounces 85 percent lean ground beef
4 ounces ground pork
¼ cup grated Parmesan cheese, plus extra for serving
2 tablespoons minced fresh parsley
1 large egg yolk
1 garlic clove, minced
¾ teaspoon salt
⅛ teaspoon pepper
Vegetable oil

Tomato Sauce and Pasta

2 tablespoons extra-virgin olive oil
1 garlic clove, minced
1 (28-ounce) can crushed tomatoes
1 tablespoon minced fresh basil
Salt and pepper
1 pound spaghetti

1. *For the meatballs:* Using fork, mash bread and buttermilk in large bowl. Let stand for 10 minutes. Add beef, pork, Parmesan, parsley, egg yolk, garlic, salt, and pepper to bowl and mix together with your hands. Pinch off and lightly shape mixture into 1½-inch round meatballs (about 14 meatballs total).

2. Add oil to 12-inch skillet until it measures ¼ inch deep. Heat oil over medium-high heat until shimmering. Carefully add meatballs in single layer and cook until well browned on all sides, about 10 minutes. Using slotted spoon, transfer meatballs to paper towel–lined plate. Discard remaining oil.

3. *For the tomato sauce and pasta:* Heat oil and garlic in now-empty skillet over medium heat. Cook, stirring often and scraping up any browned bits, until garlic turns golden but not brown, about 3 minutes. Stir in tomatoes, bring to simmer, and cook until sauce thickens, about 10 minutes. Stir in basil and season with salt and pepper to taste. Gently nestle meatballs into sauce, bring back to simmer, and cook, turning meatballs occasionally, until heated through, about 5 minutes. (Sauce and meatballs can be refrigerated for up to 2 days.)

4. While sauce cooks, bring 4 quarts water to boil in large pot. Add pasta and 1 tablespoon salt and cook, stirring often, until al dente. Reserve ½ cup cooking water, then drain pasta and return it to pot. Add 1 cup sauce (without meatballs) to pasta and toss to combine. Adjust consistency with reserved cooking water as needed. Transfer pasta to serving platter, top with additional tomato sauce and meatballs, and serve, passing extra Parmesan separately.

GETTING FLAVORFUL, MOIST MEATBALLS

1. Mash bread pieces and buttermilk together with fork. Let stand until smooth paste forms, about 10 minutes.

2. Add beef, pork, Parmesan, parsley, egg yolk, garlic, salt, and pepper to bowl and mix with your hands until roughly combined. Lightly shape into 1½-inch round meatballs.

RESCUING VEGETABLE LASAGNA

BRYAN ROOF, *September/October 2011*

There's no reason why a vegetable lasagna made with the classic trio of eggplant, zucchini, and summer squash should be any less satisfying than a meat-based casserole, especially when the produce is in season and locally grown. But I've rarely cooked one that I've been moved to make again. Some versions look tempting enough with a topcoat of bubbly cheese and thick tomato gravy, but cutting out a square of it invariably reveals trouble at the core. Often placed between the pasta sheets raw, the zucchini and squash turn out steamy and limp, flooding the dish with their juices—or, in some instances, undercooked and crunchy. Then there's the eggplant, which is typically not only soggy, but greasy from prefrying. Add to that the usual patches of dry, grainy ricotta and it's a wonder this dish ever became an Italian American standard.

So what would it take to make a full-flavored lasagna with vegetables that could stand up to—not wash out—the cheese and sauce? Ridding the produce of some of its moisture and boosting its flavor before adding it to the dish would be steps in the right direction.

We precook the vegetables and create a no-cook white sauce for a simple, rich vegetable lasagna.

SHEDDING WATER

I first focused my efforts on the most unruly element: the eggplant. Besides being full of water, eggplant is very porous and readily soaks up liquid (or oil). It therefore requires some sort of pretreatment that not only rids the fruit of water but also breaks down its absorbent air pockets. Fortunately, the test kitchen had already devised an effective—and novel—approach to both problems in another recipe: salting the eggplant and then microwaving it. Salt pulls water out of the fruit at the same time the microwave causes it to steam. Microwaving also collapses the eggplant's air pockets, leaving the flesh shrunken, wrinkled, and less prone to absorbing oil or liquid. Following this method, I cut the eggplant into ½-inch cubes, sprinkled them with 1 teaspoon of salt, and placed the pieces on a double layer of coffee filters. (The filters absorb moisture so that liquid doesn't pool on the plate.) I then microwaved the pieces for 10 minutes. When I sautéed this eggplant to give it more flavor and color, it hardly picked up any oil at all.

I considered salting the zucchini and yellow squash to remove their excess water, but I was fairly certain that a turn in the skillet would burn off enough liquid and deepen their flavor. I cut the squashes (1 pound of each) into ½-inch cubes and, to save myself an extra step, combined them with the microwaved eggplant. I then sautéed the mixture in two batches with minced garlic and healthy dashes of salt and pepper. About 7 minutes later, the vegetables had developed good color and picked up some garlicky flavor, but I wondered if I could do better. I minced a few more cloves of garlic, this time letting the bits soak in a tablespoon of olive oil along with some minced fresh thyme. Added to the skillet as each batch of vegetables finished cooking, this supergarlicky, herbal-infused mixture gave the eggplant and squash so much flavor that they were good enough to eat straight from the pan.

Now it was time to see how the vegetables would fare in the lasagna. I made a placeholder tomato sauce by briefly simmering crushed tomatoes with garlic, olive oil, basil, and a dash of pepper flakes. I then layered a dozen no-boil noodles (our favorite alternative to fresh pasta) with the sauce, the sautéed eggplant and vegetables, and generous helpings of ricotta, mozzarella, and nutty Parmesan cheese. I baked the casserole in a 375-degree oven until golden and bubbly.

The good news was that starting with precooked vegetables allowed me to cut the baking time from the usual hour-plus down to about 35 minutes. But improvements were still needed here and there. Instead of acting as a creamy binder, the ricotta had cooked up into grainy slicks, and some tasters wanted the dairy element to be even richer. Plus, we all agreed that the tomato sauce tasted a bit flat.

ON THE SAUCES

I had one quick idea about the ricotta, thanks to the efforts of another colleague who'd encountered similar graininess when he tried incorporating the tiny, pebbly curds into baked ziti. To solve the problem, he substituted cottage cheese, which boasts a creamier consistency (not to mention slightly tangier flavor), for the ricotta. When I made the switch with my next batch, everyone agreed that things were looking up, but that the cheese was still a bit dry and lean-tasting. In fact, this round of testing convinced me that what we all really wanted was the richness and creaminess of a béchamel sauce, the classic roux-thickened milk mixture found in countless meat and vegetable lasagna recipes. My only hesitation was that it involved extra work. I didn't want to add more fuss to the dish by cooking a third element, so I tried a lazy man's approach and whipped up a no-cook white sauce by whisking together 1 cup each of milk and cottage cheese with a generous 2 cups of Parmesan and a couple of minced garlic cloves.

I wasn't expecting much from this experiment, but the results were surprisingly good. All that cheese produced a "sauce" that was considerably richer, if still a bit thin and curdled. The first problem I easily fixed by swapping the milk for an equal amount of heavy cream. The second took a bit more experimentation, but a glossy, silky-smooth sauce finally came together after I whisked 1 teaspoon of cornstarch in with the other dairy ingredients. (When the starch granules in cornstarch absorb water and swell, they get in the way of the dairy proteins and prevent them from clumping together in curds.)

As for the tomato sauce, I couldn't help but wonder if a similar no-cook approach might liven up its dull flavor—and save a few extra minutes at the stove. I prepared another batch, this time simply stirring together the ingredients and adding the sauce to the casserole without simmering it first. The results were better than ever. Even after baking and cooling, the sauce still tasted bright, punching up the filling with just enough acidity.

FINAL FLOURISHES

And yet balancing the complexity of the dairy-rich "béchamel" sauce with the fruity tomato sauce didn't quite perk up tasters' interest in the filling. I needed something bolder and fresher to complement the eggplant, zucchini, and squash. Rummaging through the refrigerator for ideas, I spotted a jar of kalamata olives. A handful of these, chopped, added meaty texture and a briny, salty jolt of flavor. For freshness, I added a bag of baby spinach, which took no time to sauté in a touch of olive oil until wilted and then drain before layering into the filling. My final touch was a generous amount of chopped fresh basil leaves sprinkled on the casserole right before serving. Each of these additions was small, but they made a big difference in the flavor of the dish.

At last, this lasagna more than had it all with its rich flavors, creamy cheese, and substantial texture—along with a summery brightness that set it apart from the meat kind. I had to restrain a smile when I saw that even the most dedicated meat lovers among my tasters couldn't help but come back for more.

Vegetable Lasagna

SERVES 8 TO 10

Part-skim mozzarella can also be used in this recipe, but avoid preshredded cheese, as it does not melt well. We prefer kosher salt because it clings best to the eggplant. If using table salt, reduce the amounts by half.

Tomato Sauce

1 (28-ounce) can crushed tomatoes
¼ cup finely chopped fresh basil
2 tablespoons extra-virgin olive oil
2 garlic cloves, minced
1 teaspoon kosher salt
¼ teaspoon red pepper flakes

Cream Sauce

8 ounces (1 cup) whole-milk cottage cheese
4 ounces Parmesan cheese, grated (2 cups)
1 cup heavy cream
2 garlic cloves, minced
1 teaspoon cornstarch
½ teaspoon kosher salt
½ teaspoon pepper

Filling and Noodles

1½ pounds eggplant, peeled and cut into ½-inch pieces
Kosher salt and pepper
1 pound zucchini, cut into ½-inch pieces
1 pound yellow summer squash, cut into ½-inch pieces
5 tablespoons plus 1 teaspoon extra-virgin olive oil
4 garlic cloves, minced
1 tablespoon minced fresh thyme
12 ounces (12 cups) baby spinach
12 no-boil lasagna noodles
½ cup pitted kalamata olives, minced
12 ounces whole-milk mozzarella cheese, shredded (3 cups)
2 tablespoons chopped fresh basil

1. *For the tomato sauce:* Whisk all ingredients together in bowl; set aside.
2. *For the cream sauce:* Whisk all ingredients together in second bowl; set aside.
3. *For the filling and noodles:* Adjust oven rack to middle position and heat oven to 375 degrees. Toss eggplant with 1 teaspoon salt in large bowl. Line large plate with double layer of coffee filters and lightly spray with vegetable oil spray. Spread eggplant in even layer over coffee filters; wipe out and reserve bowl. Microwave eggplant until dry to touch and slightly shriveled, about 10 minutes, tossing halfway through microwaving. Let cool slightly. Return eggplant to bowl and toss with zucchini and summer squash.
4. Combine 1 tablespoon oil, garlic, and thyme in small bowl. Heat 2 tablespoons oil in 12-inch nonstick skillet over medium-high heat until shimmering. Add half of eggplant mixture, ¼ teaspoon salt, and ¼ teaspoon pepper and cook, stirring occasionally, until vegetables are lightly browned, about 7 minutes. Push vegetables to sides of skillet. Add half of garlic mixture to center and cook, mashing mixture into pan, until fragrant, about 30 seconds. Stir garlic mixture into vegetables and transfer to medium bowl. Repeat with 2 tablespoons oil, remaining eggplant mixture, and remaining garlic mixture; transfer to bowl.
5. Heat remaining 1 teaspoon oil in now-empty skillet over medium-high heat until shimmering. Add spinach and cook, stirring frequently, until wilted, about 3 minutes. Transfer spinach to paper towel–lined plate and let drain for 2 minutes. Stir into eggplant mixture. (Filling can be refrigerated for up to 24 hours.)
6. Grease 13 by 9-inch baking dish. Spread 1 cup tomato sauce evenly over bottom of dish. Arrange 4 noodles on top of sauce (noodles will overlap). Spread half of vegetable mixture evenly over noodles, followed by ¼ cup olives. Spoon half of cream sauce over top and sprinkle with 1 cup mozzarella. Repeat layering with 4 noodles, 1 cup tomato sauce, remaining vegetable mixture, remaining ¼ cup olives, remaining cream sauce, and 1 cup mozzarella. For final layer, arrange remaining 4 noodles on top and cover completely with remaining tomato sauce. Sprinkle remaining 1 cup mozzarella evenly over tomato sauce.
7. Cover dish tightly with aluminum foil that has been sprayed with oil spray and bake until edges are just bubbling, about 35 minutes, rotating dish halfway through baking. Let lasagna cool for 25 minutes, sprinkle with basil, and serve.

STREAMLINING MANICOTTI

REBECCA HAYS, *January/February 2007*

I have a love/hate relationship with manicotti. Well-made versions of this Italian American classic—pasta tubes stuffed with rich ricotta filling and blanketed with tomato sauce—can be eminently satisfying. So what's not to love? Putting it all together. For such a straightforward collection of ingredients (after all, manicotti is just a compilation of pasta, cheese, and tomato sauce), the preparation is surprisingly fussy. Blanching, shocking, draining, and stuffing slippery pasta tubes require more patience (and time) than I usually have. In addition, a survey of manicotti recipes proved that most recipe writers don't get the filling right; too often, the ricotta-based mixture turns out bland and runny.

TEST TUBES

Testing started with the pasta component. Cheese-stuffed pastas have been consumed in Italy since medieval times, and traditional recipes used either homemade *crespelle* (thin, eggy, crêpe-like pancakes) or rectangular sheets of homemade pasta as wrappers for the filling. (Both are terrific, though neither fit into my streamlined schematic.) Over time, most Italian American recipes evolved to use ready-made dried pasta tubes, which are parboiled, shocked in ice water to stop the cooking, drained, and stuffed with ricotta filling. It was on this approach that I focused my attention.

Some recipes require a pastry bag for filling the long, hollow cylinders with ricotta; others explain how to snip the corner from a zipper-lock bag to create a mock pastry bag. Many recipes take a different approach altogether, suggesting a small soupspoon for stuffing the tubes. With a bowl of basic ricotta filling at my side, I gave each method a try. The pastry bag was messy but workable. However, many cooks don't own a pastry bag, and I didn't want to write a recipe requiring a specialty tool. Using a zipper-lock bag to force the ricotta into a slick parboiled pasta tube was maddening; most of the cheese oozed out of the bag, with an embarrassingly small amount actually making it into the tube. The soupspoon was equally frustrating; I eventually gave up on it and used my fingers instead. A colleague suggested slitting a blanched noodle lengthwise, packing it with filling, and putting the stuffed tube into a casserole seam side down. Not bad, but I still had to blanch, shock, and drain the noodles.

I found a "quick" recipe that seemed worth trying on the back of one of the manicotti boxes. It called for stuffing uncooked pasta tubes with ricotta, covering them with a watery sauce, then baking. Filling raw pasta tubes was marginally easier than stuffing parboiled noodles, though a few shattered along the way. Still, I followed the recipe through, watering down a jar of tomato sauce with a cup of boiling water and pouring it over the manicotti. After 45 minutes in the oven, this manicotti was inedible, with some of the pasta shells remaining uncooked and the pink, watered-down sauce tasting, well, like water.

Rolling soaked no-boil lasagna noodles around a cheesy filling is easier than stuffing pasta tubes.

Nearly at my wit's end, I remembered the crespelle and fresh pasta sheets. Spreading the filling onto a flat wrapper had to be easier than cramming it into a floppy tube. I wondered if I could use store-bought crêpes instead of crespelle, but they were far too sugary. Fresh pasta sheets aren't sold at many supermarkets. Then I thought of no-boil lasagna noodles. What if I softened the noodles in water, turning them into pliable sheets of pasta? This method worked like a charm. After a quick soak in boiling water, no-boil lasagna noodles could be spread with filling and rolled up in a few easy minutes.

THE BIG CHEESE

It was a given that ricotta would serve as the base for the filling, and I discovered that part-skim ricotta provided an ideal level of richness, allowing the other flavors to shine.

Shredded low-moisture mozzarella and Parmesan are typical additions to the filling, but I wondered if other cheeses might fare better. After testing cream cheese, fresh mozzarella, fontina, Asiago, pecorino, and aged provolone, I decided to stick with tradition, opting for mozzarella and Parmesan.

Without eggs, the filling separates, becoming loose and watery. After experimenting with various amounts of whole eggs and yolks, I settled on two whole eggs. But eggs alone didn't completely ward off a runny filling. The proper amounts of mozzarella and Parmesan also proved key; specifically, a generous amount of mozzarella was necessary.

As for seasonings, a few specks of parsley plus salt and pepper are the norms. Looking for improvement, I explored other options, eventually settling on a combination of fresh parsley and basil.

FINISHING TOUCHES

A slow-cooked tomato sauce didn't fit into my streamlining goal, so I was relieved when tasters preferred the bright, fresh flavor of a 15-minute sauce made with olive oil, garlic, and diced canned tomatoes pureed in a food processor to give the sauce body quickly. I punched up my quick recipe with fresh basil leaves and a dash of red pepper flakes.

Finally, most baked pasta dishes benefit from a browned, cheesy topping. The best approach was to add a light sprinkling of Parmesan, passing the casserole under the broiler before serving. This, at last, was manicotti that won my complete affection: great tasting and easy to prepare.

Baked Manicotti

SERVES 6 TO 8

If your baking dish isn't broiler-safe, brown the manicotti at 500 degrees for about 10 minutes. Note that some products contain only 12 no-boil noodles per package; this recipe requires 16 noodles.

Tomato Sauce

2 (28-ounce) cans diced tomatoes
2 tablespoons extra-virgin olive oil
3 garlic cloves, minced
½ teaspoon red pepper flakes (optional)
Salt
2 tablespoons chopped fresh basil

Cheese Filling

24 ounces (3 cups) part-skim ricotta cheese
8 ounces mozzarella cheese, shredded (2 cups)
4 ounces Parmesan cheese, grated (2 cups)
2 large eggs
2 tablespoons chopped fresh parsley
2 tablespoons chopped fresh basil
¾ teaspoon salt
½ teaspoon pepper
16 no-boil lasagna noodles

1. ***For the tomato sauce:*** Pulse 1 can tomatoes in food processor until coarsely chopped, 3 to 4 pulses; transfer to bowl. Repeat with remaining 1 can tomatoes; transfer to bowl.

2. Heat oil, garlic, and pepper flakes, if using, in large saucepan over medium heat. Cook, stirring often, until garlic turns golden but not brown, about 3 minutes. Stir in chopped tomatoes and ½ teaspoon salt, bring to simmer, and cook until thickened slightly, about 15 minutes. Stir in basil and season with salt to taste.

3. ***For the cheese filling:*** Combine ricotta, mozzarella, 1 cup Parmesan, eggs, parsley, basil, salt, and pepper in bowl.

4. Adjust oven rack to middle position and heat oven to 375 degrees. Pour 2 inches boiling water into 13 by 9-inch broiler-safe baking dish. Slip noodles into water, one at a time, and soak until pliable, about 5 minutes, separating noodles with tip of paring knife to prevent sticking. Remove noodles from water and place in single layer on clean dish towels; blot dry. Discard water and dry dish.

5. Spread 1½ cups sauce evenly over bottom of dish. Using soupspoon, spread ¼ cup cheese mixture evenly onto bottom three-quarters of each noodle (with short side facing you), leaving top quarter of noodle exposed. Roll each noodle into tube shape and arrange in dish seam side down. Top evenly with remaining sauce, making sure that noodles are completely covered.

6. Cover dish tightly with aluminum foil and bake until bubbling, about 40 minutes, rotating dish halfway through baking. Remove dish from oven and remove foil. Adjust oven rack 6 inches from broiler element and heat broiler. Sprinkle manicotti evenly with remaining 1 cup Parmesan. Broil until cheese is spotty brown, 4 to 6 minutes. Let manicotti cool for 15 minutes before serving.

variations

Baked Manicotti with Sausage

Cook 1 pound hot or sweet Italian sausage, casings removed, in 2 tablespoons olive oil in large saucepan over medium-high heat, breaking sausage into ½-inch pieces with wooden spoon, until no longer pink, about 6 minutes. Omit olive oil in sauce and cook remaining sauce ingredients in saucepan with sausage.

Baked Manicotti Puttanesca

Cook 3 rinsed and minced anchovy fillets with oil, garlic, and pepper flakes. Add ¼ cup pitted kalamata olives, quartered, and 2 tablespoons rinsed capers to cheese filling.

Baked Manicotti with Spinach

Add one 10-ounce package frozen chopped spinach, thawed, squeezed dry, and chopped fine, and pinch ground nutmeg to cheese filling. Increase salt in filling to 1 teaspoon.

MAKING MANICOTTI

In our streamlined recipe, the ricotta filling is spread onto softened no-boil lasagna noodles, eliminating the slippery task of stuffing parboiled manicotti shells.

1. Soak no-boil lasagna noodles in boiling water for 5 minutes until pliable, using tip of paring knife to separate noodles and prevent sticking.

2. Using soupspoon, spread about ¼ cup filling onto three-quarters of each noodle, leaving top quarter of noodle exposed.

3. Roll each noodle by hand and place in baking dish, seam side down.

PAD THAI AT HOME

ANNIE PETITO, *November/December 2016*

I once pulled out all the stops to make an entirely authentic version of pad thai, and the result was a real stunner: tender rice noodles entwined in a sweet, sour, salty sauce and stir-fried with garlic, shallot, sweet shrimp, soft curds of scrambled egg, and nuggets of tofu. Chopped dried shrimp and pungent preserved daikon radish contributed intense flavor and chewy, crunchy textures that made me think I'd been transported to Bangkok. Chopped roasted peanuts, crisp bean sprouts, and garlic chives scattered over the top ensured that every bite was as exciting as the next.

My only quibbles? After all that work, the recipe yielded only two servings. Also, although it was incredibly satisfying to eat, my homemade pad thai had required a lot of forethought. Sourcing ingredients like dried shrimp and preserved radish demanded an excursion to an Asian market. Instead, could I create a satisfying version of pad thai using mostly everyday ingredients?

THE BASICS

Thankfully, the dried rice noodles that form the base of pad thai are available at most supermarkets. Having dealt with rice noodles before, I knew exactly how to treat them. I put 8 ounces in a bowl with boiling water and let them sit until they were pliant, about 8 minutes. After draining and rinsing the noodles with cold water, I tossed them with oil for antistick insurance.

With the noodles sorted out, I moved on to the sauce. The interplay of salty, sweet, and sour tastes is the primary characteristic of pad thai. These flavors typically come from pungent, saline fish sauce; caramel-like palm sugar; and sour, fruity tamarind. Fish sauce is now widely available, so it would need no substitute. Next up: thick palm sugar disks. Rather than hunt them down, I tested brown and white sugar. Finding no real flavor difference, I opted to use white.

Tamarind, a fruit that grows as a round, brown pod, is also available as pure tamarind concentrate. I was committed to using everyday ingredients in my recipe, but after some testing I concluded that tamarind is essential to pad thai and is worth seeking out. Happily, tamarind is increasingly available in the Asian or Latin section of supermarkets. I chose the juice concentrate, since it is easier to work with.

On to the protein. Pad thai typically includes three types: firm tofu, shrimp, and eggs. To keep the ingredient list manageable, I omitted tofu and added more of the latter two. One pound of large shrimp and four beaten eggs were adequate.

Most recipes call for adding the many ingredients in pad thai to the skillet sequentially. But to avoid overcrowding the pan, the volume of food must be kept low, so only one or two servings can be produced. By cooking in batches rather than gradually adding ingredients to the skillet, I could make enough to serve four. I started with minced garlic and scallion whites (instead of the usual shallot since I planned on using the scallion greens in place of relatively obscure garlic chives) and then mixed in the shrimp and eggs. Once they were cooked, I transferred them to a bowl and stir-fried the noodles and sauce. I tossed in a handful of bean sprouts and the green parts of the scallions, and the dish was ready to be garnished with lime and chopped peanuts.

FAKE IT 'TIL YOU MAKE IT

My pad thai was now in very good shape, but I pined for those salty bits of chewy dried shrimp and crunchy preserved daikon that help make it unique.

Hoping to replicate the daikon, which has a crunchy texture akin to pickled cabbage, I thought of similar salty, pickled options: everything from sauerkraut (too vinegary) to pickles (too briny) to dried apricots that I brined (too sweet and sticky). In the end, the most successful option was, not too surprisingly, fresh radishes. Soaking matchsticks of red radish in a warm solution of salt, sugar, and water created a fresh, crunchy, salty mix-in.

Next, I considered the dried shrimp. In Thailand, the tiny shellfish are peeled, salted, and dried in the sun, giving them a meaty flavor and a firm, chewy texture. In Thai cooking, they are typically fried and used as a garnish or seasoning. My thought was to use a portion of the shrimp I was already calling for—just treated in a different manner. I cut a handful of shrimp into small bits and gently cooked them with the scallions and garlic, hoping to create a kind of shrimp paste. However, the shrimp pieces just plumped as they cooked, making them indistinguishable from the rest.

We achieve authentic flavor using supermarket ingredients like sugar, fish sauce, and tamarind juice concentrate.

To produce a better facsimile, I would have to overcook the shrimp. Doing so in a skillet set over low heat took 20 minutes, so I turned to the microwave. I nuked shrimp pieces until they were shriveled and then fried the nuggets in the skillet until they were golden. I continued with the recipe as before, tossing in my makeshift pickled radishes and dried shrimp. Both were huge hits, giving my pad thai authentic character.

THAI'ING IT ALL TOGETHER

Typically pad thai is served with condiments such as fish sauce, sugar, Thai chile powder, and vinegar. Instead, I stirred thinly sliced serrano chiles into white vinegar, which brightened all the other flavors.

My pad thai boasted all the right flavors and textures, and I could have it almost any time I wanted.

Everyday Pad Thai

SERVES 4

Since pad thai cooks very quickly, prepare everything before you begin to cook. Use the time during which the radishes and noodles soak to prepare the other ingredients. We recommend using a tamarind juice concentrate made in Thailand in this recipe. If you cannot find tamarind, substitute 1½ tablespoons lime juice and 1½ tablespoons water and omit the lime wedges.

Chile Vinegar

- **⅓ cup distilled white vinegar**
- **1 serrano chile, stemmed and sliced into thin rings**

Stir-Fry

- **Salt**
- **Sugar**
- **2 radishes, trimmed and cut into 1½-inch by ¼-inch matchsticks**
- **8 ounces (¼-inch-wide) rice noodles**
- **3 tablespoons plus 2 teaspoons vegetable oil**
- **¼ cup fish sauce**
- **3 tablespoons tamarind juice concentrate**
- **1 pound large shrimp (26 to 30 per pound), peeled and deveined**
- **4 scallions, white and light green parts minced, dark green parts cut into 1-inch lengths**
- **1 garlic clove, minced**
- **4 large eggs, beaten**
- **4 ounces (2 cups) bean sprouts**
- **¼ cup roasted unsalted peanuts, chopped coarse**
- **Lime wedges**

1. *For the chile vinegar:* Combine vinegar and chile in bowl and let stand at room temperature for at least 15 minutes.
2. *For the stir-fry:* Combine ¼ cup water, ½ teaspoon salt, and ¼ teaspoon sugar in small bowl. Microwave until steaming, about 30 seconds. Add radishes and let stand for 15 minutes. Drain and pat dry with paper towels.
3. Bring 6 cups water to boil. Place noodles in large bowl. Pour boiling water over noodles. Stir, then let soak until noodles are almost tender, about 8 minutes, stirring once halfway through soaking. Drain noodles and rinse with cold water. Drain noodles well, then toss with 2 teaspoons oil.
4. Combine fish sauce, tamarind concentrate, and 3 tablespoons sugar in bowl and whisk until sugar is dissolved. Set sauce aside.
5. Remove tails from 4 shrimp. Cut shrimp in half lengthwise, then cut each half into ½-inch pieces. Toss shrimp pieces with ⅛ teaspoon salt and ⅛ teaspoon sugar. Arrange pieces in single layer on large plate and microwave at 50 percent power until shrimp are dried and have reduced in size by half, 4 to 5 minutes. (Check halfway through microwaving and separate any pieces that may have stuck together.)
6. Heat 2 teaspoons oil in 12-inch nonstick skillet over medium heat until shimmering. Add dried shrimp and cook, stirring frequently, until golden brown and crispy, 3 to 5 minutes. Transfer to large bowl.
7. Heat 1 teaspoon oil in now-empty skillet over medium heat until shimmering. Add minced scallions and garlic and cook, stirring constantly, until garlic is golden brown, about 1 minute. Transfer to bowl with dried shrimp.
8. Heat 2 teaspoons oil in now-empty skillet over high heat until just smoking. Add remaining whole shrimp and spread into even layer. Cook, without stirring, until shrimp turn opaque and brown around edges, 2 to 3 minutes, flipping halfway through cooking. Push shrimp to sides of skillet. Add 2 teaspoons oil to center, then add eggs to center. Using rubber spatula, stir eggs gently and cook until set but still wet. Stir eggs into shrimp and continue to cook, breaking up large pieces of egg, until eggs are fully cooked, 30 to 60 seconds longer. Transfer shrimp-egg mixture to bowl with scallion-garlic mixture and dried shrimp.
9. Heat remaining 2 teaspoons oil in now-empty skillet over high heat until just smoking. Add noodles and sauce and toss with tongs to coat. Cook, stirring and tossing often, until noodles are tender and have absorbed sauce, 2 to 4 minutes. Transfer noodles to bowl with shrimp mixture. Add 2 teaspoons chile vinegar, drained radishes, scallion greens, and bean sprouts and toss to combine.
10. Transfer to platter and sprinkle with peanuts. Serve immediately, passing lime wedges and remaining chile vinegar separately.

DIY DRIED SHRIMP

Small dried shrimp, which are firm and chewy when reconstituted, add savory depth to many Asian dishes. Since they're not readily available in most supermarkets, we created a faux version using fresh shrimp. This is how we did it:

Cut shrimp in half lengthwise, then cut each half into ½-inch pieces. Toss with salt and sugar, then microwave until shrimp are dried and have reduced in size by half. Cook shrimp pieces in oil until they turn golden brown and crispy.

ALL ABOUT TAMARIND

The tart, fruity flavor of tamarind is essential for authentic-tasting pad thai. The fruit is sold in a variety of forms, from fresh pods to bricks of pulp to pure concentrate and powder. The pods must be opened to remove the seedy pulp; the bricks require soaking and straining. Concentrate is used straight from the container, as is tamarind powder.

When we tasted the options while developing our recipe, we liked the fresh flavor of pods or pulp, but they required the most preparation. Tamarind powder was easy to use but had a faint flavor. Tamarind juice concentrate offered the best of both worlds: tangy, fresh flavor and ease of use. Look for tamarind juice concentrate manufactured in Thailand, which is thinner and tastes brighter than the paste concentrate produced in other countries. (If all you can find is a paste concentrate, mix 1½ tablespoons with 1½ tablespoons hot water to use it in our Everyday Pad Thai recipe.)

FRESH PODS
Too much prep

JUICE CONCENTRATE
Easy to use

SESAME NOODLES WITH CHICKEN

JULIA COLLIN DAVISON, *September/October 2004*

Much like a Chinese finger trap that lures by appearing to be a toy, sesame noodles are not what they seem. You may think of them as merely a humble bowl of cold noodles, but don't be fooled—just one bite and you're hooked on these toothsome noodles with shreds of tender chicken, all tossed with the fresh sesame sauce.

The real problem is, good versions of this dish can be hard to find. The cold noodles have a habit of turning gummy, the chicken often dries out, and the sauce is notorious for turning bland and pasty. I wanted a recipe that could not only quell a serious craving but could do it fast.

Though drawn to the softer texture of fresh Asian-style noodles, I conceded that dried spaghetti could serve as a second-string substitute. The trouble with both types of noodle, however, was that after being cooked and chilled, they gelled into a rubbery skein. After trying a number of ways to avoid this, I found it necessary to rinse the noodles under cold tap water directly after cooking. This not only cooled the hot noodles immediately but also washed away much of their sticky starch. To further forestall any clumping, I tossed the rinsed noodles with a little oil.

Pureeing chunky peanut butter with toasted sesame seeds makes a smooth, bold-flavored sauce base.

Boneless, skinless chicken breasts are quick to cook and easy to shred; the real question is how to cook them. The microwave seemed easy in theory, but I found the rate of cooking difficult to monitor—30 seconds meant the difference between underdone and overdone. Many recipes suggested poaching the chicken in water or broth, but this chicken had a washed-out flavor. Nor was roasting the answer; it caused the outer meat to dry out before the interior was fully cooked. Cooking under both gas and electric broilers, however, worked perfectly. The chicken cooked through in minutes, retaining much of its moisture and flavor.

To be authentic, the sesame sauce should be made with an Asian sesame paste (not to be confused with Middle Eastern tahini), but most recipes substitute peanut butter because it's easier to find. Somewhat surprisingly, tasters preferred chunky peanut butter over smooth, describing its flavor as fresh and more peanutty. I had been making the sauce in a blender and realized that the chunky bits of peanuts were being freshly ground into the sauce, producing a cleaner, stronger flavor.

I found the flavors of both fresh garlic and ginger necessary, along with soy sauce, rice vinegar, hot sauce, and brown sugar. I then stumbled on the obvious way to keep the sauce from being too thick or pasty: Thin it out with water.

Although the sauce was tasting pretty good, tasters still complained that there was not enough sesame flavor. Tossing the rinsed pasta with toasted sesame oil helped a bit, as did garnishing the noodles with toasted sesame seeds. But tasters were still not satisfied; they wanted more. Finally, I tried adding some of the toasted sesame seeds to the sauce. Blended into the sauce along with the chunky peanut butter, the sesame seeds added the final kick of authentic sesame flavor we were all hankering for.

Sesame Noodles with Shredded Chicken

SERVES 4

We prefer the flavor and texture of chunky peanut butter here; however, creamy peanut butter can be used. If you cannot find fresh Chinese egg noodles, substitute 12 ounces dried spaghetti or linguine.

5 tablespoons soy sauce
¼ cup chunky peanut butter
¼ cup sesame seeds, toasted
2 tablespoons rice vinegar
2 tablespoons packed light brown sugar
1 tablespoon grated fresh ginger
2 garlic cloves, minced
1 teaspoon hot sauce
½ cup hot water
4 (6-ounce) boneless, skinless chicken breasts, trimmed
Salt and pepper
1 pound fresh Chinese noodles
2 tablespoons toasted sesame oil
4 scallions, sliced thin on bias
1 carrot, peeled and grated

1. Puree soy sauce, peanut butter, 3 tablespoons sesame seeds, vinegar, sugar, ginger, garlic, and hot sauce in blender until smooth, about 30 seconds. With machine running, add hot water, 1 tablespoon at a time, until sauce has consistency of heavy cream (you may not need entire amount of water).
2. Adjust oven rack 6 inches from broiler element and heat broiler. Spray broiler pan top with vegetable oil spray. Pat chicken dry with paper towels, season with salt and pepper, and lay on prepared pan. Broil chicken until lightly browned and registers 160 degrees, 10 to 15 minutes, flipping chicken over halfway through broiling time. Transfer chicken to cutting board, let cool slightly, then shred into bite-size pieces.
3. Meanwhile, bring 4 quarts water to boil in large pot. Add noodles and 1 tablespoon salt and cook, stirring often, until tender. Drain noodles, rinse with cold water, and drain again, leaving noodles slightly wet. Transfer to large bowl and toss with oil. Add shredded chicken, scallions, carrot, and sauce and toss to combine. Sprinkle with remaining 1 tablespoon sesame seeds and serve.

Adzuki
Flageolet
Jacob's Cattle
Pinto
Garbanzo
Rice Bean
Steuben Yellow Eye
Scarlet Runner
Appaloosa
Kidney
Cannellini
Black-Eyed Pea

RICE, GRAINS, AND BEANS

EXPLORING RICE PILAF

ANNE YAMANAKA, *March/April 2000*

A few years ago when eating in a Persian restaurant, I became instantly enamored of its rice pilaf. Fragrant and fluffy, perfectly steamed, tender but still retaining an al dente quality, this was the type of rice I loved. Still better, this rice had gained flavor and texture from the other, more intensely flavored ingredients that had been added to it. Excited, I decided to find the best way to make rice pilaf that was this good in my own kitchen.

My first step was to define rice pilaf. According to most culinary sources, it is simply long-grain rice that has been cooked in hot oil or butter before being simmered in hot liquid, typically either water or stock. In Middle Eastern cuisines, however, the term pilaf also refers to a more substantial dish in which the rice is cooked in this manner and then flavored with other ingredients—spices, nuts, dried fruits, and/or chicken or other meat. To avoid confusion, I decided to call the simple master recipe for my dish "pilaf-style" rice, designating the flavored versions as rice pilaf.

I also discovered in my research that there are many different ways to cook rice pilaf. Most of these methods were traditions from the Middle East, from which this dish hails. Most recipes stipulated that the rice had to be soaked or at least rinsed prior to cooking in order to produce a finished rice with very separate, very fluffy grains, the characteristic that virtually defines the dish. With my recipes in hand, I started testing.

Rinsing the rice before cooking and then letting it steam covered with a towel after simmering produces fluffy, separate grains.

RIGHT RICE, RIGHT RATIO

The logical first step in this process was to isolate the best type of rice for pilaf. I limited my testing to long-grain rice, since medium and short-grain rice inherently produce a rather sticky, starchy product and I was looking for fluffy, separate grains. I came upon a number of different choices: plain long-grain white rice, converted rice, instant rice, jasmine, basmati, and Texmati (basmati rice grown domestically in Texas). I cooked them each according to a standard, stripped-down recipe for rice pilaf, altering the ratio of liquid to rice according to each variety when necessary.

Each type of rice was slightly different in flavor, texture, and appearance. Worst of the lot was the instant rice, which was textureless and mushy and had very little rice flavor. The converted rice had a very strong, off-putting flavor, while the jasmine rice, though delicious, was a little too sticky for pilaf. Plain long-grain white rice worked well, but basmati rice was even better: each grain was separate and long and fluffy, and the rice had a fresh, delicate fragrance. Though the Texmati produced similar results, it cost three times as much as the basmati per pound, making the basmati rice the logical choice. That said, I would add that you can use plain long-grain rice if basmati is not available.

In culinary school I was taught that the proper rice to liquid ratio for long-grain white rice is 1 to 2, but many cooks use less water, so I decided to figure it out for myself. After testing every possibility, from 1:1 to 1:2, I found that I got the best rice using 1⅔ cups of water for every cup of rice. To make this easier to remember, as well as easier to measure, I increased the rice by half to 1½ cups and the liquid to 2½ cups.

GIVE IT A RINSE

With my rice to water ratio set, I was ready to test the traditional methods for making pilaf, which called for rinsing, soaking, or parboiling the rice before cooking it in fat and simmering it to tenderness. Each recipe declared one of these preparatory steps to be essential in producing rice with distinct, separate grains that were light and fluffy.

I began by parboiling the rice for 3 minutes in a large quantity of water, as you would pasta, then draining it and proceeding to sauté and cook it. This resulted in bloated, waterlogged grains of rice.

Rinsing the rice, on the other hand, made a substantial difference, particularly with basmati rice. I simply covered 1½ cups of rice with water, gently moved the grains around using my fingers, and drained the water from the rice. I repeated this process about four or five times until the rinsing water was clear enough for me to see the grains distinctly. I then drained the rice and cooked it in oil and liquid (decreased to 2¼ cups to compensate for the water that had been absorbed by or adhered to the grains during rinsing). The resulting rice was less hard and more tender, and it had a slightly shinier, smoother appearance.

I also tested soaking the rice before cooking it. I rinsed three batches of basmati rice and soaked them for 5 minutes, 1 hour, and overnight, respectively. The batch that soaked for 5 minutes was no better than the one that had only been rinsed. Soaking the rice for an hour proved to be a still greater waste of time, since it wasn't perceptibly different from the rinsed-only version. While the rice that was soaked overnight was better than the rinsed-only rice, the difference was subtle, and the extra step required so much forethought that I opted for the simpler step of merely rinsing.

Thus far, I had allowed the rice to steam an additional 10 minutes after being removed from the heat to ensure that the moisture was distributed throughout. I wondered if a longer or shorter steaming time would make a big difference in the resulting pilaf. I made a few batches of pilaf, allowing the rice to steam for 5 minutes, 10 minutes, and 15 minutes. The rice that steamed for 5 minutes was heavy and wet. The batch that steamed for 15 minutes was the lightest and least watery. I also decided to try placing a clean dish towel between the pan and the lid right after I took the rice off the stove. What I found was that this produced the best results of all, while

reducing the steaming time to only 10 minutes. The towel prevents condensation and absorbs the excess water in the pan during steaming, producing drier, fluffier rice.

FAT AND FLAVORINGS

In culinary school, we were taught to use just enough fat to cover the grains of rice with oil, about 1 tablespoon per cup of rice. I was therefore surprised to see that many Middle Eastern recipes called for as much as ¼ cup of butter per cup of rice. I decided to do a test of my own to determine the optimal amount of fat. Using butter (since I like the extra flavor and richness that it lends to the rice), I tried from 1 to 4 tablespoons per 1½ cups of rice. Three tablespoons was best: The rice was buttery and rich without being overwhelmingly so, and each grain was more distinct than when cooked with less fat.

I also wondered if sautéing the rice for different amounts of time would make a difference, so I sautéed the rice over medium heat for 1 minute, 3 minutes, and 5 minutes. The pan of rice that was sautéed for 5 minutes was much less tender than the other two. It also had picked up a strong nutty flavor. When sautéed for 1 minute, the rice simply tasted steamed. The batch sautéed for 3 minutes was the best, with a light nutty flavor and tender texture.

At the end comes the fun part—adding the flavorings, seasonings, and other ingredients that give the pilaf its distinctive character. You need to pay attention when you add these ingredients, though, since different types work best when added at different stages. Dried spices, minced ginger, and garlic, for example, are best sautéed briefly in the fat before the raw rice is added to the pan, while fresh herbs and toasted nuts should be added to the pilaf just before serving to maximize freshness, texture (in the case of nuts), and flavor. Dried fruits such as currants can be added just before steaming the rice, which gives them enough time to heat and become plump.

Simple Pilaf-Style Rice

SERVES 4

You will need a saucepan with a tight-fitting lid for this recipe. Olive oil can be substituted for the butter. If using a nonstick pan, feel free to use less butter—a tablespoon or two will be plenty. If you prefer, the onion can be omitted. Or use a minced shallot or two instead.

1½ cups basmati or other long-grain white rice
1½ teaspoons salt
Pinch pepper
3 tablespoons unsalted butter
1 small onion, chopped fine

1. Place rice in bowl and cover with water by 2 inches; using your hands, gently swish grains to release excess starch. Carefully pour off water, leaving rice in bowl. Repeat 4 to 5 times, until water runs almost clear. Drain rice in fine-mesh strainer.
2. Bring 2¼ cups water to boil, covered, in small saucepan over medium-high heat. Add salt and pepper and cover to keep hot. Meanwhile, melt butter in large saucepan over medium heat. Add onion and cook until softened but not browned, about 4 minutes. Add rice and stir to coat grains with butter; cook until edges of grains begin to turn translucent, about 3 minutes. Stir hot seasoned water into rice. Return to boil, then reduce heat to low, cover, and cook until all liquid is absorbed, 16 to 18 minutes. Off heat, remove lid, fold dish towel in half, and place over saucepan; replace lid. Let stand for 10 minutes. Fluff rice with fork and serve.

variations

Rice Pilaf with Currants and Pine Nuts

Add 2 minced garlic cloves, ½ teaspoon ground turmeric, and ¼ teaspoon ground cinnamon to softened onion and cook until fragrant, about 30 seconds. When rice is off heat, before covering saucepan with towel, sprinkle ¼ cup currants over top of rice (do not mix in). When fluffing rice with fork, toss in ¼ cup toasted pine nuts.

Indian-Spiced Rice Pilaf with Dates and Parsley

Add 2 minced garlic cloves, 1 tablespoon grated fresh ginger, ¼ teaspoon ground cinnamon, and ¼ teaspoon ground cardamom to softened onion and cook until fragrant, about 30 seconds. When fluffing rice with fork, toss in ½ cup chopped dates and 3 tablespoons minced fresh parsley.

Saffron Rice Pilaf with Apricots and Almonds

Add ½ teaspoon saffron with onion in step 2. When rice is off heat, before covering saucepan with towel, sprinkle ½ cup finely chopped dried apricots over top of rice (do not mix in). When fluffing rice with fork, toss in ½ cup toasted slivered almonds.

DOUBLING RICE PILAF? DON'T DOUBLE THE WATER

If you try to simply double the recipe for our Simple Pilaf-Style Rice, you will end up with a layer of mushy rice on the bottom of the pot. The reason: Rice-to-water ratios can't be scaled up proportionally. Rice absorbs water in a 1:1 ratio, no matter the volume. So in the master recipe, which calls for 1½ cups of rice and 2¼ cups of water, the rice absorbs 1½ cups of water. The remaining ¾ cup of water evaporates. But here's the catch: The amount of water that evaporates doesn't double when the amount of rice is doubled. When you cook a double batch of rice using the same conditions—the same large pot and lid and on the same stove burner over low heat—as you'd use for a single batch, the same quantity of water will evaporate: ¾ cup. So simply doubling the recipe leads to mushy rice because there is an excess of water in the pot. The bottom line: To double our rice pilaf recipe, use 3 cups of rice and only 3¾ cups of water.

PERFECTING RICE AND PASTA PILAF

ANDREW JANJIGIAN, *May/June 2014*

For some, rice and pasta pilaf conjures up images of streetcars ascending steep hills to the tune of that familiar TV jingle. But for me, it's not the "San Francisco Treat" that comes to mind but Sunday dinners at my Armenian grandmother's. As it turns out, the two memories are not so disparate: Rice-A-Roni owes its existence to a fateful meeting in 1940s San Francisco. Lois DeDomenico, daughter of Italian immigrants, learned to make rice and pasta pilaf from her Armenian landlady, Pailadzo Captanian. The dish became a staple of the DeDomenico household and would eventually inspire Lois's husband, Tom, whose family owned a pasta factory, to develop a commercial version. They named the product after its two main ingredients—rice and macaroni (pasta)—and the rest is history.

The original dish is a simple affair: A fistful of pasta (usually vermicelli) is broken into short pieces and toasted in butter. Finely chopped onion and/or minced garlic is added next, followed by basmati rice. Once the grains are coated in fat, chicken broth is poured in. After simmering, the pilaf is often allowed to sit covered with a dish towel under the lid to absorb steam—a trick that yields superfluffy results. In a well-executed version, the rice and pasta are tender and separate, boasting rich depth from the butter and nuttiness from the toasted noodles.

Soaking the rice ensures that the grains finish cooking at the same time as the pasta.

Sadly, I never learned my grandmother's recipe, and the cookbook versions I tried fell short, with either mushy, overcooked vermicelli or sticky, overly firm rice. Using both garlic and onion (shredded on a box grater so that it would add flavor but not a distracting texture), I patched together a recipe and mostly resolved the under- or overcooked rice problem simply by nailing the appropriate amount of liquid: 2½ cups to 1½ cups rice and ½ cup pasta.

But even with this ratio, my pilaf was plagued by a thin layer of somewhat raw, crunchy rice just beneath the pasta, which always floated to the top of the pot during simmering. What's more, the pasta was too soft and mushy. The quicker-cooking vermicelli seemed to absorb broth more rapidly than the rice, thereby denying the rice that surrounded it sufficient liquid to cook through. My theory was confirmed when I reduced the water by ¼ cup and deliberately left the pasta out of a batch: The rice cooked up tender as could be.

Adding more broth would make the dish soggy. Stirring during cooking helped, but plenty of grains still emerged underdone.

I needed every last grain of rice to absorb the broth at the same rate as the pasta did. I considered removing the toasted vermicelli from the pot, starting the rice, and then adding back the pasta when the rice was nearly tender, but that seemed unwieldy. Then I came up with a more viable solution: soaking. Starches absorb water at relatively low temperatures, so I guessed that I could hydrate, or sort of parcook, the rice in hot tap water ahead of time. Sure enough, when I saturated the grains in hot water for 15 minutes before continuing with the recipe, the finished rice and pasta both had an ideal tender texture.

With my foolproof approach at hand, I developed a few flavorful variations. This side dish brought me right back to my grandmother's kitchen.

Rice and Pasta Pilaf

SERVES 4 TO 6

Use long, straight vermicelli or vermicelli nests. Grate the onion on the large holes of a box grater.

1½ cups basmati or other long-grain white rice
3 tablespoons unsalted butter
2 ounces vermicelli, broken into 1-inch pieces
1 onion, grated
1 garlic clove, minced
2½ cups chicken broth
1¼ teaspoons salt
3 tablespoons minced fresh parsley

1. Place rice in medium bowl and cover with hot tap water by 2 inches; let stand for 15 minutes.
2. Using your hands, gently swish grains to release excess starch. Carefully pour off water, leaving rice in bowl. Add cold tap water to rice and pour off water. Repeat adding and pouring off cold water 4 to 5 times, until water runs almost clear. Drain rice in fine-mesh strainer.
3. Melt butter in saucepan over medium heat. Add pasta and cook, stirring occasionally, until browned, about 3 minutes. Add onion and garlic and cook, stirring occasionally, until onion is softened but not browned, about 4 minutes. Add rice and cook, stirring occasionally, until edges of rice begin to turn translucent, about 3 minutes. Add broth and salt and bring to boil. Reduce heat to low, cover, and cook until all liquid is absorbed, about 10 minutes. Off heat, remove lid, fold dish towel in half, and place over saucepan; replace lid. Let stand for 10 minutes. Fluff rice with fork, stir in parsley, and serve.

variations

Herbed Rice and Pasta Pilaf

Stir ¼ cup plain whole-milk yogurt, ¼ cup minced fresh dill, and ¼ cup minced fresh chives into pilaf with parsley.

Rice and Pasta Pilaf with Crispy Shallots and Pistachios

Omit garlic and onion. Place 3 thinly sliced shallots and ½ cup olive oil in large saucepan. Cook over medium heat, stirring constantly, until shallots are golden and crispy, 6 to 10 minutes. Using slotted spoon, transfer shallots to paper towel–lined plate. Leave oil in pan; omit butter and toast pasta in shallot oil. Add 2 teaspoons ground coriander and half of shallots to pan with broth. Omit parsley and stir ½ cup chopped fresh mint; ½ cup shelled pistachios, toasted and chopped coarse; and 1 tablespoon lemon juice into fluffed rice. Sprinkle remaining shallots over rice before serving.

Rice and Pasta Pilaf with Golden Raisins and Almonds

Place ½ cup golden raisins in bowl and cover with boiling water by 1 inch. Let stand until plump, about 5 minutes. Drain and set aside. Add 2 bay leaves and 1 teaspoon ground cardamom to pot with chicken broth. Discard bay leaves and stir in raisins and ½ cup slivered almonds, toasted and chopped coarse, with parsley.

Rice and Pasta Pilaf with Pomegranate and Walnuts

Omit onion and garlic. Add 2 tablespoons grated fresh ginger to pan with rice. Add ½ teaspoon ground cumin with chicken broth. Omit parsley and stir ½ cup walnuts, toasted and chopped coarse; ½ cup pomegranate seeds; ½ cup chopped fresh cilantro; and 1 tablespoon lemon juice into fluffed rice.

NEATLY BREAKING LONG STRANDS OF PASTA

Our Rice and Pasta Pilaf calls for vermicelli that has been broken into 1-inch pieces. Here's a way to break the strand pasta without causing short pieces to fly every which way in the kitchen.

1. Place pasta in dish towel and fold sides of towel over pasta with 3- to 4-inch overlap at both ends.

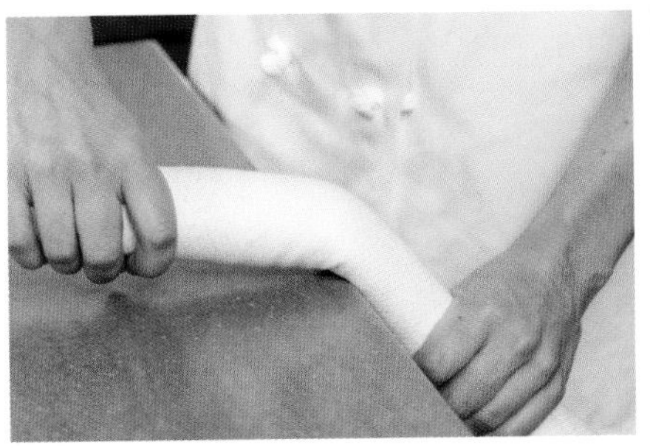

2. Holding ends of towel firmly, center rolled bundle on edge of counter and push down to break pasta. Repeat until pasta is broken into 1-inch pieces.

SEEKING OUT AUTHENTIC BASMATI

Basmati rice is the traditional choice for rice and pasta pilaf, but supermarket shelves teem with a multitude of boxes, bags, and burlap sacks labeled "basmati." True basmati can only come from India or Pakistan, and must meet standards for grain dimension, amylose content, and grain elongation during cooking, as well as for aroma. Unlike American basmati, authentic basmati is aged for a minimum of a year (and often much longer) before packaging. Aging dehydrates the rice, so the cooked grains expand greatly in length—more so than any other long-grain rice.

MAKING RICE AND PASTA PILAF

To make sure that both the rice and the pasta in our pilaf are done at the same time, we first soak the rice briefly in hot water and then rinse it of excess starch. To cook the pilaf, we start by toasting the pasta and rice, then add liquid. Covering with a dish towel at the end absorbs moisture.

1. Toast pasta in melted butter until browned, then add onion and garlic. Add rice and cook, stirring occasionally, until edges of rice begin to turn translucent.

2. Add broth, bring to boil, then reduce heat to low, cover, and cook until liquid is absorbed, about 10 minutes.

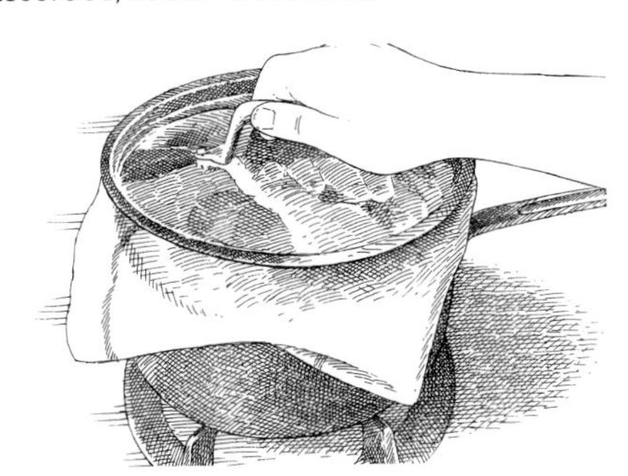

3. Off heat, place folded dish towel under lid and let stand for 10 minutes. Fluff with fork and stir in parsley.

FOOLPROOF BROWN RICE

REBECCA HAYS, *May/June 2004*

Most cooks I know shun brown rice, classifying it as wholesome yet unappealing sustenance for penniless vegetarians, practitioners of macrobiotics, and the like. But I'm not sure why. I find it ultimately satisfying, with a nutty, gutsy flavor and more textural personality—slightly sticky and just a bit chewy—than white rice. An ideal version should be easy to come by: Just throw rice and water in a pot and set the timer, right? Yet cooks who have attempted to prepare brown rice know it isn't so simple. My habit, born of impatience, is to crank up the flame in an effort to hurry along the slow-cooking grains (brown rice takes roughly twice as long to cook as white), which inevitably leads to a burnt pot and crunchy rice. Adding plenty of water isn't the remedy; excess liquid swells the rice into a gelatinous mass.

I pulled out an expensive, heavy-bottomed pot with a tight-fitting lid (many recipes caution against using inadequate cookware), fiddled with the traditional absorption method (cooking the rice with just enough water), and eventually landed on a workable recipe. Yet when I tested the recipe with less than ideal equipment—namely, a flimsy pan with an ill-fitting lid—I was back to burnt, undercooked rice. With the very best pot and a top-notch stove, it is possible to cook brown rice properly, but I wanted a surefire method that would work no matter the cook, no matter the equipment.

The even, encircling heat of the oven guarantees perfectly cooked brown rice every time.

I wondered if the microwave might work well in this instance, given that it cooks food indirectly, without a burner. Sadly, it delivered inconsistent results, with one batch turning brittle and another, prepared in a different microwave, too sticky. A rice cooker yielded faultless brown rice on the first try, but many Americans don't own one.

I set out to construct a homemade cooker that would approximate the controlled, indirect heat of a rice cooker—and so began to consider the merits of cooking the rice in the oven. I'd have more precise temperature control, and I hoped that the oven's encircling heat would eliminate the risk of scorching. My first try yielded extremely promising results: With the pan tightly covered with aluminum foil, the rice steamed to near perfection. Fine-tuning the amount of water, I settled on a ratio similar to that used for our white rice recipe: 2⅓ cups of water to 1½ cups of rice, falling well short of the 2:1 water-to-rice ratio advised by most rice producers and nearly every recipe I consulted. Perhaps that is why so much brown rice turns out sodden and overcooked.

My next task was to spruce up the recipe by bringing out the nutty flavor of the otherwise plain grains. Toasting the rice dry in the oven imparted a slight off-flavor. When I sautéed the rice in fat before baking, the grains frayed slightly; tasters preferred rice made by adding fat to the cooking water. A small amount (2 teaspoons) of either butter or oil adds mild flavor while keeping the rice fluffy.

To reduce what was a long baking time of 90 minutes at 350 degrees, I tried starting with boiling water instead of cold tap water and raising the oven to 375 degrees. These steps reduced the baking time to a reasonable 1 hour. (A hotter oven caused some of the fragile grains to explode.)

No more scorched or mushy brown rice for me, and no more worrying about finding just the right pan or adjusting the stovetop to produce just the right level of heat. Now I can serve good brown rice anytime, even to a meat lover.

Foolproof Oven-Baked Brown Rice

SERVES 4 TO 6

For an accurate measurement of boiling water, bring a full kettle of water to a boil and then measure out the desired amount. Medium or short-grain brown rice can be substituted for the long-grain rice.

2⅓ cups boiling water
1½ cups long-grain brown rice, rinsed
2 teaspoons unsalted butter or vegetable oil
Salt and pepper

1. Adjust oven rack to middle position and heat oven to 375 degrees. Combine boiling water, rice, butter, and ½ teaspoon salt in 8-inch square baking dish. Cover dish tightly with double layer of aluminum foil. Bake until liquid is absorbed and rice is tender, about 1 hour.
2. Remove dish from oven, uncover, and fluff rice with fork, scraping up any rice that has stuck to bottom. Cover dish with clean dish towel and let rice sit for 5 minutes. Season with salt and pepper to taste, and serve.

variation

Brown Rice with Parmesan, Lemon, and Herbs

Increase butter to 2 tablespoons and melt in 10-inch nonstick skillet over medium heat. Add 1 finely chopped small onion and cook until translucent, about 3 minutes; set aside. Substitute chicken broth for water and reduce salt to ⅛ teaspoon. Stir onion mixture into rice after adding broth. Cover and bake rice as directed. Remove foil; stir in ½ cup grated Parmesan cheese, ¼ cup minced fresh parsley, ¼ cup chopped fresh basil, 1 teaspoon grated lemon zest, ½ teaspoon lemon juice, and ⅛ teaspoon pepper before covering with dish towel.

ALMOST HANDS-FREE RISOTTO

ANDREA GEARY, *May/June 2010*

Cooking a pot of long-grain rice is simple: Bring your ingredients to a simmer, cover the pot, and wait. Risotto is the exact opposite. Accepted wisdom dictates near-constant stirring to achieve the perfect texture: tender grains with a slight bite in the center, bound together in a light, creamy sauce. Here's why stirring is critical: As the rice cooks, it releases starch granules, which absorb liquid and expand, thickening the broth to a rich consistency. Constantly stirring the pot jostles the rice grains against one another, agitating them and promoting the release of more starch granules from their exterior.

But frankly, most of us have neither the time nor the patience for all that stirring. That's why, several years ago, we came up with an easier method. It starts out just like a traditional risotto recipe: Sweat the aromatics in a saucepan until softened, add 2 cups of Arborio rice, toast the grains in the hot fat for a few minutes, and pour in dry white wine, stirring until the liquid is just absorbed. Then, rather than adding the broth in traditional half-cup intervals, we add roughly half the liquid—3 cups of broth and water—all at once and simmer for a full 12 minutes, with only a few stirs during the process. Finally, for the last 9 minutes, we resume the traditional method, slowly adding the remaining broth while stirring constantly. The resulting risotto turns out every bit as creamy and al dente as those stirred nonstop for 30 minutes.

How does it work? Once it starts bubbling, all that liquid added at the beginning jostles the rice grains in much the same way as constant stirring, accelerating the release of starch. But now, I wanted to see if I could eliminate the final 9-minute stir and still deliver a perfect pot of risotto.

THE RIGHT RICE

A short-grained rice like Arborio is ideal for risotto because of its high starch content; other varieties simply aren't starchy enough to properly thicken the sauce. What's more, the starches at the very center don't break down as readily as in other varieties, allowing the rice to maintain a firm, al dente center, even as the exterior becomes tender.

With all that going for it, the right rice paired with the right ratio of liquid should all but cook itself into a velvety dish without the aid of stirring. But one batch prepared according to our existing method, minus the final stirring step, left me with a pot of rice that was overcooked and mushy on the bottom, chalky and wet on top.

I had only so many variables to consider here, so I started with the liquid. What if I added 5 cups from the start? That way, I reasoned, the contents of the pot would be very fluid for the first 15 to 20 minutes of cooking, allowing the rice to bob around and cook more evenly with minimal stirring on my part. Only when the rice released enough starch and the sauce started to thicken up, impeding fluidity, would I need to resume stirring to ensure even cooking. I was pleasantly surprised by the outcome, though quite a few crunchy bits of uncooked rice from the cooler top of the pan had lingered. But I was getting somewhere.

DUTCH AND COVER

As I thought more about it, I realized that simply adding more liquid at the start wasn't enough; I needed to keep that moist heat evenly distributed from top to bottom through the duration of cooking. I needed my cooking vessel to do more of the legwork—and my saucepan wasn't cutting it.

A Dutch oven, on the other hand, has a thick, heavy bottom, deep sides, and a tight-fitting lid—all of which are meant to trap and distribute heat as evenly as possible, which seemed ideal. I cooked up a new batch, covering it as soon as I added my liquid. Traditionally, the lid is left off because risotto requires constant stirring, but here, I was free to use the lid to my advantage, ensuring, I hoped, that the top of the rice would stay as hot as the bottom. The first 19 minutes of cooking were easy—I had to lift the lid only twice for a quick stir—but after that, the liquid once again turned too viscous for the rice (still undercooked at this stage) to move around the pot without some manual assistance. Even over low heat, the rice still needed at least 5 minutes of constant stirring to turn uniformly al dente.

Adding most of the liquid at the beginning of cooking agitates the rice and decreases the need to stir.

Conceptually, this uneven heat problem was not unlike a challenge we faced when developing our recipe for Slow-Roasted Beef (page 106). Aiming to cook the roast as gently and evenly as possible, we turn the heat way down—and then shut the oven off completely, leaving the beef to rest in the still-warm environment until it crawls up to temperature. Here, the pot functions in much the same way, retaining heat long after it comes off the burner. If the risotto required its final stirring because the bottom was still cooking faster than the top, what if I removed the Dutch oven from the burner during the final few minutes? Without sitting over a direct flame, the rice should turn perfectly al dente just from the retained heat.

I made one last batch. This time, after the initial 19-minute covered cooking period, I gave the risotto a quick 3-minute stir to get the sauce to the right consistency, followed by a 5-minute, covered, off-heat rest. When I removed the lid, a big plume of steam escaped, indicating that my rice was indeed still hot throughout. I stirred in extra butter, a few herbs, and a squeeze of lemon juice, and had a perfectly creamy, velvety, and just barely chewy risotto—without going stir-crazy.

Almost Hands-Free Risotto with Parmesan and Herbs

SERVES 6

This recipe is more hands-off than traditional risotto recipes, but it does require precise timing. For that reason, we strongly recommend using a timer. The consistency of risotto is largely a matter of personal taste; if you prefer a looser texture, add more of the hot broth mixture in step 4.

5 cups chicken broth
1½ cups water
4 tablespoons unsalted butter
1 large onion, chopped fine
Salt and pepper
1 garlic clove, minced
2 cups Arborio rice
1 cup dry white wine
2 ounces Parmesan cheese, grated (1 cup)
2 tablespoons chopped fresh parsley
2 tablespoons chopped fresh chives
1 teaspoon lemon juice

1. Bring broth and water to boil in large saucepan over high heat. Reduce heat to medium-low to maintain gentle simmer.
2. Melt 2 tablespoons butter in Dutch oven over medium heat. Add onion and ¾ teaspoon salt and cook, stirring frequently, until onion is softened, 5 to 7 minutes. Add garlic and stir until fragrant, about 30 seconds. Add rice and cook, stirring frequently, until grains are translucent around edges, about 3 minutes.
3. Add wine and cook, stirring constantly, until fully absorbed, 2 to 3 minutes. Stir 5 cups hot broth mixture into rice; reduce heat to medium-low, cover, and simmer until almost all liquid has been absorbed and rice is just al dente, 16 to 19 minutes, stirring twice during cooking.
4. Add ¾ cup hot broth mixture and stir gently and constantly until risotto becomes creamy, about 3 minutes. Stir in Parmesan. Off heat, cover and let stand for 5 minutes. Stir in parsley, chives, lemon juice, and remaining 2 tablespoons butter. Adjust consistency with remaining hot broth mixture as needed. Season with salt and pepper to taste, and serve immediately.

variation

Almost Hands-Free Risotto with Chicken and Herbs

SERVES 6

Adding chicken breasts to the risotto turns a side dish into a main course. The thinner ends of the chicken breasts may be fully cooked by the time the broth mixture is added, with the thicker ends finishing about 5 minutes later.

5 cups chicken broth
2 cups water
1 tablespoon olive oil
2 (12-ounce) bone-in split chicken breasts, trimmed and halved crosswise
4 tablespoons unsalted butter
1 large onion, chopped fine
Salt and pepper
1 garlic clove, minced
2 cups Arborio rice
1 cup dry white wine
2 ounces Parmesan cheese, grated (1 cup)
2 tablespoons chopped fresh parsley
2 tablespoons chopped fresh chives
1 teaspoon lemon juice

1. Bring broth and water to boil in large saucepan over high heat. Reduce heat to medium-low to maintain gentle simmer.
2. Heat oil in Dutch oven over medium heat until just smoking. Add chicken, skin side down, and cook, without moving chicken, until golden brown, 4 to 6 minutes. Flip chicken and cook until second side is lightly browned, about 2 minutes. Transfer chicken to saucepan of simmering broth mixture and cook until chicken registers 160 degrees, 10 to 15 minutes. Transfer chicken to large plate.
3. Melt 2 tablespoons butter in now-empty Dutch oven over medium heat. Add onion and ¾ teaspoon salt and cook, stirring frequently, until onion is softened, 5 to 7 minutes. Add garlic and stir until fragrant, about 30 seconds. Add rice and cook, stirring frequently, until grains are translucent around edges, about 3 minutes.
4. Add wine and cook, stirring constantly, until fully absorbed, 2 to 3 minutes. Stir 5 cups hot broth mixture into rice; reduce heat to medium-low, cover, and simmer until almost all liquid has been absorbed and rice is just al dente, 16 to 19 minutes, stirring twice during cooking.
5. Add ¾ cup hot broth mixture and stir gently and constantly until risotto becomes creamy, about 3 minutes. Stir in Parmesan. Off heat, cover and let stand for 5 minutes.
6. Meanwhile, discard skin and bones from chicken and shred chicken into bite-size pieces. Gently stir parsley, chives, lemon juice, chicken, and remaining 2 tablespoons butter into risotto. Adjust consistency with remaining hot broth mixture as needed. Season with salt and pepper to taste, and serve immediately.

SECRETS TO ALMOST HANDS-FREE RISOTTO

1. **ADD LOTS OF LIQUID AND PUT A LID ON IT** A full 5 cups of liquid added at the start of cooking agitates the rice grains much like stirring, accelerating the release of creamy starch. Covering the pot helps distribute the heat evenly.

2. **STIR, THEN REST** A brief stir followed by a 5-minute rest provides additional insurance that the rice will be perfectly al dente, from the top of the pot to the bottom.

NO-FUSS CREAMY POLENTA

YVONNE RUPERTI, *March/April 2010*

When it comes to peasant roots, it doesn't get much humbler than polenta. This simple, hearty dish of long-cooked cornmeal dates back to 16th-century Rome, where *polenta sulla tavola* was poured directly onto the table to soak up flavors from previous meals. These days, polenta passes for haute restaurant cuisine. Its nutty corn flavor is equally satisfying, whether embellished with simple butter and cheese or served as a base for everything from braised veal shanks to an exotic mushroom ragout. Most modern-day preparations take one of two forms: warm, porridge-like spoon food or cooked grains that are cooled until firm, then cut into squares to grill or fry. Both have their merits, but when the cold weather sets in, a bowl of the soothing, silky-textured stuff can't be beat.

The recipe sounds easy enough: Boil water, whisk in cornmeal, and stir until the gruel-like concoction has softened. But the devil is in the details: Depending on the grind, polenta can take up to an hour to cook, and if you don't stir it almost constantly during this time, it forms intractable clumps. Surely, after five centuries, it was time to find a better way.

CORNMEAL 101

Here's what's going on in a pot of polenta: When the starchy part of the corn kernels (the endosperm) comes in contact with hot water, it eventually absorbs liquid, swells, and bursts, releasing starch in a process known as gelatinization. At the same time, the grains soften, losing their gritty texture. But the tough pieces of endosperm require plenty of time and heat for the water to break through. And the pot must be stirred constantly; if polenta heats unevenly (such as in the hotter spots at the bottom of the pan), some of its starch gelatinizes much faster than the rest, forming little pockets of fully cooked polenta. This starch is so sticky that once these pockets form, it's nearly impossible to fully break them up again. Stirring ensures that the entire pot cooks evenly, preventing lumps from forming in the first place.

You can shortcut the cooking and stirring with parboiled "instant" brands that are ready in just a few minutes, but tasters bemoaned these samples, complaining that they cooked up gluey, with lackluster flavor. It was time for a tour of cornmeal options. The typical supermarket offers a bewildering assortment of products, and their labels only confuse matters further. First, the same exact dried ground corn can be called anything from yellow grits to polenta to corn semolina. Labels also advertise "fine," "medium," and "coarse" grinds, but I quickly discovered that no standards for these definitions exist, and one manufacturer's medium grind might be another's heartiest coarse option. Then there's the choice between whole-grain and degerminated corn (which is treated before grinding to remove both the hull and the germ but leaves the endosperm intact). With all this confusing nomenclature, I decided my best bet was to try everything and come up with my own system for identifying what worked best.

After testing a half-dozen styles, I eventually settled on the couscous-size grains of coarse-ground degerminated cornmeal (often labeled "yellow grits"); they delivered the hearty yet soft texture I was looking for, plus plenty of nutty corn flavor.

THINKING INSIDE THE GRAIN

The only downside: The large, coarse grains took a full hour to cook through, during which time the mixture grew overly thick and my arm started to ache from stirring. I had been sticking to the typical 4:1 ratio of water to cornmeal. After experimenting, I found a 5:1 ratio (or a full 7½ cups of water for 1½ cups of cornmeal) worked far better, producing just the right loose consistency.

Now for the hard part: whittling down the 1-hour cooking time and decreasing the stirring. The rate at which water penetrates the corn is proportional to temperature, but raising the heat, even in a heavy-bottomed pot, burned the polenta.

Maybe the key wasn't in the cooking method, but in the cornmeal itself. There had to be a way to give that water a head start on penetrating the grains. Would soaking the cornmeal overnight help, the way it does with dried beans? I combined the cornmeal and water the night before, then cooked them together the next day. The results were uninspiring. While the grains did seem to absorb some of the liquid, this small improvement didn't alter the cooking time enough to make this extra step worth it.

A pinch of baking soda makes for beautifully creamy polenta without the need for constant stirring.

Casting about for ideas, I came back to beans. The goal in cooking dried beans and dried corn is essentially identical. In a bean, water has to penetrate the hard outer skin to gelatinize the starch within. In a corn kernel, the water has to penetrate the endosperm. To soften bean skins and speed up cooking, some cooks advocate adding baking soda to the cooking liquid. Would this same ingredient work for cornmeal?

In my next batch of polenta, I added ¼ teaspoon baking soda to the water as soon as it came to a boil. To my delight, the polenta cooked up in 20 minutes flat. But the baking soda acted so effectively that the cooked porridge turned gluey, and had a strange, toasted, chemical flavor. Obviously, ¼ teaspoon of soda was too much; even half that was excessive. Just a pinch turned out to be plenty—it produced polenta that still cooked in 30 minutes without any gluey texture or objectionable flavors.

The solution for cutting back on the stirring time came to me by accident. I'd just whisked the cornmeal into the boiling water when I got called away from the kitchen. Without thinking, I threw a lid on the pot (the traditional method is to leave the polenta uncovered), turned the heat down to its lowest level, and left the polenta to sputter untouched for nearly the entire 30 minutes. Rushing back to the stove, I expected to find a clumpy, burnt-on-the-bottom mess. To my surprise, I found perfectly creamy polenta when I lifted the lid. The baking soda must have helped the granules break down and release their starch in a uniform way so that the bottom layer didn't cook any faster than the top. And the combination of covering the pot and adjusting the heat to low, wispy flames cooked the polenta so gently and evenly that the result was lump-free, even without vigorous stirring.

I repeated this new approach, finding that after one relatively brief whisk as soon as the ingredients went in and another, shorter one 5 minutes later, I didn't even have to lift the lid until it was time to add the cheese. A full 2 cups of grated Parmesan plus a pair of butter pats stirred in at the last minute gave this humble mush enough nutty tang and richness to make it a satisfying dish, with or without a topping—and with the barest amount of effort.

HOMEMADE FLAME TAMER

Our recipe for Creamy Parmesan Polenta relies on heat so low it barely disturbs the pot's contents. A flame tamer can help to ensure that the heat is as gentle as possible.

Squeeze a 3-foot length of aluminum foil into a ½-inch rope. Twist the rope into a ring the size of the burner.

Creamy Parmesan Polenta

SERVES 4 TO 6

Coarse-ground degerminated cornmeal, such as yellow grits, works best in this recipe. Avoid instant and quick-cooking products as well as whole-grain, stone-ground, and regular cornmeal. Do not omit the baking soda—it reduces the cooking time and makes for a creamier polenta. The polenta should do little more than emit wisps of steam. If it bubbles or sputters even slightly after the first 10 minutes, the heat is too high and you may need a flame tamer. A flame tamer can be found at most kitchen supply stores; alternatively, you can fashion your own from a ring of foil. For a main course, serve the polenta with a topping (recipes follow) or with a wedge of rich cheese or a meat sauce. Served plain, the polenta makes a great accompaniment to stews and braises.

7½ cups water
Salt and pepper
Pinch baking soda
1½ cups coarse-ground cornmeal
4 ounces Parmesan cheese, grated (2 cups), plus extra for serving
2 tablespoons unsalted butter

1. Bring water to boil in heavy-bottomed large saucepan over medium-high heat. Stir in 1½ teaspoons salt and baking soda. Slowly pour cornmeal into water in steady stream while stirring back and forth with wooden spoon or rubber spatula. Bring mixture to boil, stirring constantly, about 1 minute. Reduce heat to lowest possible setting and cover saucepan.
2. After 5 minutes, whisk polenta to smooth out any lumps that may have formed, about 15 seconds. (Make sure to scrape down sides and bottom of saucepan.) Cover and continue to cook, without stirring, until grains of polenta are tender but slightly al dente, about 25 minutes longer. (Polenta should be loose and barely hold its shape but will continue to thicken as it cools.)
3. Off heat, stir in Parmesan and butter and season with pepper to taste. Let polenta stand, covered, for 5 minutes. Serve, passing extra Parmesan separately.

accompaniments

Broccoli Rabe, Sun-Dried Tomato, and Pine Nut Topping

SERVES 4 TO 6

1½ cup oil-packed sun-dried tomatoes, chopped coarse
3 tablespoons extra-virgin olive oil
6 garlic cloves, minced
½ teaspoon red pepper flakes
Salt and pepper
1 pound broccoli rabe, trimmed and cut into 1½-inch pieces
¼ cup chicken or vegetable broth
2 tablespoons pine nuts, toasted
¼ cup grated Parmesan cheese

Cook sun-dried tomatoes, oil, garlic, pepper flakes, and ½ teaspoon salt in 12-inch nonstick skillet over medium-high heat, stirring frequently, until garlic is slightly toasted, about 2 minutes. Add broccoli rabe and broth, cover, and cook until broccoli rabe turns bright green, about 2 minutes. Uncover and cook, stirring frequently, until most of broth has evaporated, about 3 minutes. Season with salt and pepper to taste. Spoon mixture over individual portions of polenta and top with pine nuts and Parmesan. Serve.

Sautéed Cherry Tomato and Fresh Mozzarella Topping

SERVES 4 TO 6

3 tablespoons extra-virgin olive oil
2 garlic cloves, sliced thin
Pinch red pepper flakes
Pinch sugar
1½ pounds cherry tomatoes, halved
Salt and pepper
3 ounces fresh mozzarella cheese, shredded (¾ cup)
2 tablespoons shredded fresh basil

Cook oil, garlic, pepper flakes, and sugar in 12-inch nonstick skillet over medium-high heat until fragrant and sizzling, about 1 minute. Stir in tomatoes and cook until just beginning to soften, about 1 minute. Season with salt and pepper to taste. Spoon mixture over individual portions of polenta and top with mozzarella and basil. Serve.

INTRODUCING FARRO RISOTTO

STEVE DUNN, *May/June 2016*

Risotto has been a staple in American restaurants and home kitchens for years, but farrotto has only recently gained a footing stateside. As the name suggests, it's a twist on the classic Italian rice-based dish, made with farro, an ancient form of wheat that's been grown in Italy for centuries and that boasts a nutty flavor and a tender chew. Using this whole grain instead of rice yields a more robust dish that still cooks relatively quickly and functions well as a blank slate for any type of flavor addition—from cheese and herbs to meats and vegetables. There's just one pitfall to farrotto: bran. Arborio or carnaroli rices have been stripped of their bran layer and thus readily give up their amylopectin, the starch molecule that makes risotto creamy. Farro retains most of its bran (how much depends on whether it's been "pearled," or had its bran at least partially rubbed away), which gives it bite and earthy flavor but also traps the starch inside the grain. Hence, most farrottos lack risotto's velvety body and cohesion. I wanted both: the distinct flavor and chew of farro with the creamy consistency of risotto.

My instinct was to first try pearled farro; since it has less bran, it might cook up creamier. I had a leg up on a basic cooking method, which I'd borrow from our Almost Hands-Free Risotto with Parmesan and Herbs (page 334). The trick in that recipe is to add most of the liquid up front, rather than in several stages, which helps the grains cook evenly so that you need to stir only a couple of times rather than constantly. We also use a lidded Dutch oven, which helps trap and distribute the heat evenly so every grain is tender.

Pulsing the farro in a blender before cooking allows it to release some of its trapped starch, producing a creamy-textured dish.

To start, I softened onion and garlic in butter, added the farro to toast in the fat, and finally added the liquid. But the pearled farro not only lacked the robust flavor of whole farro but also resulted in farrotto that was too thin. I would have to stick with whole farro.

My breakthrough came from an outlier farrotto recipe, which called for "cracking" the farro before cooking by soaking the grains overnight to soften them and then blitzing them in a food processor. This gave the starch an escape route and yielded a silkier dish. The only drawback was that lengthy soak.

I tried skipping the soak, and I also tried a hot soak to see if I could soften the grains quickly. In both cases the hard grains just danced around the processor bowl without breaking. Switching to a blender created a vortex that drew the unsoaked grains into the blade. Six pulses cracked about half of them so that there was plenty of starch but still enough chew.

Seasoned with Parmesan, herbs, and lemon juice, my farrotto was hearty and flavorful—and more satisfying than any risotto I've eaten.

Parmesan Farrotto

SERVES 6

We prefer the flavor and texture of whole farro. Do not use quick-cooking or pearled farro. The consistency of farrotto is a matter of personal taste; if you prefer a looser texture, add more of the hot broth mixture in step 6.

1½ cups whole farro
3 cups chicken broth
3 cups water
4 tablespoons unsalted butter
½ onion, chopped fine
1 garlic clove, minced
2 teaspoons minced fresh thyme
Salt and pepper
2 ounces Parmesan, grated (1 cup)
2 tablespoons minced fresh parsley
2 teaspoons lemon juice

1. Pulse farro in blender until about half of grains are broken into smaller pieces, about 6 pulses.
2. Bring broth and water to boil in medium saucepan over high heat. Reduce heat to medium-low to maintain gentle simmer.
3. Melt 2 tablespoons butter in large Dutch oven over medium-low heat. Add onion and cook, stirring frequently, until softened, 3 to 4 minutes. Add garlic and stir until fragrant, about 30 seconds. Add farro and cook, stirring frequently, until grains are lightly toasted, about 3 minutes.
4. Stir 5 cups hot broth mixture into farro mixture, reduce heat to low, cover, and cook until almost all liquid has been absorbed and farro is just al dente, about 25 minutes, stirring twice during cooking.
5. Add thyme, 1 teaspoon salt, and ¾ teaspoon pepper and continue to cook, stirring constantly, until farro becomes creamy, about 5 minutes.
6. Remove pot from heat. Stir in Parmesan, parsley, lemon juice, and remaining 2 tablespoons butter. Season with salt and pepper to taste. Adjust consistency with remaining hot broth mixture as needed. Serve immediately.

ORZO PILAF

MATTHEW CARD, *May/June 2003*

Pilaf made with orzo, the rice-shaped pasta, is culinary sleight of hand at its finest. What look to be giant grains of rice reveal their true nature after just one bite, presenting a firm-yet-tender texture that is far removed from rice's dull chew. Unfortunately, most of the versions I've tasted have been bland at best—little more than a generic starch used to bulk up a meal. I wanted to design a better pilaf, finessed in technique and strong in flavor; all in all, an orzo pilaf worth the effort.

A survey of orzo pilaf recipes yielded mixed results and little insight. Technique, for the most part, cleaved close to standard pilaf procedure: Sauté the orzo briefly with aromatics, then simmer in a covered pot until tender. Flavors ran the gamut from bland to overwrought. I quickly made a decision to focus on technique and keep the flavors of my pilaf simple. Returning to the "orzo as rice" conceit, I borrowed the clean, classic flavors of Parmesan risotto: butter, alliums, white wine, broth, and cheese.

Toasting the orzo before adding the cooking liquid ups the flavor in this simple yet elegant side dish.

I tested two preparation methods head to head: cooking the orzo as I would rice, covered over a low flame, and cooking as I would pasta, in an abundance of water at a raging boil. Cooked as rice, the orzo failed to fully hydrate and was chalky, though attractively creamy. Cooked as pasta, the orzo was al dente in a fraction of the time but it tasted bland. Because neither method seemed ideal, I turned to a hybrid cooking method.

Starting with an uncovered pan, I sautéed the orzo with butter and onions and then added the liquid. High heat yielded unevenly cooked orzo and a sticky mess on the pan bottom. Low heat produced creamy but too-soft orzo. Moderate heat yielded just what I wanted: firm, slick orzo lightly napped with a creamy coating.

While the texture was ideal, the flavor was still bland. As I was already sautéing the orzo, I wondered if I could simply extend the time it spent browning in the butter. The results were stunning. Toasted light brown, the pasta was now nutty, sweet, and notably "wheatier" in flavor. I toasted several batches of orzo to varying degrees of doneness—pale yellow to a deep mahogany—and realized that, as with caramel, the darker the color, the richer the flavor (shy of burning, of course). Tasters most enjoyed orzo taken to golden brown. Attentive stirring while toasting was crucial to prevent scorching.

With the technique down, it was quick work to finesse the risotto-inspired flavors I had chosen. Olive oil and vegetable oil couldn't touch butter's nutty, sweet charm. For alliums, I tried onion, shallot, and garlic, but none provided enough depth solo. Onion and shallot proved redundant, but onion and garlic gave the dish both low-end sweetness and full-range depth. Dry white wine is a classic flavor in risotto, but I tossed dry vermouth into the tasting as well. Tasters unanimously preferred the latter's fuller, herbaceous flavor. For cooking liquid, I limited the choices to canned broth. Beef tasted tinny; my tasters much preferred chicken broth.

Finely grated Parmesan melted quickly and made the pilaf creamier. A pinch of nutmeg—an Italian secret in cream sauces—pointed up the cheese's nuttiness. For a bit of green to perk things up, I tried a handful of different herbs. Each added a distinct note, but in the end I chose an easier route and simply tossed in frozen peas. The pilaf's ambient heat warmed them through and magnified the peas' glossy green hue.

Toasted Orzo with Peas and Parmesan

SERVES 6 TO 8

We prefer dry vermouth here, but you can substitute dry white wine, if desired.

2 tablespoons unsalted butter
1 onion, chopped fine
Salt and pepper
2 garlic cloves, minced
1 pound orzo
3½ cups chicken broth
¾ cup dry vermouth or dry white wine
1¾ cups frozen peas
2 ounces Parmesan cheese, grated (1 cup)
Pinch ground nutmeg

1. Melt butter in 12-inch nonstick skillet over medium-high heat. Add onion and ¾ teaspoon salt and cook, stirring frequently, until onion has softened and is beginning to brown, 5 to 7 minutes. Add garlic and cook until fragrant, about 30 seconds. Add orzo and cook, stirring frequently, until most of orzo is lightly browned and golden, 5 to 6 minutes. Off heat, add broth and vermouth. Bring to boil over medium-high heat; reduce heat to medium-low and simmer, stirring occasionally, until all liquid has been absorbed and orzo is tender, 10 to 15 minutes.
2. Stir in peas, Parmesan, and nutmeg. Off heat, let stand until peas are heated through, about 2 minutes. Season with salt and pepper to taste, and serve.

variation

Toasted Orzo with Fennel, Orange, and Olives

Add 1 small fennel bulb, stalks discarded, halved, cored, and cut into ¼-inch dice, ¾ teaspoon fennel seeds, and pinch red pepper flakes along with onion. Add 1 teaspoon grated orange zest along with garlic and substitute ½ cup coarsely chopped olives for peas.

A BETTER WAY TO COOK COUSCOUS

MARCUS WALSER, *January/February 2011*

Although couscous traditionally functions as a sauce absorber beneath North African stews and braises, it works equally well as a lighter, quicker alternative to everyday side dishes like rice pilaf and mashed potatoes. The tiny grains of pasta, made by rubbing together moistened semolina granules, readily adapt to any number of flavorful add-ins—from grassy fresh herbs like cilantro and parsley to heady spices like cumin and coriander and sweeter elements like raisins and dates. Best of all, the whole operation, from box to bowl, takes about 5 minutes.

At least that's what the back-of-the-box instructions say. I quickly realized that such convenience comes at a cost. No matter how precisely I followed the directions—measure and boil water, stir in couscous, cover and let stand off heat for 5 minutes, fluff with fork—the results were discouragingly similar to wet sand: bland, blown-out pebbles that stuck together in clumps. And it wasn't just one brand's poor instruction. Every box I bought spelled out the same steps.

We briefly sauté the couscous in butter to boost its flavor and ensure that the grains cook up fluffy.

I'm no expert on North African cuisine, but I'd read enough about couscous to know that it has far more potential than my efforts were suggesting. Then, as I was researching how the grains are made, I realized my problem: the box—both its contents and its cooking instructions. According to traditional couscous-making practices, the uncooked grains are steamed twice in a double boiler–shaped vessel called a *couscoussière*, from which the grains emerge fluffy and separate. The commercial staple we find on grocery store shelves, however, is far more processed: The grains are flash-steamed and dried before packaging. When exposed to the rigors of further cooking, this parcooked couscous—more or less a convenience product—turns to mush. That's why the box instructions are so simple: A quick reconstitution in boiling water is all the grains can stand.

To bring some much-needed flavor to the dish, I tried dry-toasting the grains in the pan and then stirring in boiling water—to no avail: The pasta grains burned before they had a chance to develop any real flavor. Then I recalled a popular trick used on another grain that, without some finesse, can also cook up woefully bland: rice. The "pilaf method" calls for briefly sautéing the grains in hot fat before liquid is introduced. So for my next batch of couscous, I melted a small amount of butter, which, as I'd hoped, coated the grains nicely, allowing them to brown gently and uniformly and helping them cook up fluffy and separate. To bump up the flavor even further, I replaced half of the water with chicken broth. Now I was getting somewhere: After absorbing the hot stock-based liquid, the couscous grains were flavorful enough to stand on the plate without a sauce.

I figured my work was just about done—until I spied the two dirty pans in the sink. Given that the dish took all of 5 minutes to cook, I was determined to do better when it came to cleanup. Then it dawned on me: Since my saucepan was already hot from toasting the grains, why not simply add room-temperature liquid to it instead of going to the trouble to heat the liquid in a separate pan? Sure enough, that did it. The residual heat from the pan boiled the liquid almost instantly—it was like deglazing a skillet after searing. On went the lid, and after a brief rest and a quick fluff with a fork, my couscous was perfect.

Basic Couscous

SERVES 4 TO 6

Do not substitute large-grain couscous (also known as Israeli couscous) in this recipe; it requires a much different cooking method. Use a large fork to fluff the couscous grains; a spoon or spatula can mash its light texture.

2 tablespoons unsalted butter
2 cups couscous
1 cup water
1 cup chicken broth
Salt and pepper

1. Melt butter in medium saucepan over medium-high heat. Add couscous and cook, stirring frequently, until grains are just beginning to brown, about 5 minutes.

2. Add water, broth, and 1 teaspoon salt; stir briefly to combine, cover, and remove saucepan from heat. Let stand until grains are tender, about 7 minutes. Uncover and fluff grains with fork. Season with pepper to taste, and serve.

variations

Couscous with Dates and Pistachios

Increase butter to 3 tablespoons and add ½ cup chopped dates, 1 tablespoon finely grated fresh ginger, and ½ teaspoon ground cardamom to saucepan with couscous in step 1. Increase water to 1¼ cups. Stir ¾ cup toasted chopped pistachios, 3 tablespoons minced fresh cilantro, and 2 teaspoons lemon juice into couscous before serving.

Couscous with Dried Cherries and Pecans

Increase butter to 3 tablespoons and add ½ cup chopped dried cherries, 2 minced garlic cloves, ¾ teaspoon garam masala, and ⅛ teaspoon cayenne pepper to saucepan with couscous in step 1. Increase water to 1¼ cups. Stir ¾ cup toasted chopped pecans, 2 thinly sliced scallions, and 2 teaspoons lemon juice into couscous before serving.

QUINOA PILAF FOR NONBELIEVERS

DAN SOUZA, *January/February 2014*

In the span of a decade, quinoa, a seed with humble South American roots, has gone from obscurity to mass consumption in America. I've always assumed its rapid ascent is mainly due to awareness of its health benefits (it's a nearly complete protein that's rich in fiber). While in theory the cooked grain (almost no one calls quinoa a seed) has an appealingly nutty flavor and crunchy texture, in practice it more often turns into a mushy mess with washed-out flavor and an underlying bitterness.

Pilaf recipes that call for cooking the grain with onion and other flavorings don't help matters. If it's blown out and mushy, quinoa pilaf is no better than the plain boiled grain on its own. I was determined to develop a foolproof approach to quinoa pilaf that I'd want to make not because it was healthy but because it tasted great.

My first clue as to what might go wrong with the usual quinoa pilaf surfaced as soon as I gathered up recipes to try. All called for softening onion in butter or oil, adding quinoa to the pan and toasting it in the same fat, then pouring in liquid, and simmering covered until the grains were cooked through and the liquid was absorbed. Almost without exception, these recipes used a 2:1 ratio of liquid to quinoa. Could that be the problem?

To find out, I put together a basic working recipe: Soften finely chopped onion in butter in a saucepan, stir in quinoa and water, cover, and cook until tender. I then tested a range of water-to-quinoa ratios and found that, while 2 to 1 might be the common rule, 1 to 1 was nearly perfect. To allow for evaporation, I tweaked this ratio just slightly, using a bit more water than quinoa (1¾ cups water to 1½ cups quinoa). After about 20 minutes of covered simmering, the quinoa was tender, with a satisfying bite.

Or at least most of it was. There was a ½-inch ring of overcooked seeds around the pot's circumference. The heat of the pot was cooking the outer grains faster than the interior ones. To even things out, my first thought was to stir the quinoa halfway through cooking, but I feared that I would turn my pilaf into a starchy mess, as so easily happens with rice. But I needn't have worried. A few gentle stirs at the midway point gave me perfectly cooked quinoa, with no ill effects. Why? While quinoa is quite starchy—more so than long-grain white rice—it also contains twice the protein of white rice. That protein is key, as it essentially traps the starch in place so you can stir it without creating a gummy mess.

Dry-toasting the quinoa and using a nearly 1:1 ratio of grains to water produces flavorful and tender quinoa pilaf.

The texture of the quinoa improved further when I let it rest, covered, for 10 minutes before fluffing. This allowed the grains to finish cooking gently and firm up, making them less prone to clumping.

It was time to think about the toasting step. While the majority of quinoa on the market has been debittered, some bitter-tasting compounds (called saponins) remain on the exterior. We have found that toasting quinoa in fat can exacerbate this bitterness, so I opted to dry-toast the grains in the pan before sautéing the onion. After about 5 minutes in the pan, the quinoa smelled like popcorn. This batch was nutty and rich-tasting, without any bitterness.

I finished the quinoa simply, with herbs and lemon juice, ensuring that my quinoa stayed in the spotlight—right where it belonged.

Quinoa Pilaf

SERVES 4 TO 6

If you buy unwashed quinoa, rinse it and then spread it out over a clean dish towel to dry for 15 minutes before cooking.

1½ cups prewashed white quinoa
2 tablespoons unsalted butter or extra-virgin olive oil
1 small onion, chopped fine
¾ teaspoon salt
1¾ cups water
3 tablespoons chopped fresh cilantro, parsley, chives, mint, or tarragon
1 tablespoon lemon juice

1. Toast quinoa in medium saucepan over medium-high heat, stirring frequently, until quinoa is very fragrant and makes continuous popping sound, 5 to 7 minutes; transfer to bowl.
2. Add butter to now-empty saucepan and melt over medium-low heat. Add onion and salt and cook, stirring frequently, until onion is softened and light golden, 5 to 7 minutes.
3. Stir in water and toasted quinoa, increase heat to medium-high, and bring to simmer. Cover, reduce heat to low, and simmer until grains are just tender and liquid is absorbed, 18 to 20 minutes, stirring once halfway through cooking. Remove pan from heat and let sit, covered, for 10 minutes.
4. Fluff quinoa with fork, stir in herbs and lemon juice, and serve.

variation

Quinoa Pilaf with Chipotle, Queso Fresco, and Peanuts

Add 1 teaspoon chipotle chile powder and ¼ teaspoon ground cumin with onion and salt. Substitute ½ cup crumbled queso fresco; ½ cup roasted unsalted peanuts, chopped coarse; and 2 thinly sliced scallions for herbs. Substitute 4 teaspoons lime juice for lemon juice.

RESCUING TABBOULEH

SUSAN LIGHT, *July/August 2012*

Tabbouleh has long been a meze staple in the Middle East, but these days it can be found in the refrigerator case of virtually every American supermarket. Its brief (and healthful) ingredient list explains its popularity: Chopped fresh parsley and mint, tomatoes, onion, and bits of nutty bulgur are tossed with lemon and olive oil for a refreshing appetizer or side dish. It all sounds easy enough, but most versions are hopelessly soggy, with flavor that is either too bold or too bland.

Another problem is that there's no agreement on the correct proportions for tabbouleh. Middle Eastern cooks favor loads of parsley (75 to 90 percent of the salad), employing a sprinkle of bulgur as a texturally interesting garnish. Most American recipes invert the proportions, creating an insipid pilaf smattered with herbs. I decided to take a middle-of-the-road approach for a dish that would feature a hefty amount of parsley as well as a decent amount of bulgur.

Soaking the bulgur in some of the liquid from the tomatoes, plus a bit of lemon juice, enhances its flavor.

Bulgur needs only to be reconstituted in cool water, but specific advice on how to prepare the grains is all over the map. Rehydration times range from 5 minutes all the way up to several hours, and while some recipes call for just enough liquid to plump the grains, others soak the bulgur in lots of water and then squeeze out the excess.

Working with ½ cup of medium-grind bulgur, I experimented with innumerable permutations of time and amount of water. I found that the grains required at least 90 minutes to tenderize fully. And the less liquid I used, the better the texture. Excess water only made the grains heavy, damp, and bland. A mere ¼ cup of liquid was enough for ½ cup of dried bulgur. With my method settled, I switched to soaking the bulgur in lemon juice instead of water, as some cookbooks recommend.

Next up: parsley. One and a half cups of chopped parsley and ½ cup of chopped mint still put the emphasis on the bright, peppery parsley but didn't discount the lemony bulgur and refreshing mint.

As for the rest of the salad, 6 tablespoons of extra-virgin olive oil tempered the tart lemon juice, and three chopped ripe tomatoes and two sliced scallions (preferred over onion) rounded out the mix. A smidge of cayenne pepper added zing. Tasters soundly rejected garlic and cucumbers, complaining that they detracted from the salad's clean flavor and overall texture.

Tasters were now happy with the texture, but the flavors weren't cohesive—my method wasn't giving them time to blend. To solve this, I reworked my method to give the bulgur a chance to absorb any liquid—namely, olive oil and juices from the tomatoes—in the salad. Soaking the bulgur for 30 to 40 minutes, until it began to soften, and then combining it with the remaining ingredients and letting it sit for an hour until fully tender gave everything time to mingle.

I had just one final issue to deal with. Depending on variety, the tomatoes' liquid sometimes diluted the salad's flavor and made it soupy. The solution? Tossing the tomatoes in salt and letting them drain in a colander drew out their moisture, precluding sogginess. Plus, I could use the savory liquid to soak the bulgur, thereby upping its flavor. I used 2 tablespoons of the tomato liquid (along with an equal amount of lemon juice) to soak the bulgur, whisking the remaining 2 tablespoons of lemon juice with oil for the dressing. At last, here was tabbouleh with fresh, penetrating flavor and a light texture.

Tabbouleh

SERVES 4

Don't confuse bulgur with cracked wheat, which has a much longer cooking time and will not work in this recipe. Serve the salad with the crisp inner leaves of romaine lettuce and wedges of pita bread.

3 tomatoes, cored and cut into ½-inch pieces
Salt and pepper
½ cup medium-grind bulgur, rinsed
¼ cup lemon juice (2 lemons)
6 tablespoons extra-virgin olive oil
⅛ teaspoon cayenne pepper
1½ cups minced fresh parsley
½ cup minced fresh mint
2 scallions, sliced thin

1. Toss tomatoes with ¼ teaspoon salt in fine-mesh strainer set over bowl and let drain, tossing occasionally, for 30 minutes; reserve 2 tablespoons drained tomato juice. Toss bulgur with 2 tablespoons lemon juice and reserved tomato juice in bowl and let sit until grains begin to soften, 30 to 40 minutes.
2. Whisk remaining 2 tablespoons lemon juice, oil, cayenne, and ¼ teaspoon salt together in large bowl. Add tomatoes, bulgur, parsley, mint, and scallions and toss gently to combine. Cover and let sit at room temperature until flavors have blended and bulgur is tender, about 1 hour. Before serving, toss salad to recombine and season with salt and pepper to taste.

variation

Spiced Tabbouleh

Add ¼ teaspoon ground cinnamon and ¼ teaspoon ground allspice to dressing with cayenne.

REALLY GOOD LENTIL SALAD

ANDREW JANJIGIAN, *September/October 2011*

Lentils may not get points for glamour, but when properly cooked and dressed up in a salad with bright vinaigrette and herbs, nuts, and cheeses, the legumes' earthy, almost meaty depth and firm-tender bite make a satisfying side dish for almost any meal.

The trouble is, perfectly cooked lentils are never a given. Too often, either their skins burst and their flesh disintegrates into starchy mush or they don't cook through completely and retain chewy skin and a hard, crunchy core. Before I started adding accoutrements, I had to nail down a reliable way to produce tender, buttery lentils with soft, unbroken skins. And because the tiny, shape-retaining French green lentils we favor can be hard to come by, I was also determined to develop an approach that would yield perfect results with whatever lentil variety my supermarket had to offer.

An hour-long soak in a warm brine and salt in the cooking water produces lentils with creamy centers and soft, tender skins.

Fortunately, the test kitchen's previous work with bean cookery gave me a good idea of how to improve the skins. We've discovered that, odd as it may sound, brining beans overnight softens their outer shells and makes them less likely to burst. The explanation is twofold: As the beans soak, the sodium ions from the salt replace some of the calcium and magnesium ions in the skins. By replacing some of the mineral ions, the sodium ions weaken the pectin in the skins, allowing more water to penetrate and leading to a more pliable, forgiving texture. But with beans, brining requires an overnight rest to be most effective. Fortunately, due to the lentils' smaller, flatter shape, I found that just a few hours of brining dramatically cuts down on blowouts. I also had another idea for hastening the process: Since heat speeds up all chemical reactions, I managed to reduce that time to just an hour by using warm water in the salt solution.

Another way to further reduce blowouts would be to cook the lentils as gently as possible. But I could see that even my stovetop's low setting still agitated the lentils too vigorously. I decided to try the oven, hoping that its indirect heat would get the job done more gently—and it did. And while the oven did increase the cooking time from less than 30 minutes to nearly an hour, the results were worth the wait: Virtually all of the lentil skins were tender yet intact.

Despite the lentils' soft, perfect skins, their insides tended to be mushy, not creamy. It occurred to me that I could try another very simple trick with salt: adding it to the cooking water. Many bean recipes (including ours) shy away from adding salt during cooking because it produces firmer interiors that can be gritty. Here's why: While a brine's impact is mainly confined to the skin, heat (from cooking) affects the inside of the bean, causing sodium ions to move to the interior, where they slow the starches' ability to absorb water. But a firmed-up texture was exactly what my mushy lentils needed. Could a problem for beans prove to be the solution for lentils? Sure enough, when I added ½ teaspoon of salt to the cooking water, the lentils went from mushy to firm yet creamy.

I had just one remaining task to tackle: enriching the flavor of the lentils. Swapping some of the cooking water for chicken broth solved the problem. Finally, I had tender, flavorful lentils that were ready for the spotlight.

Lentil Salad with Olives, Mint, and Feta

SERVES 4 TO 6

French green lentils, or lentilles du Puy, *are our preferred choice for this recipe, but it works with any type of lentil except red or yellow. Brining helps keep the lentils intact, but if you don't have time, they'll still taste good without it. The salad can be served warm or at room temperature.*

Salt and pepper
1 cup lentils, picked over and rinsed
5 garlic cloves, lightly crushed and peeled
1 bay leaf
5 tablespoons extra-virgin olive oil
3 tablespoons white wine vinegar
½ cup pitted kalamata olives, chopped coarse
1 large shallot, minced
½ cup chopped fresh mint
1 ounce feta cheese, crumbled (¼ cup)

1. Dissolve 1 teaspoon salt in 1 quart warm water (about 110 degrees) in bowl. Add lentils and soak at room temperature for 1 hour. Drain well.
2. Adjust oven rack to middle position and heat oven to 325 degrees. Combine lentils, 1 quart water, garlic, bay leaf, and ½ teaspoon salt in medium ovensafe saucepan. Cover, transfer saucepan to oven, and cook until lentils are tender but remain intact, 40 minutes to 1 hour.
3. Drain lentils well, discarding garlic and bay leaf. In large bowl, whisk oil and vinegar together. Add lentils, olives, and shallot and toss to combine. Season with salt and pepper to taste.
4. Transfer to serving dish, gently stir in mint, and sprinkle with feta. Serve warm or at room temperature.

DRUNKEN BEANS

ANDREW JANJIGIAN, *January/February 2015*

Soupy beans, or *frijoles de la olla*, are a staple at most Mexican tables and for good reason. The humble preparation, which supposedly derives from the bean suppers that caballeros cooked over fires on the range, typically consists of beans, a bit of pork or lard, and just a few herbs and aromatics like onion, chiles, and maybe tomato. Once the flavors meld and the cooking liquid thickens slightly from the beans' starches, the dish is as satisfying as a rich stew. Add a side of rice and you've got a meal.

There are numerous iterations, but my favorite might be *frijoles borrachos*, or drunken beans, in which pinto beans are cooked with beer or tequila. The alcohol should be subtle, lending the pot brighter, more complex flavor than beans cooked in water alone. And yet, when I've made the dish at home, the alcohol tastes either overwhelmingly bitter, raw, and boozy or is so faint that I can't tell it's there. I've also never gotten the consistency of the liquid quite right—that is, thickened just enough that it's brothy, not watery.

I set my sights on a pot that featured creamy, intact beans and a cooking-liquid-turned-broth that wasn't awash in alcohol but that offered more depth than a batch of plain old pintos.

Adding tequila at the beginning of cooking and beer partway through offers complex, not boozy, flavor.

HUMBLE BEGINNINGS

My first step was to nail down the basics of Mexican pot beans. I knew that canned beans were out here, since this recipe requires a full-flavored bean cooking liquid that only dried beans can impart. Step one was to soak the dried beans overnight in salty water—an adjustment we make to the usual plain-water soak because we've learned that sodium weakens the pectin in the beans' skins and, thus, helps them soften more quickly. For the pork element, I chose bacon; plenty of recipes called for it, and its smoky depth would ratchet up the flavor of the dish. I browned a few sliced strips in a Dutch oven. Setting aside the meat, I left the rendered fat to sauté the aromatics: a chopped onion and a couple of poblano chiles, plus minced garlic. Once they had softened, I added the drained beans, a few cups of water, bay leaves, and salt and slid the vessel into a low (275-degree) oven, where the beans would simmer gently for the better part of an hour—no need to stir them or take the risk that they'd burst.

HOP TO IT

I gave the beans an hour head start before adding the beer. Though some recipes call for incorporating it from the start of cooking, we've learned that cooking dried beans with acidic ingredients (and beer is definitely acidic) strengthens the pectin in the beans' skins and prevents them from fully softening. As for what type of beer to use, recipes were divided between dark and light Mexican lagers, but I reached for the former, figuring that a full-flavored pot of beans would surely require a full-flavored brew. I used 1 cup, splitting the difference between recipes that called for a full 12-ounce bottle and those that went with just a few ounces. I slid the pot back into the oven to meld the flavors and thicken the liquid. But the results I returned to half an hour later weren't what I was hoping for. Most noticeable was the beer's bitter flavor. The extra liquid had also thinned out the broth so that it lacked body.

I figured that reducing the amount of beer would thereby reduce the bitterness and the volume of liquid, too. But when I used just ½ cup, the "drunken" flavor was lost. Next, I tried cooking a full cup by itself before adding it to the pot when the beans were done cooking, hoping to increase its flavor and drive off some bitterness. Wrong again. The reduced beer tasted more bitter than ever, and some research explained why: The compounds responsible for the complex aroma and flavor of beer are highly volatile and dissipate quickly when boiled, while those that contribute bitterness are more stable and, in the absence of other flavors, become more pronounced. Given that, I tried adding the beer to the pot just before serving. This did help the beer retain a more complex flavor, but it also retained more of its raw-tasting alcohol.

A COCKTAIL OF FLAVOR

I decided to switch gears and try tequila instead, since I'd seen it used in a number of recipes. I made more batches of beans, adding varying amounts of the liquor—from a few tablespoons all the way up to ½ cup. Further research told me that the flavor compounds in tequila are very stable and thus wouldn't be affected by a long simmer, so I added the tequila at the beginning of cooking to allow more time for some of the alcohol to evaporate.

In small amounts, the tequila's smoky-sweetness was very subtle, so I went with ½ cup, which added noticeable complexity. That said, my tasters and I all missed the beer's malty flavor, so I decided to use both types of alcohol. But this time I'd try a lighter (read: less bitter-tasting) lager.

Working up another batch, I poured in the tequila at the outset of cooking, but waited an hour to add the beer, as I had in my first test. This time I got the booze flavor just right: faint bitterness and maltiness from the beer, with a deeper underpinning of flavor from the tequila. To underscore the pot's fresh and sweet flavors, I took a cue from other Mexican dishes and added a bundle of cilantro stems (I'd use the leaves from the bunch as a garnish) along with the bay leaves and a generous ¼ cup of tomato paste with the beer.

The only lingering issue: the too-thin broth. The low oven wasn't reducing the liquid enough, so when I pulled out the pot to add the beer, I simply moved it to the stove where it would simmer more rapidly. My only hesitation was that the beans might jostle and break down, but happily they held their shape, releasing just enough starch to turn the cooking liquid into a satisfying broth.

My drunken beans were still simple to prepare, but with two sources of alcohol; just the right depth from the bacon (I used the cooked pieces as a garnish), aromatics, and tomato paste; and a last touch of lime juice, chopped cilantro, and crumbled cheese, they were also incredibly satisfying.

PERFECT BEANS—AND BROTH—START SLOW AND FINISH STRONG

We like to cook beans in the oven because its heat is more even and gentle than that of the stovetop. Since the cooking liquid is a key component in our Drunken Beans, we follow up the stint in the oven with a hard simmer on the stove. The higher, more direct heat jostles the beans, causing them to release starches that give the cooking liquid pleasant body.

You'd think that this vigorous simmer would also cause blowouts—exactly what we'd been avoiding by moving the initial cooking to the oven. But it didn't, because the beans fully cook in the oven—their flesh becomes saturated and their skins softened and flexible—and are therefore less vulnerable to blowing out. Just as you can simmer canned beans in a pot of soup with minimal blowouts, we found that our oven-cooked beans could be simmered without breaking down.

START IN OVEN
Gentle cooking softens skins, saturates interiors.

FINISH ON STOVE
High heat causes starches to release into liquids.

Drunken Beans

SERVES 6 AS A MAIN DISH

You'll get fewer blowouts if you soak the beans overnight, but if you are pressed for time, they can be quick-brined. In step 1, combine the salt, water, and beans in a large Dutch oven and bring to a boil over high heat. Remove from the heat, cover, and let stand for 1 hour. Drain and rinse the beans and proceed with the recipe. Serve with rice. Feta cheese can be used in place of the Cotija.

Salt
1 pound (2½ cups) dried pinto beans, picked over and rinsed
30 sprigs fresh cilantro (1 bunch)
4 slices bacon, cut into ¼-inch pieces
1 onion, chopped fine
2 poblano chiles, stemmed, seeded, and chopped fine
3 garlic cloves, minced
½ cup tequila
2 bay leaves
1 cup Mexican lager
¼ cup tomato paste
2 limes, quartered
2 ounces Cotija cheese, crumbled (½ cup)

1. Dissolve 3 tablespoons salt in 4 quarts cold water in large bowl or container. Add beans and soak at room temperature for at least 8 hours or up to 24 hours. Drain and rinse well.

2. Adjust oven rack to lower-middle position and heat oven to 275 degrees. Pick leaves from 20 cilantro sprigs (reserve stems), chop fine, and refrigerate until needed. Using kitchen twine, tie remaining 10 cilantro sprigs and reserved stems into bundle.

3. Cook bacon in Dutch oven over medium heat, stirring occasionally, until crisp, 5 to 8 minutes. Using slotted spoon, transfer bacon to paper towel–lined bowl and set aside. Add onion, poblanos, and garlic to fat in pot and cook, stirring frequently, until vegetables are softened, 6 to 7 minutes. Remove from heat. Add tequila and cook until evaporated, 3 to 4 minutes. Return to heat. Increase heat to high; stir in 3½ cups water, bay leaves, 1 teaspoon salt, beans, and cilantro bundle; and bring to boil. Cover, transfer to oven, and cook until beans are just soft, 45 minutes to 1 hour.

4. Remove pot from oven. Discard bay leaves and cilantro bundle. Stir in beer and tomato paste and bring to simmer over medium-low heat. Simmer vigorously, stirring frequently, until liquid is thick and beans are fully tender, about 30 minutes. Season with salt to taste. Serve, passing chopped cilantro, lime wedges, Cotija, and reserved bacon separately.

WHY LOTS OF ALCOHOL DOESN'T MAKE BEANS BOOZY

Adding ½ cup of tequila and a cup of beer to our Drunken Beans lends the dish subtly bright, complex flavor and doesn't make the final product as boozy as you might think. That's because we add the tequila before—rather than with—the other liquids and allow it to evaporate completely before adding first water and then beer. This allows all the tequila's alcohol to burn off.

Here's why: When alcohol and water cook together, they form an azeotrope—a mixture of two different liquids that behaves as if it were a single compound. Because alcohol and water have a strong affinity for one another, it's not possible for alcohol molecules to evaporate without some water molecules present, and vice versa. This means that even though alcohol's boiling point is lower than water's, it will never fully boil off unless all the water does, too. The upshot: As long as there is water in the pot, there will also be alcohol.

We demonstrated this by making two batches of our Drunken Beans. In one batch we incorporated the tequila together with the other liquids; in the other it was added on its own (as per our recipe). When the alcohol content of both batches was measured by a lab, the batch in which the tequila had been added on its own contained 0.35 percent alcohol (from the beer, which we add partway through cooking), while the alcohol in the batch in which all the liquids were added simultaneously was 0.77 percent, more than double the amount.

CUBAN BLACK BEANS AND RICE

YVONNE RUPERTI, *March/April 2011*

Rice and beans has always been a sustenance dish to me—satisfying, surely, but a bit mundane. So I was intrigued when a friend returned from a trip to Miami and raved about a Cuban version in which black beans and rice are cooked together with aromatic vegetables, spices, and pork to create either a hearty main course or a flavorful side dish. Traditionally called *Moros y Cristianos*, this dish is unique in that the rice is cooked in the inky concentrated liquid leftover from cooking the beans, which renders the grains just as flavorful. This was definitely a dish I wanted to cook at home.

Most of the recipes that I found followed the same method: Sauté pork (usually salt pork or bacon) in a Dutch oven until crisp; lightly brown aromatic vegetables and spices in the rendered fat; then stir in uncooked rice, followed by the already cooked black beans and their cooking liquid. Cover and gently simmer until the liquid has been absorbed and the rice is tender.

Sounded easy enough. But after cooking up a few pots, my problems became clear: Sometimes I had bland rice studded with insipid beans—hardly worth the effort. Other times I ended up with poorly cooked rice: either a moist, gluey mash or grains scorched on the bottom but still undercooked on the top (the liquid having boiled away). My goal: a dish that was not just richly flavorful, but foolproof.

FLAVOR MAKERS

To get the flavor right, I knew I needed to perfect the *sofrito*. This mixture of aromatic vegetables, spices, and herbs is a cornerstone of Latin cooking and the starting point for this dish. The specific elements in the mix differ from one Latin cuisine to another, but a Cuban sofrito usually consists of a "holy trinity" of onion, green pepper, and garlic, typically flavored with cumin and oregano.

I quickly found that pureeing the vegetables for the sofrito before combining them with the beans and rice was not the way to go here; the resulting paste muddied the texture of the dish and eliminated the possibility of browning the sofrito in a skillet first. Chopping the vegetables (or pulsing them in a food processor) was a better option. After crisping 6 ounces of diced salt pork (bacon made an acceptable substitute), I added the onion, pepper, cumin, and oregano, and sautéed the sofrito for 15 minutes in the rendered fat and a splash of extra-virgin olive oil until the mixture was golden brown and flavorful. Then I added some garlic to the mix.

The only problem? There just wasn't enough of that rich flavor. I needed this sofrito to be the backbone for a big pot of beans and rice, not just give it a mild overtone. Increasing the spices helped, but only to a point; overdoing it made the dish dusty and harsh. I thought that doubling the amount of sofrito would do the trick—and flavorwise, it did—but the sheer volume of moist vegetables weighed down the rice and beans in a kind of sofrito sludge. Did all of the veggies have to go directly into the sofrito? Since I had been precooking the soaked beans in plain water, I wondered if I could use the extra veggies to infuse the beans and thereby increase the overall flavor of the dish. With that in mind, I put half an onion, half a green pepper, half a garlic head, and bay leaves in with the beans to simmer. When the beans were just cooked, I sampled them. It turned out to be a good idea—both the beans and their cooking liquid were fullflavored and would lend that quality to the rice as well. The results were even better when I swapped half of the water for chicken broth.

RESCUING THE RICE

With the flavor of the dish where I wanted it, I turned to the rice. The traditional step of rinsing the rice before cooking washed off the excess starch from the grains and helped prevent them from turning sticky and clumping together.

The gentle heat of the oven ensures that every grain of rice is cooked through and infused with flavor.

Fixing the scorched-yet-undercooked rice was a little trickier. It's a fine line between gummy rice and undercooked rice because the beans, sofrito, and pork all add moisture to the pot. I tinkered around a bit with extra liquid; after a few sodden pots of beans and rice, I found that 2½ cups was the correct amount of bean liquid to get 1½ cups of rice cooked through in about 30 minutes. But even at the lowest heat setting, I found that the mixture at the bottom of the pot was still scorching while the rice grains at the top remained almost crunchy. The problem made sense: With the stove's flame hitting only the underside of the pot, the bottom layer of rice burned while the grains at the top barely cooked at all. That's when I recalled our oven-baked rice technique, in which the all-around, indirect heat cooks the pot's contents gently and evenly. I brought the rice, beans, and liquid (including a splash of red wine vinegar for brightness) to a simmer, gave the mixture a stir, covered the vessel, and slid it into a 350-degree oven. After about the same time as it took to cook on the stove, I removed the pot, fluffed the contents with a fork, and let it sit for 5 minutes. Finally, perfectly cooked rice from top to bottom.

As a final touch, a sprinkling of thinly sliced scallions and a squeeze of lime brought the dish to life. Forget about packing your bags—this was a taste of Cuba that you could make in any kitchen.

Cuban-Style Black Beans and Rice

SERVES 6 TO 8

It is important to use lean—not fatty—salt pork. If you can't find lean salt pork, substitute six slices of bacon. If using bacon, decrease the cooking time in step 4 to 8 minutes. For a vegetarian version, substitute water for the chicken broth and omit the salt pork. Add 1 tablespoon of tomato paste with the vegetables in step 4 and increase the amount of salt in step 5 to 1½ teaspoons.

Salt
1 cup dried black beans, picked over and rinsed
2 cups chicken broth
2 large green bell peppers, halved, stemmed, and seeded
1 large onion, halved at equator and peeled, root end left intact
1 head garlic, 5 cloves minced, rest of head halved at equator with skin left intact
2 bay leaves
1½ cups long-grain white rice
2 tablespoons olive oil
6 ounces lean salt pork, cut into ¼-inch pieces
4 teaspoons ground cumin
1 tablespoon minced fresh oregano
2 tablespoons red wine vinegar
2 scallions, sliced thin
Lime wedges

1. Dissolve 1½ tablespoons salt in 2 quarts cold water in large bowl or container. Add beans and soak at room temperature for at least 8 hours or up to 24 hours. Drain and rinse well.
2. In Dutch oven, stir together beans, 2 cups water, broth, 1 bell pepper half, 1 onion half (with root end), halved garlic head, bay leaves, and 1 teaspoon salt. Bring to simmer over medium-high heat, cover, and reduce heat to low. Cook until beans are just soft, 30 to 35 minutes. Using tongs, discard bell pepper, onion, garlic, and bay leaves. Drain beans in colander set over large bowl, reserving 2½ cups bean cooking liquid. (If you don't have enough bean cooking liquid, add water to equal 2½ cups.) Do not clean pot.
3. Adjust oven rack to middle position and heat oven to 350 degrees. Place rice in large fine-mesh strainer and rinse under cold running water until water runs clear, about 1½ minutes. Shake strainer vigorously to remove all excess water; set rice aside. Cut remaining bell peppers and remaining onion half into 2-inch pieces and pulse in food processor until broken into rough ¼-inch pieces, about 8 pulses, scraping down sides of bowl as needed; set vegetables aside.
4. In now-empty pot, heat 1 tablespoon oil and salt pork over medium-low heat and cook, stirring frequently, until lightly browned and rendered, 15 to 20 minutes. Add remaining 1 tablespoon oil, chopped bell peppers and onion, cumin, and oregano. Increase heat to medium and continue to cook, stirring frequently, until vegetables are softened and beginning to brown, 10 to 15 minutes longer. Add minced garlic and cook, stirring constantly, until fragrant, about 1 minute. Add rice and stir to coat, about 30 seconds.
5. Stir in beans, reserved bean cooking liquid, vinegar, and ½ teaspoon salt. Increase heat to medium-high and bring to simmer. Cover and transfer to oven. Cook until liquid is absorbed and rice is tender, about 30 minutes. Fluff with fork and let rest, uncovered, for 5 minutes. Serve, passing scallions and lime wedges separately.

WHAT'S A SOFRITO?

A *sofrito* serves as the fundamental flavor base for many Cuban dishes, including this one. The combination of onion, green pepper, and garlic (and often cumin and oregano) is a close relative of the French *mirepoix*, which features onion, carrot, and celery.

CUBAN FLAVOR BASE

GETTING DEEPLY FLAVORED BLACK BEANS AND RICE

A threefold method guarantees the most flavorful black beans and rice.

1. **ENRICH BEANS** Simmering the beans in water and broth bolstered with bell pepper, onion, and garlic adds extra flavor.

2. **DEEPEN SOFRITO FLAVOR** Lightly browning the sofrito and spices with the rendered salt pork adds complex, meaty flavor.

3. **ADD BEAN COOKING LIQUID** Cooking the rice and beans in the reserved bean cooking liquid plus red wine vinegar imbues the dish with flavor.

Kale
Rutabaga
Dinosaur Kale
Turnip
Cabbage
Brussels Sprouts
Cauliflower
Broccoli Rabe
White Kohlrabi
Broccoli
Purple Kohlrabi
Mustard Greens

VEGETABLE SIDES

THE BEST WAY TO COOK ARTICHOKES

ADAM RIED, *May/June 2014*

Steaming is the classic way to cook an artichoke: The vegetable goes into the pot whole, so there's almost no prep work involved, which keeps the method dead simple. But cooking an artichoke in water washes out the vegetable's delicate nuttiness; plus, some diners are as daunted by an untrimmed artichoke as they are by manhandling a lobster at the table.

A dry-heat method like roasting seemed like a much better approach. With a bit of knife work upfront, you can get concentrated nutty richness and an almost entirely edible product: a velvety stem and heart surrounded by fully tender inner leaves and soft outer leaves that are chewy at the top with a patch of creamy meat at their base—the part you scrape off with your teeth. But artichokes can dry and toughen easily in the oven, so I would need to come up with a foolproof roasting method to achieve that ideal.

Artichokes range considerably in size, but I decided to stick with widely available medium (8- to 10-ounce) specimens. Larger artichokes can be tough and fibrous; smaller ones make for more prep work.

Before I started in on my roasting method, I trimmed away the woody exterior of the stems, split the bulbs down the middle, and scooped out the chokes. I next submerged the halved artichokes in lemon water to prevent them from oxidizing and discoloring. While I hoped this step might be unnecessary since the artichokes would be browning in the oven, a quick test convinced me it was worth doing. When artichokes oxidize, they develop drab gray-brown patches that are unlike the deep, rich brown color produced by caramelization and the Maillard reaction.

Artichokes are prone to drying out because their leaves open and separate as they cook, exposing much more surface area and allowing their moisture to evaporate quickly. They're also fibrous, which means the texture of the inner leaves quickly goes from softly chewy to leathery. Those factors compelled me to start with a hybrid steaming-roasting technique. I arranged the halves cut side down in a 3-quart baking dish (the taller sides of which would trap more moisture than a rimmed baking sheet) and then crimped aluminum foil over the dish, creating a steam chamber out of the moisture escaping from the artichokes that I hoped would soften even the more-fibrous outer leaves and preserve more of their flavor since they'd be steaming in their own "juice." I let the artichokes steam for about 15 minutes in a 475-degree oven, at which point I pulled off the foil and let them roast for another 10 to 15 minutes so that the moisture would burn off, allowing the artichokes to develop deeper color and flavor.

Our hybrid steam-and-roast method yields artichokes that are tender, deeply flavorful, and nicely browned.

Though the artichokes' inner leaves, stems, and hearts were just about tender, the meat on some of the outer leaves was rather dry and chewy. Clearly, the artichokes needed to retain more moisture, so for my next test, I tried leaving the foil on the baking dish for the full 25 minutes. The artichokes' color wasn't as burnished as it had been, but the slight cosmetic compromise was worth the artichokes' considerably better texture. The inner leaves, stems, and hearts were fully tender, while the outer layers were a notch shy of softly chewy. These artichokes also had a noticeably more concentrated and nutty flavor.

Steaming may be traditional, but with a roasting technique that produces results that are more flavorful—and almost entirely edible—I can't imagine ever going back.

Roasted Artichokes

SERVES 4

If your artichokes are larger than 8 to 10 ounces, strip away another layer or two of the toughest outer leaves.

1 lemon, plus lemon wedges for serving
4 artichokes (8 to 10 ounces each)
3 tablespoons extra-virgin olive oil
Salt and pepper

1. Adjust oven rack to lower-middle position and heat oven to 475 degrees. Cut lemon in half, squeeze halves into 2 quarts water, and drop in spent halves.
2. Cut off most of stem of 1 artichoke, leaving about ¾ inch attached. Cut off top quarter. Pull tough outer leaves downward toward stem and break off at base; continue until first 3 or 4 rows of leaves have been removed. Using paring knife, trim outer layer of stem and rough areas around base, removing any dark green parts. Cut artichoke in half lengthwise. Using spoon, remove fuzzy choke. Pull out inner, tiny purple-tinged leaves, leaving small cavity in center of each half. Drop prepped halves into lemon water. Repeat with remaining artichokes.
3. Brush 13 by 9-inch baking dish with 1 tablespoon oil. Remove artichokes from lemon water, shaking off some excess lemon water (some should be left clinging to leaves). Toss artichokes with remaining 2 tablespoons oil and ¾ teaspoon salt and season with pepper, gently working some oil and seasonings between leaves. Arrange artichoke halves cut side down in baking dish and cover tightly with aluminum foil.
4. Roast until cut sides of artichokes start to brown and both bases and leaves are tender when poked with tip of paring knife, 25 to 30 minutes. Transfer artichokes to serving dish. Serve artichokes warm or at room temperature, passing lemon wedges separately.

ROASTED GREEN BEANS

REBECCA HAYS, *November/December 2005*

Delicate and slender, garden-fresh haricots verts need only a few minutes of steaming, a pat of butter, and a sprinkle of salt and pepper to be ready for the table. In fact, they are so sweet, crisp, and tender that it's not uncommon to eat them raw. Take the same route with mature supermarket green beans, however, and you'll regret it. Unlike their lithe cousins, overgrown store-bought beans are often tough and dull, demanding special treatment.

Italians solve the problem with braising; gentle, moist cooking has a tenderizing effect. But the stovetop can get awfully crowded as dinnertime approaches—especially during the holidays. Roasting is commonplace for hardy root vegetables like potatoes and carrots, but the technique can be used to cook other vegetables, too. Would a stint in the oven have a positive effect on out-of-season green beans?

Just 20 minutes of roasting transforms tough supermarket specimens into tender, deeply caramelized beans.

I had my answer when an embarrassingly simple test produced outstanding results. Roasted in a hot oven with only oil, salt, and pepper, an entire baking sheet of beans disappeared faster than French fries. Repeated tests confirmed that roasting consistently transforms geriatric specimens into deeply browned, full-flavored beauties. Here's why: As green beans mature, their fibers toughen and their sugars are converted into starch. The hot, dry heat of the oven helps reverse the aging process. Fibers break down and an enzymatic reaction causes the starch to turn back into sugar, restoring sweetness. Roasting also encourages the Maillard reaction (a chemical response that creates flavor through browning), a benefit lost with moist cooking methods.

The technique needed a few refinements. Those rare roasted-green-bean recipes that I found called for at least 2 tablespoons of oil per pound of beans, but I favored a more restrained approach. A single tablespoon of oil encouraged browning without making the beans slick and greasy. And after testing multiple time and temperature combinations, 20 minutes (with a quick stir at the halfway point) in a 450-degree oven proved optimal.

Now it was time to experiment with variations. But their development was not without missteps: Aromatics (like garlic) added at the outset scorched. The solution wasn't to lower the heat (the beans didn't brown well enough) but to add these ingredients halfway through roasting. When liquid seasonings (like balsamic vinegar) slid right off the beans onto the baking sheet, I included a spoonful of sticky sweetener (honey) to create an appealing glaze, a move that incidentally encouraged even more browning. Last, a smattering of flavorful toppings added after cooking provided complexity.

Roasted Green Beans

SERVES 4

1 pound green beans, trimmed
1 tablespoon olive oil
Salt and pepper

1. Adjust oven rack to middle position and heat oven to 450 degrees. Line rimmed baking sheet with aluminum foil and spread green beans on prepared sheet. Drizzle green beans with oil, sprinkle with ½ teaspoon salt, and toss to coat; spread green beans in even layer. Transfer sheet to oven and roast for 10 minutes.
2. Remove sheet from oven. Using tongs, toss green beans, then spread into even layer. Continue to roast until green beans are dark brown in spots and have started to shrivel, 10 to 12 minutes. Season with salt and pepper to taste, and serve.

variations

Roasted Green Beans with Red Onion and Walnuts

Whisk together 1 tablespoon balsamic vinegar, 1 teaspoon honey, 1 teaspoon minced fresh thyme, and 2 minced garlic cloves in small bowl; set aside. Toss ½ red onion, cut into ½-inch-thick-wedges, with green beans in step 1. In step 2, toss balsamic-honey mixture with beans and onions before returning to oven. Sprinkle with ⅓ cup toasted chopped walnuts before serving.

Roasted Sesame Green Beans

Whisk together ½ teaspoon toasted sesame oil, 2 teaspoons honey, ¼ teaspoon red pepper flakes, and 3 minced garlic cloves in small bowl; set vinaigrette aside. In step 2, toss vinaigrette with beans before returning to oven. Sprinkle with 4 teaspoons toasted sesame seeds before serving.

Roasted Green Beans with Sun-Dried Tomatoes, Goat Cheese, and Olives

SERVES 4

½ cup oil-packed sun-dried tomatoes, rinsed, patted dry, and chopped coarse
½ cup pitted kalamata olives, chopped
1 tablespoon lemon juice
2 teaspoons minced fresh oregano
1 teaspoon extra-virgin olive oil
1 recipe Roasted Green Beans
Salt and pepper
2 ounces goat cheese, crumbled (½ cup)

Whisk sun-dried tomatoes, olives, lemon juice, oregano, and oil together in medium bowl. Add green beans and toss well to combine. Season with salt and pepper to taste, top with goat cheese, and serve.

A NEW WAY OF COOKING BEETS

CELESTE ROGERS, *March/April 2013*

Beets are packed with complex earthy sweetness, but preparing them is no small feat. Roasting concentrates their flavor but can take more than 90 minutes—way too long for a weeknight side dish. Boiling shaves off time, but the beets leach tons of flavor into the water. Not wanting to pour flavor down the drain or wait longer than an hour, I went in search of a more streamlined approach to bringing out the best in beets.

Most quick-cooking beet recipes begin by cutting the beets down to bite size. While this reduces the roasting time to less than a half-hour, peeling and cutting the rock-hard raw beets is a tedious and messy task.

What about the epitome of speed and convenience—the microwave? Although whole beets became tender in just 12 minutes, their skins were impossible to remove without some arm strength and a vegetable peeler. This is because the microwave heats the outermost inch of food so fast that moisture in the beet flesh doesn't have time to evaporate and cause the flesh to shrink and separate slightly from the skin—the key to easy removal.

Braising the beets in a small amount of liquid creates the base for a flavorful sauce to finish the dish.

I knew I would have to use a more traditional method, and boiling had the most potential for speed. Halving the raw beets before placing them in a saucepan with about a quart of water to cover (turning a blind eye to any consequential flavor loss for now) cost less than a minute but shaved 10 to 15 minutes off the cooking time typically required for whole beets. As an added benefit, the halved beets cooled to handling temperature faster than whole beets and shed their peels just as easily.

To avoid losing the flavor in the cooking water, I decided to reduce the vibrant "beet broth" to about a tablespoon and use it to build a dressing. Unfortunately, reducing a quart of water took upwards of 25 minutes.

Cooking the beets in less liquid to begin with made sense; a mere 1¼ cups was enough to submerge a small portion of each beet and provide ample steam. This effectively switched my method from boiling to braising. For even cooking, I needed to make certain that the beets were in a single layer, so I switched from a large saucepan to a broader straight-sided skillet. (A Dutch oven worked, too.) Now the leftover braising liquid reduced in just 5 minutes flat.

To play up the earthy sweetness of the beets and introduce a complementary acidity, I added a tablespoon of light brown sugar and 3 tablespoons of vinegar to the beet reduction. Just 1 more minute of cooking gave the resultant sweet-and-sour sauce enough body to coat the peeled wedges. Thin slices of shallot underscored the savory depth, while toasted nuts, aromatic citrus zest, and fresh herbs added just enough contrast without overshadowing the robust beet flavor. Armed with a simple method that cost me less than an hour, I was ready to add beets to my midweek vegetable roster.

Beets with Lemon and Almonds

SERVES 4 TO 6

To ensure even cooking, we recommend using beets that are of similar size—roughly 2 to 3 inches in diameter. The beets can be served warm or at room temperature. If serving at room temperature, wait to sprinkle with almonds and herbs until right before serving.

1½ pounds beets, trimmed and halved horizontally
1¼ cups water
Salt and pepper
3 tablespoons distilled white vinegar
1 tablespoon packed light brown sugar
1 shallot, sliced thin
1 teaspoon grated lemon zest
½ cup whole almonds, toasted and chopped
2 tablespoons chopped fresh mint
1 teaspoon chopped fresh thyme

1. Place beets, cut side down, in single layer in 11-inch straight-sided sauté pan or Dutch oven. Add water and ¼ teaspoon salt; bring to simmer over high heat. Reduce heat to low, cover, and simmer until beets are tender and tip of paring knife inserted into beets meets no resistance, 45 to 50 minutes.
2. Transfer beets to cutting board. Increase heat to medium-high and reduce cooking liquid, stirring occasionally, until pan is almost dry, 5 to 6 minutes. Add vinegar and sugar; return to boil; and cook, stirring constantly with heat-resistant spatula, until spatula leaves wide trail when dragged through glaze, 1 to 2 minutes. Remove pan from heat.
3. When beets are cool enough to handle, rub off skins with paper towel or dish towel and cut into ½-inch wedges. Add beets, shallot, lemon zest, ½ teaspoon salt, and ¼ teaspoon pepper to glaze and toss to coat. Transfer beets to serving dish; sprinkle with almonds, mint, and thyme; and serve.

variations

Beets with Lime and Pepitas

Omit thyme. Substitute lime zest for lemon zest, toasted pepitas for almonds, and cilantro for mint.

Beets with Orange and Walnuts

Substitute orange zest for lemon zest; walnuts, toasted and chopped, for almonds; and parsley for mint.

BROILED BROCCOLI RABE

STEVE DUNN, *September/October 2016*

In the past I rarely, if ever, cooked broccoli rabe. (Rabe, or rapini, as it's known in Italy where the vegetable is a mainstay in the cuisine, is actually more closely related to spicy turnips than to regular, more-mellow broccoli.) While I'm a fan of this green's bitter, mustardy bite, I seem to be in the minority on this. As a result, the majority of recipes you find jump through hoops to subdue its characteristic flavor. One of the most popular approaches calls for chopping, blanching, shocking, draining, and sautéing the pieces with strong-flavored aromatics—a lengthy ordeal that wipes out just about any trace of the green's pungency and leaves you with a sink full of dirty dishes.

I wanted to figure out an efficient way to temper rabe's bitterness but not eliminate it entirely. And since this green would offer much more character than most vegetables, it would need little or no dressing before it hit the plate.

Broccoli rabe gets its bitter flavor from enzymes that are stored mainly in its florets and that get released when the plant is cut or chewed.

Broiling broccoli rabe browns the vegetable, creating sweetness and taming bitterness.

The upshot of this was that the way in which I cut the rabe seemed likely to be at least as important as how I cooked it. I proved this with a quick side-by-side test: I divided a bunch of rabe in half and fully chopped one portion, florets and all. Then, I cut the remaining stalks roughly where the leaves and florets start to branch off from the stems, leaving the leafy parts intact, and cut the stem segments (where less of the bitter-tasting enzyme resides) into bite-size pieces. I simply sautéed both batches and took a taste. Sure enough, the intact pieces were considerably more mellow. It also turns out that there was another factor at play: The high heat of cooking deactivates one of the enzymes in the vegetable and thus stops the reaction that contributes most of the bitter flavor in the first place.

I could have stopped right there and created a recipe for sautéing chopped stems and whole leaves and florets, but I'd found a few recipes that called for roasting the rabe, which was an interesting alternative. I hoped that the rabe would brown deeply and take on a rich caramelized flavor that would balance out the remaining bitterness. I prepared another batch using my new cutting technique, tossing them with simple flavorings and roasting them on a rimmed baking sheet in a 400-degree oven.

After 10 minutes, the rabe had caramelized nicely, and the leaves now also offered a delicate crunch—that part was good. But texturally, the stems had suffered, turning soft and stringy by the time they had browned.

Part of the problem was that the water droplets left over from washing the rabe were taking a long time to burn off and therefore delaying browning. Going forward, I got serious about drying the greens by rolling them in clean dish towels to blot away as much moisture as possible. I also cranked the heat to 450, but even then the stems were limp by the time they were browned.

It was time to take it up a notch to the broiler. I adjusted the oven rack 4 inches from the heating element, popped in another batch, and kept a close watch. I tossed them halfway through to make sure they cooked evenly. A few minutes later, the results were perfect: lightly charred, crisp leaves and florets and perfectly crisp-tender stalks.

Broiled Broccoli Rabe

SERVES 4

3 tablespoons extra-virgin olive oil
1 pound broccoli rabe
1 garlic clove, minced
¾ teaspoon kosher salt
¼ teaspoon red pepper flakes
Lemon wedges

1. Adjust oven rack 4 inches from broiler element and heat broiler. Brush rimmed baking sheet with 1 tablespoon oil.
2. Trim and discard bottom 1 inch of broccoli rabe stems. Wash broccoli rabe with cold water, then dry with clean dish towel. Cut tops (leaves and florets) from stems, then cut stems into 1-inch pieces (keep tops whole). Transfer broccoli rabe to prepared sheet.
3. Combine remaining 2 tablespoons oil, garlic, salt, and pepper flakes in small bowl. Pour oil mixture over broccoli rabe and toss to combine.
4. Broil until half of leaves are well browned, 2 to 2½ minutes. Using tongs, toss to expose unbrowned leaves. Return sheet to oven and continue to broil until most leaves are lightly charred and stems are crisp-tender, 2 to 2½ minutes longer. Transfer to serving platter and serve immediately, passing lemon wedges.

NIPPING BITTERNESS IN THE BUD

Cutting and chewing broccoli rabe releases compounds that are bitter. Since more of these compounds are in the florets, we leave the leafy part whole. Broiling the rabe also reduces bitterness, as heat exposure deactivates the enzyme (myrosinase) that causes the bitterness.

WARM BRUSSELS SPROUT SALADS

LAN LAM, *November/December 2015*

Though most often sautéed or roasted, raw Brussels sprouts make a great salad green. Slicing the sprouts thin and letting them sit in the dressing helps tenderize the tough leaves and brightens their pungent flavor. Sprouts also take well to punchy dressings and bold additions.

But thin-slicing the sprouts is tedious—and they can literally be a lot to chew on. I was able to streamline the shredding process with an assembly line approach: Rather than trimming, halving, and slicing the sprouts one by one, I worked through all the trimming, then the halving, and so forth.

Still, the sprouts were very dense to eat; a handful of bitter but more tender radicchio was just the thing to break up the salad's slaw-like density and add complexity.

Tossing thinly sliced Brussels sprouts with a warm vinaigrette tenderizes the tough leaves and gives them bold flavor.

Softening raw Brussels sprouts with a regular dressing takes about 30 minutes, but what if I dressed them with a warm vinaigrette? Surely the heat would wilt them faster, and a warm dressing would give me options other than oil as a base, since the fat is heated. This seemed like a perfect opportunity to use my favorite Brussels sprouts partner: bacon.

While I crisped a few chopped slices in a skillet, I used the microwave to lightly pickle some thinly sliced shallots and then I whisked the shallot mixture into the bacon. Adding the greens right to the skillet meant they were warmed not just by the dressing but also by the pan's residual heat.

Now for some bold additions—toasted almonds and shaved Parmesan for the bacon version and dried cranberries, toasted hazelnuts, and Manchego for another variation with brown butter. These salads are as complex as they are elegant and will play a starring role on my holiday table.

Brussels Sprout Salad with Warm Bacon Vinaigrette

SERVES 6

A food processor's slicing blade can be used to slice the Brussels sprouts, but the salad will be less tender.

¼ cup red wine vinegar
1 tablespoon whole-grain mustard
1 teaspoon sugar
Salt and pepper
1 shallot, halved through root end and sliced thin crosswise
4 slices bacon, cut into ½-inch pieces
1½ pounds Brussels sprouts, trimmed, halved, and sliced thin
1½ cups finely shredded radicchio, long strands cut into bite-size lengths
2 ounces Parmesan, shaved into thin strips using vegetable peeler
¼ cup sliced almonds, toasted

1. Whisk vinegar, mustard, sugar, and ¼ teaspoon salt together in bowl. Add shallot, cover tightly with plastic wrap, and microwave until steaming, 30 to 60 seconds. Stir briefly to submerge shallot. Cover and let cool to room temperature, about 15 minutes.
2. Cook bacon in 12-inch skillet over medium heat, stirring frequently, until crisp and well rendered, 6 to 8 minutes. Off heat, whisk in shallot mixture. Add Brussels sprouts and radicchio and toss with tongs until dressing is evenly distributed and sprouts darken slightly, 1 to 2 minutes. Transfer to serving bowl. Add Parmesan and almonds and toss to combine. Season with salt and pepper to taste, and serve immediately.

variation

Brussels Sprout Salad with Warm Brown Butter Vinaigrette

SERVES 6

A food processor's slicing blade can be used to slice the Brussels sprouts, but the salad will be less tender.

¼ cup lemon juice
1 tablespoon whole-grain mustard
1 teaspoon sugar
Salt and pepper
1 shallot, halved through root end and sliced thin crosswise
¼ cup dried cranberries
5 tablespoons unsalted butter
⅓ cup hazelnuts, toasted, skinned, and chopped
1½ pounds Brussels sprouts, trimmed, halved, and sliced thin
1½ cups baby arugula, chopped
4 ounces Manchego cheese, shaved into thin strips using vegetable peeler

1. Whisk lemon juice, mustard, sugar, and ¼ teaspoon salt together in bowl. Add shallot and cranberries, cover tightly with plastic wrap, and microwave until steaming, 30 to 60 seconds. Stir briefly to submerge shallot and cranberries. Let cool to room temperature, about 15 minutes.
2. Melt butter in 12-inch skillet over medium heat. Add hazelnuts and cook, stirring frequently, until butter is dark golden brown, 3 to 5 minutes. Off heat, whisk in shallot mixture. Add Brussels sprouts and arugula and toss with tongs until dressing is evenly distributed and sprouts darken slightly, 1 to 2 minutes. Transfer to serving bowl. Add Manchego and toss to combine. Season with salt and pepper to taste, and serve immediately.

SLOW-COOKED WHOLE CARROTS

KEITH DRESSER, *January/February 2015*

As a chef, I get particular enjoyment from dining out: It's my chance to keep up with the ever-changing culinary landscape by experiencing cutting-edge techniques and trendy ingredients. But at home I rarely have the desire to re-create restaurant food. (Who has the time to whip up a frothy bacon emulsion or labor over a batch of green apple taffy?) Still, every so often I come across a dish or approach that I absolutely have to try in my own kitchen. The most recent was a gorgeous platter of slow-cooked whole carrots. Fork-tender and without a hint of mushiness, they had a dense, almost meaty quality to them. And the carrot flavor was superconcentrated: sweet and pure, but still earthy. I pictured these carrots as an accompaniment to everything from a holiday beef tenderloin to a basic roast chicken.

A search for recipes that would produce similar results generated a lot of slow-roasted and braised carrots, but none came close to what I had been served. The roasted carrots boasted plenty of sweetness and browning, but this obscured their true flavor. Braised carrots inevitably took on the flavor of whatever liquid they were cooked in. I wanted carrots that tasted like carrots, not like chicken broth or white wine. I would need to use another cooking method to spotlight the carrots in the best possible way.

Slow, gentle cooking produces beautifully fork-tender carrots with concentrated sweetness.

SAVING SWEETNESS

I got my bearings by slowly simmering 12 whole peeled carrots of similar size in a full saucepan of salted water (about 6 cups) until they were tender. This test shed light on two issues. The first was inconsistent cooking: By the time the thick end of the carrot was tender, the thinner tapered end was mushy and waterlogged. The second was that the carrots had been robbed of their inherent sweetness. Simmering had drawn out the soluble sugar in the vegetable, and all of that sugar flowed down the drain when I poured off the cooking water.

The latter problem would be solved by coming up with an approach that didn't call for discarding the cooking water. Switching from a saucepan to a skillet (whose shallow sides would facilitate evaporation) and reducing the amount of water to just 3 cups were my first moves. I arranged the carrots in a single layer and simmered them uncovered until all the water evaporated and the carrots were fully tender when I pierced them with a paring knife, which took about 45 minutes. Adding a tablespoon of butter to the water at the beginning of simmering, in combination with the sugar released from the carrots, reduced to a light glaze that coated the carrots with a handsome sheen.

Unfortunately, even with this specialized method, the inconsistent doneness from the thick end of the carrot to the narrow end remained. I experimented with squirting some lemon juice into the water, hoping that its acid would firm up the pectin in the carrots and balance out the textural inconsistencies. The good news: It worked. The bad: In order for the lemon juice to have an effect, I needed to squeeze in so much of it that it buried the carrots' sweetness.

PECTIN POWER

Looking for a better solution, I was reminded of a phenomenon called "persistent firmness." Here's how it works: Precooking certain fruits or vegetables at a low temperature sparks an enzymatic reaction that helps the produce remain tender-firm during a second cooking phase at a higher temperature. If I could use persistent firmness to my advantage in this recipe, it would mean that the thin ends of the carrots wouldn't turn mushy while the thicker ends fully cooked through.

To put the science to the test, I outfitted my skillet with a probe thermometer, brought 3 cups of salted water (along with the pat of butter) to a boil, removed the skillet from the heat, arranged the carrots in a single layer in the water, covered the skillet, and let the carrots stand for 20 minutes. During this time, the water clocked in at 135 to 150 degrees, in the ideal range for the enzymatic reaction to work its magic. After 20 minutes, I removed the lid and switched over to my newly developed cooking method, returning the carrots to the heat and simmering them until the water evaporated. These carrots were fully tender, yet they still boasted a firm, meaty texture.

The carrots were now just about perfect, but I did notice that the top sides of some of them were occasionally a little underdone. I suspected that because I was using a relatively small amount of water, the level was falling below the tops of the carrots before they had time to become tender. Covering the pan only slowed evaporation. Partially covering the skillet was a no-go since it might not be the same for every pot. Rolling the carrots during cooking to promote even cooking was a pain in the neck and imperfect at best: Some of the carrots inevitably rolled back into their initial positions, thwarting my efforts.

That's when I thought of a trick I'd learned in restaurant kitchens: using a cartouche—a piece of parchment paper that sits directly on the food as it cooks, regulating the reduction of moisture in cooking. I topped my next batch of carrots with a cartouche and was happy to find that it solved the problem. The paper allowed the perfect rate of evaporation but also trapped more of the escaping steam and kept it concentrated on top of the carrots, ensuring perfectly tender, evenly cooked results.

These carrots, with their firm, tender texture and pure carrot flavor, didn't need any embellishment. But to make them real showstoppers, I dressed them up a bit. I settled on easy relishes that could be whipped up while the carrots cooked. These toppings, made with bold ingredients like sherry vinegar, olives, fresh herbs, and nuts, packed a punch that complemented the carrots' sweet, earthy flavor. I may not be a restaurant chef anymore, but no one will know that from eating these carrots.

Slow-Cooked Whole Carrots

SERVES 4 TO 6

Use carrots that measure ¾ to 1¼ inches across at the thickest end. The carrots can be served plain, but we recommend topping them with one of our relishes (recipes follow).

3 cups water
1 tablespoon unsalted butter
½ teaspoon salt
12 carrots (1½ to 1¾ pounds), peeled

1. Fold 12-inch square of parchment paper into quarters to create 6-inch square. Fold bottom right corner of square to top left corner to create triangle. Fold triangle again, right side over left, to create narrow triangle. Cut off ¼ inch of tip of triangle to create small hole. Cut base of triangle straight across where it measures 5 inches from hole. Open paper round.
2. Bring water, butter, and salt to simmer in 12-inch skillet over high heat. Remove pan from heat, add carrots in single layer, and place parchment round on top of carrots. Cover skillet and let stand for 20 minutes.
3. Remove lid from skillet, leaving parchment round in place, and bring to simmer over high heat. Reduce heat to medium-low and simmer until almost all water has evaporated and carrots are very tender, about 45 minutes. Discard parchment round, increase heat to medium-high, and continue to cook carrots, shaking pan frequently, until they are lightly glazed and no water remains in skillet, 2 to 4 minutes longer. Transfer carrots to platter and serve.

relishes

Green Olive and Golden Raisin Relish

MAKES ABOUT 1 CUP

⅓ cup golden raisins
1 tablespoon water
⅔ cup pitted green olives, chopped
1 shallot, minced
2 tablespoons extra-virgin olive oil
1 tablespoon red wine vinegar
½ teaspoon ground fennel
¼ teaspoon salt

Microwave raisins and water in bowl until steaming, about 1 minute. Cover and let stand until raisins are plump, about 5 minutes. Add olives, shallot, oil, vinegar, fennel, and salt to plumped raisins and stir to combine.

Pine Nut Relish

MAKES ABOUT ¾ CUP

Pine nuts burn easily, so be sure to shake the pan frequently while toasting them.

⅓ cup pine nuts, toasted
1 shallot, minced
1 tablespoon sherry vinegar
1 tablespoon minced fresh parsley
1 teaspoon honey
½ teaspoon minced fresh rosemary
¼ teaspoon smoked paprika
¼ teaspoon salt
Pinch cayenne pepper

Combine all ingredients in bowl.

Red Pepper and Almond Relish

MAKES ABOUT ¾ CUP

½ cup finely chopped jarred roasted red peppers
¼ cup slivered almonds, toasted and chopped coarse
2 tablespoons extra-virgin olive oil
2 tablespoons minced fresh parsley
1 tablespoon white wine vinegar
1 teaspoon minced fresh oregano
¼ teaspoon salt

Combine all ingredients in bowl.

MAKING A PARCHMENT LID (CARTOUCHE)

1. Fold 12-inch square of parchment into quarters to create 6-inch square.

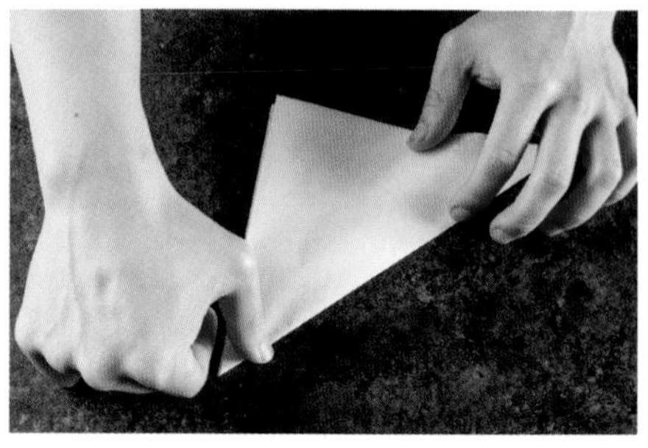

2. With openings at top and right sides, fold bottom right corner of square to top left corner.

3. Fold triangle again, right side over left, to create narrow triangle.

4. Cut off ¼ inch of tip to create hole. Cut base of triangle straight across where it measures 5 inches from hole.

TWO WAYS WITH CAULIFLOWER

EVA KATZ, *March/April 1998*

One of my most vivid childhood culinary memories is soggy, overcooked cauliflower flooded with congealing neon-yellow cheese. At that time, I was definitely only interested in the gooey cheese, and the cauliflower always got left on my plate. Until I started cooking for this article, my opinion of cauliflower had not changed that much. But after several days in the kitchen, I was pleased to discover that when properly cooked and imaginatively flavored, cauliflower can be nutty, slightly sweet, and absolutely delicious.

I spent those first few days trying to develop a quick stovetop method for cooking this oft-overcooked vegetable. During my first round at the stove, I observed that cauliflower is very porous. This can work to its advantage or disadvantage, depending on what the cauliflower absorbs during cooking. I identified two basic cooking methods that went hand-in-hand with this observation. In the first method the cauliflower is fully cooked by boiling, steaming, or microwaving and then tossed with a light vinaigrette or sautéed briefly in butter or oil with simple flavorings. In this scenario, keeping the water out is key. In the second method the cauliflower is flavored as it cooks, which means that you want to get liquid in. My goal was to test the variables for both methods and devise two different recipes.

I first worked on perfecting the "cook first, flavor later" technique. I began by comparing boiling, steaming, and microwaving. The boiled cauliflower tasted watery regardless of how long I boiled it. The microwaved cauliflower (cooked on full power for 6 minutes and left to stand for 3 minutes) had a sweet, nutty flavor, but the florets cooked unevenly. Steaming the cauliflower for 7 to 8 minutes, on the other hand, produced evenly cooked florets with a clean, bright, sweet flavor.

To confirm that steamed cauliflower was less watery than the boiled version, I compared the raw and cooked weights of cauliflower cooked by each method. With steaming, there was no weight increase. With boiling, the cauliflower gained approximately 10 percent of its original weight.

Next I moved to the "flavor while cooking" approach. The basic technique was braising, which involves cooking with a small amount of liquid in a covered container. I hoped that the cooking liquid—my foe in the previous method—would now become my friend. But how was this best done? Should the cauliflower simply be braised with no previous cooking? Or should it be steamed or sautéed first, then finished by braising?

Steaming brings out cauliflower's fresh, sweet flavors; browning and braising intensify its nutty taste.

After testing these three methods I immediately realized the benefits of sautéing the cauliflower first. Braising the dense vegetable with no precooking simply took too long. When I partially cooked the cauliflower by steaming it and then braised it, the taste was lackluster and flat. Sautéing it for 7 minutes on medium-high heat and then braising it, however, intensified the cauliflower's naturally mild flavors. Not only did the cauliflower absorb the flavors from the braising liquid, but the browned cauliflower also tasted wonderfully smoky and earthy.

Cooking cauliflower too long can release unpleasant sulfur-containing compounds that break down when exposed to heat. To avoid this problem, I found it best to cut the cauliflower into 1-inch pieces, which cook quite quickly. With the brown-and-braise method, I also liked how the cut surface of the florets lay flat in my sauté pan. The cut surfaces browned beautifully and the sweetness of the florets was pronounced.

CUTTING CAULIFLOWER INTO FLORETS

Cutting the cauliflower into small pieces ensures that the florets cook quickly and evenly, minimizing the sulfurous flavor that can develop if cauliflower is cooked for too long.

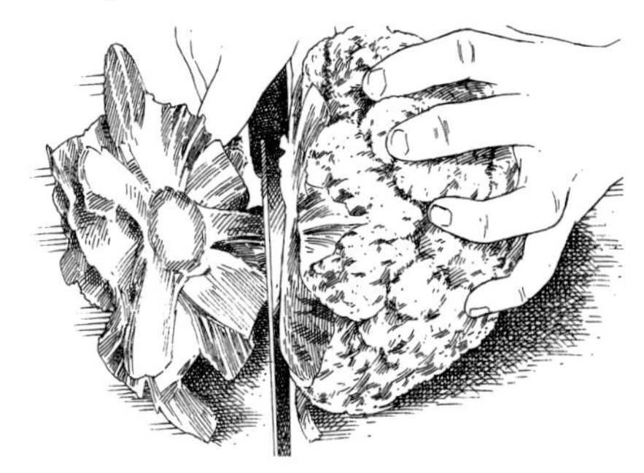

1. Start by pulling off outer leaves and trimming off stem near base of head.

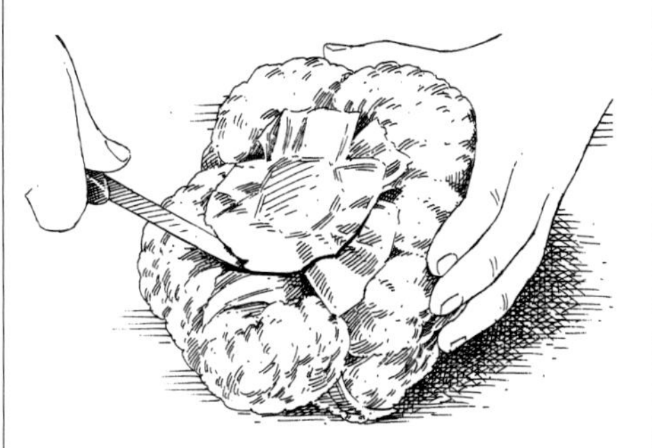

2. Turn cauliflower upside down and use sharp knife to cut around and remove core.

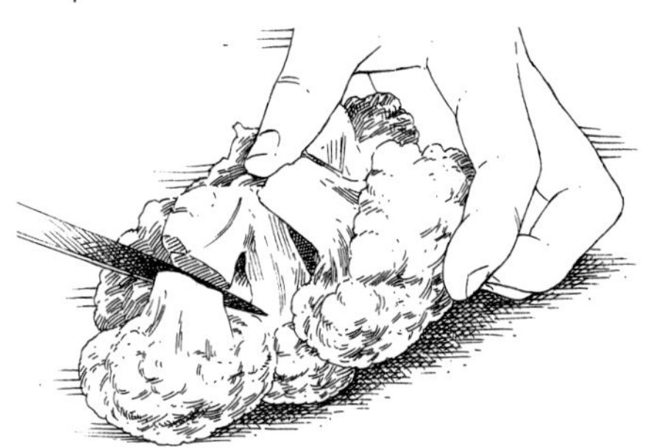

3. Using tip of chef's knife, separate florets from inner stem, then cut florets into 1-inch pieces.

Steamed Cauliflower

SERVES 4

Steamed cauliflower is best complemented by mild seasonings or the simple flavors of the recipe that follows.

1 head cauliflower (2 pounds), cored and cut into 1-inch florets

Fit large saucepan with steamer basket. Add water, keeping level below basket. Bring water to boil, add cauliflower florets, reduce heat to medium, and cover. Steam until florets are tender but still offer some resistance when poked with paring knife, 7 to 8 minutes. Remove cauliflower from basket and serve.

variation

Steamed Cauliflower with Bread Crumbs, Capers, and Chopped Eggs

SERVES 4

Crumble the hard-cooked egg by pressing it through a sieve.

2 tablespoons unsalted butter
3 tablespoons dry bread crumbs
1 recipe Steamed Cauliflower
1 Easy-Peel Hard-Cooked Egg (page 8), crumbled fine
2 tablespoons minced fresh parsley
2 tablespoons capers, rinsed
1½ tablespoons lemon juice
Salt and pepper

Melt butter in 12-inch skillet over medium heat, add bread crumbs, and cook, stirring occasionally, until lightly browned, about 5 minutes. Add cauliflower and cook until heated through, about 1 minute. Add egg, parsley, capers, and lemon juice and toss lightly to distribute. Season with salt and pepper to taste, and serve immediately.

Browned and Braised Cauliflower with Garlic, Ginger, and Soy

SERVES 4

The stronger flavor of browned cauliflower stands up well to bolder, more complex flavor combinations, such as these Asian flavorings.

1½ tablespoons vegetable oil
1 head cauliflower (2 pounds), cored and cut into 1-inch florets
2 tablespoons grated fresh ginger
2 garlic cloves, minced
1 teaspoon toasted sesame oil
¼ cup water
2 tablespoons soy sauce
2 tablespoons rice vinegar
1 tablespoon dry sherry
2 scallions, minced
Pepper

1. Heat vegetable oil in 12-inch skillet over medium-high heat until just smoking. Add cauliflower and cook, stirring occasionally, until beginning to brown, 6 to 7 minutes.
2. Clear center of skillet and add ginger, garlic, and sesame oil. Cook, mashing mixture into pan, until fragrant, about 1 minute. Stir ginger mixture into cauliflower and cook 30 seconds more. Reduce heat to low and add water, soy sauce, vinegar, and sherry. Cover and cook until florets are tender but still offer some resistance when poked with paring knife, 4 to 5 minutes. Add scallions and toss lightly to distribute. Season with pepper to taste, and serve immediately.

variation

Browned and Braised Cauliflower with Indian Spices

SERVES 4

Cooking the spices for a minute or two removes their raw edge and allows their flavors to deepen.

1½ tablespoons vegetable oil
1 head cauliflower (2 pounds), cored and cut into 1-inch florets
½ onion, sliced thin
1 teaspoon ground cumin
1 teaspoon ground coriander
1 teaspoon ground turmeric
¼ teaspoon red pepper flakes
¼ cup plain yogurt
¼ cup water
1 tablespoon lime juice
½ cup frozen green peas, thawed (optional)
¼ cup chopped fresh cilantro
Salt and pepper

1. Heat oil in 12-inch skillet over medium-high heat until just smoking. Add cauliflower and cook, stirring occasionally, until beginning to soften, 2 to 3 minutes. Add onion and continue cooking until florets begin to brown and onion softens, about 4 minutes longer.
2. Stir in cumin, coriander, turmeric, and pepper flakes and cook until spices begin to toast and are fragrant, about 1 to 2 minutes. Reduce heat to low and add yogurt, water, and lime juice. Cover and cook until flavors meld, about 4 minutes. Add peas, if using, and cilantro and toss to combine. Cover and cook until florets are fully tender but offer some resistance when poked with paring knife, about 2 minutes more. Season with salt and pepper to taste, and serve immediately.

PERFECT BOILED CORN

LAN LAM, *September/October 2016*

I almost didn't pursue a boiled corn recipe. I'd never consulted one, and as one of my colleagues asked dubiously, what was wrong with the usual method? Bring a pot of water to a boil, drop in the ears, and wait. When the kernels turn bright yellow, they're done.

But then I thought about how rarely I've produced perfectly crisp, juicy corn. Usually, I pull the ears out too early and the kernels are underdone and starchy, or I let them sit in the cooling water while I get the rest of dinner ready and find that they've shriveled and turned to mush. I decided to figure out a method that delivers perfect results every time.

For perfect corn on the cob every time, we drop it in boiling water—then turn off the heat.

First, I took a close look at exactly what happens to corn as it cooks. There are two key variables at play: the starches and the pectin. When raw, the liquid inside the kernels (referred to as the "milk") is chalky, thanks to the presence of raw starches. As corn heats, those starches absorb water, swell, and gelatinize, and the starchy liquid becomes seemingly smoother, silkier, and more translucent. Simultaneously, the pectin (which is essentially glue holding together the cell walls inside each kernel) dissolves, and the cell walls no longer stick together, so the corn softens. The more pectin that dissolves, the mushier the corn becomes.

All of this meant that the key to perfectly cooked corn would be pinpointing when the starches had gelatinized but the pectin hadn't dissolved so much that the kernels lost their crisp bite. Fortunately, I was able to attach temperatures to these phases: Corn starch begins to gelatinize at 144 degrees, while pectin starts dissolving at 176 degrees and does so rapidly at 194 degrees. Using those temperatures as parameters, I would aim for a doneness zone of 150 to 170 degrees—hot enough to cook the starches quickly but cool enough to keep the majority of the pectin intact.

Figuring that the only way to guarantee consistent results would be to cook a certain number of ears in a measured amount of water for a certain amount of time, I settled on six ears and began testing various amounts of boiling water and cooking times. But sometimes the corn would cook perfectly, and other times it would be under- or overdone. I realized that the problem was the varying sizes of the ears. Depending on the total weight of corn in the pot, the water temperature dropped accordingly, and the cooking time varied.

I didn't want to call for specific size ears, but I could ensure that the water never got hot enough to overcook the corn in the first place. The idea is based on sous vide cooking, where food cooks in a water bath set at a specific temperature and can get only as hot as that temperature. We've hacked that technique in the past by bringing water to a boil, adding the item(s), and shutting off the heat. The food increases in temperature as the water temperature decreases, until an equilibrium is reached; the final temperature depends on the relative amounts of water and food.

So I experimented: I dropped six ears of various sizes into 3, 4, and 5 quarts of boiling water; shut off the heat; and let them sit between 10 and 30 minutes. About a dozen batches later, I'd nailed the formula: six ears of any size in 4 quarts of cooling water yielded snappy kernels every time.

As an added bonus, I could achieve these results whether I left the corn in the water for 10 minutes or 30 minutes, since the water temperature continued to drop and the corn would never overcook—an advantage for those who eat two ears but don't want to pull both from the water at the same time. My method was more reliable and also more forgiving than not using a recipe at all.

Foolproof Boiled Corn

SERVES 4 TO 6

6 ears corn, husks and silk removed
Unsalted butter, softened
Salt and pepper

1. Bring 4 quarts water to boil in large Dutch oven. Turn off heat, add corn to water, cover, and let stand for at least 10 minutes or up to 30 minutes.
2. Transfer corn to large platter and serve immediately, passing butter, salt, and pepper separately.

accompaniments

Chili-Lime Salt

MAKES 3 TABLESPOONS

This spice mix can be refrigerated for up to one week.

2 tablespoons kosher salt
4 teaspoons chili powder
¾ teaspoon grated lime zest

Combine all ingredients in small bowl.

Cumin-Sesame Salt

MAKES 3 TABLESPOONS

1 tablespoon cumin seeds
1 tablespoon sesame seeds
1 tablespoon kosher salt

Toast cumin seeds and sesame seeds in 8-inch skillet over medium heat, stirring occasionally, until fragrant and sesame seeds are golden brown, 3 to 4 minutes. Transfer mixture to cutting board and let cool for 2 minutes. Mince mixture fine until well combined. Transfer mixture to small bowl and stir in salt.

CHINESE SMASHED CUCUMBERS

KEITH DRESSER, *July/August 2017*

My longtime definition of cucumber salad—cool, crisp slices tossed with a tangy vinaigrette or a sour cream dressing—was recently upended when, at a Sichuan restaurant, I was presented with a plate of large, craggy, skin-on cucumber pieces sparingly coated with dressing. The cukes had a crunchy, almost pickle-like texture and hinted at garlic and sesame, with mild acidity and touches of sweetness and salinity. The simple preparation proved to be an ideal accompaniment to the rich, spicy food. The dish, called *pai huang gua*, is drop-dead easy to make. Smash the cukes with a skillet or rolling pin (or, as is traditional, with the flat side of a Chinese cleaver). Once they're smashed, tear them into rough pieces and briefly salt them to expel excess water. Finally, dress the chunks with a quick vinaigrette of soy sauce, vinegar, minced garlic, and sesame oil.

Why smash the cukes? I found a couple of reasons. The first was speed. When I treated equal amounts of smashed versus chopped cucumbers with salt and measured the amount of liquid each batch exuded, the smashed cucumbers were crisp and had lost about 5 percent of their water weight after only 15 minutes. It took the chopped cucumbers four times as long to shed the same amount of water.

This refreshing take on cucumber salad replaces slicing with smashing, which encourages the cucumbers to soak up the flavorful dressing.

The second benefit was textural. Smashing breaks up the vegetable in a haphazard way that exposes more surface area than chopping or slicing, so more vinaigrette can adhere. A colleague compared dressing smooth cut cucumbers to spilling water on a laminate floor—virtually nothing was absorbed. The smashed cucumbers, on the other hand, acted like a shag carpet, sucking up almost every drop.

As for the best type of cuke, I dismissed American cucumbers, finding their thick, wax-coated skins too tough. That left nearly seedless English cucumbers, pickling cucumbers, or small Persian cucumbers. All had thin, crisp skins, but the pickling type can have a lot of seeds and the Persian type lacked a thick layer of flesh and was therefore missing the refreshing crispness of the English variety, my ultimate choice.

Regarding the dressing, soy sauce, garlic, and toasted sesame oil provided a complex base that I accented with sugar, but what really made it special was Chinese black vinegar, which is made by fermenting rice.

And there I had it: an all-new (and more interesting) take on cucumber salad.

CHINESE BLACK VINEGAR

Black vinegar is made primarily from rice and wheat bran and is aged in earthenware crocks to develop complexity. Products labeled "black vinegar" range greatly in flavor. We prefer vinegars labeled *Chinkiang* (or *Zhenjiang*), which are similar from brand to brand.

Smashed Cucumbers (Pai Huang Gua)

SERVES 4

We recommend using Chinese Chinkiang (or Zhenjiang) black vinegar in this dish for its complex flavor. If you can't find it, you can substitute 2 teaspoons of rice vinegar and 1 teaspoon of balsamic vinegar. A rasp-style grater makes quick work of turning the garlic into a paste.

2 (14-ounce) English cucumbers
1½ teaspoons kosher salt
4 teaspoons Chinese black vinegar
1 teaspoon garlic, minced to paste
1 tablespoon soy sauce
2 teaspoons toasted sesame oil
1 teaspoon sugar
1 teaspoon sesame seeds, toasted

1. Trim and discard ends from cucumbers. Cut each cucumber crosswise into 3 equal lengths. Place pieces in large zipper-lock bag and seal bag. Using small skillet or rolling pin, firmly but gently smash cucumbers until flattened and split lengthwise into 3 to 4 spears each. Tear spears into rough 1- to 1½-inch pieces and transfer to colander set in large bowl. Toss cucumbers with salt and let stand for at least 15 minutes or up to 30 minutes.
2. While cucumbers sit, whisk vinegar and garlic together in small bowl; let stand for at least 5 minutes or up to 15 minutes.
3. Whisk soy sauce, oil, and sugar into vinegar mixture until sugar has dissolved. Transfer cucumbers to medium bowl and discard any extracted liquid. Add dressing and sesame seeds to cucumbers and toss to combine. Serve immediately.

THE PERFECT BAKED POTATO

LAN LAM, *January/February 2016*

Baking a potato is about as basic as cooking gets—so basic, in fact, that it doesn't even seem to require a recipe. Simply stick a russet in a moderately hot oven directly on the rack, and after about an hour, give it a squeeze. If it's still firm, bake it longer; if it gives to pressure, it's done.

The beauty of that method is its simplicity, but how often does it produce a truly great baked potato? In my experience, almost never. Whether the center is dense and gummy or the skin is soggy, shriveled, or chewy, the best I can do is slather on as much butter or sour cream as possible to cover up the flaws.

I want more from a baked potato than a dense or desiccated log of starch, and I was determined to examine every variable to nail down ideal results. That meant a fluffy interior encased in thin, crisp skin.

DEGREES OF DONENESS

Russets are the classic choice for baked potatoes because they're a dry, floury variety, meaning they contain a relatively high amount (20 to 22 percent) of starch. (So-called in-between varieties like Yukon Golds, or waxy types like Red Bliss, contain 16 to 18 percent and about 16 percent starch, respectively.) The more starch a potato contains, the more water from inside the potato can be absorbed during baking. As the starch granules swell with water within the spud's cell walls, they eventually force the cells to separate into clumps that result in the texture we perceive as dry and fluffy.

But when exactly does a potato reach that dry and fluffy stage—the point at which it is done? Taking a closer look at the bake-until-it's-squeezable approach would at least give me a baseline temperature to work from, so I pricked an 8-ounce russet a few times with a fork and placed it in a 400-degree oven. Once the exterior had softened, I cut slits to open up the potato and stuck an instant-read thermometer in several places. The outer ½ inch or so, which was soft enough to squeeze but not quite fluffy, registered 195 degrees, while the dense core, which was clearly underdone, was 175 degrees. From there, I baked off several more potatoes, placing probes at exterior points in each and removing them from the oven at different temperatures. At 200 degrees the outer edge was light and fluffy, while the core was just tender, but at 205 degrees the whites of the potatoes were at their best: fluffy from edge to center. A few more tests revealed that the method was somewhat forgiving; I could bake the potatoes as high as 212 degrees and still achieve perfectly light and fluffy results. The only hitch, I discovered, was that it was crucial to cut the potatoes open immediately after baking to let steam escape; if they sat for even 10 minutes, they retained more water than potatoes that were opened immediately and turned dense and gummy even after cooking to 205 degrees.

WORKING FROM THE INSIDE OUT

Now that I knew exactly when the potato was cooked through, I wanted to see how fast I could get it there. Microwaving the potatoes would surely speed up the cooking, I assumed. But further tests proved that this was actually the worst approach. Whether I used the microwave alone or in tandem with the oven, the potatoes always cooked unevenly and were often gummy and dense. Why? Because microwaves heat potatoes very unevenly, rendering some portions fully cooked while others are still rock-hard.

Back to the oven. The potatoes took between 60 and 80 minutes to cook through at 400 degrees, so I hoped that cranking the heat up to 500 would hasten things. Unfortunately, this caused the outer portion of the potato to overbrown and almost char in spots, leading to a slightly burned flavor. Going forward, I turned the oven temperature down notch by notch and eventually found 450 degrees for 45 minutes or so to be the sweet spot—the interior was soft and light, the skin nicely browned. Now I just had to see about crisping it up.

SKIN CARE

Since frying potatoes in oil crisps and browns their exteriors, I hoped that coating the russets' skin with oil might do the same as they baked. But as it turned out, painting the spuds with vegetable oil (1 tablespoon coated four potatoes nicely) and then baking them yielded disappointingly soft and chewy skins. The problem was that the oil created a barrier on the skin's exterior that prevented moisture from escaping, so the skins weren't able to dry out and crisp.

The better method was to apply the oil once the potatoes were cooked, by which point the skins had dehydrated considerably. Returning them to the oven for 10 more minutes rendered them deep brown and crisp (the extra time increases the interior temperature of the potatoes by just 2 or 3 degrees).

A dunk in salted water before baking and a brush of oil at the end produces well-seasoned potatoes with fluffy interiors and crisp skins.

I was very pleased with my method, which really wasn't much more work than baking a potato without a recipe. But one variable lingered: seasoning. Sure, I'd sprinkle salt and pepper on the potato at the table, but what I really wanted was even seasoning all over. My first attempt, brining the potatoes for 1 hour before baking, delivered skins with fantastic flavor, but did I really have to add that much more time to the method? Instead, I tried simply wetting the raw potatoes and sprinkling them with salt—and when that failed (the salt crystals didn't stick), I simply dunked the potatoes in salty water. The flavor was just as full and even as that of the brined potatoes, but this step added mere seconds to my recipe. The last tweak I made, baking the potatoes on a rack set in a rimmed baking sheet, prevented drips of salt and water from staining the bottom of my oven and allowed the hot air to circulate evenly around the potatoes during baking.

Crisp and thoroughly seasoned on the outside and light and fluffy within, my baked potatoes were perfect as-is, though nobody disagreed that a pat of butter or sour cream was in order. And for the times when I wanted a real showstopper of a side dish (or even a main course with a salad), I put together a few simple toppings that could be made while the potatoes baked. Topped with a creamy egg salad–like mixture or herbed goat cheese, these spuds were an unqualified hit at the dinner table.

Best Baked Potatoes

SERVES 4

Open up the potatoes immediately after removal from the oven in step 3 so steam can escape. Top them as desired, or with one of our toppings (recipes follow).

Salt and pepper
4 (7- to 9-ounce) russet potatoes, unpeeled, each lightly pricked with fork in 6 places
1 tablespoon vegetable oil

1. Adjust oven rack to middle position and heat oven to 450 degrees. Dissolve 2 tablespoons salt in ½ cup water in large bowl. Place potatoes in bowl and toss so exteriors of potatoes are evenly moistened. Transfer potatoes to wire rack set in rimmed baking sheet and bake until center of largest potato registers 205 degrees, 45 minutes to 1 hour.
2. Remove potatoes from oven and brush tops and sides with oil. Return potatoes to oven and continue to bake for 10 minutes.
3. Remove potatoes from oven and, using paring knife, make 2 slits, forming X, in each potato. Using clean dish towel, hold ends and squeeze slightly to push flesh up and out. Season with salt and pepper to taste. Serve immediately.

accompaniments

Creamy Egg Topping

MAKES 1 CUP

Leftover topping makes a great sandwich filling.

3 Easy-Peel Hard-Cooked Eggs (page 8), chopped
¼ cup sour cream
1½ tablespoons minced cornichons
1 tablespoon minced fresh parsley
1 tablespoon Dijon mustard
1 tablespoon capers, rinsed and minced
1 tablespoon minced shallot
Salt and pepper

Stir all ingredients together and season with salt and pepper to taste.

Herbed Goat Cheese Topping

MAKES ¾ CUP

4 ounces goat cheese, softened
2 tablespoons extra-virgin olive oil
2 tablespoons minced fresh parsley
1 tablespoon minced shallot
½ teaspoon grated lemon zest
Salt and pepper

Mash goat cheese with fork. Stir in oil, parsley, shallot, and lemon zest. Season with salt and pepper to taste.

Smoked Trout Topping

MAKES 1 CUP

We prefer trout for this recipe, but any hot-smoked fish, such as salmon or bluefish, may be substituted.

5 ounces smoked trout, chopped
⅓ cup crème fraîche
2 tablespoons minced fresh chives
4 teaspoons minced shallot
1¼ teaspoons grated lemon zest plus ¾ teaspoon lemon juice
Salt and pepper

Stir all ingredients together and season with salt and pepper to taste.

MUST YOU PRICK?

Everyone knows that you have to prick potatoes before baking them so steam doesn't build up inside and cause them to explode. Well, we baked 40 potatoes without doing this, and not one exploded. But since it takes so little effort, here's one time we'll err on the side of caution. It could be the 41st one that explodes.

WE'RE NOT KIDDING ABOUT THE THERMOMETER!

It might sound fussy to take the temperature of a baked potato to see if the center has reached 205 degrees, but it's the only way to guarantee that you're getting a uniformly fluffy interior. The usual approach to checking for doneness, squeezing the potato, doesn't work because while the outer edge might feel soft, the center is likely dense and firm. This cross section shows how different the texture (and temperature) can be from the surface to the center.

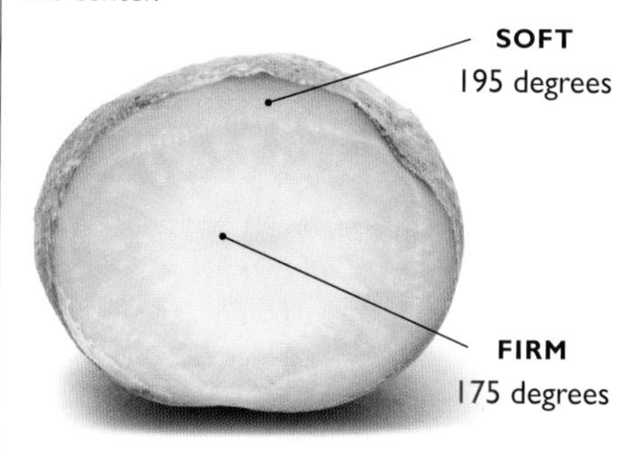

WHY YOU SHOULDN'T MICROWAVE

A microwave might seem like a fast way to "bake" a potato, but we found two reasons why it's actually the worst approach. First, microwaves heat foods very unevenly, so some parts of the potato might rapidly reach 205 degrees while others get to only 180 degrees. Second, rapidly heating a potato causes pressure to build and cell walls to burst, releasing starch molecules that glue together the broken cell walls.

A NEW WAY TO COOK POTATOES

DAN SOUZA, *May/June 2013*

I love the versatility of waxy potatoes like Red Bliss. Steamed whole, they turn tender and creamy—perfect canvases for tossing with butter and fresh herbs. They also take well to halving and roasting, which browns their cut surfaces. So when I came across recipes for braised new potatoes, I wondered if this approach, which pairs dry heat for browning with moist heat for simmering, would yield the best of both worlds. In fact, I thought there might be a third benefit to braising Since many recipes call for simmering the spuds in chicken broth, I reasoned that the potatoes would soak up all that flavorful liquid like little savory sponges. All in all, it sounded like a promising—and super-simple—alternative method for cooking waxy potatoes.

CHARTING A NEW COURSE

Except it wasn't that simple. To my surprise, the recipes I made were failures. Any flavor that the potatoes might have picked up from the chicken broth was barely discernible—even after I'd halved or thin-sliced the spuds to expose their flesh to the cooking liquid. Worse, the typical brown-and-then-simmer approach to braising had been a bust, as all the flavorful brown color that the potatoes developed during searing washed off by the time they had cooked through in the liquid.

But by this point, I was fixated on braised potatoes and convinced that if I could revise the technique, the results would surely be ideal. Enter my first change: ditching the chicken broth, since there was no point in using broth if it wasn't considerably improving the potatoes' flavor. Instead, I would use heavily salted water. (While most of the aromatic flavor molecules in chicken are fat-soluble and won't penetrate water-filled potatoes, salt is water-soluble and will seep into the spuds' flesh.) I halved 1½ pounds of small red potatoes—enough to feed at least four—placed them cut side down in an oiled 12-inch skillet, and turned the dial to medium-high. Once they'd browned, I reexamined the steaming step by adding 2 cups of seasoned water (to evenly cover the surface of the pan), covering the pan, and leaving the potatoes to braise until tender. Removing the lid revealed potatoes with smooth and creamy interiors. But their cut sides were wan in appearance—and flavor.

That's when I realized I should reverse the order of operations and brown the potatoes after simmering them to guarantee good browning. I moved ahead with this plan and, once the potatoes were tender, carefully drained off the water, added some oil to the dry pan, and let the pieces brown over high heat. This time, my colleagues assured me that I was getting somewhere, as the salt had thoroughly seasoned the spuds and searing after simmering had produced the rich, deeply flavorful browning that I'd had in mind.

The downside was that straining off simmering water from a large skillet was cumbersome, and rearranging each of the hot potato halves cut side down to ensure that they browned properly was fussy—too fussy for a simple side dish. When a colleague suggested that I simply simmer the potatoes uncovered so that the water would evaporate, I was skeptical. The time it would take to simmer off a full 2 cups of liquid would certainly mean overcooking the spuds. But at that point, I didn't have any better ideas, so I decided to give it a shot.

It did, in fact, take about 35 minutes for the water to cook off, at which point I expected to find a mushy, overcooked mess. Imagine my surprise, then, when I stuck a fork into a few of the potatoes and found that they were holding together just fine. More than that, these potatoes were remarkably silky and smooth—by far the best texture I'd produced to date. Pleased by the results, I researched an explanation and learned that if low-starch potatoes like Red Bliss are cooked long enough, they exude a fluid gel that keeps the potato "glued" together and also gives the impression of extreme creaminess.

Still, my newfound cooking method for waxy potatoes wasn't entirely without fault. In my excitement over these ultracreamy spuds, I'd ignored that their undersides, now in contact with a dry, hot skillet, were stuck fast to the pan and scorched.

We simmer small red potatoes to velvety tenderness in a covered pan, then uncover them and cook off the liquid so they can brown.

EASTERN INSPIRATION

The more I thought about it, the more I realized that my recipe shared the basic framework of a classic Chinese dish: potstickers. After browning these flat-sided dumplings in an oil-coated skillet, you add water and simmer them until the water evaporates and the dumplings once again make contact with the skillet and crisp in the oil. The main difference was that with potstickers, the oil goes in at the beginning. I wondered if adding the fat earlier in the potato-cooking process might gloss the potatoes and prevent them from sticking after the water evaporated.

So I combined everything—water, salt, potatoes, and a few tablespoons of oil—in the skillet and brought it to a simmer. After a few minutes of covered cooking (which ensured that any sections of unsubmerged potato would steam), I removed the lid and cranked the burner to medium-high. My hope was that, just as with potstickers, the water would evaporate and leave the oil and potatoes alone in the pan to brown. About 15 minutes later, I got my wish. As the last few wisps of steam escaped, the oil sizzled and the potatoes developed rich color—but I knew that I could do even better if I switched from oil to butter. Indeed, the protein in the butter's milk solids magnified the effects of browning (known as the Maillard reaction) and left the potatoes significantly richer and more complex-tasting. Even better, as I poked a fork into the velvety pieces, every bit of their deeply browned surface pulled away cleanly from the pan's surface. I was thrilled with this unlikely approach to potato cookery. All I had left to do was jazz up the potatoes' earthy flavor.

BUTTERY FINISH

Tossing a few sprigs of thyme into the pan during the covered simmering step was an easy way to add some herbal depth (thyme is soluble in both water and fat), but garlic was trickier. Though a natural partner with potatoes, garlic burned when added while the spuds browned, and stirring in raw minced garlic at the end led to a flavor that was unpalatably sharp. Instead, I simmered whole cloves with the potatoes to mellow their bite before mincing them into a paste, which I stirred into the finished potatoes. Tasters loved the now-mellow garlic's flavor, not to mention the body that it lent to the sauce. After a few grinds of black pepper, a squeeze of fresh lemon juice, and a sprinkling of minced chives, these spuds had it all: creamy, well-seasoned interiors; flavorful browned exteriors; and a heady sauce. (I also worked up a variation with Dijon mustard and tarragon.) Best of all, I'd done little hands-on cooking and dirtied just one pan.

SIMMERED 'N' SEARED—IN ONE PAN

Our new approach to cooking waxy potatoes produces spuds with super-creamy interiors and nicely browned patinas.

Braise the potatoes in a covered skillet until they soften, then remove the lid to evaporate the liquid. The browning butter eventually gives the potatoes rich color and flavor.

Braised Red Potatoes with Lemon and Chives

SERVES 4 TO 6

Use small red potatoes measuring about 1½ inches in diameter.

1½ pounds small red potatoes, unpeeled, halved
2 cups water
3 tablespoons unsalted butter
3 garlic cloves, peeled
3 sprigs fresh thyme
¾ teaspoon salt
1 teaspoon lemon juice
¼ teaspoon pepper
2 tablespoons minced fresh chives

1. Arrange potatoes in single layer, cut side down, in 12-inch nonstick skillet. Add water, butter, garlic, thyme, and salt and bring to simmer over medium-high heat. Reduce heat to medium, cover, and simmer until potatoes are just tender, about 15 minutes.
2. Remove lid and use slotted spoon to transfer garlic to cutting board; discard thyme. Increase heat to medium-high and vigorously simmer, swirling pan occasionally, until water evaporates and butter starts to sizzle, 15 to 20 minutes. When cool enough to handle, mince garlic to paste. Transfer paste to bowl and stir in lemon juice and pepper.
3. Continue to cook potatoes, swirling pan frequently, until butter browns and cut sides of potatoes turn spotty brown, 4 to 6 minutes longer. Off heat, add garlic mixture and chives and toss to thoroughly coat. Serve immediately.

variation

Braised Red Potatoes with Dijon and Tarragon

Substitute 2 teaspoons Dijon mustard for lemon juice and 1 tablespoon minced fresh tarragon for chives.

THE BENEFITS OF OVERCOOKING WAXY POTATOES

The rules for cooking potatoes seem pretty straightforward: Undercook them and they'll stay intact; overcook them and they'll break down into crumbly bits. But while developing our Braised Red Potatoes with Lemon and Chives recipe, I allowed a batch of halved red potatoes to simmer for 35 minutes (by which point I expected them to be overcooked) and noticed that they not only stayed intact but actually cooked up incredibly creamy and smooth. Had I been wrong about the effects of overcooking potatoes in general, or was there something different about the low-starch red kind?

EXPERIMENT I prepared two batches of my working recipe, one with low-starch red potatoes and another with high-starch russets (quartering these larger spuds) and simmering each for 35 minutes.

RESULTS Just as they had before, the red potatoes held their shape and boasted remarkably silky interiors. The russets, however, broke down and turned crumbly and mushy.

EXPLANATION A little-known but key difference between waxy potatoes (red or new potatoes) and starchy potatoes (russets) is that they contain different ratios of two different starches: amylopectin and amylose. Waxy potatoes contain very little amylose; as they cook, the starch granules in waxy potatoes burst, releasing very sticky amylopectin, which in essence glues the potato structure together, giving the impression of creaminess. In a russet or other starchy potato, there is a higher ratio of the second starch—amylose—which is made up of smaller molecules that are less sticky. Despite the fact that, overall, russets contain more starch than do waxy potatoes (hence they are often described as being "high starch"), russets simply fall apart once overcooked since most of the starch is the less sticky amylose.

ULTIMATE OVEN FRIES

JULIA COLLIN DAVISON, *January/February 2004*

Low fat is never a good excuse for lousy food, and oven fries should be no exception. Abysmal flavor and texture just aren't worth the savings in calories, especially when these "lite" fries taste like overroasted potatoes with thick, leathery crusts and hollow interiors. In other cases, they are limp, whitish, mealy, and bland—a complete failure in all respects. Yet easy and clean oven cooking—as opposed to deep-frying in a pot of hot, splattering oil—is such an engaging proposition that I decided to enlist temporarily in the low-fat army to see if I could make an oven fry worth eating on its own terms. If it didn't have a golden, crisp crust and a richly creamy interior, I was going back to the deep fryer.

I started off by baking five recipes from "healthy" cookbooks. The simplest called for cutting the potatoes into wedges and tossing them with oil before spreading them on a baking sheet. Other recipes called for cutting the potatoes more precisely into squared fries and then took off in different directions, leading me to toss the fries in egg whites, rinse them under running water, soak them in ice water, or steam them on the stovetop before baking. Yet another recipe called for preheating the baking sheet to crisp the crusts (and caused me two forearm burns). Yet no matter what the technique, these recipes produced fries that were either pale, soggy, and hopelessly stuck to the pan or incredibly crusty and tough. Still, aspects of each held promise. Some of the sickly looking examples had creamy interiors, while the tougher ones were perfectly golden and slid effortlessly off the pan. I decided that the place to start was at the beginning: what type of potato to use and how to cut it.

THE RUDIMENTARY FRY

First off, I tested russet, Yukon Gold, and boiling potatoes. The Yukon Gold and boiling potatoes couldn't hold a candle to the russets, with their hearty flavor and facility for turning golden brown. Tasters also liked the ample size and easy preparation of potatoes cut into wedges as opposed to the fussy and wasteful option of trimming potatoes down into squared, fast-food-fry wannabes.

Next I tried baking the fries at 400, 425, 450, 475, and 500 degrees. At lower temperatures, the fries didn't brown sufficiently. The 500-degree oven was a bit too hot and burned the fries at the edges. Baking at 475 degrees was best, but the fries still needed a deeper golden color and a crispier texture. Adjusting the oven rack to the lower-middle position was only moderately helpful, but moving it to the lowest position made for a significant improvement in the fries. The intense heat from the bottom of the oven browned them quickly and evenly, which, in turn, prevented the interiors from overcooking and melding into the crust (thereby becoming the unlikable hollow fry). Lightweight baking sheets can't handle this extreme temperature, so a heavy pan is a must.

Up until now, I had been simply tossing the potatoes with oil, salt, and pepper before spreading them out on the baking sheet. Turning my attention to the amount of oil, I found the differences between 1 and 6 tablespoons to be astounding. Any fewer than 5 tablespoons left some of the fries uncoated and caused them to bake up dry and tough; any more than 5 tablespoons made them disagreeably greasy. Exactly 5 tablespoons, however, ensured that each wedge was evenly coated with oil as it baked. To guarantee even distribution of oil, I found it best to spread 4 tablespoons on the baking sheet and to toss the raw fries with the fifth. Slightly glistening as they emerge from the oven, the fries require a brief drain on paper towels to keep them from tasting oily. Although 5 tablespoons is much less oil than the couple of quarts or more called for when deep-frying potatoes, I felt my oven fries no longer qualified as "low fat." Then again, neither did they qualify as pale, soggy, or dry.

Olive oil tasted slightly bitter and out of place, while the mild flavor of vegetable oil and the slight nuttiness of peanut oil (which we prefer to use when deep-frying) both worked well. Although the fries were now sticking to the pan far less than before, I was still plagued by the occasional stuck-on fry until I discovered one last trick. Rather than tossing the potatoes with salt and pepper, I sprinkled the seasonings over the oiled baking sheet. Acting like little ball bearings, the grains of salt and pepper kept the potatoes from sticking to the pan without getting in the way of browning.

Letting potato wedges soak in hot water for a few minutes before baking ensures creamy centers and crisp exteriors.

SOAKED, STEAMED, AND PAMPERED

Even though I had nailed down the basic method for cooking the fries, they were still beset with crusts that were too thick and interiors that were unappealingly mealy. Wondering what would happen if I steamed the fries before baking them (a technique I'd seen in a few other recipes), I steamed one batch on top of the stove in a steamer basket and another in the oven by covering the baking sheet tightly with foil. Little did I suspect that this seemingly odd method would deliver just the thing I had been after: an oven fry with the creamy, smooth core of an authentic french fry. Steaming on the stovetop had been a counter-clogging, time-consuming affair, but wrapping a baking sheet with foil was easy. The foil trapped the potatoes' natural moisture as they steamed themselves in the oven, and it then came off so the crusts could crisp for the balance of cooking. Five minutes of steaming was just right, turning the dry, starchy centers of the fries to a soft, creamy consistency without interfering with browning.

Now the only problem remaining was the crust. Steaming, although beneficial for the interior, turned the already thick crust even tougher; this was a far cry from the thin, brittle crust of a good french fry. To solve this problem, I decided to try the techniques of rinsing and soaking, which are often employed when making french fries. Rinsing the raw fries under running water made for a slightly more delicate crust, but soaking them for about an hour in cold tap water was pure magic. Slowly turning the water cloudy as they soaked, the fries emerged from the oven with thin, shatteringly crisp crusts and interiors more velvety than any oven fry I had tasted. But perhaps the biggest surprise came when I tried soaking the fries in water at different temperatures: ice cold, cold from the tap, and hot from the tap. The ice water took hours to become cloudy, the cold tap water took about 1 hour, and the hot tap water a convenient 10 minutes, which meant that I could peel, cut, and soak the potatoes in roughly the same time it took to heat up the oven.

With an ultracrisp shell, a velvety smooth core, and a nearly authentic french-fry flavor, these excellent oven fries were nearly indistinguishable from their deep-fried counterparts. I fooled several people in the test kitchen, and I know I won't be heating up 2 quarts of peanut oil the next time I get a hankering for fries.

Oven Fries

SERVES 4

Use a heavy-duty rimmed baking sheet for this recipe because the intense heat of the oven may cause lightweight pans to warp. Nonstick baking sheets work great with this recipe.

3 large russet potatoes, unpeeled, each quartered lengthwise and cut into 10 to 12 evenly sized wedges
5 tablespoons vegetable oil
Salt and pepper

1. Adjust oven rack to lowest position and heat oven to 475 degrees. Place potatoes in large bowl, cover with hot tap water, and let soak for 10 minutes. Meanwhile, coat heavy-duty rimmed baking sheet with ¼ cup oil. Sprinkle baking sheet evenly with ¾ teaspoon salt and ¼ teaspoon pepper.
2. Drain potatoes, spread over paper towels, and thoroughly pat dry. Toss dried potatoes with remaining 1 tablespoon oil. Arrange potatoes with either cut side facing down in single layer on prepared baking sheet. Cover sheet tightly with aluminum foil and bake for 5 minutes.
3. Remove foil and continue to bake until sides of potatoes touching pan are crusty and golden, 15 to 20 minutes, rotating baking sheet after 10 minutes.
4. Using metal spatula, scrape potato wedges loose from pan and flip over. Continue to bake until fries are golden and crisp on both sides, 10 to 15 minutes, rotating pan as needed for even browning. Transfer fries to paper towel–lined baking sheet. Season with salt to taste and serve.

THE POWER OF SOAKING

Experts agree (just ask McDonald's or our test cooks) that russet potatoes are the best variety for frying—either in a vat of bubbling oil or on a baking sheet in the oven. Unlike other potato varieties, russets produce fries with light, ethereal centers, but they are not perfect.

Russets can produce excessively thick crusts and somewhat dry interiors. The thick crust is caused by the browning of simple sugars in the russet, and the best way to remove some of the surface sugar is to soak the potatoes in water. The water has an added benefit. Potato starches gelatinize completely during cooking. The water introduced during soaking improves the creaminess and smoothness by working its way between the strands of gelatin starch. The final result is a fry that has a good surface crunch married to a smooth interior.

A HOT BATH WORKS WONDERS

CUTTING POTATOES INTO WEDGES

1. Quarter potatoes lengthwise.

2. Slice each quarter into 2 or 3 wedges.

EASIER FRENCH FRIES

MATTHEW CARD, *July/August 2009*

While everyone loves crisp, salt-flecked French fries, few of us like to cook them. Sure, the ingredient list is simple—nothing more than potatoes, oil, and salt—but success depends on precision. The traditional method requires rinsing the sliced spuds to remove excess surface starch that can cause sticking, soaking them in ice water to encourage more even cooking, and then deep-frying them in a vat of oil—not once but twice—at incrementally hotter temperatures. Finally, the fries must be drained, blotted, and salted. This process is time-consuming and potentially hazardous, not to mention messy—oil will splatter near and far. When the craving strikes, it's simpler to head out to a local bistro (or, dare I say, McDonald's) than into the kitchen.

Over the years, many cooks have sought to make an "easier" French fry and failed, producing fries that were either limp and soggy or leathery and mealy. But I didn't let this dismal track record stop me. I was determined to find a way to make crisp, slender fries with a tender interior and earthy potato flavor, and without the rigmarole.

OUT OF THE POT, INTO THE OVEN

I began by doing some research to make sure I understood the science behind deep-fried potatoes. Spuds are composed mainly of starch and water. When they hit hot oil, moisture on the surface turns to steam, and oil gradually takes the place of escaping water. As the potato surface becomes hotter, the starch at these outermost layers forms a crust, and the browning reactions that create greater depth of flavor and crispness begin to occur. You typically need very hot oil to ensure a good crisp crust (near 350 degrees), but unless you precook the fries in moderately hot oil first (no more than 325 degrees), the fries crisp long before they can cook through and expel sufficient moisture from their centers. The result: fries that quickly turn limp and soggy once out of the fryer.

This quandary explains double-frying, a method first popularized by Parisian street vendors in the mid-19th century: The potatoes are submerged in moderately hot oil to cook through and then quickly finished in hotter oil to render them golden and crisp.

So-called oven frying—the potatoes are tossed in a small amount of oil and roasted at a high temperature—is a route cooks often take to avoid the mess and bother of deep-frying. But this approach usually calls for thicker wedges of potato that never achieve the crispness of thinner, deep- fried batons. Simply cutting the spuds (I used russets, our favorite for both French fries and oven fries) into thin lengths and roasting them like thicker wedges yielded tough, desiccated, spottily browned results. With enough testing, I could surely achieve a better outcome. But would it be worth it? The dry heat of an oven and a vessel of hot oil are two very different cooking environments (and one can never entirely replicate the other). Even the best oven fry was sure to have a heartier texture than the shatteringly crisp crust of the true fry that I was after. I decided to move on.

UNCOMMON COLD START

I was pondering what to do next when a colleague passed along an impossibly simple-sounding fry recipe from food writer Jeffrey Steingarten. Based on a method attributed to Michelin-starred French über-chef Joël Robuchon, it skips the rinsing and soaking steps, then calls for something even more heretical: The spuds are submerged in a few cups of room-temperature (or "cold") oil, rather than quarts of hot grease, and fried over high heat until browned. I had to try it.

I combined 2½ pounds of ½-inch-thick, peeled russet batons with just enough peanut oil to cover them (6 cups) in a Dutch oven, our preferred vessel for deep frying. I cranked up the heat and about 25 minutes later pulled out golden fries that looked identical to classic fries and tasted pretty darn good, albeit a little tough in texture.

Intrigued, I approached our science editor for more information. He surmised that by starting with cold oil, I gave the potato interior an opportunity to soften and cook through before the exterior started to crisp. And despite the fact that the temperature of the oil never got as hot as in the classic method (I found it maxed out at around 280 degrees), it was still high enough to trigger the same reactions that led to a golden, nicely crisped crust.

Starting our fries in cold oil gives the interiors a chance to soften before the exteriors crisp.

As for the slight toughness, he thought the russet's starchiness might be the culprit. Starchiness is an asset for the typical double-fry method—the starch granules from the outermost layers of the potato swell, burst, and form a glue-like substance that solidifies into a crisp crust. However, with a longer cooking time, too many starch granules were bursting, leading to an overly thick crust that was more leathery than crisp.

If starchy potatoes were the problem, why not start with a less starchy spud? I sliced up a couple pounds of Yukon Golds, which also have more water than russets, and proceeded with my working recipe. They worked well, really well. The exterior was crisp—well within the ballpark of a double-fry fry—with none of the toughness of russets, and the interior was creamy. Clearly, the moister, less starchy composition of the Yukon Golds could better withstand the long cooking time of this approach. Plus, Yukon Golds have such a thin skin that they could be used unpeeled, making the recipe even easier.

I was nearly done, but I still wondered: If my cold-start fries were spending longer in oil than the classic method, why didn't they seem greasier? After cooking fries by each method, I sent the results to a lab—and found that the cold-start fries contained about a third less oil.

Encouraged that these fries were not only easier to make but also lower in fat, I moved on to resolve the one remaining predicament: fries sticking to the bottom of the pot (and each other). Rinsing or soaking the potato batons before they went into the pot had no effect. In the conventional deep-fry approach, sticking can be addressed by stirring the potatoes throughout cooking, but with this new method, the Yukons (which soften significantly during the early part of cooking) were so fragile that any disturbance caused them to break apart. I found that if I didn't touch the spuds for 20 minutes after putting them in the pot, enough of a crust formed so that I could stir them with no ill effect. I also determined that thinner ¼-inch fries were less likely to stick (and tasters liked their higher ratio of crispy crust to creamy interior).

For a final touch, I took a moment to stir together two creamy dipping sauces as alternatives to ketchup. Finally, I had perfect French fries that were remarkably easy to cook in a minimal amount of oil. The only hard part was restraining myself from devouring an entire batch on my own.

Easier French Fries

SERVES 3 TO 4

This recipe will not work with sweet potatoes or russets. We prefer peanut oil for frying, but vegetable oil can be substituted. Flavoring the oil with bacon fat gives the fries a mild, meaty flavor, but omitting it will not affect the final texture of the fries. Use a Dutch oven that holds 6 quarts or more for this recipe. Serve with ketchup or one of our dipping sauces (recipes follow).

6 cups peanut oil
¼ cup bacon fat, strained (optional)
2½ pounds Yukon Gold potatoes, unpeeled, sides squared, and cut lengthwise into ¼-inch-thick fries
Kosher salt

1. Set wire rack in rimmed baking sheet, line with triple layer of paper towels, and set aside. Combine oil, fat, if using, and potatoes in large Dutch oven. Cook over high heat until oil has reached rolling boil, about 5 minutes. Continue to cook, without stirring, until potatoes are limp but exteriors are beginning to firm, about 15 minutes.
2. Using tongs, stir potatoes, gently scraping up any that stick, and continue to cook, stirring occasionally, until golden and crispy, 5 to 10 minutes longer. Using skimmer or slotted spoon, transfer fries to prepared wire rack. Season with salt to taste, and serve immediately.

accompaniments

Belgian-Style Dipping Sauce

MAKES ABOUT ½ CUP

In Belgium, mayonnaise-based dipping sauces for fries are standard. Hot sauce gives this dipping sauce a bit of a kick.

5 tablespoons mayonnaise
3 tablespoons ketchup
1 garlic clove, minced
½ teaspoon hot sauce
¼ teaspoon salt

Whisk all ingredients together in small bowl.

Chive and Black Pepper Dipping Sauce

MAKES ABOUT ½ CUP

5 tablespoons mayonnaise
3 tablespoons sour cream
2 tablespoons chopped fresh chives
1½ teaspoons lemon juice
¼ teaspoon salt
¼ teaspoon pepper

Whisk all ingredients together in small bowl.

KEYS TO EASIER CRISP FRENCH FRIES

The classic technique for French fries involves several labor-intensive steps, including deep-frying twice in quarts of hot oil. Our method calls for just one round of frying and a lot less oil.

1. **LESS OIL** Our fries cook in just 6 cups of oil instead of 2 or 3 quarts.

2. **COLD START** Beginning with room-temperature oil gives the fries time to cook through before their exteriors crisp.

3. **ONE FRY** The potatoes are fried only once, for about 25 minutes, rather than twice.

ULTIMATE FRENCH MASHED POTATOES

STEVE DUNN, *November/December 2016*

In the early 1980s, Parisian chef Joël Robuchon turned mashed potatoes into an utterly sublime experience by employing two hallmarks of French cooking: tireless attention to detail and a whole lot of butter.

His method: Boil 2 pounds of whole unpeeled potatoes and then peel them while hot before passing them through a food mill. Next, incorporate a full pound of cold butter, 1 tablespoon at a time, by beating vigorously with a wooden spoon—a 10-minute, arm-numbing process. Finally, thin the puree with warm milk and pass it repeatedly through a tamis (a flat, drum-shaped ultrafine sieve). Robuchon's painstaking efforts produced the ultimate example of *pommes purée*, ethereally smooth and laden with butter.

Cooking peeled potatoes in a mixture of milk and butter makes this traditionally labor-intensive puree much simpler.

While I love Robuchon's recipe, the scandalous fat content and the drudgery of sieving make it unrealistic for a home cook. But if I could streamline the process and cut back somewhat on the fat, it would be a dish I'd love to make for special occasions.

In France, the puree is made with La Ratte potatoes, medium-starch fingerlings. I used Yukon Golds, a close substitute. For my first go, I cut the amount of butter in half and poured in extra milk to compensate; I used a food mill, but I skipped the tamis.

Was the resulting puree as gloriously smooth as Robuchon's? Perhaps not, but tasters still called it "pillow-soft," so I happily gave up any thoughts of trying to jury-rig a tamis. That said, the potatoes did lack the richness of Robuchon's version. Adding butter back a little at a time, I found that 2½ sticks elevated these spuds to pommes purée status: a rich, silky step above regular mashed potatoes.

Now that I had experienced beating cold butter into potatoes, I was eager to find a way around it. How about melting the butter? Sadly, with so much of it in the mix, the butter and potatoes didn't fully integrate, so the puree was separated and greasy.

Setting that problem temporarily aside, I turned my attention to the literal pain of peeling hot potatoes. I compared a puree made with peeled and diced potatoes (rinsed to remove surface starch) to one made with whole, skin-on spuds. The latter required more than a cup of milk to achieve the proper silken consistency. However, the peeled, diced potatoes absorbed so much cooking water that they could accommodate only ½ cup of milk. The result? A weaker-tasting mash. This got me thinking: Why not peel them and cook them in the milk and butter? I gave it a try, reserving the buttery cooking milk and whisking it into the milled potatoes. The puree was velvety-smooth and tasted rich and buttery. What's more, it was not at all separated or greasy. This was a double victory: no more beating in cold butter or peeling hot potatoes.

Why did this result in a cohesive puree? Potato starch is critical for helping fat emulsify with potatoes, but when peeled potatoes are boiled in water, much of their starch is released and eventually poured down the drain. With too little starch in the mix, the melted butter struggles to form an emulsion with the wet spuds, resulting in a slick, greasy puree. When the potatoes are cooked directly in the milk and butter, none of the released starch gets lost, so it helps the butter emulsify with the water in the potatoes.

In the end, my simplified recipe delivered a rich, silky-smooth mash while allowing me to wave *au revoir* to an exhausted arm.

French-Style Mashed Potatoes (Pommes Purée)

SERVES 8

When serving, keep the richness in mind. A small dollop on each plate should suffice.

2 pounds Yukon Gold potatoes, peeled and cut into 1-inch pieces
20 tablespoons (2½ sticks) unsalted butter
1⅓ cups whole milk
Salt and white pepper

1. Place potatoes in fine-mesh strainer and rinse under cold running water until water runs clear. Set aside to drain.
2. Heat butter, milk, and 1 teaspoon salt in large saucepan over low heat until butter has melted. Add potatoes, increase heat to medium-low, and cook until liquid just starts to boil. Reduce heat to low, partially cover, and gently simmer until paring knife can be slipped into and out of centers of potatoes with no resistance, 30 to 40 minutes, stirring every 10 minutes.
3. Drain potatoes in fine-mesh strainer set over large bowl, reserving cooking liquid. Wipe out saucepan. Return cooking liquid to saucepan and place saucepan over low heat.
4. Set food mill fitted with finest disk over saucepan. Working in batches, transfer potatoes to hopper and process. Using whisk, recombine potatoes and cooking liquid until smooth, 10 to 15 seconds (potatoes should almost be pourable). Season with salt and pepper to taste, and serve immediately.

TRADITIONAL POTATO LATKES

LISA WEISS, *November/December 1997*

For many years, beginning as newlyweds, my husband and I attended the family Passover Seder at his grandmother Rose's house. Often she would serve latkes as a side dish to the roast turkey or braised brisket. Rose would grate the potatoes coarsely by hand, put them through the meat grinder with the onions, add eggs and matzo, and then cook and serve them immediately from the frying pan.

Like Grandma Rose's, the latkes of my dreams are somewhat thick, golden, very crisp on the outside, with a creamy potato center. To figure out how to make these ideal latkes, I had to find the best potato, the best grating method, and the best frying technique.

I began with the potatoes, which can be classified in three categories, according to their starch content. I tested russets, which are high starch; Yukon Golds, which have a medium starch content; and red potatoes, which are low starch. The russet potato pancakes had a pleasantly pronounced potato flavor and a dry texture. The red potato latkes were very creamy, almost gluey on the inside. Pancakes made with he Yukon Golds were an attractive deep yellow-gold color, tasted somewhat sweet and mild, and were creamy in texture, but not gluey or sticky. Everyone who tried the Yukon Gold latkes judged them superior in taste.

Some people feel that latkes made with potatoes grated by hand on a box grater are superior to those made with potatoes grated in a food processor. I tried both methods and found a negligible difference in texture between the two. I did, however, discover a very useful two-step grating procedure.

For the first step, I put the peeled potatoes through the feed tube of the food processor, using the coarse shredding blade. I then removed about half to two-thirds of the shreds and placed them in a separate mixing bowl. Next, I inserted the metal blade, added chunks of onion to the shreds left in the processor bowl, and processed the mixture in spurts until I had a very coarse puree, each piece being no larger than ⅛ inch. Then I combined the pureed potatoes and onions with the shredded potatoes.

This two-step procedure gave me latkes that had some larger shreds that cooked up quite crisp along the perimeters while the center portion was thicker and chewier, like a traditional pancake. This, I discovered, was the best of both latke worlds: crispy and lacy along the edges but still thick and chewy in the middle.

A similar result can be obtained without a food processor. First, grate the potatoes on the largest holes of a box grater and place half of them in a sieve set over a bowl. Then, using a chef's knife, chop the other half of the grated potatoes and all of the onions into a fine ⅛-inch dice. Mix this with the larger shreds and proceed with the recipe.

After I pressed the potatoes in a fine sieve to remove their moisture, I set them aside. I allowed the mixing bowl with the potato water to sit for a minute and then very slowly poured off the potato water that had accumulated. At the bottom of the bowl there was a layer of thick, white potato starch. In all of my tests that were successful, this starch proved helpful in binding the latkes, whether or not flour or matzo meal was added.

THE BIG QUESTION: FRYING

Now I began to test the most crucial part of the whole process—frying. First I tested three different frying mediums: a combination of chicken fat (schmaltz) and vegetable oil; solid vegetable shortening (Crisco); and good-quality liquid vegetable oil.

The chicken fat and vegetable combination was impractical; chicken fat is not readily available. Grandma Rose swore by solid vegetable shortening, but it reached its smoke point much more quickly than the liquid vegetable oil and it was difficult to add more shortening to the frying pan to maintain a consistent depth through several batches. Fresh, high-quality liquid vegetable oil, such as corn, peanut, safflower or a combination, proved to be the perfect oil for frying latkes.

I tried cooking my latkes in several depths of oil, from ½ inch to only ¹⁄₁₆ inch, and I found that more oil does not necessarily result in oilier pancakes, if the oil is at the right temperature. It is much easier to regulate the temperature of the oil if you have at least ¼ inch of oil in the pan, and that was the minimum amount for very thin pancakes. Also, if the oil is deep enough from the start you don't have to add oil in between batches as frequently.

A two-step potato grating technique yields latkes that are crispy around the edges but still creamy in the center, with serious potato flavor.

The temperature of the oil is crucial to frying the perfect latke. However, this is the one category that defies absolute analysis, because it is really difficult to accurately measure the temperature of oil that is only ¼ inch deep. The key is to have the oil really hot, but not smoking, when the latkes go in. The temperature of the oil will decrease with the addition of more batter, but should be kept at a constant lively bubble throughout the cooking of all the pancakes. When the oil is hot enough to start frying, it begins to shimmer on the surface and appears kind of wavy. If it is smoking, it's too hot and the heat should be turned down. I tested the oil initially by dropping in about a teaspoon of batter and observing how quickly it cooked. If it browned in under a minute, the oil was too hot. Two minutes was just about right.

HOLD AND FREEZE? YES!

With every batch of latkes I made, I held some in a 200-degree oven and tried a bite every 5 to 10 minutes. With every bite after the first one, the latkes tasted progressively more old and chewy. I concluded that you

cannot hold latkes for more than 10 minutes at the most. They may still be hot, but the taste diminishes and the texture deteriorates so much that after all the trouble you have gone to preparing them, you might as well have chosen something else to cook.

I did discover, however, that latkes that have been left to cool at room temperature for a few hours and then reheated in a 375-degree oven for about 5 minutes are the next best thing to freshly fried.

I also reserved some of my good latke batches for the freezer. I placed them on a parchment-lined baking sheet and allowed them to freeze for about 15 minutes before I placed them in zipper-lock freezer bags. When I was ready to serve the latkes, I reheated them on a baking sheet in the middle of a 375-degree oven for about 8 minutes per side. All my tasters agreed that there was only a slight difference in quality compared to the freshly fried.

ONION'S SULFUR PREVENTS BROWNING

Traditional cooks have always sworn that alternating the grating of potatoes with onions helped to prevent the potatoes from darkening. This was one theory that proved true: Potatoes grated alone darkened much faster than those grated with onions. Browning occurs because, as potato cells are exposed to air after slicing, certain enzymes add oxygen to phenol compounds found in the potato cells. This process creates a harmless but unsightly brown pigment known as melanin.

There are a number of ways to retard this browning, including cooking, coating the cut surfaces with acid such as lemon juice, or covering the cut food with an airtight coating of plastic wrap. Commercial processing plants often use certain sulfur compounds to prevent browning because these compounds inhibit the action of the enzymes that cause browning. Onions, as it turns out, contain several of these sulfur compounds, which not only lend onions their distinct odor, but also act to prevent browning of any cut fruits or vegetables that the onions come into contact with.

Thick And Creamy Potato Latkes

MAKES APPROXIMATELY 14 (3-INCH) PANCAKES

We prefer Yukon Gold potatoes here but russet potatoes will also work. Matzo meal is a traditional binder, though we found that the texture of the pancakes does not suffer without it. Applesauce and sour cream are classic accompaniments for potato latkes.

2 pounds Yukon Gold or russet potatoes, peeled
1 onion, cut into 8 wedges
1 large egg
4 scallions, minced
3 tablespoons minced fresh parsley
2 tablespoons matzo meal (optional)
Salt and pepper
1 cup vegetable oil

1. Grate potatoes in food processor fitted with coarse shredding blade. Place half of grated potatoes in fine-mesh strainer set over bowl and reserve. Fit food processor with steel blade, add onions, and pulse with remaining potatoes until coarsely chopped, 5 or 6 pulses. Mix with reserved potato shreds and press against sieve to drain as much liquid as possible into bowl below. Let potato liquid sit until starch settles to bottom, about 1 minute. Pour off liquid, leaving starch in bowl. Add egg and whisk to combine, then mix in potato mixture; scallions; parsley; matzo meal, if using; and salt and pepper to taste, into starch.
2. Set wire rack in rimmed baking sheet and line with triple layer of paper towels; set aside. Pour oil into 12-inch skillet to depth of ¼ inch and heat over medium-high heat until shimmering. Gently squeeze ¼ cup potato mixture to remove excess liquid, shape into ½-inch-thick disk, and place in oil. Press gently with nonstick spatula to compact latke; repeat until 5 latkes are in skillet.
3. Maintaining heat so fat bubbles around latke edges, fry until golden brown on bottom and edges, about 3 minutes. Using spatula, flip latkes and continue frying until golden brown all over, about 3 minutes more. Transfer to prepared wire rack to drain. Repeat with remaining potato mixture, returning oil to medium-high heat between each batch and replacing oil after every second batch. Season with salt and pepper to taste, and serve immediately.

GETTING LATKES TO STAY TOGETHER

Removing most of the potatoes' moisture is essential for cohesive latkes, but we reserve some of the starch to help bind our pancakes together.

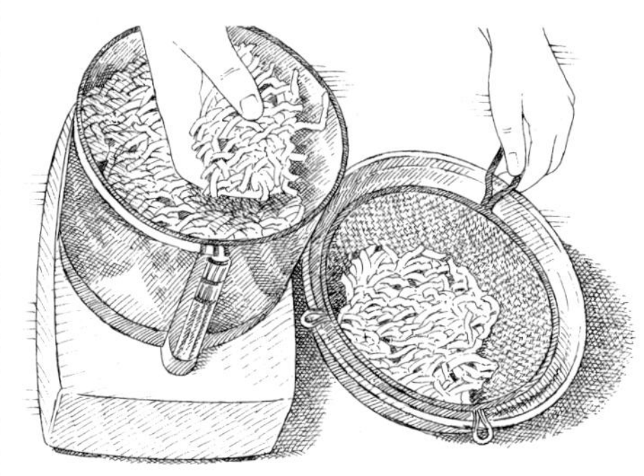

1. Shred potatoes using food processor and set half in fine-mesh strainer. Pulse remaining potatoes with onions, then transfer to strainer with reserved potatoes.

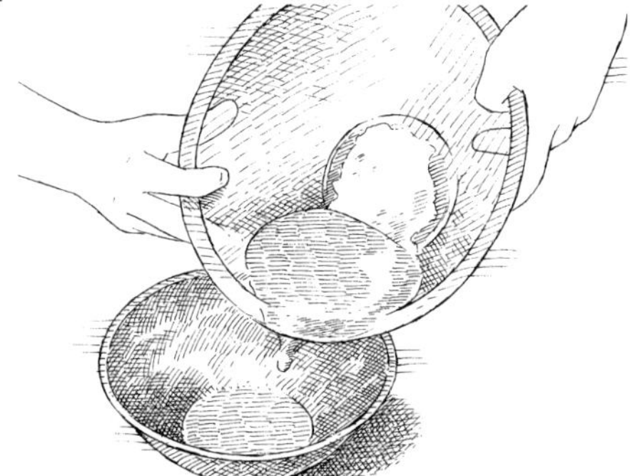

2. Press potato-onion mixture to release as much liquid as possible, then let liquid sit for 1 minute so starch settles. Pour off liquid, reserving starch.

FRENCH POTATO SALAD

REBECCA HAYS WITH MEG SUZUKI, *July/August 2002*

American-style potato salad, thickly dressed with mayonnaise and sweet pickle relish, is archetypal picnic fare and will always have a place on summer tables. But I've cooked (and eaten) piles of it over the years, and these days I yearn for something lighter and fresher to serve with grilled fish, chicken, and even meat. In my mind, French potato salad is just the ticket. Having little in common with its American counterpart, French potato salad is served warm or at room temperature and is composed of sliced potatoes glistening with olive oil, white wine vinegar, and plenty of fresh herbs.

I expected quick success with this seemingly simple recipe—how hard could it be to boil a few potatoes and toss them in vinaigrette? I sliced the hot potatoes, dressed them while they were still warm (warm potatoes are more absorbent than cool ones), and then served them up to my tasters. The salad looked mangled, as the warm potatoes consistently broke apart upon slicing. I had chosen not to peel the potatoes for the sake of convenience and beauty, but the potato skins inevitably tore, leaving unsightly streaks. And the salad didn't taste much better than it looked. Despite an assertively seasoned vinaigrette, the potatoes themselves were uniformly bland. Another irksome point was that it was hard to tell when the potatoes were done. Unevenly sized potatoes made it difficult to avoid some over- or undercooked potatoes in the finished dish. This wasn't going to be as easy as I thought.

TATTERED TATERS

My first task was to put a stop to homely salads made from jagged, broken potatoes with ripped skins. I tried shocking the whole potatoes after cooking, slicing the potatoes with a serrated knife, and starting the potatoes in boiling instead of cold water, none of which worked. It was proving impossible to slice a just-cooked potato without having it fall apart, and I kept burning my fingers on the hot potatoes.

Up to this point, I was using low starch/high moisture red potatoes, the most common choice for salads. I backtracked, wondering if russet, all-purpose, or Yukon Golds would be better-behaved. This lead was a dead end. None of the potatoes held together when sliced, nor could they compete with the sweet, earthy flavor and (potentially) good looks of the red potatoes.

Slicing the potatoes before cooking, then dressing them while they're hot are the keys to this bistro classic.

I reevaluated my cooking technique. I had been boiling the potatoes whole, the idea being that the skins prevent potato starch from leaching out into the water, and slicing them while warm. On a whim, I sliced some potatoes before cooking. This, surprisingly, did the trick. The potato slices emerged unbroken and with their skins intact. They had a clean (not starchy) taste, were evenly cooked, and held together perfectly, unlike those that had been cooked whole before being sliced. This one simple change in technique eliminated the frustrating (and sometimes painful) task of slicing hot potatoes. Plus, I now had no need to find uniformly sized potatoes to ensure even cooking. (I just needed to cut the potatoes into slices of uniform thickness.) I also found I could perfectly season the cut potatoes while they cooked by adding a hefty amount of salt to the cooking water.

DRESSING UP

I shifted my focus to the vinaigrette and its usual suspects: olive oil, white wine vinegar, herbs, mustard, minced onion, chicken stock, and white wine. Because my initial tests had produced relatively dull salads, I decided to experiment with each component until I found a surefire way to pump up the flavor. The first improvement came by using slightly more vinegar, since these bland potatoes could handle extra acid. I especially loved the sharp flavor notes added by champagne vinegar. As for the olive oil, extra-virgin worked well. However, my tasters rejected expensive fruity olive oils for their overpowering nature.

I liked the extra moisture and layer of complexity that chicken stock and wine added (salads made strictly with oil and vinegar were a tad dry), but it seemed wasteful to uncork a bottle only to use a few tablespoons. I found a solution to this problem and a revelation when I consulted Julia Child's *The Way to Cook* (1989). She suggests adding some of the potato cooking water to the vinaigrette, a quick and frugal solution that also adds plenty of potato flavor and a nice touch of saltiness. Two teaspoons of Dijon mustard and a sprinkle of freshly ground black pepper perked things up, while the gentle assertiveness of one minced shallot and a blanched garlic clove (raw garlic was too harsh) added even more depth. As for the fresh herbs, I tested chives, dill, basil, parsley, tarragon, and chervil. But an inherently French *fines herbes* mixture seemed appropriate: Chives, parsley, tarragon, and chervil make up this classic quartet with anise undertones.

The last problem was how to toss the cooked, warm potatoes with the vinaigrette without damaging the slices. The solution was simple: I laid the potatoes in a single layer on a baking sheet and then poured the vinaigrette over them. Spreading out the potatoes also allowed them to cool off a bit, preventing residual cooking and potential mushiness. While I waited for the vinaigrette to soak into the potatoes, I had just enough time to chop the herbs and shallots before sprinkling them on the finished salad. Adding the herbs just before serving guarded against wilting and darkening.

French Potato Salad with Dijon and Fines Herbes

SERVES 4 TO 6

If fresh chervil isn't available, substitute an additional ½ tablespoon of minced parsley and an additional ½ teaspoon of tarragon. Use small red potatoes measuring 1 to 2 inches in diameter.

2 pounds small red potatoes, unpeeled, sliced ¼ inch thick
2 tablespoons salt
1 garlic clove, peeled and threaded on skewer
¼ cup extra-virgin olive oil
1½ tablespoons white wine vinegar or Champagne vinegar
2 teaspoons Dijon mustard
½ teaspoon pepper
1 small shallot, minced
1 tablespoon minced fresh chervil
1 tablespoon minced fresh parsley
1 tablespoon minced fresh chives
1 teaspoon minced fresh tarragon

1. Place potatoes in large saucepan, add water to cover by 1 inch, and bring to boil over high heat. Add salt, reduce heat to simmer, and cook until potatoes are tender and paring knife can be slipped in and out of potatoes with little resistance, about 6 minutes.

2. While potatoes are cooking, lower skewered garlic into simmering water and blanch for 45 seconds. Run garlic under cold running water, then remove from skewer and mince.

3. Reserve ¼ cup cooking water, then drain potatoes and arrange in tight single layer in rimmed baking sheet. Whisk oil, minced garlic, vinegar, mustard, pepper, and reserved potato cooking water together in bowl, then drizzle over potatoes. Let potatoes sit until flavors meld, about 10 minutes. (Potatoes can be refrigerated for up to 8 hours; return to room temperature before serving.)

4. Transfer potatoes to large bowl. Combine shallot and herbs in small bowl, then sprinkle over potatoes and gently toss to coat using rubber spatula. Serve.

variations

French Potato Salad with Fennel, Tomatoes, and Olives

If desired, chop 1 tablespoon of the fennel fronds and add it to the salad with the parsley.

Omit chervil, chives, and tarragon. Increase parsley amount to 3 tablespoons. Add ½ fennel bulb, sliced thin, 1 cored and chopped tomato, and ¼ cup pitted oil-cured black olives, quartered, to salad with shallots and parsley.

French Potato Salad with Radishes, Cornichons, and Capers

Omit chervil, parsley, chives, and tarragon. Substitute 2 tablespoons minced red onion for shallot. Add 2 thinly sliced red radishes, ¼ cup rinsed capers, and ¼ cup thinly sliced cornichons to salad with onion.

French Potato Salad with Arugula, Roquefort, and Walnuts

Omit herbs and toss dressed potatoes with ½ cup walnuts, toasted and chopped coarse, 1 cup crumbled Roquefort cheese, and 3 ounces baby arugula, torn into bite-size pieces (3 cups) along with shallot in step 4.

DRESSING THE POTATOES

Dressing the potatoes while they're still warm helps them absorb more of the vinaigrette's flavor.

After potatoes have been thoroughly drained, spread them out on rimmed baking sheet and drizzle evenly with vinaigrette.

KEEPING POTATO SALAD SAFE

Mayonnaise has gotten a bad reputation, being blamed for spoiled potato salads and upset stomachs after many summer picnics and barbecues. You may think that switching from a mayonnaise-based dressing to a vinaigrette will protect your potato salad (and your family) from food poisoning. Think again.

The main ingredients in mayonnaise are raw eggs, vegetable oil, and an acid (usually vinegar or lemon juice). The eggs used in commercially made mayonnaise have been pasteurized to kill salmonella and other bacteria. Its high acidity is another safeguard; because bacteria do not fare well in acidic environments, the lemon juice or vinegar inhibits bacterial growth. Mayonnaise, even when homemade, is rarely the problem unless it contains very little acid. It's the potatoes that are more likely to go bad.

The bacteria usually responsible for spoiled potato salad are *Bacillus cereus* and *Staphylococcus aureus* (commonly known as staph). Both are found in soil and dust, and they thrive on starchy, low-acid foods like rice, pasta, and potatoes. If they find their way into your potato salad via an unwashed cutting board or contaminated hands, they can wreak havoc on your digestive system.

Most foodborne bacteria grow well at temperatures between 40 and 140 degrees Fahrenheit. This is known as the temperature danger zone, and if contaminated food remains in this zone for too long, the bacteria can produce enough toxins to make you sick. The U.S. Food and Drug Administration (FDA) recommends refrigerating food within 2 hours of its preparation, or 1 hour if the room temperature is above 90 degrees. Heat from the sun is often what causes the trouble at summer picnics.

Although the high acid content of the vinaigrette for our French potato salad might slow bacteria growth, it's best to play it safe and follow the FDA's guideline. Don't leave the potato salad out for more than 2 hours; promptly refrigerate any leftovers.

WALKAWAY RATATOUILLE

ANNIE PETITO, *July/August 2016*

Ratatouille is a rustic Provençal specialty that transforms late-summer produce—tomatoes, eggplant, zucchini, and bell peppers—by simmering the vegetables, scented with garlic, onion, and herbs, until they have softened into a rich stew. It's a satisfying dish that can be served as an accompaniment or even turned into a light main course by topping it with an egg, sandwiching it between slices of bread, or spooning it over pasta or rice.

The problem with ratatouille boils down to one thing: water. More specifically, each of the primary ingredients contains more than 90 percent water. If all that liquid isn't dealt with somehow, you end up with a wet, pulpy mess of ingredients that are indistinguishable in taste, color, and texture.

To remedy this, many cooks complicate what is already a prep-heavy dish (cutting multiple pounds of vegetables into ¼- or ½-inch pieces is the norm). Techniques like salting, microwaving, and pressing are often used to extract excess moisture. The individual vegetables are then typically sautéed in batches to create some flavorful browning before being simmered to cook off more water.

Recipes that skip these steps and call for simply throwing everything into a pot on the stove fared exactly as I anticipated: They were soggy, mushy, and bland. Surely I could come up with a more hands-off approach that would hold ratatouille to its rustic roots but still deliver complex flavor and tender-yet-firm texture.

OVEN ME TENDER

I definitely wanted to skip any type of pre-treatment, and that meant finding a method that could efficiently draw out moisture during cooking. On the stovetop, the heat must be kept low in order to avoid burning the food on the bottom of the pot, but this also means that liquid does not readily evaporate. How about using the oven, where the ambient dry heat would evaporate moisture with less risk of burning?

Roasting the vegetables in batches on baking sheets would be almost as bothersome as sautéing each vegetable individually, so I limited myself to using only a Dutch oven and started with the least amount of chopping that I thought I could get away with. I cut onions, plum tomatoes (meatier than round types, with less watery gel), bell peppers, and zucchini into quarters and an eggplant into eighths, figuring that large pieces would retain their shape and texture better than small ones. I tossed the vegetables with olive oil, salt, and pepper (I'd fiddle with other seasonings later) and slid the Dutch oven, uncovered, into a 400-degree oven. Sure enough, after about 2 hours, the moisture had mostly evaporated and the top layer of vegetables was deeply caramelized. But I wasn't done yet.

The secret to great yet easy ratatouille is to overcook some of the vegetables, barely cook the others—and let the oven do the work.

It had taken so long for any significant amount of moisture to evaporate from the vegetables that some of them (like the zucchini) were blown out and overcooked. What's more, any intact pieces were unwieldy to eat. I reduced the vegetable size to more manageable 1-inch chunks, which would cook more quickly but still wouldn't require too much time at the cutting board. I also decided to jump-start the cooking of the onions on the stovetop, which would cut down the oven time and would give me the opportunity to sauté some smashed garlic cloves before I stirred in the remaining vegetables. These procedural tweaks cut the oven time in half, but even after I stirred partway through, the more delicate vegetables were overdone by the time any browning happened.

The eggplant had even begun to disintegrate, leaving its soft pulp and slivers of peel behind. That was unacceptable. Or was it? If eggplant cooks long enough, its flesh becomes downright silky. Perhaps, I thought, I should embrace eggplant's texture and allow it to break down completely. It just might make for a creamy sauce to unify the stew.

COOKING IN STAGES

I decided to peel the eggplant to create a smooth sauce with no distractions, and since tomatoes supply so much juice, I added them (also peeled) to the pot with the sautéed onions, garlic, and herbs and seasonings, knowing that their moisture would evaporate for even more concentrated flavor. I would hold the quicker-cooking zucchini and bell peppers back until near the end of the cooking time.

I put my plan into action. After 40 minutes in the oven, the eggplant, onions, and tomatoes were so meltingly soft that they yielded to gentle smashing with a potato masher, turning them into the velvety sauce that I had envisioned. What's more, most of the onions and eggplant had become so deeply browned and full of concentrated flavor that I wouldn't need to worry about getting color on the zucchini and bell peppers. Giving these later additions just a short time in the pot would maintain some pleasing bite to contrast with the smooth sauce.

I stirred in the zucchini and bell peppers and returned the pot to the oven for 20 minutes. When I checked, a few pieces of zucchini were still on the cusp of being done, but rather than return the pot to the oven, I simply covered it and let it rest for 10 minutes. Now a paring knife just slipped in and out of the pieces.

I noticed that the pot had a dark ring of fond around the inside edge. When left to sit with the lid on, the steam moistened the fond, so I could easily scrape the browned bits back into the ratatouille, making for a simple but robust flavor boost. For spice and heady fragrance, I also added red pepper flakes, a bay leaf, and herbes de Provence (a French blend usually consisting of dried basil, fennel, lavender, marjoram, rosemary, savory, and thyme). In fact, the dish now tasted so rich that I felt that some freshening up was in order.

The intensely caramelized, almost jammy quality of the ratatouille needed a touch of acid. Although entirely untraditional, a splash of sherry vinegar helped wake up the flavors of the sweet vegetables. Finally, just before serving, I stirred in chopped fresh basil and parsley and gave the stew a glossy drizzle of extra-virgin olive oil. And there it was, a ratatouille that was simultaneously flavorful and easy to make.

SEASON AS YOU GO

To give salt time to migrate into food for even seasoning and fully developed flavor, don't wait until the end of cooking to season. Here, we add salt each time we put vegetables in the pot.

SECRETS TO FASTER, MORE FLAVORFUL RATATOUILLE

Classic ratatouille recipes call for cutting vegetables into small pieces, pretreating them to remove moisture, and then cooking them in batches on the stovetop. Our streamlined oven method eliminates the need for batch cooking and pretreatments—plus, it tastes better.

STREAMLINE THE PREP Chop the onions into chunks and smash the garlic cloves instead of mincing them. A brief stovetop sauté cuts down on oven time.

GIVE SOME VEGETABLES A HEAD START Add the eggplant and tomatoes and then transfer the pot to the oven where moisture evaporates and flavors concentrate.

MAKE AN EGGPLANT MUSH Cook eggplant long enough and it becomes soft and creamy. We exploit this trait by mashing the eggplant (along with tomatoes and onions) into a velvety sauce.

FINISH WITH FRESHNESS Added to the pot toward the end of cooking, zucchini and bell peppers maintain freshness and bite.

Walkaway Ratatouille

SERVES 6 TO 8

This dish is best prepared using ripe, in-season tomatoes. If good tomatoes are not available, substitute one 28-ounce can of whole peeled tomatoes that have been drained and chopped coarse. Ratatouille can be served as an accompaniment to meat or fish. It can also be served on its own with crusty bread, topped with an egg, or over pasta or rice. This dish can be served warm, at room temperature, or chilled.

⅓ cup plus 1 tablespoon extra-virgin olive oil
2 large onions, cut into 1-inch pieces
8 large garlic cloves, peeled and smashed
Salt and pepper
1½ teaspoons herbes de Provence
¼ teaspoon red pepper flakes
1 bay leaf
1½ pounds eggplant, peeled and cut into 1-inch pieces
2 pounds plum tomatoes, peeled, cored, and chopped coarse
2 small zucchini, halved lengthwise and cut into 1-inch pieces
1 red bell pepper, stemmed, seeded, and cut into 1-inch pieces
1 yellow bell pepper, stemmed, seeded, and cut into 1-inch pieces
2 tablespoons chopped fresh basil
1 tablespoon minced fresh parsley
1 tablespoon sherry vinegar

1. Adjust oven rack to middle position and heat oven to 400 degrees. Heat ⅓ cup oil in Dutch oven over medium-high heat until shimmering. Add onions, garlic, 1 teaspoon salt, and ¼ teaspoon pepper and cook, stirring occasionally, until onions are translucent and starting to soften, about 10 minutes. Add herbes de Provence, pepper flakes, and bay leaf and cook, stirring frequently, for 1 minute. Stir in eggplant and tomatoes. Sprinkle with ½ teaspoon salt and ¼ teaspoon pepper and stir to combine. Transfer pot to oven and cook, uncovered, until vegetables are very tender and spotty brown, 40 to 45 minutes.
2. Remove pot from oven and, using potato masher or heavy wooden spoon, smash and stir eggplant mixture until broken down to sauce-like consistency. Stir in zucchini, bell peppers, ¼ teaspoon salt, and ¼ teaspoon pepper and return to oven. Cook, uncovered, until zucchini and bell peppers are just tender, 20 to 25 minutes.
3. Remove pot from oven, cover, and let stand until zucchini is translucent and easily pierced with tip of paring knife, 10 to 15 minutes. Using wooden spoon, scrape any browned bits from sides of pot and stir back into ratatouille. Discard bay leaf. Stir in 1 tablespoon basil, parsley, and vinegar. Season with salt and pepper to taste. Transfer to large platter, drizzle with remaining 1 tablespoon oil, sprinkle with remaining 1 tablespoon basil, and serve.

BETTER BROWNING IN THE OVEN

In a liquid-y dish like ratatouille, the vegetables can brown only when most of the moisture has evaporated. That's because the exteriors of the vegetables must rise beyond the boiling point of water (212 degrees) to about 300 degrees, the temperature at which browning occurs. On the stovetop, this can take a long time if the heat must be kept low to avoid scorching. However, in the dry, ambient heat of the oven, evaporation and subsequent browning happen quickly, especially since we sauté the onions and garlic in the pot on the stovetop first, preheating the pot before it goes into the oven. Another benefit of oven cookery is that as moisture evaporates, a dark, flavorful fond develops around the inside edge of the pot. Such a fond would take much longer to develop over the low flame of the stovetop.

HOW TO COOK ACORN SQUASH

REBECCA HAYS, *September/October 2004*

The popularity of acorn squash has always mystified me. After what seems like eons in the oven, it inevitably lands on the table with little flavor and a dry, grainy texture. Perhaps the appeal resides in its spherical shape—the hollowed-out halves are perfect receptacles for melted butter and sugar—but this feature doesn't make up for the dry, cottony flesh. Yet acorn squash can be outright delicious when prepared properly. At its best, it is characterized by a sweet, almost nutty taste and moist, smooth flesh. Could I solve this culinary challenge and do it relatively quickly?

HIGH-TECH(NIQUE)

Most cookbook authors recommend baking acorn squash in a covered dish, while a few suggest somewhat unconventional methods, including steaming, boiling, and braising. Steamed and boiled chunks of peeled squash cooked quickly but turned out waterlogged. Braising resulted in a soggy, stringy texture. The baked squash was just as expected: dry, very dry.

We use the microwave and the broiler to get acorn squash with tender, sweet flesh and flavorful browning in only 20 minutes.

I was running out of hope until I found a recipe that suggested microwaving, a cooking method we usually avoid here in the test kitchen because of its finicky nature and its poor powers of flavor enhancement. Nonetheless, I shoved aside my concerns and nuked a couple of squashes. When I tasted a forkful, I became a believer. The texture was tender and silky-smooth, with nary a trace of dryness or stringiness. I was so surprised (and pleased) with the results that I repeated the test once, and then again. When subsequent tries produced identical outcomes, I seemed to have no choice but to use the microwave to cook the squash.

Hammering out the details was easy: Microwave on high power for 20 minutes (give or take a few, depending on the model used), and the squash is perfectly cooked. It was best to halve and seed the squashes before cooking; whole pierced squashes cooked unevenly. Last, I learned that when added before cooking, salt seemed to better permeate the squash. Now I had a 20-minute recipe and vastly improved results.

Why was the microwave such a success? As microwaves (which are electromagnetic), enter food, water molecules in the food begin to vibrate, and this activity generates heat evenly and efficiently, for quick cooking. In effect, the microwave was steaming the squash in its own juices.

SWEET STUFF

Finally, I tackled the flavoring for the squash. My colleagues wanted a classic butter and sugar glaze. Dark brown sugar is the most common choice and was named the best sweetener. I limited the amount of sugar to 3 tablespoons—enough to provide ample sweetness but not so much that I'd be tempted to serve the squash with a scoop of vanilla ice cream. An equal amount of butter made the best complement.

One problem remained. The squash was lacking the sticky, caramelized glaze that forms when it is baked. Passing the buttered and sugared squash halves under the broiler for a few minutes after microwaving was the way to go. Many cooks have the habit of simply placing a pat of butter in each cavity and then adding a coating of sugar, but a better method was to melt the two ingredients, along with a pinch of salt, on the stovetop for a smooth, cohesive mixture.

By using the microwave and broiler, I was now able to produce squash with great texture and flavor. Not bad for 20 minutes' work.

ARE ALL MICROWAVES CREATED EQUAL?

Because every cook's microwave oven varies in size, wattage, type, and age, I was concerned about writing a recipe using equipment whose power is difficult to quantify. Would microwaving on "high" power produce consistent results among different machines? I was doubtful.

The amount of microwave energy absorbed by a food is a function of the cooking time, power (watts), portion size, and the amount of water in the food to be cooked (the energy produced by the microwave is absorbed primarily by water). Roughly speaking, the more watts, the faster food will cook. Theoretically, a microwave with 1,000 watts of power would cook the same volume of food twice as quickly as a machine with 500 watts.

To gauge real-life differences, I sent armfuls of acorn squashes and bags of microwave popcorn (an easy gauge of cooking power) home with my colleagues to cook in their microwaves. When they reported back, I found that differences in cooking times correlated roughly—though not reliably—to the power of the microwave used. For example, popcorn took 3 minutes and 45 seconds in the only 700-watt microwave tested, while the same brand of popcorn was ready in just 2 minutes in several 1,100-watt models. The same thing held true for squash, with cooking times running from a low of 15 minutes in several powerful microwaves to a high of 27 minutes in the same weak 700-watt microwave.

What to do, then, when cooking the squash in your microwave? Check the label inside the machine (or your owner's manual) to determine its wattage. If your microwave runs on fewer than 900 watts of power, you will likely need to increase the cooking time by a few minutes. If you own a high-wattage machine (more than 1,100 watts), you may need to decrease the cooking time. That said, it always pays to use your senses, not a timer, to judge when food is ready.

Acorn Squash with Brown Sugar

SERVES 4

Squashes smaller than 1½ pounds will likely cook faster, so begin checking for doneness a few minutes early. Conversely, larger squashes will take slightly longer. However, keep in mind that the cooking time is largely dependent on the microwave. If microwaving the squash in Pyrex, the manufacturer recommends adding water to the dish (or bowl) prior to cooking. If you are cooking the squash in a bowl, you will need one that holds about 4 quarts.

2 acorn squashes (1½ pounds each), halved pole to pole and seeded
Salt
3 tablespoons unsalted butter
3 tablespoons packed dark brown sugar

1. Sprinkle squash halves with salt and place cut sides down in 13 by 9-inch baking dish or arrange halves in large bowl so that cut sides face out. If using Pyrex, add ¼ cup water to dish or bowl. Cover and microwave until squash flesh is very tender and offers no resistance when poked with paring knife, 15 to 25 minutes. Remove baking dish or bowl from microwave and set on clean, dry surface (avoid damp or cold surfaces).

2. While squashes are cooking, adjust oven rack 6 inches from broiler element and heat broiler. Melt butter, brown sugar, and ⅛ teaspoon salt in small saucepan over low heat, whisking occasionally, until combined.

3. Using tongs, transfer cooked squash halves, cut side up, to rimmed baking sheet. Spoon portion of butter mixture onto each squash half. Broil until brown and caramelized, 5 to 8 minutes, rotating baking sheet as necessary and removing squash halves as they are done. Serve immediately.

variation

Acorn Squash with Rosemary–Dried Fig Compote

While squash is cooking, combine 1 cup orange juice, 4 chopped dried black figs, 1 tablespoon packed dark brown sugar, ½ teaspoon minced fresh rosemary, ¼ teaspoon pepper, and ⅛ teaspoon salt in small saucepan. Simmer over medium-high heat, stirring occasionally, until syrupy and liquid is reduced to about 3 tablespoons, 15 to 20 minutes. Stir in 1 tablespoon unsalted butter. Substitute fig compote for butter mixture.

HOW TO BUY AND STORE ACORN SQUASH

Acorn squashes can vary significantly in quality, depending on where they are purchased, how they are stored, and how old they are. They may be richly flavored, with deep, golden orange flesh, or spongy and pale.

SEASON Acorn squashes are domestically in season from July through November. When purchased in the off-season, they are usually imported from Mexico and are likely to be more expensive. Squashes that had spent weeks in transit cooked up dehydrated, fibrous, and pasty in the test kitchen.

WEIGHT Each squash should be hard and heavy for its size, an indication that it contains a lot of moisture and has not been sitting on the supermarket produce shelf for weeks.

COLOR The most popular variety of acorn squash is green, though gold and white varieties are spottily available. Gold or orange tinges on the rind of green squashes are not indicators of ripeness but rather a mark of where the fruit touched the ground during growing (and was therefore untouched by sunlight).

STORAGE Acorn squashes should be stored at cool room temperature, not in the refrigerator. When we stored squashes for a few weeks in the refrigerator, chill damage set in, causing the flavor and texture to deteriorate.

GETTING SQUASH READY TO MICROWAVE

If your microwave is spacious enough to accommodate it, a 13 by 9-inch microwave-safe baking dish works well for containing the squash halves. Otherwise, a large, wide microwave-safe bowl can be used. If using a bowl, position the halves with cut sides facing out.

CUTTING ACORN SQUASH

1. Position knife on rind of squash.

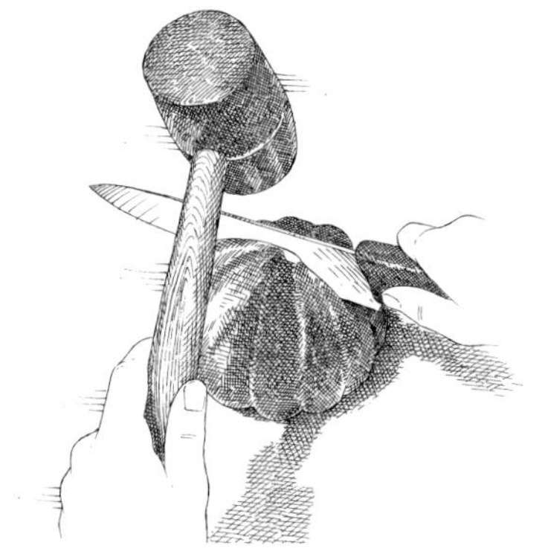

2. Strike back of knife with rubber mallet to drive knife into squash. Continue to hit knife with mallet until knife cuts through squash.

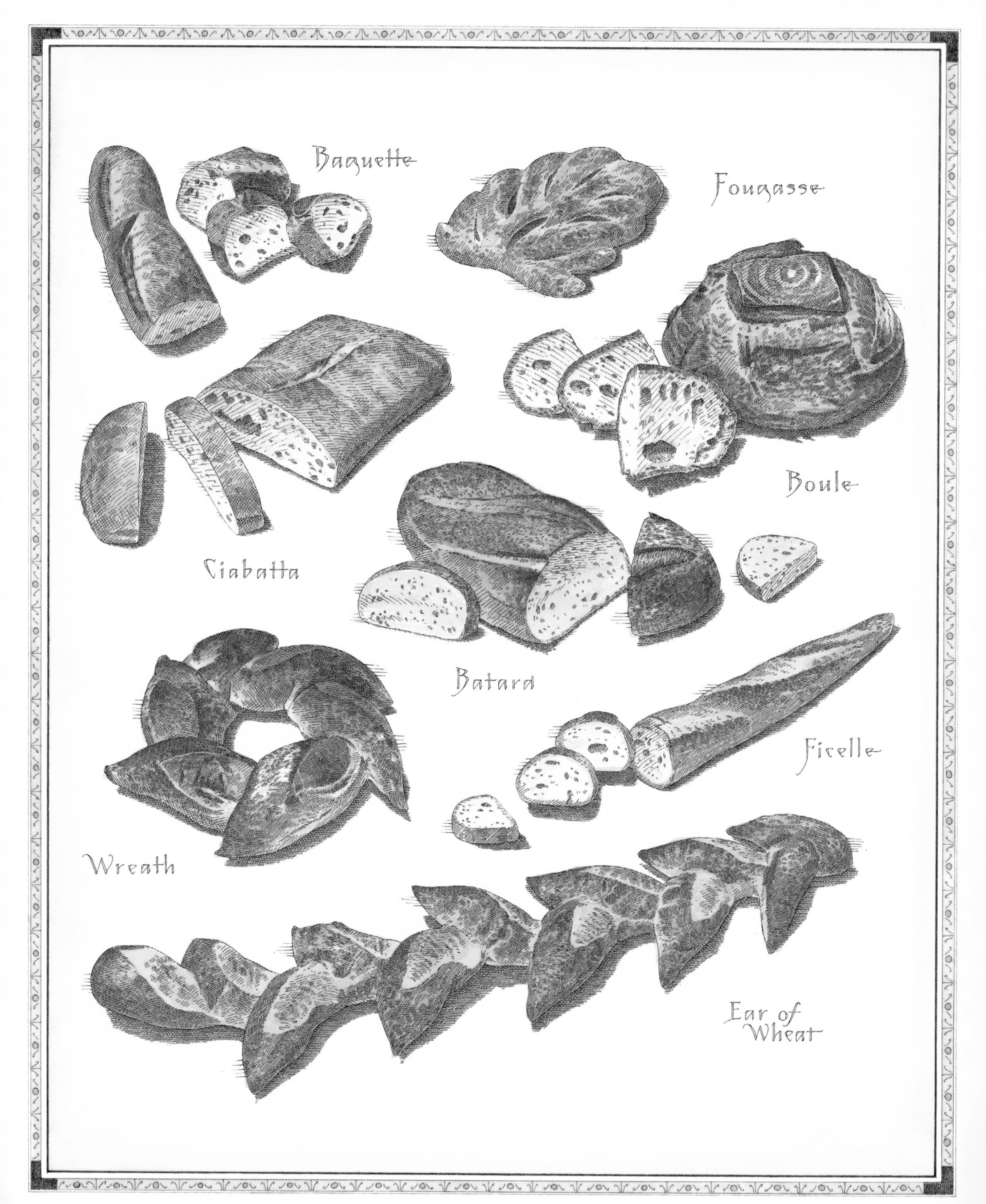
Baguette
Fougasse
Boule
Ciabatta
Batard
Ficelle
Wreath
Ear of Wheat

BREADS

ULTIMATE FLAKY BISCUITS

ANDREW JANJIGIAN, *September/October 2015*

From the enormous soft and fluffy Southern cat head to the simple drop, I love biscuits of all kinds. But my current obsession is a specimen I've recently found in several restaurants. It's crisp and crunchy on the outside but tender and light as air inside, with flaky strata that peel apart like sheets of buttery paper in a way that rivals a croissant. No, this is not an everyday biscuit; it's an ethereal, once-in-a-while treat rich enough that there's no need to spread on any extra butter, just a slathering of jam, if that. But when I tried recipes billed as "rich and tender flaky biscuits," very few lived up to the promise, and those that did required a lengthy process of folding the dough and letting it rest that was as much work as making croissants. I set out to see what I could do to produce my ideal flaky biscuit with considerably less fuss.

A FLAKY FOUNDATION

Despite the failures, those early tests did help sort out a few things. First, I'd use only butter rather than a mixture of butter and shortening. Shortening lacks flavor, and I also found that it inhibited the formation of distinct layers. As in pie crusts, leaving distinct pieces of fat in the dough (what many recipes refer to as "pea-size" pieces) is key to producing flakiness. As the biscuits cook, the bits of fat melt into the dough, leaving small voids. Then, as the water in the dough turns to steam, it expands these gaps and creates layers. The problem with shortening is that it has a soft texture and tends to combine with the flour rather than stay distinct like butter. Most recipes I found called for 2 to 4 tablespoons of fat per cup of flour; I suspected that I could squeeze in more. I settled on 16 tablespoons butter to 3 cups flour—a little more than 5 tablespoons per cup.

As for the type of flour, unlike ultratender, fluffy Southern-style biscuits that demand a specialty low-protein flour (generally 7 to 8 percent) like White Lily, my early tests confirmed that flaky biscuits are better off made with all-purpose flour. This is because all-purpose flour has a little more protein (10 to 12 percent), and when combined with water, the protein in flour produces gluten. The more protein, the more gluten, which translates to a biscuit dough with more strength that can bake up with distinct, structured layers rather than cakey and fluffy. I tried bread flour (which is closer to 13 percent protein) but found that it created an overly strong gluten network that produced tough biscuits. The best results came from using King Arthur all-purpose flour, which is 12 percent protein.

Grated butter, a series of folds, and a brief rest in the fridge produce the flakiest, most tender biscuits.

I also determined that I'd use buttermilk rather than milk for its distinctive tang, a touch of sugar for complexity, a little baking soda to enhance browning and add some lift, and, finally, baking powder for additional lift. As for shaping, I settled on square biscuits. Round biscuits were pretty, but they left too much scrap dough and rerolling those scraps produced biscuits that were tough. Shaping the dough into a square slab and then cutting that into squared-off biscuits was fast and meant no rerolling—and no waste.

CUT THE FAT

I moved on to the heart of the matter: mixing and shaping. Many biscuit recipes require that you spend a lot of effort getting the butter into small, even, pea-size pieces by cutting it into the dry ingredients using a dough cutter, a pair of knives, a food processor, or your hands. The problem with most of these approaches is that it's far too easy to over- or underdo it, both of which hamper flakiness. I found that the most consistent method was to grate the butter using the large holes of a box grater, a trick I picked up from our recipe for Blueberry Scones.

Of course, the effort is moot if these shreds of butter soften during mixing and shaping. To avoid that, I froze the butter for 30 minutes before grating it. And to get around the awkwardness of grating the stubs, I saved the last tablespoon of each stick to melt and brush on the tops of the biscuits just before baking them, which would improve crisping and browning.

BETWEEN THE FOLDS

The grated butter helped create some layering but not nearly as much as I was after. In pie dough, leaving the butter in small pieces is sufficient to get the right flaky effect, but that's because pie dough contains far less liquid (and far more butter) and is rolled out thin, a pair of factors that inherently smears the butter into thin sheets among floury layers. But in a wet, minimally rolled-out slab of biscuit dough, the butter pieces just float randomly in the mixture like raisins in a muffin batter. And that's where folding comes in. This process starts with rolling out the dough into a large, thin rectangle and then folding it into thirds like a letter. You then press the dough together to seal the package tightly, turn it 90 degrees, and repeat. The special thing about folding dough is that the technique works by multiplication, not addition. Each fold doesn't simply give you one more layer; it creates an exponentially greater number of layers because it's a trifold every single time, not a single fold.

Folding my biscuit dough, at least in the early stages, was a messy affair: It started out shaggy and crumbly—anything but a cohesive mass—and it seemed like I wasn't really doing anything useful. But slowly and surely, the dry bits and the wet bits came together; by the fourth fold, the process was pretty tidy. The interesting thing was, I found in subsequent tests that the messier—and less mixed—the dough was in the beginning, the better. Even in those first few messy "folds," the slivers of butter were getting pressed and stretched into thinner and thinner sheets among clumps of wet and dry dough. If I mixed the dough in the bowl to the point where it was uniform before I folded it (which is what most recipes call for) or if I added more liquid to help bring the dough together, I ended up with layers that were less defined.

Some recipes call for letting the dough rest for as long as 30 minutes after every set of folds. This is because with each set the gluten in the dough gets stronger, making the dough increasingly harder to roll out. But because my dough wasn't cohesive for the first few sets of folds, gluten didn't develop at the same pace, and I could make five folds without any resting.

When I cut this dough into squares, each biscuit looked like the side view of a book, with layers that pulled away from one another dramatically during baking—just the effect I'd hoped for. There was only one problem: Most of the biscuits were coming out of the oven lopsided. In fact, of the nine biscuits the recipe produced, only the one cut from the center of the dough came out square and level.

I realized that the edges of the dough slab were being compressed during the rolling and folding process. Trimming away ¼ inch from the perimeter of the dough before cutting the biscuits took care of that, but the biscuits were still a bit wonky. By the fifth fold, the layers of dough were taut like stretched rubber bands. Once the layers started to separate in the oven, this tension caused them to slip and slide in different directions, leaving the biscuits lopsided. A single 30-minute rest in the refrigerator—a far cry from the multiple rests other recipes required—gave them time to relax. With that, I had buttery, superflaky biscuits that consistently rose up tall and true.

Flaky Buttermilk Biscuits

MAKES 9 BISCUITS

We prefer King Arthur all-purpose flour for this recipe, but other brands will work. Use sticks of butter. In hot or humid environments, chill the flour mixture, grater, and work bowls before use. The dough will start out very crumbly and dry in pockets but will be smooth by the end of the folding process; do not be tempted to add extra buttermilk. Flour the counter and the top of the dough as needed to prevent sticking, but be careful not to incorporate large pockets of flour into the dough when folding.

3 cups (15 ounces) King Arthur all-purpose flour
2 tablespoons sugar
4 teaspoons baking powder
½ teaspoon baking soda
1½ teaspoons salt
16 tablespoons (2 sticks) unsalted butter, frozen for 30 minutes
1¼ cups buttermilk, chilled

1. Line rimmed baking sheet with parchment paper and set aside. Whisk flour, sugar, baking powder, baking soda, and salt together in large bowl. Coat sticks of butter in flour mixture, then grate 7 tablespoons from each stick on large holes of box grater directly into flour mixture. Toss gently to combine. Set aside remaining 2 tablespoons butter.
2. Add buttermilk to flour mixture and fold with spatula until just combined (dough will look dry). Transfer dough to liberally floured counter. Dust surface of dough with flour; using your floured hands, press dough into rough 7-inch square.
3. Roll dough into 12 by 9-inch rectangle with short side parallel to edge of counter. Starting at bottom of dough, fold into thirds like business letter, using bench scraper or metal spatula to release dough from counter. Press top of dough firmly to seal folds. Turn dough 90 degrees clockwise. Repeat rolling into 12 by 9-inch rectangle, folding into thirds, and turning clockwise 4 more times, for total of 5 sets of folds. After last set of folds, roll dough into 8½-inch square about 1 inch thick. Transfer dough to prepared sheet, cover with plastic wrap, and refrigerate for 30 minutes. Adjust oven rack to upper-middle position and heat oven to 400 degrees.
4. Transfer dough to lightly floured cutting board. Using sharp, floured chef's knife, trim ¼ inch of dough from each side of square and discard. Cut remaining dough into 9 squares, flouring knife after each cut. Arrange biscuits at least 1 inch apart on sheet. Melt reserved butter; brush tops of biscuits with melted butter.
5. Bake until tops are golden brown, 22 to 25 minutes, rotating sheet halfway through baking. Transfer biscuits to wire rack and let cool for 15 minutes before serving.

TO AVOID SLUMPS, RELAX AND TRIM

Folding the dough multiple times creates great layering—but it also compresses the edges and causes tension that makes the layers separate and slide in different directions in the oven. Our fixes: We let the dough relax for 30 minutes in the fridge after folding and then trim away the compressed edges before cutting the dough into individual biscuits.

PREVENTABLE FLAW
Slumping is easily fixed by letting the dough rest.

THE FLUFFIEST DINNER ROLLS

ANDREA GEARY, *January/February 2016*

I used to think that the Old Testament adage "There is nothing new under the sun" could be applied to bread baking. Most "new" bread recipes are actually just modern twists on established recipes or resurrections of bygone techniques. So I was intrigued when I read about *tangzhong*, an oddball bread-making technique that originated in Japan and was popularized by pastry chef Yvonne Chen in the early 2000s.

Instead of simply combining the dry and wet ingredients and kneading as you would to make a conventional loaf, you begin by cooking a portion of the flour and liquid to form a pudding-like paste that you then let cool and mix into the dough. Fans of the method claim not only that it produces bread with a particularly moist, airy, feathery crumb but also that the loaf remains fresh and soft longer than conventional bread.

Curious, I made a popular published Japanese milk bread recipe (a soft, rich sandwich loaf with a snow-white crumb that's a staple in Asian bakeries) that employs the tangzhong method and was immediately won over: The dough was soft and silky, and its pillowy crumb was made up of delicate, almost croissant-like sheets. Eating it gave me the kind of satisfaction I get from a really good dinner roll—except that this bread was even fluffier and, as promised, maintained its impressively moist, plush crumb over the next couple of days.

So, what if I applied this Japanese technique to my usual pull-apart dinner roll recipe? If it worked, it could potentially yield the best dinner rolls I'd ever made and give them a perk that most rolls don't have: make-ahead potential.

WELL HYDRATED

In the recipes I found that employ the tangzhong method, the paste is about 5 parts liquid to 1 part flour and makes up 15 to 20 percent of the total dough weight. My standard dinner roll recipe yields 25 ounces of dough, so to make about 5 ounces of paste, I whisked together ½ cup of water and 3 tablespoons of bread flour in a saucepan. As I stirred the mixture over medium heat, its consistency went from heavy cream to thick pudding. I set the paste aside to cool while I added the remaining ingredients to the stand mixer bowl: 2 cups of bread flour, instant yeast, a little sugar and salt, 4 tablespoons of softened butter, an egg, and ¼ cup milk. Then I added the cooled paste and started mixing. But after 3 minutes, I knew something was wrong: The dough, which is usually slightly sticky and workable, was dry and tight.

Incorporating a cooked flour paste into the dough creates soft, superfluffy rolls that can be made in advance.

I knew this wasn't typical for a tangzhong dough; the Japanese milk loaf dough I'd made had been soft and smooth. The discrepancy lay in the hydrations of the two doughs: My standard dough had a hydration of 60 percent (meaning there were 6 parts liquid to every 10 parts flour), while the hydration of the Japanese milk bread was 80 percent, which I later learned was typical for a dough using the tangzhong method. Ordinarily, that much liquid would make a dough slack, sticky, and hard to shape, but not so with my milk bread.

I made another batch of rolls with a hot-water paste, but this time I added extra milk (½ cup total) to the dough to bring the hydration to 80 percent. Sure enough, the dough was soft and silky, not sticky, and held its shape nicely after kneading.

So why wasn't it a sticky mess? In a standard dough, where you mix cold water and flour, most of the water is not absorbed, so the stickiness you feel is so-called free water. But flour can absorb twice as much hot water as cold water. Heating the water for the paste allows it to be fully absorbed by the flour; in essence, a portion of what would be free water in a standard dough gets locked away. Thus, when the flour paste is mixed with the rest of the ingredients, the dough is smooth, not sticky.

From there, I knocked the air out of the doubled dough to eliminate large air bubbles and encourage a fine crumb, portioned it into 12 pieces, rolled each into a taut ball, and arranged the rolls in a greased cake pan to rise. Baked at 375 degrees until they were deep golden brown, these rolls were moist and flavorful—but they were a bit squat and the crumb was coarse.

BUILDING STRENGTH

A close look at some tangzhong recipes revealed my mistake: I had added more moisture to my dough without building any additional structure to support the greater expansion of steam produced by the extra water. So I made a few changes. First, I added an autolyse—a brief resting period between mixing and kneading the dough that alters the gluten-forming proteins so they can link up more effectively. Withholding sugar and salt until after the autolyse makes this little power nap even more effective, since those ingredients would otherwise slow the alteration of the proteins. Second, I waited until the second half of the kneading period—when the gluten was well established—to add the butter, since fat makes the gluten strands slippery and unable to "grab" each other to form a network. I also streamlined my method by microwaving the flour paste; roughly 60 seconds on high did the trick. And rather than wait for the hot paste to cool (so it wouldn't kill the yeast on contact), I added it to cold milk and whisked them together until the mixture was merely warm.

My rolls were now lighter and boasted a finer crumb, but those gossamer-thin layers were still missing, and I wondered if altering my shaping method might help.

When dough is kneaded, the flour proteins link up in a fairly random way. Rounding each portion of dough into a tight ball, as you typically would when shaping dinner rolls, organizes the proteins on the exterior into a kind of membrane (bakers call this a "gluten cloak") but does not affect the proteins on the interior, which remain random. The Japanese milk bread's shaping method was elaborate, and now I suspected that it was the key to the bread's delicate vertical layers. To shape that loaf, I had divided the dough into four pieces, rolled each one into a rectangle, and folded each rectangle into thirds like a business letter; I then flattened each piece of dough out again and rolled it up again like a jelly roll before nestling it into the loaf pan with the others.

Because I was shaping 12 dinner rolls instead of four larger dough pieces, I tried a simplified version, flattening each piece into a long, narrow rectangle before rolling it up and placing it in the pan. When the rolls had doubled, they looked especially smooth and plump, thanks to the strong gluten development. I baked them to a deep golden brown, removed them from the pan, and brushed them with ½ tablespoon of melted butter.

When I pulled one roll from the round, it separated from the others cleanly, and I delightedly peeled away layer after delicate layer. The combined effect of the added liquid in the flour paste, the well-developed gluten, and the unusual shaping had given me the ideal dinner roll: moist, tender, and particularly fluffy. The most convincing part of all: The rolls were great the next day when I refreshed them in the oven, a real bonus when making them for a holiday dinner.

Fluffy Dinner Rolls

MAKES 12 ROLLS

We strongly recommend weighing the flour for the dough. The slight tackiness of the dough aids in flattening and stretching it in step 5, so do not dust your counter with flour. This recipe requires letting the dough rest for at least 2 hours before baking. The rolls can be made a day ahead. To refresh them before serving, wrap them in aluminum foil and heat them in a 350-degree oven for 15 minutes.

Flour Paste

½ cup water
3 tablespoons bread flour

Dough

½ cup cold milk
1 large egg
2 cups (11 ounces) bread flour
1½ teaspoons instant or rapid-rise yeast
2 tablespoons sugar
1 teaspoon salt
4 tablespoons unsalted butter, softened, plus ½ tablespoon, melted

1. *For the flour paste:* Whisk water and flour together in small bowl until no lumps remain. Microwave, whisking every 20 seconds, until mixture thickens to stiff, smooth, pudding-like consistency that forms mound when dropped from end of whisk into bowl, 40 to 80 seconds.
2. *For the dough:* In bowl of stand mixer, whisk flour paste and milk together until smooth. Add egg and whisk until incorporated. Add flour and yeast. Fit stand mixer with dough hook and mix on low speed until all flour is moistened, 1 to 2 minutes. Let stand for 15 minutes.
3. Add sugar and salt and mix on medium-low speed for 5 minutes. With mixer running, add softened butter, 1 tablespoon at a time. Continue to mix on medium-low speed 5 minutes longer, scraping down dough hook and sides of bowl occasionally (dough will stick to bottom of bowl).
4. Transfer dough to very lightly floured counter. Knead briefly to form ball and transfer, seam side down, to lightly greased bowl; lightly coat surface of dough with vegetable oil spray and cover with plastic wrap. Let rise until doubled in volume, about 1 hour.
5. Grease 9-inch round cake pan and set aside. Transfer dough to counter. Press dough gently but firmly to expel all air. Pat and stretch dough to form 8 by 9-inch rectangle with short side facing you. Cut dough lengthwise into 4 equal strips and cut each strip crosswise into 3 equal pieces. Working with 1 piece at a time, stretch and press dough gently to form 8 by 2-inch strip. Starting on short side, roll dough to form snug cylinder and arrange shaped rolls seam side down in prepared pan, placing 10 rolls around edge of pan, pointing inward, and remaining 2 rolls in center. Cover with plastic and let rise until doubled, 45 minutes to 1 hour.
6. When rolls are nearly doubled, adjust oven rack to lowest position and heat oven to 375 degrees. Bake rolls until deep golden brown, 25 to 30 minutes. Let rolls cool in pan on wire rack for 3 minutes; invert rolls onto rack, then reinvert. Brush tops and sides of rolls with melted butter. Let rolls cool for at least 20 minutes before serving.

WHAT IS THIS THING CALLED TANGZHONG?

The *tangzhong* method calls for briefly cooking a portion of the flour and water to make a paste, which is then combined with the rest of the ingredients. By using hot water, we can actually add more liquid to the dough because flour can absorb twice as much hot water as cold water. The superhydrated dough yields rolls that are not just moist but also fluffy because the water converts to steam, which acts as a leavening agent, creating rise. The extra water also increases gluten development, giving the bread the structure it needs to contain the steam rather than letting it escape.

HOT WATER PASTE
The paste should be stiff and smooth.

PERFECT STICKY BUNS

ANDREA GEARY, *May/June 2016*

I once made sticky buns at home, and I enjoyed every step of the baking process, from rolling the spiced sugar filling up in the firm, smooth dough to nestling the tidy spirals in the nutty caramel topping to flipping the baked buns onto a platter and watching the glaze drip down the sides. But when it came to the final step—actually eating a bun—I felt betrayed.

Even when slightly warm, the bread part was drier and tougher than I had anticipated, and the topping was so firm that I feared for my fillings. A few hours later, the buns were downright hard from top to bottom, but it didn't really matter. They were so overwhelmingly sweet that finishing one had been a feat, and I couldn't muster enough enthusiasm to repeat the experience.

When I was finally ready to attempt sticky buns again, I set some firm goals: This time around the bread would be moist, soft, and fluffy, and the topping would be substantial enough to sit atop the buns without sinking in but not so hard that it stuck in my teeth. And, of course, I'd keep the overall sweetness in check so that I could eat an entire bun.

A HARD CASE

Most sticky bun recipes follow a common procedure: First, you make a yeast dough, and while it rises you mix up a filling and a topping. The filling is often just sugar and a bit of spice but may also include ingredients such as softened butter, dried fruit, and chopped nuts. The topping usually involves cooking butter and sugar and maybe honey or maple syrup together in a saucepan, pouring the mixture into a baking pan, and scattering the surface with nuts. You flatten the risen dough into a rectangle, sprinkle the filling over it, and roll it up like a jelly roll. Cut the dough cylinder into pieces, place them in the pan, let them rise, and then bake, flip, and enjoy (in theory).

I chose simple formulas to act as placeholders for the filling and topping so I could concentrate on creating a dough that would bake up soft and light. I started with a couple of basic yeast doughs made with flour, milk, sugar, butter, and eggs, as well as some that included ingredients like rolled oats and instant mashed potatoes for their purported moisture-retaining qualities.

In dough form, each of these was pleasantly smooth and springy, a joy to work with. Unfortunately, all of the recipes—even those with oats and mashed potatoes—yielded buns that were drier and harder than my ideal. I was quickly learning that, while firm, smooth doughs are the least sticky and as such the easiest to shape, they inevitably yield tight, tough bread.

Fair enough. I was willing to struggle with a slack, sticky dough if it gave me the light, moist results I was after, so I mixed together a buttery, eggy brioche dough. As expected, its softness made it difficult to roll into a cylinder, and when I sliced it into pieces, they stuck to the knife, which left them mangled. But that's not what discouraged me. When baked, the rich, sugar-filled brioche topped with buttery, nutty caramel was just too much of a good thing. I couldn't finish a full portion.

It seemed that the three qualities I wanted most in a dough—easy to work with, not too rich, light and fluffy when baked—were incompatible. And then I realized that I had tackled a similar problem a few months earlier.

LIGHTEN UP

While developing a recipe for dinner rolls (see page 410), I had learned about an interesting Asian bread-baking technique called *tangzhong*, in which a portion of the flour and liquid in a recipe is cooked together until it forms a pudding-like gel, which is then added to the bread dough. This allows you to add more liquid to the dough, yet the added water doesn't make the dough sticky or difficult to work with because that precooked gel traps it. The extra water converts to steam during baking, which made my rolls fluffy and light. And with a fraction of the eggs and butter found in a rich brioche and just a few tablespoons of sugar, they aren't too decadent.

Easy to work with? Light and moist without too much richness? Obviously the sticky bun–tangzhong marriage was meant to be.

Given that sticky buns are a bit of work and something that you tend to make for an occasion, I wanted to make enough to fill a 13 by 9-inch pan, so I increased my dinner roll recipe by one-third. I cooked a small amount of flour and water together in the microwave until it had formed a smooth paste and then whisked the mixture with milk to cool it down to ensure that it wouldn't kill the yeast. I stirred in eggs, flour, and instant yeast and let the mixture rest for 15 minutes before adding some salt and a modest amount of sugar. I then let the mixer knead the dough for 5 minutes. Next, I added some softened butter and mixed for 5 minutes more before setting the dough aside to rise while I made the filling and topping.

> *A highly hydrated dough makes for fluffy, soft buns; dark corn syrup and water create a gooey but not-too-sweet topping.*

Why wait to add the salt and sugar? They are hygroscopic, which means they attract water and would divert moisture away from the flour, delaying the formation of gluten. Pausing before adding salt and sugar allows the gluten-forming proteins to fully hydrate so that they can link up and create structure, giving the buns height and lightness when baked. And because my sticky buns would have a heavy topping to support, a sound structure would be crucial.

I turned the risen dough out onto the counter and patted and stretched it to form a rectangle, a technique I found easier and more effective than rolling this soft dough with a pin. I sprinkled on the filling, rolled the dough into a tight cylinder, and sliced it into portions using a length of dental floss, which kept the pieces neat and round. I transferred the pieces to the pan, let them rise, and then baked them.

When I retrieved the buns from the oven, I found that almost every one had blossomed into a tall cone shape, but otherwise, these moist, fluffy buns were a success. After a few more tests, I realized that the dough expanded so much when it baked that it had nowhere to go but up. Keeping the cylinder a little looser produced tall but level buns.

TOPPED OFF

It was time to examine the filling and topping. My placeholder filling was just ¾ cup of sugar and 1 teaspoon of cinnamon. It tasted okay, but the dry, loose mixture had a tendency to roll and shift over the surface of the dough when I formed the cylinder, which left some pieces with less filling than others.

Some bakers encourage the filling to stick by brushing the dough with melted butter (a little rich) or water (a bit messy) or by mixing butter into the filling and smearing it over the dough (rich, messy, and also a pain). Instead, I switched to using dark brown sugar; its moistness helped it stick to the tacky dough, so I could roll it up easily.

The topping required a little more trial and error. My placeholder was a mixture of brown sugar, butter, honey, and cream that was cooked in a saucepan, poured into the baking pan, and covered evenly with a layer of chopped pecans. It baked up a bit too firm, and I wasn't crazy about the assertive flavor of the honey or the overall sweetness.

The first thing to go was the saucepan. I simply melted the butter in a bowl in the microwave and then stirred the other ingredients into it. Next, I substituted dark corn syrup for the honey. Because it contains water, it produced a softer texture than I'd get with just granulated or brown sugar; plus, the sugar in corn syrup is fully dissolved, which helped avoid grainy results. It gave me a topping that was a little less sweet and also a little less distinctive, so it didn't overpower the cinnamon in the filling or the pleasant yeastiness of the bread.

But that cream bothered me. I was using just 2 tablespoons, so it was hardly worth buying a carton, but eliminating it made the topping even firmer. And then it occurred to me: Cream is mostly water and fat, and my buttery topping was hardly lacking in the fat department. Substituting water for the cream did the trick and, by decreasing the fat and increasing the liquid with this swap, I created a topping that was substantial, gooey, and sticky—yet not too firm.

Though I'd typically make these buns to give to a crowd, they're now so fluffy and light that the prospect of keeping more than one for myself is pretty tempting.

THE IDEAL STICKY BUN

Most sticky buns are dense and dry, with a filling that's fussy to work with and a topping so sticky that chewing it makes your jaw ache. Plus, the whole package is usually so rich that you can't finish an entire bun. Here's how we made a better bun.

FILLING THAT STAYS INSIDE Moist brown sugar doesn't scatter like granulated when the dough is rolled.

SOFT, FLUFFY BREAD Adding extra water to our dough creates more steam, which results in more lift and a lighter bun.

STICKY BUT NOT HARD TOPPING Corn syrup and water help keep the topping soft.

NOT TOO SWEET OR TOO RICH Keeping the eggs and sugar in the dough to a minimum means you can eat a whole bun.

HOW WE GOT TO MOIST STICKY BUNS

Our ideal was a light, moist bun that wasn't too rich or sweet, so we could eat the whole thing without regret. Here's how we got there.

TEST 1 Make a basic yeasted dough.
WHY WE TRIED IT Most are not too sticky, which makes them easy to work with.
RESULT The buns were dense and dry.

TEST 2 Replace some flour with rolled oats.
WHY WE TRIED IT We hoped the oats would help retain moisture and soften the buns.
RESULT No improvement.

TEST 3 Add mashed potatoes.
WHY WE TRIED IT Instant mashed potatoes also have moisture-retaining properties for the promise of a softer bun.
RESULT No improvement.

TEST 4 Add eggs and butter.
WHY WE TRIED IT Eggs and butter add fat; eggs also add water.
RESULT The buns were tender but too rich; the dough was overly sticky.

TEST 5 Add a cooked flour-and-water paste.
WHY WE TRIED IT Also known as *tangzhong*, this technique allowed us to add more water without making the dough too wet.
RESULT The buns were light and moist; the dough was simple to roll and cut.

A cooked flour-and-water paste is the best route to moist yet fluffy buns.

Sticky Buns

MAKES 12 BUNS

These buns take about 4 hours to make from start to finish. For dough that is easy to work with and produces light, fluffy buns, we strongly recommend that you measure the flour for the dough by weight. The slight tackiness of the dough aids in flattening and stretching it in step 6, so resist the urge to use a lot of dusting flour. Rolling the dough cylinder tightly in step 7 will result in misshapen rolls; keep the cylinder a bit slack. Bake these buns in a metal, not glass or ceramic, baking pan. We like dark corn syrup and pecans here, but light corn syrup may be used, and the nuts may be omitted, if desired.

Flour Paste

⅔ cup water
¼ cup (1⅓ ounces) bread flour

Dough

⅔ cup milk
1 large egg plus 1 large yolk
2¾ cups (15⅛ ounces) bread flour
2 teaspoons instant or rapid-rise yeast
3 tablespoons granulated sugar
1½ teaspoons salt
6 tablespoons unsalted butter, softened

Topping

6 tablespoons unsalted butter, melted
½ cup packed (3½ ounces) dark brown sugar
¼ cup (1¾ ounces) granulated sugar
¼ cup dark corn syrup
¼ teaspoon salt
2 tablespoons water
1 cup pecans, toasted and chopped (optional)

Filling

¾ cup packed (5¼ ounces) dark brown sugar
1 teaspoon ground cinnamon

1. ***For the flour paste:*** Whisk water and flour together in small bowl until no lumps remain. Microwave, whisking every 25 seconds, until mixture thickens to stiff, smooth, pudding-like consistency that forms mound when dropped from end of whisk into bowl, 50 to 75 seconds.
2. ***For the dough:*** In bowl of stand mixer, whisk flour paste and milk together until smooth. Add egg and yolk and whisk until incorporated. Add flour and yeast. Fit stand mixer with dough hook and mix on low speed until all flour is moistened, 1 to 2 minutes. Let stand for 15 minutes. Add sugar and salt and mix on medium-low speed for 5 minutes. Stop mixer and add butter. Continue to mix on medium-low speed for 5 minutes longer, scraping down dough hook and sides of bowl halfway through (dough will stick to bottom of bowl).
3. Transfer dough to lightly floured counter. Knead briefly to form ball and transfer seam side down to lightly greased bowl; lightly coat surface of dough with vegetable oil spray and cover bowl with plastic wrap. Let dough rise until just doubled in volume, 40 minutes to 1 hour.
4. ***For the topping:*** While dough rises, grease 13 by 9-inch metal baking pan. Whisk melted butter, brown sugar, granulated sugar, corn syrup, and salt together in medium bowl until smooth. Add water and whisk until incorporated. Pour mixture into prepared pan and tilt pan to cover bottom. Sprinkle evenly with pecans, if using.
5. ***For the filling:*** Stir sugar and cinnamon in small bowl until thoroughly combined; set aside.
6. Turn out dough onto lightly floured counter. Press dough gently but firmly to expel air. Working from center toward edge, pat and stretch dough to form 18 by 15-inch rectangle with long edge nearest you. Sprinkle filling over dough, leaving 1-inch border along top edge; smooth filling into even layer with your hand, then gently press mixture into dough to adhere.
7. Beginning with long edge nearest you, roll dough into cylinder, taking care not to roll too tightly. Pinch seam to seal and roll cylinder seam side down. Mark gently with knife to create 12 equal portions. To slice, hold strand of dental floss taut and slide underneath cylinder, stopping at first mark. Cross ends of floss over each other and pull. Slice cylinder into 12 portions and transfer, cut sides down, to prepared baking pan. Cover tightly with plastic wrap and let rise until buns are puffy and touching one another, 40 minutes to 1 hour. (Buns may be refrigerated immediately after shaping for up to 14 hours. To bake, remove baking pan from refrigerator and let sit until buns are puffy and touching one another, 1 to 1½ hours.) Meanwhile, adjust oven racks to lowest and lower-middle positions. Place rimmed baking sheet on lower rack to catch any drips and heat oven to 375 degrees.
8. Bake buns on upper rack until golden brown, about 20 minutes. Tent with aluminum foil and bake until center of dough registers at least 200 degrees, 10 to 15 minutes longer. Remove foil and let buns cool in pan on wire rack for 5 minutes. Place rimmed baking sheet over buns and carefully invert. Remove pan and let buns cool for 5 minutes. Using spoon, scoop any glaze on baking sheet onto buns. Let cool for at least 10 minutes longer before serving.

USE THE CORRECT PAN

If a recipe specifies a particular pan—metal or glass—don't be tempted to swap one for the other. Each material conducts heat at a different rate, and baking for more or less time to account for that difference won't give you identical results. Case in point: Our Sticky Buns recipe calls for a metal baking pan. When we tried baking the buns in a glass baking dish, which conducts heat more slowly than a metal pan, we had to extend the baking time by 10 minutes to ensure that the buns in the center of the dish were done. But since glass retains heat longer than metal, the buns on the edges of the dish turned dry and hard. For best results, stick with the pan the recipe calls for.

THESE BUNS PALE IN COMPARISON
Our buns baked in glass instead of metal were pale and undercooked in the center.

THE BEST CINNAMON SWIRL BREAD

DAN SOUZA, *March/April 2012*

Cinnamon swirl bread always sounds terrifically appealing in theory, but until recently, I've ended up being disappointed every time I've tried it. My ideal is a fluffy, delicate crumb that's studded with plump raisins and laced with a substantial swirl of gooey cinnamon sugar. But most versions I've sampled are either austere white sandwich loaves rolled up with a bare sprinkle of cinnamon and sugar or overly sweet breads ruined by gobs of filling oozing from the cracks.

When I finally stumbled upon cinnamon bread nirvana, it was in the unlikeliest of places: Tokyo's Narita Airport. After one bite of a lightly toasted slice of swirl bread that I'd bought at a bakery kiosk, I realized I'd found it. Beneath the lightly crisp exterior, the crumb was so springy, moist, and feathery it could be pulled into cotton candy–like strands. This style of milky-sweet Japanese white sandwich bread, called *shokupan*, proved the perfect foil for a sweet, viscous spiral, which, in this case, was red-bean paste. I vowed to figure out a cinnamon swirl version with raisins once I was back home.

TURNING JAPANESE

I decided to focus first on the bread and worry about incorporating the swirl and the raisins later. But when recipes for shokupan written in English proved hard to come by, I sought out an expert: Takeo Sakan, head baker at Boston's acclaimed Japonaise Bakery & Café. To help better understand how shokupan is made, we compared it with American sandwich bread. The two styles share a number of the same ingredients: flour, yeast, salt, water, milk, sugar, and butter. Shokupan, however, boasts considerably more fat (roughly twice as much butter, plus an egg) and more sugar, which accounts for its particularly tender crumb. Another major difference: Shokupan contains more gluten—the network of proteins that builds structure and allows bread to rise high and retain its springy crumb. To achieve that result, Sakan relies on a combination of thorough kneading and specialty high-gluten flour, which contains even more of the structure-building proteins than regular bread flour. It's that marriage of particularly strong gluten and tenderizers like fat and sugar that produces shokupan's airy-yet-sturdy crumb.

I took careful notes and returned to the test kitchen emboldened to mix up my own version. There was one change to Sakan's recipe I'd make immediately, however: Since the high-gluten flour he used requires mail-ordering, I'd have to stick with bread flour and worry about making up for the lack of gluten later. Otherwise, I followed his lead: I mixed the flour with yeast, sugar, and nonfat dry milk powder; added water (1½ cups) plus an egg and 8 tablespoons of softened butter for richness; and kneaded the mixture in a stand mixer for a few minutes until it formed a cohesive mass. After letting the dough rest for about 20 minutes, I added the salt and then let the mixer knead the dough for a longer stretch—about 10 minutes, by which time the dough was smoother and more workable. I mixed in a generous handful of golden raisins (which are more plump and moist than dark raisins) and left the dough to proof in a turned-off oven. Because warm, humid air stimulates yeast activity and speeds rise time, I'd placed a loaf pan of boiling water on the oven floor, simulating the proof boxes used by professional bakers. Forty-five minutes later, I patted the dough into a rectangle, sprinkled a placeholder cinnamon sugar filling over the surface, rolled it into a spiral, fitted it into a loaf pan, and let it proof for another 45 minutes. I brushed the dough with an egg wash for shine and baked it until the crust was dark brown.

But while the color of the bread was handsome, the crumb itself was far from ideal. Among other problems, I couldn't replicate the bread's hallmark lift and airy texture. In fact, I could tell something had gone wrong as soon as I'd mixed up the dough. Unlike the springy, elastic mass that Sakan had made, mine was slack and easily extensible. The reason, no doubt, had a lot to do with the lower-protein bread flour.

Using a series of folds and letting the dough rest before adding the butter gives it enough structure to hold in the sweet filling.

ON THE RISE

I had one solution in mind to strengthen the dough: Work in more air. While you might think of oxygen as merely providing lift to baked goods, it's also the driving force behind gluten development, enabling the proteins in flour to cross-link and form a tightly bonded network. The more oxygen the dough gets, the tighter the bonds will be, and the stronger the gluten network. My first test: introducing two sets of "folds" into the process. By deflating the dough and folding it back onto itself several times, I incorporated more air into it, thereby encouraging the bread to expand and rise more. I also increased the kneading time to about 15 minutes, rendering it even more elastic and better able to trap gas for a taller rise. This bread baked up noticeably higher, but still not as tall as the shokupan loaves I'd tasted.

Leaving the technique alone for the moment, I scanned my ingredient list for other ways to boost the bread's height. When I got to the butter, I paused. I knew that incorporating it into the dough at the outset was coating the flour proteins with fat, preventing them from bonding and inhibiting gluten formation. A better method, I reasoned, would be to knead the dough almost completely to develop gluten and then work in some softened butter during the final minutes of kneading. The idea worked, save for the soft butter pieces smearing into the dough and not incorporating evenly. Tossing the pieces with a tablespoon of flour before letting them soften helped the dough grip the butter and pull it into the dough. The resulting loaf was gorgeously lofty—by far the best yet. It would serve as the perfect counterpoint for my next challenge: a gooey cinnamon sugar swirl.

MIND THE GAP

I thought perfecting a thick cinnamon swirl would be the easy part of making this bread—until my first attempt at incorporating it. The bread rose beautifully tall during the first half of baking and then sprung a leak and spewed molten cinnamon sugar from its crevices. When I sliced it open, I discovering a mangled mix of dense bread, huge gaps, and puddles of filling—all perennial problems with swirled breads.

Our science editor explained: All of these issues boil down to the fact that the sugary filling and bread don't readily bind. During proofing, the gas produced by the yeast leaks from the dough into the spiral, and because it has no place to go, the gas pushes apart the layers of dough. This separation becomes more distinct during baking, when steam also fills the gaps. At the same time, all that pressure compresses the dough, further widening the trails for the cinnamon sugar filling to flow to the bottom of the bread and eventually burst through its seam.

What I needed, then, was a way to encourage binding between the swirl and the dough. I added a slew of different ingredients to the filling to see if any would help it adhere: flour, eggs, pectin, corn syrup, pureed raisins, cooked caramel, crushed cinnamon cereal, and ground-up nuts. Most of the loaves still baked up with comically large gaps. In desperation, I even went so far as to make a second dough spiked with cinnamon and roll that up with the regular dough. That took care of the gapping problem but also did away with the gooey filling.

That's when I realized that adding extra ingredients to the swirl might not be as effective as examining the ingredients I already had in it. Up to this point, the filling consisted of ½ cup of granulated sugar and 1 tablespoon of ground cinnamon per loaf. I baked more loaves, this time trading the granulated stuff for confectioners' sugar as well as tripling the cinnamon. These loaves showed significant improvement: When confectioners' sugar absorbs water from the dough, it immediately dissolves, forming a sticky paste. This paste is thickened by the cornstarch in the confectioners' sugar along with the abundance of carbohydrates in the cinnamon. The thickened paste doesn't pool at the bottom of the bread as readily and is sticky enough to help bind the layers as the bread expands during proofing.

This was by far the best loaf I had made to date, but unfortunately, I couldn't always replicate it; I still got the occasional spewing leak or gaping hole. Lightly spraying the dough with water before and after dusting on the filling helped the paste form even more quickly, but it wasn't enough.

FROM RUSSIA WITH LOAVES

I started to wonder if there was anything I could do during shaping to help the situation. Since gas trapped between the layers of dough was the trigger for the gapping, perhaps what I needed was to provide a way for it to escape. I tested a multitude of different shaping techniques that created crevices in the dough that would allow gas to escape, including monkey bread and braids. The easiest of these shaping methods, which cut down on gapping and leaking considerably, was an attractive weave called a Russian braid. To make it, I sprinkled the filling over the dough, rolled it into a cylinder just as before, and then halved it lengthwise to reveal the striations of dough and filling. I then stretched these two halves slightly and twisted them together (keeping the cut surfaces facing up to expose the nice-looking striations). Any gas that would have been trapped between the layers was able to escape, and the bread baked up tightly seamed and beautifully marbled. To prevent any risk of burning the raisins or the bread's sugary surface, I pushed the exposed pieces of fruit into the braid and tented the loaves with aluminum foil halfway through baking.

This was the bread I'd always envisioned: a burnished crust encasing springy, airy, slightly sweet bread streaked with thick lines of gooey cinnamon filling.

WEAVING A TIGHT CINNAMON SWIRL BREAD, RUSSIAN-STYLE

The benefit of a Russian braid is that the twisted shape tightly seals the pieces of dough together while providing plenty of escape routes for the excess air that would otherwise create tunnels in the loaf.

CUT LENGTHWISE Using bench scraper or sharp chef's knife, cut filled dough in half lengthwise. Turn halves so cut sides are facing up.

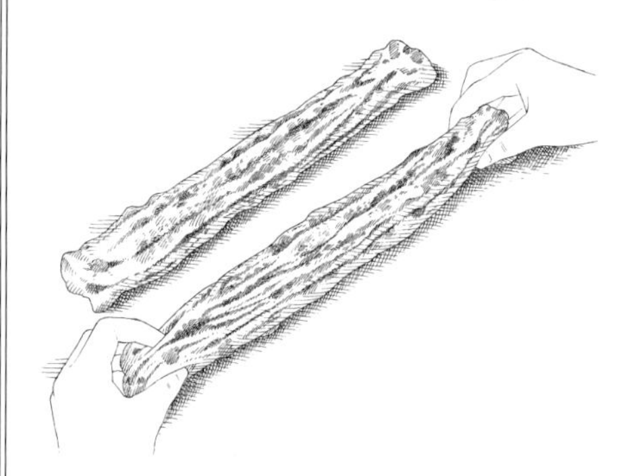

STRETCH With cut sides up, stretch each half into 14-inch length, then pinch ends together.

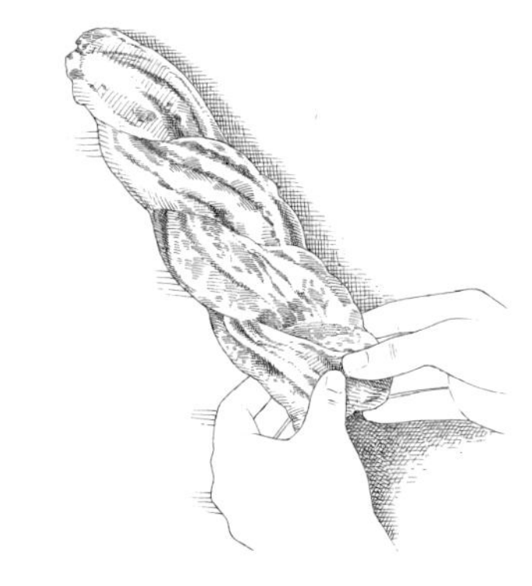

FOLD AND PINCH Take left strip of dough and lay it over right strip of dough. Repeat, keeping cut sides face up, until pieces are tightly twisted. Pinch ends together.

Cinnamon Swirl Bread

MAKES 2 LOAVES

To achieve the proper dough consistency, make sure to weigh your ingredients. The dough will appear very wet and sticky until the final few minutes of kneading; do not be tempted to add supplemental flour. The test kitchen's preferred loaf pan measures 8½ by 4½ inches; if using 9 by 5-inch loaf pans, start checking for doneness 5 minutes early. To make ahead, store the baked and cooled loaves in a double layer of plastic wrap at room temperature for up to two days. To freeze the bread for up to one month, wrap it with an additional layer of aluminum foil.

Dough

- 8 tablespoons unsalted butter
- 3¾ cups (20 ounces) bread flour, plus extra for work surface
- ¾ cup (2¾ ounces) nonfat dry milk powder
- ⅓ cup (2⅓ ounces) granulated sugar
- 1 tablespoon instant or rapid-rise yeast
- 1½ cups (12 ounces) warm water (110 degrees)
- 1 large egg, lightly beaten
- 1½ teaspoons salt
- 1½ cups (7½ ounces) golden raisins

Filling

- 1 cup (4 ounces) confectioners' sugar
- 3 tablespoons ground cinnamon
- 1 teaspoon vanilla extract
- ½ teaspoon salt

1 large egg, lightly beaten with pinch of salt

1. *For the dough:* Cut butter into 32 pieces and toss with 1 tablespoon flour; set aside to soften while mixing dough. Whisk remaining flour, milk powder, sugar, and yeast together in bowl of stand mixer. Using stand mixer fitted with dough hook, add water and egg and mix on medium-low speed until cohesive mass forms, about 2 minutes, scraping down bowl if necessary. Cover mixing bowl with plastic wrap and let stand for 20 minutes.
2. Adjust oven rack to middle position and place loaf or cake pan on bottom of oven. Remove plastic from mixer bowl, add salt, and mix on medium-low speed until dough is smooth and elastic and clears sides of bowl, 7 to 15 minutes. With mixer running, add butter, few pieces at a time, and continue to knead until butter is fully incorporated and dough is smooth and elastic and clears sides of bowl, 3 to 5 minutes longer. Add raisins and mix until incorporated, 30 to 60 seconds. Transfer dough to large greased bowl and, using bowl scraper or rubber spatula, fold dough over itself by gently lifting and folding edge of dough toward middle. Turn bowl 90 degrees; fold again. Turn bowl and fold dough 6 more times (total of 8 folds). Cover tightly with plastic and transfer to middle rack of oven. Pour 3 cups boiling water into loaf pan in oven, close oven door, and allow dough to rise for 45 minutes.
3. Remove bowl from oven and gently press down on center of dough to deflate. Repeat folding step (making total of 8 folds), re-cover, and return to oven until doubled in volume, about 45 minutes.
4. *For the filling:* Whisk filling ingredients together until well combined; set aside.
5. Grease two 8½ by 4½-inch loaf pans. Transfer dough to lightly floured counter and divide into 2 pieces. Working with 1 piece of dough, pat into rough 6 by 11-inch rectangle. With short side facing you, fold long sides in like business letter to form 3 by 11-inch rectangle. Roll dough away from you into ball. Dust ball with flour and flatten with rolling pin into 7 by 18-inch rectangle with even ¼-inch thickness. Using spray bottle, spray dough lightly with water. Sprinkle half of filling mixture evenly over dough, leaving ¼-inch border on sides and ¾-inch border on top and bottom; spray filling lightly with water. (Filling should be speckled with water over entire surface.) With short side facing you, roll dough away from you into firm cylinder. Turn loaf seam side up and pinch closed; pinch ends closed. Dust loaf lightly on all sides with flour and let rest for 10 minutes. Repeat with second ball of dough and remaining filling.
6. Working with 1 loaf at a time, use bench scraper to cut loaf in half lengthwise; turn halves so cut sides are facing up. Gently stretch each half into 14-inch length. Line up pieces of dough and pinch 2 ends of strips together. Take piece on left and lay over piece on right. Repeat, keeping cut side up, until pieces of dough are tightly twisted. Pinch ends together. Transfer loaf, cut side up, to prepared loaf pan; push any exposed raisins into seams of braid. Cover loaves loosely with plastic, return to oven, and allow to rise for 45 minutes. Remove loaves and water pan from oven; heat oven to 350 degrees. Allow loaves to rise at room temperature until almost doubled in size, about 45 minutes longer (top of loaves should rise about 1 inch over lip of pan).
7. Brush loaves with egg mixture. Bake until crust is well browned, about 25 minutes. Reduce oven temperature to 325 degrees, tent loaves with aluminum foil, and continue to bake until internal temperature registers 200 degrees, 15 to 25 minutes longer.
8. Transfer pans to wire rack and let cool for 5 minutes. Remove loaves from pans, return to rack, and cool to room temperature before slicing and serving, about 2 hours.

A BETTER BASE FOR CINNAMON SWIRL BREAD

The usual base for cinnamon swirl bread is American sandwich bread, but we looked to a different source: *shokupan*, Japan's version of the same loaf. Shokupan relies on lots of fat, highprotein flour, and thorough kneading to create a crumb that's feathery light yet still strong enough to support a gooey cinnamon filling.

JAPANESE SHOKUPAN

REALLY GOOD PUMPKIN BREAD

LAN LAM, *September/October 2012*

After testing a half-dozen recipes for pumpkin bread, I found myself thinking of it as the John Doe of quick breads: No loaf was remarkably bad—and none was remarkably good. They were all just fine.

So when I set out to make a great one, I knew I'd need a bread that had just the right texture—neither too dense nor too cakey—and a rich pumpkin flavor that was properly tempered with sweetness and gently enhanced rather than obscured by spices.

While you might think that the best pumpkin bread would begin with from-scratch pumpkin puree, I found a loaf made with from-scratch puree only marginally better than one made with canned—and it was a lot more work. But I was definitely going to have to do something to improve the canned puree, since it had noticeable metallic, raw flavors. After I failed in my attempts to mask that canned flavor by using more spices or adding molasses or prune puree (the spices overwhelmed the pumpkin flavor, while the other two just tasted slightly odd), I wondered if I was overthinking the problem: The puree tasted raw, so why not cook it? I dumped a can of the puree into a saucepan and stirred it over medium heat until it barely began to caramelize. I then cooled it down and quickly stirred together another batch of bread using the cooked puree. Tasters marveled at the rich, full pumpkin flavor of this loaf.

Precooking canned pumpkin puree and adding a bit of cream cheese yields a loaf with deep yet balanced flavor.

However, the texture of these loaves was a little dense and dry. By cooking down the pumpkin I had driven off some of the moisture, so I added a bit of buttermilk. But caramelizing the puree had also increased its sweetness, throwing off the balance of flavors. I needed to add a bit of tanginess. Since gently tangy cream cheese is often slathered onto slices of pumpkin bread, I tried directly incorporating it into the batter. I didn't even have to dirty a stand mixer to do it—I simply cut a block of cream cheese into small chunks, tossed them into the pan with the hot puree, and stirred—the lumps became streaks that melted away with a few swirls of the spatula, achieving the dual goals of melting the cream cheese and cooling the puree.

Could I simplify even further and just stir everything together in the saucepan? I cracked my eggs into the measuring cup with the buttermilk, gave them a quick whisk and then stirred them into the puree. The dry ingredients were easy to mix in. And happily, these loaves had perfectly balanced flavor plus just the texture I was after: moist but not greasy, with a crumb that was neither cakey nor dense.

For some textural contrast, I topped the bread with a simple streusel. John Doe no longer, this was a pumpkin bread to make you sit up and take notice.

Pumpkin Bread

MAKES 2 LOAVES

The test kitchen's preferred loaf pan measures 8½ by 4½ inches; if using 9 by 5-inch loaf pans, start checking for doneness 5 minutes early.

Topping

5 tablespoons packed (2¼ ounces) light brown sugar
1 tablespoon all-purpose flour
1 tablespoon unsalted butter, softened
1 teaspoon ground cinnamon
⅛ teaspoon salt

Bread

2 cups (10 ounces) all-purpose flour
1½ teaspoons baking powder
½ teaspoon baking soda
1 (15-ounce) can unsweetened pumpkin puree
1 teaspoon salt
1½ teaspoons ground cinnamon
¼ teaspoon ground nutmeg
⅛ teaspoon ground cloves
1 cup (7 ounces) granulated sugar
1 cup packed (7 ounces) light brown sugar
½ cup vegetable oil
4 ounces cream cheese, cut into 12 pieces
4 large eggs
¼ cup buttermilk
1 cup walnuts, toasted and chopped fine

1. ***For the topping:*** Using your fingers, mix all ingredients together in bowl until well combined and topping resembles wet sand; set aside.
2. ***For the bread:*** Adjust oven rack to middle position and heat oven to 350 degrees. Grease two 8½ by 4½-inch loaf pans. Whisk flour, baking powder, and baking soda together in bowl.
3. Combine pumpkin puree, salt, cinnamon, nutmeg, and cloves in large saucepan over medium heat. Cook mixture, stirring constantly, until reduced to 1½ cups, 6 to 8 minutes. Remove pot from heat; stir in granulated sugar, brown sugar, oil, and cream cheese until combined. Let mixture stand for 5 minutes. Whisk until no visible pieces of cream cheese remain and mixture is homogeneous.
4. Whisk together eggs and buttermilk. Add egg mixture to pumpkin mixture and whisk to combine. Fold flour mixture into pumpkin mixture until combined (some small lumps of flour are OK). Fold walnuts into batter. Scrape batter into prepared pans. Sprinkle topping evenly over top of each loaf. Bake until skewer inserted in center of loaf comes out clean, 45 to 50 minutes. Let breads cool in pans on wire rack for 20 minutes. Remove breads from pans and let cool for at least 1½ hours. Serve warm or at room temperature.

ULTIMATE BANANA BREAD

ANDREA GEARY, *July/August 2010*

The tradition of banana bread–baking is more heavily steeped in parsimony than indulgence: When bananas get covered with brownish-black spots, the frugal alternative to pitching them in the trash has always been to mash them up, add them to a quick bread batter, and bake.

I'm all for thrift in the kitchen, but I've yet to come across a banana bread recipe that actually makes me glad I saved those overripe specimens. Depending on the fat-to-flour ratio—and just how spotty those bananas really were—the crumb varies from cottony and tough to dense and damp, with a typically overbaked ring crusting over the exterior. Even more discouraging, all that ripe banana flavor somehow seems to vaporize during baking, leaving me with a ho-hum loaf that just begs for the added oomph of chocolate chips, coconut, rum, or gobs of cream cheese slathered on top. Without upsetting the humble charms of this bread, what would it take to create a moist, tender loaf that really tasted like bananas?

CONCENTRATION CONSTERNATION

Just to reacquaint myself with the core problems, I cherry-picked a few promising-looking recipes to make in the test kitchen, most of which followed a formula along these lines: Combine mashed, ripe bananas with vegetable oil, eggs, and sugar; fold that into a dry mix of flour, baking soda, and salt; and scrape the batter into a loaf pan before popping it into a 350-degree oven for about an hour. I suppose the breads were passable as PTA-meeting handouts—sweet-smelling and pleasant enough to eat while warm and fresh—but their banana flavor was utterly forgettable.

Except for one loaf, that is. With a stature that was a good half-inch shorter than the other breads and an interior crumb that could only be described as wet, it wasn't much to look at. (One taster actually used the word "sludgy.") But it took only a couple of bites before my colleagues and I were returning for seconds, declaring that this loaf had unprecedented true fruit flavor. Why the drastic difference? Simple: This recipe called for roughly the same amount of flour, sugar, fat, and eggs as all the others, but twice the number of bananas—six instead of the usual three. Their effect was both a blessing and a curse: Doubling the bananas may have doubled the flavor, but it also oversaturated the batter. My task was clear—figure out how to cram as many bananas as possible into the loaf without sinking its cake-like structure.

We pack our banana bread with tons of banana flavor by reducing the bananas' liquid, getting rid of moisture while concentrating flavor.

Since it was clear that simply mashing up more bananas to add to the batter compromised the crumb, I decided to limit myself to three pieces and try alternative avenues to ratcheting up the flavor. A few of the more inventive recipes I came across stirred crushed banana chips into the batter; presumably, the chips' toasty, concentrated flavor would pick up where the fresh fruit left off. Wrong. The loaf I made with ½ cup of ground chips had no more flavor than previous batches; in fact, it was even a bit drier. Turns out, banana chips are made from underripe bananas (because they withstand processing better than ripe fruit), and underripe bananas are largely composed of moisture-absorbing starch. Scratch that off the list.

If banana chips were too dehydrated, maybe the answer to bigger banana flavor was to start at the source—actual ripe bananas—and drain their liquid myself. That way, I'd get all the benefits of the fruit's creamy sweetness and be able to control the moisture level. Flipping through the test kitchen archives for ideas, I came across a recipe for low-fat banana bread, where we discovered that roasting the fruit not only helped some of the excess moisture evaporate, but also concentrated its rich brown-sugar notes. My goal was to remove enough moisture so that two more bananas (for a total of five) wouldn't overwhelm the batter. Unsure how much moisture would escape through the skin, I roasted batches of bananas three different ways—peels intact, peels split, and peels removed—and then incorporated them into the batter. No matter what the roasting method, five bananas still produced an unacceptably wet loaf, so I scaled back to four bananas. This time around, the split-peel loaf stood out for a nice, moist (but not pudding-like) crumb and a fruity flavor that was a significant step up from any threebanana loaf I'd made. But roasting tacked 45 minutes onto the recipe. And were four bananas really as high as I could go?

LIQUID ASSET

My patience with this process was growing thin. Then a thrifty colleague mentioned that in lieu of throwing out bananas too ripe to eat, she saves them in the freezer, though she has seen them exude quite a lot of liquid when thawed. Armed with this promising nugget, I thawed some very ripe bananas I had stored in the freezer; sure enough, five of them yielded around ⅔ cup of liquid. I pureed the fruit, added it to my bread, and was rewarded with a flavor-packed loaf boasting a moist, fully baked crumb. My enthusiasm was renewed—until I realized this discovery would be moot if I had no frozen ripe bananas at the ready.

I had no choice but to return to trying to cook off extra moisture. This time around, I moved my efforts out of the oven and onto the stove: I tried simmering the mashed bananas as well as dicing and sautéing them—but the direct heat in both attempts gave the fruit an overcooked, jammy flavor. I was stumped until I remembered a solution for removing moisture from waterlogged eggplant: microwaving it. I placed five bananas in a glass bowl and zapped them on high power for about

5 minutes, then transferred the now-pulpy fruit to a sieve to drain. Bingo! This caused them to release as much liquid as the thawed frozen bananas. Furthermore, since the bananas were heated for only a short time, they didn't take on the overly cooked flavor of the simmered puree or sautéed bananas.

But what to do about the banana liquid I'd collected? I couldn't bear the thought of pouring all that sweet flavor down the drain. (In cooking terms, it seemed as blasphemous as throwing away the fond.) I transferred this liquid to a saucepan, cooked it down to 2 ounces, and then added it back to the mashed bananas (along with another ¼ cup of flour to compensate for the extra liquid). As crazy as it sounded to extract banana liquid only to put it back (albeit in concentrated form), the result was a revelation. Not only did this step infuse the bread with ripe, intensely fruity banana flavor, it also assuaged my frugal Yankee conscience. Furthermore, the extra moisture in the batter helped to create a crumb that was tender through and through, without being framed by overly crusty sides.

THE SIXTH SENSE

With the flavor problem solved, a few minor tweaks completed the recipe: I exchanged the granulated sugar for light brown sugar, finding that the latter's molasses notes better complemented the bananas. A teaspoon of vanilla rounded out the bananas' faintly boozy, rum-like flavor, as did swapping out the oil for the nutty richness of butter. I also added ½ cup of toasted walnuts to the batter, finding that their crunch provided a pleasing contrast to the rich, moist crumb.

This banana bread was a true showpiece, from its deep golden crust all the way through to the center's velvety crumb, yet lingering in the back of my mind was the urge to actually double the number of bananas in the conventional recipe. Wondering if the crust might benefit from a little embellishment, I sliced a sixth banana and shingled it on top of the batter. A final sprinkle of sugar helped the buttery slices caramelize and gave the loaf an enticingly crisp, crunchy top. I now make a point of always having a bunch of ripe bananas waiting in the wings.

Ultimate Banana Bread

MAKES 1 LOAF

Be sure to use very ripe, heavily speckled (or even black) bananas in this recipe. The test kitchen's preferred loaf pan measures 8½ by 4½ inches; if using a 9 by 5-inch loaf pan, start checking for doneness 5 minutes early.

1¾ cups (8¾ ounces) all-purpose flour
1 teaspoon baking soda
½ teaspoon salt
6 very ripe large bananas (2¼ pounds), peeled
8 tablespoons unsalted butter, melted and cooled
2 large eggs
¾ cup packed (5¼ ounces) light brown sugar
1 teaspoon vanilla extract
½ cup walnuts, toasted and chopped coarse (optional)
2 teaspoons granulated sugar

1. Adjust oven rack to middle position and heat oven to 350 degrees. Grease 8½ by 4½-inch loaf pan. Whisk flour, baking soda, and salt together in large bowl.
2. Place 5 bananas in separate bowl, cover, and microwave until bananas are soft and have released liquid, about 5 minutes. Drain bananas in fine-mesh strainer set over medium bowl, stirring occasionally, for 15 minutes; you should have ½ to ¾ cup liquid.
3. Transfer drained liquid to medium saucepan and cook over medium-high heat until reduced to ¼ cup, about 5 minutes. Return drained bananas to bowl. Stir reduced liquid into bananas and mash with potato masher until mostly smooth. Whisk in butter, eggs, brown sugar, and vanilla.
4. Pour banana mixture into flour mixture and stir until just combined, with some streaks of flour remaining. Gently fold in walnuts, if using. Scrape batter into prepared loaf pan and smooth top. Slice remaining banana on bias into ¼-inch-thick slices and shingle down both sides of loaf pan, leaving center clear to ensure even rise. Sprinkle granulated sugar over top.
5. Bake until skewer inserted in center comes out clean, 55 minutes to 1¼ hours, rotating pan halfway through baking. Let loaf cool in pan for 15 minutes, then turn out onto wire rack and continue to cool. Serve warm or at room temperature.

WHO KNEW? BANANAS HAVE JUICE

Typical banana bread contains just three pieces of fruit. Here's how we upped the number to five without turning the loaf into pudding.

1. **EXTRACT JUICE, THEN STRAIN** Microwaving ripe bananas for 5 minutes causes them to release "juice," which we strain out using a fine-mesh strainer.

2. **REDUCE THE JUICE** Reducing the banana liquid yields a concentrated liquor, intensifying flavor without making the loaf wet.

QUICK CHEESE BREAD

REBECCA HAYS, *May/June 2004*

Cheese bread sounds like a great idea, a pairing of two of America's favorite foods. Unlike pizza, wherein bread dough is merely topped with cheese, a true cheese bread involves a more intimate relationship, going well beyond the quick blind date in which the two ingredients are merely thrown together and then heated. Good cheese bread displays a subtle balance of flavor and texture, neither party getting the upper hand. But most of the recipes I tested offered the worst of both worlds: dry bread and no cheese flavor.

The quickest (and easiest) recipe I came across was a chemically leavened bread that I mixed up in 10 minutes; the most difficult required a trip to a cheese shop plus a 48-hour time investment. Made with yeast, this bread was fantastic, and I will likely make it again when I have a spare weekend. But for most purposes, cheese bread ought to be quick.

I baked a half-dozen more quick recipes, but the results were awful—tough and devoid of cheese flavor. My colleagues yearned for a moist, hearty bread with bits of cheese throughout, plus a cheesy crust. My first step toward this end was to create a working recipe that consisted of 3 cups flour, 1 tablespoon baking powder, 6 tablespoons melted butter, 2 cups milk, and one egg. For the cheese, I chose shredded cheddar, the most frequently used type in my stack of recipes. My working recipe had lots of problems, but I could now methodically test every variable.

CONSTRUCTING THE BREAD

I first experimented with different flours, making one loaf with all-purpose, another with bread flour, and yet another with half bread and half all-purpose flour. A few tasters noticed that the breads made with the higher-protein bread flour were slightly rubbery, but though the difference was not that dramatic, all-purpose was clearly the best, and most convenient, choice.

Buttermilk is a common ingredient in quick breads, and it produced a decent loaf. Skim milk was too watery and produced a crumbly, dry loaf. The whole milk version was the best, though, with a creamier, cleaner, cheesier flavor.

I next tinkered with the amount of butter, which was preferred over oil for its flavor. Starting with 6 tablespoons, I worked my way down to a mere 3, putting an end to greasiness. Less fat also pushed the bread away from the texture of a delicate cake and toward that of a hearty muffin. The single egg I'd been using turned out to be just right. When I omitted it, the loaf failed to rise properly and had little structure. Loaves made with more than one egg were beautifully golden but tasted like quiche.

For maximum flavor, this bread has cheese baked into the top and bottom crusts as well as the dough itself.

So far so good, but I was falling short in the texture department. Because I wanted a rich loaf, similar to a good banana bread, I replaced a portion of the milk in each of two breads with scoops of yogurt and sour cream, respectively. Given that this was cheese bread, it also seemed logical to try cottage cheese, cream cheese, goat cheese, and ricotta. In the end, most tasters chose the sour cream–based bread. It was rich and moist without being greasy, just what I'd been aiming for. The sour cream also added a nip of tartness to the bread, offsetting the richness of the cheese without overpowering it.

It was time to decide on the leavening: baking soda or baking powder. To do its job, baking soda needs an acidic ingredient (such as the lactic acid in sour cream), while baking powder is self-reliant, essentially composed of baking soda plus one or two acids. I made two breads, one with 1 tablespoon baking powder (this was a heavy batter that needed a decent amount of powder for proper leavening) and a second with ¾ teaspoon baking soda. (One teaspoon of baking powder contains ¼ teaspoon of baking soda.) Both breads rose into beautiful domed loaves, but the bread made with baking powder was preferred, possessing a more complex flavor.

Curious about these findings, I had the pH levels of the finished breads tested and discovered that the bread made with baking powder was quite acidic, with a pH of 5.8, whereas the bread made with baking soda was actually alkaline, with a pH of 8.3. The reason? The baking soda had neutralized the lactic acid in the sour cream, whereas the baking powder, which brings its own acid to the mix, had not. The acid was giving the bread more flavor.

WORKING IN THE CHEESE

Test results showed that small chunks, not shreds, were best, as they melted into luscious, cheesy pockets. In terms of the cheese itself, I tested five supermarket offerings: extra-sharp cheddar, Muenster, Asiago, Gruyère, and Monterey Jack. Cheddar and Asiago were the leaders of the pack, with Muenster and Monterey Jack being too mild and Gruyère too pungent (although I liked this last cheese in a variation made with bacon). Excess cheese weighed down the bread, causing it to collapse. With a modest 4 ounces of cheese, the bread had plenty of flavor but still rose to its full potential.

The final problem: getting rich flavor and color on the top crust. The solution was a topping of shredded nutty, salty Parmesan. A colleague suggested that I coat the bottom of the pan with cheese as well, thus doubling the cheesy exterior. Now every bite was packed with flavor. The Parmesan also turned the crust a deep bronze color.

In the end, my cheese bread tasted like recipes that required considerable preparation time, but this recipe was oven-ready after just 15 minutes of hands-on work.

Quick Cheese Bread

MAKES 1 LOAF

Use the large holes of a box grater to shred the Parmesan. A mild Asiago, crumbled into ¼- to ½-inch pieces, can be used instead of the cheddar. (Aged Asiago that is as firm as Parmesan is too sharp and pungent.) If, when testing the bread for doneness, the toothpick comes out with what looks like uncooked batter clinging to it, try again in a different but still central spot. (A toothpick hitting a pocket of melted cheese may give a false indication.) The bread is best when made with whole milk, but it will taste fine if you have only 2 percent low-fat milk on hand; do not use skim milk. The test kitchen's preferred loaf pan measures 8½ by 4½ inches; if you use a 9 by 5-inch loaf pan, start checking for doneness 5 minutes early.

3 ounces Parmesan cheese, shredded (1 cup)
2½ cups (12½ ounces) all-purpose flour
1 tablespoon baking powder
1 teaspoon salt
⅛ teaspoon cayenne pepper
⅛ teaspoon pepper
4 ounces extra-sharp cheddar cheese, cut into ½-inch cubes (1 cup)
1 cup whole milk
½ cup sour cream
3 tablespoons unsalted butter, melted and cooled
1 large egg, lightly beaten

1. Adjust oven rack to middle position and heat oven to 350 degrees. Spray 8½ by 4½-inch loaf pan with vegetable oil spray, then sprinkle ½ cup Parmesan evenly in bottom of pan.
2. Whisk flour, baking powder, salt, cayenne, and pepper together in large bowl. Using rubber spatula, stir in cheddar, breaking up clumps, until cheese is coated with flour. Whisk milk, sour cream, melted butter, and egg together in medium bowl. Gently fold milk mixture into flour mixture until just combined (batter will be heavy and thick; do not overmix). Transfer batter to prepared pan; spread to sides of pan and smooth top with rubber spatula. Sprinkle remaining ½ cup Parmesan evenly over surface.
3. Bake until deep golden brown and toothpick inserted in center comes out clean, 45 to 50 minutes, rotating pan halfway through baking. Let loaf cool in pan on wire rack for 5 minutes. Remove loaf from pan and let cool on wire rack for 45 minutes before serving.

variations

Quick Cheese Bread with Bacon, Onion, and Gruyère

Cook 5 slices bacon, cut into ½-inch pieces, in 10-inch nonstick skillet over medium heat, stirring occasionally, until crispy, 5 to 7 minutes. Using slotted spoon, transfer bacon to paper towel–lined plate and pour off all but 3 tablespoons fat from skillet. Add ½ cup finely chopped onion to skillet and cook, stirring frequently, until softened, about 3 minutes. Substitute Gruyère for cheddar and omit butter. Add bacon and onion to flour mixture with cheese in step 2.

Quick Cheese Muffins

MAKES 12 MUFFINS

Adjust oven rack to middle position and heat oven to 375 degrees. Reduce Parmesan cheese to 2 ounces and cut cheddar into ¼-inch cubes. Spray 12-cup muffin tin with vegetable oil spray, then sprinkle each muffin cup with about 1 teaspoon grated Parmesan cheese, tapping and shaking pan so that cheese evenly coats sides and bottom of each cup. Prepare batter as directed. Using ice cream scoop or large spoon, divide batter evenly among prepared muffin cups, dropping batter to form mounds (do not level or flatten batter). Sprinkle remaining Parmesan evenly over surface of batter. Reduce baking time to 20 to 25 minutes, rotating muffin tin halfway through baking. Let muffins cool in tin on wire rack for 5 minutes, then invert muffins onto wire rack, turn right side up, and continue to let cool until warm, about 30 minutes.

MAKING CHEESE BREAD

1. Coat bottom of greased loaf pan with Parmesan cheese to create flavorful crust.

2. Add cubed cheese to bowl with dry ingredients and mix well, breaking apart pieces that clump.

3. Whisk wet ingredients in second bowl. Pour into bowl with dry ingredients and fold until combined.

4. Scrape batter into prepared pan, sprinkle with remaining Parmesan, and bake.

FRESH CORN CORNBREAD

BRIDGET LANCASTER, *July/August 2013*

Cornbread falls into two main styles: the sweet, cakey Northern type and the crusty, savory kind more often found in Southern kitchens. Each has its die-hard fans, but—let's face the facts—neither tastes much like corn. This is because most cornbreads are made with cornmeal alone, and no fresh corn at all. Furthermore, the so-called "field" or "dent" corn used to make cornmeal is far starchier (read: less flavorful) than the sweet corn grown to eat off the cob.

But getting real corn flavor in cornbread wouldn't be as simple as tossing some fresh-cut kernels into the batter. When I tried, I found that I needed to add at least 2 whole cups of kernels for the corn flavor to really shine, and since fresh kernels are full of moisture, the crumb of the cornbread was now riddled with unpleasant gummy pockets. What's more, the kernels turned chewy and tough as the bread baked. But I was determined to find a way to get true sweet corn flavor in cornbread.

For a cornbread that actually tastes like sweet corn, not cornmeal, the secret is cooking down pureed fresh corn until it becomes corn butter.

CORN STALKER

I decided to work on the cornbread base first. The little bit of sweetener added to Northern-style versions helped fresh corn flavor break through, so I settled on that archetype. For my working recipe, I used slightly more cornmeal than flour and decided to abandon fine-ground cornmeal in favor of the stone-ground type, which contains both the hull and the oil-rich germ of the corn kernel. The upshot: a more rustic texture and fuller flavor. For the liquid component, I would stick with traditional tangy buttermilk. Three tablespoons of melted butter and two eggs provided richness, and baking the cornbread in a cast-iron skillet allowed it to develop a brown, crisp crust.

With the batter figured out, I turned back to the problems of the fresh corn. I wondered if I could get rid of the unpleasantly steamed, chewy texture of the kernels by soaking them in a solution of water and baking soda before adding them to the batter—a technique we recently used to tenderize kernels for a fresh corn salsa. (The baking soda helps soften the hulls of the kernels.) Sure enough, the kernels were tender—until they were baked in the bread and the heat of the oven toughened them right back up. And I still had the issue of all those wet, gummy pockets. Out of ideas, I was idly flipping through cookbooks when I came across a recipe for "corn butter" made by pureeing fresh kernels and then reducing the mixture on the stove until thick. I tried it using three large ears of corn and found that the puree thickened and turned deep yellow in minutes, transforming into a "butter" packed with concentrated corn flavor. While the recipes I found used the corn butter as a spread, I added the reduced puree right to a batch of batter, baked it—and rejoiced. My cornbread tasted like real corn, without any distracting chewiness.

Since cooking the corn puree drove off moisture, my bread no longer had gummy pockets, but now the bread was almost too dry and even a little crumbly—a result of the large amount of natural cornstarch (released by pureeing the kernels) that was now absorbing moisture in the batter. This problem was easy to solve by increasing the amount of fat in the batter: an extra egg yolk and 2 more tablespoons of butter did the trick.

Moist, tender, and bursting with corn flavor, my cornbread tasted like a bite of corn on the cob.

Fresh Corn Cornbread

SERVES 6 TO 8

We prefer to use a well-seasoned cast-iron skillet in this recipe, but an ovensafe 10-inch skillet can be used in its place. Alternatively, in step 4 you can add 1 tablespoon of butter to a 9-inch cake pan and place it in the oven until the butter melts, about 3 minutes.

1⅓ cups (6⅔ ounces) stone-ground cornmeal
1 cup (5 ounces) all-purpose flour
2 tablespoons sugar
1½ teaspoons baking powder
¼ teaspoon baking soda
1¼ teaspoons salt
3 ears corn, kernels cut from cobs (2¼ cups)
6 tablespoons unsalted butter, cut into 6 pieces
1 cup buttermilk
2 large eggs plus 1 large yolk

1. Adjust oven rack to middle position and heat oven to 400 degrees. Whisk cornmeal, flour, sugar, baking powder, baking soda, and salt together in large bowl.
2. Process corn kernels in blender until very smooth, about 2 minutes. Transfer puree to medium saucepan (you should have about 1½ cups). Cook puree over medium heat, stirring constantly, until very thick and deep yellow and it measures ¾ cup, 5 to 8 minutes.
3. Remove pan from heat. Add 5 tablespoons butter and whisk until melted and incorporated. Add buttermilk and whisk until incorporated. Add eggs and yolk and whisk until incorporated. Transfer corn mixture to bowl with cornmeal mixture and, using rubber spatula, fold together until just combined.
4. Melt remaining 1 tablespoon butter in 10-inch cast-iron skillet over medium heat. Scrape batter into skillet and spread into even layer. Bake until top is golden brown and toothpick inserted in center comes out clean, 23 to 28 minutes. Let cool on wire rack for 5 minutes. Remove cornbread from skillet and let cool for 20 minutes before cutting into wedges and serving.

EASY SANDWICH BREAD

ANDREA GEARY, *January/February 2014*

A freshly baked loaf of bread is one of life's great pleasures. But these days, most people don't have 4 hours to devote to mixing dough, waiting for it to rise for an hour or so—twice—plus kneading (even if it's the stand mixer approach of most recipes today), shaping, and baking. While I can appreciate the classic bread-making process, I wondered: Could I find a way to make a yeasted loaf of bread in about half of the time? Furthermore, could I possibly avoid, or at least shortcut, some of the work?

I began by scouring cookbooks and websites for clever bread-making tricks and came across an old-fashioned type of loaf: batter bread. As its name implies, the yeasted loaf begins with a fluid batter (not a thick dough) that's made of all-purpose flour, yeast, salt, sugar, and quite a bit of water. Since its hydration level is so high (80 to 85 percent), the batter is beaten with a paddle instead of a dough hook (usually for about 5 minutes) and is transferred straight from the mixing bowl to a prepared loaf pan, no shaping required. And some recipes call for only one rise rather than the two needed to make most traditional loaves. They all promised tender loaves with great flavor—homemade sandwich bread without all the work. Was it too good to be true?

Using a moderate amount of water and leaving the salt out of our dough until the second rise allows our bread to build structure fast.

Well, yes and no. The few batter bread recipes I tried featured quick and easy aspects—less time being kneaded in the mixer (some even relied on just a wooden spoon and bowl), abbreviated or fewer proofs, and no shaping—that met my requirements. But that speed and simplicity came at a price. The loaves were generally squat and dumpy-looking, with bumpy, sunken tops instead of smooth, tender domes. Slicing revealed damp, fragile interiors that were exceedingly yeasty but otherwise bland. I wanted great-tasting bread with a soft, uniform crumb sturdy enough to support sandwich fillings. To get a loaf that justified even a modest effort, I'd have to make some serious modifications.

BUILDING CHARACTER

I decided to solve the easiest problem first: that single-note yeast flavor. For quick rising, all the batter bread recipes that I found rely on more than twice as much yeast as traditional loaf recipes do: 2¼ teaspoons versus 1 teaspoon. But all that yeast was giving the breads an overly yeasty, not "bready," flavor. Nevertheless, I was committed to sticking with the large amount since it made such a huge time savings.

My strategy was to cover up part of the yeastiness by working in some more flavorful ingredients. Adding a few tablespoons of melted butter was a good start, and substituting whole-wheat flour for a portion of the all-purpose flour provided nutty, wheaty depth. I also traded the sugar for 1 tablespoon of honey, which contributed complexity, and, because heat causes honey to break down into simple sugars that encourage browning, it also gave the crust more color.

Next up: building that complexity. In traditional bread, complexity develops by way of fermentation, which happens during the first and second rises. In these two proofing stages (each of which takes about an hour) the yeast consumes the sugars that are created as the starches in the flour break down, producing the gases essential for making the dough rise. Along the way, a multitude of flavorful byproducts are generated: sugars, acids, and alcohol. Knowing this, I decided I couldn't get by with just one rise. Two 20-minute proofs—one after mixing the batter and one after transferring it to the pan—would allow for some flavor development.

My bread, which was coming together in about 90 minutes, now had quite a bit more depth, and the yeast flavor was much less noticeable than in previous versions. But it still wasn't winning points for its damp, fragile texture or sunken appearance.

NETWORK FAILURE

Yeasted breads derive their light, airy structure from gluten, a stretchy protein network that forms only when wheat flour is combined with water. That network traps the gases given off by the yeast, inflating the dough and causing it to rise. (If the gluten structure is weak, the network can't hold enough gas and the bread will collapse in the heat of the oven.) When a dough is initially mixed, the proteins that form the network are weak and disorganized. They need to align in order to link up and acquire strength. Given enough time, they will line up on their own, or they can be physically encouraged to do so by kneading.

You'd think that my bread would have had a strong gluten network since I had been beating the batter in the mixer for 5 minutes. Yet the loaf's inadequate volume, sunken top, and fragile crumb suggested otherwise.

Before launching an in-depth investigation into the disappointing structure and crumb, I made a quick adjustment: I swapped the all-purpose flour for higher-protein bread flour. More gluten-forming proteins in the bread-flour dough would surely result in a more robust structure. This switch was a step in the right direction, but my loaf still had a long way to go.

My batter had so much water in it that the loaf was damp. Maybe that was too much liquid? The hydration level of a dough (or batter, in this case) affects gluten strength: Generally, the more water, the stronger and more extensible the gluten strands are and the better able they are to provide support. That translates into a sturdier, airier bread. But there's a tipping point: Unless you are

planning on a long fermentation—which I wasn't—too much water can actually inhibit the formation of gluten. I had been using 1¾ cups warm water (using warm, rather than room-temperature, water helps jump-start the yeast's activity, ensuring a faster rise). Guessing that my existing batter was too wet, I reduced the water in my next batch to 1¼ cups.

I beat the batter for 5 minutes on medium speed, then set it aside to rise. (The hydration level was still notably high; the dough was still pourable.) After 20 minutes, I transferred the mixture to a greased loaf pan, smoothed the top with a spatula, and let it rise again briefly before baking it. After the loaf cooled, I evaluated it for signs of improvement. It had a better top: not quite domed, but at least it wasn't lumpy or sunken. When I sliced it, I found a crumb that was not as damp as those of my earlier versions, but it was still fragile. I had made modest progress but not enough.

In other test kitchen bread recipes, we have waited to add the salt until later in the mixing process. Why? Salt inhibits both the ability of flour to absorb water and the activity of the enzymes that break down proteins to begin the process of forming gluten. By delaying the addition of salt, I hoped that my bread would develop a stronger gluten network. I mixed the flours, yeast, honey, water, and butter until everything was combined and let the batter rise for 20 minutes. Then I added the salt (dissolved in 2 tablespoons of water for even distribution) and proceeded with mixing, rising, and so on.

At last I had a complete success. The resulting loaf was crowned with a rounded top, and the crumb was more resilient and no longer wet. I had a flavorful sandwich bread that could be made start to finish in about 90 minutes. To highlight my crowning achievement, I brushed the risen loaf with a shine-enhancing egg wash before baking. As a finishing touch, I brushed the warm loaf with melted butter after turning it out on the cooling rack, which augmented the sheen and made the thin crust even more tender and delicious.

This bread is so easy and quick that fitting it into my schedule will be no problem.

Easy Sandwich Bread

MAKES 1 LOAF

The test kitchen's preferred loaf pan measures 8½ by 4½ inches; if using a 9 by 5-inch loaf pan, start checking for doneness 5 minutes early. To prevent the loaf from deflating as it rises, do not let the batter come in contact with the plastic wrap. This loaf is best eaten the day it is made, but leftovers may be wrapped in plastic wrap and stored for up to two days at room temperature or frozen for up to one month.

2 cups (11 ounces) bread flour
6 tablespoons (2 ounces) whole-wheat flour
2¼ teaspoons instant or rapid-rise yeast
1¼ cups plus 2 tablespoons warm water (120 degrees)
3 tablespoons unsalted butter, melted
1 tablespoon honey
¾ teaspoon salt
1 large egg, lightly beaten with 1 teaspoon water and pinch salt

1. In bowl of stand mixer, whisk bread flour, whole-wheat flour, and yeast together. Add 1¼ cups warm water, 2 tablespoons melted butter, and honey. Fit stand mixer with paddle and mix on low speed for 1 minute. Increase speed to medium and mix for 2 minutes. Scrape down bowl and paddle with greased rubber spatula. Continue to mix 2 minutes longer. Remove bowl and paddle from mixer. Scrape down bowl and paddle, leaving paddle in batter. Cover with plastic wrap and let batter rise in warm place until doubled in size, about 20 minutes.

2. Adjust oven rack to lower-middle position and heat oven to 375 degrees. Spray 8½ by 4½-inch loaf pan with vegetable oil spray. Dissolve salt in remaining 2 tablespoons warm water. When batter has doubled, attach bowl and paddle to mixer. Add salt-water mixture and mix on low speed until water is mostly incorporated, about 40 seconds. Increase speed to medium and mix until thoroughly combined, about 1 minute, scraping down paddle if necessary. Transfer batter to prepared pan and smooth surface with greased rubber spatula. Cover with plastic wrap and leave in warm place until batter reaches ½ inch below edge of pan, 15 to 20 minutes. Uncover and let rise until center of batter is level with edge of pan, 5 to 10 minutes.

3. Gently brush top of risen loaf with egg mixture. Bake until deep golden brown and loaf registers 208 to 210 degrees, 40 to 45 minutes. Using dish towels, carefully invert bread onto wire rack. Reinvert loaf and brush top and sides with remaining 1 tablespoon melted butter. Let cool completely before slicing and serving.

POURABLE DOUGH

The dough for this sandwich bread is so wet that it is actually more like a batter. After a brief first rise, you simply pour it straight from the mixer bowl into the loaf pan—you couldn't shape it even if you tried.

KEYS TO FASTER AND EASIER BREAD

While most breads require several hours, ours takes only 90 minutes from start to finish. Here's how we did it.

MORE YEAST
Lots of yeast means a faster rise—20 minutes versus up to 2 hours for a standard loaf.

HIGHER HYDRATION
More water in the dough (up to a point) enhances gluten structure without requiring as much kneading; it also results in pourable dough that doesn't need shaping.

PADDLE ATTACHMENT
Using a paddle instead of a dough hook allows for more aggressive, faster kneading.

EASY MULTIGRAIN SANDWICH BREAD

ERIKA BRUCE, *March/April 2006*

When it comes to multigrain bread, there are two distinct styles: the rustic free-form loaf found in artisan bakeries and your basic sandwich loaf. While the hearty, rustic loaves sport a thick, crunchy crust and a flavorful, chewy interior, re-creating this version at home requires lots of time (for an overnight sponge) and special equipment (a superhot oven, a baking stone, and so on).

Sandwich-style multigrain bread, on the other hand, requires only a loaf pan and a modest amount of effort. The problem is that the hearty, multigrain flavor is usually sacrificed for the light, tender texture that is well suited to sandwiches, and you end up with all fluff and no substance. Even the small amount of effort necessary to make this loaf should yield something tastier than presliced supermarket bread.

After digging through cookbooks geared more toward the bread hobbyist than the casual cook, I found a few recipes that held promise. Lengthy ingredient lists, which included obscure grains, called for an excursion to the natural foods store, but the techniques were straightforward enough. Unfortunately, these doughs—full of heavy grains and whole-grain flours—baked into poorly risen loaves, dense and heavy as bricks. I wanted a lighter loaf, tender enough for a sandwich yet with the sweet, nutty, complex flavor of bakery bread.

GLUTEN FOR PUNISHMENT

Using instant yeast for a quick rise, I started with our basic whole-wheat sandwich bread recipe, calling for 6 cups of flour (roughly half whole-wheat and half all-purpose), 2½ cups of water, ¼ cup of honey, and a tablespoon of salt. I replaced some of the flour with a generous cup of mixed grains (I'd work out the precise components later). The result was one dense and heavy loaf. It was obvious that the added grains were the problem. I knew that the sharp flakes of bran in whole-wheat flour can actually slice through and weaken the matrix of gluten—a protein made when flour and water are mixed—that gives all breads their strength and structure. Apparently, the rough-edged grains were having the same effect. That plus their added weight were impeding the development of gluten. To get the light texture I was after, the bread needed more gluten.

Because the protein content of any flour is an indicator of how much gluten it will produce, I thought first to switch out all-purpose flour (protein content of 10 to 12 percent) for bread flour (12 percent or more). But this only made the bread chewier, not less dense. Next I tried reducing the whole-wheat flour to half of the amount of all-purpose; any less meant sacrificing flavor. (While whole-wheat flour has a high protein content—about 14 percent—its density, like its bran flakes, can impede gluten development.) This step did alleviate some of the denseness, but the bread still felt heavy and dry. I added melted butter, which lubricated and tenderized the dough, but it didn't create more lift. I went so far as to add vital wheat gluten (made by stripping away most components of flour, leaving behind a whopping 75 to 80 percent pure protein). At last, I sliced into a well-risen loaf with a light, feathery crumb, but the wheat gluten left behind a bitter aftertaste. Frustrated, I moved on to kneading in hopes of finding a solution.

WORKING IT OUT

While the purist mode of some multigrain recipes requires kneading the dough by hand, I wanted to avoid a full workout. I pulled out my trusty stand mixer and mixed the dough on medium-high speed in an effort to kick-start the gluten development (gluten, once hydrated, is stretched and strengthened via mechanical action). But the texture was crumbly. I tried lowering the mixer speed and experimenting with timing: After 3 minutes of mixing, the bread hardly rose in the pans; after 5 minutes, the loaves had better height. I kept mixing until the dough became very elastic and bounced back when I poked it, a total of about 10 minutes. This dough rose well and sported a mediumholed, albeit still crumbly, texture.

For a light and flavorful multigrain loaf, we turn to an unexpected source: seven-grain hot cereal mix.

Next, I ran through the gamut of traditional bread-mixing techniques to see if any proved helpful. Some recipes call for punching down the dough after the first rise, a step that redistributes the sugars (broken-down starches) that feed the yeast and get it working more rapidly. But speeding up the yeast action served only to give the bread a boozy flavor (alcohol is a byproduct of yeast metabolism). I then decided to try an autolyse, a resting period just after the initial mixing of water and flour that gives the flour time to hydrate. This step proved vital, ramping up the development of gluten (which depends on water) and making the dough less tacky and so easier to work with and the baked loaf less crumbly. The bread now had a nice chew, without being tough.

AGAINST THE GRAIN

I was ready to tackle the grains. Driving all over town collecting one obscure grain here and another there was an onerous task. Could I pare down the list without losing the multidimensional flavor profile? I started with basic grains that were available at the supermarket: cornmeal, rolled oats, and rye flour. But this abridged grain mixture produced a loaf that was more of a muddy-tasting rye

than a sweet, earthy multigrain bread. I returned to the supermarket in search of other options. As I scanned the shelves of steel-cut oats and Cream of Wheat in the hot cereal section, my eyes fell upon a package of seven-grain cereal, a handy mixture of ground whole grains, including the hard-to-find varieties. I quickly snatched up a package and headed back to the kitchen to see if it could deliver flavor as well as convenience.

Sure enough, the complexity was there—from the nutty flax seed to the tangy rye and sweet wheat—but some of the grains remained distractingly hard and crunchy, even after baking. I tried soaking them for up to 24 hours before mixing them into the dough, but they seemed impervious to room-temperature water. Because these grains were meant to make a hot cereal, I tried cooking them per the package instructions, allowing the mixture to cool before adding my yeast, flours, and salt. But this dough was soupy and wet, requiring a startling 2 cups of additional flour before it became manageable.

Not discouraged, I tried using only the amount of water already called for in my bread recipe, bringing it to a boil, and pouring it over the grains. Once cooled, this thick porridge produced a dough with the right moisture content and a baked loaf with grains that added interesting textural contrast without cracking any teeth.

Now the only thing missing from my bread was the welcome (gentle) crunch of seeds. I tried poppy and sesame, but they were too small and got lost in the mix of grains. Sunflower and pumpkin seeds were better able to distinguish themselves from the crowd and added a nutty richness as well. Last, I rolled the shaped loaves in oats to give them a finished, professional look. While my tasters had undoubtedly suffered through plenty of barely edible loaves, in the end they could hardly believe that the ones they were eating hadn't been smuggled in from the bakery down the street. Not bad for just a few hours in the kitchen.

Multigrain Bread

MAKES 2 LOAVES

Don't confuse the seven-grain hot cereal mix called for in this recipe with boxed, cold breakfast cereals that may also be labeled "seven-grain." Do not substitute instant oats in this recipe. For an accurate measurement of boiling water, bring a full kettle of water to a boil and then measure out the desired amount. The test kitchen's preferred loaf pan measures 8½ by 4½ inches; if using 9 by 5-inch loaf pans, start checking for doneness 5 minutes early.

1¼ cups (6¼ ounces) seven-grain hot cereal mix
2½ cups boiling water
3 cups (15 ounces) all-purpose flour, plus extra as needed
1½ cups (8¼ ounces) whole-wheat flour
¼ cup honey
4 tablespoons unsalted butter, melted and cooled
2½ teaspoons instant or rapid-rise yeast
1 tablespoon salt
¾ cup unsalted pepitas or sunflower seeds
½ cup (1½ ounces) old-fashioned rolled oats or quick oats
Vegetable oil spray

1. Place cereal mix in bowl of stand mixer. Pour boiling water over cereal mix and let stand, stirring occasionally, until mixture cools to 100 degrees and resembles thick porridge, about 1 hour. Whisk all-purpose flour and whole-wheat flour together in separate bowl.
2. Fit stand mixer with dough hook; add honey, butter, and yeast to cooled grain mixture; and mix on low speed until combined. Add flour mixture, ½ cup at a time, and mix until cohesive mass starts to form, 1½ to 2 minutes. Cover bowl with plastic wrap and let dough rest for 20 minutes. Add salt to dough and knead on medium-low speed until dough clears sides of bowl, 3 to 4 minutes (if it does not clear sides, add extra 2 to 3 tablespoons all-purpose flour and knead until it does); continue to knead dough for 5 minutes longer. Add pepitas and knead for another 15 seconds. Transfer dough to lightly floured counter and knead by hand until pepitas are evenly dispersed and dough forms smooth, round ball, about 30 seconds. Transfer dough to large, lightly greased bowl; cover bowl tightly with plastic and let dough rise at room temperature until nearly doubled in size, 45 minutes to 1 hour.
3. Grease two 8½ by 4½-inch loaf pans. Spread oats on rimmed baking sheet. Transfer dough to lightly floured counter and divide in half with bench scraper. Press 1 piece of dough into 9 by 6-inch rectangle, with short side facing you. Roll dough toward you into firm cylinder, keeping dough taut by tucking it under itself as you go. Turn cylinder seam side up and pinch it closed. Repeat with second piece of dough. Spray cylinders lightly with oil spray and roll in oats to coat evenly; place coated cylinders seam side down in prepared pans, pressing gently into corners. Cover pans loosely with greased plastic and let dough rise at room temperature until nearly doubled in size, 30 to 40 minutes. (Dough should barely spring back when poked with your knuckle.)
4. Thirty minutes before baking, adjust oven rack to middle position and heat oven to 375 degrees. Bake until loaves register 200 degrees, 35 to 40 minutes. Let loaves cool in pans on wire rack for 5 minutes. Remove loaves from pans and let cool completely on rack, about 2 hours, before slicing and serving. (Bread can be wrapped in double layer of plastic and stored at room temperature for up to 2 days. Wrapped in additional layer of aluminum foil, bread can be frozen for up to 1 month.)

NO-KNEAD BREAD 2.0

J. KENJI LOPEZ-ALT, *January/February 2008*

In November 2006, *New York Times* writer Mark Bittman published a recipe developed by Jim Lahey of the Sullivan Street Bakery in Manhattan that promised to shake up the world of home baking. The recipe did the seemingly impossible. It allowed the average home cook to bake a loaf of bread that looked like it had been produced in a professional bakery. The recipe, which instantly won legions of followers, was exceedingly simple: Combine a few cups of flour, a tiny amount of yeast, and a little salt in a bowl; stir in some water until the ingredients just come together; and leave the dough to rise. After 12 to 18 hours, the dough is turned a couple of times, shaped, risen, and baked in a Dutch oven. An hour later, out comes the most beautiful loaf most people have ever baked at home—and all with no kneading.

At first, it seemed unlikely that there was anything to improve upon here. The recipe was remarkably easy and worlds better than other no-fuss breads. But there were some complaints amid all the praise. I decided to give the existing recipe to five inexperienced bakers to see what (if any) issues arose, and noticed a problem even before we sliced into them. While all were beautifully browned and crisp, the loaves varied wildly in size and shape, ranging from rounded mounds to flat, irregular blobs. And though the crusts were extraordinary—better than any I'd ever produced—the flavor fell flat in every sample. It simply did not capture the complex yeasty, tangy flavor of a true artisanal loaf. I wondered if I could make this bread more consistent and better-tasting.

ANALYZING AUTOLYSIS

I decided to tackle the problem of shape first. Thanks to the ingenious use of a Dutch oven, the bread always acquired a dark, crisp crust, but the loaves took on a disconcertingly broad range of forms. After watching testers make the recipe a few times, I realized what the problem was: The dough's wetness was making it too delicate to handle. Though it was well risen before baking, it was deflating on its way into the pot. In addition, because of its high moisture content, the dough was spreading out over the bottom of the pot before it could firm up properly. I analyzed the no-knead recipe and found that its dough is 85 percent hydrated—meaning that for every 10 ounces of flour, there are 8.5 ounces of water. Most rustic breads, on the other hand, max out at around 80 percent hydration, and standard sandwich breads hover between 60 percent and 75 percent hydration. This got me to thinking: What would happen if I reduced the water?

To find out, I made a batch of dough in which I cut the hydration to 70 percent. Sure enough, this dough was much easier to handle and emerged from the oven well risen and perfectly shaped. But instead of having an open, airy crumb structure, this loaf was dense and chewy, with rubbery pockets of unleavened flour. So more moisture led to an open but squat loaf and less moisture led to a high but dense loaf. Was there a way to reconcile these two extremes?

Many bread recipes call for a rest period after adding water to the flour but before kneading. This rest is called "autolysis" (although most bakers use the French term autolyse). In most recipes, autolysis is just 20 to 30 minutes, but the no-knead bread calls for something completely out of the ordinary: a 12-hour rest. I hoped I could analyze the mechanics of this lengthy autolysis to help me solve the textural problem.

The ultimate goal of making bread dough is to create gluten, a strong network of cross-linked proteins that traps air bubbles and stretches as the dough bakes, creating the bubbly, chewy crumb structure that is the signature of a good loaf. In order to form these cross-links, the proteins in the flour need to be aligned next to each other. Imagine the proteins as bundled-up balls of yarn you are trying to tie together into one longer piece, which you'll then sew together into a wider sheet. In their balled-up state, it's not possible to tie them together; first you have to untangle and straighten them out. This straightening out and aligning is usually accomplished by kneading.

But untangling and stretching out short pieces of yarn is much easier than untangling entire balls. This is where autolysis comes in. As the dough autolyzes, enzymes naturally present in wheat act like scissors, cutting the balled-up proteins into smaller segments that are easier to straighten during kneading. This is why dough that has undergone autolysis requires much less kneading than freshly made dough. And here's where the hydration level comes in: The more water there is, the more efficiently the cut-and-link process takes place.

A lower hydration level and 1 minute of kneading makes this revolutionary method even better.

So this was the explanation for how the no-knead bread recipe published in *The New York Times* worked. With 85 percent hydration and a 12-hour rest, the dough was so wet and had autolyzed for so long that the enzymes had broken the proteins down into extremely small pieces. These pieces were so small that, even without kneading, they could stretch out and cross-link during fermentation and the brief turning step. At 70 percent hydration, there simply was not enough water in my dough for the enzymes to act as efficiently as they had in the original recipe. As a result, many of the proteins in my finished bread were still in a semiballed-up state, giving my bread an overly chewy texture.

What if the secret was actually adding some kneading? I knew that even at a relatively dry 70 percent hydration, the proteins in my dough had already been broken down

significantly by the long autolysis. All they probably needed was a little kneading to untangle and create an airy, light crumb.

This time, I gave the rested dough the bare minimum of kneads—adding just 1 minute to the no-knead recipe—and continued exactly as I had before. The dough emerged from the oven beautifully browned and perfectly shaped. After letting it cool, I cut into it to reveal an ideal crumb structure. And I found that since such a small amount of kneading could develop gluten in such a forceful manner, I could reduce the minimum time of the rest period from 12 hours to 8 hours.

NO SUBSTITUTE FOR FLAVOR

Now that I had bread with a great shape and texture, I turned my attention to solving the problem of the loaf's lackluster taste. How could I get the complex, almost tangy flavors of bakery breads made with fermented starters?

Since I was partially looking for acidity and tang, I started by adding vinegar. The majority of bottled vinegars are 5 percent solutions of acetic acid—the same acid produced by bacteria during dough fermentation. Since other vinegars would introduce undesirable flavors to the bread, I experimented with different amounts of distilled white vinegar, settling on one tablespoon.

What I needed now was a concentrated shot of yeasty flavor. Luckily, beyond bread, there is another commonly available substance that relies on yeast for flavor: beer.

After testing different types, I discovered that light American-style lagers gave the loaf a distinct "bready" (not "beery") aroma that could fool anyone who had not seen the lager go into the dough. It turns out that the yeast in lagers is treated in a way that closely resembles the way yeast acts in dough, resulting in the production of similar flavor compounds.

Through the simplest of tweaks—less hydration, the addition of vinegar and beer, and a few seconds of kneading—I had a loaf of bread that looked and tasted incredible.

Almost No-Knead Bread

MAKES 1 ROUND LOAF

Although an enameled cast-iron Dutch oven will yield the best results, the recipe also works in a regular cast-iron Dutch oven or heavy stockpot. Check the knob on your Dutch oven lid, as not all are ovensafe to 425 degrees; look for inexpensive replacement knobs from the manufacturer (or try using a metal drawer handle from a hardware store). This dough rises best in a warm kitchen—at least 68 degrees.

3 cups (15 ounces) all-purpose flour
1½ teaspoons salt
¼ teaspoon instant or rapid-rise yeast
¾ cup water, room temperature
6 tablespoons mild-flavored lager, such as Budweiser, room temperature
1 tablespoon distilled white vinegar
Vegetable oil spray

1. Whisk flour, salt, and yeast together in large bowl. Add water, beer, and vinegar. Using rubber spatula, fold mixture, scraping up dry flour from bottom of bowl, until shaggy ball forms. Cover bowl with plastic wrap and let sit at room temperature for at least 8 hours or up to 18 hours.

2. Lay 18 by 12-inch sheet of parchment paper on counter and coat lightly with oil spray. Transfer dough to lightly floured counter and knead by hand 10 to 15 times. Shape dough into ball by pulling edges into middle. Transfer loaf, seam side down, to center of greased parchment paper. Using parchment paper as sling, gently lower dough into heavy-bottomed Dutch oven. Mist dough lightly with oil spray, cover loosely with plastic, and let rise at room temperature until doubled in size, about 2 hours. (Dough should barely spring back when poked with your knuckle.)

3. Adjust oven rack to middle position. Lightly flour top of loaf. Using sharp serrated knife, cut ½-inch-deep X into top of loaf. Cover pot and place in oven. Heat oven to 425 degrees. Once oven reaches 425 degrees, bake for 30 minutes.

4. Remove lid and continue to bake until crust is deep golden brown and loaf registers 210 degrees, 20 to 30 minutes longer. Carefully remove loaf from pot using parchment sling and transfer to wire rack, discarding parchment. Let cool completely, about 2 hours, before serving. (Bread is best eaten on day it is baked but will keep, wrapped in double layer of plastic and stored at room temperature, for up to 2 days. To recrisp crust, place unwrapped bread in 450-degree oven for 6 to 8 minutes.)

variations

Almost No-Knead Bread with Olives, Rosemary, and Parmesan

Add 2 cups finely grated Parmesan and 1 tablespoon minced fresh rosemary to flour mixture in step 1. Add 1 cup chopped pitted green olives with water.

Almost No-Knead Cranberry-Pecan Bread

Add ½ cup dried cranberries and ½ cup toasted pecans to flour mixture in step 1.

Almost No-Knead Seeded Rye Bread

Substitute 1 cup plus 2 tablespoons rye flour for 1¼ cups plus 2 tablespoons all-purpose flour. Add 2 tablespoons caraway seeds to flour mixture in step 1.

Almost No-Knead Whole-Wheat Bread

Substitute 1 cup whole-wheat flour for 1 cup all-purpose flour. Stir 2 tablespoons honey into water before adding it to flour mixture in step 1.

FOOLPROOF BRIOCHE

ANDREW JANJIGIAN, *March/April 2013*

Well-made brioche is something of a miracle: Despite being laden with butter and eggs, it manages to avoid the density of a pound cake and turn out incredibly light and airy. Yet this gossamer-wing texture still provides brioche with enough structure to serve as a base for a sandwich, a slice of toast slathered with jam, or even the foundation for bread pudding. But achieving these results is a balancing act—and a tricky one at that.

Most butter-enriched doughs, like those for sandwich bread or dinner rolls, contain between 10 and 20 percent butter. The average brioche recipe brings the ratio up to 50 percent (or 5 parts butter to 10 parts flour). Because fat lubricates the wheat proteins in the flour, any amount at all will inhibit their ability to form gluten, the network of cross-linked proteins that gives bread its structure. The more fat the greater the interference. This can make brioche incredibly tender—or it can cause the dough to separate into a greasy mess.

The typical brioche method goes as follows: After a sponge of flour, yeast, and water sits overnight in order to ferment and build flavor, additional flour, yeast, and water, as well as salt, sugar, and several eggs, are added, and the mixture is kneaded in a stand mixer until a strong gluten network has begun to form. The next step is to add butter, softened to just the right temperature, a few tablespoons at a time. Only after one portion is fully incorporated into the dough is the next added. This painstaking process, which can take more than 20 minutes, is necessary to ensure that the butter is completely and evenly combined without causing the dough to separate. Next, the dough is left to rise at room temperature for a few hours and then chilled in the refrigerator for anywhere from an hour to overnight to firm up the butter—an essential step when shaping a sticky, wet dough. Once cold, the dough is shaped into loaves, left to rise yet again, and—at long last—baked. Phew.

My goal: to make tender, plush brioche with butter-rich flavor but no butter-induced headache.

BUTTER UP

Though tempting, I knew that dumping everything (butter included) together at the start and letting the stand mixer knead it all into submission wouldn't work. All that softened butter would coat the wheat proteins (which normally come together to form gluten as soon as water is added to the mix) so thoroughly that no amount of kneading would develop sufficient structure.

To simplify this rich loaf, we eliminate the step of carefully kneading in softened butter in favor of melted butter and an extended rest period.

But what about cold butter? Cut into the flour before adding other ingredients, the solid little chunks surely wouldn't coat the proteins as readily as softened fat, making it possible to develop at least some gluten—or so I hoped.

Using a respectable 45 percent fat-to-flour ratio and simplifying things by leaving out the sponge, I began by cutting cold butter into flour in a food processor. After transferring the mixture to the bowl of a stand mixer, I threw in the yeast, sugar, and salt. With the dough hook turning, I gradually added some water and a few beaten eggs. The dough was quite wet but still had a surprising amount of structure. After putting the dough through the usual steps—proof, chill, proof—I baked it, fingers crossed.

The results? Not great, but not half bad either. The interior crumb was far too open, with large, irregular holes, and the bread had a cottony, crumbly texture, both of which suggested that it needed more gluten development. But its having any structure at all meant that I was onto something.

KNEADLESSLY COMPLICATED

A familiar approach popped to mind: the "no-knead" bread technique first popularized by Mark Bittman and Jim Lahey in *The New York Times*, which we adapted for our Almost No-Knead Bread (page 438). Basically, you combine all your ingredients and let the mixture sit for hours. During this long rest, enzymes naturally present in wheat help untangle the wheat proteins that eventually come together to form an organized gluten network. This allows the dough to stitch itself together into a loaf containing plenty of structure with only a bit of stirring and a couple of folds—no actual kneading required. The key to this technique is a very wet dough (the more water the more efficient the enzymes). And happily, brioche dough is highly hydrated.

I gave the no-knead approach a whirl, cutting the butter into the flour in the food processor like before but then simply mixing the liquid ingredients into the dry ones and stirring with a wooden spoon. This produced a dough that was soupy—exactly what I wanted. I covered it and let it sit at room temperature while it proofed, giving it a series of folds at 30-minute intervals to encourage the gluten to form. As I'd hoped, after several hours, the dough had just as much strength as the previous machine-kneaded one. Even better: After being chilled, shaped, and proofed a second time, it baked up just as nicely. Feeling emboldened, I wondered if I could eliminate the food processor step as well. So this time, I melted the butter, let it cool, then whisked it into the egg and milk mixture before adding the liquid to the dry ingredients. This simplification produced a loaf that was indistinguishable from the one in which I'd cut the butter into the flour first.

STRUCTURAL ENGINEERING

Still, my loaves remained cottony and open-crumbed—a sure sign that they needed more gluten than my hand-mixed method could provide on its own. But I had a few tricks up my sleeve.

First, the flour: Since its protein content is directly related to its ability to form gluten (the more protein it has the more structure it can provide to the dough), it was no shock that brioche made with flour containing the highest amount of protein—bread flour—was the clear winner.

Next, I'd let the dough sit even longer, a process that would not only increase gluten development but also add more flavor, since it would give the starches in the dough more time to ferment (a role normally played by a sponge). Gluten development and fermentation are slowed but not halted by cold temperatures, so I'd also extend the dough's second rest in the fridge (where it wouldn't run the risk of overproofing and collapsing), giving it even more strength. Sure enough, brioche made from dough that was allowed to rest overnight in the fridge was much improved: It had a more finely textured and resilient crumb than any previous versions, as well as a more complex flavor.

Lastly, I gave some consideration to my shaping method. Until now, I'd been forming the dough into a single long loaf. I realized that I could add even more strength and structure to the dough by dividing it in two and shaping each half into a tight, round ball instead. Placed side by side in the pan, the two balls merged during rising and baking to form a single loaf. Even this little bit of extra manipulation made the crumb a bit finer and more uniform. And if shaping them once was good, I figured that twice might be even better. After letting the dough rounds rest, I patted them flat once more and then reshaped them into tight balls. As expected, the interior crumb was fine-textured, uniform, and resilient but still delicate.

Finally, I had a reliable and relatively hands-off brioche recipe that could hold its own against those from the best bakeries in town.

No-Knead Brioche

MAKES 2 LOAVES

If you don't have a baking stone, bake the bread on a preheated rimmed baking sheet. The test kitchen's preferred loaf pan measures 8½ by 4½ inches; if using 9 by 5-inch loaf pans, start checking for doneness 5 minutes early.

3¼ cups (17¾ ounces) bread flour
2¼ teaspoons instant or rapid-rise yeast
Salt
7 large eggs
½ cup water, room temperature
⅓ cup (2⅓ ounces) sugar
16 tablespoons unsalted butter, melted and cooled slightly

1. Whisk flour, yeast, and 1½ teaspoons salt together in large bowl. Whisk 6 eggs, water, and sugar together in medium bowl until sugar has dissolved. Whisk in butter until smooth. Add egg mixture to flour mixture and stir with wooden spoon until uniform mass forms and no dry flour remains, about 1 minute. Cover bowl with plastic wrap and let stand for 10 minutes.

2. Holding edge of dough with your fingertips, fold dough over itself by gently lifting and folding edge of dough toward middle. Turn bowl 45 degrees; fold again. Turn bowl and fold dough 6 more times (total of 8 folds). Cover with plastic and let rise for 30 minutes. Repeat folding and rising every 30 minutes, 3 more times. After fourth set of folds, cover bowl tightly with plastic and refrigerate for at least 16 hours or up to 48 hours.

3. Transfer dough to well-floured counter and divide into 4 pieces. Working with 1 piece of dough at a time, pat dough into 4-inch disk. Working around circumference of dough, fold edges of dough toward center until ball forms. Flip dough over and, without applying pressure, move your hands in small circular motions to form dough into smooth, taut round. (If dough sticks to your hands, lightly dust top of dough with flour.) Repeat with remaining dough. Cover dough rounds loosely with plastic and let rest for 5 minutes.

4. Grease two 8½ by 4½-inch loaf pans. After 5 minutes, flip each dough ball so seam side is facing up, pat into 4-inch disk, and repeat rounding step. Place 2 rounds, seam side down, side by side into prepared pans and press gently into corners. Cover loaves loosely with plastic and let rise at room temperature until almost doubled in size (dough should rise to about ½ inch below top edge of pan), 1½ to 2 hours. Thirty minutes before baking, adjust oven rack to middle position, place baking stone on rack, and heat oven to 350 degrees.

5. Beat remaining 1 egg with pinch salt. Remove plastic and brush loaves gently with egg. Set loaf pans on stone and bake until golden brown and internal temperature registers 190 degrees, 35 to 45 minutes, rotating pans halfway through baking. Transfer pans to wire rack and let cool for 5 minutes. Remove loaves from pans, return to wire rack, and let cool completely before slicing and serving, about 2 hours.

MELTED BUTTER EASES THE WAY

Traditionally, making a rich dough like brioche means adding softened butter tablespoon by tablespoon to already-kneaded dough. It's a painstaking process, but if the butter isn't added slowly, the dough can break into a greasy mess. With our simpler "no-knead" technique, however, the dough (which must be very wet) sits for a long time, stitching itself together to form gluten without any help from a mixer. With kneading out of the equation, we were able to simply melt the butter and add it all at once.

FOLDING THE DOUGH

Gently lift edge of dough and fold it over itself. Turn bowl 45 degrees and repeat until you've made full circle (total of 8 folds).

FOOLPROOF THIN-CRUST PIZZA

ANDREW JANJIGIAN, *January/February 2011*

Pizza was the first food I learned to make as a kid, and I've been determined to perfect it ever since. Over the years, my dogged pursuit of the ideal crust—thin, crisp, and spottily charred on the exterior; tender yet chewy within—has led me into exhaustive research and experiments, and even compelled me to extremes. I've been known to override the lock on my oven during its white-hot cleaning cycle. I've even built a wood-fired oven in my backyard.

But despite those efforts, I had yet to produce a recipe that was both reliable and reasonable for someone baking in a conventional oven. After the 10 to 12 minutes necessary to crisp the crust, the interior inevitably turns dry and tough. Plus, the raw dough itself is a devil to work with: Too wet and it becomes sticky; too dry and it's a stiff, dense wad. And forget stretching it into a neat circle; most of the time it either rips or springs back like a rubber band. If I were really going to bring home the kind of pizza I've come to crave when dining out, I'd have to take each element back to the drawing board.

TESTING THE WATER

Like other lean doughs, pizza tends to have a short ingredient list (often just flour, water, salt, and yeast), so each element counts for a lot. Flour was the obvious first consideration, and I opted for high-protein (about 13 percent by weight) bread flour. It's a typical choice when a chewy, nicely tanned crust is the goal, since the proteins both encourage gluten development and brown easily.

The other major factor is the hydration level of the dough—in other words, the weight of the water in relation to the weight of the flour. From my recent work on focaccia, I knew that low-hydration doughs (55 to 70 percent water) generally result in the type of tight, even crumb you might find in sandwich bread, whereas a higher hydration (70 percent and up) produces the looser, airier, more bubbly crumb typical of rustic artisan-style breads. Figuring my goal was somewhere in the middle, I started my testing by mixing together five moderately wet doughs (from 58 to 67 percent hydration), kneading all the ingredients with our preferred food-processor method. (A more conventional stand-mixer method might take 15 to 20 minutes before the dough turns into a shiny, elastic mass, but we've recently found that a food processor turns out comparably kneaded results in less than 2 minutes.) I let the dough proof at room temperature for a few hours, shaped and topped the pies with our quick no-cook pizza sauce (a placeholder at this stage) and a generous handful of shredded mozzarella, and shuttled them onto blazing hot (500-degree) baking stones to cook. I pulled them out roughly 10 minutes later, once the crusts had puffed up a bit and blistered in spots and the cheese was melted and spotty brown.

An extended fermentation in the fridge gives our pizza dough complex flavor with minimal effort; baking on a high rack ensures great browning.

Just as I'd expected, the lower-hydration doughs were not only stiff and difficult to shape into even rounds when raw, but also tough to chew once baked. But really wet doughs weren't ideal either; though they emerged significantly more tender from the oven, all that water had made the raw dough so sticky and soft that it tended to tear when stretched. The best of the bunch fell at about 61 percent—enough to stretch easily without ripping or sticking to my fingers and retain moisture as it baked. With further experimentation, I found that I could raise the hydration level to 63 percent and still be able to handle this stickier dough by adding a little extra flour to the exterior as I shaped and stretched the pie. Such a judicious use of "bench flour" allowed me to increase the hydration of the dough while still maintaining the ability to shape it easily.

COLD STORAGE

With this dough I had a good jumping-off point, but pizza perfection was still a long way away. First off, instead of being thin and just a bit floppy, like a good parlor pie, my crust was bready and overinflated—more like focaccia than pizza—even when stretched as thinly as possible. Even more troubling, the dough was lacking in flavor, save for a strong yeastiness.

Simply dialing back on the yeast seemed like an obvious test—and did help deflate the too-puffy crust just a bit. But it also wiped out what little flavor the dough started with. Since keeping the yeast to a minimum was a given, I clearly needed an altogether different approach to fermentation.

First, a little background on the relationship between fermentation and dough's texture and flavor. When dough is first mixed, tiny "seed" bubbles form that expand with carbon dioxide at two different junctures: once when the bread is proofed and again when a last burst of carbon dioxide is produced during the first few minutes of baking. The larger the bubbles in the dough prior to baking, the more open and puffy the final dough will be. One way to minimize the size of the bubbles is to chill the dough as it proofs. Aside from producing finer, tighter air bubbles, cold fermentation has the added benefit of creating more flavorful dough. Why? Because at lower temperatures, yeast produces less carbon dioxide and more of the initial side products of fermentation: flavorful sugars, alcohol, and acids.

With that in mind, I mixed up a new batch of dough and immediately placed it in the refrigerator to proof. The next day, I pulled it out, divided and shaped it into rounds, and let it warm to room temperature while I preheated my baking stone. I was skeptical at first; unlike the room temperature–proofed batch, this dough looked pretty unremarkable,

showing none of the telltale signs of active fermentation such as an airy, bubbly structure. But one sniff of its heady, slightly boozy aroma clearly indicated that plenty had been happening beneath the surface. Furthermore, this tighter, smoother mass of dough proved much easier to work with, pulling effortlessly into a circle that gradually tapered in thickness from edge to center. I shouldn't have been surprised by this latter development. Besides slowing carbon dioxide production, chilling dough slows down gluten development so that dough literally stays looser, making it easier to stretch and hold its shape without snapping back. And the pizza it produced? Vastly better than previous attempts: Though not perfect, the dough was more complexly flavored and crisp than any other pie I'd made, with an interior that boasted decent tenderness and chew. Even the rim offered just the right degree of puffiness and functioned as an ample handle.

I had to wonder: If 24 hours of cold fermentation had such a dramatic effect on the dough, what would happen if I left it in the fridge even longer? Three days later, I had my answer. I'd mixed together and chilled a batch of dough each day over a 72-hour period, and the pizza bake-off proved that its flavor improved as time went by. (Push the fermentation beyond three days, however, and the yeast finally starts to produce a surplus of carbon dioxide, rendering the dough puffy.) True, cold fermented dough wasn't exactly quick, but the recipe was a snap to make. Plus, the long rest wasn't altogether inconvenient; with a little planning, this dough had great make-ahead potential.

HOT STONE

But the crust's crispness—or lack thereof—continued to nag me. Adding a tablespoon of oil to the dough helped a bit, but not enough. I had one other idea about how to encourage more crunch and color: sugar. We often sprinkle a spoonful over poultry skin to help it darken and crisp up in the oven, and I saw no reason the same trick couldn't be used here. I worked 2 teaspoons into the dough and, sure enough, the next pizza I pulled from the oven was tinged a slightly deeper shade of brown. But it still wasn't enough.

The real problem was the same one I'd been trying to address with all of my radical pizza-baking experiments over the years: Home ovens simply don't get hot enough to produce a deeply browned crust before the interior crumb dries out and toughens. The best solution has always been the hottest setting on the oven dial and a pizza stone, which soaks up the radiating heat like a sponge. Following that logic, most recipes call for the stone to be placed as low in the oven as possible, where it gets maximum exposure to the main heating element. But when I thought about it, that technique didn't really make sense—and I even had an industry clue to prove it: commercial pizza ovens. These wide, shallow chambers quickly reflect heat from the floor back onto the top of the pie as it cooks, preventing the crust from drying out before the toppings have browned. Obviously I couldn't alter the shape of my oven—but I could move the stone up closer to the top to narrow the gap between the stone and the ceiling. After a series of tests with thermocouples and an infrared thermometer, I found the best position for the stone is really as close to the top of the oven as possible—about 4 inches or so from the ceiling, which left just enough headroom to comfortably house the pie. When I pulled this latest attempt from my newfangled setup, the results were a revelation: Everything had baked in sync, producing a pizza that was thoroughly crisp, well browned on both top and bottom, and slightly chewy, just like a good parlor slice.

TO TOP IT OFF

All I had left to do was tweak the toppings. A splash of red wine vinegar gave my no-cook sauce a jolt of flavor. As for the cheese, I supplemented the creamy, stretchy mozzarella with a fistful of sharp, salty, finely grated Parmesan. And that's where I stopped. Of course, additional toppings are fine (provided one doesn't use too heavy a hand); but for me, this simple-to-make, simply dressed pie bakes up perfect as-is.

TOPPING TIPS

We like our Thin-Crust Pizza simply dressed with tomato sauce and handfuls of shredded mozzarella and Parmesan, but additional toppings are always an option—provided they're prepared correctly and added judiciously. (An overloaded pie will bake up soggy.) Here are a few guidelines for how to handle different types of toppings:

HEARTY VEGETABLES Aim for a maximum of 6 ounces per pie, spread out in a single layer. Vegetables such as onions, peppers, and mushrooms should be thinly sliced and lightly sautéed (or microwaved for a minute or two along with a little olive oil) before using.

DELICATE VEGETABLES AND HERBS Leafy greens and herbs like spinach and basil are best placed beneath the cheese to protect them or added raw to the fully cooked pizza.

MEATS Proteins (no more than 4 ounces per pie) should be precooked and drained to remove excess fat. We like to poach meats like sausage (broken up into ½-inch chunks), pepperoni, or ground beef for 4 to 5 minutes in a wide skillet along with ¼ cup of water, which helps to render the fat while keeping the meat moist.

SHRINK YOUR HEADROOM

Baking the pizza on the top rack—rather than the usual approach of placing it near the bottom of a home oven—means heat will hit the top of the pie, browning the toppings before the crust overcooks.

Thin-Crust Pizza

MAKES TWO 13-INCH PIZZAS

If you don't have a baking stone, bake the pizzas on an overturned and preheated rimmed baking sheet. You can shape the second dough round while the first pizza bakes, but don't add the toppings until just before baking. You will need a pizza peel for this recipe. It is important to use ice water in the dough to prevent it from overheating in the food processor. Semolina flour is ideal for dusting the peel; use it in place of bread flour if you have it. The sauce will yield more than needed in the recipe; extra sauce can be refrigerated for up to one week or frozen for up to one month.

Dough

3 cups (16½ ounces) bread flour
2 teaspoons sugar
½ teaspoon instant or rapid-rise yeast
1⅓ cups ice water
1 tablespoon vegetable oil
1½ teaspoons salt

Sauce

1 (28-ounce) can whole peeled tomatoes, drained
1 tablespoon extra-virgin olive oil
1 teaspoon red wine vinegar
2 garlic cloves, minced
1 teaspoon salt
1 teaspoon dried oregano
¼ teaspoon pepper

1 ounce Parmesan cheese, grated fine (½ cup)
8 ounces whole-milk mozzarella, shredded (2 cups)

1. *For the dough:* Process flour, sugar, and yeast in food processor (fitted with dough blade if possible) until combined, about 5 seconds. With processor running, slowly add water and process until dough is just combined and no dry flour remains, about 10 seconds. Let dough stand for 10 minutes.

2. Add oil and salt to dough and process until dough forms satiny, sticky ball that clears sides of bowl, 30 to 60 seconds. Transfer dough to lightly oiled counter and knead briefly by hand until smooth, about 1 minute. Shape dough into tight ball and transfer to large, lightly oiled bowl; cover bowl tightly with plastic wrap and refrigerate dough for at least 24 hours or up to 3 days.

3. *For the sauce:* Process all ingredients in clean, dry workbowl of food processor until smooth, about 30 seconds. Transfer sauce to bowl and refrigerate until ready to use.

4. One hour before baking, adjust oven rack 4 to 5 inches from broiler element, set baking stone on rack, and heat oven to 500 degrees. Transfer dough to clean counter and divide in half with bench scraper. Form each piece of dough into smooth, tight ball. Space balls at least 3 inches apart on lightly greased baking sheet. Cover sheet loosely with plastic coated with vegetable oil spray; let dough stand for 1 hour.

5. Coat 1 dough ball generously with flour and place on well-floured counter (keep other ball covered). Using your fingertips, gently flatten dough into 8-inch disk, leaving 1 inch of outer edge slightly thicker than center. Using your hands, gently stretch disk into 12-inch round, working along edges and giving disk quarter turns. Transfer dough to well-floured pizza peel and stretch into 13-inch round. Using back of spoon or ladle, spread ½ cup sauce in thin layer over surface of dough, leaving ¼-inch border around edge. Sprinkle ¼ cup Parmesan evenly over sauce, followed by 1 cup mozzarella. Carefully slide pizza onto baking stone and bake until crust is well browned and cheese is bubbly and beginning to brown, 10 to 12 minutes, rotating pizza halfway through baking. Transfer pizza to wire rack and let cool for 5 minutes before slicing and serving.

6. Repeat process of shaping, topping, and baking with remaining dough and toppings.

SHAPING THIN-CRUST PIZZA DOUGH

1. **DIVIDE** Once dough has fermented in fridge, halve dough and shape into balls. Place on lightly oiled baking sheet and cover with oiled plastic wrap. Let rest for 1 hour to allow dough to return to room temperature.

2. **FLATTEN** On well-floured surface and using your fingertips, gently flatten dough into 8-inch disk, leaving outer edge slightly thicker than center to create fatter "handle."

3. **STRETCH** With your hands, stretch dough into 12-inch round, working along edges and giving dough quarter turns. Transfer to well-floured peel and stretch to 13-inch round.

Peanut Butter
Hermit
Black & White
Oatmeal Raisin
Jam Thumbprint
Graham Cracker
Molasses
Chocolate Sandwich
Chocolate Chip
Snickerdoodle

COOKIES AND BARS

THE PERFECT CHOCOLATE CHIP COOKIE

CHARLES KELSEY, *May/June 2009*

Since Nestlé first printed the recipe for Toll House cookies on the back of chocolate chip bags in 1939, generations of cooks have packed them into lunches, taken them to bake sales, and kept them on hand for snacking—arguably more so than any other kind of cookie. I've also made countless batches over the years. The recipe is easy: Cream butter and sugar (half white, half brown), add two eggs and vanilla, and mix in all-purpose flour, salt, baking soda, some chopped nuts, and the chips. Drop tablespoons of dough on a cookie sheet, bake at 375 for 10 minutes, and you're done.

With its cakey texture and sweet, buttery flavor, the Toll House cookie certainly has its appeal. But in my opinion, a truly great cookie offers real complexity. My ideal has always been a cookie that's moist and chewy on the inside and crisp at the edges, with deep notes of toffee and butterscotch to balance its sweetness. Could I achieve the perfect specimen?

NOT-SO-COOKIE-CUTTER TECHNIQUES

I'm not the first to think the Toll House cookie could stand improvement. *The New York Times* published a recipe inspired by famed New York City pastry chef Jacques Torres trumpeting an unusual tactic for creating more complex flavor: letting the dough rest for a full 24 hours before baking. The rest enables the flour to fully absorb moisture from the eggs, leading to drier dough that, theoretically, caramelizes more quickly in the oven and achieves richer flavor. When I tried the recipe, tasters found that it did have a slightly deeper toffee taste than the Toll House cookie—but not nearly enough to warrant the inconvenience of a 24-hour rest.

Several Boston-area bakeries employ their own dough-resting techniques: Joanne Chang at Flour Bakery swears by a rest of two or three days. At Clear Flour Bread, they portion and freeze the dough before baking, a trick that prevents the dough from spreading too much (and that keeps the center of the cookie moist and chewy). These are fine ideas for professional bakers but impractical for time-pressed home cooks.

Other pastry chefs rely on "pet" ingredients. Following the lead of Christina Tosi at Manhattan's Momofuku Bakery and Milk Bar, I added milk powder to one batch. Tosi finds that it brings depth; I found that it made the cookies taste milky. I also experimented with tapioca powder, brown rice flour, and xanthan gum for chew. In each case, tasters were unanimous: No thanks.

I wasn't having luck on the flavor or chewiness front, but an approach for increasing crispiness from the Toll House creator herself, Ruth Wakefield, seemed worth trying: In a variation on her chocolate chip cookie recipe published in *Toll House Tried and True Recipes* (1940), Wakefield swaps all-purpose flour for cake flour. But the swap yielded a cookie so crumbly that it practically disintegrated after one bite, since cake flour has less protein than all-purpose flour. Protein is one of the building blocks of gluten, which gives baked goods their structure. The less protein, the less structure, and thus the more crumbly the end product.

EXAMINING THE ELEMENTS

It was time to come up with my own ideas. Since small tweaks in a baking recipe can translate into big differences, I would break down the Toll House recipe and see what changes I could invoke by playing around with ingredients and proportions.

I decided to start by tackling texture, first zeroing in on the impact of the fat. I knew that I wanted to stick with butter—vegetable shortening and oil could never compete with its rich flavor. The Toll House recipe calls for creaming the butter with the sugar, which creates tiny air bubbles that bring a cakey lift to cookies. When developing a recipe for Brown Sugar Cookies (page 459), I discovered that melting the butter before combining it with the other ingredients led to a chewier texture. Butter contains up to 18 percent water. When butter melts, the water separates from the fat and interacts with the proteins in flour to create more structure-enhancing gluten. Melting the butter created a relative abundance of water (more than 3 tablespoons), for cookies that tasters found noticeably chewier. And since I was melting butter, I saw an opportunity to brown it, a technique that can add nutty flavor. Sure enough, it worked. But since browning burns off some of butter's moisture, I made sure not to brown all of it.

For cookies that are crisp at the edges and chewy in the middle, we up the ratio of brown sugar and let the batter rest before baking.

Next ingredient: sugar. Besides adding sweetness, sugar affects texture. White sugar lends crispiness, while brown sugar, which is hygroscopic (meaning it attracts and retains water), enhances chewiness. Cookies made with all brown sugar were nearly floppy. I got the best results when I simply used a bit more brown sugar than granulated.

Next came flour. I already knew that cake flour wouldn't work. What if I tried bread flour, with its higher protein content? This was going too far: The cookies were dense and chewy. In the end, cutting back on the all-purpose flour by ½ cup allowed the chewiness contributed by the brown sugar to come to the fore. The only problem: With less flour, the cookies were a little greasy. To resolve the issue, I decreased the butter by 2 tablespoons.

Finally, I was ready to evaluate the role of eggs. I knew from experience that egg whites, which contain much of the protein in the egg, tend to create cakey texture in baked goods—not what I was after. What's more, as the cookies bake, any white that isn't fully absorbed in the batter readily dries out, which can leave a cookie crumbly. Eliminating one egg white resulted in cookies that were supremely moist and chewy.

WAITING FOR BETTER FLAVOR

I had achieved chewiness, but the crisp edges and deep toffee flavor were still missing. That's when batch number 43 came along.

In the middle of stirring together the butter, sugar, and eggs, I stopped to take a phone call. Ten minutes later, the sugars had dissolved and the mixture had turned thick and shiny. I didn't think much of it until I pulled the finished cookies from the oven. Instead of having the smooth, matte surface of the previous batches, these emerged with a glossy sheen and an alluring craggy surface. One bite revealed deep, toffee-like flavor. And these cookies finally had just the texture I was aiming for: crisp on the outside and chewy within. When I made the cookies bigger (3 tablespoons versus the single tablespoon called for in the Toll House recipe), the contrast was even greater.

Our science editor theorized that allowing the sugar to rest in the liquids meant that more of it dissolved before baking. The dissolved sugar caramelizes more easily, creating toffee flavors and influencing texture. I kept the resting period, maximizing the effect with some occasional whisking.

Now I just had to finesse the baking time and temperature. With caramelization in mind, I kept the oven hot: 375 degrees, the same as for Toll House cookies. Watching the oven carefully, I baked the cookies until they were golden brown, just set at the edges, and soft in the center, between 10 and 14 minutes.

After more than 700 cookies baked, my cookies were crisp and chewy and gooey with chocolate, with a complex medley of sweet, buttery, toffee flavors. I held one more blind tasting, pitting my cookie against the Toll House classic. The verdict? My cookies weren't just better—they were perfect.

Perfect Chocolate Chip Cookies

MAKES 16 COOKIES

Avoid using a nonstick skillet to brown the butter; the dark color of the nonstick coating makes it difficult to gauge when the butter is sufficiently browned. Use fresh, moist brown sugar instead of hardened brown sugar, which will make the cookies dry.

1¾ cups (8¾ ounces) all-purpose flour
½ teaspoon baking soda
14 tablespoons unsalted butter
¾ cup packed (5¼ ounces) dark brown sugar
½ cup (3½ ounces) granulated sugar
2 teaspoons vanilla extract
1 teaspoon salt
1 large egg plus 1 large yolk
1¼ cups (7½ ounces) semisweet chocolate chips or chunks
¾ cup pecans or walnuts, toasted and chopped (optional)

1. Adjust oven rack to middle position and heat oven to 375 degrees. Line 2 rimmed baking sheets with parchment paper. Whisk flour and baking soda together in medium bowl; set aside.

2. Melt 10 tablespoons butter in 10-inch skillet over medium-high heat. Continue to cook, swirling pan constantly, until butter is dark golden brown and has nutty aroma, 1 to 3 minutes. Transfer browned butter to large heatproof bowl. Add remaining 4 tablespoons butter and stir until completely melted.

3. Add brown sugar, granulated sugar, vanilla, and salt to melted butter; whisk until fully incorporated. Add egg and yolk; whisk until mixture is smooth with no sugar lumps remaining, about 30 seconds. Let mixture stand for 3 minutes, then whisk for 30 seconds. Repeat process of resting and whisking 2 more times until mixture is thick, smooth, and shiny. Using rubber spatula, stir in flour mixture until just combined, about 1 minute. Stir in chocolate chips and pecans, if using. Give dough final stir to ensure no flour pockets remain and ingredients are evenly distributed.

4. Working with 3 tablespoons dough at a time, roll into balls and space them 2 inches apart on prepared sheets. Bake, 1 sheet at a time, until cookies are golden brown, still puffy, and edges have begun to set but centers are soft, 10 to 14 minutes, rotating sheet halfway through baking. Let cookies cool completely on sheets on wire racks before serving. (Cookies can be stored in zipperlock bag for up to 3 days.)

DON'T BAKE TWO TRAYS AT ONCE

Baking two trays at a time may be convenient, but it leads to uneven cooking. The cookies on the top tray are often browner around the edges than those on the bottom, even when rotated halfway through cooking.

TOP RACK

BOTTOM RACK

CLASSIC CHEWY OATMEAL COOKIES

ANDREA GEARY, *September/October 2016*

Why does the man on the Quaker oatmeal package look so smug? Maybe it's because he's the cunning perpetrator of a wildly successful cookie con. The evidence is anecdotal but persuasive: When I asked several friends to share their favorite family recipe for oatmeal cookies, many produced (often unbeknownst to them) the recipe from the Quaker Oatmeal website, Quaker's Best Oatmeal Cookies. The guy on the canister has apparently cornered the market, but do his cookies really deserve all the love?

The recipe goes like this: Use a mixer to cream the butter and sugar and then add an egg and some vanilla. Stir in some flour, leavening, salt (oddly optional in this recipe), spices (a generous amount), and old-fashioned rolled oats, and then spoon the mixture onto baking sheets. As they bake, the cookies fill the house with the heady scents of butter and cinnamon.

Replacing some of the butter in our oatmeal cookies with vegetable oil and adding an egg yolk creates great chew.

One bite of a cooled cookie, though, and the problems were apparent: The Quaker standby was crumbly at the edges and dry and cakey in the middle. Plus, the abundant spices overpowered the subtle flavor of the oats. I wanted a cookie with a crispy edge; a dense, chewy middle; and true oaty flavor. I was confident I could attain these goals and, in doing so, topple the oatmeal cookie kingpin. But I wasn't above using his recipe as a starting point.

MIXED UP

I planned to make the salt mandatory instead of optional and to tone down the spices, but other than that I saw no reason to change the key ingredients in the Quaker recipe at this point—they each played a role—so I turned my attention to the ingredient proportions.

Most of those seemed OK, too. Only one, the 2½ sticks of butter, stood out as scandalously extravagant. The only cookie I know that has such a high proportion of butter to flour is shortbread, and that was definitely not the texture I was after. Instead, I placed a more reasonable 1½ sticks of softened butter in the mixer bowl. The brown sugar, granulated sugar, egg, vanilla, flour, and baking soda amounts all remained the same. But because I wanted just a hint of spice, I cut the cinnamon back to a mere ¼ teaspoon and eliminated the nutmeg altogether.

All was going well until it was time to add the oats. The mixture was simply too dry to accommodate all of them; I ended up with something that resembled crumble topping more than it did cookie dough.

I abandoned that batch and started over, keeping the butter to 1½ sticks but reducing the flour to 1 cup. This worked better: The cookies weren't as dry, and with less flour in the mix, the flavor of the oats stood out more.

Unfortunately, these cookies tasted a bit tinny. They also seemed rather lean, and the cakey texture remained. The metallic flavor, I knew, was coming from the baking soda—a full teaspoon was too much for the reduced amount of flour, especially now that there wasn't as much spice to hide behind. The excess soda might have been contributing to the cakey texture, too, but I suspected something else was at play.

The whole point of creaming butter and sugar when baking is to seed the softened butter with millions of tiny air bubbles. When the alkaline leavener reacts with acidic ingredients in the dough to produce carbon dioxide, the gas inflates the air bubbles, producing a light texture. If I wanted flatter, less cakey cookies, I probably didn't need—or want—the mixer.

But combining the butter and sugar by hand sounded like a chore. Then it occurred to me: If I wasn't whipping air into it, there was no need for the butter to be solid. Instead, I melted it. Eliminating the creaming step made the recipe easier and, along with cutting the baking soda amount in half, produced cookies that were flatter and denser in a good way. They were still a bit lean, but I didn't want to increase the butter because of the textural issues, so I'd need to enrich them in another way. And they still weren't as chewy as I wanted.

FAT FACTOR

Luckily, I had some experience with making baked goods chewy, having developed our recipe for Chewy Brownies (page 474). The key lies in the chemistry of fats. Both saturated fats (such as butter) and unsaturated fats (such as vegetable oil) consist of long chains of carbon atoms strung together with hydrogen atoms attached to them. The carbon chains in saturated fats have the maximum number of hydrogen atoms attached, so they can pack together more closely into a solid like butter. Unsaturated fats have fewer hydrogen atoms attached, so the chains pack more loosely and thus remain fluid, like vegetable oil. The right combination of loosely and tightly packed chains will produce the ideal chewy texture. When developing my brownie recipe, I learned that 3 parts unsaturated fat to 1 part saturated fat was the magic ratio.

Would the same hold true for my oatmeal cookies? With 12 tablespoons of butter (which is mostly saturated fat) and 1 egg, the fat in my recipe was currently 35 percent unsaturated and 65 percent saturated. For my next batch of cookies, I switched out 8 tablespoons of butter for ½ cup of vegetable oil. I also added an extra egg yolk for richness. Now the cookies had 71 percent unsaturated fat and 29 percent saturated, which was much closer to that 3:1 ideal.

So how were they? Crispy on the edges and chewy in the middle, the texture was at last spot-on. But with so much of the butter replaced by neutral-tasting vegetable oil, they were a bit bland and boring. The recipe would need a few more tweaks.

If I had only 4 tablespoons of butter to work with, I was determined to get as much flavor out of it as I could, so I cooked it in a skillet until it was fragrant and the milk solids had turned a dark golden brown before transferring it to the mixing bowl. And rather than increasing the amount of cinnamon, I added the ¼ teaspoon to the warm browned butter to let it bloom, making its flavor rounder and more complex. Correct seasoning is every bit as important in sweets as it is in savory dishes; for my last adjustment, I bumped up the salt to ¾ teaspoon.

The three tweaks were, in combination, surprisingly effective. My cookies now had not only the right texture but also a rich, toasty flavor: buttery, sweet oats with a subtle spice background. A small handful of raisins stirred into the last batch of dough added pops of bright flavor and reinforced the cookies' chew. Knowing that they're a controversial addition, I kept them optional in the recipe.

The Quaker guy no longer has the best recipe, so I guess I'll have to come up with another reason for his smug expression now. Maybe it's the hat.

Classic Chewy Oatmeal Cookies

MAKES 20 COOKIES

Regular old-fashioned rolled oats work best in this recipe. Do not use extra-thick rolled oats; they will bake up tough in the cookies. For cookies with just the right amount of spread and chew, we strongly recommend that you weigh your ingredients. If you omit the raisins, the recipe will yield 18 cookies.

1 cup (5 ounces) all-purpose flour
¾ teaspoon salt
½ teaspoon baking soda
4 tablespoons unsalted butter
¼ teaspoon ground cinnamon
¾ cup packed (5¼ ounces) dark brown sugar
½ cup (3½ ounces) granulated sugar
½ cup vegetable oil
1 large egg plus 1 large yolk
1 teaspoon vanilla extract
3 cups (9 ounces) old-fashioned rolled oats
½ cup raisins (optional)

1. Adjust oven rack to middle position and heat oven to 375 degrees. Line 2 rimmed baking sheets with parchment paper. Whisk flour, salt, and baking soda together in medium bowl; set aside.

2. Melt butter in 8-inch skillet over medium-high heat, swirling pan occasionally, until foaming subsides. Continue to cook, stirring and scraping bottom of pan with heat-resistant spatula, until milk solids are dark golden brown and butter has nutty aroma, 1 to 2 minutes. Immediately transfer browned butter to large heatproof bowl, scraping skillet with spatula. Stir in cinnamon.

3. Add brown sugar, granulated sugar, and oil to bowl with butter and whisk until combined. Add egg and yolk and vanilla and whisk until mixture is smooth. Using wooden spoon or spatula, stir in flour mixture until fully combined, about 1 minute. Add oats and raisins, if using, and stir until evenly distributed (mixture will be stiff).

4. Divide dough into 20 portions, each about 3 tablespoons (or use #24 scoop). Arrange dough balls 2 inches apart on prepared sheets, 10 dough balls per sheet. Using your damp hand, press each ball into 2½-inch disk.

5. Bake, 1 sheet at a time, until cookie edges are set and lightly browned and centers are still soft but not wet, 8 to 10 minutes, rotating sheet halfway through baking. Let cookies cool on sheet on wire rack for 5 minutes; using wide metal spatula, transfer cookies to wire rack and let cool completely before serving.

FOR A CHEWY COOKIE, CUT THE (SATURATED) FAT

When our cookies were coming out cakey and tender rather than dense and chewy, we knew to look at the fat—specifically, the types of fat we were using and their proportion to each other. More saturated fat (e.g., butter) will produce baked goods with a tender texture, while more unsaturated fat (e.g., vegetable oil) leads to a chewier baked good. We were using all butter up to this point, so swapping in vegetable oil for some of that butter (and adding another egg yolk) gave us a ratio of about 3 parts unsaturated fat to 1 part saturated—and cookies that met our chewy, dense ideal.

NO MIXER? NO NEED

A lot of oatmeal cookie recipes, including Quaker's Best Oatmeal Cookies, call for using a mixer, but we realized that hauling one out was not only unnecessary but even counterproductive. Mixers are great for incorporating air into cake batters, but that's exactly what you don't want for a dense, chewy oatmeal cookie. So we skipped the mixer and simply stirred our dough together in a bowl. And since we didn't need to whip air into the butter, there was no reason for it to stay in solid form. Melting it made for easier mixing and also gave us the chance to brown it for a flavor boost that enhanced the oaty flavor.

FOOLPROOF SUGAR COOKIES

ANDREA GEARY, *November/December 2010*

The first challenge for every prospective test cook at *Cook's Illustrated* is to bake a batch of chewy sugar cookies under the watchful eye of the test kitchen director. The task looks simple enough: Cream the fat with sugar; mix in egg and vanilla, followed by the dry ingredients (flour, sugar, salt, and leavener); roll balls of dough in sugar; and bake. But more often than not, the resulting cookies range from stunted and humped to flat and brittle, with smooth rather than crackly tops. With no nuts, raisins, or chunks of chocolate to provide distraction, such flaws become all the more glaring. Indeed, the sugar cookie has been the downfall of many a hopeful applicant.

The truth is, making a just-right version of this humble cookie is far from easy. I was determined to engineer a recipe that would produce my ideal, every time: crisp at the edges, soft and chewy in the center, crackly-crisp on top—and, of course, richly flavorful.

WHY THE COOKIE CRUMBLES

I already had a leg up in the chewiness department. While developing our recipe for Chewy Brownies (page 474), I learned that the key to a truly chewy texture is all in the fat. For optimal chew, a recipe must contain both saturated and unsaturated fat in a ratio of approximately 1 to 3. When combined, the two types of fat molecules form a sturdier crystalline structure that requires more force to chew through than the structure formed from a high proportion of saturated fats.

Right away I could eliminate the majority of recipes I'd found in my research; almost all called for butter alone. Butter is predominantly—but not entirely—a saturated fat, and an all-butter cookie actually contains approximately 2 parts saturated fat to 1 part unsaturated fat. For optimal chew, I needed to reverse that ratio and then some.

I got to work adjusting the fat in the recipe that I'd singled out as a baseline for "soft and chewy" sugar cookies. I knocked down the recipe's 8 ounces (16 tablespoons) of butter to 3 ounces (6 tablespoons) and added 5 ounces of mostly unsaturated vegetable oil, which gave me a fat content that was approximately 25 percent saturated and 75 percent unsaturated.

With so little butter in the recipe, there was not enough solid fat to hold the air, so creaming it with the sugar no longer made sense. Instead, I melted the butter and whisked it with the sugar. This simple switch proved to be a boon in more ways than one. First, it eliminated one of the trickier aspects of baking sugar cookies: ensuring that the solid butter is just the right temperature. Second, melted butter would aid in my quest for chewiness: When liquefied, the small amount of water in butter mixes with the flour to form gluten, which makes for chewier cookies. Finally, with creaming out of the equation, I'd no longer need to pull out my stand mixer; I could mix all the ingredients by hand.

But there was a downside to swapping butter for oil. The two doses of liquid fat made the dough so soft that it was practically pourable. Plus, now that I was no longer creaming, there wasn't enough air in the dough, and the cookies were baking up too flat. I spent the next several tests readjusting my ingredients. More flour helped build up structure, while another ½ teaspoon of baking powder added lift. To keep the cookies from being too dry and biscuitlike, I ramped up the sugar, salt, and vanilla and added a tiny bit of milk.

With this new formula, the chewiness of my cookies was spot-on. But I still had a few problems, two of which were mainly cosmetic: The cookies had gone from too flat to a bit more domed than I liked, and they didn't have much of that appealingly crackly top that makes a sugar cookie distinctive. But most important, trading more than half the rich butter for neutral-tasting vegetable oil had plagued the cookies with a one-dimensional sweetness.

SUGAR FIX

There was no use reducing the amount of sugar: Given the choice between blandness and one-note sweetness, I'd take the latter. Instead, I wondered if I could add something to take the edge off all that sugariness. I thought an acidic ingredient like lemon juice or zest might work. But such assertive citrus flavor took the cookies out of the "sugar" category and dropped them squarely into the lemon family. We often add buttermilk, sour cream, or yogurt to muffins and cakes to round out their flavors. But when I tried each of these in place of the milk in my recipe, I couldn't add more than a tablespoon of any one before it upset the precarious moisture balance, leading to dough that was too soft.

The secret to achieving balanced sweetness in our sugar cookies is adding a little bit of cream cheese.

I scanned the supermarket dairy aisle and zeroed in on cream cheese, wondering if it would enrich the dough's flavor without adding much liquid. Of course, the trade-off would be my perfect chewiness ratio: Cream cheese has less than one-third the fat of vegetable oil, but most of it is saturated. With every ounce I added, I would be chipping away at my carefully calibrated ratio of fats, so I traded 1 ounce of oil for a modest 2 ounces of cream cheese. The saturated-fat content increased from 25 percent to 32 percent—and I was thrilled to find that the difference didn't markedly affect the cookies' texture. But flavorwise, the effect of the cream cheese was dramatic, and my tasters' faces lit up as they bit into this latest batch.

There was more good news: With acidic cream cheese in the mix, I could now add baking soda to the dough. As long as there's an acidic ingredient present, baking soda has all sorts of special powers, including the ability to solve my other two pesky problems: slightly humped cookies and not enough crackle. Just ½ teaspoon produced cookies that looked as good as they tasted.

SATISFACTION GUARANTEED

The recipe was in good shape: The butter-oil combination led to satisfying chew, the liquid fats made the dough easy to mix by hand, the cream cheese provided a subtle contrast to the sugar, and the baking soda ensured a crackly top and a nicely rounded shape. But when a friend tried it out, I was dismayed to find that her cookies spread all over the pan to form one giant confection.

I asked her to walk me through her process—and realized I'd taken a crucial test kitchen technique for granted. When baking, we measure our ingredients by weight, but like many home cooks, my friend had measured hers by volume. In the past, we've found that weights of volume-measured ingredients can vary by as much as 20 percent, a particular hazard when too little flour is measured. While a bit too much flour isn't a catastrophe, too little means more flour proteins get coated in fat and can't form structure-building gluten. The result: cookies that spread and bake up flat. For a truly foolproof recipe, I needed to provide some wiggle room. The solution turned out to be as simple as cutting back a little on the fat, so there would never be too much to go around. Reducing the butter was out of the question—I didn't want to lose its rich flavor. Instead, I took the oil down from ½ cup to ⅓ cup.

This change, of course, rejiggered my fat ratios, with the saturated fat now totaling 36 percent and the unsaturated fat 64 percent—closer to a 1:2 ratio than a 1:3 ratio, but still almost the reverse of the all-butter recipe I began with. Happily, while the cookies were not quite as chewy as before, they still had far more chew than any sugar cookie I'd ever eaten.

The only outstanding problem? With such an easy, truly foolproof chewy sugar cookie recipe on record, the test kitchen director will have to find something more challenging to spring on job applicants.

Chewy Sugar Cookies

MAKES ABOUT 24 COOKIES

The final dough will be slightly softer than most cookie doughs. For best results, handle the dough as briefly and gently as possible when shaping the cookies. Overworking the dough will result in flatter cookies.

2¼ cups (11¼ ounces) all-purpose flour
1 teaspoon baking powder
½ teaspoon baking soda
½ teaspoon salt
1½ cups (10½ ounces) sugar, plus ⅓ cup for rolling
2 ounces cream cheese, cut into 8 pieces
6 tablespoons unsalted butter, melted and still warm
⅓ cup vegetable oil
1 large egg
1 tablespoon whole milk
2 teaspoons vanilla extract

1. Adjust oven rack to middle position and heat oven to 350 degrees. Line 2 baking sheets with parchment paper. Whisk flour, baking powder, baking soda, and salt together in medium bowl. Set aside.
2. Place 1½ cups sugar and cream cheese in large bowl. Spread remaining ⅓ cup sugar in shallow dish and set aside. Pour melted butter over sugar and cream cheese and whisk to combine (some small lumps of cream cheese will remain). Whisk in oil until incorporated. Add egg, milk, and vanilla; continue to whisk until smooth. Add flour mixture and mix with rubber spatula until soft, homogeneous dough forms.
3. Working with 2 tablespoons dough at a time, roll into balls. Working in batches, roll half of dough balls in sugar in shallow dish to coat, then space them evenly on prepared sheet. Repeat with remaining dough balls and second prepared sheet. Using bottom of greased measuring cup, flatten dough balls until 2 inches in diameter. Sprinkle tops of cookies evenly with sugar remaining in shallow dish, using 2 teaspoons for each sheet. (Discard remaining sugar.)
4. Bake, 1 sheet at a time, until edges of cookies are set and just beginning to brown, 11 to 13 minutes, rotating sheet halfway through baking. Let cookies cool on sheet for 5 minutes, then transfer to wire rack and let cool completely before serving.

variations

Chewy Chai-Spice Sugar Cookies

Add ¼ teaspoon ground cinnamon, ¼ teaspoon ground ginger, ¼ teaspoon ground cardamom, ¼ teaspoon ground cloves, and pinch pepper to sugar–cream cheese mixture and reduce vanilla to 1 teaspoon.

Chewy Coconut-Lime Sugar Cookies

Whisk ½ cup sweetened shredded coconut, chopped fine, into flour mixture in step 1. Add 1 teaspoon finely grated lime zest to sugar–cream cheese mixture and substitute 1 tablespoon lime juice for vanilla.

SECRET WEAPONS FOR TASTE AND TEXTURE

Sugar cookies can be cloyingly sweet, and are rarely chewy. These two ingredients helped us create the best flavor and chewy texture.

CREAM CHEESE Cream cheese is an ingredient not often included in sugar cookies. But we found that it helps cut their one-note sweetness and round out their flavors.

OIL All-butter sugar cookies may have rich taste, but they never boast real chew. Swapping some of the butter, which is mainly a saturated fat, for unsaturated vegetable oil boosts chewiness considerably. Why? The two types of fat create a sturdier structure that requires more force to chew through.

BROWN SUGAR COOKIES

CHARLES KELSEY, *March/April 2007*

I'm not one for fancy cookies. No special nuts, exotic flavor extracts, or intricate decorating for me. I prefer simple cookies done well. Take sugar cookies, for example: Made of nothing more than butter, sugar, flour, eggs, and leavener, they're rich and buttery with a crisp sugary exterior. Big results from pantry ingredients . . . now that's what I like.

But a sugar cookie can seem too simple—even dull—at times. I love the butterscotch, vanilla, and caramel flavors that brown sugar gives coffee cakes and other baked goods. Could I replace the granulated sugar in a sugar cookie with brown sugar and create a simple cookie that was actually exciting? I had a clear vision of this cookie. It would be oversized, with a crackling crisp exterior and a chewy interior. And, like Mick Jagger, this cookie would scream "brown sugar."

I found a half-dozen recipes and got to work. Although they looked similar on paper, the baked cookies ranged in style from bite-size puffs with a soft, cakey texture to thin disks with a short crumb. This first round of testing reminded me that cookies are deceptively difficult. Yes, most recipes can be executed by a young child, but even the tiniest alteration will make a significant difference in flavor and, especially, texture. To construct my ideal brown sugar cookie, I would need to brush up on the science of cookie making.

BASIC COOKIE CONSTRUCTION

Most sugar cookie recipes start by creaming softened butter with sugar until fluffy, beating in an egg or two, and then adding the dry ingredients (flour, baking powder, and salt). Vanilla is often incorporated along the way.

Butter was the obvious choice for optimal flavor, but creaming the fat and sugar beat tiny air bubbles into the dough and the resulting cookies were cakey and tender—not what I had in mind. I tried cutting the butter into the flour (like you do when making pie dough), but this method produced crumbly cookies with a texture akin to shortbread. When I melted the butter, the cookies finally had the chewy texture I wanted.

So why does melted butter make chewy cookies? Butter is actually 20 percent water and 80 percent fat. When melted, the water and fat separate and the proteins in the flour absorb some of the water and begin to form gluten, the protein that gives baked goods, including breads, their structure and chew.

Cookies made with melted butter and an entire 1-pound box of brown sugar had plenty of flavor, but these taffy-textured confections threatened to pull out my expensive dental work. Using dark brown sugar rather than light brown sugar allowed me to get more flavor from less sugar. Cookies made with 1¾ cups dark brown sugar had the best texture and decent flavor. I decided to nail down the rest of my recipe before circling back to flavor issues.

Browning the butter enhances the deep flavor of brown sugar; rolling the dough balls in more brown sugar adds additional flavor and texture.

Eggs add richness and structure to cookies. A single egg didn't provide enough of the latter—the cookies were too candy-like. Thinking that two eggs would solve the problem, I was surprised when a test batch turned out dry and cakey. Splitting the difference, I added one whole egg plus a yolk and was pleased with the results.

Too much flour gave the cookies a homogenous texture; too little and that candy-like chew reemerged. Two cups flour, plus a couple extra tablespoons, was the perfect match for the amounts of butter, sugar, and egg I'd chosen.

The choice of leavener is probably the most confusing part of any cookie recipe. Sugar cookies typically contain baking powder—a mixture of baking soda and a weak acid (calcium acid phosphate) that is activated by moisture and heat. The soda and acid create gas bubbles, which expand cookies and other baked goods. However, many baked goods with brown sugar call for baking soda. While granulated sugar is neutral, dark brown sugar can be slightly acidic. When I used baking soda by itself, the cookies had an open, coarse crumb and craggy top. Tasters loved the craggy top but not the coarse crumb. When I used baking powder by itself, the cookies had a finer, tighter crumb but the craggy top disappeared. After a dozen rounds of testing, I found that ¼ teaspoon of baking powder mixed with ½ teaspoon of baking soda moderated the coarseness of the crumb without compromising the craggy tops.

BROWNING AROUND

I had now developed a good cookie, but could I eke out even more brown sugar flavor? Riffing off a classic sugar cookie technique, I tried rolling the dough balls in brown sugar before baking them. The brown sugar clumped in some spots, but overall the crackling sugar exterior added good crunch and flavor. Cutting the brown sugar with granulated sugar solved the clumping problem.

To further ramp up the brown sugar flavor, I tested maple syrup, molasses, and vanilla extract. The maple and molasses were overpowering and masked the cookies' butterscotch flavor, but 1 tablespoon of vanilla extract properly reinforced the brown sugar flavor. A healthy dose of table salt (½ teaspoon) balanced the sweetness and helped accentuate the more interesting flavor components in brown sugar. But my biggest success came from an unlikely refinement.

Browned butter sauces add nutty flavor to delicate fish and pasta dishes. I wondered if browning the melted butter would add the same nutty flavor to my cookies. My tasters thought the complex nuttiness added by the browned butter made a substantial difference.

I noticed that cookies made with browned butter were slightly drier than cookies made with melted butter; some of the water in the butter was evaporating when I browned it. Adding an extra 2 tablespoons of butter and browning most (but not all) of the butter restored the chewy texture to my cookies.

FINAL BAKING TESTS

I tried a range of baking temperatures between 300 and 400 degrees Fahrenheit and found that right down the middle (350 degrees) gave me the most consistent results. I had hoped to bake two sheets at the same time, but even with rotating and changing tray positions at different times during baking, I could not get two-tray baking to work. Some of the cookies had the right texture, but others were inexplicably dry. Baking one tray at a time allows for even heat distribution and ensures that every cookie has the same texture.

My final recipe relies on pantry staples and delivers big brown sugar flavor. And although my technique isn't difficult (the cookies can be in the oven after just 15 minutes of work), it did require me to learn some chemistry and physics. After baking 1,200 brown sugar cookies, I think I've earned advanced degrees in both subjects.

CHECKING DONENESS

Achieving the proper texture—crisp at the edges and chewy in the middle—is critical to this recipe. Because the cookies are so dark, it's hard to judge doneness by color. Instead, gently press halfway between the edge and center of the cookie. When it's done, it will form an indent with slight resistance. Check early and err on the side of underdone.

Brown Sugar Cookies

MAKES 24 COOKIES

Use fresh, moist brown sugar for cookies with the best texture.

14 tablespoons unsalted butter
2 cups plus 2 tablespoons (10⅔ ounces) all-purpose flour
½ teaspoon baking soda
¼ teaspoon baking powder
1¾ cups packed (12¼ ounces) dark brown sugar, plus ¼ cup for rolling
½ teaspoon salt
1 large egg plus 1 large yolk
1 tablespoon vanilla extract
¼ cup (1¾ ounces) granulated sugar

1. Melt 10 tablespoons butter in 10-inch skillet over medium-high heat. Continue to cook, swirling skillet constantly, until butter is dark golden brown and has nutty aroma, 1 to 3 minutes. Transfer browned butter to large bowl and stir in remaining 4 tablespoons butter until melted; let cool for 15 minutes.
2. Meanwhile, adjust oven rack to middle position and heat oven to 350 degrees. Line 2 baking sheets with parchment paper. Whisk flour, baking soda, and baking powder together in bowl.
3. Whisk 1¾ cups brown sugar and salt into cooled browned butter until smooth and no lumps remain, about 30 seconds. Whisk in egg and yolk and vanilla until incorporated, about 30 seconds. Using rubber spatula, stir in flour mixture until just combined, about 1 minute.
4. Combine remaining ¼ cup brown sugar and granulated sugar in shallow dish. Working with 2 tablespoons dough at a time, roll into balls, then roll in sugar to coat; space dough balls 2 inches apart on prepared sheets. (Dough balls can be frozen for up to 1 month; bake frozen dough balls on 1 baking sheet set inside second sheet in 325-degree oven for 20 to 25 minutes.)
5. Bake cookies, 1 sheet at a time, until edges have begun to set but centers are still soft, puffy, and cracked (cookies will look raw between cracks and seem underdone), 12 to 14 minutes, rotating sheet halfway through baking. Let cookies cool on sheet for 5 minutes, then transfer to wire rack. Let cookies cool completely before serving.

BUILDING BIG BROWN SUGAR FLAVOR

Dark brown sugar was an obvious place to begin our efforts to create a cookie with a bold, nutty, butterscotch flavor. A whole tablespoon of vanilla helped, but everyone in the test kitchen was surprised how much impact browning the butter had on the flavor of these cookies.

DARK BROWN SUGAR

LOTS OF VANILLA

BROWNED BUTTER

GETTING THE COOKIES YOU WANT

Cookie making is simple given the number of key ingredients in a typical recipe, but the slightest alteration can have a major impact. By adjusting any of the key ingredients, you can change the texture of any cookie recipe.

IF YOU WANT...	ADD...	EXPLANATION
Chewy cookies	Melted butter	Butter is 20 percent water. Melting helps water in butter mix with flour to form gluten.
Thin, candy-like cookies	More sugar	Sugar becomes fluid in the oven and helps cookies spread.
Cakey cookies	More eggs	Yolks make cookies rich, and whites cause cookies to puff and dry out.
An open, coarse crumb and craggy top	Baking soda	Baking soda reacts quickly with acidic ingredients (such as brown sugar) to create lots of gas bubbles.
A fine, tight crumb and smooth top	Baking powder	Baking powder works slowly and allows for an even rise.

PEANUT BUTTER SANDWICH COOKIES

ANDREA GEARY, *March/April 2012*

Being a peanut butter cookie is a lot like being a lady: If you have to announce that you are, you aren't. I admit to taking liberties with Margaret Thatcher's famous line (she drew a parallel between being powerful and being a lady), but to a peanut butter obsessive like me, that distinguishing crosshatch on top of a traditional peanut butter cookie feels like a cheat. A cookie shouldn't have to rely on a homey hieroglyph to proclaim its identity. Great flavor speaks for itself.

Their looks aside, I've always had another issue with peanut butter cookies: The raw dough tastes better than the baked treats. This is because in the presence of heat, the starch granules in flour soak up peanut flavor molecules like a sponge, reducing their aroma and limiting their ability to interact with our tastebuds. The upshot is that a traditional peanut butter cookie becomes flavor challenged as soon as it hits the oven. As I mulled over the facts, it occurred to me that a sandwich cookie—that is, two peanut butter cookies enclosing a filling made primarily with uncooked (read: full-flavored) peanut butter—might be the ideal delivery system for the strong flavor that I craved.

The cookies themselves would have to be quite thin and flat (so you could comfortably eat two of them sandwiched with filling) as well as crunchy, to contrast with the creamy center. As for that smooth filling, it had to be substantial enough that it wouldn't squish out the sides of the cookies with each bite. I also wanted my cookies to have the simplicity of a drop cookie: no chilling of the dough, no slicing, no rolling, and no cutting.

STARTING IN THE MIDDLE

Because a good sandwich cookie is all about balanced flavors and textures, I knew that the filling would influence my cookie and vice versa. I chose to start with the simpler filling. Most recipes call for blending peanut butter and confectioners' sugar (granulated sugar remains too gritty and doesn't provide much thickening power) with a creamy element, such as butter, cream cheese, heavy cream, or even marshmallow crème. I settled on butter, which provided the silkiest consistency and allowed for the purest peanut butter flavor. I softened 3 tablespoons of butter with ¾ cup of creamy peanut butter in the microwave and then, to keep the peanut flavor in the forefront, stirred in a modest ½ cup of confectioners' sugar.

This low-sugar filling tasted great, but it was far too soft, squirting out from my placeholder cookies as soon as I pressed them together. To thicken things up, I ultimately found that I had to double the sugar amount, for a filling that was very sweet. For a perfectly balanced whole, I would have to counter with a significantly less sweet cookie frame.

These cookies boast intense peanut flavor and a perfectly flat, crisp texture thanks to toasted crushed peanuts and extra baking soda.

CRUNCH TIME

Setting the filling aside, I put together a dough with 3 tablespoons of butter, ½ cup of peanut butter, two eggs, 1 cup of sugar, 2 cups of flour, and ½ teaspoon each of baking soda and salt. After portioning the dough and baking it at 350 degrees for about 12 minutes, I had cookies that weren't bad for a first try, offering just the right degree of sweetness to complement the sugary filling. But they were too thick and soft. I wanted more spread, more crunch, and—if I could pack it in—more peanut flavor.

My first change was to scrap one of the eggs (they contribute protein that traps air and makes baked goods cakey), replacing it with 3 tablespoons of milk. I knew that other factors influence how much cookie dough will spread in the oven: sugar (more sugar equals more spread) and moisture level (more moisture leads to a looser dough that spreads more readily). I'd already established that I couldn't make the dough any sweeter, so my only option was to increase the moisture level by cutting back on flour. Since my goal was also a super-nutty-tasting cookie, I decided to replace a full cup of flour with finely chopped peanuts, which would absorb far less moisture as well as add welcome crunch and peanut flavor. These changes helped, but the cookies still weren't spreading enough.

What would happen if I actually took out all of the flour? The idea wasn't without precedent. Flourless peanut butter cookie recipes abound on the Internet, and I'd always been curious about them. I eliminated the flour and, to my surprise, found that the resulting cookies were not that much thinner or flatter, though they tasted great. They were also far too crumbly. I added flour back incrementally, finding that a ratio of ¾ cup flour to the ½ cup of peanut butter created relatively thin, nutty-tasting cookies that were still sturdy enough to serve as a shell for the filling. Finally, to get them thinner, I relied on brute force: After portioning the dough on the baking sheet, I used my wet hand to squash it into even 2-inch rounds.

I was almost there, but I had one final trick up my sleeve: tinkering with the baking soda. In other cookie recipes, we have found that adding extra soda causes the bubbles within dough to inflate so rapidly that they burst before the cookies set, leaving the cookies flatter than they would be with less soda. A mere ¼ teaspoon of baking soda would be sufficient to leaven the ¾ cup of flour in my recipe; when I quadrupled that amount to a full teaspoon, the cookies quickly puffed up

in the oven and then deflated. Voilà: greater spread, just as I had hoped. In addition, these cookies boasted a coarser, more open crumb, which provided extra routes through which moisture could escape. This left the cookies even drier and crunchier—a better foil for the creamy filling.

SPREAD 'EM

With my creamy, peanutty filling and ultra-crunchy cookies ready to go, it was time to put the two components together. But on my first few maddening attempts, the cookies shattered into pieces as I tried to spread the firm filling. I resisted the urge to loosen the filling with more butter, lest it squish out from between the cookies, making the package impossible to eat with any degree of decorum. Then I realized that it was a matter of timing: If I prepared the filling right before assembly, it could be easily scooped and squished between the cookies while it was still warm from the microwave—no painstaking spreading necessary—after which it would cool and set to an ideal firm texture.

At last, I had a cookie with a simple, understated appearance that delivered the powerful peanut wallop promised (but rarely provided) by those pretenders sporting the traditional fork marks.

Peanut Butter Sandwich Cookies

MAKES 24 COOKIES

Do not use unsalted peanut butter for this recipe.

Cookies

- 1¼ cups (6¼ ounces) raw peanuts, toasted and cooled
- ¾ cup (3¾ ounces) all-purpose flour
- 1 teaspoon baking soda
- ½ teaspoon salt
- 3 tablespoons unsalted butter, melted
- ½ cup creamy peanut butter
- ½ cup (3½ ounces) granulated sugar
- ½ cup packed (3½ ounces) light brown sugar
- 3 tablespoons whole milk
- 1 large egg

Filling

- ¾ cup creamy peanut butter
- 3 tablespoons unsalted butter
- 1 cup (4 ounces) confectioners' sugar

1. *For the cookies:* Adjust oven racks to upper-middle and lower-middle positions and heat oven to 350 degrees. Line 2 baking sheets with parchment paper. Pulse peanuts in food processor until finely chopped, about 8 pulses. Whisk flour, baking soda, and salt together in bowl. Whisk melted butter, peanut butter, granulated sugar, brown sugar, milk, and egg together in second bowl. Stir flour mixture into peanut butter mixture with rubber spatula until combined. Stir in peanuts until evenly distributed.
2. Using 1-tablespoon measure or #60 scoop, evenly space 12 mounds on each prepared baking sheet. Using your damp hand, flatten mounds until 2 inches in diameter.
3. Bake until deep golden brown and firm to touch, 15 to 18 minutes, switching and rotating sheets halfway through baking. Let cookies cool on sheets for 5 minutes. Transfer cookies to wire rack and let cool completely, about 30 minutes. Repeat portioning and baking remaining dough.
4. *For the filling:* Microwave peanut butter and butter until butter is melted and warm, about 40 seconds. Using rubber spatula, stir in confectioners' sugar until combined.
5. *To assemble:* Place 24 cookies upside down on work surface. Place 1 level tablespoon (or #60 scoop) warm filling in center of each cookie. Place second cookie on top of filling, right side up, pressing gently until filling spreads to edges. Allow filling to set for 1 hour before serving. (Assembled cookies can be stored in airtight container for up to 3 days.)

FILLING COOKIES EVENLY

One of our goals for our Peanut Butter Sandwich Cookies was to get a filling that would spread evenly but not ooze out the sides. Here's how we did it.

SCOOP IT WARM Using a #60 scoop or a 1-tablespoon measure, portion warm filling onto the bottom cookies (turned upside down).

SQUISH IT GENTLY Rather than smearing the filling with a knife or offset spatula, top it with a second cookie and press gently until it spreads to the edges.

variations

Peanut Butter Sandwich Cookies with Honey-Cinnamon Filling

Omit butter from filling. Stir 5 tablespoons honey and ½ teaspoon ground cinnamon into warm peanut butter before adding confectioners' sugar.

Peanut Butter Sandwich Cookies with Milk Chocolate Filling

Reduce peanut butter to ½ cup and omit butter from filling. Stir 6 ounces finely chopped milk chocolate into warm peanut butter until melted, microwaving for 10 seconds at a time if necessary, before adding confectioners' sugar.

NUT CRESCENT COOKIES

DAWN YANAGIHARA, *November/December 1998*

Baking cookies has become a holiday tradition—as has the disposal of those with so little appeal that they go uneaten, even during a season of unabashed overindulgence. In my house, after the fruitcake, the first cookies to bite the dust are the balls and crescents coated in a pasty layer of melting confectioners' sugar. I have come to expect these cookies to be no more than stale, dry, floury, flavorless little chokeballs. They always fall short of the buttery, nutty, slightly crisp, slightly crumbly, melt-in-your-mouth nuggets they should be.

But that is a shame. Nut crescents are very much an "adult" cookie, low on sweetness, simple in flavor, and the perfect accompaniment to a cup of coffee or tea. When they are well-made, they are delicious, and I wanted to devise a recipe that would yield cookies that are eagerly awaited every holiday season, much like my mother's sugar cookies.

Superfine sugar and a combination of finely chopped and ground nuts yield tender, delicate, nutty cookies.

I gathered recipe after recipe from large, authoritative books and small, pamphlet-sized publications. These cookies, round and crescent-shaped, go by different names: Viennese crescents, butterballs, and Mexican wedding cakes, as well as almond, pecan, or walnut crescents. All the recipes are surprisingly similar, differing mainly in the amount and type of sugar and nuts. The standard ratio of butter to flour is 1 cup to 2 cups, with the flour in a few instances going as low as 1¾ cup and as high as 2½ cups. Across the board, the ingredients are simple: flour, sugar, butter, and nuts. Some add vanilla extract and salt. I chose four recipes and, with the input of a few tasters, formed a composite recipe to serve as the springboard for my testing.

FLOUR AND SWEETNESS

Flour was my starting point. I certainly didn't need to go very far. Cookies made with 2 cups of all-purpose flour to 1 cup of butter were right on. The dough was easy to shape and handle, and the baked cookies were tender, delicate, and shapely. Any less flour and the rich cookies spread and lost some form in the oven; any more and they were dry and floury. I tried cake flour and cornstarch in place of some flour, thinking that one or another would provide extra tenderness. Both were failures. The resulting cookies lacked body and structure and disintegrated unpleasantly in the mouth.

Next I zeroed in on sugar. I liked the sweetness of the cookies I had been making, but needed to discover the effects of granulated, confectioners', and superfine sugar. Granulated sugar yielded a cookie that was tasty, but coarse in both texture and appearance. Cookies made with confectioners' sugar were very tender, light, and fine-textured. Superfine, however, proved superior, producing cookies that were delicate, lightly crisp, and superbly tender, with a true melt-in-your-mouth quality. In a side-by-side tasting, the cookies made with superfine sugar were nuttier and purer in flavor, while the cornstarch in the confectioners' sugar bogged down the flavor and left a faint pastiness in the mouth.

As I tinkered with the amount of sugar, I had to keep in mind that these cookies are coated in confectioners' sugar after they are baked. One-third of a cup gives them a mildly sweet edge when they're eaten plain, but it's the roll in confectioners' sugar that gives them their finished look and just the right amount of extra sweetness.

When to give the baked cookies their coat of confectioners' sugar is a matter of some debate. Some recipes said to dust or dip them when they're still hot or warm. The sugar melts a bit, and then they're usually given a second coat to even out their appearance and form a thicker coating. But I didn't like the layer of melting moistened confectioners' sugar, concealed or not. It formed a thin skin that was pasty and gummy and didn't dissolve on the tongue with the same finesse as a fine, powdery coat. I found it better to wait until the cookies had cooled to room temperature before coating them with confectioners' sugar.

Sifting sugar over the cooled cookies was tedious, and I wasn't able to achieve a heavy enough coating on the tops—or any at all on the bottoms. What worked much better was simply rolling them in confectioners' sugar. One coat resulted in a rather thin layer that was a bit spotty, but a second roll covered any blemishes, giving them an attractive, thick, powdery white coating.

If not served immediately, the cookies may lose a little in looks due to handling and storage. This problem can be easily solved by reserving the second coat of confectioners' sugar until just before serving.

NUT CASE

During the nut testing, I concluded that what affected the cookies most was not the taste of the nuts but whether they were oily or dry. I found that when they were ground, the two types of nuts affected the cookies in different ways.

The flavor of oily nuts like walnuts and pecans is strong and distinct. These nuts are easier to chop and grind and, when finely ground, become quite oily. This is a definite advantage when making nut crescents, because the dough becomes softer and the resulting cookies are incredibly tender and delicate. Dry nuts like almonds and hazelnuts are rather subdued by comparison. Toasting brings out their maximum flavor and crunchiness. Although these nuts are somewhat difficult to chop, that is the best form to use them in. Ground dry nuts did very little, if

anything at all, to the texture of the cookies. Don't get me wrong: The almond and hazelnut cookies are delicious—they just don't melt in your mouth with the same abandon as the pecan and walnut ones.

In a recipe using 1 cup of butter and 2 cups of flour, various bakers called for anywhere from ½ cup to a hefty 2 cups of nuts, either roughly chopped, finely chopped, or ground. I wanted to cram as much nut flavor as I could into these cookies, but I found that 2 cups of ground nuts made them a tad greasy, while 1½ cups didn't give as much flavor as I was hoping for, so 1¾ cups was a happy compromise.

Chopped nuts were too coarse for the fine texture of the crescents and were quickly dismissed. Ground nuts, on the other hand, warranted further investigation. Oily ground nuts were flavorful, and because grinding really brought out the oils, they actually tenderized the cookies. I thought, though, that using a combination of ground and finely chopped nuts might tenderize, be flavorful, and add a pleasant bite. Hands down, a combo of 1 cup of finely chopped and ¾ cup of ground nuts was the tasters' choice.

I had, up to this point, baked over 30 batches of cookies. I pressed on, however, knowing that I was very close.

TAKING SHAPE

Recipes suggested baking temperatures ranging from a ridiculously low 300 degrees to a hot 400. At 375 degrees, the cookies browned too quickly, while at 300, they never achieved a nice golden hue, even after nearly half an hour of baking. Clearly the answer lay somewhere in between. My cookie-baking experience told me that many delicate, rich doughs like to bake at lower temperatures, and these cookies were no exception. Cookies baked at 350 degrees were good, but those baked at 325 degrees had a smoother, finer appearance, and were more tender and evenly textured and colored.

Whether you give them as gifts or keep them, these are cookies for eating, and not for the trash. The fruitcake may be a little lonely from now on.

Pecan or Walnut Crescent Cookies

MAKES ABOUT 48 COOKIES

If you can't find superfine sugar, process granulated sugar in a food processor for 30 seconds.

2 cups (10 ounces) all-purpose flour
2 cups (8 ounces) pecans or walnuts, chopped fine
½ teaspoon salt
16 tablespoons unsalted butter, softened
⅓ cup (2½ ounces) superfine sugar
1½ teaspoons vanilla extract
1½ cups (6 ounces) confectioners' sugar

1. Adjust oven racks to upper-middle and lower-middle positions and heat oven to 325 degrees. Line 2 baking sheets with parchment paper.
2. Whisk flour, 1 cup pecans, and salt together in medium bowl; set aside. Process remaining 1 cup pecans in food processor until they are texture of coarse cornmeal, 10 to 15 seconds (do not overprocess). Stir pecans into flour mixture and set aside.
3. Using stand mixer fitted with paddle, beat butter and superfine sugar at medium-low speed until light and fluffy, about 2 minutes; add vanilla, scraping down bowl as needed. Add flour mixture and beat on low speed until dough just begins to come together but still looks scrappy, about 15 seconds. Scrape down bowl as needed; continue beating until dough is cohesive, 6 to 9 seconds longer. Do not overbeat.
4. Working with 1 tablespoon dough at a time, roll into balls. Roll each ball of dough between your palms into rope that measures 3 inches long. Place ropes on prepared baking sheets and turn up ends to form crescent shape. Bake until tops of cookies are pale golden and bottoms are just beginning to brown, 17 to 19 minutes, switching and rotating baking sheets halfway through baking.
5. Let cookies cool on baking sheets for 2 minutes; transfer cookies to wire rack and let cool completely. Place confectioners' sugar in shallow baking dish. Working with 3 or 4 cookies at a time, roll cookies in sugar to coat thoroughly; gently shake off excess. (Cookies can be stored in airtight container for up to 5 days.) Before serving, roll cookies in confectioners' sugar again to ensure thick coating and tap off excess.

variation

Almond or Hazelnut Crescent Cookies

Almonds can be used raw, for cookies that are light in both color and flavor, or toasted, to enhance the almond flavor and darken the crescents.

Substitute 1¾ cups whole blanched almonds (toasted, if desired) or 2 cups skinned toasted hazelnuts for pecans or walnuts. If using almonds, add ½ teaspoon almond extract along with vanilla extract.

SHAPING THE COOKIES

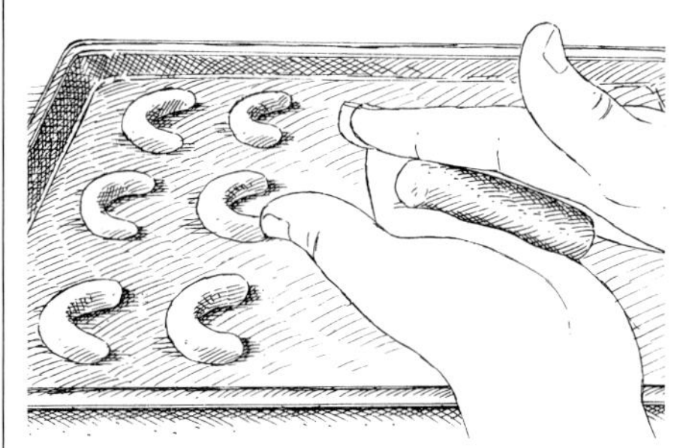

1. Roll dough balls between your palms to form 3-inch-long ropes.

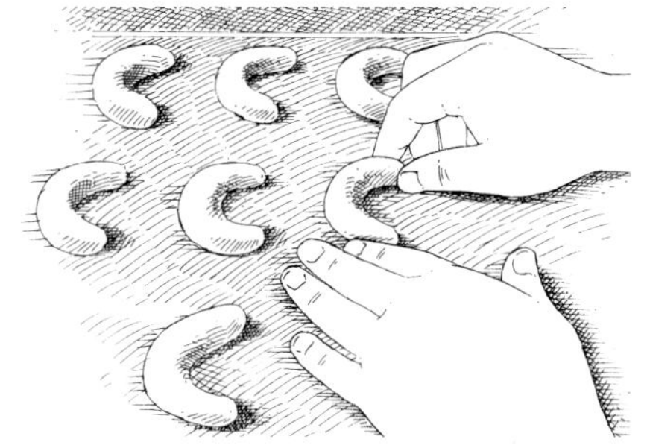

2. Place ropes on prepared baking sheets and turn up ends to form crescent shapes.

THE BEST SHORTBREAD

J. KENJI LOPEZ-ALT, *November/December 2009*

If your experience with shortbread is limited to bland, chalky specimens from tins, you might wonder how this plain-looking bar (which dates back to at least 12th-century Scotland) came to be one of the British Isles' most famous tea cakes. But when shortbread is made well, it's easy to understand why it earned a reputation as a favorite of high-ranking palates from Mary, Queen of Scots, to Elizabeth II. The best versions are an alluring tawny brown with a pure, buttery richness. Shortbread's distinctive sandy texture distinguishes it from the simple crispness of its cousin, the American butter cookie, while its moderate sweetness makes it easy to go back for seconds.

Shortbread originated as a way to turn leftover oat bread into something more special: The scraps were sprinkled with sugar and left to harden overnight in an oven still hot from the day's baking. By the 16th century, wheat flour had replaced oat bread in the recipe, and this biscuit morphed from a foodstuff of commoners into the more refined confection prized by nobility.

For shortbread with an ultrafine, sandy texture, we add some ground oats and let the cookies finish baking in a turned-off oven.

The basics haven't changed much over the past five centuries: Combine flour, sugar, butter, and salt and then pat the dough into a round and bake. But the recipes I unearthed varied in their proportions. Some called for equal parts butter and flour, and some for 1 part butter to 1 parts flour; several included unlikely ingredients like rice flour or cornstarch. Results were also all over the map. While some cookies fell apart in my hand, others were sturdy and crispy to a fault, and still others turned out either greasy or overly airy and cake-like. Moreover, nearly every version suffered from some degree of uneven cooking and overbrowning.

IN THE MIX

To get my bearings, I decided to limit my ingredients to the basic four before tinkering with extras. As for proportions, I ruled out a 1:1 ratio of butter to flour after preliminary tests proved that this was too greasy. I settled on a more moderate 1:2 ratio, with two sticks of butter, 2 cups of all-purpose flour, ⅔ cup of sugar, and ¼ teaspoon of salt.

As for mixing method, I would need to test the most traditional approach, which is akin to making pie crust: Cut the butter and dry ingredients together until they form wet crumbs and then pack the crumbs together into a dough. I also made two batches using more modern methods. For one, I creamed the butter and sugar in a stand mixer before adding the flour; for the other, I employed reverse creaming, mixing the flour and sugar before adding the butter.

Next, I formed cookies from my three doughs. Shortbread traditionally takes one of three shapes: individual round cookies; rectangular "fingers"; or one large circle with a hole cut in the center and then scored into wedges, called "petticoat tails" because the uncut cookie resembles a dressmaker's pattern. Pursuing the petticoat shape (for no reason except that it was reportedly the shape favored by Mary, Queen of Scots), I pressed the dough into a 9-inch disk, used a biscuit cutter to remove a hole from the center, and placed the shortbread in a 450-degree oven for a few minutes. Following the usual high-low baking protocol called for in shortbread recipes, I then reduced the oven to 300 degrees and continued to bake the cookies for an hour before scoring and cooling them.

I evaluated the results. The traditional, packed-crumb method produced cookies that were crumbly in some spots and brittle in others. Regular creaming incorporated too much air into the dough, making for soft, airy, cake-like cookies. Reverse creaming, which creates less aeration, yielded the most reliable results and was clearly the way to go. Tweaking the recipe, I reduced the butter, from 16 to 14 tablespoons, which resulted in a dough that was pliable and had plenty of buttery flavor but did not exude grease during baking. I also traded the white sugar for confectioners' sugar to smooth out an objectionable granular texture. Although my basic ingredients and mixing technique now seemed to be in order, the shortbread cookies were somewhat tough, and they were not as crisp as I wanted.

TOUGH COOKIE

Two factors played into my texture problem: gluten and moisture. Gluten, the protein matrix that lends baked goods structure and chew, forms naturally when liquid and all-purpose flour are combined, even with minimal kneading. The liquid in my recipe was coming from the butter, which contains 20 percent water—just enough to make my cookies tough. In addition, cookies can become truly crisp and crumbly only if they are perfectly dry. My goals, then, were to limit gluten development and to help the cookies dry out completely.

I first tried baking a batch entirely at 450 degrees, hoping the higher temperature would drive moisture from the cookies, but the edges started overbrowning after just 10 minutes, while the inner portion remained wet. I tried again, baking a second batch at 450 degrees for 5 minutes (to help set the dough) and then lowering the temperature to 250 degrees. This was better but still not perfect.

Early shortbread was made by leaving the dough in a still-warm oven heated only by dying embers. What if I briefly baked the shortbread, shut off the oven, and left it inside until it was completely dry? With just 15 minutes or so of "real" baking in a hot oven—and an hour with the oven

turned off—the results were striking: This batch was dry through and through, with an even, golden-brown exterior.

With the moisture issue resolved, I shifted my focus to the toughness caused by excess gluten development. Various 21st-century recipes have tried to solve this problem by substituting low-protein, gluten-free rice flour for some of the all-purpose flour. I gave it a try. The rice-flour shortbread's crumbly texture looked promising, but when I took a bite, I realized that reducing the all-purpose flour had also made the cookies woefully bland. Cornstarch (another gluten-free ingredient used in some modern recipes) yielded equally insipid results.

Scanning the test kitchen's shelves, I spotted a possible solution: old-fashioned oats. Oats have a nice nutty flavor and contain few of the proteins necessary for gluten development; on top of that, they're traditional to early shortbread recipes. I ground some oats to a powder in a spice grinder and substituted ¾ cup of this oat flour for some of the all-purpose flour in my recipe. The resulting cookies had a promising crisp and crumbly texture, but the oats muted the buttery flavor. Still, I knew that I was on the right track. For my next batch, I used less oat flour and supplemented it with a modest amount of cornstarch. This worked handsomely. The cookies were now perfectly crispy, with an appealing hint of oat flavor.

SO LONG, SPREADING

I had one last problem to solve: spreading. As buttery shortbread bakes, it expands, losing its shape as the edges flatten out. I tried baking the dough in a traditional shortbread mold with ½-inch-high sides, but it still widened into an amorphous mass. Clearly, the dough needed a substantial barrier to keep its edges corralled. My solution? A springform pan collar. I set the closed collar on a parchment-lined baking sheet, patted the dough into it, and then opened the collar to give the cookie about half an inch to spread out.

With my baking method perfected, I put together a gussied-up variation, dipping a pistachio-studded version in melted chocolate. History had repeated itself, and I now had some of the finest shortbread of its time.

Best Shortbread

MAKES 16 WEDGES

Use the collar of a springform pan to form the shortbread into an even round. Mold the shortbread with the collar in the closed position, then open the collar, but leave it in place. This allows the shortbread to expand slightly but keeps it from spreading too far. The extracted round of dough in step 2 is baked alongside the rest of the shortbread.

½ cup (1½ ounces) old-fashioned rolled oats
1½ cups (7½ ounces) all-purpose flour
⅔ cup (2⅔ ounces) confectioners' sugar
¼ cup (1 ounce) cornstarch
½ teaspoon salt
14 tablespoons unsalted butter, cut into ⅛-inch-thick slices and chilled

1. Adjust oven rack to middle position and heat oven to 450 degrees. Pulse oats in spice grinder or blender until reduced to fine powder, about 10 pulses (you should have ¼ to ⅓ cup oat flour). Using stand mixer fitted with paddle, mix oat flour, all-purpose flour, sugar, cornstarch, and salt on low speed until combined, about 5 seconds. Add butter to dry ingredients and continue to mix until dough just forms and pulls away from sides of bowl, 5 to 10 minutes.

2. Line baking sheet with parchment paper. Place upside-down (grooved edge should be at top) collar of 9- or 9½-inch springform pan on prepared sheet (do not use springform pan bottom). Press dough into collar in even ½-inch-thick layer, smoothing top of dough with back of spoon. Place 2-inch biscuit cutter in center of dough and cut out center. Place extracted round alongside springform collar on sheet and replace cutter in center of dough. Open springform collar, but leave it in place.

3. Bake shortbread for 5 minutes, then reduce oven temperature to 250 degrees. Continue to bake until edges turn pale golden, 10 to 15 minutes longer. Remove sheet from oven; turn off oven. Remove springform pan collar; use chef's knife to score surface of shortbread into 16 even wedges, cutting halfway through shortbread. Using wooden skewer, poke 8 to 10 holes in each wedge. Return shortbread to oven and prop door open with handle of wooden spoon, leaving 1-inch gap at top. Let shortbread dry in turned-off oven until pale golden in center (shortbread should be firm but giving to touch), about 1 hour.

4. Transfer sheet to wire rack; let shortbread cool completely. Cut shortbread at scored marks to separate and serve. (Shortbread can be wrapped tightly in plastic wrap and stored at room temperature for up to 1 week.)

variations

Chocolate-Dipped Pistachio Shortbread

Add ½ cup finely chopped toasted pistachios to dry ingredients in step 1. Bake and cool shortbread as directed. Once shortbread is cool, melt 8 ounces finely chopped bittersweet chocolate in small heatproof bowl set over saucepan filled with 1 inch of barely simmering water, making sure that water does not touch bottom of bowl and stirring occasionally until smooth. Off heat; stir in additional 2 ounces finely chopped bittersweet chocolate until smooth. Carefully dip base of each wedge in chocolate, allowing chocolate to come halfway up cookie. Scrape off excess with finger and place on parchment-lined rimmed baking sheet. Refrigerate until chocolate sets, about 15 minutes.

Ginger Shortbread

Turbinado sugar is commonly sold as Sugar in the Raw. Demerara sugar, sanding sugar, or another coarse sugar can be substituted.

Add ½ cup chopped crystallized ginger to dry ingredients in step 1. Sprinkle shortbread with 1 tablespoon turbinado sugar after poking holes in shortbread in step 3.

Toasted Oat Shortbread

To toast the oats, heat them in an 8-inch skillet over medium-high heat until light golden brown, 5 to 8 minutes.

Add ½ cup toasted oats to dry ingredients in step 1. Sprinkle ½ teaspoon sea salt evenly over surface of dough before baking.

BETTER HOLIDAY SUGAR COOKIES

ANDREW JANJIGIAN, *November/December 2017*

Are roll-and-cut sugar cookies a fun, festive project? Not in my kitchen: They've always been a maddening chore with nothing but floury, shapeless disappointments to show for the effort. Most recipes require you to haul out a stand mixer to cream sugar and softened butter before mixing in the remaining ingredients and then to refrigerate the dough before rolling, cutting, and baking. The lump of dough is always stiff after chilling, so it's challenging to roll. Many of the cookies puff during baking, which leaves them uneven or with indistinct outlines. What's more, they're often hard and dense rather than simply sturdy.

I wanted to turn things around with a dough that would be easy—maybe even fun—to work with. It would be firm enough to shape with cookie cutters and to carry frosting and other decorations after baking. The cookies would bake up crisp and flat, with sharp edges, and they would have a satisfying, buttery flavor.

THE WAY THE COOKIE CRUMBLES

I began with a recipe that had decent flavor. It called for beating two sticks of softened butter with 1 cup of sugar; mixing in 2½ cups of flour, an egg, salt, and vanilla; and then chilling the dough before rolling, cutting, and baking. The cookies were buttery and just sweet enough, but they had a slightly granular texture and tended to puff in the oven, leaving them bumpy and uneven.

Graininess can come from an excess of sugar, but reducing the sugar by ⅓ cup upset the flavor. Instead, I tried replacing the granulated sugar with confectioners' sugar, but this turned the cookies somewhat chalky and hard rather than crisp. However, superfine sugar (granulated sugar that has been ground to a fine—but not powdery—consistency) was just the ticket: fine enough to smooth out any graininess but coarse enough to maintain a slightly open crumb. And happily, superfine sugar is a cinch to make by pulverizing granulated sugar in a food processor.

To address the cookies' puffiness, I examined the creaming step, the goal of which is to incorporate air. It makes sense for a soft, cakey cookie, but was it detrimental to one that I wanted to be flat and even? For my next batch, I briefly mixed the sugar and butter until just combined. Sure enough, these cookies baked up entirely flat.

But they were now a little dense, begging for a tiny amount of air. I turned to baking soda and baking powder; ¼ teaspoon of each produced flat cookies with a crisp yet sturdy texture.

Combining superfine sugar and cold butter in the food processor makes this dough easy to work with.

ROLLING IN DOUGH

Now it was time to address my other issue with roll-and-cut cookies—the need to chill the dough before rolling it, which inevitably leads to strong-arming a cold, hardened lump into submission. Refrigerating the dough for a shorter time wasn't an option, since it wouldn't have time to chill evenly. And rolling the dough straightaway was out of the question because I was using softened butter—a must for easy combining in a stand mixer—which produced a soft dough that would cling to a rolling pin. I needed a dough made with cold butter.

That meant I would need to "plasticize" the butter, or soften it while keeping it cold, so that my dough would roll out without ripping or sticking. Croissant bakers plasticize blocks of butter by pounding them with a rolling pin. I didn't want to beat butter by hand, but I could use the food processor. Unlike the paddle of a stand mixer, which would struggle to soften cold butter quickly, the fast, ultrasharp blades of a food processor could turn it malleable.

I processed the sugar and then added chunks of cold butter and combined them into a smooth paste. I whizzed in the egg and vanilla, plus a smidge of almond extract for an unidentifiable flavor boost, and then added the dry ingredients. The dough was pliable but not soft or sticky.

I halved the dough and placed each portion between sheets of parchment paper to help prevent sticking. It rolled out like a dream. To ensure easy cutting and clean, well-defined edges, I still needed to chill the dough, so I placed it in the refrigerator for 1½ hours. By eliminating the need to bring the butter to room temperature, skipping creaming, and making the dough easy to roll, I'd shaved off some time—and plenty of effort—from the recipe.

I'd been baking the cookies at 350 degrees on the middle rack, but the edges of the cookies around the perimeter of the sheet were dark brown by the time the center ones were golden. The fix was three-pronged. One: I reduced the oven temperature to 300 degrees; more-gradual baking evened the color. Two: I lowered the oven rack, so the cookies baked from the bottom up. This meant that they browned nicely on their undersides (for hidden flavor) while remaining lighter on top. Three: I used a rimless cookie sheet instead of a rimmed baking sheet. This promoted air circulation, so the cookies baked more evenly.

A ROYAL FINISH

For decoration, I decided to use royal icing, which tasted good and firmed up nicely. Named for its use on Queen Victoria's cake at her marriage to Prince Albert in 1840, this mix of whipped egg whites and sugar sets into a dry coating with a matte surface. I added vanilla and salt to my version. Piped or poured onto the cooled cookies, it was a joyful finish to the best—and easiest—cut-out cookies I'd ever made.

Easy Holiday Sugar Cookies

MAKES ABOUT FORTY 2½-INCH COOKIES

For the dough to have the proper consistency when rolling, make sure to use cold butter directly from the refrigerator. In step 3, use a rolling pin and a combination of rolling and a pushing or smearing motion to form the soft dough into an oval. A rimless cookie sheet helps achieve evenly baked cookies; if you don't have one, use an overturned rimmed baking sheet. Dough scraps can be combined and rerolled once, though the cookies will be slightly less tender. If desired, stir one or two drops of food coloring into the icing. For a pourable icing, whisk in milk, 1 teaspoon at a time, until the desired consistency is reached. You can also decorate the shapes with sanding sugar or sprinkles before baking.

Cookies

1 large egg
1 teaspoon vanilla extract
¾ teaspoon salt
¼ teaspoon almond extract
2½ cups (12½ ounces) all-purpose flour
¼ teaspoon baking powder
¼ teaspoon baking soda
1 cup (7 ounces) granulated sugar
16 tablespoons unsalted butter, cut into ½-inch pieces and chilled

Royal Icing

2⅔ cups (10⅔ ounces) confectioners' sugar
2 large egg whites
½ teaspoon vanilla extract
⅛ teaspoon salt

1. ***For the cookies:*** Whisk egg, vanilla, salt, and almond extract together in small bowl. Whisk flour, baking powder, and baking soda together in second bowl.

2. Process sugar in food processor until finely ground, about 30 seconds. Add butter and process until uniform mass forms and no large pieces of butter are visible, about 30 seconds, scraping down sides of bowl as needed. Add egg mixture and process until smooth and paste-like, about 10 seconds. Add flour mixture and process until no dry flour remains but mixture remains crumbly, about 30 seconds, scraping down sides of bowl as needed.

3. Turn out dough onto counter and knead gently by hand until smooth, about 10 seconds. Divide dough in half. Place 1 piece of dough in center of large sheet of parchment paper and press into 7 by 9-inch oval. Place second large sheet of parchment over dough and roll dough into 10 by 14-inch oval of even ⅛-inch thickness. Transfer dough with parchment to rimmed baking sheet. Repeat pressing and rolling with second piece of dough, then stack on top of first piece on sheet. Refrigerate until dough is firm, at least 1½ hours (or freeze for 30 minutes). (Rolled dough can be wrapped in plastic wrap and refrigerated for up to 5 days.)

4. Adjust oven rack to lower-middle position and heat oven to 300 degrees. Line rimless cookie sheet with parchment. Working with 1 piece of rolled dough, gently peel off top layer of parchment. Replace parchment, loosely covering dough. (Peeling off parchment and returning it will make cutting and removing cookies easier.) Turn over dough and parchment and gently peel off and discard second piece of parchment. Using cookie cutter, cut dough into shapes. Transfer shapes to prepared cookie sheet, spacing them about ½ inch apart. Bake until cookies are lightly and evenly browned around edges, 14 to 17 minutes, rotating sheet halfway through baking. Let cookies cool on sheet for 5 minutes. Using wide metal spatula, transfer cookies to wire rack and let cool completely. Repeat cutting and baking with remaining dough. (Dough scraps can be patted together, rerolled, and chilled once before cutting and baking.)

5. ***For the royal icing:*** Using stand mixer fitted with whisk attachment, whip all ingredients on medium-low speed until combined, about 1 minute. Increase speed to medium-high and whip until glossy, soft peaks form, 3 to 4 minutes, scraping down bowl as needed.

6. Spread icing onto cooled cookies. Let icing dry completely, about 1½ hours, before serving.

LOOSEN PARCHMENT SO COOKIES DON'T STICK

After chilling the rolled-out dough between sheets of parchment paper, we peel back and replace the top sheet of parchment before flipping the dough over. The loosened parchment won't stick to the undersides of the cut-out cookie shapes when we transfer them to a baking sheet.

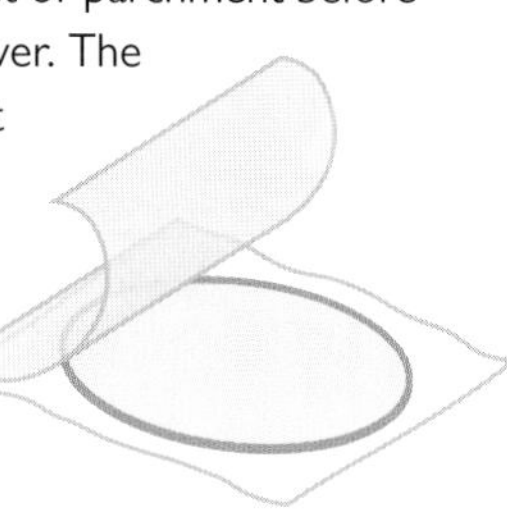

REVAMPING SUGAR COOKIES

A number of updates to the usual approach resulted in better, easier cookies.

COLD BUTTER instead of softened butter means dough is firm enough to be rolled immediately after mixing.

SUPERFINE SUGAR made by processing granulated sugar in food processor smooths out graininess but still allows for open crumb.

SHARP BLADES OF FOOD PROCESSOR rapidly whiz cold ingredients into malleable dough.

ROLL, THEN CHILL method eliminates need to battle cold, hard lump of dough into thin sheet.

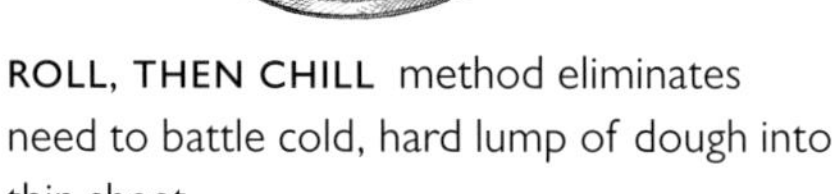

CRACKING THE CODE TO CHEWY BROWNIES

ANDREA GEARY, *March/April 2010*

Confession: I consider myself a from-scratch, hands-on, all-natural kind of cook, but I love a good box-mix brownie. It was a dicey admission to make to my colleagues, all serious cooks themselves, as we discussed the brownies we crave most. Then one ally voiced her support, and another followed. Pretty soon, any previous high-minded idea of what makes a brownie truly irresistible had been eclipsed by the collective memory of versions from a cardboard box.

True, nobody was gushing over their chemical sweetness—everyone agreed that box-mix brownies are all about texture. My goal was clear: a homemade brownie with the chewiness (and the shiny, crisp, crackly top) to rival box-mix versions—but flush with a rich, deep, chocolate flavor.

BROWNIE POINTS

To start, I rounded up as many brownie recipes as I could find with "chewy" in the title, but not one of the recipes could actually lay claim to such a quality. The issue was that all brownie recipes, regardless of texture, are composed of the same basic ingredients: fat (usually butter), eggs, salt, sugar, vanilla, flour (typically all-purpose), and, of course, chocolate (most often from an unsweetened bar). Producing a fudgy brownie or a cakey one boils down to manipulating the ratio of fat and chocolate to flour. But the ratios called for in the "chewy" brownie recipes I consulted (on average, about 4 ounces of chocolate, 8 ounces of butter, and 5 ounces of flour) tended to produce brownies that were merely soft, not chewy. Their mixing techniques, another possible way to introduce chewiness, weren't helping either: While a few called for creaming the butter and sugar, most simply required melting the chocolate and butter; stirring in the sugar, eggs, and vanilla; and folding in the flour.

I resumed my recipe hunt, keeping an eye out for any unusual techniques or ingredients. I tried one that called for cooking the sugar and butter into a caramel, which I folded into the other ingredients, but these lacked chewiness. I tried baking brownies on a pizza stone (the theory being that the burst of bottom heat would melt the sugars, imparting chew) as well as underbaking brownies and then chilling them in an ice bath. Alas, the pizza-stone brownie turned out as soft as previous attempts, and the underbaked specimen was … underbaked.

For better-than-box-mix brownies, we use both butter and vegetable oil for the best texture, and three kinds of chocolate for intense flavor.

Clearly, to create a brownie with a truly chewy texture, I was on my own. Taking a break from baking, I tried to think of other baked goods that are heavy on chew. Brown sugar cookies came to mind. Because brown sugar and corn syrup are both hygroscopic (i.e., they attract and retain water), cookie dough containing high levels of these ingredients bakes up moister and chewier than the exact same cookie dough made with white sugar, which is less hygroscopic.

So, I took one of the chewier brownie recipes I found, which called for 4 ounces of unsweetened chocolate, two sticks of butter, 1 cup of flour, two eggs, and 2 cups of sugar, and replaced the white sugar with a combination of brown sugar and corn syrup. Not only did it do nothing for texture, it also managed to lose the shiny, crackly crust; in its place emerged a dull, matte, cake-like finish. Regular sugar would have to stay.

I consulted our science editor to see if he knew of any tricks that box-mix brownies use to achieve their chewiness. His answer completely changed the direction of my research: "high-tech shortening system."

BEAT THE SYSTEM

It turns out that the whole key to the texture of a box-mix brownie resides in the types and amounts of fat it includes, and manufacturers have spent years coming up with the right formulation.

Fat can be divided into two broad types—saturated and unsaturated. Predominantly saturated fats such as shortening and lard are solid even at room temperature. Unsaturated fats, such as vegetable oils, are liquid at room temperature. The right combination—the shortening system—is what gives box-mix brownies their unique texture.

Brownie mixes come with the saturated-fat component, which is broken down into tiny, powdery crystals. When a cook adds unsaturated vegetable oil to this mix, the liquid fat and powdered solid fat combine in a ratio designed to deliver maximum chew. To get the same chew at home, I would have to discover the perfect proportion of liquid to solid fat without the aid of the high-tech fats used by brownie-mix manufacturers.

REACHING A SATURATION POINT

I started by identifying all the sources of fat in my recipe: butter, melted chocolate, and egg yolks. I'd keep the butter as my saturated fat—it would be a more flavorful choice than vegetable shortening. To simplify my calculations, I eliminated the melted chocolate and used cocoa powder, which contains very little fat by comparison. Once I figured out the ideal fat ratios, I'd put the bar chocolate back in. For an unsaturated fat, I stuck to vegetable oil.

Next I devised a series of recipes that all had roughly the same amount of total fat, but with varying ratios of butter to vegetable

oil. I found that brownies that contained mostly saturated fat baked up quite tender and not at all chewy, while brownies made with mostly unsaturated fat were the chewier ones. Finally, after extensive trial and error, I hit on the magic formula to produce the chewiest brownie: 29 percent saturated fat to 71 percent unsaturated—or about a 1:3 ratio. The box-mix numbers virtually mirrored my results, with 28 percent saturated fat to 72 percent unsaturated.

But problems persisted: While chewy, my brownies were greasy, and with cocoa powder as the sole source of chocolate, their flavor was predictably lackluster.

GREASE, BE GONE

I attacked the greasiness first. Emulsifiers can help prevent fats from separating and leaking out during baking. I thought back to the test kitchen's recipe for vinaigrette, in which we found that mayonnaise—an emulsion itself—was able to keep the dressing from separating because of its emulsifiers. Delving deeper, I identified the active emulsifier in the mayonnaise as lecithin, a phospholipid that occurs naturally in egg yolks. The addition of two extra yolks to my recipe in exchange for a little oil made greasiness a thing of the past.

Now for chocolate flavor. Loath to tamper with my fine-tuned fat ratio, I first tried tweaks that wouldn't affect the fats. Espresso powder deepens chocolate flavor without imparting a strong coffee taste. Stirring 1½ teaspoons into the boiling water along with the cocoa helped, but I knew I could do better.

Research revealed that although the total fat in unsweetened chocolate is lower per ounce than in an equivalent amount of butter, it contains a similar ratio of saturated to unsaturated fat. By replacing 2 tablespoons of butter (or 1 ounce) with 2 ounces of unsweetened chocolate, I could stay very close to the ideal fat ratio.

Finally, to pack in still more chocolate flavor, I incorporated a full 6 ounces of bittersweet chocolate chunks—since they didn't melt until the batter started baking, they didn't affect the texture. The result: chewy, fudgy bars with gooey pockets of melted chocolate, no industrial processing needed.

Chewy Brownies

MAKES 24 BROWNIES

For the chewiest texture, it is important to let the brownies cool thoroughly before cutting. If your baking dish is glass, cool the brownies for 10 minutes, then remove them promptly from the pan (otherwise, the superior heat retention of glass can lead to overbaking).

- **⅓ cup (1 ounce) Dutch-processed cocoa**
- **1½ teaspoons instant espresso powder (optional)**
- **½ cup plus 2 tablespoons boiling water**
- **2 ounces unsweetened chocolate, chopped fine**
- **½ cup plus 2 tablespoons vegetable oil**
- **4 tablespoons unsalted butter, melted**
- **2 large eggs plus 2 large yolks**
- **2 teaspoons vanilla extract**
- **2½ cups (17½ ounces) sugar**
- **1¾ cups (8¾ ounces) all-purpose flour**
- **¾ teaspoon salt**
- **6 ounces bittersweet chocolate, cut into ½-inch pieces**

1. Adjust oven rack to lowest position and heat oven to 350 degrees. Make foil sling for 13 by 9-inch baking pan by folding 2 long sheets of aluminum foil; first sheet should be 13 inches wide, and second sheet should be 9 inches wide. Lay sheets of foil in pan perpendicular to each other, with extra foil hanging over edges of pan. Push foil into corners and up sides of pan, smoothing foil flush to pan, and grease foil.

2. Whisk cocoa, espresso powder, if using, and boiling water together in large bowl until smooth. Add unsweetened chocolate and whisk until chocolate is melted. Whisk in oil and melted butter. (Mixture may look curdled.) Whisk in eggs, yolks, and vanilla until smooth and homogeneous. Whisk in sugar until fully incorporated. Add flour and salt and mix with rubber spatula until combined. Fold in chocolate pieces.

3. Scrape batter into prepared pan and smooth top. Bake brownies until toothpick inserted halfway between edge and center comes out with few moist crumbs attached, 30 to 35 minutes, rotating pan halfway through baking. Let brownies cool in pan for 1½ hours.

4. Using foil overhang, lift brownies from pan. Transfer to wire rack and let cool completely, about 1 hour. Cut into 24 squares and serve.

BAKING BROWNIES WITH A SHINY, CRACKLY TOP

A glossy, crackly top is one of the hallmarks of a great brownie, but achieving it can be elusive. Can the type of sweetener you use help?

THE EXPERIMENT We baked three batches of brownies, one sweetened with granulated sugar, another with brown sugar, and a third with brown sugar and corn syrup.

THE RESULTS Only the brownies made with granulated sugar took on an attractive crackly sheen. The other batches had a dull, matte finish.

THE EXPLANATION Why does granulated sugar work best? It's all due to what might be deemed "special effects." Whether on its own or in combination with corn syrup, brown sugar forms crystals on the surface of the cooling brownie. Crystals reflect light in a diffuse way, creating a matte effect. The pure sucrose in granulated sugar, on the other hand, forms a smooth, glass-like surface as it cools that reflects light in a focused way, for a shiny effect. As for the crackly crust, its formation depends on sugar molecules rising to the surface of the batter and drying out during baking. Since both brown sugar and corn syrup contain more moisture than granulated sugar, the surface of brownies made with either of these sweeteners never dries out enough for a crisp crust to form.

BROWN SUGAR
Dull, Matte Finish

WHITE SUGAR
Shiny, Crackly Finish

BUILDING A BETTER BLONDIE

MATTHEW CARD, *July/August 2005*

A fashion editor once said that style lies in the ability to walk across a room without having anyone notice you. What speaks for fashion, I believe, also holds true for food. Brownies, with their brash, full-frontal chocolate flavor, are the plunging necklines of baking, whereas the more subtle, butterscotch-flavored blondies have real timeless style. Of course, subtle elegance in baking is hard to come by, and that's why blondies are often greasy, cakey, and bland. Nobody ever said style was easy.

Despite these differences, brownies and blondies are cut from similar cloth. Each includes a simple list of ingredients: flour, eggs, butter, sugar (light brown for blondies), vanilla, and salt. Brownies require the addition of melted chocolate, whereas blondie recipes call for including nuts and chocolate chips.

After I baked off a slew of remarkably similar recipes, it was clear that proportions made all the difference. Cloyingly sweet, bland, crumbly, greasy—all of these ills were readily apparent with only slight variations in ingredient amounts. I also discovered that producing great chewy texture along with good flavor was no mean feat: Having one seemed to preclude the other. I'd need to find my way around this discouraging discovery.

Blondies are prepared in two very distinct styles. The first calls for melted butter to be mixed with sugar and eggs before the dry ingredients are folded in. The second requires creaming butter and sugar until fluffy and then adding the eggs and dry ingredients. Tasters preferred melted butter versions for their dense, chewy texture (the creamed versions were too cakey). As a bonus, this approach was also simpler.

BATTER MATTERS

Most blondie recipes have close to a 1:1 ratio of light brown sugar to all-purpose flour—much more flour than is typically included in brownie recipes. The reason? Chocolate (or lack thereof). Chocolate, like flour, contains starch, and it also acts as an emulsifier, helping hold brownie batter together. When I reduced the flour to the proportions common in brownie recipes (closer to a 3:1 ratio of sugar to flour), the blondies turned into a greasy puddle. Additional testing simply left me back where I had started: using equal parts sugar and flour.

Mixing and matching sugars—adding portions of dark brown sugar or granulated sugar to the light brown sugar—did not improve the recipe. Neither did adding liquid sugars like molasses or dark corn syrup. As it turned out, light brown sugar, the choice in most recipes, worked best.

I had been using two sticks of butter (which I had melted and briefly let cool), which helped produce a pleasant chewy texture—but also made the blondies greasy. I reduced the butter a tablespoon at a time until I reached the tipping point—12 tablespoons—below which flavor and texture were compromised. I had also noticed that blondie recipes tend to call for fewer eggs than brownie recipes, and I soon found out why. More than two eggs put the texture into the "rubbery" category.

I had made some progress, but my blondies were still squat and dense, in dire need of a lift. Baking powder was the obvious answer. One teaspoon provided the lift and also contributed to the elusive chewiness I was after.

Timing also appeared to be crucial. I was baking the blondies at 350 degrees—no other temperature worked as well. When I removed them from the oven too soon, they had the pale, sticky sweetness and gummy texture of cookie dough. However, if removed too late, the blondies dried out. It seemed the usual signifiers of an adequately baked bar cookie—the cooked dough pulls away from the sides of the pan, a toothpick comes out clean—did not apply to blondies. Better indicators were color and texture: a light golden brown top that looked shiny and cracked.

ODDS AND ENDS

Now that my blondies had the proper texture, it was time to tweak their flavor. It came as no surprise that my recipe was largely improved by a dash of vanilla. I found that 1½ teaspoons gave the blondies just the right balanced aromatic flavor. As for the nuts, most recipes favor walnuts, although pecans are not unusual. Tasters liked both and were ultimately split in making a choice, so I've left it up to the baker. Either way, everyone agreed that browning the nuts before adding them to the dough boosted the flavor significantly. I also found that stovetop toasting (in a dry skillet) produced only faint coloring with spotty singeing; a more thorough oven toasting was the better approach.

Decreasing the amount of butter and adding toasted nuts and white chocolate chips produces blondies with great texture and dynamic flavor.

As with the choice of nuts, the test kitchen was split on the addition of chocolate chips. Half the tasters thought that chips muddied the flavors, while the rest preferred a bit of culinary counterpoint. I also tested butterscotch chips, a common addition, but one tasting confirmed my suspicion that any flavor they added would be artificial—no thanks. While buying the butterscotch chips, I picked up a bag of white chocolate chips as well. A bit to my surprise, the white chocolate chips did indeed enrich the flavor and became a key component in the recipe that everyone in the test kitchen could agree on.

Here was my final batch of blondies: chewy without being dense, sweet without being cloying, and sufficiently interesting (with the addition of nuts and white chocolate chips) to hold one's attention beyond just one bar. Now that's the kind of style I like.

Blondies

MAKES 36 BARS

Do not overbake the blondies; they dry out easily and will turn hard.

1½ cups (7½ ounces) all-purpose flour
1 teaspoon baking powder
½ teaspoon salt
1½ cups packed (10½ ounces) light brown sugar
12 tablespoons unsalted butter, melted and cooled
2 large eggs
1½ teaspoons vanilla extract
1 cup pecans or walnuts, toasted and chopped coarse
½ cup (3 ounces) semisweet chocolate chips
½ cup (3 ounces) white chocolate chips

1. Adjust oven rack to middle position and heat oven to 350 degrees. Make foil sling for 13 by 9-inch baking pan by folding 2 long sheets of aluminum foil; first sheet should be 9 inches wide and second sheet should be 13 inches wide. Lay sheets of foil in pan perpendicular to each other, with extra foil hanging over edges of pan. Push foil into corners and up sides of pan, smoothing foil flush to pan. Grease foil.
2. Whisk flour, baking powder, and salt together in medium bowl; set aside.
3. Whisk sugar and melted butter together in medium bowl until combined. Add eggs and vanilla and mix well. Using rubber spatula, fold flour mixture into egg mixture until just combined. Do not overmix. Fold in pecans and semisweet and white chocolate chips.
4. Transfer batter to prepared pan, smoothing top with rubber spatula. Bake until top is shiny and cracked and feels firm to touch, 22 to 25 minutes, rotating pan halfway through baking. Transfer pan to wire rack and let cool completely. Loosen edges with paring knife; using foil overhang, lift blondies out of pan. Cut into 36 bars and serve.

variation

Congo Bars

Keep a close eye on the coconut as it toasts because it can burn easily. Sweetened coconut is not a suitable substitute here.

Toast 1½ cups unsweetened shredded coconut on rimmed baking sheet, stirring 2 or 3 times, until light golden, 5 to 7 minutes. Proceed with recipe as directed, adding coconut with chocolate in step 3.

RAISING THE BAR

Chocolate adds more than just flavor to brownies. It contains a fair amount of starch that helps brownies hold their shape. Because blondies contain just chips (no melted chocolate), this recipe requires more flour than a brownie recipe.

MEASURE IT RIGHT

With their simple ingredient list, even a tablespoon too much or too little flour can have an impact on our Blondies. Here's how to measure accurately.

PREFERRED Weigh flour
For the greatest accuracy, weigh flour before using it. Put a bowl on a scale, hit the "tare" button to set the scale to zero, and scoop the flour into the bowl.

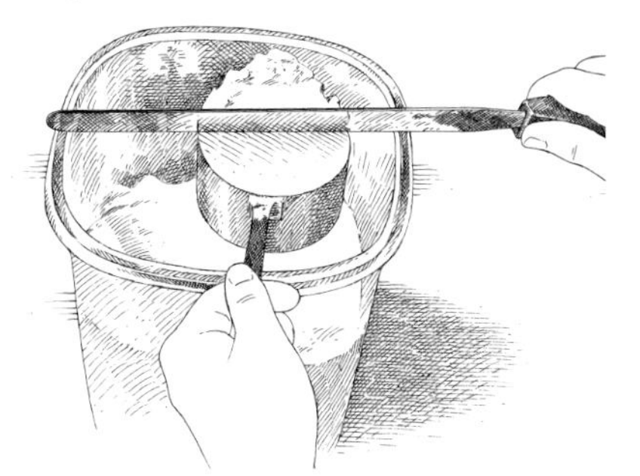

SECOND-BEST Dip and sweep
Dip a dry measuring cup into the flour, sweeping away excess flour with a flat edge. This method yields more accurate results than spooning flour into a measuring cup.

MAKING A FOIL SLING

Lining the pan with a foil sling before baking prevents sticking and makes it easy to get bar cookies out of the pan. Once cool, lift the bars from the pan, transfer to a cutting board, and cut into pieces.

1. Fold long sheet of foil so it is 9 inches wide. Lay in pan, pushing foil into corners and up sides.

2. Fold second long sheet of foil so it is 13 inches wide. Lay perpendicular to first sheet. Smooth foil flush to pan, allowing extra to hang over sides.

THE BEST RASPBERRY BARS

ERIKA BRUCE, *September/October 2005*

What you look for in a raspberry bar is neither refined flavor nor stately appearance but the homey comfort of a triple-decker: sturdy base, jam center, and crisp streusel on top. The secret of this bar cookie's simplicity is the dough, which serves as both bottom crust and—with a modification or two—pebbly topping. But a great-tasting raspberry bar requires just the right balance of bright, tangy fruit filling and rich, buttery shortbread. Unfortunately, I've had my fair share of raspberry squares that were more crumb sandwich than bar cookie. Worse than the loose crumbs was the meager layer of raspberry jam attempting feebly to hold it all together—so overcooked and leathery that the fruit flavor was gone. I was determined to find the perfect harmony of dough, fruit, and topping.

The first thing I discovered was that the economical use of a single dough for both the top and the bottom crust was, alas, problematic. The same dough responsible for a firm and sturdy bottom layer yielded a topping that was sandy and dry. Some recipe writers get around this problem by assembling two separate mixtures for the top and bottom layers, but I was loath to make more work for myself. My goal was to create a plain and simple shortbread-like bottom crust and then somehow customize a portion of this dough to end up with a successful streusel topping.

For the bottom crust, I started with a basic shortbread recipe—a simple mixture of flour, sugar, salt, and what I thought was a healthy dose of softened butter (12 tablespoons). But this crust turned out dense and chewy. I tested several methods to tenderize it, including chilling the butter before mixing it with the flour (as with biscuit or pie dough) and adding baking powder, lemon juice, or cornstarch but in the end, the answer was quite simple: increase the butter to 16 tablespoons.

But even this butter-rich dough wasn't up to the task of forming a neat-crumbed topping for the jam. While streusel is generally on the loose side, I wanted a more cohesive topping. Adding an extra 2 tablespoons of butter (rubbed into the dough with my fingers) produced hazelnut-size crumbs that melded in the oven yet remained light and crunchy. All I had to do now was add sugar and spices. Light brown sugar lent a distinct sweetness, but spices were deemed unnecessary for these fruity bars. Instead, tasters opted for a few oats and chopped nuts for more interesting dimensions of flavor and texture.

We make raspberry bars that are tender, fruity, and crunchy by adding plenty of butter to the crust and topping and using fresh fruit along with jam for the filling.

Plain old raspberry jam was the filling of choice for most recipes, but tasters liked brighter, fruitier preserves better. Yet even the preserves lost significant flavor when cooked again in the raspberry bars. I added a dash of lemon juice with the hope that it would brighten the filling. This kept the deadening heat of the oven in check, but it didn't fool one taster into believing there were fresh berries anywhere near these bars. The logical solution? Add fresh berries to get fresh berry flavor. But berries alone produced a mouth-puckeringly tart bar. Clearly, the viscous, sweet preserves were essential to the filling. I found success with a combination of preserves and fresh berries (lightly mashed for easier spreading), which produced a well-rounded flavor and a wonderfully moist consistency.

MAKING EVEN BAR COOKIES

There are two tricks for cutting perfect square or rectangular bars. The first is using the foil sling to lift the bars from the pan before cutting. Haphazardly scoring bars while in the pan makes for uneven edges that can crumble. Cutting outside of the pan makes even lines from edge to edge. And if you want your bars to be precise, don't just eyeball them before cutting; use a ruler to cut rows and columns at even intervals.

JAMS, JELLIES, AND PRESERVES

Fruity bar cookies such as our Raspberry Streusel Bars include a layer of jam. We also often use it to fill thumbprints and sandwich cookies. Is jam interchangeable with other fruit spreads? Jam is made from crushed or finely chopped fruit, which is cooked with pectin and sugar until the pieces of fruit are almost formless and the mixture is thickened. Preserves are similar, but they contain whole pieces or large chunks of fruit. Jam's good fruit flavor and relatively smooth texture make it our first choice for baking. Avoid jelly; it has a wan, overly sweet taste since it's made from just fruit juice, sugar, and pectin, so we reserve it for glazing desserts.

Raspberry Streusel Bars

MAKES 24 BARS

Frozen raspberries can be substituted for fresh, but be sure to defrost them before using. Quick oats will work, but the bars will be less chewy and flavorful; do not use instant oats.

2½ cups (12½ ounces) all-purpose flour
⅔ cup (4⅔ ounces) granulated sugar
½ teaspoon salt
18 tablespoons (2¼ sticks) unsalted butter, cut into 18 pieces and softened
½ cup (1½ ounces) old-fashioned rolled oats
½ cup pecans, toasted and chopped fine
¼ cup packed (1¾ ounces) light brown sugar
¾ cup raspberry jam
3¾ ounces (¾ cup) fresh raspberries
1 tablespoon lemon juice

1. Adjust oven rack to middle position and heat oven to 375 degrees. Make foil sling for 13 by 9-inch baking pan by folding 2 long sheets of aluminum foil; first sheet should be 13 inches wide and second sheet should be 9 inches wide. Lay sheets of foil in pan perpendicular to each other, with extra foil hanging over edges of pan. Push foil into corners and up sides of pan, smoothing foil flush to pan. Grease foil.
2. Whisk flour, granulated sugar, and salt together in bowl of stand mixer. Fit mixer with paddle and beat in 16 tablespoons butter, 1 piece at a time, on medium-low speed until mixture resembles damp sand, 1 to 1½ minutes. Set aside 1¼ cups mixture in bowl for topping.
3. Sprinkle remaining flour mixture into prepared pan and press firmly into even layer. Bake until edges of crust begin to brown, 14 to 18 minutes, rotating pan halfway through baking. (Crust must still be hot when filling is added.)
4. Meanwhile, stir oats, pecans, and brown sugar into reserved topping mixture. Add remaining 2 tablespoons butter and pinch mixture between your fingers into clumps of streusel. Using fork, mash jam, raspberries, and lemon juice in small bowl until few berry pieces remain.
5. Spread berry mixture evenly over hot crust, then sprinkle with streusel. Bake until filling is bubbling and topping is deep golden brown, 22 to 25 minutes, rotating pan halfway through baking.
6. Let bars cool completely in pan on wire rack, about 2 hours. Using foil overhang, remove bars from pan. Cut into 24 bars before serving. (Uncut bars can be frozen for up to 1 month; let wrapped bars thaw at room temperature for 4 hours before serving.)

variations

Strawberry Streusel Bars

Thawed frozen strawberries will also work here.

Substitute strawberry jam and chopped fresh strawberries for the raspberry jam and raspberries.

Blueberry Streusel Bars

Thawed frozen blueberries will also work here.

Substitute blueberry jam and fresh blueberries for the raspberry jam and raspberries.

WASHING BERRIES

Washing berries before you use them is always a safe practice, and we think that the best way to wash them is to place the berries in a colander and rinse them gently under running water for at least 30 seconds. As for drying them, we've tested a variety of methods and have found that a salad spinner lined with a buffering layer of paper towels is the best approach.

As for storage, berries are prone to growing mold and rotting quickly. If the berries aren't to be used immediately, we recommend cleaning the berries with a mild vinegar solution (3 cups water mixed with 1 cup white vinegar), which will destroy the bacteria, before drying them and storing them in a paper towel–lined airtight container.

MAKING RASPBERRY BARS

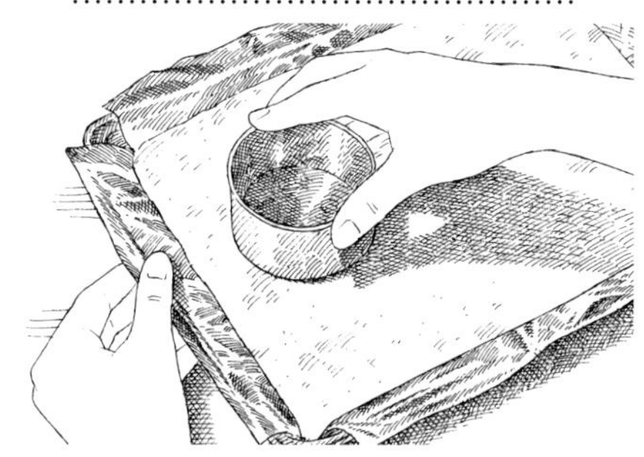

1. Press bottom crust firmly and evenly into foil-lined pan.

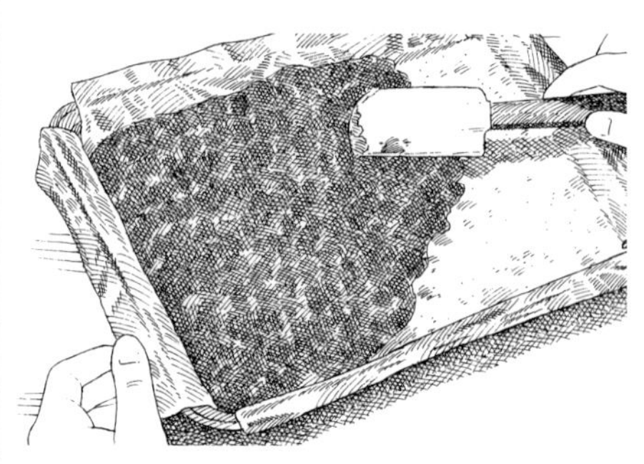

2. Spread fruit filling over hot bottom crust with spatula.

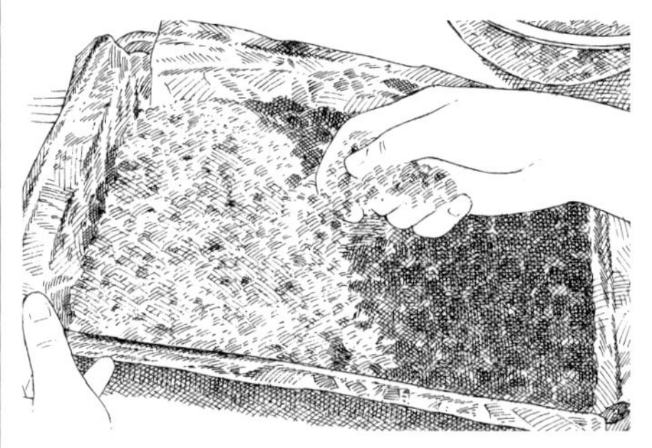

3. Sprinkle streusel evenly over filling, but resist urge to press it in.

FRESH FRUIT MAKES THE DIFFERENCE

We added fresh raspberries to preserves to get a cohesive filling that remained bright and full of raspberry flavor, even after baking.

REINVENTING PECAN BARS

ANNIE PETITO, *November/December 2015*

Most pecan bars take their cue from pecan pie, with a single layer of nuts dominated by a thick, gooey, ultrasweet filling sitting atop a pat-in-the-pan crust. I'm not opposed to that style, but it's mainly about the filling and only a little about the nuts. As a lover of nuts (pecans especially), I've always thought it would be great to have a bar that emphasized the star ingredient.

The closest I've come are recipes that ditch the rich, egg-based custard in favor of a toffee-like topping. These call for heating sugar and butter together until thickened, stirring in the nuts, and spreading the mixture over a parbaked crust before popping it into the oven. But when I tried a few such approaches, I found that the resulting bars still had a one-note sweetness that distracted from the pecans—and there were never enough pecans in the first place. My ideal was a pecan bar featuring a buttery crust piled high with nuts held in place not by a filling, per se, but by a not-too-sweet glaze whose only jobs were to enhance the flavor of the pecans and glue them to the crust. For that kind of a bar, I was on my own.

GOING NUTS

I started with a placeholder crust, a food processor–blended mixture of flour, sugar, salt, and cold butter that I borrowed from our archives and scaled up to fit a 13 by 9-inch pan (you can never have too many cookies on hand during the holidays). I patted the sandy dough into the pan and parbaked it for 20 minutes at 350 degrees until the crust was light brown—standard procedure to prevent a wet filling from seeping in and making it soggy.

Since I wanted a topping that was all about the nuts, I wondered what would happen if I simply tossed the pecans with corn syrup, which is one-third less sweet than granulated sugar, before spreading them over the crust. I tried this, stirring ½ cup into a relatively modest 2 cups of chopped pecans, which I toasted first to enhance their rich flavor. But it was a bust, as the corn syrup's flat taste did nothing to bring out the flavor of the nuts, and now the bar wasn't sweet enough overall. Next, I experimented with maple syrup, thinking its caramel-like flavors might complement the pecans, heating it with some butter to cut some of the sweetness and bring extra nuttiness to the glaze. Its flavors matched nicely with the pecans, but the syrup dried out and crystallized in the oven, making the topping crusty with an unappealing matte finish. Honey didn't work either. Though it produced a moist, glossy, slightly chewy topping that my tasters liked for its texture, its prominent flavor was a distraction from the pecans. Ultimately, I landed on a combination of corn syrup and brown sugar, the latter's molasses-like notes a good match for the pecans. I heated ½ cup of corn syrup and ¾ cup of brown sugar with 7 tablespoons of butter on the stove until the mixture was bubbly and syrupy; I then took the glaze off the heat and stirred in vanilla extract to add complexity, followed by the pecans. This glaze had a lot going for it: It was glossy and stayed slightly moist and chewy in the oven. But its sweetness still dominated the pecans. I wondered if I could fix that simply by increasing the amount of nuts, which had been my goal anyway.

I upped the nuts from 2 cups to 3 cups and left them in halves, which gave them a more impressive presence. This worked so well to offset the glaze's sweetness that I added another cup. The nuts were now the main event of the topping, enhanced but not overpowered by the glaze. There was another bonus: With this many pecans, the nuts did not sit neatly in a single layer on the crust but were more haphazardly layered on top of one another, allowing for a variety of textures—some nuts were chewy, sitting directly in a slick of glaze, while those sitting on the very top were crisp.

CRUST CONTROL

With the topping settled, I turned my attention back to the crust. I'd been using the food processor to cut the cold butter into the flour, but it occurred to me that there was an even easier crust I could use. In our French Apple Tart (page 497), we make an easy press-in crust using melted butter instead of chilled, stirring it right into the dry ingredients. Buttery and sturdy, this shortbread-like crust was ideal for the pecan topping and a snap to make.

Swapping the traditional custard filling for a mixture of brown sugar, corn syrup, and butter streamlines this classic recipe.

I had an additional thought: Now that the topping was barely wet at all, did I even need to parbake the crust? I tried skipping this step, spreading the hot topping over the unbaked crust and baking it for 20 minutes. When I turned the bars out of the pan, I found that the bottom of the crust was still pale and slightly pliable. Baking the bars on the bottom rack and for a little longer produced a crust that was evenly golden, but it also created a new problem: Since the bars were closer to the heat source, more moisture was evaporating from the topping, which was getting crunchy and brittle in parts, especially at the edges.

Up until now I had been boiling the glaze on the stove before adding the nuts. If I didn't do that, I thought, maybe enough moisture would stay in the glaze to keep the topping more pliable. Plus, it would make the recipe even quicker. It was worth trying.

For my next test, I combined the brown sugar, corn syrup, vanilla, and salt in a bowl. I melted the butter separately and then stirred it, piping hot, into the mixture so the sugar would melt, continuing to stir until the mixture was homogeneous and glossy. But it was so thick that after I stirred in the nuts, there was no question of spreading it evenly across the crust. All I could do was push it to the edges as best I could, leaving patches of crust bare. I was sure this was a dead end, but as I watched the bars cook, I could see the thick brown sugar mixture begin to melt. After 25 minutes, the topping was bubbling across the crust, and all the empty spots were completely coated.

Once the bars were cooled, I turned them out of the pan. They were golden brown on the bottom, with a glossy, even sheen on top. I trimmed the edges to neaten them up and cut them into squares. The bars were chewy and moist, not overly sweet, and loaded with pecans. For a final touch, I sprinkled the bars with flake sea salt as they came out of the oven.

TOPPING CLUMPS? NOT TO WORRY

To streamline our Ultranutty Pecan Bars recipe, we skipped the step of heating the topping on the stovetop. Instead, we simply stirred together a mixture of brown sugar, corn syrup, melted butter, vanilla and salt, folded in our toasted pecans, and spread the thick mixture as best we could over the crust. Don't worry if there are bare patches: The topping melts during baking, distributing itself evenly over the crust and covering up all of the bare spots.

Ultranutty Pecan Bars

MAKES 24 BARS

Use pecan halves, not pieces. The edges of the bars will be slightly firmer than the center. If desired, trim ¼ inch from the edges before cutting into bars.

Crust

1¾ cups (8¾ ounces) all-purpose flour
6 tablespoons (2⅔ ounces) granulated sugar
½ teaspoon salt
8 tablespoons unsalted butter, melted

Topping

¾ cup packed (5¼ ounces) light brown sugar
½ cup light corn syrup
7 tablespoons unsalted butter, melted and hot
1 teaspoon vanilla extract
½ teaspoon salt
4 cups (1 pound) pecan halves, toasted
½ teaspoon flake sea salt (optional)

1. *For the crust:* Adjust oven rack to lowest position and heat oven to 350 degrees. Make foil sling for 13 by 9-inch baking pan by folding 2 long sheets of aluminum foil; first sheet should be 13 inches wide and second sheet should be 9 inches wide. Lay sheets of foil in pan perpendicular to each other, with extra foil hanging over edges of pan. Push foil into corners and up sides of pan, smoothing foil flush to pan. Lightly spray foil with vegetable oil spray.

2. Whisk flour, sugar, and salt together in medium bowl. Add melted butter and stir with wooden spoon until dough begins to form. Using your hands, continue to combine until no dry flour remains and small portion of dough holds together when squeezed in palm of your hand. Evenly scatter tablespoon-size pieces of dough over surface of pan. Using your fingertips and palm of your hand, press and smooth dough into even thickness in bottom of pan.

3. *For the topping:* Whisk sugar, corn syrup, melted butter, vanilla, and salt in medium bowl until smooth (mixture will look separated at first but will become homogeneous), about 20 seconds. Fold pecans into sugar mixture until nuts are evenly coated.

4. Pour topping over crust. Using spatula, spread topping over crust, pushing to edges and into corners (there will be bare patches). Bake until topping is evenly distributed and rapidly bubbling across entire surface, 23 to 25 minutes.

5. Transfer pan to wire rack and lightly sprinkle with flake sea salt, if using. Let bars cool completely in pan on rack, about 1½ hours. Using foil overhang, lift bars out of pan and transfer to cutting board. Cut into 24 bars and serve. (Bars can be stored at room temperature for up to 5 days.)

HOW TO TOAST NUTS

Nuts toast more evenly in the oven, but the stovetop is more convenient for small amounts.

IN THE OVEN Spread nuts in single layer on rimmed baking sheet and toast in 350-degree oven until fragrant and slightly darkened, 8 to 12 minutes, shaking sheet halfway through.

ON THE STOVETOP Place nuts in single layer in dry skillet set over medium heat and toast, stirring frequently, until fragrant and slightly darkened, 3 to 5 minutes.

Pain
au Chocolat
Tarte aux Fruits
Mille-Feuille
Chausson
aux Pommes
Tarte au Citron
Dôme au Chocolat
Éclair
Palmier
Croissant

DESSERTS

BEST BLUEBERRY COBBLER

ERIN MCMURRER WITH MEG SUZUKI, *July/August 2002*

I have always been a huge fan of baked fruit desserts, especially cobblers. What could be better than a hot and bubbly fruit filling matched with tender biscuits? As simple (and appealing) as this sounds, why do so many of us end up with a filling that is sickeningly sweet and overspiced? Why is the filling so often runny, or, on the flip side, so thick and gloppy? Why are the biscuits, the most common choice of topping for cobblers, too dense, dry, and heavy? My goal was to create a filling in which the blueberries (my choice for fruit) were allowed to cook until lightly thickened. I wanted their natural sweetness to sing a cappella without being overshadowed by a symphony of sugar and spice. The biscuits would stand tall with structure, be crisp on the outside and light and buttery on the inside, and complement the filling. Most important, it had to be easy.

THE FILLING GOES FIRST

The basic ingredients found in most cobbler fillings are fruit, sugar, thickener (flour, arrowroot, cornstarch, potato starch, or tapioca), and flavorings (lemon zest, spices, etc.). The fruit and sugar are easy: Take fresh blueberries and add enough sugar such that the fruit neither remains puckery nor turns saccharine. For 6 cups of berries, I found ½ cup sugar to be ideal—and far less than the conventional amount of sugar, which in some recipes exceeds 2 cups.

A cornstarch-thickened filling topped with cornmeal and buttermilk–enhanced biscuits makes for a speedy and intensely flavored cobbler.

Some recipes swear by one thickener and warn that other choices will ruin the filling. I found this to be partly true. Tasters were all in agreement that flour—the most common choice in recipes—gave the fruit filling an unappealing starchy texture. Most tasters agreed that tapioca thickened the berry juices nicely, but the soft beads of starch left in the fruit's juices knocked out this contender. (Also, when exposed to direct heat, as in a cobbler, the tapioca that remains near the surface of the fruit quickly turns as hard as Tic-Tacs.) Arrowroot worked beautifully, but this starch is far too expensive and can be difficult to find. Cornstarch, the winner, thickened the juices without altering the blueberry flavor or leaving any visible traces of starch behind.

Lemon juice as well as grated lemon zest brightened the fruit flavor, and, as for spices, everyone preferred cinnamon. Other flavors simply got in the way.

NOT YOUR AVERAGE TOPPING

For the topping, my guiding principle was ease of preparation. A biscuit topping was the way to go, and I had my choice of two types: dropped and rolled. Most rolled biscuit recipes call for cold butter cut into dry ingredients with a pastry blender, two knives, or sometimes a food processor, after which the dough is rolled and cut. The dropped biscuits looked more promising (translation: easier)—mix the dry ingredients, mix the wet ingredients, mix the two together, and drop (over fruit). Sounded good to me!

To be sure that my tasters agreed, I made two cobblers, one with rolled and one with dropped biscuits. The dropped biscuits, light and rustic in appearance, received the positive comments I was looking for but needed some work. To start, I had to fine-tune the ingredients, which included flour, sugar, leavener, milk, eggs, butter/shortening, and flavorings. I immediately eliminated eggs from the list because they made the biscuits a tad heavy. As for dairy, heavy cream was too rich, whereas milk and half-and-half lacked depth of flavor. I finally tested buttermilk, which delivered a much-needed flavor boost as well as a lighter, fluffier texture. As for the choice of fat, butter was in and Crisco was out—butter tasted much better. Next I wanted to test melted butter versus cold butter. Although I had been using melted butter in the dropped biscuits, I wondered if cold butter would yield better results, as some sources suggested. I melted butter for one batch and cut cold butter into the dry ingredients (with a food processor) for another. The difference was nil, so melting, the easier method, was the winner.

I soon discovered that the big problem with drop biscuits is getting them to cook through. (The batter is wetter than rolled biscuit dough and therefore has a propensity for remaining doughy.) No matter how long I left the biscuits on the berry topping in a 400-degree oven, they never baked through, turning browner and browner on top while remaining doughy on the bottom. I realized that what the biscuits needed might be a blast of heat from below—that is, from the berries. I tried baking the berries alone in a moderate 375-degree oven for 25 minutes and then dropped and baked the biscuit dough on top. Bingo! The heat from the bubbling berries helped to cook the biscuits from underneath, while the dry heat of the oven cooked the biscuits from above.

There was one final detail to perfect. I wanted the biscuits to be more crisp on the outside and to have a deeper hue. This was easily achieved by bumping the oven to 425 degrees when I added the biscuits. A sprinkling of cinnamon sugar on the dropped biscuit dough added just a bit more crunch.

Blueberry Cobbler

SERVES 6 TO 8

While the blueberries are baking, prepare the ingredients for the topping, but do not stir the wet ingredients into the dry ingredients until just before the berries come out of the oven. A standard or deep-dish 9-inch pie plate works well for this recipe; however, an 8-inch square baking dish can also be used. Serve with vanilla ice cream or whipped cream. To reheat leftovers, put the cobbler in a 350-degree oven for 10 to 15 minutes, until heated through.

Filling

½ cup (3½ ounces) sugar
1 tablespoon cornstarch
Pinch ground cinnamon
Pinch salt
30 ounces (6 cups) blueberries
1½ teaspoons grated lemon zest plus 1 tablespoon juice

Biscuit Topping

1 cup (5 ounces) all-purpose flour
¼ cup (1¾ ounces) sugar, plus 2 teaspoons for sprinkling
2 tablespoons stone-ground cornmeal
2 teaspoons baking powder
¼ teaspoon baking soda
¼ teaspoon salt
⅓ cup buttermilk
4 tablespoons unsalted butter, melted
½ teaspoon vanilla extract
⅛ teaspoon ground cinnamon

1. *For the filling:* Adjust oven rack to lower-middle position and heat oven to 375 degrees. Line rimmed baking sheet with aluminum foil. Whisk sugar, cornstarch, cinnamon, and salt together in large bowl. Add blueberries and mix gently until evenly coated; add lemon zest and juice and mix until combined. Transfer mixture to 9-inch pie plate, place plate on prepared sheet, and bake until filling is bubbling around edges, about 25 minutes.

2. *For the biscuit topping:* Meanwhile, whisk flour, ¼ cup sugar, cornmeal, baking powder, baking soda, and salt together in large bowl. Whisk buttermilk, melted butter, and vanilla together in small bowl. Combine cinnamon and remaining 2 teaspoons sugar in small bowl and set aside. One minute before blueberries come out of oven, add buttermilk mixture to flour mixture; stir until just combined and no dry pockets remain.

3. After removing blueberries from oven, increase oven temperature to 425 degrees. Divide dough into 8 equal pieces and place them on hot filling, spacing them at least ½ inch apart (they should not touch). Sprinkle dough mounds evenly with cinnamon sugar. Bake until filling is bubbling and biscuits are golden brown on top and cooked through, 15 to 18 minutes, rotating pie plate halfway through baking. Let cool on wire rack for 20 minutes; serve warm.

variations

Blueberry Cobbler with Gingered Biscuits

Add 3 tablespoons minced crystallized ginger to flour mixture and substitute ⅛ teaspoon ground ginger for cinnamon in sugar for sprinkling on biscuits.

All-Season Blueberry Cobbler

Thaw 30 ounces frozen blueberries in colander set over bowl to catch juice. Transfer juice (you should have about 1 cup) to small saucepan; simmer over medium heat until syrupy and thick enough to coat back of spoon, about 10 minutes. Mix syrup with blueberries and other filling ingredients; increase baking time for filling to 30 minutes and increase baking time in step 3 to 20 to 22 minutes.

GETTING EVENLY BAKED BISCUITS

Dropping the biscuits onto a hot filling heats them from the bottom, ensuring they cook through.

1. While berries bake, whisk dry ingredients in large bowl. Whisk together wet ingredients in separate small bowl. One minute before berries come out of oven, add buttermilk mixture to flour mixture and stir until just combined.

2. Take berries out of oven and increase temperature to 425 degrees. Divide dough into 8 pieces and drop onto hot filling, spacing biscuits at least ½ inch apart (they should not touch). Sprinkle with cinnamon sugar.

3. Bake until filling is bubbling and biscuits are golden brown and cooked through, 15 to 18 minutes.

SUMMER PUDDING

DAWN YANAGIHARA, *July/August 1999*

If any food speaks of the summer, summer pudding does. Ripe, fragrant, lightly sweetened berries are gently cooked to coax out their juices, which then soak and soften slices of bread to make them meld with the fruit. Served chilled, summer pudding is incredibly fresh and refreshing. Last summer, I came home from a farmer's market with half a flat of strawberries that I'd purchased for a dollar. Not enough to preserve, I thought, but a great chance to make a summer pudding. With some raspberries, blueberries, and old bread from the freezer, I easily threw one together. I was pleased with this first attempt, but the pudding was a bit too sweet for me, and the bread seemed to stand apart from the fruit, as if it were just a casing. Improving upon it, I knew, would be an easy task. I wanted sweet-tart berries and bread that melded right into them.

In a typical summer pudding, berries fill a bowl or mold of some sort that has been neatly lined with crustless bread. Well, trimming the crusts is easy, but trimming the bread to fit the mold and lining the bowl with it is fussy. After having made a couple of puddings, I quickly grew tired of this technique—it seemed to undermine the simplicity of the dessert. I came across a couple of recipes that called for layering the bread right in with the berries instead of using it to line the bowl. Not only is this bread-on-the-inside method easier, but a summer pudding made in this fashion looks spectacular—the berries on the outside are like brilliant jewels. Meanwhile, the layers of bread on the inside almost melt into the fruit.

My next adjustment to this recipe was losing the bowl as a mold. I switched instead to making individual summer puddings in ramekins. I found them to be hardly more labor-intensive in assembly than a single large pudding. Sure, you have to cut out rounds of bread to fit the ramekins, but a cookie cutter makes easy work of it, and individual servings transform this humble dessert into an elegant one. The individual puddings are also easily served—simply unmold one onto a plate, no slicing or scooping involved. I also found I could use a loaf pan to make a single large pudding; its rectangular shape requires less trimming of bread slices.

With the form set, I moved on to the ingredients. For the 4 pints of berries I was using, ¾ cup of sugar was a good amount. Lemon juice, I found, perked up the berry flavors and rounded them out. I then sought alternatives to cooking the fruit in an attempt to preserve its freshness. I mashed first some and then all of the berries with sugar. I tried cooking only a portion of the fruit with sugar. I macerated the berries with sugar. None of these methods worked. These puddings, even after being weighted and chilled overnight, had an unwelcome crunchy, raw quality. The berries need a gentle cooking to make their texture more yielding, more pudding-like, if you will. But don't worry—5 minutes is all it takes, not even long enough to heat up the kitchen.

Next I investigated the bread. I tried six different kinds as well as pound cake (for which I was secretly rooting). Hearty, coarse-textured sandwich bread and a rustic French loaf were too tough and tasted fermented and yeasty. Very soft, pillowy sandwich bread became soggy and lifeless when soaked with juice. The pound cake, imbued with berry juice, turned into wet sand and had the textural appeal of sawdust. A good-quality white sandwich bread with a bit of heft was good, but there were two very clear winners: challah and potato bread. Their even, tight-crumbed, tender texture and light sweetness were a perfect match for the berries.

Most summer pudding recipes call for stale bread. And for good reason. Fresh bread, I found, when soaked with those berry juices, turns to mush. You might not think this would be so noticeable with the bread layered between all those berries, but every single taster remarked that the pudding made with fresh bread was soggy and gummy. On the other hand, stale bread absorbs some of the juices and melds with the berries yet still maintains some structural integrity. Rather than waiting for bread to stale, however, I simply baked the slices in the oven at a very low temperature until they were dry to the touch but still somewhat pliable.

Cooking the berries for just 5 minutes and then layering them with dried slices of potato bread makes for an elegant and bright dessert.

Probably the oddest thing about summer pudding is the fact that it is weighted as it chills. What, I wondered, does this do for the texture? And how long does the pudding need to chill? I made several batches and chilled them with and without weights for 4, 8, 24, and 30 hours. The puddings chilled for 4 hours tasted of underripe fruit. The bread was barely soaked through, and the berries barely clung together. At 8 hours the puddings were at their peak: the berries tasted fresh and held together, while the bread melted right into them. Twenty-four hours and the puddings were still good, though a hairsbreadth duller in color and flavor. After 30 hours the puddings were well past their prime and began to smell and taste fermented.

No matter how long they chilled, the summer puddings without weights were loose—they didn't hold together after unmolding. The fruit was less cohesive and the puddings less pleasurable to eat.

No pound cake, no butter. Just bright, fresh summer berries made into the perfect summer dessert. Topped with a healthy dollop of whipped cream, what could be better?

Individual Summer Berry Puddings

SERVES 6

For this recipe, you will need six 6-ounce ramekins and a round cookie cutter of slightly smaller diameter than the ramekins. If you don't have the right-size cutter, use a paring knife and the bottom of a ramekin (most ramekins taper toward the bottom) as a guide for trimming the rounds. Top with whipped cream, if desired.

12 slices potato bread, challah, or hearty white sandwich bread
1¼ pounds strawberries, hulled and sliced (4 cups)
10 ounces (2 cups) raspberries
5 ounces (1 cup) blackberries
5 ounces (1 cup) blueberries
¾ cup (5¼ ounces) sugar
2 tablespoons lemon juice

1. Adjust oven rack to middle position and heat oven to 200 degrees. Place bread in single layer on rimmed baking sheet and bake until dry but not brittle, about 1 hour, flipping slices once and rotating sheet halfway through baking. Set aside to cool.
2. Combine strawberries, raspberries, blackberries, blueberries, and sugar in large saucepan and cook over medium heat, stirring occasionally, until berries begin to release their juices and sugar has dissolved, about 5 minutes. Off heat, stir in lemon juice; let cool to room temperature.
3. Spray six 6-ounce ramekins with vegetable oil spray and place on rimmed baking sheet. Use cookie cutter to cut out 12 bread rounds that are slightly smaller in diameter than ramekins.
4. Using slotted spoon, place ¼ cup fruit mixture in each ramekin. Lightly soak 1 bread round in fruit juice in saucepan and place on top of fruit in ramekin; repeat with 5 more bread rounds and remaining ramekins. Divide remaining fruit among ramekins, about ½ cup per ramekin. Lightly soak 1 bread round in fruit juice and place on top of fruit in ramekin (it should sit above lip of ramekin); repeat with remaining 5 bread rounds and remaining ramekins. Pour remaining fruit juice over bread and cover ramekins loosely with plastic wrap. Place second baking sheet on top of ramekins and weight with heavy cans. Refrigerate puddings for at least 8 hours or up to 24 hours.
5. Remove cans and baking sheet and uncover puddings. Loosen puddings by running paring knife around edge of each ramekin, unmold into individual bowls, and serve immediately.

variation

Large Summer Berry Pudding

SERVES 6 TO 8

Because there is no need to cut out rounds for this version, you will need only about eight slices of bread, depending on their size.

Trim crusts from toasted bread and trim slices to fit in single layer in loaf pan (you will need about 2½ slices per layer; there will be three layers). Spray 9 by 5-inch loaf pan with vegetable oil spray, line with plastic wrap, and place on rimmed baking sheet. Using slotted spoon, spread about 2 cups fruit mixture evenly over bottom of prepared pan. Lightly soak enough bread slices for 1 layer in fruit juice in saucepan and place on top of fruit. Repeat with 2 more layers of fruit and bread. Pour remaining fruit juice over bread and cover loosely with plastic wrap. Place second baking sheet on top of loaf pan and weight it with heavy cans. Refrigerate pudding as directed. When ready to serve, invert pudding onto serving platter, remove loaf pan and plastic, slice, and serve.

ASSEMBLING INDIVIDUAL SUMMER BERRY PUDDINGS

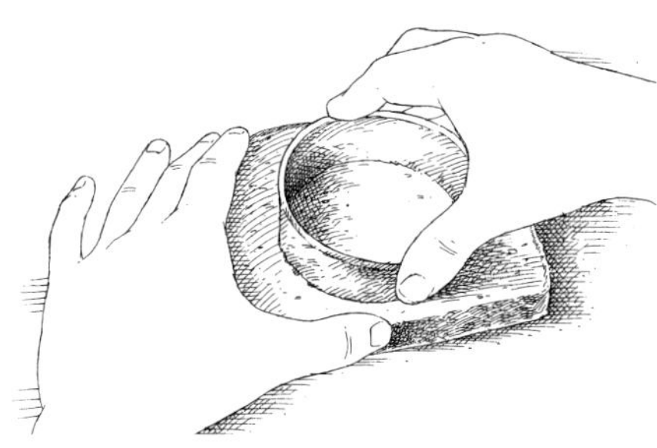

1. Cut out rounds of bread with cookie cutter.

2. Use slotted spoon to place about ¼-cup portions of fruit into greased 6-ounce ramekins.

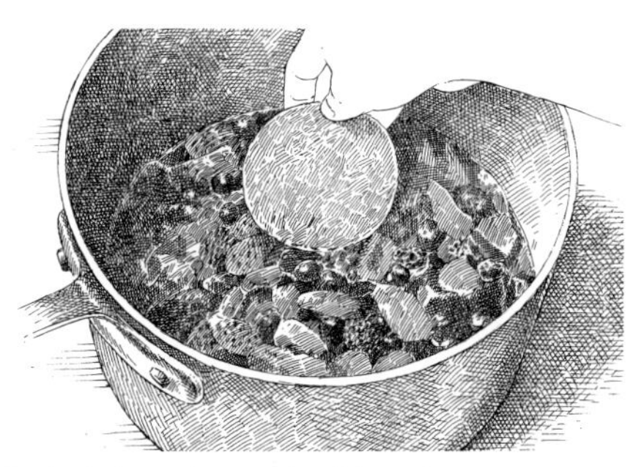

3. Lightly soak rounds of bread in berry juice and layer with fruit in each ramekin. Repeat layering with remaining fruit and bread rounds.

4. Cover filled ramekins with plastic wrap. Place cookie sheet on top, then weight with several heavy cans.

MODERN FRESH FRUIT TART

LAN LAM, *July/August 2017*

A fresh fruit tart is the showpiece of a bakery pastry case. With its clean crust edge and ornate arrangement of fruit glistening with glaze, this dessert is beautiful and conveys a sense of occasion. But anyone who has served one knows that the pretty presentation falls apart when the knife meets the tart. Instead of neat wedges, you get shards of pastry oozing messy fruit and juice-stained filling. That's a disappointing end for a dessert that started out so impressive and required several hours to make.

I set out to reconceptualize the classic fresh fruit tart from crust to crown. I wanted the crust and filling to be sturdy and stable enough to retain their form when cut, and I wanted to streamline their preparation. That might mean departing from tradition, but as long as the tart looked pretty and featured a buttery crust complementing a satiny filling and bright, sweet, juicy fruit, I was ready for new ideas.

CRUST EASE

Plenty of published recipes touted innovative approaches to the fresh fruit tart, starting with the crust. The most promising one traded the traditional pâte sucrée—in which cold butter is worked into flour and sugar, chilled, and rolled out—for a simpler pat-in-the-pan crust. This style of crust calls for simply melting the butter and stirring it into the flour mixture to create a pliable dough that is easily pressed into the pan and baked. I tried one such recipe: While the result was crisp and cookie-like rather than flaky, it still made a nice contrast to the creamy filling.

I had one tweak in mind: Since I would be melting the butter anyway, I'd try browning it to give the pastry a richer, nuttier character. But because browning the butter cooked off its water, this produced a sandy, cracked crust. There wasn't enough moisture for the proteins in the flour to form the gluten necessary to hold the crust together. Adding a couple of tablespoons of water to the browned butter before mixing it with the dry ingredients fixed the problem: The dough was more cohesive and, after 30 minutes in a 350-degree oven, formed a crust that held together.

On to the filling. I wasn't keen on the traditional pastry cream: It's fussy to make and tends to ooze from the crust when sliced. What I needed was something that was thick and creamy from the get-go. Mascarpone, the creamy, tangy-sweet fresh cheese that's the star of tiramisù and many other Italian desserts, seemed like a good option. Sweetened with a little sugar and spread over the tart shell, it was a workable starting point, but it still wasn't dense enough to hold its shape when sliced. Thickeners such as gelatin, pectin, and cornstarch required either cooking or hydrating in liquid to be effective, as well as several hours to set up. A colleague had a better idea: white chocolate. I could melt it in the microwave and stir it into the mascarpone. Since white chocolate is solid at room temperature, it would firm up the filling as it cooled.

I melted white baking chips (they resulted in a firmer texture than white chocolate, which contains cocoa butter) in the microwave, adding ¼ cup of heavy cream so the mixture would blend smoothly into the cheese. When the filling was homogeneous, I smoothed it into the cooled crust, gently pressed in the fruit while the filling was still slightly warm (once cooled completely it would be too firm to hold the fruit neatly), brushed on a jam glaze, and refrigerated the tart for 30 minutes so the filling would set. I then allowed the tart to sit at room temperature for 15 minutes before slicing it.

The filling was satiny and, thanks to the baking chips, nicely firm. To give it a little more oomph, I added bright, fruity lime juice, which—despite being a liquid—wouldn't loosen the filling. Instead, the acid would act on the cream's proteins, causing them to thicken; meanwhile, the cream's fat would prevent any graininess.

Since heating the lime juice would drive off its bright flavor, I stirred it in with the mascarpone; it paired beautifully with the rich cheese and white chocolate. For even more lime flavor, I added a teaspoon of zest, heating it with the chocolate and cream to draw out its flavor-packed oils.

For neat slicing and serving, we use mascarpone and white baking chips in the filling and arrange the fruit in wedges.

EDIBLE ARRANGEMENTS

I decided to top the tart with an appealing, summery combo of berries and ripe peaches, peeled and cut into thin slices. But before I placed the fruit on the filling, I thought carefully about how to arrange it. Many tarts feature fruit organized in concentric circles. These look great when whole, but since you have to cut through the fruit when slicing, it winds up mangled. Why not arrange the fruit so that the knife could slip between pieces?

First, I spaced eight berries around the outer edge of the tart, which I then used as guides to help me evenly arrange eight sets of three slightly overlapping peach slices so that they radiated from the center of the tart to its outer edge. The peach slices would serve as cutting guides for eight wedges. Next, I artfully arranged a mix of berries on each wedge. The final touch: I made a quick glaze using apricot preserves that I thinned with lime juice for easy dabbing.

The crisp, sturdy, rich crust; satiny yet stable filling; and bright-tasting fruit added up to a classic showpiece with modern flavor. Best of all, it was quick to make, and each slice looked just as polished and professional as the whole tart.

Fresh Fruit Tart

SERVES 8

This recipe calls for extra berries to account for any bruising. Ripe, unpeeled nectarines can be substituted for the peaches, if desired. Use white baking chips here and not white chocolate bars, which contain cocoa butter and will result in a loose filling. Use a light hand when dabbing on the glaze; too much force will dislodge the fruit. If the glaze begins to solidify while dabbing, microwave it for 5 to 10 seconds.

Crust

1⅓ cups (6⅔ ounces) all-purpose flour
¼ cup (1¾ ounces) sugar
⅛ teaspoon salt
10 tablespoons unsalted butter
2 tablespoons water

Tart

⅓ cup (2 ounces) white baking chips
¼ cup heavy cream
1 teaspoon grated lime zest plus 7 teaspoons juice (2 limes)
Pinch salt
6 ounces (¾ cup) mascarpone cheese, room temperature
2 ripe peaches, peeled
20 ounces (4 cups) raspberries, blackberries, and blueberries
⅓ cup apricot preserves

1. *For the crust:* Adjust oven rack to middle position and heat oven to 350 degrees. Whisk flour, sugar, and salt together in bowl. Melt butter in small saucepan over medium-high heat, swirling saucepan occasionally, until foaming subsides. Cook, stirring and scraping bottom of saucepan with heatproof spatula, until milk solids are dark golden brown and butter has nutty aroma, 1 to 3 minutes. Remove saucepan from heat and add water. When bubbling subsides, transfer butter to bowl with flour mixture and stir until well combined. Transfer dough to 9-inch tart pan with removable bottom and let dough rest until just warm, about 10 minutes.

2. Use your hands to evenly press and smooth dough over bottom and up side of pan (using two-thirds of dough for bottom crust and remaining third for side). Place pan on wire rack set in rimmed baking sheet and bake until crust is golden brown, 25 to 30 minutes, rotating pan halfway through baking. Let crust cool completely, about 1 hour. (Cooled crust can be wrapped loosely in plastic wrap and stored at room temperature for up to 24 hours.)

3. *For the tart:* Microwave baking chips, cream, lime zest, and salt in medium bowl, stirring every 10 seconds, until baking chips are melted, 30 to 60 seconds. Whisk in one-third of mascarpone, then whisk in 6 teaspoons lime juice and remaining mascarpone until smooth. Transfer filling to tart shell and spread into even layer.

4. Place peach, stem side down, on cutting board. Placing knife just to side of pit, cut down to remove 1 side of peach. Turn peach 180 degrees and cut off opposite side. Cut off remaining 2 sides. Place pieces cut side down and slice ¼ inch thick. Repeat with second peach. Select best 24 slices.

5. Evenly space 8 berries around outer edge of tart. Using berries as guide, arrange 8 sets of 3 peach slices in filling, slightly overlapping slices with rounded sides up, starting at center and ending on right side of each berry. Arrange remaining berries in attractive pattern between peach slices, covering as much of filling as possible and keeping fruit in even layer.

6. Microwave preserves and remaining 1 teaspoon lime juice in small bowl until fluid, 20 to 30 seconds. Strain mixture through fine-mesh strainer. Using pastry brush, gently dab mixture over fruit, avoiding crust. Refrigerate tart for 30 minutes.

7. Remove outer metal ring of tart pan. Slide thin metal spatula between tart and pan bottom to loosen tart, then carefully slide tart onto serving platter. Let tart sit at room temperature for 15 minutes. Using peaches as guide, cut tart into wedges and serve. (Tart can be refrigerated for up to 24 hours. If refrigerated for more than 1 hour, let tart sit at room temperature for 1 hour before serving.)

MAKE AN EDIBLE SLICING GUIDE

Strategically arranging the fruit isn't all about looks. It can make it easier to cut clean slices, too.

1. Evenly arrange 8 berries around outer edge of tart.

2. Arrange 8 sets of 3 overlapping peach slices from center to edge of tart on right side of each berry.

3. Arrange remaining berries in attractive pattern between peach slices in even layer to cover filling.

FRENCH APPLE TART

ANDREA GEARY, *November/December 2014*

Classic and elegant, a traditional French *tarte aux pommes* is a visually stunning dessert that has intense fruit flavor and varied textures, yet is made with just a few basic ingredients. In its simplest form, this tart consists of crisp pastry shell that's filled with a concentrated apple puree and then topped with a spiraling fan of paper-thin apple slices. It's usually finished with a delicate glaze that caramelizes during baking, providing an extra layer of flavor.

But poor structure is the fatal flaw of many a handsome apple tart; overly tough apple slices and mushy crusts abound. Plus, the dessert's overall flavor can be a bit one-dimensional. Still, I was drawn to this showstopper dessert that could be made with a short list of pantry staples. My challenge would be perfecting each component to produce a gorgeous tart with lively, intense apple flavor and a crust that stayed crisp.

For an apple tart with both integrity and beauty, we use melted rather than chilled butter in the crust and parcook the apples for the topping.

A STRONG FOUNDATION

For a dough that would hold its shape and maintain a crisp texture even after being filled with the puree, I started by preparing the three classic French pastry options and filling them with a placeholder puree: five peeled and cored Golden Delicious apples (widely available, and good quality year round) cooked with a splash of water until soft, mashed with a potato masher, and reduced until thick.

My first attempt was with frozen puff pastry, which I rolled thin and parbaked to dry it out and firm it up. But the dough shrank, and its texture softened beneath the wet puree. On to the next.

Following a classic recipe for *pâte brisée* (essentially the French equivalent of flaky American pie dough), I used the food processor to pulse cold butter into flour until the mixture formed a coarse meal. I drizzled in a little water, then chilled the dough, rolled it out, fit it into the tart pan, chilled it again, lined the dough with parchment, weighed it down with pie weights, parbaked it, removed the parchment and weights, and baked it until it was crisp. All that work is supposed to keep the dough from shrinking—and this shell did hold its shape nicely. But the puree still turned the pastry soggy.

Lastly, I tried a *pâte sucrée*. This pastry typically contains more sugar than the previous doughs, but the most significant difference is that the butter is thoroughly worked into the flour, which limits the development of gluten—the strong elastic network that forms when flour proteins are moistened with water. Less gluten translates to pastry that is less prone to shrinking and that bakes up with a finer, shorter crumb.

I worked the butter into the dry ingredients until the mixture looked like sand, then bound it with an egg (typical in pâte sucrée recipes). I chilled, rolled, chilled, and baked as before—but I skipped the pie weights, since the dough wasn't likely to shrink.

Indeed, this crust baked up plenty sturdy, and it didn't sog out when I filled it with the puree. But it puffed slightly during baking, and frankly, all that chilling and rolling was tiresome. There had to be an easier way.

CRUNCH TIME

Eliminating the egg would mitigate the cookie-like lift, but without the egg's moisture, I would need another liquid component to bind the dry ingredients with the cold butter. I didn't want to add water, since that would encourage gluten development. But what if I turned the butter (which contains very little water) into a liquid by melting it?

Stirring melted butter into the dry ingredients produced a promisingly cohesive dough that was so malleable, I didn't need to roll it—I could simply press it into the pan. Then I chilled it and baked it.

This was by far the easiest pastry I'd ever made. The crust baked up perfectly sturdy and was no longer puffed, but crisp and delicate like shortbread—and stayed that way even when filled with the puree. Subsequent streamlining tests showed that I didn't even have to chill this modified pâte sucrée before baking; the sides of the tart pan were shallow enough that the pastry didn't slump. Now to improve that placeholder puree.

AMPING UP APPLESAUCE

My apple filling had to have concentrated fruit flavor and enough body to hold its shape on a fork. The latter goal I'd almost met by cooking down the puree until it had a texture and flavor somewhere between applesauce and apple butter. Moving this operation from a saucepan to a wider covered skillet helped water from the fruit evaporate faster.

For more distinctive flavor, I took a cue from Julia Child's recipe for tarte aux pommes, in which she adds butter and apricot preserves to her puree. Tasters applauded this richer, brighter-tasting filling. The preserves also contributed pectin, which helped the filling firm up even more.

TOPPING IT OFF

Finally, I needed to find a way to simplify the shingling of the apples on top—a painstaking task, especially when trying to brush the delicately placed apples with a shiny glaze. (Luckily, the glaze itself was simple: I just brushed the top with the brightly flavored apricot preserves I was already using in the filling.) To add to my frustrations, the apple slices never became tender enough for me to cut the tart without their resisting and becoming dislodged. I tried baking the tart longer, brushing the slices with water or melted butter, and covering the tart with foil for part of the baking time so the slices

might soften in the trapped steam—none of which worked.

In the end, I swapped the wafer-thin apple slices for more generous slices and sautéed them for 10 minutes to jump-start the softening before placing them on the tart. As for the spiral shingling, I decided to forgo this fussy tradition and came up with a more easygoing, but still sophisticated, rosette pattern made by placing the apple slices in concentric circles. The parcooking had made the slices conveniently pliable, so there was no awkwardness toward the center of the arrangement; I simply bent the pieces and slipped them into place.

Once the tart was baked, I applied the glaze. Encouragingly, these sturdier pieces stayed put when I brushed them with the strained jam. Then I briefly ran the tart under the broiler to get the burnished finish that characterizes this French showpiece.

The rosette design made this tart look a bit different from classic French versions, but it was every bit as elegant. And thanks to the now-tender glazed apple slices, the rich puree, and the crisp—not to mention utterly simple and foolproof—crust, every slice of the tart that I cut was picture-perfect.

MAKING A ROSETTE

1. Arrange most of parcooked apple slices in tightly overlapping concentric circles.

2. Bend remaining slices to fit in center.

French Apple Tart

SERVES 8

You may have extra apple slices after arranging the apples in step 6. If you don't have a potato masher, you can puree the apples in a food processor. For the best flavor and texture, be sure to bake the crust thoroughly until it is deep golden brown. To ensure that the outer ring of the pan releases easily from the tart, avoid getting apple puree and apricot glaze on the crust. The tart is best served the day it is assembled, but the baked crust, apple slices, and apple puree can be made up to 24 hours in advance. Apple slices and apple puree should be refrigerated separately in airtight containers. Assemble tart with refrigerated apple slices and puree and bake as directed, adding 5 minutes to baking time.

Crust

1⅓ cups (6⅔ ounces) all-purpose flour
5 tablespoons (2¼ ounces) sugar
½ teaspoon salt
10 tablespoons unsalted butter, melted

Filling

10 Golden Delicious apples (8 ounces each), peeled and cored
3 tablespoons unsalted butter
1 tablespoon water
½ cup apricot preserves
¼ teaspoon salt

1. *For the crust:* Adjust 1 oven rack to lowest position and second rack 5 to 6 inches from broiler element. Heat oven to 350 degrees. Whisk flour, sugar, and salt together in bowl. Add melted butter and stir with wooden spoon until dough forms. Using your hands, press two-thirds of dough into bottom of 9-inch tart pan with removable bottom. Press remaining dough into fluted sides of pan. Press and smooth dough with your hands to even thickness. Place pan on wire rack set in rimmed baking sheet and bake on lowest rack, until crust is deep golden brown and firm to touch, 30 to 35 minutes, rotating pan halfway through baking. Set aside until ready to fill.

2. *For the filling:* Cut 5 apples lengthwise into quarters and cut each quarter lengthwise into 4 slices. Melt 1 tablespoon butter in 12-inch skillet over medium heat. Add apple slices and water and toss to combine. Cover and cook, stirring occasionally, until apples begin to turn translucent and are slightly pliable, 3 to 5 minutes. Transfer apples to large plate, spread into single layer, and set aside to cool. Do not clean skillet.

3. While apples cook, microwave apricot preserves until fluid, about 30 seconds. Strain preserves through fine-mesh strainer into small bowl, reserving solids. Set aside 3 tablespoons strained preserves for brushing tart.

4. Cut remaining 5 apples into ½-inch-thick wedges. Melt remaining 2 tablespoons butter in now-empty skillet over medium heat. Add remaining apricot preserves, reserved apricot solids, apple wedges, and salt. Cover and cook, stirring occasionally, until apples are very soft, about 10 minutes.

5. Mash apples to puree with potato masher. Continue to cook, stirring occasionally, until puree is reduced to 2 cups, about 5 minutes.

6. Transfer apple puree to baked tart shell and smooth surface. Select 5 thinnest slices of sautéed apple and set aside. Starting at outer edge of tart, arrange remaining slices, tightly overlapping, in concentric circles. Bend reserved slices to fit in center. Bake tart, still on wire rack in sheet, on lowest rack, for 30 minutes. Remove tart from oven and heat broiler.

7. While broiler heats, warm reserved preserves in microwave until fluid, about 20 seconds. Brush evenly over surface of apples, avoiding tart crust. Broil tart, checking every 30 seconds and turning as necessary, until apples are attractively caramelized, 1 to 3 minutes. Let tart cool for at least 1½ hours. Remove outer metal ring of tart pan, slide thin metal spatula between tart and pan bottom, and carefully slide tart onto serving platter. Cut into wedges and serve.

FOOLPROOF ALL-BUTTER PIE DOUGH

ANDREA GEARY, *January/February 2018*

Outside the kitchen I'm sometimes a bit of a klutz, but give me a rolling pin and a lump of traditional all-butter pie dough—the kind that's dry and brittle and exhibits an alarming tendency to crack—and I'll dazzle you with my proficiency and grace as I roll it into a flawless circle. It's a skill that's taken me decades to acquire, and practicing it makes me feel like a high priestess of pastry. Happily, that feeling of accomplishment became accessible to even the most inexperienced bakers in 2010 when we developed our Foolproof Pie Dough, which is soft and moist and a dream to roll out and bakes up flaky and tender. But as great as that recipe is, I've never been 100 percent converted from my traditional ways.

UPENDING PIE TRADITION

The 2010 recipe controls the ability of the flour in the dough to absorb water. That's important because water bonds with protein in flour to form gluten, the elastic network that gives baked goods their structure. If there's too little water, the dough will be crumbly and impossible to roll and the baked crust will fall apart; too much water and the dough will roll out easily, but it may shrink when it bakes and will certainly be tough.

To appreciate just how revolutionary the 2010 recipe is, it's helpful to recall the way that pie dough has been made for centuries: You start by combining flour, salt, and sugar, then cut in cold butter until it's broken into pea-size nuggets. Then you add water and mix until the dough comes together in a crumbly mass with visible bits of butter strewn throughout.

But our 2010 dough spurns tradition: Using a food processor, you mix 1½ cups of flour with some sugar and salt before adding 1½ sticks of cold butter and ½ cup of shortening (often added to pie doughs to increase flakiness); you continue processing until the fat and the dry ingredients form a smooth paste. Next you pulse in the remaining cup of flour until you have a bunch of flour-covered chunks of dough and a small amount of free flour.

Finally, you transfer the dough to a bowl and stir in ¼ cup of water and ¼ cup of vodka to bring it all together. Why vodka? Because it's 60 percent water and 40 percent alcohol, and alcohol doesn't activate gluten. So replacing some of the water with vodka gives you the freedom to add enough liquid to make a moist, supple dough without the risk of forming excess gluten.

We process some of the butter with the flour and grate the rest into the dough to create a crust that bakes up tender, crisp, and shatteringly flaky.

TAKING THE ALL-BUTTER ROUTE

I've made plenty of pies with the 2010 dough, but honestly, I'm not crazy about using vodka and shortening. I don't always have spirits on hand, and I prefer the richer flavor and cleaner mouthfeel of an all-butter pie crust. So I was intrigued when food writer J. Kenji Lopez-Alt, who developed the original recipe while working at *Cook's Illustrated*, went on to create a shortening- and vodka-free version of the dough for the website Serious Eats. How could it work?

Quite well, actually. The new recipe called for just 6 tablespoons of water—the ¼ cup (4 tablespoons) called for in the original recipe plus 2 additional tablespoons to replicate the water content in ¼ cup of vodka. Even with less water, I found the dough only a little harder to roll out than the original, and it baked up just as tender and flaky.

Turns out that the quirky mixing method was much more important than I'd initially realized. Thoroughly processing a lot of the flour with all the fat effectively waterproofed that portion of the flour, making it difficult for its proteins to hydrate enough to form gluten. Only the remaining cup of flour that was pulsed into the paste was left unprotected and therefore available to be hydrated. The result was a limited gluten network, which produced a very tender crust even without the vodka.

And how did Lopez-Alt's recipe work so well even without shortening? Well, shortening can be valuable in pie dough because it's pliable even when cold, so it flattens into thin sheets under the force of the rolling pin more readily than cold, brittle butter does. But the flour-and-butter paste in this dough also rolls out more easily than butter alone would, so with the paste mixing method there's no shortening required.

A GRATE SOLUTION

There's no denying that the mixing method is a real game changer, but the crust it produces has a couple of faults. When I make pie dough the old-fashioned way I always get a nice sharp edge and a shatteringly flaky crust, but the edges of crusts made using the paste method usually slump a bit in the oven, even when I'm hypervigilant about chilling the formed crust. And that flakiness, which looks so impressive when you break the crust apart, doesn't hold up when you eat it. The crust is a bit too tender, so the flakes disintegrate too readily on the palate.

Luckily, I thought I might know a way to fix both problems with one solution: I made a dough with a full ½ cup of water. My hope was that it would actually produce a little more gluten, thus giving the baked crust more structure and true crispness.

With all that water, the dough was as easy to roll as the vodka crust had been, and the slightly increased gluten gave the baked

crust a more defined edge. But the crust was still a bit too tender for my taste. Maybe the best way to decrease the tenderizing effect of the butter was simply to decrease the butter.

I had been using two-and-a-half sticks of butter to equal the amount of fat in the vodka pie crust. I tried cutting back to an even two sticks, but that crust baked up hard and tough and felt stale right out of the oven. It was just too lean; I'd have to bring the butter back up to two-and-a-half sticks.

But something was bugging me: I'd made plenty of traditionally mixed all-butter pie crusts with an equally high proportion of fat. These doughs were challenging to roll out but the finished crusts always boasted just the right balance of crispness and tenderness. Why was this one so delicate?

And then I realized: In the traditional method much of the butter is left in discrete pieces that enrich the dough without compromising gluten development, but in my new crust, every bit of the butter was worked in. Perhaps the answer was to use the same amount of butter overall but to use less butter in the paste and to make sure that some of the butter remained in pieces.

Cutting the butter into very small pieces wasn't feasible, but what if I grated it? I gave it a try, shredding 4 tablespoons of butter on a box grater. To ensure that those pieces stayed firm enough not to mix with the flour, I froze them. Meanwhile, I processed the remaining two sticks into the dry ingredients. After breaking up the paste, I pulsed in the remaining flour, transferred the mixture to a bowl, and tossed in the grated butter. Finally, I folded in ½ cup of ice water, which was absorbed by the dry flour that coated the dough chunks and the grated butter.

After a 2-hour chill, the dough rolled out beautifully. The fat-rich paste and the shredded butter–flour mixture swirled together, and, once baked, the crust held a perfect, crisp edge and was rich-tasting while being both tender and truly flaky.

Now that I have an all-butter pie dough that's a cinch to roll out, I'm ready to adopt a new tradition.

Foolproof All-Butter Dough for Double-Crust Pie

MAKES ONE 9-INCH DOUBLE CRUST

Be sure to weigh the flour for this recipe. In the mixing stage, this dough will be more moist than most pie doughs, but as it chills it will absorb a lot of excess moisture. Roll the dough on a well-floured counter.

20 tablespoons (2½ sticks) unsalted butter, chilled
2½ cups (12½ ounces) all-purpose flour
2 tablespoons sugar
1 teaspoon salt
½ cup ice water

1. Grate 4 tablespoons butter on large holes of box grater and place in freezer. Cut remaining 16 tablespoons butter into ½-inch cubes.
2. Pulse 1½ cups flour, sugar, and salt in food processor until combined, 2 pulses. Add cubed butter and process until homogeneous paste forms, 40 to 50 seconds. Using your hands, carefully break paste into 2-inch chunks and redistribute evenly around processor blade. Add remaining 1 cup flour and pulse until mixture is broken into pieces no larger than 1 inch (most pieces will be much smaller), 4 to 5 pulses. Transfer mixture to medium bowl. Add grated butter and toss until butter pieces are separated and coated with flour.
3. Sprinkle ¼ cup ice water over mixture. Toss with rubber spatula until mixture is evenly moistened. Sprinkle remaining ¼ cup ice water over mixture and toss to combine. Press dough with spatula until dough sticks together. Use spatula to divide dough into 2 portions. Transfer each portion to sheet of plastic wrap. Working with 1 portion at a time, draw edges of plastic over dough and press firmly on sides and top to form compact, fissure-free mass. Wrap in plastic and form into 5-inch disk. Repeat with remaining portion; refrigerate dough for at least 2 hours or up to 2 days. Let chilled dough sit on counter to soften slightly, about 10 minutes, before rolling. (Wrapped dough can be frozen for up to 1 month. If frozen, let dough thaw completely on counter before rolling.)

variation

Foolproof All-Butter Dough for Single-Crust Pie

MAKES ONE 9-INCH SINGLE CRUST

Be sure to weigh the flour for this recipe. This dough will be more moist than most pie doughs, but as it chills it will absorb a lot of excess moisture. Roll the dough on a well-floured counter.

10 tablespoons unsalted butter, chilled
1¼ cups (6¼ ounces) all-purpose flour
1 tablespoon sugar
½ teaspoon salt
¼ cup ice water

1. Grate 2 tablespoons butter on large holes of box grater and place in freezer. Cut remaining 8 tablespoons butter into ½-inch cubes.
2. Pulse ¾ cup flour, sugar, and salt in food processor until combined, 2 pulses. Add cubed butter and process until homogeneous paste forms, about 30 seconds. Using your hands, carefully break paste into 2-inch chunks and redistribute evenly around processor blade. Add remaining ½ cup flour and pulse until mixture is broken into pieces no larger than 1 inch (most pieces will be much smaller), 4 to 5 pulses. Transfer mixture to medium bowl. Add grated butter and toss until butter pieces are separated and coated with flour.
3. Sprinkle 2 tablespoons ice water over mixture. Toss with rubber spatula until mixture is evenly moistened. Sprinkle remaining 2 tablespoons ice water over mixture and toss to combine. Press dough with spatula until dough sticks together. Transfer dough to sheet of plastic wrap. Draw edges of plastic over dough and press firmly on sides and top to form compact, fissure-free mass. Wrap in plastic and form into 5-inch disk. Refrigerate dough for at least 2 hours or up to 2 days. Let chilled dough sit on counter to soften slightly, about 10 minutes, before rolling. (Wrapped dough can be frozen for up to 1 month. If frozen, let dough thaw completely on counter before rolling.)

BUILDING A BETTER DEEP-DISH APPLE PIE

ERIKA BRUCE, *September/October 2005*

Deep-dish apple pies were traditionally baked without a bottom crust in casserole dishes, the generous filling blanketed with a layer of thick, flaky pastry. Nowadays, it is more common to find double-crust deep-dish apple pies, with the apples nestled between two layers of pastry. Unfortunately, these pies often bear little resemblance to their name, instead looking suspiciously like your standard apple pie. But I didn't want a thin slice of plain old apple pie; I wanted a towering wedge of tender, juicy apples, fully framed by a buttery, flaky crust.

After foraging for recipes that met my specifications for deep-dish—a minimum of 4 pounds of apples as opposed to the meager 2 pounds in a standard pie—I realized that, while a standard apple pie may be juicy, most deep-dish pies are downright flooded with liquid. As a result, the bottom crust becomes a pale, soggy mess. In addition, the crowd of apples tends to cook unevenly, with mushy edges surrounding a crunchy center. Less serious—but no less annoying—is the gaping hole left between the apples (which shrink considerably) and the arching top crust, which makes it impossible to slice and serve a neat piece of pie.

Sautéing the apples on the stovetop before loading them into the crust eliminates excess moisture and prevents gaps in the finished pie.

After a week of rescue efforts, I had made little progress. My failed attempts included slicing the apples into thick chunks and thin slices, cutting large vents in the pie dough before baking to promote steam release, and baking the pies at different temperatures. I tried moving the pie to the very bottom rack of the oven. No matter what I tried, I was confronted with a soupy filling and soggy crust. To sop up the copious amount of liquid, I added a thickening agent. But so much thickener (flour or cornstarch) was required to dam the flood that it muddied the bright flavor of the apples.

THE PECTIN PROBLEM

During my research, I had come across recipes that called for sautéing the apples before assembling them in the pie, the idea being to both extract juice and cook the apples more evenly. Although this logic seemed counterintuitive (how could cooking the apples twice cause them to become anything but insipid and mushy?), I forged ahead. After browning the apples in a hot skillet (in two batches to accommodate the large volume), I made yet another pie and then crossed my fingers. As expected, the apples were disappointingly mealy and soft, especially the exteriors, which had been seared in the hot pan. But this pie did deliver on a couple of counts: In addition to the absence of juice flooding the bottom of the pie plate, it offered a nicely browned bottom crust.

Could I keep the apples from disintegrating if I tried this method with a gentler hand? I dumped the whole mound into a large Dutch oven along with some granulated sugar (to flavor the apples and extract moisture) and then covered the pot to promote more even cooking. With frequent stirring over a medium flame for 15 to 20 minutes, the apples were tender yet still held their shape. After cooling the apples (so the butter in the crust would not melt immediately) and draining them, I baked the pie, which was again free of excess juice and sported the same browned bottom as before. This time, however, the apples weren't mealy—they were miraculously tender.

After some digging, I discovered that apples undergo a significant structural change when held at moderately warm temperatures for 20 to 30 minutes. Between 120 and 140 degrees, the pectin is converted into a more heat-stable form. (While pectin provides structure in the raw fruit, it breaks down under the high heat of sautéing.) Once an adequate amount of pectin has been stabilized at low heat (as it apparently was on the stovetop), the apples can tolerate the heat from additional cooking (in the pie and in the oven) without becoming excessively soft.

To top it off, because the apples were shrinking before going into the pie rather than after, I had inadvertently solved the problem of the maddening gap, too. The top crust now remained united with the rest of the pie, and slicing was a breeze.

GETTING IN DEEP

Finally, with a cooking technique that produced picture-perfect results, it was time to adjust flavors. I snuck in another pound of apples (bringing the total to 5 pounds) to compensate for the bulk lost during stovetop cooking. Tart apples, such as Granny Smiths and Empires, were well liked for their brash flavor, but it was a one-dimensional profile. To achieve a fuller, more balanced flavor, I found it necessary to add a sweeter variety, such as Golden Delicious or Braeburn. Another important factor in choosing the right apple was texture. Even over the gentle heat of the stovetop, softer varieties such as McIntosh broke down and turned to mush.

With the right combination of apples, heavy flavorings were gratuitous. Some light brown sugar and granulated sugar, as well as a pinch of salt and a squeeze of lemon juice, heightened the flavor of the apples. After sampling the gamut of spices, tasters were content with just an unimposing hint of cinnamon. The perfect slice was no longer a deep-dish apple pie in the sky but a reality, sitting up nice and tall on my plate.

Deep-Dish Apple Pie

SERVES 8

If desired, you can substitute tart Empire or Cortland apples for the Granny Smith apples and sweet Jonagold, Fuji, or Braeburn apples for the Golden Delicious apples here.

- **1 recipe Foolproof All-Butter Dough for Double-Crust Pie (page 500)**
- **2½ pounds Granny Smith apples, peeled, cored, halved, and sliced ¼ inch thick**
- **2½ pounds Golden Delicious apples, peeled, cored, halved, and sliced ¼ inch thick**
- **½ cup (3½ ounces) plus 1 tablespoon granulated sugar**
- **¼ cup packed (1¾ ounces) light brown sugar**
- **½ teaspoon grated lemon zest plus 1 tablespoon juice**
- **¼ teaspoon salt**
- **⅛ teaspoon ground cinnamon**
- **1 large egg white, lightly beaten**

1. Roll 1 disk of dough into 12-inch circle on floured counter. Loosely roll dough around rolling pin and gently unroll it onto 9-inch pie plate, letting excess dough hang over edge. Ease dough into plate by gently lifting edge of dough with your hand while pressing into plate bottom with your other hand. Wrap dough-lined plate loosely in plastic wrap and refrigerate until dough is firm, about 30 minutes.

2. Roll other disk of dough into 12-inch circle on floured counter, then transfer to parchment paper–lined baking sheet; cover with plastic and refrigerate for 30 minutes.

3. Toss apples, ½ cup granulated sugar, brown sugar, lemon zest, salt, and cinnamon together in Dutch oven. Cover and cook over medium heat, stirring often, until apples are tender when poked with fork but still hold their shape, 15 to 20 minutes. Transfer apples and their juice to rimmed baking sheet and let cool completely, about 30 minutes.

4. Adjust oven rack to lowest position and heat oven to 425 degrees. Drain cooled apples thoroughly in colander set over bowl; reserve ¼ cup juice. Stir lemon juice into reserved juice.

5. Transfer apples to dough-lined plate, mounding them slightly in middle, and drizzle with apple juice mixture. Loosely roll remaining dough round around rolling pin and gently unroll it onto filling. Trim overhang to ½ inch beyond lip of plate. Pinch edges of top and bottom crusts firmly together. Tuck overhang under itself; folded edge should be flush with edge of plate. Crimp dough evenly around edge of plate using your fingers. Cut four 2-inch slits in top of dough. Brush surface with beaten egg white and sprinkle evenly with remaining 1 tablespoon granulated sugar.

6. Place pie on rimmed baking sheet and bake until crust is light golden brown, about 25 minutes. Reduce oven temperature to 375 degrees, rotate sheet, and continue to bake until juices are bubbling and crust is deep golden brown, 30 to 40 minutes longer. Let pie cool on wire rack until filling has set, about 2 hours; serve slightly warm or at room temperature.

THE INCREDIBLE SHRINKING APPLE

When raw apples are used in a deep-dish pie, they shrink to almost nothing, leaving a huge gap between the top crust and the filling. Precooking the apples eliminates the shrinking problem and actually helps the apples hold their shape once baked in the pie. This seems counterintuitive, but here's what happens: When the apples are gently heated, their pectin is converted into a heat-stable form that prevents the apples from becoming mushy when cooked further in the oven. The key is to keep the temperature of the apples below 140 degrees during this precooking stage. Rather than cooking the apples in a skillet (where they are likely to become too hot), it's best to gently heat the apples and seasonings in a large covered Dutch oven.

COOK BEFORE BAKING Precooking the apples converts their pectin into a heat-stable form that prevents them from becoming mushy—even after being cooked twice.

VARIETY MAKES A BETTER PIE

A combination of sweet and tart apples works best in pie. These six varieties, all of which retain their shape when cooked, were our favorites in kitchen tests.

SWEET

GOLDEN DELICIOUS
Sweet with buttery undertones

BRAEBURN
Takes on a pear-like flavor when baked

JONAGOLD
Intensely sweet and buttery

TART

GRANNY SMITH
Vibrantly tart, holds shape best

EMPIRE
Strong, complex, cider-like flavor

CORTLAND
Similar to Empire, but more tart than complex

FRESH PEACH PIE

ANDREW JANJIGIAN, *September/October 2013*

While the almost-impossible juiciness of a ripe peach is the source of the fruit's magnificence, it's also the reason that fresh peaches can be tricky to use in pies. The hallmark of any fresh fruit pie is fresh fruit flavor, but ripe peaches exude so much juice that they require an excess of flavor-dampening binders to create a filling that isn't soup. Fresh peaches can also differ dramatically in water content, so figuring out how much thickener to add can be a guessing game from one pie to the next. Finally, ripe peaches are delicate, easily disintegrating into mush when baked.

I wanted to make a peach pie with tender yet intact fruit, and I wanted it to slice cleanly without being the least bit muddled, gluey, grainy, or cloudy.

For a cohesive filling with bright, clean flavor, we add a combination of pectin and cornstarch and mash a small portion of the peaches.

CREATING A CRUST

Before I could nail down the filling, I'd need a reliable crust. Experimenting with a few recipes taught me one thing: The fillings in pies with lattice-top crusts had far better consistencies than those in pies with solid tops, since the crosshatch allows moisture to evaporate during cooking.

The pliability of a typical double-crust pie dough makes it challenging to weave into a lattice; when making a lattice, it's helpful to have a dough with a little more structure. Luckily, we have such a dough in our archives. A little extra water and a little less fat help create a sturdy dough that can withstand some extra handling. Just as important, this dough still manages to bake up tender and taste rich and buttery.

I also wanted to simplify the mechanics of building the lattice itself, which usually requires practice to create neat, professional-looking results, but I wanted a lattice that a novice baker could do perfectly. The best approach I found came from our Linzertorte, which skips the weaving in favor of simply laying one strip over the previous one in a pattern that allows some of the strips to appear woven. Freezing the strips for 30 minutes before creating the lattice made them easier to handle.

BOUND AND UNBOUND

Now it was time to get down to the fruit. Most recipes I'd tested called for tossing thinly sliced peaches with sugar and spices before throwing them into the pie crust and then putting the pie into the oven. But I'd noted that the peaches handled this way shed a lot of moisture before they even reached the oven, thanks to the sugar's osmotic action on the slices. Sugar is hygroscopic—meaning it easily attracts water to itself—making it superbly capable of pulling juice out of the peaches' cells. If I was going to gain control over the consistency of the filling, that's where I'd need to start. Since osmosis occurs on the surface, one obvious tweak would be to make the peach slices relatively large to minimize total surface area. So instead of slicing the peaches thin, I cut them into quarters and then cut each of these into thick—but still bite-size—1-inch chunks.

I also let the sugared peaches macerate for a bit and then drained off the juice before tossing the fruit into the pie, adding back only enough juice to moisten—not flood—the filling. This would allow me to control how much liquid the peaches contributed from batch to batch. I tossed 3 pounds of peaches with ½ cup of sugar, 1 tablespoon of lemon juice, and a pinch of salt. When I drained the peaches 30 minutes later, they yielded more than ½ cup of juice. I settled on using just ½ cup to moisten the filling. To this I added just enough cinnamon and nutmeg to accent the flavor of the peaches without overshadowing it.

Now it was time to experiment with thickeners that would tighten up the fruit and juice while maintaining the illusion that nothing was in the pie but fresh peaches. Flour left the filling grainy and cloudy, while tapioca pearls never completely dispersed, leaving visible beads of gel behind. (Grinding the rock-hard tapioca pearls into finer grains helped but was a pain.) Potato starch and cornstarch each worked admirably up to a point, but after that they did not eliminate further runniness so much as turn the filling murky and gluey. More important, all these starches dulled the flavor of the peaches.

Maybe adding starch was not the best approach. I thought about apple pie, which barely needs any thickener to create a filling that slices cleanly. Apples are less juicy than peaches, but they also contain lots of pectin, which helps them hold on to their moisture and remain intact during baking. For my next test I stirred some pectin into my reserved peach juice, heated the mixture briefly on the stove, and then folded it into the peach chunks. This filling turned out smooth and clear and tasted brightly of peaches. But it was still runnier than I wanted. Adding more pectin would only make the filling bouncy. Then I thought back to our recipe for Fresh Strawberry Pie, which uses a combination of pectin and cornstarch. Could I find the sweet spot using both thickeners? Yes: Two tablespoons of pectin and 1 tablespoon of cornstarch left me with a filling that was smooth, clear, and moist without being soupy.

One problem remained: a tendency for the peach chunks to fall out of the pie slices. To fix this, I mashed a small amount of the macerated peaches to a coarse pulp with a fork and used it as a form of mortar to eliminate gaps and stabilize the filling.

At last, I had a fresh peach pie that looked perfect, tasted of fresh peaches, and sliced neatly.

Fresh Peach Pie

SERVES 8

If your peaches are too soft to withstand the pressure of a peeler, cut a shallow X in the bottom of the fruit, blanch them in a pot of simmering water for 15 seconds, and then shock them in a bowl of ice water before peeling.

3 pounds peaches, peeled, quartered, and pitted, each quarter cut into thirds
½ cup (3½ ounces) plus 3 tablespoons sugar
1 teaspoon grated lemon zest plus 1 tablespoon juice
⅛ teaspoon salt
2 tablespoons low- or no-sugar-needed fruit pectin
¼ teaspoon ground cinnamon
Pinch ground nutmeg
1 recipe Pie Dough for Lattice-Top Pie (recipe follows)
1 tablespoon cornstarch

1. Toss peaches, ½ cup sugar, lemon zest and juice, and salt in medium bowl. Let stand at room temperature for at least 30 minutes or up to 1 hour. Combine pectin, cinnamon, nutmeg, and 2 tablespoons sugar in small bowl and set aside.
2. Remove dough from refrigerator. Before rolling out dough, let it sit on counter to soften slightly, about 10 minutes. Roll 1 disk of dough into 12-inch circle on lightly floured counter. Transfer to parchment paper–lined baking sheet. With pizza wheel, fluted pastry wheel, or paring knife, cut round into ten 1¼-inch-wide strips. Freeze strips on sheet until firm, about 30 minutes.
3. Adjust oven rack to lowest position, place rimmed baking sheet on rack, and heat oven to 425 degrees. Roll other disk of dough into 12-inch circle on lightly floured counter. Loosely roll dough around rolling pin and gently unroll it onto 9-inch pie plate, letting excess dough hang over edge. Ease dough into plate by gently lifting edge of dough with your hand while pressing into plate bottom with your other hand. Leave any dough that overhangs plate in place. Wrap dough-lined pie plate loosely in plastic wrap and refrigerate until dough is firm, about 30 minutes.
4. Meanwhile, transfer 1 cup peach mixture to small bowl and mash with fork until coarse paste forms. Drain remaining peach mixture in colander set in large bowl. Transfer peach juice to liquid measuring cup (you should have about ½ cup liquid; if liquid measures more than ½ cup, discard remainder). Return peach pieces to bowl and toss with cornstarch. Transfer peach juice to 12-inch skillet, add pectin mixture, and whisk until combined. Cook over medium heat, stirring occasionally, until slightly thickened and pectin is dissolved (liquid should become less cloudy), 3 to 5 minutes. Remove skillet from heat, add peach pieces and peach paste, and toss to combine.
5. Transfer peach mixture to dough-lined pie plate. Remove dough strips from freezer; if too stiff to be workable, let stand at room temperature until malleable and softened slightly but still very cold. Lay 2 longest strips across center of pie perpendicular to each other. Using 4 shortest strips, lay 2 strips across pie parallel to 1 center strip and 2 strips parallel to other center strip, near edges of pie; you should have 6 strips in place. Using remaining 4 strips, lay each one across pie parallel and equidistant from center and edge strips. If dough becomes too soft to work with, refrigerate pie and dough strips until dough firms up.
6. Trim overhang to ½ inch beyond lip of pie plate. Press edges of bottom crust and lattice strips together and fold under. Folded edge should be flush with edge of pie plate. Crimp dough evenly around edge of pie using your fingers. Using spray bottle, evenly mist lattice with water and sprinkle with remaining 1 tablespoon sugar.
7. Place pie on preheated sheet and bake until crust is set and begins to brown, about 25 minutes. Rotate pie and reduce oven temperature to 375 degrees; continue to bake until crust is deep golden brown and filling is bubbly at center, 25 to 30 minutes longer. Let cool on wire rack for 3 hours before serving.

dough

Pie Dough for Lattice-Top Pie

FOR ONE 9-INCH LATTICE-TOP PIE

3 cups (15 ounces) all-purpose flour
2 tablespoons sugar
1 teaspoon salt
7 tablespoons vegetable shortening, cut into ½-inch pieces and chilled
10 tablespoons unsalted butter, cut into ¼-inch pieces and frozen for 30 minutes
10–12 tablespoons ice water

1. Process flour, sugar, and salt in food processor until combined, about 5 seconds. Scatter shortening over top and process until mixture resembles coarse cornmeal, about 10 seconds. Scatter butter over top and pulse until mixture resembles coarse crumbs, about 10 pulses. Transfer to bowl.
2. Sprinkle 5 tablespoons ice water over flour mixture. With rubber spatula, use folding motion to evenly combine water and flour mixture. Sprinkle 5 tablespoons ice water over mixture and continue using folding motion to combine until small portion of dough holds together when squeezed in palm of your hand, adding up to 2 tablespoons remaining ice water if necessary. (Dough should feel quite moist.) Turn out dough onto clean, dry counter and gently press together into cohesive ball. Divide dough into 2 even pieces and flatten each into 4-inch disk. Wrap disks tightly in plastic wrap and refrigerate for 1 hour or up to 2 days.

PEELING PEACHES

A sharp serrated peeler can make quick work of peeling soft, ripe fruit. If you don't have one, you can blanch the fruit in boiling water. Score the bottom of the peach with an X before dropping it into the water. After 30 to 60 seconds, watch the skin around the X for signs of splitting and tearing. Remove the peach from the boiling water with a slotted spoon and plunge it into an ice bath to stop the cooking. Once the peach has cooled, pull it from the ice water and use a paring knife to help peel back the slippery skin, starting at the X. It should come off in large strips.

REINVENTING SWEET CHERRY PIE

YVONNE RUPERTI, *July/August 2010*

I've often wondered why apple pie beat out cherry as our national dessert. At their best, cherry pies are juicier, more colorful, and, in my opinion, just plain tastier than apple. It all boils down to a matter of availability. You can find decent apples year-round in even the most meagerly stocked supermarket, but cherry season is cruelly short—just a brief blossoming period during the early summer. And even when cherries are available, chances are they're a sweet variety (usually crimson-colored Bing or red-yellow-blushed Rainier), not the rare, ruby-hued sour species prized for jams and pie-making.

What makes sour cherries such prime candidates for baking (most people find them too tart for snacking purposes) is their soft, juicy flesh and bright, punchy flavor that neither oven heat nor sugar can dull. Plumper sweet cherries, on the other hand, have mellower flavors and meaty, firm flesh—traits that make them ideal for eating straight off the stem but don't translate well to baking. My challenge was obvious: Develop a recipe for sweet cherry pie with all the intense, jammy flavor and softened but still intact fruit texture of the best sour cherry pie.

SWEET AND SOUR

Before I abandoned sour cherries altogether, I needed to get my hands on one batch to help me understand how they function in pie compared with their sweeter cousins. With help from the U.S. Postal Service, I obtained a few pounds of the tart variety from an online retailer, baked them into a pie, and tasted it side by side with one made of supermarket sweet cherries. The difference was night-and-day. Compared with the sour cherry pie's bracing acidity, the sweet cherry pie's taste was beyond sweet; it was downright cloying. Even more problematic, the sweet cherries' drier, relatively dense flesh failed to break down completely (even after an hour or more of baking) and resulted in a filling that called to mind slightly softened jumbo marbles, not fruit.

So I had two issues to resolve: taming the cherries' sweetness, and getting them to break down to the proper juicy texture. To get my bearings, I made another pie. I combined 2 pounds of pitted fresh Bing cherries and 1 cup of sugar, stirred in 3 tablespoons of ground tapioca (tasters' preferred thickener in earlier tests), poured the filling into a shell, and wove a traditional lattice-top crust to show off the fruit's jewel-like shine. After it had baked and cooled, I offered my colleagues a bite. As I expected, nobody could taste past the sweetness. Figuring all that sugar wasn't helping, I tried cutting back a few tablespoons at a time, but that only created a new problem: Since sugar draws moisture out of the cherries through osmosis, less of it made for a less juicy filling. A half-cup was as low as I could go without completely ruining the texture, but the filling still verged on candy sweetness.

By pureeing some of the cherries with plums and skipping the lattice crust, we create a flavorful and juicy pie with sweet cherries.

My only other option was to add another ingredient to offset the sweetness. A couple of splashes of bourbon—a classic pairing with cherries—helped, as did the acidity of fresh lemon juice, but these were minor tweaks, and adding more of either just made the pies taste boozy or citrusy. I even tried vinegar, hoping to more closely mimic the tartness of sour cherries, but tasters objected to the sharpness of even the smallest drop. As a last-ditch effort, I tried introducing alternative fruits: super-t art fresh cranberries (too bitter), tangy red grapes (too musty), and dried sour cherries (too chewy).

None of these ideas panned out, but the concept did get me thinking about other types of fruit. Cherries fall into the stone-fruit category, along with peaches, nectarines, and plums. Sweet-fleshed peaches and nectarines wouldn't help me, but the tartness of plums might be worth a shot. For my next pie, I sliced a couple of plums into the filling, but their flesh was just as dense and resilient as the cherries'. No problem, I thought; this was nothing my trusty food processor couldn't fix. I made another pie, this time pureeing the plums and mixing the resulting pulp with the cherries. Perfect! The flavor, now tangy and complex, was spot on, and nobody suspected my secret.

SEALING IN THE JUICES

Now that I'd crossed one challenge off my list, I was ready to tackle the sweet cherries' overly firm texture. The problem was two-fold: Not only were the cherries refusing to break down, as a result they also weren't releasing enough juice to amply moisten the filling. As it turned out, the culprit was cellulose, the main structural component of fruit cells: Compared with sour cherries, the sweet variety contains a full 30 percent more cellulose, making the flesh more rigid.

Without a way to rid the cherries of that extra structure, I'd have to rely on more conventional techniques to soften the flesh. I was already macerating them in sugar before baking to help draw out some of their juices, but with their relatively thick skin, this technique wasn't effective. Halving them helped considerably, since their juice was very easily drawn out of the exposed fleshy centers. Even better, the cut cherries collapsed more readily and turned out markedly softer in the finished pie, save for a few too many solid chunks. By tossing a portion of them (1 cup) into the food processor along with the plums (and straining the chewy skins out of the resulting pulp), I got a filling that was ideally soft, if a bit dry, and studded with a few still-intact cherry pieces. As a bonus, the pies I tested using a good

brand of frozen sweet cherries—an easier alternative to pitting dozens of the fresh variety—baked up equally well, making this an any-season dessert.

I'd hoped that mashing and precooking the cherries with sugar would help release some fruit juices, but this technique actually caused moisture to evaporate through the crust's ventilated top as it baked, leading to a drier pie. Then I realized: My problem wasn't the fruit itself, but the lattice crust. Juice-gushing sour cherry and berry pies may benefit from the extra evaporation of a woven crust, but with these cherries I needed to keep a tighter lid on the available moisture. Rolling out a traditional disk of dough, I fitted it to the bottom pastry, neatly sealed the edges, and slid the whole assembly onto a baking sheet before putting it in the oven to ensure that the bottom crust crisped up before the fruit filling could seep through. An hour or so later, out came a gorgeously golden-brown, perfectly juicy (but not runny) pie. When my tasters began to line up for second helpings, I knew I'd finally gotten cherry pie in apple-pie order.

Sweet Cherry Pie

SERVES 8

Grind the tapioca to a powder in a spice grinder or mini food processor. You can substitute 2 pounds of frozen sweet cherries for the fresh cherries. If you are using frozen fruit, measure it frozen, but let it thaw before filling the pie. If not, you run the risk of partially cooked fruit and undissolved tapioca.

- 1 recipe Foolproof All-Butter Dough for Double-Crust Pie (page 500)
- 2 red plums, quartered and pitted
- 2½ pounds fresh sweet cherries, pitted and halved
- ½ cup (3½ ounces) sugar
- 2 tablespoons instant tapioca, ground
- 1 tablespoon lemon juice
- 2 teaspoons bourbon (optional)
- ⅛ teaspoon salt
- ⅛ teaspoon ground cinnamon (optional)
- 2 tablespoons unsalted butter, cut into ¼-inch pieces
- 1 large egg, lightly beaten with 1 teaspoon water

1. Roll 1 disk of dough into 12-inch circle on floured counter. Loosely roll dough around rolling pin and gently unroll it onto 9-inch pie plate, letting excess dough hang over edge. Ease dough into plate by gently lifting edge of dough with your hand while pressing into plate bottom with your other hand. Wrap dough-lined plate loosely in plastic wrap and refrigerate until dough is firm, about 30 minutes. Roll other disk of dough into 12-inch circle on lightly floured counter, then transfer to parchment paper–lined baking sheet; cover with plastic and refrigerate for 30 minutes.
2. Adjust oven rack to lowest position and heat oven to 400 degrees. Process plums and 1 cup cherries in food processor until smooth, about 1 minute, scraping down sides of bowl as necessary. Strain puree through fine-mesh strainer into large bowl, pressing on solids to extract as much liquid as possible; discard solids. Stir remaining cherries; sugar; tapioca; lemon juice; bourbon, if using; salt; and cinnamon, if using, into puree. Let stand for 15 minutes.
3. Spread cherry mixture with its juices into dough-lined plate and scatter butter over top. Loosely roll remaining dough round around rolling pin and gently unroll it onto filling. Trim overhang to ½ inch beyond lip of plate. Pinch edges of top and bottom crusts firmly together. Tuck overhang under itself; folded edge should be flush with edge of plate. Crimp dough evenly around edge of plate using your fingers. Cut eight 1-inch slits in top of dough. Brush surface with egg mixture. Freeze pie for 20 minutes.
4. Place pie on rimmed baking sheet and bake until crust is light golden brown, about 30 minutes. Reduce oven temperature to 350 degrees, rotate sheet, and continue to bake until juices are bubbling and crust is deep golden brown, 35 to 50 minutes longer. Let pie cool completely on wire rack to allow juices to thicken, 2 to 3 hours. Serve.

KEYS TO JUICY, SWEET-TART CHERRY PIE

While some fruits (such as blueberries) gush excess juice when baked into a pie, sweet cherries such as Bing suffer the opposite problem: Their firm, meaty flesh holds on to juice and can lead to a too-dry filling.

1. **HALVE CHERRIES** Halving the cherries exposes their dense, meaty flesh and helps them release more juice than if left whole.

2. **GET PLUMMY** To add tartness and juiciness, puree 1 cup cherries with two plums. Strain, adding the liquid to the halved cherries and discarding the solids.

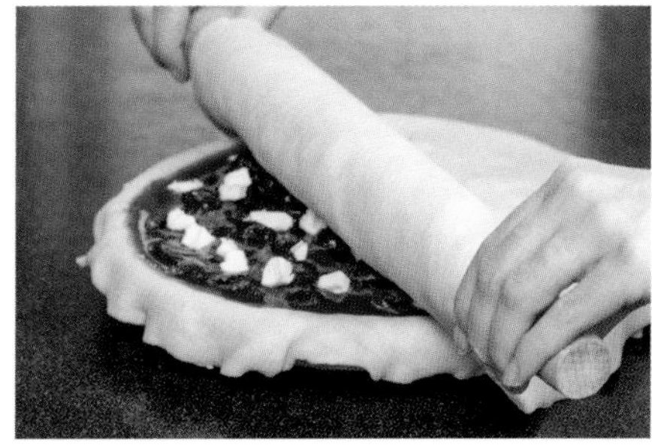

3. **SKIP THE LATTICE** A traditional lattice crust allows too much moisture to evaporate during baking; a closed crust helps keep juices inside.

CLASSIC PECAN PIE

STEPHEN SCHMIDT, *November/December 1995*

William Faulkner once said, "You don't love because; you love despite." I love pecan pie more than most any other pie, despite its deep-seated problems. First off, the filling is just too sweet, both in an absolute sense and in relation to the other flavors of the pie. Can you taste the nuts? The buttery crust? Probably not; the sticky-sweet filling runs roughshod over the other components. As for that filling, it's either curdled and separated or half-baked and soggy enough to prevent the bottom crust from baking. The pie I love, despite it all, can be wonderfully soft and smooth—almost like a cream pie—and is topped with a crunchy layer of pecans.

IN THE DETAILS

Pecan pies are prepared in a pretty uniform fashion. Corn syrup, sugar (granulated or brown), eggs, butter, and flavorings are mixed together, poured into a flaky pie shell, topped with pecans, and baked. Simple-sounding, perhaps, but each step includes various choices that will make or break the pie.

After testing a variety of different recipes, I was able to make some important decisions. The most successful recipes I tried called for partially baking the crust before adding the filling—an extra step, perhaps, but well worth it, because it ensured a well-browned, crisp crust. As for the filling, recipes were remarkably consistent, varying only in the details. That said, some did include thickeners like flour or cornstarch for stabilization, but I thought that the starchiness diminished the filling's silky texture. For baking the assembled pie, a hot oven spelled disaster: The pies baked above 375 degrees set firm around the edges long before the center was even warmed through. Clearly, more moderate temperatures were in order. And finally, toasted pecans tasted a whole lot better than those left untoasted.

After all the problems I saw in my initial testing, I was most concerned with the texture of the filling; flavor would follow. I chose my favorite filling from those I had tested and set to work trying different oven temperatures and rack placements. While I knew that high-temperature baking was off the table, I quickly learned that too low could be just as bad. The filling took so long to firm up at 250 degrees that it rendered the formerly crisp brown crust soggy. Furthermore, the filling tended to separate, with a jelly-like layer on the bottom and a frothy cap on top. Above 300 degrees, however, the filling cooked in distinct concentric rings: The closer to the center, the softer it was.

TIME AND TEMPERATURE

Feeling a little flummoxed, I began looking at custard pie recipes to see how they solved the problems I couldn't seem to overcome. One thing I was really surprised to learn was how early some recipes called for the pie to be pulled from the oven. I followed the instructions despite my apprehension and the pie's jiggly tremor. As the pie cooled on the wire rack, a wonderful transformation occurred. The jiggly filling set up to the silky, smooth-as-could-be texture I sought. It appeared that the residual heat of the filling, pulled by conduction, cooked the center through. What was as loose as an egg white when pulled from the oven set up to a silky, tender filling a few hours later.

Another recipe I found tweaked the method further by heating the filling before pouring it into the crust. And the crust was hot, too—straight from the oven. These steps gave the cooking process a head start, and the results were the best yet, with the silkiest, most even texture and the crispiest crust, because the filling set up so fast in the oven.

With all this new information, I eagerly applied my findings to my pecan pie filling and produced the best pie yet. The flavor, however, still needed a little work. Hoping to mitigate the sweetness, I scaled back the amount of corn syrup typically used. I also chose dark brown sugar over granulated for its earthy, faintly bitter flavor. Butter added lushness to the filling, but too much made it greasy. After starting with one whole stick, I found that I preferred a filling with a little less—just 6 tablespoons total. Vanilla improved the filling's flavor and brought out the pecans' sweetness. I thought a teaspoon or so would do it, but a whopping tablespoon proved best. A generous ½ teaspoon of salt heightened the flavors and tied everything together.

Partially baking the crust and parcooking the filling before assembling the pie produces a silky filling and crisp crust.

I was thrilled with the pie but for one thing: the pecans. Left whole, they were too much of a mouthful, and I had difficulty cutting through them with a fork as I ate. Finely chopped nuts were easier to slice through and eat. This pecan pie is easy to love—without qualification. Still, there are many people who find pecan pie intrinsically too sweet. To them I recommend the soft, custard-like Maple Pecan Pie variation that follows—it might just be my favorite pie in the whole world.

Classic Pecan Pie

SERVES 8

The crust must still be warm when the filling is added. Serve with vanilla ice cream or whipped cream, if desired.

1 recipe Foolproof All-Butter Dough for Single-Crust Pie (page 500)
6 tablespoons unsalted butter, cut into 1-inch pieces
1 cup packed (7 ounces) **dark brown sugar**
½ teaspoon salt
3 large eggs
¾ cup light corn syrup
1 tablespoon vanilla extract
2 cups pecans, toasted and chopped fine

1. Adjust oven rack to lowest position and heat oven to 425 degrees. Roll dough into 12-inch circle on floured counter. Loosely roll dough around rolling pin and gently unroll it onto 9-inch pie plate, letting excess dough hang over edge. Ease dough into plate by gently lifting edge of dough with your hand while pressing into plate bottom with your other hand. Wrap dough-lined plate loosely in plastic wrap and refrigerate until dough is firm, about 30 minutes.

2. Trim overhang to ½ inch beyond lip of plate. Tuck overhang under itself; folded edge should be flush with edge of plate. Crimp dough evenly around edge of plate using your fingers. Wrap dough-lined plate loosely in plastic and refrigerate until dough is firm, about 15 minutes.

3. Line chilled pie shell with parchment paper or double layer of aluminum foil, covering edges to prevent burning, and fill with pie weights. Bake until pie dough looks dry and is pale in color, about 15 minutes, rotating plate halfway through baking. Remove parchment and weights and continue to bake crust until golden brown, 4 to 7 minutes longer. Transfer plate to wire rack. (Crust must still be warm when filling is added.)

4. While pie shell is baking, melt butter in heatproof bowl set in skillet of barely simmering water. Remove bowl from skillet and stir in sugar and salt until butter is absorbed. Whisk in eggs, then corn syrup and vanilla until smooth. Return bowl to skillet and stir until mixture is shiny, hot to touch, and registers 130 degrees. Off heat, stir in pecans.

5. As soon as crust comes out of oven, adjust oven rack to lower-middle position and reduce oven temperature to 275 degrees. Pour pecan mixture into warm crust. Bake pie on rimmed baking sheet until filling looks set but yields like gelatin when gently pressed with back of spoon, 50 minutes to 1 hour, rotating sheet halfway through baking. Let pie cool on wire rack until filling has set, about 2 hours; serve slightly warm or at room temperature. (Cooled pie can be wrapped tightly in plastic and stored at room temperature for up to 2 days. To serve warm, let cool as directed, then transfer to 250-degree oven for about 15 minutes before serving.)

CRIMPING A SINGLE CRUST PIE SHELL

Our easy crimping technique makes a decorative, sturdy edge.

1. Use scissors to trim overhanging dough to uniform ½ inch, then tuck dough under to form thick, even edge on lip of pie plate.

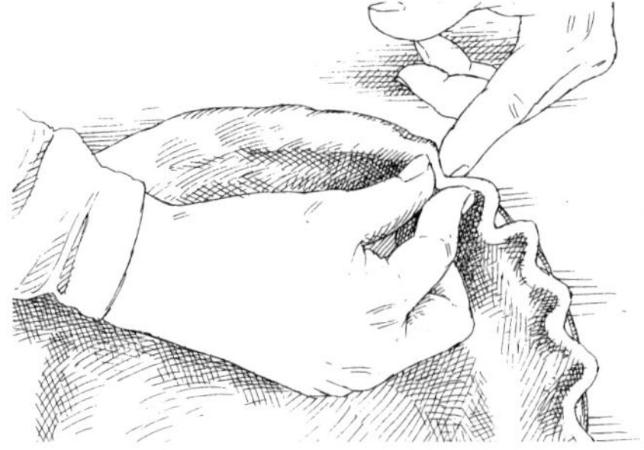

2. Use both hands to pinch dough into ridges, working around perimeter.

variations

Maple Pecan Pie

Maple syrup yields a more custard-like pie. Toasted walnuts can be substituted for the pecans. Use dark amber maple syrup here.

In step 4, decrease butter to 4 tablespoons and pecans to 1½ cups. Substitute ½ cup granulated sugar for brown sugar and 1 cup maple syrup for corn syrup and vanilla.

Buttermilk Pecan Pie with Raisins

Substitute 1½ cups granulated sugar for brown sugar and ⅔ cup buttermilk for corn syrup and vanilla. Reduce pecans to ½ cup and stir into filling with ½ cup finely chopped raisins.

CORN SYRUP QUANDARY

Is Karo corn syrup the same thing as the high-fructose corn syrup (HFCS) ubiquitous in soft drinks and other processed foods? In a word, no. Corn syrup (the most popular brand being Karo, introduced in 1902) is made by adding enzymes to a mixture of cornstarch and water to break the long starch strands into glucose molecules. It's valuable in candy making because it discourages crystallization; it also helps baked goods retain moisture. And because it is less sweet than granulated sugar, corn syrup makes an excellent addition to savory glazes, contributing body and sticking power.

High-fructose corn syrup is a newer product, coming onto the market in the 1960s. It is made by putting regular corn syrup through an additional enzymatic process that converts a portion of the glucose molecules into fructose, boosting its sweetness to a level even higher than that of cane sugar. Because HFCS is considerably less expensive than cane sugar, it is widely used in processed foods, but it is not sold directly to consumers.

GOOD STUFF

REVISITING PUMPKIN PIE

FRANCISCO J. ROBERT, *November/December 2008*

Serving pumpkin pie at Thanksgiving is an exercise in futility. After a rich, filling repast, the last part of the ritual appears, problematic as ever: grainy, canned pumpkin–custard encased in a soggy crust. If pumpkin pie is so important that it wouldn't be a holiday without it, why not make it a first-class dessert? The test kitchen's recipe from 20 years ago was good, but lately we've found it overspiced and dense. I set out to turn this classic holiday dessert into more than an obligatory endnote.

PUMPING UP PUMPKIN FLAVOR

All too often, pumpkin pie does a poor job of showcasing the flavor of its star ingredient. I knew using fresh pumpkin wouldn't help; we've found that very few tasters can distinguish between fresh and canned pumpkin once it's baked in a pie—and cooking a fresh pumpkin is a lot of work. The real problem is that pumpkin, fresh or canned, contains a lot of moisture, which ultimately dilutes the pie's flavor. This point was driven home when I wrapped the contents of a can of pumpkin puree in cheesecloth and left it in a colander to drain overnight. By the next morning, the pumpkin had released copious amounts of intensely flavored liquid.

Adding sweet potatoes to the pie filling gives it surprising depth, and precooking the filling blooms the spices and concentrates flavor.

To maximize that flavor, it made sense to concentrate the pumpkin's liquid rather than just remove it. I took a cue from our 1993 recipe, in which we found cooking the pumpkin on the stovetop to be beneficial. I emptied a can of puree into a saucepan along with some sugar and spices and then cranked up the heat. I whisked in some dairy and eggs and poured the filling into a prebaked pie shell. Cooking the pumpkin not only improved its flavor but the hot filling also allowed the custard to firm up quickly in the oven, preventing it from soaking into the crust and turning it soggy. But I wasn't done: Tasters still complained about an overabundance of spices.

After a few rounds of testing, I singled out just nutmeg, cinnamon, and ginger as essential. Substituting a couple of teaspoons of freshly grated ginger for the dry equivalent imparted a bright, almost fruity flavor to the pie. To intensify the flavor of the ginger and spices, I bloomed them by cooking them along with the pumpkin puree. I also experimented with different sweeteners; in the end, tasters favored a combination of white sugar and a small amount of maple syrup, which added a layer of complexity. But not enough complexity—tasters still craved a more flavorful pie.

On a whim, I borrowed a few roasted sweet potatoes that a colleague was testing for a side dish and mashed them into my pumpkin mixture without telling anyone. Tasters immediately recognized a new and deeper flavor in the pie. I had hit on a secret ingredient! But I didn't really want to take the time to roast the sweet potatoes for this effect. Would it work just as well to microwave them? I tried this, and my tasters liked this pie just as much. Could I streamline the method even further and use canned sweet potatoes? I drained the sugar syrup from a can of candied sweet potatoes (commonly labeled yams) and cooked them with the canned pumpkin. Once again, my tasters loved the pie and never guessed the true source of the flavor.

THE SEARCH FOR A SILKY TEXTURE

With richly flavored filling at hand, it was time to tackle the texture. For a creamy, sliceable, not-too-dense pie, my goal was to eliminate the graininess that plagues most custard. To achieve this, I first played with the type of dairy and quantity of eggs. Whole milk yielded a looser pie than one made with cream, but tasters found the latter too rich. Using equal amounts of whole milk and cream provided balance. But this filling was barely sliceable, and using extra whole eggs to firm it up just made the pie taste too eggy. Since the white contains most of the water in an egg, I replaced a few of the whole eggs with yolks to firm up the custard, settling on a ratio of 3 whole eggs to 2 yolks. I then whisked the milk, cream, and eggs with some vanilla into the cooked pumpkin–sweet potato mixture and passed the filling through a fine-mesh strainer to remove any stringy bits, ensuring a smooth texture.

Most pumpkin pie recipes call for a high oven temperature to expedite cooking time. But baking any custard at high heat has its dangers. Once the temperature of custard rises above 175 degrees, it curdles, turning the filling coarse and grainy. This is exactly what happened when I baked the pie at 425 degrees, the temperature recommended by most recipes. Lowering the temperature to 350 degrees wasn't the solution: I now had a pie that was curdled and overcooked at the outer edges but still underdone in the center. I tried the opposite extreme and baked the pie at 300 degrees, a temperature that would give me a wide margin of safety. The problem was that for the pie to cook through, I needed to leave it in the oven for nearly 2 hours. What if I combined both approaches: a high initial oven temperature for 10 minutes to give the already-warm filling a blast of heat, followed by a gentle 300 degrees for the remainder of the baking time? Not only did this reduce the total baking time to less than an hour, but the dual temperatures produced a creamy pie fully and evenly cooked from edge to center.

Hundreds of pies later, I had a pumpkin pie destined to be a new classic: velvety smooth, packed with pumpkin flavor, and redolent with just enough fragrant spices.

Pumpkin Pie

SERVES 8

Make sure to buy unsweetened canned pumpkin; avoid pumpkin pie mix. If candied sweet potatoes or yams are unavailable, regular canned sweet potatoes or yams can be substituted. When the pie is properly baked, the center 2 inches of the pie should look firm but jiggle slightly. The pie finishes cooking with residual heat; to ensure that the filling sets, let it cool at room temperature and not in the refrigerator. Do not cool this fully baked crust; the crust and filling must both be warm when the filling is added. Serve with whipped cream.

1 recipe Foolproof All-Butter Dough for Single-Crust Pie (page 500)
1 cup heavy cream
1 cup whole milk
3 large eggs plus 2 large yolks
1 teaspoon vanilla extract
1 (15-ounce) can unsweetened pumpkin puree
1 cup drained candied sweet potatoes or yams
¾ cup (5¼ ounces) sugar
¼ cup maple syrup
2 teaspoons grated fresh ginger
1 teaspoon salt
½ teaspoon ground cinnamon
¼ teaspoon ground nutmeg

1. Adjust oven rack to lowest position and heat oven to 425 degrees. Roll dough into 12-inch circle on floured counter. Loosely roll dough around rolling pin and gently unroll it onto 9-inch pie plate, letting excess dough hang over edge. Ease dough into plate by gently lifting edge of dough with your hand while pressing into plate bottom with your other hand. Wrap dough-lined plate loosely in plastic wrap and refrigerate until dough is firm, about 30 minutes.

2. Trim overhang to ½ inch beyond lip of plate. Tuck overhang under itself; folded edge should be flush with edge of plate. Crimp dough evenly around edge of plate using your fingers. Wrap dough-lined plate loosely in plastic and refrigerate until dough is firm, about 15 minutes.

3. Line chilled pie shell with parchment paper or double layer of aluminum foil, covering edges to prevent burning, and fill with pie weights. Bake until pie dough looks dry and is pale in color, about 15 minutes, rotating plate halfway through baking. Remove parchment and weights and continue to bake crust until golden brown, 4 to 7 minutes longer. Transfer plate to wire rack. (Crust must still be warm when filling is added.) Reduce oven temperature to 400 degrees.

4. While pie shell is baking, whisk cream, milk, eggs and yolks, and vanilla together in bowl. Bring pumpkin puree, sweet potatoes, sugar, maple syrup, ginger, salt, cinnamon, and nutmeg to simmer in large saucepan and cook, stirring constantly and mashing sweet potatoes against sides of pot, until thick and shiny, 15 to 20 minutes.

5. Remove saucepan from heat and whisk in cream mixture until fully incorporated. Strain mixture through fine-mesh strainer into bowl, using back of ladle or spatula to press solids through strainer. Whisk mixture, then pour into warm prebaked pie crust.

6. Place pie on rimmed baking sheet and bake for 10 minutes. Reduce oven temperature to 300 degrees and continue to bake until edges of pie are set and center registers 175 degrees, 20 to 35 minutes longer. Let pie cool on wire rack to room temperature, about 3 hours. Serve.

KEY FLAVORING INGREDIENTS

SWEET POTATOES
Sweet potatoes intensify the pie's flavor.

FRESH GINGER
Grated ginger packs more punch than dried ginger.

MAPLE SYRUP
Maple syrup boosts pumpkin's natural sweetness.

KEEPING CUSTARD FROM CURDLING

Many recipes call for baking pumpkin pie at 425 degrees, but this can curdle the delicate custard. Baking at too low a temperature, however, simply takes too long. For a creamy pie that's fully and evenly cooked from edge to center, we give the filling a brief blast of heat at 400 degrees and then finish the pie in a gentle, 300-degree oven.

OVERCOOKED
A pie baked at 425 degrees the whole time curdles and becomes watery and grainy.

SILKY SMOOTH
Starting the pie at 400 degrees and finishing it at 300 degrees allows it to bake without curdling.

COOKING THE FILLING

Simmering the filling for pumpkin pie is an unusual step, but its benefit is threefold. First, cooking the pumpkin and sweet potatoes drives off moisture and concentrates their flavor. Second, cooking the spices along with the pumpkin allows their flavors to bloom. Third, heating the filling allows it to firm up quickly in the oven rather than soak into the pastry and cause the crust to become soggy.

KEY LIME PIE IN MINUTES

STEPHEN SCHMIDT, *March/April 1997*

I will start with a confession. Until I embarked on this article, I had never made a classic key lime pie. By "classic" I mean the kind of key lime pie with a filling that consists solely of four simple ingredients: sweetened condensed milk, egg yolks, and lime juice and zest. These ingredients, when simply mixed together and poured into a pie shell, magically thicken into a filling that sets up stiff enough to slice within a couple of hours. No baking is required (though, as I will tell, I found baking an improvement). While the "magic" of the filling is easily explained, this does not gainsay the ease, convenience, and sheer fun of the recipe.

Why, then, had I never made a condensed milk key lime pie? Because the versions that I had sampled in restaurants had tasted harsh and artificial to me. I had assumed that this unpleasant flavor had something to do with the condensed milk, but once I made a classic key lime pie myself, I understood the true source. Restaurant key lime pies are prepared with bottled, reconstituted lime juice, which tastes terrible.

If, like me, you have judged, and condemned, condensed milk key lime pies on the basis of commercial offerings, I urge you to make one yourself using fresh squeezed juice. You will find the pie an entirely different experience: pungent and refreshing, yet also cool and creamy, a very satisfying dessert indeed.

The standard recipe for condensed milk key lime pie is incredibly short and simple: Beat four egg yolks, add a 14-ounce can of sweetened condensed milk, and then stir in ½ cup of lime juice and a tablespoon of grated lime zest. Pour it all into a graham cracker crust and chill it until firm, about 2 hours. Top the pie with sweetened whipped cream and serve.

It would be lovely if this recipe worked, but I found that it doesn't, at least not to my total satisfaction. Although the filling does set firm enough to yield clean-cut slices, it has a loose, "slurpy" consistency that I do not like. I tried to fix the consistency by beating the yolks until thick, as some recipes direct, but this did not help. Nor did it help to dribble in the lime juice, rather than adding it all at once, as other recipes suggest. I also made the filling with only two yolks and with no yolks at all (such "eggless" versions of the recipe do exist) but this yielded even thinner fillings.

Still, I am glad that I spent a day mixing key lime pie fillings in various ways. While in the heat of experimenting, I inadvertently threw the lime zest into a bowl in which I had already placed the egg yolks. When I whisked up the yolks, they turned green, and the whole filling ended up tinted a lovely shade of pale lime. What a great way to dispense with food coloring!

Having found the mix-and-chill method wanting, I decided to try baking the pie, as many recipes suggest. I used the same ingredients as I had before and simply baked the pie until the filling stiffened slightly, about 15 minutes in a moderate oven. The difference between the baked pie (which was really a custard) and the unbaked pie (which had merely been a clabber) was remarkable. The baked filling was thick, creamy, and unctuous, reminiscent of cream pie. It also tasted more pungent and complex than my raw fillings had, perhaps because the heat of the oven released the flavorful oils in the lime zest.

I had discovered that condensed milk key lime pie, when prepared according to the standard recipe and baked, was a delicious dessert. However, before I settled on the standard recipe, curiosity impelled me to try a couple of other recipes that I had come across in cookbooks. I had two recipes on hand that called for folding stiffly beaten egg whites into the filling: One called for three whites and the other for just one. The three-white pie surprised me. The filling was light and fluffy, as I had expected, but also slightly curdish and rich, reminiscent of cheesecake. However, I do not think that these whites-only versions are key lime pie as most people understand it; they are what might be called "fluffy key lime pies." I also tried a recipe with heavy cream but found that the filling did not stiffen on mixing, which to my mind disqualified it.

One final problem: The crust was too crumbly. I often find crumb crusts a bit too hard, even difficult to cut, and over the years, I have deduced that an excess of butter, which is the glue that holds the crumbs together, is the culprit. With this in mind, I had deliberately prepared the crust with slightly less butter than I usually use. Evidently, though, I had gone too far: A certain minimum amount of butter was essential.

Using fresh lime juice and baking the pie briefly are key to a filling with a satiny, sliceable texture.

I did some cookbook sleuthing and noticed something I had never noticed before. There was a surprising consistency in recipes for crumb crusts. To one package of cracker rectangles, crushed, most cookbook recipes call for either 5 tablespoons or 5⅓ tablespoons of butter. I experimented. I couldn't really tell the difference between crusts made with these two amounts of butter, but 4 tablespoons, the amount I had been using, was definitely too little while 6 tablespoons was definitely too much, making a tough, chewy, almost candy-like crust. There are, of course, other variables to be considered in the making of crumb crusts—underbaking, for example, causes the crusts to soak through—but I now feel that I understand the most important point in the making of this indispensable American dessert component.

Key Lime Pie

SERVES 8

Despite this pie's name, we found that most tasters couldn't tell the difference between pies made with regular supermarket limes (called Persian limes) and those made with true Key limes. Since Persian limes are easier to find and juice, we recommend using them here. This pie's steps diverge from those of other pies: You make the filling first and then prepare the crust. This is because the crust must still be warm when you add the filling.

Pie

4 large egg yolks
4 teaspoons grated lime zest plus ½ cup juice (5 limes)
1 (14-ounce) can sweetened condensed milk
1 recipe Graham Cracker Crust (recipe follows), baked and still warm

Topping (Optional)

1 cup heavy cream, chilled
¼ cup (1 ounce) confectioners' sugar

1. *For the pie:* Whisk egg yolks and lime zest together in medium bowl until mixture has light green tint, about 2 minutes. Whisk in condensed milk until smooth, then whisk in lime juice. Cover mixture and set aside at room temperature until thickened, about 30 minutes.

2. Meanwhile, prepare and bake crust. Transfer pie plate to wire rack. Do not turn off oven. (Crust must still be warm when filling is added.)

3. Pour thickened filling into warm crust. Bake until center is firm but jiggles slightly when shaken, 15 to 20 minutes. Let pie cool slightly on wire rack, about 1 hour, then cover loosely with plastic wrap and refrigerate until filling is chilled and set, about 3 hours.

4. *For the topping, if using:* Once pie is fully chilled, use stand mixer fitted with whisk attachment to whip cream and sugar on medium-low speed until foamy, about 1 minute. Increase speed to high and whip until soft peaks form, 1 to 3 minutes. Spread topping attractively over top of pie and serve.

crust

Graham Cracker Crust

MAKES ENOUGH FOR ONE 9-INCH PIE

We don't recommend using store-bought graham cracker crumbs in this recipe because they are often stale.

9 whole graham crackers, broken into 1-inch pieces
5 tablespoons unsalted butter, melted and cooled
3 tablespoons sugar

1. Adjust oven rack to middle position and heat oven to 325 degrees. Process cracker pieces in food processor to fine, even crumbs, about 30 seconds. Sprinkle melted butter and sugar over crumbs and pulse to incorporate, about 5 pulses.

2. Sprinkle mixture into 9-inch pie plate. Using bottom of dry measuring cup, press crumbs into even layer on bottom and sides of plate. Bake until crust is fragrant and beginning to brown, 13 to 18 minutes, rotating plate halfway through baking; transfer plate to wire rack.

PRESSING IN CRUMBS FOR CRUST

Making a crumb crust is a cinch compared with working with pie pastry, but unless you pack the crust properly, you risk crumbling edges during baking and slicing. Our method ensures a tight, clean edge.

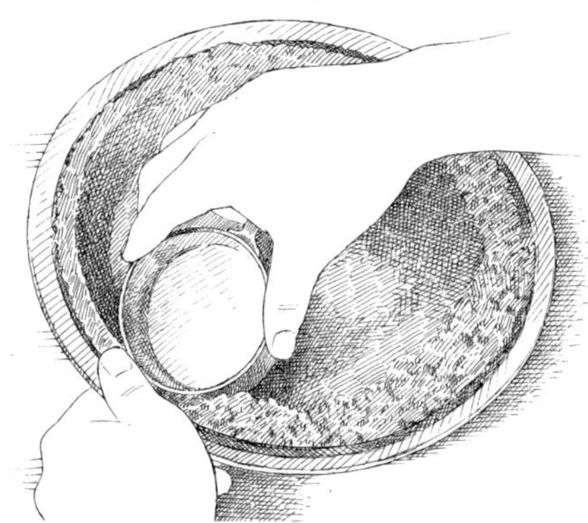

Using bottom and sides of measuring cup, press crumb mixture firmly and evenly across bottom of pie plate. Then pack crumbs against side of pie plate, using your thumb and measuring cup simultaneously.

MAKING KEY LIME PIE

Our Key Lime Pie relies on just a few ingredients and simple steps to produce a brightly flavored dessert.

1. WHISK FILLING AND LET THICKEN Whisk egg yolks and lime zest together until mixture has light green tint, about 2 minutes. Whisk in condensed milk, then whisk in lime juice. Cover mixture and let sit at room temperature until thickened, about 30 minutes.

2. POUR FILLING INTO PIE SHELL AND BAKE Pour thickened filling into warm prebaked pie crust. Bake pie until center is firm but jiggles slightly when shaken, 15 to 20 minutes.

3. CHILL BAKED PIE, THEN TOP Cover pie loosely with plastic wrap and refrigerate until filling is chilled and set, at least 3 hours or up to 24 hours. Before serving, make whipped cream and spread attractively over top of pie.

NO-WEEP LEMON MERINGUE PIE

PAM ANDERSON WITH KAREN TACK, *November/December 1994*

Most everybody loves lemon meringue pie—at least the bottom half of it. The controversial part, for cooks as well as consumers, is the meringue. Of all the people I've talked to about lemon meringue pie, I only know one person who adores the meringue. Most consider it penance to be endured for the pleasure of the filling and crust.

For cooks, meringue falls into the category of unsolved culinary mysteries. On any given day it can shrink, bead, puddle, deflate, burn, sweat, break down, or turn rubbery. Most cookbooks don't even attempt to deal with the problems of meringue. They follow the standard recipe—granulated sugar and cream of tartar beaten slowly into the egg whites—assuming, apparently, that there is no way around the flaws. After making thirtysomething lemon meringue pies, I'm not sure I blame anyone for skirting the issue. For as easy as it was to figure out the perfect lemon filling and pie crust, the meringue remains, finally, only a manageable mystery.

My goals were clear in developing the ultimate lemon meringue pie. For me that meant a pie with a crisp, flaky crust. Of course developing the perfect crust hinged on finding a weepless meringue. Even the crispiest crust will waterlog in a puddle of sugar water. I wanted a rich filling that would balance the airy meringue, without blocking the clear, lemon flavor. And I wanted the filling to be soft, but not runny; firm enough to cut, but not stiff and gelatinous. Most importantly, I wanted a meringue that didn't break down and puddle on the bottom or "tear" on top, not even (as cookbooks and old wives' tales declare it must) on rainy days.

FILLING UP

The filling in lemon meringue pie has gradually evolved over the years from a category of 17th-century English desserts called cheesecakes or curd puddings, according to cookbook author and food historian Stephen Schmidt. For the last century, however, the ingredients have remained constant: sugar, water (or sometimes milk), cornstarch (sometimes part flour), egg yolks, lemon juice (and usually zest), and a little butter. Though I made one old-fashioned curd-style filling, just to confirm that it was too rich for a pie, I mainly worked toward perfecting the cornstarch-thickened lemon filling, varying the proportions to determine each ingredient's role.

A still-hot, cornstarch-stabilized meringue is key to a topping that won't puddle or tear.

To start, I analyzed 50 or so recipes for lemon filling, and developed a formula I thought was representative of current fillings: 1½ cups sugar, 6 tablespoons cornstarch, ¼ teaspoon salt, 2 cups water, three large egg yolks, ½ cup lemon juice, 2 teaspoons lemon zest, and 2 tablespoons unsalted butter. Starting from here, I progressively made small changes. First, I made it once with water and once with milk. As is often the case, I liked a version that, in theory, existed somewhere between the two. I liked the straightforward lemon flavor of the water-based filling, but it was one-dimensional, lacking depth. The milk-based filling was rich, mellow, and delicious, but the lemon flavor was too subdued. So I thought a water-milk combination might be the answer. But to my surprise, the fillings made with this liquid combo came out butterscotch-colored. The flavor was fine; but the color was totally unacceptable. I had two other choices for enriching the pie—eggs and butter. While trying to fix the color, I also wanted to improve the pie's texture. The original was thick and Jell-O-like. I had little faith that butter would solve this problem, so I focused on eggs.

I would have considered egg proportions in the filling sooner, but the meringue stopped me. Knowing how most people feel about meringue, I decided not to overdo it. I settled on a conservative, but respectable three-white meringue. Since I wanted a neat, tidy formula—equal numbers of whites in the meringue and yolks in the filling—I wanted to limit the filling to three yolks. But after making pies with four, five, and six yolks, I realized that the pies tasted progressively richer with each yolk, and this was accomplished without the lemon flavor being compromised. Also, not only did the eggs enrich the pie, unlike the milk, they also reinforced its color.

I discovered that, up to a point, the quantity of sugar had more affect on the pie's texture than on its sweetness. The fillings of pies made with 1½ cups sugar were significantly softer than the pies made with only 1 cup. So by decreasing the sugar and increasing the egg yolks, I was able to cut back on cornstarch and achieve the firm yet tender filling I was looking for.

MERINGUE IT

Long after I had settled on the perfect filling, I was still baffled by the meringue. I couldn't find a consistently perfect meringue—one that was soft and billowy, yet firm enough to stipple nicely. And most importantly, I couldn't find one that wouldn't puddle on the bottom or bead on the top.

Stormy weather during the first two days of testing blew me off course. I attributed all my weeps and tears to the weather. After almost settling for a less-than-perfect meringue, I called food scientist Shirley Corriher, who slowly convinced me that my problems with meringue topping were not weather-related.

According to Corriher, the puddling underneath the meringue is from undercooking. The undercooked whites break down and return to their liquid state. The beading on top of the pie is from overcooking. This near-the-surface overcooking of the meringue causes the proteins in the egg white to coagulate, squeezing out the moisture which then surfaces as tears or beads. Although this double dilemma seemed insurmountable, Corriher offered several possible solutions, two of which worked.

To deal with undercooking, Corriher said the filling must be piping hot. To ensure this, she suggested I make the meringue first, then the filling.

Through the course of all my testing, fillings had been meringued hot. Once each filling was cooked, I covered its surface with plastic wrap to insulate it while making the meringue. Sometimes my meringues puddled; sometimes they didn't. I followed Corriher's suggestion to make the meringue first, but found that this delicate mixture deteriorated by the time the filling was made. So I tried another strategy. I made the filling and covered it as usual, but during the final minute or so of beating the meringue, I returned the filling to a simmer over low heat. I then poured this super-hot filling into the shell, promptly topped and sealed it with meringue, and immediately put the pie in the oven to bake. I followed this procedure with a number of differently prepared meringues and none of them puddled or wept. So, even if meringue beading or tearing is not an issue, you can at least make a lemon meringue pie with a dry bottom just by making sure the filling is really hot.

To solve the problem of overcooking, Corriher suggested that, just like the yolks in the filling, the whites in the meringue needed to be stabilized to make them more heat-tolerant. Corriher said that cornstarch, the yolk stabilizer in the filling, could also be used to strengthen the whites in the meringue. Apparently a food stylists' trick, this is done by mixing cornstarch and water and cooking it until thick. Then this paste is gradually beaten into soft-peak meringue until firm peaks form.

I found that the cornstarch mixture did not affect the flavor or texture of the meringue. After a bit more tinkering—mostly with oven time and temperature—I finally got the cornstarch-stabilized meringue to produce a virtually tearless pie, even on a hot, humid day.

Lemon Meringue Pie

SERVES 8

Make the pie crust, let it cool, and then begin work on the filling. As soon as the filling is made, press a piece of lightly greased parchment paper against the surface and then start working on the meringue topping. You want to add warm filling to the cooled pie crust and then apply the meringue topping and quickly get the pie into the oven.

1 recipe Foolproof All-Butter Dough for Single-Crust Pie (page 500)

Filling

1½ cups water
1 cup (7 ounces) sugar
¼ cup (1 ounce) cornstarch
⅛ teaspoon salt
6 large egg yolks
1 tablespoon grated lemon zest plus ½ cup juice (3 lemons)
2 tablespoons unsalted butter, cut into 2 pieces

Meringue

⅓ cup water
1 tablespoon cornstarch
4 large egg whites
½ teaspoon vanilla extract
¼ teaspoon cream of tartar
½ cup (3½ ounces) sugar

1. Adjust oven rack to lowest position and heat oven to 425 degrees. Roll dough into 12-inch circle on floured counter. Loosely roll dough around rolling pin and gently unroll it onto 9-inch pie plate, letting excess dough hang over edge. Ease dough into plate by gently lifting edge of dough with your hand while pressing into plate bottom with your other hand. Wrap dough-lined plate loosely in plastic wrap and refrigerate until dough is firm, about 30 minutes.

2. Trim overhang to ½ inch beyond lip of plate. Tuck overhang under itself; folded edge should be flush with edge of plate. Crimp dough evenly around edge of plate using your fingers. Wrap dough-lined plate loosely in plastic and refrigerate until dough is firm, about 15 minutes.

3. Line chilled pie shell with parchment paper or double layer of aluminum foil, covering edges to prevent burning, and fill with pie weights. Bake until pie dough looks dry and is light in color, 25 to 30 minutes, rotating plate halfway through baking. Remove parchment and weights and continue to bake crust until deep golden brown, 10 to 12 minutes longer. Transfer plate to wire rack. Let crust cool to room temperature.

4. ***For the filling:*** Adjust oven rack to middle position and reduce temperature to 325 degrees. Bring water, sugar, cornstarch, and salt to simmer in large saucepan over medium heat, whisking constantly. When mixture starts to turn translucent, whisk in egg yolks, two at a time. Whisk in lemon zest and juice and butter. Return mixture to brief simmer, then remove from heat. Lay sheet of lightly greased parchment paper directly on surface of filling to keep warm and prevent skin from forming.

5. ***For the meringue:*** Bring water and cornstarch to simmer in small saucepan over medium-high heat and cook, whisking occasionally, until thickened and translucent, 1 to 2 minutes. Remove from heat and let cool slightly.

6. Using stand mixer fitted with whisk attachment, whip egg whites, vanilla, and cream of tartar on medium-low speed until foamy, about 1 minute. Increase speed to medium-high and beat in sugar, 1 tablespoon at a time, until incorporated and mixture forms soft, billowy mounds. Add cornstarch mixture, 1 tablespoon at a time, and continue to beat to glossy, stiff peaks, 2 to 3 minutes.

7. Meanwhile, remove plastic from filling and return to very low heat during last minute or so of beating meringue (to ensure filling is warm).

8. Pour warm filling into cooled prebaked pie crust. Using rubber spatula, immediately distribute meringue evenly around edge and then center of pie, attaching meringue to pie crust to prevent shrinking. Using back of spoon, create attractive swirls and peaks in meringue. Bake until meringue is light golden brown, about 20 minutes. Let pie cool on wire rack until filling has set, about 2 hours. Serve.

THE MAGIC OF PUDDING CAKE

STEPHEN SCHMIDT, *January/February 1995*

Pudding cakes are basically egg custards, but with two clever improvements. Unlike ordinary egg custards, pudding cakes contain a little flour and some beaten egg whites. During baking, the beaten egg whites float to the top, forming a spongy, cake-like cap. Meanwhile, the remainder of the batter settles to the bottom to make a pudding-like layer.

Based on recipes that date back to colonial times, pudding cakes have existed in their present form for at least 150 years. Lemon and orange are the classic flavors, although other versions also appear fairly regularly. Historic and modern formulas are surprisingly similar. One cookbook that I consulted presented a version supposedly made in Shaker kitchens. Sure enough, the same recipe turned up in a Shaker cookbook that I own—but it also appeared, verbatim, in the 1975 edition of *Joy of Cooking*.

Using an extra egg white and baking in a water bath ensure that our pudding cakes have two distinct layers.

In preparing this article, I baked some 15 pudding cakes. I immediately noticed that those made with lemon or orange juice came out especially well, while those flavored in other ways tended to have flimsy, fast-dissolving tops and rubbery, dense bottoms. I eventually deduced that it was the acidity of the citrus juices that made the difference. Because the juice lightly clabbered the milk-based batter, causing it to thicken, the frothy upper layer became stiffer and more stable and thus was better able to puff. At the same time, the acidic juice undercut the thickening power of the flour, making for a more tender custard. To shore up the cake part a bit more, I tried adding an extra egg white, which worked beautifully.

As a lover of rich desserts, I could not keep myself from trying to make pudding cakes with extra butter and with cream instead of milk. I discovered, however, that the added fat caused the whipped egg whites to collapse, making for a thin top. In any case, the extra richness didn't really impr ove the desserts—in fact, it was barely discernible.

Finally, while I find baking things in a bain-marie, or water bath, just as much of a nuisance as the next person, I'm afraid that there is no way to do without it here. Because water cannot get hotter than its boiling point, it insulates the custard and prevents it from curdling. I tried baking a pudding cake without the water bath and got scrambled eggs.

Be sure to let the pudding cakes stand in the water bath for 10 minutes after removing them from the oven. Like other custards, pudding cakes need to finish cooking outside the oven; if left in the oven long enough to make their centers completely firm, pudding cakes may become rubbery and overcooked around the edges.

My pudding cakes were perfect, with two distinct layers, and I was even happier to find that my recipe could just as easily work when divided into individual ramekins or baked in a single cake pan.

WHY USE A WATER BATH?

Our Lemon Pudding Cake is baked in a water bath. Why? Using a water bath helps to protect delicate custards from cooking too quickly and drying out. The water insulates the pudding because it cannot exceed 212 degrees before converting to steam; the air temperature of the oven, on the other hand, is much higher than this. The water also helps keep the interior of the oven humid, further preventing the custard from drying out.

Lemon Pudding Cake

SERVES 6

This pudding cake can be made in six 6-ounce ramekins; a 9-inch round cake pan; or an 8-inch square cake pan. All require the same baking time.

2 tablespoons unsalted butter, softened, plus extra for pan(s)
½ cup plus 2 tablespoons (4⅓ ounces) sugar
⅛ teaspoon salt
3 large eggs, separated, plus 1 large white, room temperature
3 tablespoons all-purpose flour
2 teaspoons lemon zest plus ¼ cup juice (2 lemons)
1 cup whole milk

1. Adjust oven rack to middle position and heat oven to 325 degrees. Lightly butter pan or ramekins of choice. Lay folded dish towel in bottom of roasting pan and set pan or ramekins inside. Bring kettle of water to boil.
2. Meanwhile, in bowl mash sugar, salt, and butter together with back of wooden spoon until crumbly. Beat in egg yolks, then flour, mixing until smooth. Slowly beat in lemon zest and juice, then stir in milk.
3. Using stand mixer fitted with whisk attachment, whip egg whites on medium-low speed until foamy, about 1 minute. Increase speed to medium-high and whip until stiff peaks form, 3 to 4 minutes. Gently whisk whites into batter just until no large lumps remain.
4. Immediately ladle (don't pour) batter into pan or ramekins. Set baking pan on oven rack. Pour enough boiling water into roasting pan to come halfway up sides of baking pan or ramekins. Bake until pudding cake center is set and springs back when gently touched, about 25 minutes. Remove roasting pan from oven and let pan or ramekins continue to stand in water bath for 10 minutes. Pudding cakes can be served warm, at room temperature, or chilled.

OLIVE OIL CAKE

ANDREA GEARY, *May/June 2017*

New England, where I've lived for most of my life, is not known for its vast and fruitful olive groves. Maybe that's why I only recently learned about olive oil cake, which is commonplace in most traditional olive-producing regions of the world.

That said, I've made plenty of cakes with vegetable oil. Though most people associate cake with butter, oil is a good choice for snack cakes and quick breads; it provides moisture, tenderness, and richness without calling attention to itself. It also makes the mixing process simpler. But extra-virgin olive oil, the type often called for in recipes for olive oil cake, can be noticeably grassy, peppery, and even a little bitter. That's welcome in a salad, but in a cake?

Whipped whole eggs and ¾ cup of olive oil give this cake just enough structure and richness.

I happily discovered that the slightly savory notes of olive oil can, in fact, lend appealing complexity to a cake. But the recipes I tried varied. Some had a lot of oil and an assertive flavor and rich, dense crumb; others included a modest amount of oil and were light and spongy, with only a faint olive oil flavor. Still others had so many additional ingredients—apples, spices, citrus—that the oil's flavor was obscured. I suspect that such recipes originated not to showcase olive oil but because people wanted cake, they needed fat to make it, and the local olive oil was the fat they had on hand. But if I was going to use extra-virgin olive oil in my cake, I wanted to be able to taste it, at least a bit. I didn't want sponge-cake austerity or dense decadence but something in between. I wanted a cake that offered some intrigue but was at the same time simple.

CRUMB QUANDARY

One of the most attractive aspects of making a cake with oil rather than butter is the way it expedites the mixing process: There's no waiting for butter to come to room temperature and then beating it with sugar before you even start to add the rest of the ingredients. With many oil-based cakes, you simply whisk the dry ingredients in one bowl, whisk the wet ingredients in another, and then combine the contents of the two bowls.

So that's where I started. The dry ingredients were all-purpose flour, baking powder, and salt, and the wet ingredients were eggs, milk, and a good-quality supermarket olive oil, plus the sugar. The batter was ready to go into the oven in 5 minutes flat, and the cake came out just 40 minutes later.

This first attempt was easy to make but not easy to love. The crumb was dry and coarse, and I could detect the olive oil flavor only if I thought about it really, really hard. As for the appearance, I was okay with simplicity, but this cake looked uninvitingly plain. What I really wanted was the kind of even, fine crumb that the best butter cakes have. The problem? That texture is largely due to their being made with butter.

In a butter cake, air is whipped into the butter before it's mixed with the other ingredients. In the heat of the oven, the baking powder creates carbon dioxide, which inflates those bubbles a bit more. Those tiny bubbles are what make a butter cake fluffy and fine-textured.

But I wasn't without options for producing a similar effect in my oil cake. Although most oil cakes use the "mix wet, mix dry, and combine" method, chiffon cake is an oil cake that's mixed a bit differently. Its light and fluffy texture is achieved by whipping egg whites with some sugar to form a foam, which you then fold into the batter. Might that approach work for my olive oil cake?

I applied the chiffon method to my recipe and, at the same time, implemented a couple of ingredient adjustments: I increased the eggs from two to three for better lift and the olive oil from ½ cup to ¾ cup for more richness and moisture and a more pronounced flavor. The batter was promisingly airy and mousse-like. The cake rose impressively in the oven—but it fell when it cooled. And when I cut it open, there was a line of dense, collapsed cake in the middle. The batter was too airy to support all the fat. But I was happy with the more pronounced olive oil flavor, so I was reluctant to back down. Providing more support by switching to a tube pan, the vessel of choice for chiffon cakes, could help, but frankly I didn't want my olive oil cake to be mistaken for chiffon. Instead, I'd adjust the mixing method.

GOING ALL IN

If whipped egg whites were too airy, maybe whipping yolks, which aren't as good at holding air, would be better. I did a quick test, but the cake came out dense and squat. Whipping whole eggs, I hoped, would be the solution. I put all three eggs, both whites and yolks, in the mixer bowl with the sugar and whipped the mixture for about 4 minutes, until it was pale and airy. I added the rest of the ingredients, including a tiny bit of lemon zest to accentuate the fruitiness of the olive oil. After pouring the batter into the cake pan, I sprinkled the top liberally with granulated sugar to lend some visual appeal and textural contrast.

The whipped whole eggs did indeed provide just the right amount of lift, creating a crumb that was fine but not dense and light but not spongy. The sugar on top had coalesced into an attractively crackly crust that complemented the cake's plush texture, and the lemon zest supported the olive oil flavor without overwhelming it.

And there's one more advantage to my olive oil cake: Because it's made with liquid fat instead of solid, it will keep longer than its butter-based counterparts. It can be stored at room temperature for up to three days—in the unlikely event that it doesn't get eaten right away.

Olive Oil Cake

SERVES 8 TO 10

For the best flavor, use a fresh, high-quality extra-virgin olive oil. If your springform pan is prone to leaking, place a rimmed baking sheet on the oven floor to catch any drips. The cake will puff during baking, but settle as it cools. Leftover cake can be wrapped in plastic wrap and stored at room temperature for up to three days.

1¾ cups (8¾ ounces) all-purpose flour
1 teaspoon baking powder
¾ teaspoon salt
3 large eggs
1¼ cups (8¾ ounces) plus 2 tablespoons sugar
¼ teaspoon grated lemon zest
¾ cup extra-virgin olive oil
¾ cup milk

1. Adjust oven rack to middle position and heat oven to 350 degrees. Grease 9-inch springform pan. Whisk flour, baking powder, and salt together in bowl.
2. Using stand mixer fitted with whisk attachment, whip eggs on medium speed until foamy, about 1 minute. Add 1¼ cups sugar and lemon zest, increase speed to high, and whip until mixture is fluffy and pale yellow, about 3 minutes. Reduce speed to medium and, with mixer running, slowly pour in oil. Mix until oil is fully incorporated, about 1 minute. Add half of flour mixture and mix on low speed until incorporated, about 1 minute, scraping down bowl as needed. Add milk and mix until combined, about 30 seconds. Add remaining flour mixture and mix until just incorporated, about 1 minute, scraping down bowl as needed.
3. Transfer batter to prepared pan; sprinkle remaining 2 tablespoons sugar over entire surface. Bake until cake is deep golden brown and toothpick inserted in center comes out with few crumbs attached, 40 to 45 minutes, rotating pan halfway through baking. Transfer pan to wire rack and let cool for 15 minutes. Remove side of pan and let cake cool completely, about 1½ hours. Cut into wedges and serve.

A REAL KEEPER

Unlike butter cakes, which start to taste dry just a day after baking, oil-based cakes and tea breads can taste moist for several days. This is an illusion, since over time the starches in both types of cakes retrograde, or stale and harden into a crystalline structure, and this structure traps water within the crystals. A cake made with butter, which is solid at room temperature, will seem drier. But oil, which is liquid at room temperature, acts to retard retrogradation, causing even a days-old cake to seem moist even though it's actually not.

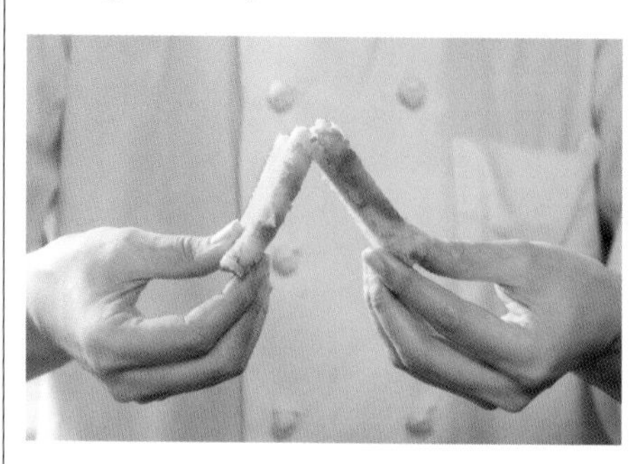

BUTTER CAKE
Dry and crumbly the day after it's baked

OIL CAKE
Seems moist and tender three days after baking

AERATING CAKE WITH EGGS

While butter cakes get their lift from air that's whipped into the butter, our olive oil cake relies on eggs. Whipped whites might be the first thing to come to mind, but you can also whip just yolks or whole eggs. We tried all three in our cake. Whipped whites made it too airy, and our cake collapsed somewhat. Whipped yolks made a squat, dense cake. Whipping whole eggs was the perfect compromise. But why?

The proteins in egg whites are better at unfurling and creating a foam than the proteins in egg yolks are, so whipped whites will be more voluminous than whipped whole eggs and certainly more voluminous than whipped yolks. But the oil in this batter is a factor, too. Oil molecules are able to displace some egg white proteins in whipped whites, which weakens the bubbles. Yolks offer some protection against this; their emulsifiers help keep the oil from interfering with the structure. Thus, whipped whole eggs are the perfect compromise because they provide some lift from the whites as well as a more stable structure from the yolks.

JUST WHITES
Ultrafluffy egg whites made a cake that was too airy and collapsed.

JUST YOLKS
Unable to hold much air, egg yolks made a squat, dense cake.

WHOLE EGGS
Whipping whole eggs provided structure and just enough lift.

SECRETS OF CHIFFON CAKE

STEPHEN SCHMIDT, *May/June 1996*

Like the Hollywood stars of the 1920s who were the first to taste Harry Baker's secret-recipe cakes, I was delighted by the uniquely light yet full richness and deep flavor of this American invention, which came to be known as the chiffon cake. To perfect this 20th-century classic, I decided to go back to Betty Crocker's version, as first put before the public by General Mills in 1948. If the original seemed in need of fixing, I would then proceed to consult the countless variations, tinkerings, and revisions that have accumulated over the years.

With the exception of the chocolate variation, all of Betty Crocker's original chiffon cakes call for 2¼ cups sifted cake flour (which translates to about 1⅔ cups measured by dip-and-sweep), 1½ cups sugar, 1 tablespoon baking powder, 1 teaspoon salt, ½ cup oil, five egg yolks, ¾ cup water or other liquid, 1 cup egg whites (seven to eight large), and ½ teaspoon cream of tartar.

I made a plain, an orange, and a walnut chiffon cake according to the original formula and found that I had three complaints. The cakes were a bit dry—cottony and fluffy rather than moist and foamy, the way I thought chiffon cakes should be—and they seemed to lack flavor, punch, pizzazz. In addition, the cakes rose a bit too high for the pan, a consequence of the downsizing of tube pans, from 18 to 16 cups, that took place around 1970.

Since fat increases perceived moistness and also transmits flavor, I thought that adding more oil might help, but it did not. An orange chiffon cake made with an additional ¼ cup of oil (up from ½ cup) turned out not only dry and flavorless but also greasy and heavy, an outcome that was as unexpected as it was disappointing.

Most of the cookbook authors whom I consulted wisely stuck with Betty's ½ cup of oil. The changes they had made usually involved the eggs. Predictably, many contemporary recipes called for reducing or eliminating the egg yolks, the idea being to produce a low-cholesterol or cholesterol-free cake. I could not fathom the health advantages of cutting back the yolks from six to two or three, so I didn't bother trying the recipes. (Assuming that the cake serves 12, the savings per person is only one-quarter to one-third yolk, around a teaspoon.)

However, the idea of using only egg whites greatly intrigued me because I thought that the result might be a sort of angel chiffon cake, easier than true angel food cake to make and, I dared hope, perhaps even more delectable. But 11 flops later, I reluctantly concluded that egg white chiffon cakes, no matter how they are made, are tough, wet, bouncy, low-rising disasters. Beware such recipes.

For a moist, tender cake that still has enough structure, decrease the flour, add extra egg yolks, and beat only some of the egg whites.

Writers more interested in taste than in health tended to increase the egg content of their chiffon cakes, particularly the whites. These recipes proved successful, but the cakes, even though they were lighter and richer than Betty Crocker's original, still struck me as dry.

I instinctively felt that adding more liquid would be a poor idea, but at this point I felt I had no choice but to try. Unfortunately, experimentation proved my instincts right. Increasing the water from ¾ cup to 1 cup made the texture gummy and heavy—and the cake still managed to taste dry.

There was now only one ingredient left to play with, the flour, and the thought of touching this one terrified me. Since the problem was dryness, the flour obviously had to be decreased, but I knew from my experience with other sponge-type cakes that decreasing the flour could have very messy consequences. I might end up with a rubbery sponge (à la my egg white chiffon experiments) or, worse, with a demonic soufflé that heaved plops of batter onto the floor of my oven.

Whenever a sponge-type cake decides to collapse or explode, the culprit is the same: a lack of structure. Since eggs as well as flour provide structure, I reasoned that I could compensate for a decrease in flour by adding an extra egg yolk.

I made an orange chiffon cake using the Betty Crocker formula but decreasing the flour by ⅓ cup and increasing the yolks from five to six. The effect was magical. Instead of being fluffy, cottony, and crumbly, the cake was wonderfully moist and so tremblingly tender that slices flopped over at the middle if cut too thin. And the moistness transmitted all of the taste that had been lacking in my first experiments.

The cake, however, was not quite perfect. Evidently the structure was borderline, and so the cake rose very high, spilling over onto the lip of the pan. This made it difficult to cut the cake free from the pan without tearing the top crust. Furthermore, because its top was humped, the cake did not sit flat when turned upside down onto a serving plate. I figured that removing an egg white would help to shrink the cake, but I feared that it might also undercut the structure to the point where the cake wouldn't rise at all. Nonetheless, I gave the idea a try. The resulting cake was lovely coming out of the oven, risen just to the top of the pan and perfectly flat—but its perfection was illusory. I hung the cake upside down to cool and started to clean up the kitchen when I heard a soft plop: My cake had fallen out of the pan.

Once I had taken a few nibbles of the mess, my fears were confirmed. The cake was pasty and overly moist. There was simply not enough structure to hold it together.

It had to have that egg white. But perhaps, I thought, using an extra egg yolk in place of that white would save the structure but prevent the excess puffiness. Unfortunately, when I tried this formula, my test cake bulged almost as much as the one I had made with five yolks and eight whites, though it didn't fall out of the pan, which meant that it had sufficient structure.

At this point a chiffon cake recipe that I had seen in Carole Walter's *Great Cakes* (1991) came to mind. Rather than whipping all the egg whites, Walter mixed some of them, unbeaten, into the dry ingredients along with the yolks, water, and oil. Thus she incorporated less air into the batter, which should, I reasoned, make for a smaller cake. I tried Walter's technique using seven eggs, two of them added whole to the batter and five of them separated with the whites beaten. Eureka! At last I had the perfect chiffon cake: moist, tender, flavorful, and just the right size for my pan.

In the original recipes for chiffon cake published by General Mills, the directions for beating the egg whites read, "WHIP until whites form *very stiff* peaks. They should be much stiffer than for angel food or meringue. DO NOT UNDERBEAT."

These instructions, with their anxiety-inducing capitalized words and italics, are well taken. If the whites are not very stiff, the cake will not rise properly, and the bottom will be heavy, dense, wet, and custard-like. Better to overbeat than underbeat. After all, if you overbeat the egg whites and they end up dry and "blocky," you can simply smudge and smear the recalcitrant blobs with the flat side of the spatula to break up the clumps.

Chiffon Cake

SERVES 12

Serve this cake as is or dust with confectioners' sugar.

1½ cups (10½ ounces) sugar
1⅓ cups (5⅓ ounces) cake flour
2 teaspoons baking powder
½ teaspoon salt
7 large eggs (2 whole, 5 separated), room temperature
¾ cup water
½ cup vegetable oil
1 tablespoon vanilla extract
½ teaspoon almond extract
½ teaspoon cream of tartar

1. Adjust oven rack to lower-middle position and heat oven to 325 degrees. Line 16-cup tube pan with parchment paper but do not grease. Whisk sugar, flour, baking powder, and salt together in large bowl. Whisk in whole eggs and yolks, water, oil, vanilla, and almond extract until batter is just smooth.
2. Using stand mixer fitted with whisk attachment, whip egg whites and cream of tartar on medium-low speed until foamy, about 1 minute. Increase speed to medium-high and whip until stiff peaks form, 3 to 4 minutes. Using large rubber spatula, fold whites into batter, smearing any stubborn pockets of egg white against side of bowl.
3. Transfer batter to prepared pan and smooth top with rubber spatula. Gently tap pan on counter to settle batter. Bake until skewer inserted in center comes out clean, 55 minutes to 1 hour 5 minutes, rotating pan halfway through baking.
4. If cake has prongs around rim for elevating cake, invert pan on them. If not, invert pan over neck of bottle or funnel so that air can circulate all around it. Let cake cool completely in pan, 2 to 3 hours.
5. Run thin knife around edge of pan to loosen cake, then gently tap pan upside down on counter to release cake. Peel off parchment and turn cake right side up onto platter. Serve. (Cake can be stored at room temperature for up to 2 days or refrigerated for up to 4 days.)

variations

Lemon Chiffon Cake

Substitute ½ teaspoon baking soda for baking powder. Reduce water to ⅔ cup, reduce vanilla to 1 teaspoon, and omit almond extract. Add 3 tablespoons grated lemon zest plus 2 tablespoons juice (3 lemons) to batter with vanilla.

Orange Chiffon Cake

Substitute 2 tablespoons grated orange zest plus ¾ cup juice (2 oranges) for water. Reduce vanilla to 1 teaspoon and omit almond extract.

Mocha-Nut Chiffon Cake

Substitute ¾ cup brewed espresso or strong coffee for water and omit almond extract. Add ½ cup finely chopped toasted walnuts and 1 ounce unsweetened grated chocolate to batter before folding in whites.

LINING A TUBE PAN WITH PARCHMENT

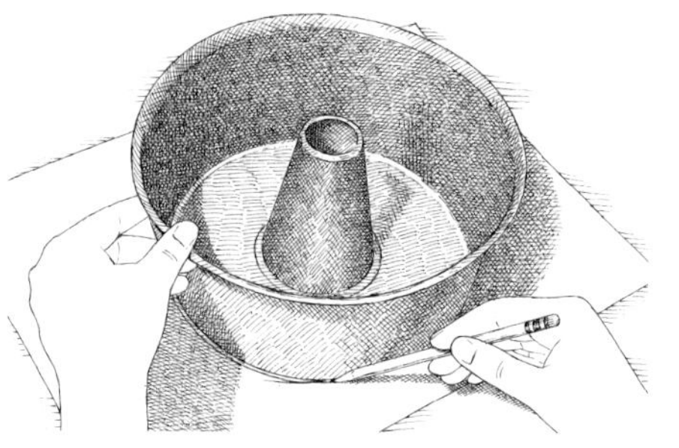

1. Starting with square of parchment larger than tube pan, place pan right side up on paper and trace around outside with pencil.

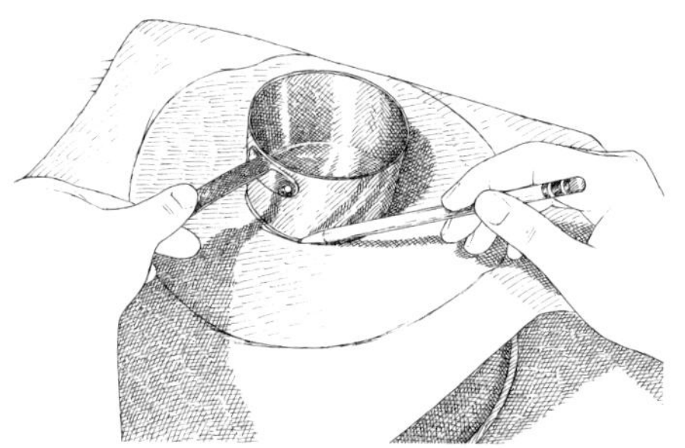

2. Turn pan upside down, place parchment on top of pan, and trace circle around measuring cup that fits opening of center hole. Cut out circles, folding parchment as needed.

SIMPLIFYING LEMON POUND CAKE

RAQUEL PELZEL, *March/April 2002*

Making a wedding cake is hard. Making a multilayered Dobos torte out of génoise sponge cake and buttercream is daunting. But lemon pound cake? Well, that's easy, isn't it? After all, it's made only of eggs, butter, sugar, flour, and lemon mixed together and baked in a loaf pan. But if it's so easy, why do pound cakes often turn out spongy, rubbery, heavy, and dry rather than fine-crumbed, rich, moist, and buttery? In addition, most pound cake recipes call for creaming the batter, a tricky method that demands the ingredients be at just the right temperature to achieve a silken cake batter. So my goal was twofold: Produce a superior pound cake while making the process as simple and foolproof as possible.

I started with a pound cake recipe developed in the *Cook's* test kitchen in 1994 that was known for being excellent in its results but finicky in its preparation. The cake was top-notch, with a submissive crumb and a golden, buttery interior. In fact, it was everything I wanted from a pound cake except for one thing—the preparation method was anything but foolproof. Made in the traditional style of creaming the butter and sugar until fluffy and pale, the method was so exacting that even the smallest diversion sent the batter over the edge into a curdled abyss. To achieve perfection, the ingredients had to be at precisely 67 degrees, the butter and sugar beaten together for exactly 5 minutes to aerate, and the eggs drizzled into the batter over a period of 3 to 5 minutes. All of these precautions were advised to eliminate the danger of "breaking" the batter (a pound cake has so many eggs that keeping them in emulsion can be tricky when using the creaming method), which can make the crust look mottled and leave the cake's interior dense and tough.

MACHINE AGE

I turned to other cake recipes for ideas. First I tried cutting softened butter into flour using a stand mixer. After the butter and flour resembled knobby crumbs, I added some of the eggs, beat the mixture until cohesive, then added the rest of the eggs and beat the batter further until thick, fluffy, and lush. We often favor this method for cakes because it produces a velvety texture and a superfine crumb. Although the pound cake batter assembled this way looked great, the baked cake was too open-grained and tender, more like a yellow cake than a pound cake.

Next I tried melting the butter, a method often used in making quick breads. The liquids are combined and the dry ingredients then mixed into the wet by hand. This method was quick and easy. Melting the butter eliminated all of the temperature issues associated with creaming. Best of all, the batter could be pulled together and put into the oven in 5 minutes.

Melted butter, baking powder, and the food processor make our lemon pound cake absolutely foolproof.

With a tight grain, a perfect swell and split in its center, and a nice, browned exterior, this cake showed promise. When I made it a second time, however, it sagged in the center. Additional tests yielded varying results. The problem may have been in the mixing method; perhaps inconsistent mixing produced inconsistent cakes. The solution? A food processor would do a better job of emulsification and also standardize the process. I added the eggs, sugar, and vanilla to the food processor bowl, combining them enough to integrate the sugar and eggs, and then I drizzled the melted butter in through the feed tube. I transferred the watery base to a large bowl, added lemon zest, and sifted in cake flour and salt, whisking these ingredients in by hand.

The method was a success. The cake had a split dome that afforded a peek inside at the marvelously yellow color of its interior. Just to be sure, I made the cake again and again, with the same results. Recognizing that some home cooks don't have a food processor, I tried the method in a blender. Although the cake was a bit more dense, the differences were so minimal that I recommend either approach. With my method determined, I focused on the cake's texture and flavor.

A MODERN POUND CAKE

My objective was to make the cake just a bit lighter, but not so light as to resemble a yellow cake. (Pound cakes are by definition heavier and more dense than layer cakes.) When I tested cake flour against all-purpose, the former was superior, making the cake more tender. But the cake still needed more lift and less sponginess.

I was at this point using two sticks of melted butter. Thinking that more butter might improve the texture, I increased the amount, but the cake turned out greasy. Next I turned to the eggs. The original *Cook's* recipe called for three eggs plus three yolks, so I tried four whole eggs instead (an equivalent liquid amount), thinking that the additional white might add some lift. The cake was better but still on the dense side. Without success, I tried adding cream (this cake turned out heavy) and reducing the flour (this one was greasy). Four whole eggs had gotten me close, but the texture was still not ideal.

In the oldest of recipes (from the 1700s), eggs were the only ingredient in pound cake that gave it lift. In the 1850s, however, many cooks began adding the new wonder ingredient—baking powder—to achieve a lighter texture and a higher rise. Although traditionalists might scoff at the addition of chemical leavening, I was willing to give it a try. With just 1 teaspoon, I instilled enough breath into the cake to produce a consistent, perfect crumb. Now that I had simplified the method and achieved the right texture, it was time to concentrate on lemon flavor.

LEMON LAWS

In all of my prior tests, I had experienced difficulty keeping the lemon zest afloat. In cake after cake, the zest came together in large yellow clumps. The solution turned out to be simple. When the lemon zest was pulsed with the sugar before the eggs were added to the food processor bowl, the baked cake came out evenly dotted throughout with perfect specks of zest. I also added lemon juice to the batter to boost flavor.

While some prefer their lemon pound cake plain, or with only a simple shower of confectioners' sugar, I like a blast of lemon flavor. A quick glaze—made by bringing sugar and lemon juice to a boil—tasted great in the pan but failed to migrate into the nooks and crannies of the cake's crumb when simply brushed on top. I used an old trick to help the glaze on its way, poking small perforations through the cake's top crust and sides with a toothpick. The glaze now penetrated to the interior of the cake, distributing plenty of lemon flavor. Finally, I had a quick, foolproof recipe that delivered a great crumb and plenty of lemon flavor. Pound for pound, this cake's a winner.

Lemon Pound Cake

SERVES 8

You can use a blender instead of a food processor to mix the batter. To add the butter, remove the center cap of the lid so the butter can be drizzled into the whirling blender with minimal splattering. This batter looks almost like a thick pancake batter and is very fluid. This recipe calls for a loaf pan that measures 8½ by 4½ inches; if you use a 9 by 5-inch loaf pan, start checking for doneness 5 minutes earlier than advised in the recipe.

Cake

1½ cups (6 ounces) cake flour
1 teaspoon baking powder
½ teaspoon salt
16 tablespoons unsalted butter
1¼ cups (8¾ ounces) sugar
2 tablespoons grated lemon zest plus 2 teaspoons juice (2 lemons)
4 large eggs, room temperature
1½ teaspoons vanilla extract

Lemon Glaze

½ cup (3½ ounces) sugar
¼ cup lemon juice (2 lemons)

1. *For the cake:* Adjust oven rack to middle position and heat oven to 350 degrees. Grease and flour 8½ by 4½-inch loaf pan. In medium bowl, whisk together flour, baking powder, and salt; set aside.

2. Melt butter in small saucepan over medium heat. Whisk melted butter thoroughly to reincorporate any separated milk solids. Pulse sugar and lemon zest in food processor until combined, about 5 pulses. Add lemon juice, eggs, and vanilla and process until combined, about 5 seconds. With processor running, add melted butter in steady stream (this should take about 20 seconds). Transfer mixture to large bowl. Sift flour mixture over sugar mixture in 3 steps, whisking gently after each addition until just combined.

3. Pour batter into prepared pan and smooth top with rubber spatula. Bake for 15 minutes; reduce oven temperature to 325 degrees and continue baking until deep golden brown and toothpick inserted in center comes out clean, about 35 minutes, rotating pan halfway through baking. Let cake cool in pan for 10 minutes, then turn out onto wire rack. Poke cake's top and sides with toothpick. Let cake cool completely, at least 1 hour. (Cooled cake can be wrapped tightly in plastic wrap and stored at room temperature for up to 5 days.)

4. *For the lemon glaze:* While cake is cooling, bring sugar and lemon juice to boil in small saucepan, stirring occasionally to dissolve sugar. Reduce heat to low and simmer until thickened slightly, about 2 minutes. Brush top and sides of cooled cake with glaze and let glaze cool completely before serving.

GLAZING POUND CAKE

To help the glaze migrate into the cake for a true blast of lemon flavor, we poke small holes in the baked cake with a toothpick.

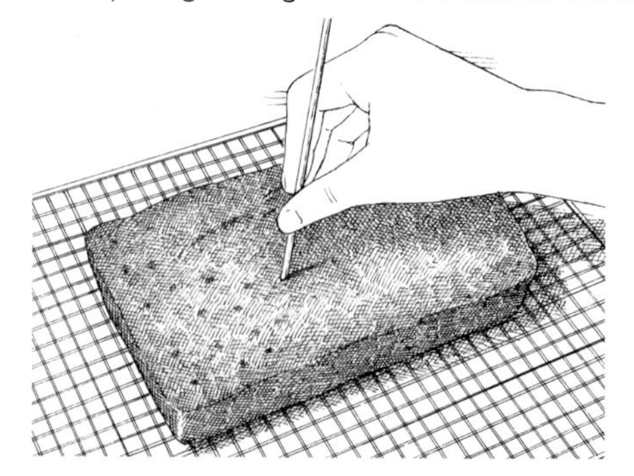

1. After removing cake from pan, poke entire top with toothpick.

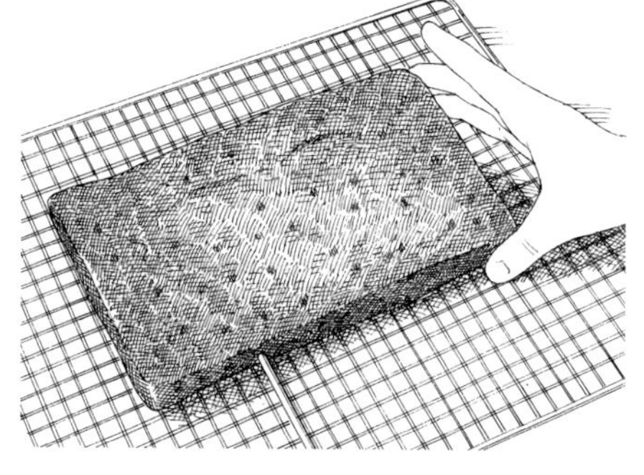

2. Poke cake on all sides with toothpick.

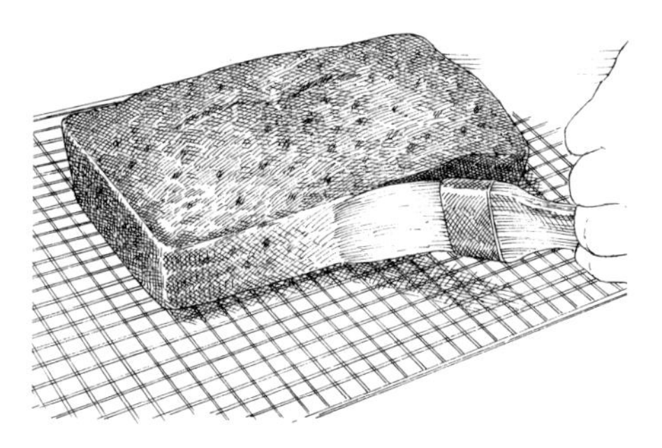

3. Brush top and sides of cooled cake with glaze. Let glaze cool to room temperature.

OLD-FASHIONED CHOCOLATE LAYER CAKE

DAVID PAZMIÑO, *March/April 2006*

While many things have been supersized in recent years, chocolate cakes have become denser, richer, and squatter. Many contemporary chocolate cakes are so intense that just a few forkfuls satisfy me. These cakes are delicious—a bad chocolate cake is hard to imagine—but sometimes I just want a piece of cake, not an overly rich confection.

When I think of the perfect chocolate cake, I remember the birthday cakes my mother made. They were tall, sweet, and chocolaty—the kind of cake you had with a glass of milk, not a demitasse of espresso. Like many mothers, mine used a cake mix, but this style of old-fashioned chocolate cake is a classic. While today's stylish cakes are dense and rich, the cake I had in mind would have a spongy but moist texture that offered a nice contrast with its thick coating of frosting.

Making a chocolate "pudding" with melted chocolate, water, cocoa powder, and sugar makes for high-impact chocolate flavor.

I knew that the mixing method would be the key to getting the right texture. Creaming—beating butter with sugar before mixing in the eggs and flour—is a very popular method for many cakes. The sugar crystals help whip air into the softened butter, which helps the cake rise in the oven. But adding melted unsweetened chocolate undid the effects of creaming, and the resulting cakes were dense and dry. I tried to lighten the load (more leavening, more eggs), but eventually I realized that this method would never produce a fluffy, tender chocolate cake.

Next up was reverse creaming. By mixing very soft butter with flour before adding any liquids, less gluten (the source of cake structure) can develop. Cake made with this technique was tender and fluffy, but too fragile to stand up to a billowy heap of frosting. I suspected that the chocolate's moisture and fat were getting in the way.

Next, I tried ribboning, a process of whipping eggs with sugar until they double in volume and then adding the butter, dry ingredients, and milk. The term refers to the ribbon-like strands that form between the whisk and the batter when the eggs and sugar are whipped. The technique is often the first step when making a French-style sponge cake, or genoise. And many of the American cake recipes I had pulled from late-19th-century cookbooks relied on this technique, since chemical leaveners (baking soda and baking powder) were not yet widely used; the egg foam aerated the cake. While I was planning on using a leavener for extra security, maybe this technique would deliver the height and the structure I wanted.

I followed the basic ribboning procedure of whipping eggs with sugar and then adding the melted chocolate and butter, followed by the dry ingredients and milk. The cake was a bit too dry and not chocolaty enough, but it had more structure and tenderness than any of the other cakes I had made. When I added a full cup of buttermilk (which won out over regular milk), I had a fairly moist cake with good structure and spongy volume. Adding cocoa powder to the flour mixture improved the chocolate flavor.

The solution to the moisture problem presented itself as I combed through chocolate cake recipes. Although some called for mixing melted unsweetened chocolate into the batter, I came across a few references to chocolate "pudding" or "custard." This wasn't a classic pudding or custard (chocolate, milk, eggs, sugar, cornstarch) but a simpler concoction of chocolate, water, and sugar. Probably used to keep the chocolate from burning, this technique was popular in the early 1900s. I found recipes using it in *The Settlement Cookbook* (1901)—one of the most important American cookbooks of its era—and in the first edition of *Joy of Cooking* (1931). Although I could find few modern references to this method, I remembered the powdered "pudding" included in some supermarket cake mixes. Maybe these cake-mix makers were onto something.

I made another cake, this time melting unsweetened chocolate and cocoa powder in hot water over a double boiler and then stirring in sugar until it dissolved. What came from the oven was the moistest cake yet, with a pronounced yet subtle chocolate flavor. It was gloriously tall, and the crumb was open and spongy yet also tender and moist—the cake I had been searching for.

I wanted a silky, voluminous frosting with good chocolate flavor to pair with my cake. Frostings fall into three categories: meringue, buttercream, and ganache. Meringue and buttercream frostings offer great volume, but don't emphasize the chocolate. Ganache is all about chocolate—it can be as simple as heated cream poured over chopped sweetened chocolate—but its texture is usually quite dense. Could I make a ganache that was soft and billowy?

I tried whipping butter into cooled ganache, but the frosting wasn't as silky and glossy as I wanted; plus, it set into a hard shell around my cake—if it didn't break first. After experimenting with various temperatures, times, and ingredients, I found the solution to be a simple reversal of the conventional ganache procedure: I poured cold (rather than heated) cream into warm melted (rather than room-temperature) chocolate, let the mixture come to room temperature, and then whipped it until fluffy.

My cake was all that I had imagined: moist, tender, and airy and perfectly balanced by a light and billowy yet creamy frosting.

Old-Fashioned Chocolate Layer Cake

SERVES 10 TO 12

For a smooth, spreadable frosting, use chopped semisweet chocolate, not chocolate chips, which contain less cocoa butter than bar chocolate does and will not melt as readily. Bittersweet chocolate that is 60 percent cacao can be substituted, but it will produce a stiffer frosting. Bittersweet chocolate with 70 percent cacao should be avoided, as it will produce a frosting that is crumbly and will not spread. For best results, do not make the frosting until the cakes are cooled, and use the frosting as soon as it is ready. If the frosting gets too cold and stiff to spread easily, wrap the mixer bowl with a dish towel soaked in hot water and mix on low speed until the frosting appears creamy and smooth.

Cake

4 ounces unsweetened chocolate, chopped coarse
½ cup hot water
¼ cup (¾ ounce) Dutch-processed cocoa powder
1¾ cups (12¼ ounces) sugar
1¾ cups (8¾ ounces) all-purpose flour
1½ teaspoons baking soda
1 teaspoon salt
1 cup buttermilk
2 teaspoons vanilla extract
4 large eggs plus 2 large yolks, room temperature
12 tablespoons unsalted butter, cut into 12 pieces and softened

Frosting

1 pound semisweet chocolate, chopped fine
8 tablespoons unsalted butter
⅓ cup (2⅓ ounces) sugar
2 tablespoons corn syrup
2 teaspoons vanilla extract
¼ teaspoon salt
1¼ cups heavy cream, chilled

1. ***For the cake:*** Adjust oven rack to middle position and heat oven to 350 degrees. Grease two 9-inch round cake pans, line with parchment paper, grease parchment, and flour pans. Combine chocolate, hot water, and cocoa in medium heatproof bowl set over saucepan filled with 1 inch barely simmering water, making sure that water does not touch bottom of bowl and stirring with heat-resistant rubber spatula until chocolate is melted, about 2 minutes. Add ½ cup sugar to chocolate mixture and stir until thick and glossy, 1 to 2 minutes. Remove bowl from heat; set aside to cool.

2. Whisk flour, baking soda, and salt together in medium bowl. In small bowl, combine buttermilk and vanilla. Using stand mixer fitted with whisk attachment, whip eggs and yolks on medium-low speed until combined, about 10 seconds. Add remaining 1¼ cups sugar, increase speed to high, and whip until light and fluffy, 2 to 3 minutes. Fit stand mixer with paddle. Add chocolate mixture to egg mixture and mix on medium speed until thoroughly combined, 30 to 45 seconds, scraping down bowl as needed. Add butter, 1 piece at a time, mixing for about 10 seconds after each addition. Add flour mixture in 3 additions, alternating with buttermilk mixture in 2 additions, mixing until incorporated after each addition (about 15 seconds) and scraping down bowl as needed. Reduce speed to medium-low and mix until batter is thoroughly combined, about 15 seconds. Give batter final stir by hand.

3. Divide batter evenly between prepared pans and smooth tops with rubber spatula. Bake until toothpick inserted in center comes out with few moist crumbs attached, 25 to 30 minutes, switching and rotating pans halfway through baking. Let cakes cool in pans on wire rack for 10 minutes. Remove cakes from pans, discarding parchment, and let cool completely on rack, about 2 hours, before frosting. (Cooled cakes can be wrapped tightly in plastic wrap and stored at room temperature for up to 24 hours. Wrapped tightly in plastic, then aluminum foil, cakes can be frozen for up to 1 month. Defrost cakes at room temperature before unwrapping and frosting.)

4. ***For the frosting:*** Melt chocolate in medium heatproof bowl set over saucepan filled with 1 inch barely simmering water, making sure that water does not touch bottom of bowl and stirring occasionally until smooth. Set aside, off heat. Meanwhile, melt butter in small saucepan over medium-low heat. Increase heat to medium; add sugar, corn syrup, vanilla, and salt; and stir with heat-resistant rubber spatula until sugar is dissolved, 4 to 5 minutes. Transfer melted chocolate and butter mixture to bowl of stand mixer. Add cream and stir with rubber spatula until thoroughly combined.

5. Fill large bowl halfway with ice and water, place mixer bowl over ice bath, and stir mixture constantly with rubber spatula until frosting is thick and just beginning to harden against sides of bowl, 1 to 2 minutes (frosting should be 70 degrees). Fit stand mixer with paddle and beat frosting on medium-high speed until frosting is light and fluffy, 1 to 2 minutes. Using rubber spatula, stir until completely smooth.

6. Line edges of cake platter with 4 strips of parchment to keep platter clean. Place 1 cake layer on platter. Spread 1½ cups frosting evenly over top, right to edge of cake. Top with second cake layer, press lightly to adhere, then spread 1½ cups frosting evenly over top. Spread remaining 2½ cups frosting evenly over sides of cake. To smooth frosting, run edge of offset spatula around cake sides and over top or create billows by pressing back of spoon into frosting and twirling spoon as you lift away. Carefully remove parchment strips before serving. (Cake can be refrigerated for up to 24 hours. Let come to room temperature before serving.)

ULTIMATE CHOCOLATE CUPCAKES

YVONNE RUPERTI, *May/June 2010*

The trend took shape almost overnight: A pastel-frosted cupcake landed a cameo on the HBO series Sex and the City, and before the owners of New York's Magnolia Bakery could blink, their single-serving sweet turned into a sugar-charged sensation. The cupcake concept—a dainty, portion-controlled, out-of-hand snack universally recognized from childhood birthday parties—was just waiting to take off, and it wasn't long before dedicated "cupcakeries" started popping up by the dozen. Now it's more than 15 years later, and the line outside Magnolia still wraps around the block.

But if cupcake appeal is all about getting the best attributes of cake in a portable package, the irony is that most of these highly specialized bakeries either can't deliver the goods—a moist, tender (but not crumbly) crumb capped with just enough creamy, not-too-sweet frosting—or they deviate from the classic model. Call me old-fashioned, but I prefer a simple, decadent, perfect chocolate cupcake any day, so that's where I decided to focus my testing.

HOW THE CUPCAKE CRUMBLES

My favorite chocolate cake features a double whammy of cocoa powder (½ cup) and melted bittersweet chocolate (3 ounces) plus the roasty, chocolate-enhancing flavor of brewed coffee (½ cup). These elements, when combined with tangy buttermilk (an appropriately less-sweet but still dairy-rich alternative to regular milk), make for a moist cake with full, unabashed chocolate intensity. Figuring that a cupcake is just a pint-size version of a cake, I mixed up the batter, portioned it into a muffin tin, and popped it into the oven. Minutes later, the tasters and I dug in—and the swooning began. Here was a chocolate cupcake that tasted like chocolate. The only problem? Piles of crumbs littering the counter as we ate. As fork food, this rich, tender cake was ideal, but eaten without utensils, it was more of a cleanup project.

I quickly identified the generous dose of cocoa and the melted chocolate as likely culprits for the cupcake's too-tender crumb. More specifically, the texture suffered from too little gluten development and too much fat. Gluten forms when proteins in flour bind together with liquid and become pliable; the more the proteins are worked into the liquid (or, in this case, the batter), the more gluten develops and the stronger the crumb. Fat (like chocolate), on the other hand, acts as a tenderizer to create a soft, delicate crumb.

Because all that cocoa powder (although very low in fat) contains no gluten-forming proteins, it works to dilute the flour, while the extra fat from the melted chocolate makes this cake too tender. Though I was loath to compromise the chocolate's intensity, I knew that I had to cut back on both chocolate components. Fifty percent less cocoa and two-thirds less bittersweet chocolate later, I had perfectly portable (if slightly dry) cupcakes—and predictably feeble chocolate flavor.

I decided that if I had to work with less chocolate, the least I could do was take advantage of the one chocolate-enhancing ingredient I was already using: coffee. Sure enough, mixing the cocoa with hot coffee eked out more chocolate flavor. When I considered the other liquid component—buttermilk—I couldn't help but wonder if I could exchange it for more of the caffeinated stuff. The effect might even benefit me twofold, I reasoned, since the richness of dairy products typically obscures other flavors (like adding cream to tomato soup); maybe the chocolate flavor would actually be cleaner and stronger without it. Hoping I was onto something, I swapped out the buttermilk and increased the amount of coffee to ¾ cup. Bingo. The chocolate flavor was noticeably more pronounced, and I was making good progress. (To activate the baking soda without the buttermilk's acid, I seamlessly added 2 teaspoons of distilled white vinegar.) But I still had another dairy ingredient to consider: butter. Trying more neutral-flavored vegetable oil in place of melted butter seemed worth a shot. The result? Not a dramatic leap flavor-wise but definitely a good move. In a side-by-side tasting, even the skeptics picked the oil-only cupcakes, citing fuller, unadulterated chocolate flavor. Even better, this batch was extra moist, which everyone agreed was a plus.

Bread flour gives our cupcakes enough structure to support an ultrachocolaty crumb and a rich ganache center.

PROTEIN SHAKE(UP)

I'd done all I could think of to boost the existing chocolate flavor when a colleague suggested a more reasonable solution: Why not toughen up the structure of the cupcake that I had? That way, I could add back the extra chocolate without tenderizing it too much. My first thought was to add an extra egg or two—although they contain fat, they also help build structure—but this made the texture rubbery. Next, I intentionally overmixed the batter to stimulate gluten development (as if I were kneading bread dough), but all that bought me was a weary arm—or so I thought. Actually, thinking about bread baking gave me a good hint, as I spied a bag of bread flour on the pantry shelf. Specifically engineered for gluten development, bread flour contains more protein than all-purpose flour and turned out a cupcake that was markedly less crumble-prone but not tough.

With newfound room for more fat in the batter, I began to add back some of the chocolate. Tablespoon by tablespoon, I traded flour for cocoa powder until the latter maxed out at ⅓ cup; I then worked the bar chocolate back up to 3 ounces for the most unapologetically chocolaty (and still sturdy) cake yet.

CENTER OF ATTENTION

And yet the chocoholic in me was holding out for something even more radical. I'd pushed the batter to its limit, but remembering an earlier attempt using chocolate chips, I missed those pockets of pure, molten chocolate in the warm cake and wondered if there was another means to that end. Perhaps a mixture that would stay almost fluid even after it cooled—such as a chocolate ganache? I microwaved a standard ganache mixture of 2 ounces of bittersweet chocolate and 2 tablespoons of heavy cream (plus 1 tablespoon of confectioners' sugar for an extra hint of sweetness), let the mixture cool until it firmed enough to scoop, and then spooned a teaspoon of it onto the cupcakes before baking. As the cupcakes baked, the ganache gently sank into the batter. In fact, the weight of the chocolate made it sink too far—a problem easily solved by thinning the ganache with 2 more tablespoons of cream. One bite into the rich cake and truffle-like center, and I knew I'd hit chocolate nirvana.

Now, about that creamy, not-too-sweet frosting. Too many of the bakery cupcakes I sampled sported swirly tufts of gritty, sicklysweet icing that cracked and disintegrated like cotton candy. I was after something a bit more refined to complement my already-rich base. Varnishing the cake with a second dose of chocolate ganache—a popular choice—actually took the chocolate intensity too far, but tasters thought that a fluffy 7-minute meringue frosting (egg whites whipped with sugar) felt insubstantial. Buttercream seemed like a reasonable compromise, but tasters vetoed the graininess of quick versions that called for simply beating butter together with confectioners' sugar.

That left me with cooked buttercreams. I opted for the Swiss meringue variety, where egg whites and granulated sugar are heated over a double boiler and then whipped with knobs of softened butter. The result is utterly silky and decadent, without the weight and greasiness of other rich frostings. I dolloped a large mound onto each cupcake and took a bite. Velvety, with just enough sweetness, this buttercream crowned the cake perfectly. After more than two months and 800 cupcakes baked, I finally had a recipe that Carrie and Miranda would ditch Magnolia for.

Ultimate Chocolate Cupcakes with Ganache Filling

MAKES 12 CUPCAKES

Use a high-quality bittersweet or semisweet chocolate for this recipe. Though we highly recommend the ganache filling, you can omit it for a more traditional cupcake.

Filling

2 ounces bittersweet chocolate, chopped fine
¼ cup heavy cream
1 tablespoon confectioners' sugar

Cupcakes

3 ounces bittersweet chocolate, chopped fine
⅓ cup (1 ounce) Dutch-processed cocoa powder
¾ cup brewed coffee, hot
¾ cup (4⅛ ounces) bread flour
¾ cup (5¼ ounces) granulated sugar
½ teaspoon salt
½ teaspoon baking soda
6 tablespoons vegetable oil
2 large eggs
2 teaspoons distilled white vinegar
1 teaspoon vanilla extract
1 recipe Creamy Chocolate Frosting (recipe follows)

1. *For the filling:* Combine chocolate, cream, and sugar in medium bowl and microwave until mixture is warm to touch, about 30 seconds. Whisk until smooth, then transfer bowl to refrigerator and let sit until just chilled, no longer than 30 minutes.
2. *For the cupcakes:* Adjust oven rack to middle position and heat oven to 350 degrees. Line 12-cup muffin tin with paper or foil liners. Place chocolate and cocoa in medium heatproof bowl. Pour coffee over mixture and let sit, covered, for 5 minutes. Whisk mixture gently until smooth, then transfer to refrigerator to cool completely, about 20 minutes.
3. Whisk flour, sugar, salt, and baking soda together in medium bowl. Whisk oil, eggs, vinegar, and vanilla into cooled chocolate mixture until smooth. Add flour mixture and whisk until smooth.
4. Divide batter evenly among prepared muffin cups. Place 1 slightly rounded teaspoon ganache filling on top of each portion of batter. Bake cupcakes until set and just firm to touch, 17 to 19 minutes, rotating muffin tin halfway through baking. Let cupcakes cool in muffin tin on wire rack for 10 minutes. Remove cupcakes from muffin tin and let cool completely before frosting, about 1 hour. (Unfrosted cupcakes can be stored at room temperature for up to 24 hours.)
5. Spread 2 to 3 tablespoons frosting over each cooled cupcake and serve.

DECORATING CUPCAKES

You don't have to be a professional baker to make cupcakes that look like they came from a bakery. Here's a simple technique for beautifully frosted cupcakes.

1. Place 2 to 3 tablespoons of frosting on each cupcake, forming thick layer. Using small offset spatula, spread to create flat top.

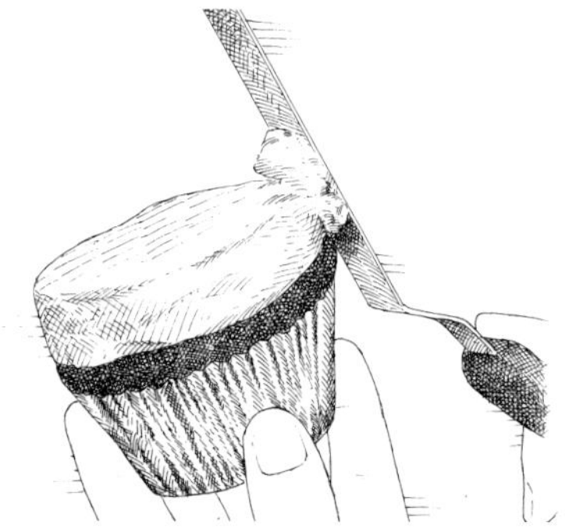

2. Using spatula, smooth edges of frosting so they are flush with sides of cupcake. Reflatten top as necessary.

frosting

Creamy Chocolate Frosting

MAKES ABOUT 2¼ CUPS

The chocolate should be cooled to between 85 and 100 degrees before being added to the frosting. If the frosting seems too soft after adding the chocolate, chill it briefly in the refrigerator and then rewhip it until creamy.

⅓ cup (2⅓ ounces) granulated sugar
2 large egg whites
Pinch salt
12 tablespoons unsalted butter, cut into 12 pieces and softened
6 ounces bittersweet chocolate, melted and cooled
½ teaspoon vanilla extract

1. Combine sugar, egg whites, and salt in bowl of stand mixer and set bowl over saucepan filled with 1 inch barely simmering water, making sure that water does not touch bottom of bowl. Whisking gently but constantly, heat mixture until slightly thickened and foamy and registers 150 degrees, 2 to 3 minutes.
2. Fit stand mixer with whisk attachment and whip mixture on medium speed until consistency of shaving cream and slightly cooled, 1 to 2 minutes. Add butter, 1 piece at a time, until smooth and creamy. (Frosting may look curdled after half of butter has been added; it will smooth with additional butter.) Once all butter is added, add cooled melted chocolate and vanilla; mix until —combined. Increase speed to medium-high and beat until light, fluffy, and thoroughly combined, about 30 seconds, scraping down whisk and bowl with rubber spatula as needed.

variations

Creamy Vanilla Frosting

Omit bittersweet chocolate and increase sugar to ½ cup. (If final frosting seems too thick, warm mixer bowl briefly over pan filled with 1 inch simmering water and beat a second time until creamy.)

Creamy Malted Milk Frosting

Reduce sugar to ¼ cup, substitute milk chocolate for bittersweet chocolate, and add ¼ cup malted milk powder to frosting with vanilla extract in step 2.

Creamy Peanut Butter Frosting

Omit bittersweet chocolate. Increase sugar to ½ cup and increase salt to ⅛ teaspoon. Add ⅔ cup creamy peanut butter to frosting with vanilla extract in step 2. Garnish cupcakes with ½ cup chopped peanuts.

INNER SECRET: SUPER-CHOCOLATY CUPCAKES

CHOCOLATE, INSIDE AND OUT After packing lots of chocolate into the batter, we raised the bar one notch higher by filling the cupcake with a dollop of truffle-like ganache.

NATURAL VERSUS DUTCH-PROCESSED COCOA POWDER

There are two types of unsweetened cocoa powder: natural and Dutch-processed. For our Ultimate Chocolate Cupcakes with Ganache Filling, we prefer Dutch-processed cocoa. So what's the difference? Dutched cocoa has been neutralized with alkali to take away some of the cacao bean's harsher, more acidic notes. But here's another, far less well-known reason: Dutched cocoas typically have far more fat than natural cocoas, sometimes twice as much. Fat adds a perception of moisture in baked goods. In addition, cocoa powders with more fat contain less starch. Why is that important? Starch absorbs free moisture in a batter, so the crumb bakes up drier. This helps explain why we found our cupcakes to be noticeably moister when made with Dutched rather than with natural cocoa powders.

KEYS TO MERINGUE-STYLE BUTTERCREAM

Whereas uncooked frostings tend to be greasy and grainy, our Swiss meringue buttercream gets its satiny-smooth texture from whisking the egg whites and sugar in a double boiler, then whipping the mixture with softened butter.

1. Whisk egg white mixture until foamy and registers 150 degrees on instant-read thermometer.

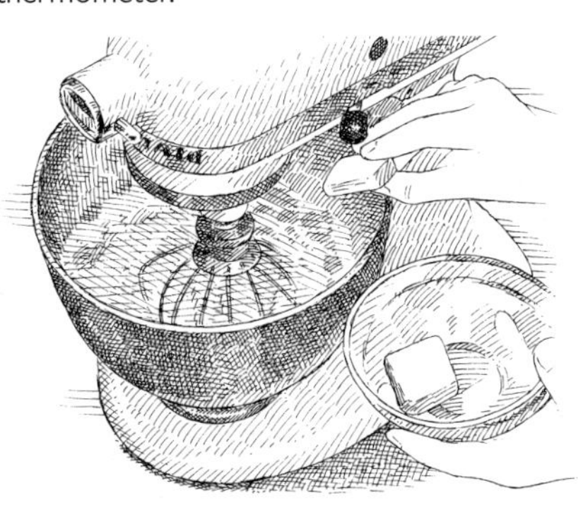

2. Beat mixture in stand mixer until slightly cooled, then slowly add softened butter.

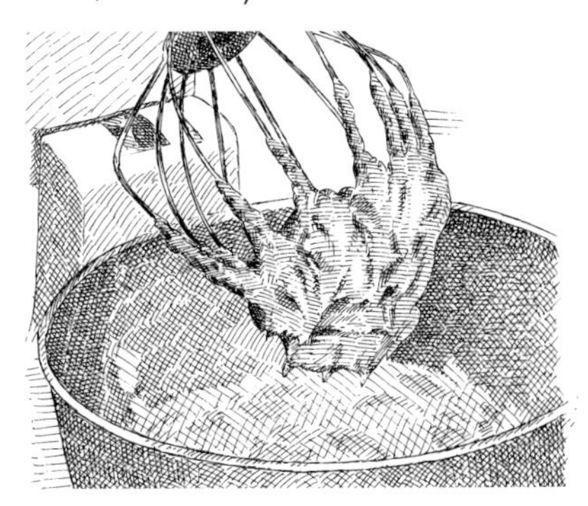

3. Add cooled melted chocolate and vanilla, then whip until light and fluffy.

THE BEST HOMEMADE FROZEN YOGURT

DAN SOUZA, *July/August 2016*

When I set out to make frozen yogurt for the first time, I thought the task would be simple. Unlike ice cream recipes, which typically call for cooking (and then cooling) a finicky custard for a base, most fro yo recipes require nothing more than throwing yogurt, sugar, and maybe a few flavorings into an ice cream maker and churning.

But these recipes were hugely disappointing: The fro yo turned out icy and rock-hard. This is partly because frozen yogurt doesn't contain yolks or cream, both of which give ice cream proportionally more fat and less water. Fat makes ice cream taste creamier and smoother, while less water means there's less of it to form ice crystals, leading to a more velvety, scoopable texture. I found a few frozen yogurt recipes that tried to improve texture by adding cream, but while these versions did turn out less icy, their tangy yogurt flavor had been muted.-

I wanted my frozen yogurt to put the fresh-tasting tartness of yogurt front and center. The challenge was to figure out how to do that and achieve a dense, creamy-smooth texture at the same time.

Lyle's Golden Syrup and gelatin are the secrets to the creamy, smooth, scoopable texture of our tangy frozen yogurt.

STRAIN AND DRAIN

The obvious thing was to try to eliminate some water from the yogurt. In my initial tests, I had been using regular whole-milk yogurt (plain was a must, since I wanted to be able to control flavorings and sweetness myself). Switching to Greek yogurt, which has had much of the liquid whey strained out, produced frozen yogurt with an oddly crumbly texture.

So I considered another option: straining regular yogurt. I spooned a quart of yogurt into a fine-mesh strainer lined with cheesecloth and set over a bowl and left it overnight. By the following morning, a generous amount of whey had drained into the bowl. The fro yo I made with this yogurt was much smoother; I knew this step was a must.

INVERTING THE PROBLEM

The next ingredient to go under my microscope was sugar. Just as in ice cream, sugar doesn't serve as a mere sweetener in frozen yogurt. It also affects the texture. Once dissolved, sugar depresses the freezing point of water, which means the more you use, the more water in the mix will stay in liquid form after churning. That translates not only to fewer ice crystals but also to a softer, more scoopable product straight from the freezer. But I didn't want to make it so sweet that the yogurt's flavor was overshadowed; I found that I could go up to a cup of sugar per quart.

I also knew from my ice cream testing that there were other sweeteners worth considering. One secret to the velvety texture of an ice cream recipe I'd developed a few years back (see page 545) was swapping out some of the granulated sugar for corn syrup. This sweetener contains starch chains that keep water molecules from joining up and forming large ice crystals. When I tried it in my frozen yogurt, it worked pretty well at minimizing iciness, but the yogurt's flavor seemed muted. A little research informed me why: Those starch chains trap flavor molecules. This wasn't a problem in tame vanilla ice cream, but in tart frozen yogurt, the dulling effect was clear.

My next thought was to try incorporating an invert sugar, which is better than granulated sugar at depressing the freezing point of water. Unlike granulated sugar, which is made up of larger sucrose molecules, invert sugar is made up of two smaller molecules, glucose and fructose. Freezingpoint depression is directly related to the number of molecules dissolved in the water. So a tablespoon of invert sugar provides twice as many sugar molecules and roughly twice as much freezing-point depression as a tablespoon of granulated sugar. Supermarket options for invert sugar include honey and agave syrup, but their distinct flavors would be distracting. Luckily, I knew of another option: Lyle's Golden Syrup. While only half invert sugar (the other half is sucrose), Lyle's worked like magic. Just 3 tablespoons (along with ¾ cup of granulated sugar) noticeably reduced the iciness.

GETTING TRAPPED

Many manufacturers add pectin, gums, or modified starches to get smoother, less icy results. These ingredients essentially trap water, which will minimize large water droplets—and thus large ice crystal formation. Pectin made the frozen yogurt taste almost fruity, but gelatin was perfect. I needed a liquid to bloom it in, so I reserved ½ cup of whey when I drained the yogurt and microwaved the whey with the gelatin to quickly dissolve the gelatin before incorporating the mixture into my base. Just 1 teaspoon of gelatin gave me the smoothest, creamiest frozen yogurt yet.

There were just a few more details to attend to. Quickly freezing the base was key, since faster freezing promotes the formation of smaller ice crystals. I refrigerated my base until it registered 40 degrees or less before churning. And in addition to churning until it looked like thick soft-serve, I also made sure it registered 21 degrees (the temperature at which roughly 50 percent of the water has frozen) for the most consistent results.

My frozen yogurt now boasted a wonderfully creamy, smooth texture as well as the distinctively tangy, fresh flavor of its namesake ingredient.